GW01605920

Thomas Finan

Collected Writings

Portrait of Thomas Finan by William A. Nathans

Thomas Finan

Collected Writings

EDITED BY:

D. VINCENT TWOMEY

First published in 2019 by

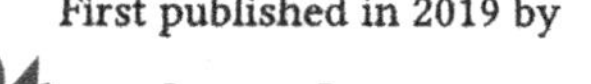

23 Merrion Square North
Dublin 2, Ireland

www.columbabooks.com

ISBN: 978-178218-360-0

Set in Linux Libertine 11/15

Cover design by Alba Esteban | Columba Books

Book design by Maria Soto | Columba Books

Cover Photo: Portrait of Thomas Finan by William A. Nathans

Printed by ScandBook, Sweden

TABLE OF CONTENTS

INTRODUCTORY NOTE

THOMAS FINAN: CHRISTIAN HUMANIST

Thomas Finan was a humanist, more precisely a Christian humanist. 'Professionally I am an *ancient* European',[1] he once proudly proclaimed. His first scholarly publication, *Hellenistic Humanism in the Book of Wisdom* (1960), was programmatic for what he would write during the following four decades. That essay opens with a question posed by the Archbishop of Paris, Cardinal Suhard: 'How much room does the meaning of God leave for the meaning of man?' This is not just a Christian problem, Finan stresses, 'it is in fact the problem of any civilization that believes in an Absolute distinct from the immediate possibilities of the visible world'. With the advent of Christianity, the problem was brought into a new, sharper definition.

Classics was his field of expertise. *Hic, pagani nos omnes*, was the first quip he made to a new lecturer on her arrival at Maynooth.[2] For Tom, as he was affectionately known to his colleagues, pagan was a noble epithet; it refers to human experience at its most primordial – God's creation in the raw, as it were – the depths of which the ancients plumbed. But he reads the ancients in the light of Christ. More precisely, he reads the ancient authors against the backdrop of the whole of western civilization which was formed by the historical encounter of reason with revelation that is Christianity. In his own words: 'St. Augustine in the fourth century made the shock discovery of the analogies between the *Logos* in Platonist philosophy and the *Logos* in St. John's Gospel. With that he put something into the European bloodstream which could only be removed by changing the blood.'[3] Tom Finan's writings on the Fathers of the Church – in particular Augustine – explore the implications of that 'shock discovery' from Justin Martyr to John Scotus Eriugena and beyond ... down to Edith Stein.

This cultural background – basically philosophical, theological, spiritual and artistic – gives his writings a unique depth, be it in exploring the Greek poets,

1 *Ireland and Europe.*

2 Dr Maeve O'Brien; see *Eklogai: Studies in Honour of Thomas Finan and Gerard Watson*, edited by Kieran McGroarty (Maynooth, 2001), vii. She describes him, accurately, as 'a real humanist with a very dry wit'.

3 *Ireland and Europe.*

the Epic of Gilgamesh, the myth of the innocent sufferer in the Greek tradition – or simply commenting on the existential dimensions of contemporary cultural developments, be it sacred art, liturgical language, Ireland's role in Europe, the artistry of Harry Clarke or the Catholicism of James Joyce.

Central to his scholarly explorations is the notion of the sublime, which he understood to incorporate (or indeed to climax in) what one could call, with due reserve, mystical experience. His primal instinct was poetic, evident even in some of his most scholarly writings, which could not infrequently be described, in his own words, as poetic prose. Accordingly, his essays on various poets and on the poetic imagination are among the most original in this collection. Why? Because for him,' ... poetry may well have this advantage, namely that, if genuine, it will always at least express some truth about the 'unchristened heart'. In poetic and religious experience alike the *regio egestatis*, the 'waste land', is as authentic as the final fulfilment in *la forma universal*.'[4]

Far from being a dry scholar, Tom was a man of passion and dry wit, for whom, as he once put it, 'life is larger than logic'.[5] His interests embraced the whole spectrum of humanistic endeavour: poetry, art, literature, philosophy, and, above all, patristic theology (including spirituality or lived theology). The topics he treated ranged from tragedy to exegesis, from poetic imagination to liturgical translations, from European culture to mysticism, all of which he approached from the perspective of Ancient Classics – reason in its primordial form, which, he knew instinctively, has to be appreciated in itself before it is illuminated, deepened, and transformed by the light of revelation.

In the course of his own intellectual odyssey, he drew fresh water from the ancient springs of European civilization (Athens, Rome and Jerusalem). In his scholarly writings, he plumbed the depths of Augustine's theology, explored the heights of Dante's poetry, and uncovered the existential concerns of the great Renaissance humanists, Thomas More and Erasmus of Rotterdam. Inspired by the same sources, he also commented in his 'occasional writings' on contemporary events, such as the entrance of Ireland into what in time became the European Union, or the transformation of his alma mater, the National Seminary of St Patrick's College, Maynooth, into a university, enabling him to recover for his contemporaries the relevance of Newman's idea of what such an institution should be.

In all his writings, be they strictly scholarly or just occasional essays or talks, he acknowledges the Christian indebtedness to the richness of Greco-Roman

4 From *The Poetic Imagination*. In a postscript to the article, he wrote: 'As it stands this paper is really no more than the record of the author's own journey up-river – undertaken at relatively short notice ...'. For this reason alone, it is worth studying to come to know the mind of Tom Finan.

5 *The Poetic Imagination*.

civilization – above all Plato and Aristotle. Their inspiration could be said to be the *cantus firmus* to all his writings. Finan was acutely aware how the ancient tragedians and philosophers could best be understood in terms of their search for, and partial discovery of Truth, more precisely, the One who is the Desired of the Nations – a theme he explicitly explored in one of his contributions to the Maynooth International Patristic Conferences. From the start, his attention was caught by the early Fathers of the Church: Justin Martyr, Clement of Alexandria and, above all, Augustine, who in their time had, as they themselves put it, 'plundered the Egyptians' – i.e. mined the great thinkers of antiquity – to plumb the depths of revelation. But revelation was not just the answer to the perennial search for truth; Greek thought had its own contribution to make. Thus, for example, while discussing the encounter of Hebrew humanism and Greek humanism as found in the Book of Wisdom, he could comment: 'It is as if the touch of Greek speculation had suddenly opened the eyes of the Hebrew to the mysteries of the created world, which he had missed in his concentration on the mysteries of God.'[6]

If Augustine was his first passion, as it were, later in life he, not surprisingly, became fascinated with the person and writings of Thomas More. For Finan, the 'attractiveness of More as man, Christian and saint, is that he was an *incarnate* spirit. He was humanist as well as saint, ... '.[7] Thomas More's wit and humour naturally appealed to him. His 'call for papers' in preparation for the Thomas More Conference he organized at Maynooth in 1998, and his introduction to the final programme were so rich in content and insight that there were published separately as articles. Interest in More led inevitably to Erasmus of Rotterdam, a fellow humanist and a fellow scholar. A paragraph of Finan's introduction to the final programme provides not only a taste of his style but also an insight into the core of his convictions: Speaking about the nature and location of this *sunmum bonum*, and of its consequent *beatitudo/eudaimonia*, he comments:

> Greek philosophy anticipated what Judeo-Christian revelation confirmed, namely that the ultimate 'law' of all things is an order of *erôs*. That *erôs* has two foci, in the Supreme Being and in the human being's unquiet heart. Plotinus as well as revelation and personal experience is behind Augustine's confession that 'You have made us oriented towards Yourself, and our hearts are restless until they rest in You' (*Confessions* I 1). Even the austerely technical Aristotle understood the Prime Mover as moving all things 'by the attraction of love' (*Metaphysics* XII 7). That remains the

6 *Hellenistic Humanism in the Book of Wisdom.*

7 *Some More Comforts.*

> supreme point of Dante's epic of Christendom – the vision of 'the Love that moves the sun and the other stars.' That transcendent point does not devalue the human being's *humanitas* and its drive towards the ideals of humanism. Rather does it provide those ideals with their classical and Judeo-Christian ground, in that 'law' whose rationale is not extrinsic constraint but liberation into harmony with the intrinsic 'order' and teleology of human beings and their world. Irenaeus of Lyon already provides the formula for that integral humanism: *gloria Dei homo vivens, vita hominis visio Dei* – the glory of God is man fully alive, the life of man is the vision of God. Pascal's 'order of charity' is in the same tradition. From Pascal also we have the best known formula for the consequences to *humanitas* of a fracture in that order: *Grandeur de l'homme* indeed but, *misère de l'homme sans Dieu* (*Pensées* 255 [165] and 73 [25], ed. Pléiade). That, of course, was already a principal theme of Greek tragedy.[8]

***

Perhaps one of the most striking characteristics of Finan's thought is his heightened sense of his own 'place' and its ancient traditions: Ireland, Celtic and modern. Since, as he attests, the universal is only found in the particular, his place of origin and his place of study are central to his identity as a man and as a writer searching for perennial – and so universal – truths. He was understandably proud to have been born in a place he called very simply 'magical': Sligo – hallowed by myth (Queen Maeve), history (St Patrick, General Humbert, etc.) and poetry (W.B.Yeats) – and to have served as a priest and professor in the National Seminary of Ireland – the Royal Catholic College of Maynooth – and later the National University of Maynooth, where, to quote his colleague Maeve O'Brien, 'Many generations of students were privileged to be taught by him because he made Maynooth a place where *"all grew friendly for a little while"* (W. B. Yeats).'[9]

His consciousness of the rich, ancient (but largely unknown) Irish tradition to which he was heir is evident not only in some of his occasional writings, such as his vision of Ireland's place in Europe or the future of Maynooth as a university, but also in his scholarly works, above all in his exploration of the uniquely Celtic colouring that distinguishes early Irish theology. This Irish Celtic flavour is highlighted in his masterly overview of Hiberno-Latin Christian literature from the fifth century (St Patrick) to the twelfth (the *Vision of Tundal*, a work which may have inspired Dante). His recovery of the originality of early Irish

8 *Renaissance Humanism and Renaissance Law*

9 Maeve O'Brien, *Eklogai*, vii.

theology, with its distinctive Celtic flavour and cosmic vision, is a welcome corrective to what is known today, misleadingly, as 'Celtic spirituality'.[10]

His occasional writings (Part Two) deserve special attention. In them, he had the freedom to be creative and original. Language is, obviously, one of his main preoccupations. His penetrating critique of the initial attempt to translate the *Novus Ordo* of the Mass into English (*The Burning of the Books*) is illuminating – and devoid of rancour. Apart from criticizing the Latin of the post-conciliar reformed liturgy itself, he elaborates on the distinction between language as communication and language as poetry, the latter alone being suited to liturgy as ritual.

Written on the eve of Ireland's entry into the European Economic Community, his essay on *Ireland and Europe* concentrates on the cultural issues at stake – and the centrality of the notion of identity, both Irish and European as well as their historical and cultural interconnections – all of which have taken on a new relevance because of recent political developments. His comments on contemporary catechesis and on the notion of mortal sin are illuminating thanks to his classical and patristic background. Visual art was another of Tom's passions, reflected here in his essay on Harry Clarke, while the inner beauty of spiritual experience and mystical experience are the subjects of his essays on visions and visionaries and on the canonization of St Edith Stein. As already mentioned, his paper on Maynooth's future as a university brings Newman home, among those cloisters where he once wandered as a valued guest. Tom's whimsical reflections on the pope's visit to Maynooth barely hide a slightly sceptical observer's restrained reflection on the historic event. Commenting on the Vigil of Prayer held the night before the visit, he observes: 'The air was mild as a Mediterranean night – a miracle some were known to have laid down as the spiritual-blackmail condition of their continued belief in the primacy of Peter and the historicity of Patrick!'

His commentary on the Apocalypse and his homilies (suitably on the end of time and the beginning of the academic year!) demonstrate how his Midas touch could turn potent dross in the hands of lesser homilists into rhetorical gold. Tom is very much at home with a fellow Irish artist, as revealed in his review article of a book on James Joyce entitled *Ulysses and the Irish God.* He brings all his impressive learning to bear on an appreciation of Joyce's take on Irish Catholicism. Speaking about Joyce 'as a superb "musician" with language', he comments: '... music has its chords and harmonics, its point, counterpoint, and polyphonic. So too has language. It *must* have, it must be intrinsic to the very

10 Thus he comments: 'There is indeed a Celtic dimension to early Irish spirituality, even if, as a relatively late-converted territory, the Irish owed much to older Christian Europe. But the "Celtic" label, like the proverbial charity, can cover a lot. And, to my limited knowledge, some of that lot is rather soft at the centre.' (*The Trinity in Early Irish Christian Writings*).

technique, when the aim of the artist is precisely that multi-layered polysemy entailed in "taking an entire culture for his verbal canvas", in drawing "a continuous parallel between contemporaneity and antiquity". Joyce is a master of that art.'[11] And I dare to say, *mutatis mutandis*, so is Finan.

***

A talk he gave in 1991 at a reunion of his primary-school classmates (previously unpublished) is a fitting epilogue to this collection of Thomas Finan's writings. It could be said to provide the key to interpreting his thought; it is perhaps best read *after* reading his collected writings. Echoing George Steiner, the talk is entitled 'Presences'. Opening the talk, he reveals his first awaking (to the sublime) that marked his life and works: 'One of my earliest memories of Stokane National School is not within the Alma Mater itself, but on the road home from it. A white, dusty road between lush verges on a brooding June afternoon, with Summer stillness all round, but inside my head the soporific buzz of a "bee-loud glade". We had been learning Yeats's "Lake Isle", and I was drugged by its music... '. In the course of his personal reminiscences, one glimpses those primordial human experiences of a sensitive and alert boy that enabled the mature man appreciate what the great minds of Western civilization expressed in sublime words when in their search for the truth of the human condition.

Thomas Finan's voice is an original and unique voice in the Irish cultural landscape. It is to be hoped that the publication of his collected writings will make him known to a new generation of scholars. I hope he will forgive me, if I end with a quotation from his own review of Joyce, now applied to his collected writings:

One may conclude then with another borrowed phrase, the one with which Apuleius prefaced his equally doubtful tale, or rather – like Joyce too – a blue rosary of tales: 'Give ear, gentle reader, you'll enjoy it.'[12]

***

In this collection, his writings are divided into two sections, which should be seen as complementary. Part One covers his more scholarly works, and Part Two his occasional writings, with the exception of two papers, which have been placed in Part One, since they function as introductions to the more scholarly

11 *Joyce and the Irish God.*

12 Ibid. And he adds, mimicking the Dubliner: 'That is to say, you'll re-joyce, and maybe even re Joyce, if you are convinced by this book's thesis re Joyce.'

articles. The scholarly articles are presented under five different headings, which are listed chronologically within each subsection: (1) Antiquity; (2) Augustine; (3) Early Irish Christian Literature; (4) Dante; (5) Renaissance. The Addendum to Part I contains a collection of quotations which evidently were of particular significance to the author. Part Two consists of articles, reviews, essays, talks, and homilies given on various occasions and grouped under the headings of (1) Controversial Topics, (2) Art & Literature, (3) Homilies, within which they are arranged in chronological order.

Finally, I wish to express my gratitude to Glenbeigh Record Management for the initial digitalization of the texts, and above all to Mark Bennett and Lisa Tierney, who painstakingly corrected the digitalized text. Both were also invaluable at the proofreading stage, as were Martin Pulbook and Michael O'Dwyer. Ultimate responsibility for the final text, however, lies with the editor. My thanks are also due to Nicholas Madden OCD, Martin Henry, Andrew Smith, David Woods, and to Anna Porter, Archivist at St Patrick's College, Maynooth, for their input at various stages in the preparation of the volume for publication. Special thanks are due to Garry O'Sullivan, Managing Director of Columba Press, for accepting this collection of previously published articles for publication, and in particular to Mags Gargan, Managing Editor, and Laura Ashcroft-Jones, editorial assitant, and the layout designers, Alba Estaban and Maria Soto, for their professionalism and patience. The Most Reverend Dr John Fleming, Bishop of Killala, and the Finan Family – above all, Canon Finan's sister, Mrs Nora Kennedy – entrusted me with the task of preparing for publication this important collection of writings from the pen of my esteemed colleague and old friend. It has been an honour and a privilege to be so closely associated with this project, as I am convinced that Tom Finan's voice is one that deserves to be heard by a wider audience than those who had the good fortune to sit at his feet in the lecture halls of his beloved Maynooth.

D. Vincent Twomey, SVD
Dublin, Feast of St Mark, 2018

A BIOGRAPHICAL NOTE[13]

Thomas Finan was born in Ballymoghany, Eniscrone, Co. Sligo, on 12 February 1931. After attending Stokane National School, he became a pupil at St Muredach's Diocesan College, Ballina, where he received his basic education in, and love for, the Classics. He entered the National Seminary, St Patrick's College, Maynooth in 1950, and after a distinguished student career (B.A. Hons in Ancient Classics, MA, BD, Honours, H Dip. in Education) was ordained to the priesthood in 1957 for the Diocese of Killala. Though he was reticent about his academic achievements while still a seminarian, he won an important international prize for a dissertation in Latin which required a special dispensation to enable him to go to Rome to receive it.[14] He also caused a stir with an article on François Mauriac in *Silhouette*, an internal seminary publication, even though he did not study French for his BA degree.[15] He undertook postgraduate studies in Paris, where he was Elève Titulaire de l'École des Hautes Études. In 1959, he was appointed Professor of Ancient Classics at Maynooth, a post he held until 1996, when he retired. His lectures covered such topics as: Roman Republican History, Virgil, Mediaeval Latin Lyric, Vitruvius and Roman Art and Architecture, Quintilian, Aeschylus, Aristotle and St Augustine (his especial love, to quote Pulbrook). He was elected Canon of St Muredach's Cathedral, Ballina. A founding member (Hon. President) of The Patristic Symposium, Maynooth, he contributed regularly to the ordinary meetings of the Symposium as well as making three major contributions at the International Patristic Conferences organized by the Patristic Symposium, Maynooth (1990, 1993, 1996). Together with Dr Clare Murphy of the *Moreanum – Amici Thomae Mori,* Université Catholique de l'Ouest, Angers, he organized the 1998 International Thomas More Conference which was held at Maynooth. After a long illness, he died on 10 June 2012. May he now be caught up in the vision of the Sublime that was the focus of his life and writings.

The Editor

13 The following is based on Dr Martin Pulbrook's appreciation in *The Irish Times* and Dr Maeve O'Brien's introduction in *Eklogai.* See the more complete biography by Denis Bergin http://avergeen9.wixsite.com/maynoothcemetery2/thomas-finan

14 Martin Pullbrook in a letter to the editor.

15 'Digging up the Past', *The Silhouette,* summer, 1957, 42–48. Tom was also editor at the time. I am grateful to Dr Michael O'Dwyer, Senior Lecturer in French, Maynooth, for this information.

Part I:

ACADEMIC

ANTIQUITY

HELLENISTIC HUMANISM IN THE BOOK OF WISDOM

'How much room does the meaning of God leave for the meaning of man?'[1] These are the terms of 'the vast problem of humanism'.[2] Although it is usual to regard it as a problem rooted in the apparent antinomies that stem from the advent of Christianity,[3] it is in fact the problem of any civilization that believes in an Absolute distinct from the immediate possibilities of the visible world.[4] What is true is that the advent of Christianity brought the elements of the question into new, sharp definition. The Incarnation is a fact of cosmic import. It must effect not merely a readjustment of the elements of profane civilization, but a radical re-estimation of the value to be assigned the profane in itself. 'Here they are, the men who are turning the world upside down ...', says the Greek of Acts, 17:6. 'It was his loving design, centred in Christ, to give history its fulfilment by resuming everything in him ...' (Eph 1:10).

These two sentences set the problem in a high relief in which it is not always seen by those who examine the Christian attitude to Greco-Roman civilization. The inevitable differences which make the early Christians an obviously foreign body in the social fabric of their time are but the outcrop of a deeper divergence of a metaphysical order.[5] A seed has been planted that will split the ancient cypress. *Ceci tuera cela.* It is the very substructure and presuppositions of the old civilization that have been undermined. And to this three-dimensional view of the problem St Paul adds the 'fourth dimension' of history. Even if linear progress – from prophecy to fulfilment, from type to reality – were not ingrained in the Judeo-Christian understanding of Time,[6] the Incarnation could not but be

1 Card. Suhard, *Pastoral Letters* (Eng. tr., London, 1955), 76.

2 Ibid., 87.

3 E.g. A. J. Toynbee, *Civilization on Trial* (London, 1948), 226; J. J. O'Meara, 'Some Thoughts on Christianity and Culture', *University Review*, vol. II, n. 1, 42, points out that long before Christianity was accepted in the West 'men had debated the values of abstention and of use...'.

4 See e.g. C. Dawson, *Enquiries into Religion and Culture* (London, 1933), 105ff; *Progress and Religion* (London, 1929), 130ff.

5 A. de Labriolle, *La Réaction Païenne* (Paris, 1934), 14.

6 A. Harnack, *The Mission and Expansion of Christianity* (London, 1908), vol. I, 15, speaks of the Judeo-Christian concept of historical teleology; cf. A. H. Chroust, 'The Metaphysics of Time and History in Early Christian Thought', *The New Scolasticism*, 19 (1945), 345.

regarded as a master-key to the meaning and direction of history. As it is, it is more than the central truth of the Christian life. It is also the *telos* of historical movement. It is the 'final meaning and the criterion of all history before and after it'.[7] Thus the problem of Christian humanism is a problem under the complementary aspects of a philosophy of history and a philosophy of values.

And at bottom these two are one. The problem in Christian humanism is the problem of Christian universalism. The Incarnation is not a fact among other facts. It is a master-idea. For those who believe that the *Logos* was made Flesh all values must be judged in relation to this supreme value, all temporal movement in relation to this fullness of time. Profane history, profane values, exist within, not independently of the Christian totality.[8]

But the Christian version of the problem, like Christianity itself, is rooted in the past. The same antinomies, under the same double aspect, are inherent in Judaism. Firstly, because it is there the lines begin to converge in the Incarnation. For the Jews all history is moving to a great fulfilment. Humanist values are determined not by the love of created beauty but by the fear of the Lord, the beginning of wisdom.[9] Secondly, because the Alexandrian Jew found himself in a situation closely analogous to that of the Christians later in the same Greco-Roman world. History and truth had seemed to centre on the Jew – the Chosen People and the predestined inheritors of the earth. How would the exclusive Jew assimilate the sudden new fact of another tradition, another corpus of values – if not as old as his own, certainly blasé in the quest for that truth which seemed to be his unique possession in the word of God? It was the great question set dramatically in 332 B.C., when Alexander, with the founding of the city that bears his name, opened the momentous locks of history through which came the confluence of two traditions that hitherto had run their parallel courses in 'total and mutual ignorance'.[10]

It was in answer to that question – for the most part implicit in a more immediately pressing apologetic purpose[11] – there were called up expressions of that Judeo-Christian universalism which makes all history a function of Judeo-Christian history, all values a function of Judeo-Christian values. On Judeo-Christian principles all history must be one – within the Judeo-Christian framework. *A fortiori* truth must be one – and Revelation is the word of God. Hence the attempt of Alexandro-Jewish apologetics – a method borrowed later by the

7 O. Cullman, *Christ and Time* (Eng. tr.), 20.

8 Cf. J. Daniélou, 'Christianisme et Histoire', *Études*, 254 (1947) : ' ... l'histoire sainte constitue en réalité l'histoire totale ...'.

9 Contrast e.g., Thucydides, 2, 40 and Proverbs 1:7.

10 Daniel-Rops, *Israel and the Ancient World* (Eng. tr., London, 1949), 245.

11 For some of the calumnies which Jewish, like Christian, apologists had to face, see e.g., Josephus, *Con. Ap.*, 2, 1ff.

Christian apologists – 'to find Plato in the Law, and ... the Law in Plato',[12] to convert him, in the phrase of Numenius,[13] into an Attic Moses.

At first this took the form of a naive historicism which tried to explain such truth and value as could not be denied to exist outside Revelation as borrowings from the more ancient books of the Jews – in particular from Moses, who became for late Judaism 'die wichtigste Gestalt der ganzen bisherigen Heilsgeschichte ...'.[14] For Eupolemus[15] he was the discoverer of the alphabet for the Jews – from whom, through the Phoenicians, the Greeks ultimately received it.[16] According to Artapanus,[17] the Greeks knew Moses as Musaeus! 'This *Moysos* was the teacher of Orpheus ... '. Among the many benefits he bestowed on mankind was philosophy.[18] Earlier than both of these was Pseudo-Aristobulus,[19] who first systematically linked Greek philosophy with the Jewish Revelation.[20]

This is tendentious history. But it is the principle that is important. History is one. Truth is one. Revelation is the cadre of that unity.[21] It is this principle which gives some significance to the long history of the theory of plagiarism in Christian apologetics – often in odd conjunction with more satisfying speculative theories of unity – notably in Justin Martyr and Clement of Alexandria.

That is the apologetic tradition to which Philo is heir. He is our most complete extra-canonical witness to Alexandro-Jewish attempts to assimilate Hellenism. He preserves the universalism we have noted as inherent in Jewish history and revelation, and gives it a new and far-reaching assertion by equiparating the Law with the highest expression of Greek civilization – philosophy. 'Whatever advantages are derived from the most approved philosophy by its students, fully as great are derived by the Jews from their laws and customs ...'.[22] Revelation is the source of all wisdom.[23] The 'word and reason of God', as embodied in the Law, is 'the true and genuine philosophy'.[24] This became Christian terminology which survives as late as Erasmus.[25]

12 C. Bigg, *The Christian Platonists of Alexandria* (Oxford, 1913), 30.

13 Apud Eusebium, *Praep. Ev.*, II, 10; Clem. Alex., *Stromata*, I, 22, *PG*, 8, 896.

14 J. Jeremias, in *Theol. Wörterbuch z. N.T.* (ed. Kittel), Bd. iv, 854, 6.

15 Floruit c.158 BC. Cf. M. J. Lagrange, *Le Judaïsme avant Jésus Christ* (Paris, 1931), 499.

16 Apud Eusebium, *Praep. Ev.*, 9, 26.

17 Before 80 BC (Lagrange, op. cit., 499).

18 Apud Eusebium, *Praep. Ev.*, 9, 27.

19 C. 100 BC (Lagrange, op. cit., 102, n. 8).

20 E. Bréhier, *Les Idées Philosophiques et Religieuses de Philon d'Alexandrie* (Paris, 1925), 48. See Eusebius, *Praep. Ev.*, 13, 12; cf. ibid., 8, 9; 9, 6; Clem. Alex., *Strom.*, I, 22, *PG*, 8, 893.

21 Cf. Daniélou, op. cit., 184.

22 *De humanitate*, 2, 386 (ed. Manjey).

23 See P. Wendland, *Die hellenistisch-römische Kultur* (Tübingen, 1912), 205.

24 *De posteritate Caini*, I, 244.

25 See L. Bouyer, *Erasmus and the Humanist Experiment* (Eng. tr., London, 1959), 142.

It is particularly meaningful in Justin[26] and Clement.[27] Its significance for Christian universalism lies in the fact that the compenetration of sacred and profane, Christian and Hellenic, in the common concept of the *Logos*, enabled them at once to annex and to break with the past and its heritage of humanism. What was good and true was Christian.[28] But it was good and true only because it was itself Christian in its ultimate principle. And it was perfectly good and completely true only as taken up into the full revelation of the *Logos* in Person at the Incarnation.

Philo does not rise to such a speculative setting, but he has advanced beyond the naive historicism of his apologetic antecedents. The Law is the true philosophy not only because it is revealed, but more fundamentally because it corresponds with reality. The Law corresponds to the world and the world to the Law.[29] The Law touches on 'the necessary principles of natural philosophy',[30] and is at all times in 'perfect consistency and accordance with nature ...'.[31] Thus while he has advanced from the antecedent *historical* monism, it is to a harmonistics in which he seeks to reconcile rather than unify the Hellenic and the Hebrew traditions. True he insists on the uniqueness and transcendence of the Jewish revelation, which contains the 'principle itself',[32] as distinct from the mere assertions of philosophy, but he leaves unsolved the problem of their ultimate relation, of the historical origin and significance of the separate Greek tradition.

In his value-theory the same uniqueness and transcendence is expressed by putting theocentric wisdom at the apex of the educational pyramid – higher still than that philosophy which had topped the pyramid of Plato. As the liberal arts in the Greek tradition have their finality in philosophy, so philosophy itself for the Jew must have its finality in the wisdom that is of the Law.[33] In this Philo is at once the heir of the Greek propaideutic theory[34] and the forerunner of the Christian adaptation of the same idea. Clement of Alexandria[35] will quote him verbatim, and Origen will outline a similar plan.[36] But for all the structural similarity with the Patristic theory his spirit is different. Even if the humanism of a Clement or an

26 See *Dialogus*, 8.

27 See e.g., *Strom.*, 2,2 (*PG*,8, 936). On this terminology see G. Bardy, 'Philosophie et Philosophe dans le Vocabulaire Chrétien des Premiers Siècles', *Revue d'Ascétique et de Mystique*, 25 (1949), 97–108.

28 See Justin, 2 *Apol.*, 13.

29 *De mundi opificio*, I, I.

30 *De Cherubim*, I, 154.

31 *De Fortitudine*, 2, 378. See Lagrange, 'Vers de *Logos* de S. Jean', *Rev. Biblique* (1923), 322.

32 *De Somn.*, I, 629.

33 *De Cong. Erud.*, I, 530.

34 On the theory of *propaideia* see H. J. Marrou, *Saint Augustin et la fin de la culture antique* (Paris, 1938), 280–283.

35 *Strom.*, I, 5 (*PG*, 8,721).

36 *Letter to Gregory*, I.

Origen must be qualified as 'sacral',[37] in that the natural is not an intermediate *end*, but is a *means* ordered directly to the supernatural, it still permits and demands a positive development of the natural powers. This openness is less discernible in Philo. Where for Clement intellectual development has a positive function in the Christian system, namely the defence and exposition of Revelation, for Philo the emphasis is on moral perfection. 'The greatest of all propositions is virtue ... '.[38] And to this ethical purpose even the liberal arts must minister.[39] As a child is to a man, so is a sophist to a *sophos*; so the liberal arts to 'real knowledge in virtue... '.[40] Spiritual perfection counts more than all humanist self-development. And this value-synthesis suffers further from the lack of a basis in a higher theory of unity between sacred and profane, which would light up the theory from within rather than impose it from without as a kind of ethics-of-experience.

Justin Martyr and Clement of Alexandria will find such a basis in the theory of the universally active *Logos*. But it is of the highest interest to find their speculative setting of the humanist question anticipated in another – this time a canonical – Alexandro-Jewish author who, earlier than Philo, is ahead of him in his solutions to both aspects of the question we have posed; who without sacrificing the uniqueness and transcendence of revelation has advanced in his theory of origins from historicism and harmonistics to a speculative monism, and in his theory of truth and value has replaced moralism by an intellectualist fusion of Hebrew theocentric wisdom with the Greek humanist ideal of anthropocentric *paideia*. He is the unknown author of the Wisdom of Solomon, belonging to the Sapiential Literature of the Bible, and among the last books of the Old Testament to be written.[41]

The Sapiential Books themselves anticipate the question of why they merit consideration in any essay on the problem of humanism. 'The knowledge of many and great things has been shown us by the Law and the Prophets and others that have followed them; for which things Israel is to be commended for doctrine and wisdom ... '.[42] If the highest aim of life may be summed up in the saying of Pindar as the effort to become 'who we are',[43] then humanism had to be important in Israel. From the very beginning she had a clear-cut definition of man, and

37 See Bouyer, op. cit., 17; J. Maritain, *Religion and Culture* (Eng. tr., London, 1931), 13.

38 *De Cong. Erud.*, I, 520.

39 *De Agricultura*, I, 303.

40 *Quod resipuit Noë*, I, 394. Cf. Bréhier, op. cit., 295; J. Drummond, *Philo Judaeus and the Jewish Alexandrian Philosophy*, vol. I (London, 1888), 260.

41 Heinisch, *Das Buch der Weisheit*, xxi, dates it 88–30 BC. Most exegetes put it between 150–50 BC (ibid., n. 5).

42 παιδείας καὶ σοφίας (Prologue to Ecclesiasticus, 1).

43 J. Maritain, *Education at the Crossroads* (New Haven, 1943), I.

therefore, by implication, of humanism.[44] '... God created man to his own image'.[45] The Sapiential Books 'may be called the documents of Israel's humanism ... '.[46] They enshrine the thoughts of her wise men, and form, as has been said, 'a *catena* of pedagogic principles without a parallel in ancient literature'.[47]

'Athens and Jerusalem perfectly embody the two opposite poles of the human mind ... '.[48] Before examining the attitude to Hellenistic humanism exhibited in the one Sapiential Book, the one book of the Bible that shows unmistakable Greek influence,[49] it will make for clearness if we characterize briefly the contrasting Greek and Hebrew conceptions of humanism.

Israel was a people with a mission. They were a people chosen, set apart, protected from pagan contamination. Even things good and lawful were forbidden them lest they impede the great purpose of their preparation. Their body politic was theocratic.[50] Their education was theocentric. 'Think of the Lord in goodness and seek him in simplicity of heart' (Wis 1:1). Its ethos was wisdom, the inculcation not of intrinsic human excellence but of the relational order between man and God. There was little reference to nature and history, no attempt to inform the mind for its own sake.[51] Education was to flower in Wisdom. And Wisdom was a communicated attribute of God. 'All wisdom is from the Lord God and hath been always with him'.[52] In man it took its origin not from the efficacy of any human technique but from the reverent recognition of the order binding creature to Creator. 'The fear of the Lord is the beginning of wisdom'.[53]

If the thoughts of Israel centred on God, those of Greece centred on man. If the ethos of Hebrew humanism was theocentric wisdom, the Greek ideal was anthropocentric *aretē* – a concept, as Marrou remarks,[54] only very lamely translated

44 See W. Jaeger, *Humanism and Theology* (Milwaukee, 1943), 18: 'The point of departure for every humanism must be its conception of human nature'.

45 Gen 1:27. See Maritain, op. cit., 8; A. J. Heschel, *Sacred Images of Man*, in *Religious Education*, vol. 53, no. 2, 97–102.

46 O. S. Rankin, *Israel's Wisdom Literature* (Edinburgh, 1936), 3.

47 *Dict. of the Bible*, vol. I, art., *Education*.

48 Daniel-Rops, op. cit., 245.

49 Ibid., 249.

50 See Josephus, *Con. Ap.*, 2.17.

51 *Dict. of the Bible*, loc. cit., col. 650. Cf. Daniel-Rops, op. cit., 249: 'Wisdom, for the Greeks, was the science that through, the intelligence, increases knowledge; for the Jew it was ... faith, and the fear of God'.

52 Sir 1:1; cf. Wisdom 6:15; Eccles 12:13.

53 Prov 1:7.

54 *Histoire de l'Éducation dans l'Antiquité* (Paris, 1948), 37. '*Areté* was the central idea of all Greek culture' (W. Jaeger, *Paideia*, Eng. tr., vol. I, Oxford, 1939, 13); 'There is no complete equivalent for the word *areté* in modern English' (ibid., 1, 2). 'Une certaine qualité de l'existence' (Marrou, *Histoire*, 37). It is a generic

as virtue. It denoted the native perfection of the human. Its content developed with the progress of philosophical ideas on man and their influence on educational and humanist theory, but constant to it is the idea of a full and harmonious development of the truly human. In Homer, the fountain-head of Greek education,[55] *aretē* summed up the ideal of the aristocratic warrior, the versatile feudal knight whose glory is αἰὲν ἀριστεύειν καὶ ὑπείροχον ἔμμεναι ἄλλων.[56] In the aristocratic Athens of the sixth and fifth centuries, education became more literary, less knightly and feudal. Athletic prowess began to take the place of the Homeric ideal of martial chivalry. *Aretē* meant *kalokagathia*,[57] the fair mind in the fair body. With the development of democracy, to which the sophists were the schoolmasters, all human energies were channelled into political life. The sophistic ideal of excellence became the *homo politicus*,[58] the careerist to whom success was more important than the means by which it was attained.[59] It was away from this relativism and back to the clear lines and eternal essences of philosophic truth that Plato tried to recall Greek idealism.[60] But it was his contemporary rival Isocrates who became the dominant influence in Hellenistic education.[61] With him Greek humanism evolved into its final predominantly literary form. The man of *aretē* was the μουσικὸς ἀνήρ, the man of developed tastes and wide sympathies – Ἀρχὴ μεγίστη τοῦ φρονεῖν τὰ γράμματα.[62]

The essential qualities of Greek and Hebrew can be crystallized and contrasted in a typical line from their respective literatures. Sophocles opens a famous hymn to man – Πολλὰ τὰ δεινὰ κοὐδὲν ἀνθρώπου δεινότερον πέλει.[63] It is man-centred[64] throughout, down to the final sad note which always haunted Greek thinking about the human situation; all things man can do – but he cannot conquer death

term, the content of which evolved with the development of ideas on man and humanism. See Jaeger, op. cit., I, 1–12, 102, 212–15, II, passim; Marrou, *Histoire*, 37, 43, 60, 72, 83, 96, 102, 106, 234.

55 Marrou, *Histoire*, 34ff; Jaeger, *Paideia*, I, 34ff. Cf. Plato, *Rep.*, 10.606e.

56 Iliad, 6.208, 11.784. In Homer's *Areté* there is possibly more of the Renaissance *virtù* than Marrou (loc. cit., 36f) is willing to admit – for a description, see R. A. Tsanoff, *The Moral Ideals of our Civilization* (London, 1947), 86. The 'will-to-power' is in fact a strain that runs through the whole of Greek history – see F. Copleston, *A History of Philosophy*, vol. I (1956), 18. For what follows, see Marrou, *Histoire*, cc. 4–7.

57 Marrou, *Histoire*, 77ff. (An ideal concerning the realization of which he is sceptical).

58 Ibid., 82ff.

59 Ibid., 87.

60 Ibid., 105.

61 Ibid., 122.

62 Quoted Marrou, *Histoire*, 140 (from Preisigke, *Sammelbuch griechischen Urkunden aus Ägypten*, 6218).

63 *Antigone*, 332.

64 See Jaeger, *Paideia*, I, p. xxiii: 'Other nations made gods ... the Greeks alone made man'. Cf. Philo (ap. Eusebium, *Praep. Ev.*, 8, 14, *PG*, 21, 673): μόνη γὰρ ἡ Ἑλλὰς ἀψευδῶς ἀνθρωπογονεῖ.

– Ἄιδα μόνον φεῦξιν οὐκ ἐπάξεται.[65] The Psalmist too has sung the praise of man[66] – he is a little less than the angels, crowned with glory and honour, set over the works of God. But his greatness only points to his insignificance in relation to him whose 'magnificence is elevated above the heavens'. 'What is man that thou art mindful of him?' 'O Lord, how admirable is thy name in the whole earth'.

What would be the reaction of the Jew when Alexandria brought humanism and divinism face to face in their apparent exclusiveness? Would he fly from the dangerous charm of Hellenism – stop his ears with ignorance?[67] Or would he attempt a premature and uncritical synthesis of two contrasting civilizations? Between the two extremes lay the middle way – of grafting on to theocentric revelation what was true and good in anthropocentric humanism. We have traced its blueprint in Philo. We shall find it in the Christians deepened and developed. We find the principle in the Book of Wisdom, already advanced beyond Philo to the speculative level on which Justin and Clement will use it. It is a principle based on the Bible itself – 'God saw all things that he had made and they were very good.'[68] It is echoed again in Wisdom – 'The first author of beauty made all these things.'[69]

These words of the author of Wisdom are more than a principle. They are themselves a symbolic fusion of Hebrew and Greek humanism. For while the argument from creature to Creator is known to the Hebrews,[70] the particular argument from beauty is Greek in its attitude of mind. 'Ein schönes Bild das schon für sich allein, ohne andere Beweise, für einen hellenistischen Verfasser unseres Buches sprechen würde; denn in keinem judäischen Schrift wird man je die Schönheit im griechischen Sinne gepriesen finden'.[71] What impressed the Hebrew mind was less the beauty than the wonder and the power of creation.[72] For the Hebrew the world was the product of creative omnipotence. For the

65 *Antigone*, 360. On the ancient attitude to death, see Möeller, *Sagesse Grecque* (Paris, 1948), 276ff. 'Le sourire grecque cache une grande austerité de l'esprit, une conscience amère de la tristesse de la vie, de la puissance de la mort' (ibid., 293). On Greek pessimism in general, see A. J. Festugiére, *L'Idéal Religieux des Grecs et l'Evangile* (Paris, 1932), 161ff. On the appositeness of the Christian answer, see e.g., S. Angus, *The Mystery Religions and Christianity*, 304ff; M. Arnold, *Pagan and Mediaeval Sentiment*, 208ff (in *Essays in Criticism* [London, 1891]).

66 Ps 8; cf. Ps 143:3–4.

67 The Homeric figure used by Clem. Alex., *Stromata*, 6, 11 (*PG*, 9,309).

68 Gen 1:31

69 Wis 13:3.

70 E.g. Ps 18:1; Is 40:26.

71 Gfrörer, *Philo und die Jüdische-Alexandrinische Philosophie*, II, 212 (apud Farrar, *The Wisdom of Solomon*, in *The Holy Bible. Apocrypha*, ed. A. Wace, vol. I, London, 1888, 407).

72 E.g., Job, cc. 36–41. Cf. Heinisch, op. cit., 256; Farrar, op. cit., 497: 'It is only after contact with the Hellenic mind that we find in Jewish writers such passages as Sir 43:9–11 … '.

Greek, who had no concept of creation,[73] the world was a *cosmos*. It exemplified the reign of reason and law.[74] In its order lay its beauty,[75] not in its power, and much less in the pathetic fallacy of an imagined sympathy with the moods of man.[76] Beauty was a by-product of structure. It was to bring them into communion with the *logos* in things that Plato would have his youths educated amid beautiful sights and sounds. ' ... Beauty, the effluence of fair works, shall flow into the eye and ear ... and insensibly draw the soul from earliest years into likeness and sympathy with the beauty of reason.'[77] Thucydides singles out the love of beauty as one of the marks of the Athenian way of life – Φιλοκαλοῦμέν τε γὰρ μετ' εὐτελείας.[78]

The argument from the imperfect beauty of the world to the supreme and uncreated beauty is Platonic. Whatever is beautiful is such because it shares in the Absolute Beauty.[79] The Symposium is the *locus classicus*. 'Beginning from obvious beauties he must for the sake of that highest beauty be ever climbing aloft as on the rungs of a ladder ... so that in the end he comes to the very essence of beauty.'[80]

Turning to the action of Wisdom in the soul, we find that she 'teacheth temperance and prudence and justice and fortitude'.[81] These are the four Platonic cardinal virtues. Plato studies them in the structure of the state because there they were 'writ large'.[82] But the most important state for Plato is that within man himself.[83] The purpose of harmony in the state was to produce harmony in the soul. There is a war against ourselves going on within us. All men are publicly one another's enemies, and each man is privately his own. The true victory is the victory over self – not the victory of repression but of harmony and reconciliation. Justice is a balancing of tensions. Among the goods of the soul: 'Wisdom is chief and leader ... and next follows temperance; and from the union of these two with courage springs justice ... '.[84]

73 See A. H. Armstrong, *An Introduction to Ancient Philosophy* (London, 1949), 168 and (on *Timaeus*), 48f; A. E. Taylor, *Plato* (London, 1926), 442–44.

74 See Festugière, *L'Idéal*, etc., 177f.

75 Cf. Aristotle, *De Part. Anim.*, 1–5, 645a 23: 'The absence of haphazard and conduciveness of everything to an end are to be found in Nature's works in the highest degree, and the resultant end ... is a form of the beautiful'.

76 See R. W. Livingstone, *The Greek Genius* (Oxford, 1915), 74f.

77 *Rep.*, 3. 401.

78 2. 40.

79 *Phaedo*, 100C.

80 212. According to Taylor, op. cit., 231, the αὐτὸ τὸ καλόν of the *Symp.* is identical with the 'form of good' of the *Rep.*

81 Wis 8:7.

82 *Rep.* 2. 268–369.

83 Ibid., 591. Cf. Marrou, *Histoire*, 119–20; Jaeger, *Paideia*, II, 347ff.

84 *Laws*, 631.

We cannot be sure how far these virtues have here the same meaning they have in Plato – they are not defined in the book. But they cannot have exactly the same meaning, because in Plato they depend on his three-fold division of the soul.[85] What is significant here is the cultural *rapprochement* indicated by the use in revelational religion of this humanist system of moral classification.

The use of Greek terminology does not by itself indicate Greek modification of the Hebrew notion of Wisdom. Content and form must be distinguished. The writer borrowed Greek philosophical expressions, 'not only because he was thinking in Greek channels but because he had the definite purpose of informing the educated Greek reader among his Hellenistic kinsmen, as also all interested Greeks, that in the Old Testament were hid treasures having some similarity with the doctrines of Greek philosophy … '.[86]

This is true in particular of 7:22 ff., where Wisdom is described in terms used by the Stoics of the world-soul. Farrar suggests that the literary form of this passage may have been influenced by a famous fragment of the Stoic Cleanthes, preserved in Clement[87] and in Eusebius,[88] in which the Good is described in a series of 26 epithets, many of which resemble those used in the Book of Wisdom. Whatever be their immediate source, many of the terms are certainly Stoic. In Wisdom is 'the spirit of understanding' – πνεῦμα νοερόν.[89] The Stoics defined God in these words, as 'intelligential spirit'.[90] Wisdom is 'subtle' – like the *nous* of Anaxagoras.[91] Wisdom 'reacheth everywhere' – διήκει δὲ καὶ χωρεῖ διὰ πάντων.[92] These are technical terms used by the Stoics to describe the universal diffusion of the immanent Deity.[93]

85 *Rep.* 4. 435. 'Zahl und Namen der Kardinaltugenden waren in jener Zeit des Eklektizismus Gemeingut aller Gebildeten … Dass der Verfesser dieselben einem bestimmten philosophischen System … entlehnt habe, kann man also nicht behaupten' (Heinisch, op. cit., 161).

86 P. Heinisch, *Theology of the Old Testament* (Minnesota, 1950), 115. Wisdom 8:7 is part of the long eulogy of Wisdom (8:2-18), which, it has been suggested (e.g. Farrar), shows literary dependence on a eulogy of personified Virtue in Xenophon's *Memorabilia*, 2.1.32ff. There are certainly parallels. Both Virtue and Wisdom are said to dwell with God (Wis 8:3); both make their subjects, though young, honoured by the old (Wis 8:10). Both confer valour in war (Wis 8:15). Heinisch (*Weisheit*, 168f) rejects any dependence, but on doctrinal grounds which would not seem to hold against a literary reminiscence.

87 *Protrepticus*, 6 (*PG*, 8, 177); *Strom.*, 5, 14 (*PG*, 9, 168).

88 *Praep. Ev.*, 13, 13 (*PG*, 21, 1121).

89 7, 22.

90 See Stobaeus, *Ecl.*, 1, 58, πνεῦμα νοερὸν καὶ πυρῶδες. Cf. Aetius, in Diels, *Doxog.*, p. 292: Ὀρίζονται δὲ τὴν τοῦ θεοῦ οὐσίαν οἱ Στωϊκοὶ οὕτως: πνεῦμα νοερὸν καὶ πυρῶδες; cf. ibid., 305.

91 7, 22, λεπτόν. The *nous* of Anaxagoras is λεπτότατόν τε πάντων χρημάτων καὶ καθαρώτατον (Diels, *Vors.*, 12). Cf. Wis 7:23–24.

92 7:24.

93 Cf. Aetius (Diels, *Doxog.*, 305) on the πνεῦμα μὲν ἐνδιῆκον δι' ὅλου τοῦ κόσμου (part of a definition of God which became classical in antiquity) – 'on le retrouve presque textuellement dans toutes les anthologies …' (Lebreton, *Theories du Logos, au début de l'ère Chrétienne*, Paris, 1906, 21).

The use of Stoic philosophical terminology does not mean that the author accepts Stoic pantheism. He shows rather that the transcendent God of the Jews is also immanent through the power of his all-pervading and ordering Wisdom. But this does modify his concept of humanism. For Wisdom, which to the Hebrew was primarily transcendent and ethical, for the author of *Wisdom* becomes also an immanent cosmological principle.[94]

For the Hebrew all wisdom is from God – 'the Lord giveth wisdom and out of his mouth cometh prudence and knowledge'.[95] There were different kinds and degrees of wisdom, from wisdom, regulator of the moral life at the highest level, down to wisdom as the source of discernment in the practical conduct of affairs.[96] But throughout it is ethical rather than speculative. 'The Jews had no philosophy, and the books which dealt ... with 'Wisdom' are too popular, too undeveloped, too loosely unsystematic to be dignified with any such title. A nation which was absorbed in the contemplation of a uniquely revealed religion had little or no need for a special philosophy'.[97] Ecclesiasticus, which so highly recommends practical wisdom, declares vain that wisdom which would know the ultimate reason of things. ' ... He that addeth knowledge addeth also labour... In unnecessary matters be not over-curious ... For many are the speculations of the sons of men, and ill imaginings lead astray.'[98] 'A rebuke to Greek philosophizing.'[99]

One of the most obvious traits of the Book of Wisdom is that it broadens this purely ethical connotation of Wisdom. 'Its abstract thought and philosophical speculation tell us that without having left Israel we are on the terrain of Hellenism. In his description of Wisdom the author exhausts the rich philosophical dictionary of Greece. For him too, as in Proverbs, Wisdom is the artificer of all, but he prefers to describe her not in the act of creating the universe but as continually active in penetrating, ordering, and renewing all things ... '.[100] Wisdom 'reacheth from end to end mightily and ordereth all things sweetly'.[101] She imparts knowledge of the inherent

94 Cf. Cornill, *Einleitung in das A.T.* (Tübingen, 1905), 260, apud Heinisch, *Weisheit*, xxxvii: 'Die hebräische Weisheit hat nicht wie die griechische Philosophie die Erkenntnis an sich zum Selbstzweck, sondern sie ist immer und überall durchaus ethisch und religiös bestimmt gedacht; ihre Probleme sind nicht theoretisch-metaphysische, sondern praktisch-religiöse'.

95 Prov 2:6.

96 See Dyson, *A Catholic Commentary on Holy Scripture*, 315a–316d.

97 Farrar, op. cit., 416; cf. *Dict. de la Bible*, V, art. *Philosophie*, col. 313: 'Il n'existe pas, à proprement parler, de philosophie hébraïque; les Hébreux reçoivent de la révélation leurs idées toutes faites.'

98 3:24.

99 Kearns, *A Catholic Commentary*, 398d.

100 Dyson, ibid., 316d.

101 8:1.

structure of the universe – 'the true knowledge of the things that are; to know the disposition of the whole world and the virtues of the elements'.[102]

The author in fact uses current scientific, as he has used current philosophical, terminology. To 'know the disposition of the whole world' is εἰδέναι σύστασιν κόσμου.[103] The term σύστασις in this sense is Platonic.[104] The 'virtue of the elements' is ἐνέργειαν στοιχείων, meaning their effective force. Empedocles was the first to reduce matter to four elements, which he called ῥιζώματα.[105] The use of στοιχεῖα in the same context gained currency from Plato.[106] Those terms would be the parlance of university circles in Alexandria where the book was written. Although the knowledge ascribed to 'Solomon' in 7:17 ff. is based on that of the real Solomon – mainly botany and natural history[107] – it is here extended to include cosmography,[108] physics,[109] astronomy,[110] rhetoric,[111] history[112] and other sciences. It is 'extended into that range of knowledge which was possessed by the most cultivated Jews of Alexandria during the two centuries before Christ'.[113]

In the Museum at Alexandria highly qualified technical and scientific instruction was given. 'On sait que la monarchie lagide dès la fin du règne de Ptolémée I Soter (323–285) avait institué dans sa capitale une remarquable organisation de la recherche scientifique; la faveur royale attirait et retenait à Alexandrie, non seulement des poètes et des lettrés, mais des savants, les plus remarquables chacun dans sa catégorie: géomètres, astronomes, médecins, historiens, critiques et grammairiens.'[114] One is surprised to learn that, in fact, it was only in a centre of higher studies like Alexandria, that Greek technical and professional education in the Hellenistic age *had not got* beyond the method of apprenticeship.[115] And even there the function of the *savants* was research rather than instruction – disinterested pursuit of knowledge made possible by state support.[116]

102 7:17.

103 Ibid.

104 See *Timaeus*, 32.

105 Text in Diels, *Vors.*, 6.

106 *Timaeus*, 48; *Theat.*, 201.

107 See 1 Kings 4:29–34.

108 7:17.

109 7:17.

110 7:19.

111 8:8.

112 8:8.

113 Farrar, op. cit., 463.

114 Marrou, *Histoire*, 201. On the Museum, see Pauly-Wissowa, *Real.-Ency.*, art. *Museion*.

115 Ibid., 263–64.

116 Ibid., 261. He has an interesting reference to the *odium philologicum* aroused by this academic well-being, quoting the *Silloi* of *Timon* (ap. *Athenaeus*, 1, 22): 'Many there be that batten in populous

The difficulties in the way of acquiring Wisdom, as expressed in 9:15, betray the influence of Greek ideas about the nature of man. Wisdom must come from God –'For the corruptible body is a load upon the soul and the earthly habitation presseth down the mind that museth upon many things.' Humanist preconceptions about the Greeks must be modified by the fact that in Greek philosophy, especially after Plato, there is a constant tendency to look on matter as evil.[117] It bred an ascetic and negative attitude to the body, as being, if not positively evil, at least a drag on the soul. Although Plato[118] did not begin this current of thinking, he did most to mould it into a system, under Orphic and Pythagorean influence.[119] The body is the tomb of the soul – σῶμα σῆμα.[120] Only asceticism can so purify the divine element in man – the soul – that it will be able to free itself from the prison of the body. Such thinking was reinforced in Hellenistic times by the influx of mystery cults and redemption religions.[121] Even a fourth-century Christian writer like Gregory Nazianzen can quote the σῶμα σῆμα[122] aphorism in the context of the Christian life. It was this way of thinking that determined the meaning and the importance of philosophy for Plato. It was more than a corpus of speculative knowledge. It was a way of life, whose business above all was the tending of the soul, to deliver it from the burden of the senses and the unreal material world of appearances.[123] Life was a rehearsal for death, a μελέτη θανάτου.[124] Wisdom 9:15 is an echo of the *Phaedo* in particular. For Plato the body is ἐμβριθὲς ... καὶ βαρὺ καὶ γεῶδες;[125] the soul is bound by its weight. For 'Solomon', the body βαρύνει ψυχήν, καὶ βρίθει τὸ γεῶδες σκῆνος νοῦν πολυφρόντιδα.[126]

Naturally the author does not believe that matter is intrinsically evil, any more than did the Greek Fathers who later used the same sources to formulate

---

Egypt, well-propped pedants who quarrel without end in the Muses' bird-cage.' Typically Greek, of course, is the notion that leisure is 'the basis of culture'. Cf. Plato, *Theaet.*, 172; Isocrates, *Areop.*, 44–45. It is symbolized in the derivation of the family of words to which the adjective 'scholastic' belongs. Although the Jews differ in this from the Greeks (cf. Josephus, *Con. Ap.*, 2, 17; Acts 18:3), the Greek idea begins to find an echo in Jewish literature of the Hellenistic period (see e.g., Sir 38:25ff.).

117 See e.g. W. R. Inge, *The Legacy of Greece* (Oxford, 1942), 45.

118 On Plato, see Festugière, *L'Idéal*, 51f; Livingstone, op. cit., 180ff.

119 Festugière, op. cit., 183. Cf. J. K. Feirleman, *Religious Platonism* (London, 1959), 47ff.

120 Plato, *Gorgias*, 493. See Burnet, *Early Greek Philosophy* (London, 1920), 78, 298.

121 Festugière, op. cit., 116ff.

122 *Ep.*, 31.

123 'Philosophy ... may be defined to be the soul's discovery of itself.' (P.E. More, *The Greek Tradition*, vol. 1 [Princeton, 1921], 37 ff., Cf. Jaeger, *Paideia*, vol. II, 37 ff.

124 *Phaedo*, 81A.

125 Ibid., 81C.

126 Wis 9:15. σκῆνος itself in this context is a Platonic term—see Clem. Alex., *Strom.*, 5, 14 (P.G. 9, 140) - γήϊνον σκῆνος.

Christian theology.[127] But he knows that the earth-bound body is a weight on the heaven-ward aspirations of the soul. And his expression of this fact is coloured by the language and the ideas of traditional Greek thinking on the same theme.

How has the author's notion of wisdom and his consequent attitude to humanism been modified by the various Greek elements we have traced in the Book of Wisdom? The details may be crystallized around the author's use of the Greek term παιδεία. The term at first denoted the actual process of education. But its meaning was amplified till in Hellenistic Greek it came to mean the cultural end-product of all that was best in the educational agencies of the time.[128] The Romans made its content more explicit when they translated it as *humanitas*[129] – the full development of the truly human. Isocrates, on whose ideas it was based, had appropriated the Platonic term φιλοσοφία for his rival educational theory.[130] But the content of the term in each is different. For Plato, philosophy is the crown of education, true knowledge and true humanism, to which all other disciplines, literary and scientific, are only preparatory. For Isocrates, the apex of the educational process is not in philosophy but in rhetoric. But it is rhetoric no longer in the formal and pragmatic sophistic sense.[131] It is the Hellenic cultural ideal, a precipitate of all the formative disciplines, among which philosophy in the technical sense is one, and not itself the culmination of all the others, as it is in Plato. In the wider cultural sense it is a comprehensive ideal of *paideia*[132] – taste, sensibility, judgement – almost Newman's ideal of philosophic knowledge.

The LXX translators used the term παιδεία to translate the Hebrew *musar*. It is used in the Book of Wisdom too, which was originally written in Greek. The Vulgate translates it *disciplina*. The Latin word might mean either 'instruction' or 'chastisement'. The commentators, however, say that the Hebrew discipline word means 'not the instruction of the intellect but the discipline or education of the

127 In particular mystical theology. See Jaeger, *Paideia*, II, 414, n. 39. Festugière, *Contemplation et Vie contemplative selon Platon* (Paris, 1950), 5. The author of Wisdom need have known the Platonic passage only at second or third hand. 'Die ähnlichkeit mit der Stelle bei Plato erklärt sich ... daraus, dass der Dialog *Phaedo* in Altertum sehr häufig gelesen wurde' (Heinisch, *Weisheit*, 188, who lists ancient passages where its influence is evident).

128 Marrou, *Histoire*, 143f.

129 'Which, since the time of Varro and Cicero at least, possessed a nobler and severer sense in addition to its early vulgar sense of humane behaviour ... It meant the process of educating man into his true form, the real and genuine human nature' (Jaeger, *Paideia*, I, xxiii). Cf. Aulus Gellius, *Noct. Att.*, 13. 17; Marrou, *Augustin*, Note A, *L'Idée de Culture et le Vocabulaire Latin*, 549f.

130 E.g., *Antidosis*, 270.

131 See Marrou, *Histoire*, 131–3.

132 So that 'the name Hellenes suggests no longer a race but an intelligence ... ' (*Panegyr.* 50).

moral nature ... '.[133] This then must be the meaning of the Greek παιδεία where it is used to translate the Hebrew *musar*. In this sense it gives an insight into the nature of that wisdom which was the ethos of Hebrew humanism, and which Hebrew education aimed at inculcating. It connoted a moral and ethical, rather than personal and intellectual, formation. In so far as it was intellectual, it was the better to ground the will in the knowledge of man's relation to God. For 'the fear of the Lord is the beginning of Wisdom'.[134] 'She will bring upon him fear and dread and trial: and she will scourge him with the affliction of her discipline, till she try him by her laws and trust his soul.'[135] Says Ecclesiasticus again: 'Who will set scourges over my thoughts and the discipline of Wisdom over my heart ... ?'[136]

Paideia, then, or *musar*, as an expression of Wisdom, shows that Wisdom to be more ethical or moral than intellectual and humanist. Its intellectual content is subordinated to the orientation of man in the right order of a theocentric world-vision. It is a concept of Wisdom which emerges clearly from the Book of Wisdom itself. According to 1:4-5, 'Wisdom will not enter into a malicious soul ... For the Holy Spirit of discipline will flee from the deceitful ... '. The word-order here connects *paideia* with πνεῦμα, not with δόλον. The context moreover suggests a moral connotation for παιδεία. This apart from the significance of the word itself: 'παιδεία, meist Übersetzung von *musar*, bedeutet Züchtigung, dann Belehrung, Zurechtweisung endlich das Resultat der Erziehung, die "Zucht" im Sinne des rechten sittlichen Verhaltens, des gottgefälligen Lebens vgl. Sap. 6:17, 7:14. '[137] In 6:17 we are told that, of Wisdom, ἀρχὴ γὰρ αὐτῆς ἡ ἀληθεστάτη παιδείας ἐπιθυμία. The adjective may be coupled with either ἀρχὴ or with ἐπιθυμία, but it will not affect the meaning of παιδείας. It is clear that *paideia* can still retain its usual sense of moral discipline. But primary here, it would seem, is an intellectual, though not yet a cultural, connotation. Heinisch interprets: ' ... über ihr Wesen, ihren Wert und den Weg, der zu ihr führt, belehrt zu werden (*paideia*) ist nötig, um die Weisheit zu gewinnen.'[138] In 7:14 it is declared that Wisdom 'is an infinite treasure to men which they that use become the friends of God, being commended for the gifts of discipline διὰ τὰς ἐκ παιδείας δωρεὰς συσταθέντες.' Heinisch distinguished the two previous passages in commenting: 'Mag *paideia* das religiös-sittlichen Leben nach Gottes Geboten bedeuten (vgl. I :5), oder aber den Unterricht über die Weisheit (6:17).'[139]

133 *Dict. of the Bible*, vol. 1, s.v. *Discipline*, cf. *Catholic Commentary*, 214d; *Int. Crit. Comment.*, on Deut. 4:36; 11:2.

134 Prov 1:7.

135 Sir 4:19.

136 Ibid., 23:2.

137 Heinisch, *Weisheit*, in loc.

138 Ibid., in loc.

139 Ibid., in loc.

Even if the following passage, in which the author prays for the power to describe Wisdom worthily, is not to be taken closely with 7:14, it cannot be left out of account in evaluating the concepts of Wisdom and *paideia* in the book as a whole. And from this point of view it seems clear that *paideia* must be given an intellectual and speculative connotation, not merely in the sense it has in 6:17, of knowing how to attain to wisdom, but in the humanist sense of an acquired body of profane learning – 'culture entendue au sens objectif, perfectif.'[140] It is expressed, in the Authorized Version, 'by the gifts that come from learning'.

It has already been noted that ideas and expressions here are taken from Greek science and philosophy. The range of knowledge ascribed to the gift of God, 'the guide of wisdom and the director of the wise'[141] is that of a contemporary Alexandrian Hellenist. As affecting the concept of humanism this implies an extension of the notion of Wisdom from a purely moral and ethical content to embrace also the subjects of profane learning. It is as if the touch of Greek speculation had suddenly opened the eyes of the Hebrew to the mysteries of the created world, which he had missed in his concentration on the mysteries of God. The quest of truth, which hitherto had studied the cosmos in its relation to the Creator, now begins to see it under the equally real aspect of its own intrinsic structure – εἰδέναι σύστασιν κόσμου.[142] Creation is not solely an exercise of Omnipotence, drawing existence out of nothingness. It is an exercise of Wisdom – reaching from end to end of the universe and ordering all things – permeating reality with law and order and harmony – the aspect of being that had most fascination for the speculative and scientific mind of the Greek.[143] 'Thou hast ordered all things in measure and number and weight', says the author of the Book of Wisdom.[144]

This lacing of Hebrew matter with the colours of Greek system is expressed *in nuce* in 2:7, where God is said to have 'made the world out of formless matter'. This is a reference back to the account of Genesis 1:2: 'And the earth was void and empty.'[145] The LXX translated the expression 'void and empty' as 'invisible and unarranged', referring to the state of primeval matter before God in his secondary act of creation had imposed order on the original chaos. The Book of Wisdom puts the same idea into the terms of Greek cosmology, according to which eternal, uncreated matter was arranged by Intelligence

140 Marrou, *Augustin*, vii.

141 Wis 7:15

142 'The intellectual curiosity which gave rise to speculations about nature ... is not characteristic of the Hebrew. Hence it is that speculative Wisdom has little place in the Sacred Books.''(Dyson, *Catholic Commentary*, 316 c). But this is precisely the advance of the Book of Wisdom.

143 See e.g., Aristotle, *De Part. Anim.*, 15, 645a.

144 Wis 11:21.

145 Hebrew *tohu wabohu*.

into a Cosmos.[146] ὕλη is the Aristotelian term for this prime matter,[147] which is called ἄμορφος by Plato.[148] This is the provenance of the expression in 11:17: κτίσασα τὸν κόσμον ἐξ ἀμόρφου ὕλης.[149]

Such are the ideas that go to make up the 'gifts of learning'. 'The stuff is still Hebrew but shot as it were with hues reflecting the light of Western speculation.'[150] In the concept of *paideia*, Hellenic and Hebrew have fused. The theocentric circle, if it has not become an ellipse with two centres, has at least extended its radius to take in the anthropocentric. The Wise Man of the Law need not be an *apaideutos*. *Chokmah*, wisdom, the gift of God that has also its finality in him, is shot through with *aretē*, the intrinsic human excellence that was the ethos of Greek humanism from Homer down.

There is another aspect to the ideas we have been considering. The *aretē*-wisdom rapprochement which they reveal is grounded not on mere sympathy, still less on the harmonizing allegorism of a Philo, or on the pseudo-historicism of an Aristobulus. The author of Wisdom preserves the unity of the sacred and the profane, in history and in truth, by an implicit theory of speculative monism.

In the third century AD, when he wishes to express the Christian universalist *Selbstbewusstsein*, that 'the barbarian philosophy is alone perfect and true',[151] Clement of Alexandria will quote Wis 7:17–22, and comment: 'Among all these he comprehends natural science which treats of all the phenomena in the world of sense. And ... he alludes also to intellectual objects ... You have in brief the professed aim of our philosophy ... '. Further, he quotes 7:16 (and 14:2) in support of a theocentric theory of philosophy and the arts.[152] 'For in his hands, "that is in his power and wisdom",[153] are both we and our words and all wisdom[154] and skill in works.' Again he uses 8:8 to describe the gnostic, and ascribes all such knowledge to Wisdom: 'Seest thou the fountain of instructions that takes its rise from Wisdom?'[155]

146 E.g., Armstrong, op. cit., 47f.

147 E.g., *Phys.*, IV 2, 209 b 11–17.

148 *Timaeus*, 51A.

149 'Also stimmt er mit der griechischen Philosophie insofern überein, als er die ἄμορφος ὕλη als das Chaos ... denkt. Damit ist aber noch nicht bewiesen den Gedankebewiesen, dass er mit dieser Vorstellung ebenso wie die griechische Philosophie den Gedanken verbindet, dass die Materie unerschaffen und ewig sei' (Heinisch, *Weisheit*, 226). This was one of the Gnostic heresies against which Christians had later to contend – cf. Clem. Alex. *Strom.* 2,16 (*PG* 8, 1012).

150 Farrar, op. cit., 407.

151 *Strom.*, 2,2 (*PG* 8, 933).

152 Strom., 6,11 (*PG* 9,313).

153 σοφία.

154 φρόνησις.

155 *Strom.*, 6, 11 (*PG* 9, 313).

The passages quoted by Clement clearly imply a speculative monism, in that they make Wisdom the source of all knowledge, profane as well as sacred. But in their context these passages become richer and more significant still. It has been noted already that 'Solomon' clothes divine and transcendent Wisdom in the attributes of Stoic immanentism. It is λεπτόν, subtle, like the *nous* of Anaxagoras. Like the Stoic *logos*, πνεῦμα μὲν ἐνδιῆκον δι' ὅλου τοῦ κόσμου, it 'reacheth everywhere' because of its purity. The Transcendent Wisdom that sits by the throne of God (9:4), now becomes also in effect the *mens agitans molem*,[156] which reaches from end to end and orders all things (8:1). She becomes the fount of the knowledge not only of God (8:4) but of the science of all the things that exist – the structure of the cosmos and the power of the elements (7:17). In the single concept of universally active Wisdom, at once transcendent in its nature and immanent in its effects, the author of Wisdom has found a principle which, while affirming Jewish universalism without having recourse to the naive theory of plagiarism, so guarantees the unity of truth in its origins and of history in its progress, that the Hebrew sage is justified in fusing his theocentric wisdom with Greek anthropocentric *paideia*.

Thus, although earlier than Philo, 'Solomon' has superseded the monistic historicism and the allegorizing harmonistics of Alexandro-Jewish apologetics with a theory of speculative monism, to which Justin and Clement are in the direct line of succession. Although Justin too, as a consequence of the fulfilment of Judaism in the Incarnation, is enabled to add a further stage to the progressive development of the theory of Christian humanism, the basic principle of his monism is identical with that of the author of the Book of Wisdom. The philosophical principle of unity, which the one finds in universally active Wisdom, the other finds in the universally active *Logos*. But the *Logos*-idea, which Justin takes from the Christian Johannine tradition, is in part a development of the Wisdom-speculation of the Old Testament and of the Book of Wisdom itself.[157]So that essentially they are both using the same principle to solve the same problem. Moreover, to make it serve their purpose, they both put this seed of unity through the same process. They fuse the transcendent *Logos* of revelation with the immanent *logos* of Stoicism[158] and the universal *nous* of Anaxagoras. The transcendent Author of the universe, the source of God-knowledge, becomes one in his effects with the

156 Virgil, *Aeneid*, 6,727.

157 A. Puech, *Les Apologistes Grecs du IIme Siècle* (Paris, 1912); Rankin, op. cit., x-xi; Heinisch, *Weisheit*, xlix f; Drummond, op. cit., I, 140–3, 226; A. L. Feder, *Justins des Martyrs Lehre von Jesus Christus*, 143–5.

158 On the Stoic *Logos*, see Lebreton, *Histoire du dogme de la Trinité*, I, 62 f; Lagrange, 'Vers le *Logos* de Saint Jean', *Rev. Bibl.*, 32 (1923), 161–76. 'Pour un Stoicien le monde est régi per la raison ... or la raison c'est le *logos* en grec'(ibid., 175). Wisdom also speaks of a *logos* (2:2; 16:12), but 'his language here does not in itself transgress Old Testament usage' (Drummond, op. cit., I, 227).

immanent principles of order, reason and law in his Creation, the *Weltvernunft* which is the source of world-knowledge, of profane science and art. In a deeper sense than Philo attained, revelation is the 'true and genuine philosophy'.

HELLENISM AND JUDEO-CHRISTIAN HISTORY IN CLEMENT OF ALEXANDRIA

Although the question which faced the early Church – the significance of Hellenism for Christianity – is a perennial question independent of historical contexts, because in essence it represents the 'vast problem of humanism', its statement is nevertheless defined by historical circumstances.[159] The abstract problem is embodied in concrete historical situations. This is particularly true in the case of Clement of Alexandria.[160] Though for Alexandria the age of the apologists has ended, the dialogue which they initiated between two worlds continues under the stress of new questions. It is from the answers to the questions forced upon Clement by the peculiar Alexandrian milieu[161] that we elicit his solution to the problem of reconciling Christian universalism – under its complementary aspects of history and values[162] – with the fact of an apparently independent tradition of profane history, and an apparently independent corpus of profane values.

Once the problem is so stated it is obvious that the meaning of Hellenism in history is a question logically prior to the meaning of Hellenic values in the Christian life. The answer to the one will to some extent determine the answer to the other. This article will therefore concentrate on Clement's notion of the function of Hellenism in history. It is not intended to be either exhaustive or speculative – the relation of Hellenism to Christianity is a many-sided problem. But as suggested elsewhere,[163] the humanist aspect of the problem is not always seen in its real dimensions. All that is attempted here is to outline what Clement actually says, in the light of an idea inherent in Christianity itself – what we

159 E. Seeberg, 'Geschichte und Geschichtsanschauung', *Zeitschr.f. Kirchengeschichte* 60 (1941), 309–31.

160 'Né vers 150, probablement à Athènes, et dans le paganisme; il ne nous a pas raconté sa conversion; on peut avec vraisemblance y voir le terme d'une longue recherche de Dieu telle que celle que nous a décrite Justin'. Died c. 215. (Fliche & Martin, *Histoire de l'Église*, II, 228ff.).

161 On Alexandria, see e.g. R. B. Tollington, *Clement of Alexandria*, I, 31–63; C. Mondésert, *Clément d'Alexandrie*, 27-45; E. de Faye, *Clément d'Alexandrie*, 10ff.

162 See T. Finan, 'Hellenistic Humanism in the Book of Wisdom', *Irish Theological Quarterly*, 27 (1960), 30–48, especially 30–1 [see above pp. 23-41].

163 Ibid.

have called Christian universalism, or the finality of the Christian event in history and the primacy of Christian truth in value-judgements.

CLEMENT AND ALEXANDRIA

Although Justin conducted a private school at Rome[164] – analogous to the philosophic schools of the time[165] – its purpose was solely the teaching of Christian doctrine.[166] It is in Alexandria, a city already famous for its schools, and the meeting-place of all the intellectual currents of the Hellenistic world,[167] that we first hear of Christian teachers who, though the penetration of Christian truth was the supreme purpose of their instruction, grounded this purpose in an integral ideal of intellectual formation towards which every branch of human knowledge, profane and sacred, was levied for contribution. In Alexandria, according to St Jerome, 'a Marco evangelista semper ecclesiastici fuere doctores, tantae prudentiae et eruditionis tam in Scripturis divinis quam in saeculari litteratura ... '.[168] Of the men who made up this supposed Christian tradition of secular learning – 'men of great ability and zeal for divine things'[169] – the first of whom there is reliable historical evidence is the Sicilian Pantaenus[170] – 'especially conspicuous, as he has been educated in the philosophical system of those called Stoics ... '.[171] According to Eusebius,[172] it is to Pantaenus as his teacher that Clement of Alexandria refers when he presents his work as 'a rough sketch of those powerful and animated words which it was my privilege to hear, as well as of blessed and truly remarkable men. Of these the one – the Ionian – was in Greece, the other in Magna Graecia ... There were others in the East ... But when I met with the last – in ability truly the first – having hunted him out in his concealment in Egypt, I found rest.'[173] In a sentence not quoted by Eusebius Clement

164 Fliche & Martin, op. cit., I, 431ff.

165 Harnack, *The Mission and Expansion of Christianity*, I, 365f.

166 Bardy, 'L'église et l'enseignement pendant les trois premiers siècles', *Revue des Sciences Religieuses*, 12 (1932), 1–28. He remarks (p. 27) 'qu'il n'y avait pas eu, a cette époque, d'école proprement chrétienne pour l'enseignement élementaire et moyen ... '. Marrou (*Histoire*, 421) notes the same surprising fact – 'aussi longtemps que dure l'antiquité, les chrétiens, sauf quelques cas exceptionnels et limités, n'ont pas créé d'écoles qui leur fussent propres ... '. Cf. Hagendahl, *Latin Fathers and the Classics*, 311.

167 'I contatti con la cultura classica, con le naturali conseguenze di chiarimento e di arricchimento del pensiero cristiano, dovevano divenire piu frequenti e piu intensi là dove più vivi operavano i fermenti dell' intelligenza antica' (Pellegrino, 'La Cultura Cristiana', *Convivium*, 22 (1954), 263).

168 Jerome, *De Viris Illustribus*, 36 (*PL*. 23. 651).

169 Eusebius, *Hist. Eccl.*, 5.11.

170 Lived c.180 (P. Chiocchetta, *Theologia della Storia*, 71).

171 Eusebius, loc. cit.

172 Cf. W. Bousset, *Jüdisch-Christlicher Schulbetrieb in Alexandria und Rom*, 263.

173 Clem., *Strom.*, 1, 1 (*PG*, 8, 700). 'On a souvent cherché a identifier les maîtres à qui Clement a été

adds: 'He, the true Sicilian bee, gathering the spoil of the flowers of the prophetic and apostolic meadow, engendered in the souls of his hearers a deathless element of knowledge (γνῶσις).'

In this rise of a Christian centre of higher culture[174] two elements may be singled out as helping to determine in the concrete the general problem of the relation of Hellenistic humanism to the Christian revelation. Firstly, the very fact of the rise of an institution of higher Christian studies implies an approach to Christian truth which is no longer that of implicit faith in the deposit of revelation. Belief is to be brought under the order of the searching and systematizing intellect. And at once the question arises where the intellect is to find its instruments – what will be its attitude to those that have been fashioned by Hellenism? Secondly, Christian penetration into the more cultivated spheres of the pagan world produced a type of Christian, and with him a problem, that was unknown to Christian apologists before Clement. It would be a questionable missionary method, even if in the abstract it were desirable, to require the cultivated convert to discard the whole apparatus of higher thinking and more sophisticated living which he brought with him from Hellenism to the Church.[175]

And yet – even if the aberrations of heresy were not there to remind her[176] – the Church was still young enough to feel the urgency in the forthright warnings of St Paul against 'these new intruding forms of speech, this quibbling knowledge that is knowledge only in name ... '.[177] How to reconcile divine truth with human learning when the Apostle himself of the Gentiles had insisted: 'Take care not to let anyone cheat you with his philosophizings, with empty fantasies drawn from human tradition, from worldly principles: they were never Christ's teaching.'[178] Add to this the peculiar Alexandrian phenomenon of the gnostic, the type

redevable de sa formation chrétienne. Il est possible que l'Ionien soit Athénagore, que l'Assyrien soit Tatien, que le judéo-chrétien soit Hégésippe ... Il semble du moins assuré que le dernier est Pantène' (Bardy, *La conversion au christianisme*, 130, n. 2).

174 I have refrained from specifying it more definitely; in the opinion of Bardy ('Aux origins de l'École d'Alexandrie', *Recherches de science religieuse*, 27 (1937), 65–90, both Pantaenus and Clement were private individuals with no official sanction. 'Die Katechetenschule in Alexandria ist spätter als Klemens gestiftet. Die Schule des Pantainos und Klemens waren freie Unternehmungen, die mit ihren persönlichen Lehrertät entstehen und mit ihr auch vergehen'. (J. Munck, *Untersuchungen über Klemens von Alexandria*, Stuttgart, 1933, 185). Origen would be the first who taught profane science in an official capacity. Cf. Bardy, 'L'église et l'enseignement pendant les trois premiers siècles', *Rev. des sc. rel.*, 12 (1932), 18.

175 See De Faye, op. cit., 120ff.; Wagner, 'Wert und Verwertung der griechischen Bildung im Urteil des Clemens von Alexandrien', *Zeitschr. f. Wissenschaftl. Theol.*, 45 (1902), 213.

176 'Haereses a philosophia subornantur' (Tertullian, *De Praescript.*, 7). See Wagner, op. cit., 217ff.

177 1 Tim 6:20.

178 Col. 2:8. Cf. Strom., 1.11 (*PG*. 8.749).

of the perfect Christian who, while presupposing faith as the foundation of the Christian life, in the Clementine ideal transcends it in a higher form of knowledge or *gnosis*[179] – and you have the elements of that interior conflict which was apparent in Christianity at the end of the second and the beginning of the third century, and expressed itself in a certain tension between the upholders of simple faith[180] and the defenders of higher learning:

> Les nouveaux convertis ... ont renié les illusions de leur paganisme ... mais d'instinct beaucoup demandent à l'Église ce qu'ils ont toujours poursuivi: une connaissance religieuse digne de leur science ... Mais si quelques esprits d'élite ressentent ces exigences et réclament du théologien ces efforts, les simples s'en effraient souvent et ne voient dans toute cette science que verbiage, dans toutes ces récherches que témérité.[181]

Among contemporary attitudes to those 'two cultures' we find the two characteristic views which divide opinion in the early Church – which indeed must always divide opinion on a lasting problem.[182] Neither view is without initial justification.[183] There can be no doubt – once the question is put in that form – which is the more important, the faith of the simple or the intellect of the learned, the ability to feel or the ability to define compunction. And Tertullian,[184] contemporary of Clement, is the Tatian of his day, for whom there is nothing in common between Athens and Jerusalem. But like poetry, more constant than the theories that try to explain it, the humanist attitude is not amenable to the logic of the absolutist – perhaps because it is itself an approach to reality which follows its own logic. For practical reasons alone the puritanical absolutism of a Tertullian would be impossible in an atmosphere like that of Alexandria, where Hellenism represented the best that was known and thought in the world, not merely the syllogistic scaffolding of the mind but an ethos of vital values which must be reconcilable with

179 Fliche & Martin, op. cit., II, p. 363. On heretical gnosis see Bigg, *Christian Platonists of Alexandria*, 53-62; De Faye, op. cit., 123ff.

180 On the 'simpliciores' see Camelot, *Foi et gnose*, 17f.; De Faye, op. cit., 126ff.

181 Fliche & Martin, op. cit., II, 361.

182 See H. I. Morrou, *Saint Augustin et la fin de la Culture Antique*, 352: 'ou ce mépris pour les valeurs culturelles proprement humaines, cette hantise des exigences de l'éternel ... elle traduit l'une des quelques options fondamentales qui se présentent à l'âme religieuse'.

183 See Pellegrino, art. cit., 269, on 'la tensione dialettica immanente alla cultura cristiana, che, ove venga meno il '*Sensus Ecclesiae*', devia nell' eresia, mentre nel cristiano che viva in pienezza la vita della Chiesa è stimolo a quell' arricchimento di chi si diceva, anche se l'intervento del magistero, o l'opera di decantazione che è frutto del tempo fara cadere certi elementi di cui da principio non si scorgeva la precarietà'.

184 On Tertullian see Bardy, art. cit., 6ff.; also his *Conversion*, 235ff.

higher intellectual truth, which Christianity could not deny, and could supersede only by transcending it and integrating it in a higher synthesis.[185] To achieve this synthesis was the effort of Clement, the disciple of Pantaenus.

> La soluzione di Clemente, figlio di pagani e convertitosi dal paganesimo, vuol essere una rivalutazione della teologia colta sopra la semplice fede dell' indotto; e, pertanto, una riabilitazione della filosofia ellenica, la quale sola ... può addestrare a una comprensione e ad un esercizio più pieno del messaggio cristiano.[186]

Thus the meaning and the historical purpose of Greek philosophy are central problems in Clement's thinking.[187] 'It is a feat fit for the gardener to pluck without injury the rose that is growing among the thorns; and for the craftsman to find out the pearl buried in the oyster's flesh ... If anyone ... wants to arrive[188] at the truth in the numerous Greek plausibilities, like the real face beneath masks, he will hunt it out with much pain.'[189] He returns to the theme again and again throughout the books of the *Stromata*. He seeks to define philosophy,[190] to distinguish it from sophistic, to determine whether it has a lasting value, above all what is its connection in the scheme of things with the revelation that has come through Christ.

It is obvious that his own prepossessions give him a sympathy towards Greek philosophy as having a part to play even in the Christian life. Regardless of whether philosophy is to be ultimately accepted or rejected, the Christian must philosophize. 'For no one can condemn a thing without first knowing it; the consequence ... is that we must philosophize.'[191] If philosophy has to be discarded, the demonstration of such a necessity is itself beneficial.[192] The Greeks must not be condemned

185 ' ... C'est la question capitale de l'époque' (De Faye, op. cit., 117).

186 Chiocchetta, op. cit., 77. 'In tal modo il Cristianesimo rispondeva coi fatti numero di gente ignorante e di schiavi divenuti discepoli di Cristo (Orig., *Con. Cels.*, 6.14) e dimostrava inconsistenti i timori del filosofo di veder scomprire dall' umanità la sapienza a causa di questi uomini che si disinteressano dei valori di cultura e di civiltà (Orig., *Con. Cels.*, 8.68)'. Pellegrino, art. cit., 263.

187 'Clément est parfaitement au courant de l'histoire de la philosophie grecque, de ses écoles et de leurs différents représentants.' Camelot, 'Clément d'Alexandrie et l'utilisation de la philosophie grecque', *Recherches sc. rel.*, 21 (1931), 541–69.

188 Reading διεληλυθέναι.

189 *Strom.*, 2.1 (*PG.* 8.933).

190 E.g. *Strom.*, 1.4 (*PG.* 8.716); 1.5 (*PG.* 8.717); 1.19 (*PG.* 8.809); 1.20 (*PG.* 8.813); 6.7 (*PG.* 9.277). With this definition cf. 6.17 (*PG.* 9.393); Paid., 2.2 (*PG.* 8.420); Philo, *De Cong. Erud.*, 1.530; Cicero, *De Off.*, 2.2.

191 *Strom.*, 6.18 (*PG.* 9.396) (from Aristotle, see Molland, 'Clem. of Alex. on the Origin of Greek Philosophy', *Symbolae Osloenses*, fasc. 15⁵16, p. 59.

192 *Strom.*, 1.2 (*PG.* 8.709).

by those who know them only on hearsay, with no basis of personal investigation. Only 'the refutation which is based on experience is entirely trustworthy'.[193] Where truth is concerned it is not the speaker that is of primary importance but what he says.[194] Clement will accept truth from any source if as truth it is authenticated. Even the arguments of those who condemn philosophy as a work of the Devil are less compelling than they think.[195] According to Scripture,[196] 'the Devil is transformed into an angel of light ...' 'But if he prophesies as an angel of light, he will speak what is true. And if he prophesies what is angelical and of the light, then he prophesies what is beneficial ... Philosophy is not then false, though the thief and the liar speak through a transformation of operation.'[197]

Nevertheless for Clement as for Justin, any truth the Greek tradition may contain proves no historical independence in face of Christian universalism. There is but one true philosophy. Christianity alone is original and complete. Only the barbarian philosophy which Christians follow is really 'perfect and true'.[198] It imparts not divine knowledge alone but the whole circle of knowledge, sacred and profane. According to 'Solomon', God as the Author of eternal Wisdom has given '"the unerring knowledge of things that exist, to know the constitution of the world",[199] and so forth ... Among all these he comprehends natural science, which treats of all the phenomena in the world of sense. And in continuation he alludes also to intellectual objects ... "And what is hidden or manifest I know; for Wisdom, the artificer of all things taught me". You have in brief the professed aim of our philosophy ... '.[200]

CHRISTIANITY THE 'TRUE PHILOSOPHY'

The designation of Christianity as a philosophy, the true and perfect philosophy, is itself in effect a proclamation of Christian universalism. The Christian synthesis must go deeper than a surface reconciliation of the tenets of Greek philosophy and Christian revelation. It is Christianity which is at once original and final – *la*

193 Ibid.: πιστὸς γὰρ εὖ μάλα ὁ μετ' ἐμπειρίας ἔλεγχος.

194 *Strom.*, 6.8 (*PG.* 9.288): οὐδὲ μὴν διὰ τὸν λέγοντα προκαταγνωστέον ἀμαθῶς καὶ τῶν λεγομένων, ... , ἀλλὰ τὰ λεγόμενα σκοπητέον, εἰ τῆς ἀληθείας ἔχεται..

195 Ibid.

196 2 Cor 11:14.

197 κατὰ μετασχηματισμὸν ἐνεργείας. Cf. *Strom.*, 1.20 (*PG.* 8.817): 'The thief possesses really what he has possessed himself of dishonestly ... '; *Strom.*, 6.17 (*PG.* 9.395), on why the Serpent is called φρόνιμος (Gen 3:1): ἐπεὶ κἀν τοῖς πονηρεύμασιν ἔστιν εὑρεῖν ἀκολουθίαν τινὰ, καὶ διάκρισιν καὶ σύνθεσιν ...

198 *Strom.*, 2.2 (*PG.* 8.933): φιλοσοφία ... τελεία τῷ ὄντι καὶ ἀληθής. On the senses of the word φιλοσοφία in Clement, see Camelot, art. cit., 541f.; Bardy, '"Philosophie" et "Philosophe" dans le vocabulaire chrétien des premiers siècles', *Rev. ascét. myst.*, 25 (1949), 97–108; de Faye, op. cit., 158ff.

199 Wis 7:17ff.

200 *Strom.*, 2.2 (*PG.* 8.936). Cf. Finan, art. cit., 46f. (= above, 40f.).

fin des choses.[201] Even though philosophy is not in fact an invention of 'the thief and the liar',[202] it is nevertheless in origin and in purpose a function of the true and perfect philosophy of the Judeo-Christian tradition.

The implications of calling Christianity the true philosophy can be understood only against the background of what philosophy meant to the Greek tradition itself. 'Bref, la philosophie qui, pour nous, n'est guère autre chose que l'étude a peu près stérile des questions métaphysiques et morales, est pour un grand nombre d'anciens une règle et une mèthode de vie … '.[203] This is true not only of the later schools which were consciously moral rather than speculative,[204] but seems to have been true from the first origins of Greek philosophy, and certainly after Plato. 'The search for truth is one which might be undertaken for more than one reason, and in fact the philosophy of the West has a twofold beginning in different quarters of the Greek world and under the impulse of different desires. The first beginning came among the Ionians, round about 600 BC, and its driving impulse seems to have been that which Aristotle sets as the beginning of all philosophy, wonder … The basic Ionian question is "I wonder why things are as they are …?" In the second beginning, in the Greek cities of South Italy during the second half of the sixth century the desire behind the search for truth was different. It was the desire for deification, for likeness to God … the basic Italian Pythagorean question is "How may I deliver myself from the body of this death, from the sorrowful weary wheel of mortal existence …?"'[205]

Pythagoreanism was a synthesis of the two ideals – the scientific ideal of Ionia, and the religious ideal of Italy and the Orphics.[206] 'The greatest purification of all is … science, and it is the man who devotes himself to that, the true philosopher, who has most effectively released himself from the wheel of birth … '.[207] Philosophy has this deeper meaning wherever the influence of Pythagoras can be traced, and especially in Plato.[208] 'That is the idea so nobly

201 J. Daniélou, 'Christianisme et histoire', *Études*, 254 (1947), 166–84.

202 *Strom*, 6.8 (*PG*. 9.288).

203 Bardy, op. cit., 47.

204 'A mésure que l'on approche de l'ère chrétienne, la philosophie incline à l'éthique' (Festugière, *L'idéal religieux des grecs et l'évangile*, 203).

205 A.H. Armstrong, *Introduction to Ancient Philosophy*, 1.

206 Cf. Festugière, op. cit., app.: 'Les origines de l'idée de Dieu chez Platon'.

207 Burnet, *Early Greek Philosophy*, 98.

208 Jaeger, 'Über Ursprung und Kreislauf des Philosophischen Lebensideals', *Sitz. der Preuss. Akad. der Wiss.* (1928), 390–421, denies that the ideal of the philosophic *bios* is earlier than Plato. 'Das Ideal des der Erkenntnis geweihten Bios ist erst eine Schöpfung Platos dessen Ethik mehrere entgegengesetzte Lebenstypen, (Bioi) aufstellt und in der "Wehe des besten Lebens" gipfelt'. (Ibid., 392). The traditional pre-Socratic representatatives 'eines eigentümlichen Lebensstils der geistigen Konzentration' are really projections on the past of post-Platonic ideals (Ibid., 387). Cf. Jaeger, 'Die Griechen und das Philosophische Lebensideal', *Zeitschr. f. Philos. Forschung*, 11 (1957), 481–96.

expressed in the Phaedo ... This way of regarding philosophy is henceforth characteristic of the best Greek thought. Aristotle is as much influenced by it as any one, as we may see from the Tenth Book of the *Ethics*,[209] and as we should see still more clearly if we possessed his *Protreptikos* in its entirety.'[210] With this work of his youth Aristotle created a literary genre which in the Graeco-Roman world formed 'tutto un ambiente di cultura',[211] and is echoed by many Christian writers.[212] In its pagan form the genre culminated in the *Hortensius* of Cicero, the reading of which was the occasion of the first conversion of St Augustine.[213]

It was not in an exclusively moral or contemplative sense that philosophy became a *bios*.[214] It embodies a complete cultural ideal. 'Elle suppose en fait une rupture avec la culture commune ... Elle suppose ... un idéal de vie qui prétend informer l'homme tout entier.'[215] It embodies one of the two rival Greek ideals of humanism, one of the expressions of their 'aspiration nostalgique vers une totalité humaine'.[216] From the moment when the two ideals of humanism, the literary and the philosophic, were formulated by Isocrates and Plato respectively, they disputed supremacy within the Greek cultural tradition.[217] An indirect illustration of the universalism implied in the humanist ideal of philosophy is contained in the fact that the upholders of the tradition of Isocrates resented the appropriation of the term philosophy by the philosophers strictly so called – 'les rhéteurs de la Seconde Sophistique, comme déjà Isocrate,[218] revendiquaient ... le beau titre de philosophe pour leur idéal de l'orateur'.[219]

209 Cf. E. Gilson, *L'esprit de la philosophie mediévale* (Paris, 1932), 30 (Première Série).

210 Burnet, op. cit., 83.

211 Lazzati, *L'Aristotele perdute e gli scrittori cristiani*, 10.

212 See the bibliography, mostly Italian, given by J.H. Waszink, 'Traces of Aristotle's Lost Dialogues in Tertullian', *Vigiliae Christianae*, I (1947), 137–49, especially 138, n. 6.

213 *Conf.*, 3, 4.

214 On the notion of *bios* see Jaeger, *Paideia*, II, p. 349; Bultmann, in *Theol. Wörterb. z. N.T.*, Bd. II, 836–8.

215 Marrou, op. cit., 283. Hence the phenomenon of 'Conversion' – μεταστροφή, περιαγωγή (Plato, *Rep.* 518 D). See Jaeger, *Humanism and Theology*, 53, 84; Ibid, *Paideia*, II, 295ff; Marrou, *Augustin*, 169-73; Ibid, *Histoire*, 283, 423; Bardy, op. cit., 46ff. Cf. A. D. Nock, *Conversion* (Oxford, 1933).

216 Marrou, op. cit., 301.

217 Ibid., 288.

218 E.g. Antidosis, 270. See Boulanger, *Aelius Aristide* (Paris, 1923), 230–1, 235–61, 236, n. 1. Cf. Cicero, *De Oratore*, 3.16. 'Il serait trés intéressant ... de rappeler l'histoire du mot philosophie', remarks Bardy, op. cit., 46, n. 1. See his own note there: his article in *Revue d'ascétique et de mystique*, 26 (1949), 97–108; J. Leclercq, 'Pour l'histoire de l'expression Philosophie Chrétienne', *Mélanges de science religieuse* (December 1952), 221–6; L. Meyer, *Saint Jean Chrysostome* (Paris, 1934), 186–92: 'Le Chrétien Parfait, Vrai Philosophe'. On the origin and use of the term within Hellenism, see e.g. Thompson's note on Plato's *Phaedrus*, 278 D; Zeller, *Pre-Socratic Philosophy*, I (Eng. tr., London, 1881), 1–6.

219 Marrou, *Histoire*, 301.

It is not an accident then that Clement calls his main work the 'Miscellany of Gnostic Notes in accordance with the True Philosophy',[220] and writes a λόγος προτρεπτικός ... to exhort all men to embrace this true and perfect, because divinely revealed, philosophy. Others have echoed protreptic themes, but Clement's is the first Christian use of the protreptic form itself. It is an implicit assertion not merely of a Christian right to co-existence, nor even of the reconcilability of Christian with philosophic truth, but of the Christian consciousness of being the new master-idea of human life in all its forms, of being the φιλοσοφία ... τελεία τῷ ὄντι καὶ ἀληθής.[221] Christian truth will not be a graft on the old stock, it will absorb the old – more, it is itself the stock from which the old is ultimately sprung. With the Christian revelation the face of Truth has appeared to those who believed in empty fables.[222] The muse-hallowed mountains of Hellas are superseded by the sacred mount of God, the mount of Truth from which will sound the new harmony, the Levitical Song, that is to replace the legends sung by the poets of old.[223] Wisdom in all its brightness is come down among men.[224] Truth, 'darting her light to the most distant points', will now 'cast her rays all around on those who are enveloped in darkness, and deliver men from delusion ... '.[225] 'And raising their eyes, and looking above, let them abandon Helicon and Cithaeron, and take up their abode in Sion. 'For out of Sion shall go forth the Law, and the word of the Lord from Jerusalem',[226] 'the celestial *Logos*, the true athlete crowned in the theatre of the whole universe'.[227]

220 *Strom.*, 6.1 (*PG.* 9.208).

221 *Strom.*, 2.2 (*PG.* 8.933). Cf. A. Puech, *Recherches sur le discours aux grecs de Tatien* (Paris, 1903), 98, quoted by Battifol in Rivière, *S. Justin et les apologistes du IIe siècle*, xiii f.: 'Les apologistes chrétiens entreprennent une tâche analogue à celle qu'avaient assumée avant eux les défenseurs de la philosophie contre les préjugées du vulgaire. Les *Discours aux Grecs ou aux Nations* sont comme une transformation chrétienne de ces *Protreptiques* ... dont on peut donner comme type *l'Hortensius* de Cicéron. Ils sont nés évidemment des besoins que créait aux chrétiens leur situation dans l'Empire, non d'une imitation voulue ... ; mais dès l'origine l'affinité entre les deux genres s'est révélée, et les apologistes eux-mêmes en ont eu le sentiment... '.

222 *Prot.*, 1 (*PG.* 8.53).

223 Ibid.

224 Ibid.

225 Ibid.

226 Is 2:3. 'Cette image d'Isaie marque immédiatement l'ampleur des vues de Clément: c'est par rapport à l'histoire du monde tout entier que doit se situer l'Incarnation' (Mondésert, *Le Protreptique*, 30).

227 *Prot.*, 1 (*PG.* 8.53): λόγος οὐράνιος, ὁ γνήσιος ἀγωνιστὴς ἐπὶ τῷ παντὸς κόσμου θεάτρῳ στεφανούμενος. Cf. *Prot.*, 10 (*PG.* 8.228); *Strom.*, 7.3 (*PG.* 9.424) (the last 'une image chère à Clement et familière à la litterature chrétienne des deux premiers siècles' – Mondésert, *Clément d'Alexandrie*, 203).

According to Lazzati[228] the imagery of music which Clement uses in the *Protreptikos* is a traditional protreptic motif. He refers to Plato's *Phaedo*, 61a ... 'e gli studi musicali rientrano nel programma di iniziazione della filosofia platonico-aristotelica ... Clemente alla musica della filosofia sostituisce il canto di Cristo'. The imagery of light[229] which he also applies to Christ belongs to the same tradition. Of the possibility that Clement owes the image to St John,[230] Lazzati declares that 'questa constatazione ... invece di porsi contro di noi finisce par essere tutta a nostro favore'.[231] The image of St John is already a conscious attempt to present Christian revelation as the fulfilment of ancient aspirations for truth – which they expressed by the metaphor of light.[232] 'Mirabile risposta per cui la nuova evangelica appare come il compimento, non solo di un desiderio che si era venuto esprimendo attraverso il popolo di Israele, ma di quei bisogni che l'universale anima dell' uomo aveva, per bocca dei sapienti, espresso.'[233] Christianity is the true philosophy, the true light – imparted by Him who is the light of the world, the true light which enlightens every man coming into the world.

CLEMENT'S ADVANCE

As indicated already, Clement's milieu made his task different from that of Justin. Justin is still an apologist, whose effort is to make contact between two worlds which in their understanding of each other are far apart.[234] Christians are a race without antecedents.[235] They must authenticate their own claims to citizen rights before raising the question of their relations with those who were born with such rights. In the Alexandrian milieu Christianity has so far penetrated the more articulate section of the Graeco-Roman world that it may be said to have won a *de facto* recognition. Christian and pagan have moved closer together. In a physical sense the City of Man and the City of God are one. The need of the moment is a *modus vivendi*. So, speaking broadly, while Justin's problem is the larger, speculative, historical problem of justifying the ways of God in history and the revelation of truth, Clement has the more delicate and complex task of integrating in

228 Op. cit., 17.

229 See *Prot.*, 11 (*PG.* 8.229).

230 E.g., 1:9.

231 Op. cit., 19.

232 Lazzati, op. cit., 18.

233 Ibid., 19.

234 'L'Apologetica cristiana dei primi tempi è ben più che un fortunato genere letterario. Essa entra nello storia del cristianesimo e della civiltà come espressione precipua del pensiero nel contatto fra due mondi ...' (M. Pellegriino, *Studi su l'antica apologetica*, V).

235 See e.g. Eusebius, *Praep. Evang.*, 1.2 (*PG.* 21.29), on the καινὴν δέ τινα καὶ ἐρήμην ἀνοδίαν of the Christians, μήτε τὰ Ἑλλήνων μήτε τὰ Ἰουδαίων φυλάττουσαν.

a single unified *Weltanschauung* the two sets of values represented by the Greek and the Judeo-Christian traditions.

The principles Clement brings to this task are basically those of Justin. 'We do not ... wholly disown Plato'.[236] And for essentially the reason given by Justin – 'Into all men whatever, especially those who are occupied with intellectual pursuits, a certain divine effluence has been instilled ... '.[237] In Clement again as in Justin unity is on the basis of Christian uniqueness and originality. The recognition accorded Hellenism is not as to an independent source of truth but to the scattered sherds of an aboriginal unity. Truth is one. While its fragments must be admitted wherever they exist, their shattered unity must be restored in the whole to which they belong. And that whole is the unity of the Christian *Logos*. Falsehood has a myriad forms but truth is one.[238] Before its great light all lesser lights must fade, as the lamp of the night before the sun.[239] It is from the theology of the eternal *Logos* that Greek philosophy has torn off its fragments of truth.[240] Its contradictions can be resolved, its unity restored only in 'the perfect *Logos*, the Truth'.[241] 'Just as the Bacchantes tore asunder the limbs of Pentheus,[242] so the sects ... of Hellenic philosophy have done with truth, and each vaunts as the whole truth the portion which has fallen to its lot. But all things are illuminated in the dawn of the true Light'.[243] Such are the main lines of Clement's synthesis. Secular history and secular truth exist within, not outside or parallel to, the corpus of Christian history and Christian truth. And, as it shall become clear in progress, Hellenism finds its own true fulfilment in the Incarnation, the central event of history for which all other moments in history prepared.

As the preamble to his main task – such divisions are not of course part of Clement's own very non-scholastic presentation – he resumes Justin's theme to ground the finality of Christian truth and Christian values in a philosophy of history in which the Christian revelation is the final purpose of historical progress. He sees Christianity not only in the breadth of its present claim to the allegiance of all men as the true and perfect philosophy, but in the perspective and the

236 *Prot.*, 6 (*PG.* 8.172); cf. Justin, 2 *Apol.* 13.

237 Ibid., (*PG.* 8.173): ἐνέστακταί τις ἀπόῤῥοια θεϊκή.

238 *Strom.*, 1.13 (*PG.* 8.753).

239 *Strom.*, 1.18 (*PG.* 8.804).

240 *Strom.*, 1.13 (*PG.* 8.756).

241 Ibid., 'Nor is there any passage in his writings which might more fittingly be chosen as an epitome of his undertaking ... ' (Tollington, op. cit., I, 334).

242 Bacchic imagery is frequent in the *Prot.* See e.g., 1 (*PG.* 8.53); 12 (*PG.* 8.240) (quotes Euripides, *Bacchae*, 918–9).

243 *Strom.*, 1.13 (*PG.* 8.753).

historical depth of the economies which prepared for its coming. Its universalism in truth and its consequent superseding of the partial truth of Hellenism, is the complement of that universalism in history which makes Christianity the final cause of all other traditions, Greek no less than Hebrew. Christianity 'is as it were the soul of history and the soul of the cosmos'.[244] If rival traditions seem more ancient it is because error has overlaid the true purpose of history and obscured its direction. However recent the song of salvation may seem, it is in reality as old as the promise of God which it fulfils. 'For "before the morning star it was",[245] and "in the beginning was the *Logos* ... ". Before the foundation of the world were we, who, because destined to be in Him, pre-existed in the eye of God before – we the rational creatures of the *Logos* of God,[246] on whose account we date from the beginning; for "in the beginning was the *Logos*".'[247]

If, as the groundwork to his integration of Hellenic and Christian values, Clement takes up again Justin's integration of Hellenic and Christian history, it is to present Justin's solution developed and deepened. Though Clement takes his stand on Justin's principles, in particular on the *Logos*, he advances beyond them – or rather vertically over them – by drawing out the implications of what had been left as undeveloped suggestions. His most significant advance is in the function he assigns to Hellenism as an economy in history. The word economy itself sums up the essence of Clement's progress over Justin. Not even in the case of the Law does Justin think in terms of an economy. Consequently the imperfections which he sees in the Law are not relative but absolute, and the Law itself cannot pertain to the primary purpose of a God to whom no inadequacy can be ascribed. And if the Law is imperfect and the punishment of sin, Hellenism is altogether a *massa damnata*, without juridical personality in the designs of Providence. Clement on the other hand not only advances to a realization of the function of the economy in history, but applies it to Hellenism as well as to the Law. They are twin stepping-stones to the Christian revelation. The significance of this principle outweighs the indeterminacy of the media by which Clement seeks to verify it in history. It is of greater consequence than any number of particular statements of attitude on disparate elements of the Greek tradition. More explicitly perhaps than any other patristic writer Clement has stated a principle which affirms the value of the secular.

---

244 Nicolas Berdyaev, *The Divine and the Human* (London, 1949), 180.

245 Ps 109:3.

246 τοῦ θεοῦ λόγου τὰ λογικὰ πλάσματα.

247 John 1:1 (*Prot.* 1, *PG.* 8.61).

PARALLELISM OF HELLENIC AND JUDEO-CHRISTIAN TRADITIONS

For Clement Scripture is 'the true light ... the truth, which shows by writing the things that are unwritten'.[248] And to Scripture he appeals for witnesses in support of the thesis that 'the Greeks ... have laid down some true opinions ... '. St Paul in particular is found to have attributed something of the truth to the Greeks, and 'is not ashamed, when discoursing for the edification of some and the shaming of others, to make use of Greek poems'.[249] Paul's most explicit evidence is in his address to the Areopagites, where, in the course of an instruction on the *theos agnostos* which the Athenians had worshipped, he quotes one of their own poets to the effect that 'We also are his offspring'.[250] 'Whence it is evident that the Apostle ... approves of what had been well spoken by the Greeks; and intimates that, by the unknown God, God the Creator was in a roundabout way[251] 'worshipped by the Greeks ... '.[252] But the integrity of Christian truth is marked at once in contrast to the fragmentary gleams of the Greeks – 'it was necessary by positive knowledge[253] to apprehend and learn Him by the Son'. Hence 'the men of highest repute among the Greeks knew God', although 'not by positive knowledge but by indirect expression'.[254] They worshipped the same God as the Christians but 'they had not learned by perfect knowledge that which was delivered by the Son'.[255] The Greeks had a vague and general grasp of what the Christian possesses in exact detail.[256] What the Christian knows the Greeks could but name.[257] Nevertheless by such light as He gave to the Greeks 'the Lord ... neither allowed those who were before the Law, nor permitted those who were unacquainted with the principles of the barbarian philosophy to be without restraint. For having furnished the one with the commandments and the other with philosophy, he shut up unbelief to the Advent. Whence[258] everyone who believes not is without excuse. For by

248 *Strom.*, 1.1 (*PG.* 8.696). 'Clément aime à établir ses doctrines par la témoignage des Écritures' (De Faye, op. cit., 165). Cf. Mondésert, op. cit., 188: 'L'Écriture ... c'est elle, en premier chef, qui inspire et guide Clément'.

249 *Strom.*, 1.14 (*PG.* 8.757); see Tit 1:12–13; 1 Cor 15:32f.

250 Acts 17:23 (Aratus). 'In quoting them thus (Aratus, and Cleanthes, in whom the same fragment is found) St Paul laid the foundation of Christian humanism'(Rand, *Founders of the Middle Ages*, 35).

251 Reading κατὰ περίφρασιν.

252 *Strom.*, 1.19 (*PG.* 8.805).

253 κατ' ἐπίγνωσιν (*PG.* 8.808).

254 *Strom.*, 6.5 (*PG.* 9.257)

255 Ibid. (*PG.* 9.260).

256 *Strom.*, 6.15 (*PG.* 9.345): ἡ γοῦν φιλοσοφία ... περιληπτικῶς θεολογεῖ, τὰ πρὸς ἀκρίβειαν δὲ καὶ τὰ ἐπὶ μέρους οὐκέτι σῴζει.

257 *Strom.*, 6.17 (*PG.* 9.380): οἱ φιλόσοφοι ... θεὸν ὀνομάζοντες οὐ γιγνώσκουσιν.

258 *Strom.*, 7.2 (*PG.* 9.413). Reading ὅθεν.

a different process of advancement, both Greek and Barbarian, He leads to the perfection which is by faith.'

UNITY OF HELLENIC AND JUDEO-CHRISTIAN TRADITIONS

So for Clement history advances on two parallel lines towards its Christian destination. But it is not sufficient to show that the Incarnation is the goal of the various economies of the past. Those economies themselves must stem from a root of unity. The parallel streams of history must flow from a single source. For Clement unity[259] is the mark of history and of truth, and the *Logos* who became incarnate must be shown to be not only the temporal heir of the economies of the past but the Principle active in those economies prior to his final and perfect revelation.

The unity of history and of the sources of truth is rooted in the transcendent unity of God.[260] As God is pre-eminently one, so must the evolution of His purpose for man, as revealed in the progress of history and the revelation of truth. But the unity of this scheme is not an artificial imposition on man in history. It corresponds with another unity – the unity of the human race itself. This was an idea already familiar to the Graeco-Roman world through the influence of Stoicism. 'Le *Logos*, étant la loi commune des hommes et des dieux, les rend concitoyens les uns des autres.'[261] It found a new and superior principle in the Incarnation, but it was the Alexandrians[262] who first elaborated its implications. There is first of all the unity of human nature, of ἀνθρωπότης, by which all souls are equal in face of the demands and the possibilities of the Christian *philosophia*:

> The individual whose life is framed as ours is may philosophize without learning,[263] whether Barbarian, whether Greek, whether slave – whether an old man, or a boy, or a woman ... Self-control is common to all human beings who have made choice of it. And we admit that the same nature exists in every race, and the same virtue ...

259 'L'unité ... est constamment affirmée par Clément comme une note transcendantale et universelle à la fois du vrai et du divin: de l'unité de Dieu, inséparable de l'unité de la verité, découle l'unité de la révélation sous ses formes diverses (Ancien et Nouveau Testament, Philosophie ...)' – Mondésert, *Clém. d'Alex.*, 206. Cf. Tollington, op. cit., 335ff.

260 See e.g., *Strom.*, 1.1 (*PG.* 8.732); 6.7 (*PG.* 9.280).

261 J. Lebreton, *Les théories du Logos au début de l'ère chrétienne*, 31.

262 Mondésert, *Clém. d'Alex.*, 193.

263 *Strom.*, 4.8 (*PG.* 8.1272). Cf. Tatian, *Adv. Gr.* 32; Justin, 1 *Apol.* 60, 2 *Apol.* 10. 'Questo motivo ritorna come un luogo commune dell' apologetica in risposta all' accusa ... di oscurantismo, lanciata contro i cristiani che reclutano i lori adepti fra le classi più umili' (Pellegrino, art. cit., 266). Cf. Minucius Felix, 16.

The abstract unity of human nature is expressed in the concrete unity of men in history – a unity of origin, progress and destiny. 'Ce n'est pas exagéré que de lire déjà, en filigrane, sous certaines de ses expressions, le mot fameux; L'Humanité est comme un seul homme ... '.[264] The lines of this historical unity of the human race Clement finds in the Scripture story of man. The race is one in its creation, in its fall, in its redemption.[265] But Clement does not leave the picture in this broad and abstract outline. The unity is made concrete and effective in the ceaseless and universal educative activity of the *Logos*, the *Paidagogos* of the whole human race. 'Our Instructor is the holy God, Jesus, the *Logos*, who is the guide of all humanity'.[266] 'The good Instructor, Wisdom, the *Logos* of the Father, cares for the whole nature of his creature ... '.[267] Not alone after the Incarnation, but from the beginning, '"in many ways and by many means"... '.[268] Man is the greatest work of the *Logos*. On him all His care is concentrated, regulating the soul by wisdom and temperance, tempering the body with beauty and proportion. Whatever there is of beauty and order in human action is the result of the inspiration of the *Logos*.[269]

It is a consequence of this two-fold unity of nature and history that, whatever variety there may be in the historical traditions of men, at bottom truth is one, and men are all indebted to one single source for its attainment.

> Eternity ... presents in an instant the future and the present, also the past ... But truth, much more powerful than limitless duration, can collect its proper germs, though they be fallen on foreign soil ... We shall find that very many of the tenets that are held by such sects as have not become wholly senseless and are not cut off from the order of nature ... though appearing unlike one another, correspond in their origin and with the truth as a whole. For they coincide in one either as a part or as a species, or a genus ... [270]

From the high and the low notes harmony is born.[271] From the odd and the even the science of numbers.[272] And in the universe, 'all the parts, though differ-

264 Mondésert, *Clém. d'Alex.*, 193.

265 *Strom.*, 3.16 (*PG.* 8.1200f.).

266 *Paid.*, 1.7 (*PG.* 8.316f).

267 *Paid.*, 1.2 (*PG.* 8.256).

268 Heb 1:1. Cf. *Strom.*, 6.7 (*PG.* 9.280).

269 *Paid.*, 1.2 (PG. 8.256): τὸ δὲ σῶμα κάλλει καὶ εὐρυθμίᾳ συνεκεράσατο, περὶ δὲ τὰς πράξεις τῆς ἀνθρωπότητος τό τε ἐν αὐταῖς κατορθοῦν καὶ τὸ εὔτακτον ἐνέπνευσεν τὸ αὐτῆς.

270 *Strom.*, 1.13 (*PG.* 8.756).

271 Ibid.

272 Ibid.

ing one from another, preserve their relation to the whole'.[273] Truth is one but it draws from many contributary streams, is elaborated by many co-operating causes. And, as co-operating, in reality they form but one cause:

> As many men drawing down the ship cannot be called many causes, but one cause consisting of many ... so also philosophy, being the search for truth, contributes to the comprehension of truth; not as being the cause of comprehension, but a cause along with others, and co-operator; perhaps also a joint cause ... By the same analogy, while truth is one, in geometry there is the truth of geometry; in music that of music; and in the right philosophy there will be Hellenic truth.[274]

The historical unity of mankind on the road to truth in its Christian culmination does not imply equal status for all the economies that prepare for it.[275] Hellenism is not a joint-cause with the Judeo-Christian tradition. Christianity, through the pre-existing *Logos*, is the master-key to history, the cistern from which flow all the conduits of truth. Christianity is the fullness of truth, as it is the finality of history. Truth is one, and many things contribute to its investigation, but 'its discovery is by the Son'.[276] The ways of wisdom are varied, leading right to the way of truth, but faith is the unique way.[277] God saves in many ways, but Christ is the 'royal and true entrance' to salvation.[278] 'The only wisdom, therefore, is the God-taught wisdom we possess; on which depend all the sources of wisdom which make conjectures at the truth'.[279] Greek philosophy 'has torn off a fragment of eternal truth ... from the theology of the ever-living *Logos*. And he who brings together again the separate fragments and makes them one, will ... contemplate the perfect *Logos*, the truth.'[280]

273 Ibid.

274 *Strom.*, 1.20 (*PG.* 8.813). Cf. *Strom.*, 6.8 (*PG.* 9.285): 'The Lord is on many waters' (Ps 28:3); not the different Covenants alone, but the modes of teaching, those among the Greeks and those among the Barbarians, conducing to righteousness.'

275 μία ... διαθήκη ... διάφορος ... τὴν δόσιν ... (*Strom.*, 6.13, *PG.* 9.328). Thus Clement obviates the risk that has been noted in Justin's universalism – 'd'effacer imprudemment les profondes divergences doctrinales ... sous des termes familiers. Cette dernière impression s'impose à quiconque étudie, dans la seconde Apologie, l'exposé que donne Justin de la théorie du Verbe Séminal appliquée au Christ'. (Fliche & Martin, op. cit., I, 443).

276 *Strom.*, 1.20 (*PG.* 8.813).

277 *Strom.*, 2.2 (*PG.* 8.933).

278 *Strom.*, 1.7 (*PG.* 8.733).

279 *Strom.*, 6.18 (*PG.* 9.400).

280 *Strom.*, 1.13 (*PG.* 8.756).

Since then there is in philosophy 'a slender spark, capable of being fanned into flame, a trace of wisdom and an impulse from God',[281] Clement has disposed of those who contend that philosophy is an invention of the Devil.[282] What is evil in itself can never be the source of good.[283] 'How absurd then is it, in those who attribute disorder and wickedness to the Devil, to make him the bestower of philosophy, a virtuous thing! For he is thus all but made more benignant to the Greeks ... than the divine providence and mind.'[284] If philosophy has been the source of virtue among men, and for this reason was given to the best of the Greeks, 'it follows that it is the work of God, whose work it is solely to do good'.[285] 'And in general terms we shall not err in alleging that all things necessary and profitable for life come to us from God, and that philosophy more especially was given to the Greeks ... '.[286]

MODE OF HELLENIC AND JUDEO-CHRISTIAN UNITY

This is Clement's theological argument in support of the divine intention behind the Greek tradition, and the consequent unity of all the sources of truth in God. 'For God is the cause of all good things.'[287] It is Clement's basic principle. God is one. The human race is one. Truth is one in the source of its revelation – using the term in the wide sense of any means by which it has been providentially determined that men should come to know the truth. Greek philosophy, then, if not on the same level as the Law, pertains no less really to the divine economy. But when Clement comes to determine how in the concrete this principle is verified, through what *media* truth is communicated by God to men, there is a great deal of uncertainty. To say that philosophy is 'the clear image of truth, a divine gift to the Greeks',[288] merely states the principle – asserted on a *priori* grounds – without specifying the mode of its operation. It is an advance from the general to the particular when he draws a distinction between what God causes κατὰ προηγούμενον, i.e. primarily and directly, and what He causes κατ' ἐπακολούθημα, i.e. indirectly and as a consequence of something else:[289]

281 *Strom.*, 1.17 (*PG.* 8.801): καθάπερ ὑπὸ Προμηθέως.

282 See above, 34–5.

283 *Strom.*, 6.17 (*PG.* 9.392).

284 Ibid.

285 Ibid.

286 *Strom.*, 6.8 (*PG.* 9.288). Cf. *Strom.*, 1.1 (*PG.* 8.708).

287 *Strom.*, 1.5 (*PG.* 8.717). Cf. *Strom.*, 1.1 (*PG.* 8.708): 'I shall show throughout the whole of these *Stromata*, that evil has an evil nature, and can never turn out the producer of aught that is good... '.

288 *Strom.*, 1.2 (*PG.* 8.709): ἀληθείας ... εἰκόνα ἐναργῆ, θείαν δωρεὰν Ἕλλησι δεδομένην.

289 'Ce sont des locutions familières à Plutarque, Sextus Empiricus et Épictète' (de Faye, op. cit.,168).

> God is the cause of all good things; but of some primarily, as of the Old and the New Testament; and of others by consequence, as philosophy. Perchance too, philosophy was given to the Greeks directly and primarily, till the Lord should call the Greeks.[290]

Here he wavers between the two possibilities ... Later he reverts to the former:

> The Greek preparatory culture, with philosophy itself, is shown to have come down from God to men, not with a definite direction, but in the way in which showers fall down on the good land, and on the dunghill and on the houses. And similarly both the grass and the wheat sprout; and the figs and any other reckless trees grow on sepulchres. And things that grow appear as a type of truths. For they enjoy the same influence of the rain. But they have not the same grace as those which spring up in rich soil, in as much as they are withered or plucked up.[291]

And he goes on to use the parable of the Sower in illustration of the varied growth of the scattered seeds of truth – depending on the quality of the soil on which they fell from the hand of the *Logos*-Sower.

There is no doubt that among the theories by which Clement tries to explain the medium of Providence in communicating the truth contained in Hellenic philosophy, quantitatively much the most important is the one already found in Justin and earlier in Alexandro-Jewish apologetics – 'one which in the eyes of modern historians is rather unworthy of a thinker like Clement'.[292] That is the theory of Greek plagiarism from the Old Testament. Since our purpose is to trace a certain development[293] in the arguments by which the universalism inherent in the Judeo-Christian revelation, and particularly in the Christian event, was reconciled with the seeming independence of the Greek humanist tradition, it is not necessary to dwell at length on an apologetic *topos* which does not represent the best thinking of Clement on the question.[294] It has, how-

290 *Strom.*, 1.5 (*PG.* 8.717).

291 *Strom.*, 1.7 (*PG.* 8.732).

292 Molland, art. cit., 63. See *Strom.*, 1.21, 2.5, 5.14. Molland, however, is not so sanguine about the 'modernity' of some of the critics of Clement – 'he is not very unlike some historians of the late-19th century who, however, found the indebtedness on the side of the Hebrews' (loc. cit.).

293 Cf. Finan, art. cit., 47f. [= above, 40f.].

294 'Hinter der Schriftstellerei des Clemens ist ... deutlich erkennbar der Lehrbetrieb der Katechetischen Schule Alexandriens aufgetaucht. Wir können sogar erkennen, dass sehr verschiedene Geister hier am Werke gewesen sind. Man hat sich in der Schule auf der einen Seite stark mit dem Thema der Abhängigkeit der griechischen Dichtkunst und Philosophie vom alten Testament beschäftigt,

ever, in Clement, as it has from the beginning, the theological interest of showing that the starting point for the patristic integration of Hellenistic humanism is the principle that the only original truth, the only providential history, is that which is Christian. Although this idea may be naively applied to history, it is itself a permanently valid Christian principle, and the necessary presupposition of any Christian solution of the problem of humanism – whether in the Greek or in any other context. That it is to this extent a serious argument in Clement's system is clear from the pains he is at to meet the charges of those who assert that Providence is the author of evil in permitting the theft of truth through foreknowledge and directing 'the issue of the audacious deed to utility'.[295] 'If strict accuracy must be employed in dealing with them, let them know that that which does not prevent what we assert to have taken place in the theft, is not a cause at all ... So in no respect is God the author of evil'.[296] On the other hand, 'it is ... the greatest achievement of divine Providence, not to allow the evil which has sprung from voluntary apostasy, to remain useless ... For it is the work of the divine wisdom ... not alone to do good ... but especially to ensure that what happens through the evils hatched by anyone, may come to a good and useful issue ...'.[297] And in further justification of Clement's use of the argument, it is to be noted that he does not always conceive of the theft in its more naive form of a personal plagiarism by Greek writers from the Books of the Jews. He speaks rather of 'some power or angel that had learned something of the truth, but abode not in it, that inspired and taught these things'. Again, 'not without the Lord's knowledge, who knew before the constitution of each essence the issues of futurity, but without His prohibition'.[298]

Another mode of the historical verification of the principle that all truth is from God, Clement bases on the argument that 'if there is instruction you must seek for the teacher'.[299] Every philosopher among the Greeks has based himself on the teaching of one who went before. Cleanthes claims Zeno as his predecessor, Metrodorus refers back to Epicurus, Theophrastus to Aristotle, Plato to Socrates.

---

hat das umfangreiche Material, das einst jüdisch–alexandrinische Apologetik und Polemik, ein Aristobul, ein Ps. Hekataios und andere gesammelt haben, weiter gegeben und nach Kraften vermehrt. Man hat sich zu diesem Zweck mit ausführlichen weltchronistischen Untersuchungen beschäftigt und so Schätze einer Gelehrsamkeit aufgehäuft, vor denen Clemens einen solchen Respekt hatte, dass er sie seinem Buche einverleibte, obwohl er eigentlich nichts vom Diebstahl der Hellenen wissen wollte' (Bousset, op. cit., 267). Cf. de Faye, op. cit., 171ff.; Wagner, art. cit., 229.

295 *Strom.*, 1.17 (*PG.* 8.797).

296 Ibid.

297 Ibid. (*PG.* 8.801).

298 Ibid. (*PG.* 8.796). Cf. *Strom.*, 7.2 (*PG.* 9.412).

299 Ibid., 6.7 (*PG.* 9.280).

Logically the argument leads back to the first generation of men.[300] 'And from that point I begin to investigate who is their teacher.'[301] It can be neither men nor angels. Not men – 'for they had not yet learned'. Not the angels – 'for in the way that angels, in virtue of being angels, speak, men do not hear ... And God is far from calling aloud in the unapproachable sanctity, separated as He is from even the archangels.' Truth is not native to the angels – they themselves have had a beginning and have had to be instructed in truth. 'It remains then, for us ascending to seek their teacher'. It can be no other than He who 'is called Wisdom by all the Prophets ... the Teacher of all created beings, the Fellow-counsellor of God, who foreknew all things'; who 'from above, from the first foundation of the world, "in many ways and many times",[302] trains and perfects ...' It is rightly said '"Call no man your teacher on earth".'[303] As then all paternity goes back to God the Creator,[304] 'so also the teaching of all good things ... goes to the Lord ... '.

It is hardly possible, remarks Molland,[305] to decide which of these solutions Clement believes in – 'as our author is extremely enigmatic'. In fact within the same chapter Clement mentions two other solutions, according to which the Greeks spoke some truths 'in consequence of being moved ... and others by human conjecture and reasoning ... '.[306] A passage in *Strom.*, 1.19, is discussed at length by Molland:[307]

> If then they say that it is by accident[308] the Greeks gave forth some utterances of the true philosophy, it is the accident of a divine economy[309] (for no one will, for the sake of the present argument with us, deify chance); or if they say it is by good fortune,[310] good fortune is not unforeseen. Or were one on the other hand to say that the Greeks possessed a natural conception[311] of these things, we know that the Creator of nature is one ... or that they had a common intellect,[312] let us reflect who is its father, and what

300 Ibid.

301 Ibid.

302 Heb 1:1. Cf. *Paid.*, 1.2 (*PG.* 8.256).

303 Mt 23:8ff.

304 Eph 3:14–15.

305 Art. cit., p. 64.

306 *Strom.*, 6.7 (*PG.* 9.77): ἃ μὲν κινούμενοι εἰρήκασιν ... τὰ δὲ ἀνθρωπίνῳ στοχασμῷ τε καὶ ἐπιλογισμῷ ...

307 Loc. cit.

308 κατὰ περίπτωσίν.

309 θείας οἰκονομίας.

310 κατὰ συντυχίαν.

311 φυσικὴν ἔννοιαν.

312 κοινὸς νοῦς.

> righteousness is in the mental economy. For were one to name 'prediction'[313] and assign as its cause 'combined utterance',[314] he specifies forms of prophecy. Further others will have it that some truths were uttered by the philosophers, in appearance.[315] The divine apostle writes accordingly respecting us: 'For now we see as through a glass';[316] knowing ourselves in it by reflection, and simultaneously contemplating ... the efficient cause, from that in us which is divine ... And by reflection and direct vision, those among the Greeks who have philosophized accurately, see God. For such, through our weakness, are our true views, as images are seen in the water, and as we see things through pellucid and transparent bodies ...

Here four alternatives are quoted by Clement. According to the first, the Greek discovery of truth was accidental – an accident however not unforeseen and therefore not unintended by Providence.[317] The second suggests a general or a natural revelation – on the lines of the natural knowledge of God which St Paul attributes to all men.[318] The third would raise the philosophers to the status of prophets – analogous to those of the Jews.[319] The fourth, as is convincingly argued[320] by Molland, refers not to 'truths ... in appearance', as it has been translated, but to the Platonic[321] notion of a reflection of eternal truth in the human mind – 'an imperfect, vague, unclear, yet true vision'.[322]

313 προαναφώνησις.

314 συνεκφώνησις.

315 κατ' ἔμφασιν.

316 βλέπομεν γὰρ νῦν ὡς δι' ἐσόπτρου ... '1 Cor 13:13 is always quoted in this form by Clement, with an inserted ὡς underlining the character of the expression being an image ...' (Molland, art. cit., 69, n. 1).

317 οὐκ ἀπρονόητος. 'Clement thinks nobody will dispute this' (Molland, art. cit., 66). For to deify chance 'is the blasphemy of Epicurus'. On Epicurus, 'the leader of Atheism' (*Strom.*, 1.1, *PG.* 8.688), see e.g. *Strom.*, 1.11 (*PG.* 8.748–9).

318 Rom 2:14; i.e., God is the ultimate source here too – 'let us investigate who is its father, and the author of that righteousness which is perceived in the distribution of this "common intellect" in all mankind' – Molland's correction of the Ante-Nicene translation of 'the somewhat enigmatic words': τίς ὁ τούτου πατὴρ ... σκοπήσωμεν.

319 'Προαναφώνησις and συνεκφώνησις are two explanations which are parallel ... The translators have made things too difficult by taking συνεκφώνησις as an explanation of προαναφώνησις' (Molland, loc. cit.). Molland translates the terms respectively as 'a pronunciation of statements coincident with ours', and 'a previous proclamation'. The term συνεκφώνησις 'hints either at the simultaneousness of Greek philosophy and Hebrew prophecy or at its coincidence in contents with the divine revelation' (Molland, loc. cit.).

320 It is worth noting that in *Strom.*, 1.17 (*PG.* 8.801), when Clement speaks of those who are wise (only) 'in appearance', he calls τοὺς δοκήσει σοφούς.

321 See e.g. *Rep.*, 6.510, 7.532.

322 Molland, art. cit., 161. Camelot, art. cit., 546 had already so interpreted the passage. Clement compares the Platonic idea with the image of St Paul. 'The divine Apostle writes this "respecting us"

What is less convincing is Molland's suggestion that Clement opts for this fourth solution.[323] Later on in the *Stromata* Clement makes a suggestion which raises philosophy to a higher level still[324] – by tracing its origin to a participated attribute of God, the 'spirit of perception',[325] which is said to have been given to the craftsmen in the Old Testament.[326] 'And this is nothing else than Understanding,[327] a faculty of the soul, capable of studying what exists ...[328] And it extends not to the arts alone but to philosophy itself'. The divine skill is of many kinds, and it pervades the whole world under the forms and appellations of the various human activities.[329] In this divine and communicated *phronēsis* philosophy is a sharer, 'partaking of a more exquisite perception'.[330] As a suggested origin for the truth contained in Greek philosophy it accords best with the general theocentric tendency of Clement to trace all knowledge to its ultimate unity in God – from Whom it is communicated to men through the agency of the *Logos*, the 'teacher of all created beings'.[331] But it cannot be pressed in face of Clement's own inconclusiveness and the unsystematic character of his work. 'Clement is a most non-scholastic thinker who does not work with clear distinctions and sharply elaborated alternatives'.[332] The finality of the tentative explanations of the principle is of less importance than the principle itself – that 'it is only possible to learn the truth either from God or from the children of God'.[333] 'And should one say that it was through human understanding that philosophy was discovered by the Greeks, still I find the Scripture saying that understanding is sent by God'.[334]

(ἐφ' ἡμῶν). In this connection "we" must mean "we human beings" not "we Christians" as distinct from other men' (Molland, art. cit., 69).

323 Art. cit., 66, 69.

324 One of Molland's arguments is that 'the three first alternatives form a climax, and we expect to find a still higher view of philosophy in the following alternative ...' (art. cit., 71).

325 πνεῦμα αἰσθήσεως.

326 Cf.Ex 28:3 (*Strom.*, 6.17 [*PG.* 9.385]).

327 φρόνησις. In Greek philosophy, especially after Aristotle, the term was distinguished from σοφία as the practical from the theoretical – see e.g. Jaeger, *Ursprung*, 400; *Aristotle* (Eng. tr., Oxford, 1934), 82ff; Cicero, *De Off.*, 1.43. But the Book of Wisdom, on which Clement elsewhere bases the same theocentric theory (see *Strom.*, 2.2, *PG.* 8.933; 6.11, *PG.* 9.313) uses both terms without clear definition – see F.W. Farrar, 'The Wisdom of Solomon' on Wis 6:15, in *The Holy Bible: Apocrypha*. Here φρόνησις is not *merely* practical – as is clear from the definition, and its equiparation with πνεῦμα αἰσθήσεως.

328 δύναμις ψυχῆς θεωρητικὴ τῶν ὄντων. (*Strom.*, 6.17, *PG.* 9.385).

329 *Strom.*, 6.17 (*PG.* 9.388).

330 Ibid.: Διαφορωτέρας ... αἰσθήσεως ... μεταλαβοῦσα.

331 See above, at n. 264, p. 56.

332 Molland, art. cit., 75.

333 *Strom.*, 6.15 (*PG.* 9.345). '... auf welchem Wege die Philosophie ... gekommen ist, ist ihm Nebensache. Die Hauptsache ist ihm, dass Gott dahinter steht ... ' (Wagner, art. cit., 239).

334 *Strom.*, 6.8 (*PG.* 9.284).

DIRECTION OF HELLENISM: THE INCARNATE *LOGOS*

Having established the unity and the divine origin of Hellenic truth Clement has yet to explain the purpose and significance of the distinct historical tradition of which it forms part.[335] And here is revealed the advance of Clement on Justin, to which reference has already been made. For Justin, too, all truth is one in its origin. The seeds of truth in Hellenism are affirmed as scattered lights of the Christian *Logos* – operative even outside the tradition which, κατά προηγούμενον, represented the pre-history of Christianity. But this *prima facie* liberalism conceals a deeper denial of Hellenism. Secular history, as distinct from the fragmentary truth it contains, represents men under the sway of demons. Such elements of truth as it preserves are at best salvaging from the wreck of the *Logos* common to all men, at worst demonic perversions of the only real and original truth. The historical tradition to which those fragments belong exists by default and not by positive divine ordinance. The seeds of truth in Hellenism are not native to its soil, they have been blown from a stock that grows in another climate. For Clement on the other hand, the secular economy is truly an economy, with a unique function, a value proper to itself. It is the second line of the double economy in which all men are led on to the fullness of time and the fullness of truth in Christ. God's care that men should come to the truth is no less universal in the theology of history that Clement constructs than it is in that of Justin;[336] but for Clement it is truth contemporary with the capacity of the recipient, truth not eternal and final but transposed into the idiom of time, striking a balance between the past and the future, not leaving 'without restraint' those 'unacquainted with the principles of the barbarian philosophy', yet leading beyond itself to the fuller revelation that is to come. 'For by a different process of advancement, both Greek and Barbarian, He leads to the perfection which is by faith.'[337] Philosophy too was 'a schoolmaster to bring the Hellenic mind, as the Law the Hebrews to Christ'.[338] It was 'a preparation, paving the way for him who is perfected in Christ'. And like its prototype, the divine revelation κατὰ προηγούμενον, philosophy has been corrupted by the primordial sower of cockle among the wheat. 'As in the barbarian philosophy, so also in the Hellenic, tares were sown by the proper husbandman of the tares; whence ... heresies grew

335 'Il sentait le besoin de s'expliquer la *raison d'être* de cette philosophie' (de Faye, op. cit., 161). Cf. Fliche & Martin, op. cit., II, 239; Camelot, 'Les idées de Clément d'Alexandrie sur l'utilisation des sciences et de la littérature profane', *Recherches sc. rel.*, 21 (1931), 39.

336 Cf. *Strom.*, 6.6 (*PG.* 9.269): 'One righteous man ... differs not, as righteous, from another ... whether he be of the Law, or a Greek. For God is not only Lord of the Jews, but of all men ...'. Cf. Camelot, 'Clément et l'utilisation de la philosophie grecque', *Recherches sc. rel.*, 21 (1931), 549: 'Clément est trop généreusement optimiste pour croire que Dieu se soit désintéressé des Gentils ... '

337 *Strom.*, 7.2. (*PG.* 9.413).

338 *Strom.*, 1.5 (*PG.* 8.720). Cf. Gal 3:24; de Faye, op. cit.,161–2.

up among us along with the productive wheat'.[339] From those 'tares' – 'existing among the Greeks as spurious fruits of the divinely bestowed philosophy', he singles out the 'impiety and voluptuousness of Epicurus', the 'voluptuous and selfish philosophy' which St Paul reprobates as 'the wisdom of this world'[340] as a result of its teaching 'the things of this world, and about it alone, and its consequent subjection ... to those who rule here'.[341]

It is solely with a view to the Christian recapitulation that Providence instituted the double pedagogy of the Law and philosophy, parallel but temporary stages in the progress of history towards a fulfilment in which, when all partial economies have served their purpose, the whole race will be in-gathered in the universalism of a prepared plan now fully realized. 'Rightly then, to the Jews belonged the Law, and to the Greeks philosophy,' but only 'until the Advent', for 'after that came the universal calling to be a peculiar people of righteousness, through the teaching which flows from faith, brought together by one Lord, the only God of both Greeks and Barbarians ... '.[342] Before the Gospel and the fullness of time there were the partial and transient provisions of the Law and the prophets for the Jews, of philosophy for the Greeks. Neither dispensation had its end in itself. The real function of both was to 'fit the ears' of the recipients for the Gospel.[343] For both, though adequate to what may be called the contemporary theological age of humanity, were defective by reference to the future. Those who lived by the Law needed faith.[344] Those who had lived by philosophy needed faith and freedom from idolatry.[345] Both became anachronisms with the Incarnation.[346] But they were not destroyed. They were taken up in a higher unity.[347] 'Those of either race who have believed, are a "peculiar people".'[348] 'With the new people God has made a new covenant',[349] distinct from and superior to both the covenants of the past:

NB

339 *Strom.*, 6.8 (*PG.* 9.289); cf. Mt 13:25ff.

340 1 Cor 2:6.

341 *Strom.*, 6.8 (*PG.* 9.289).

342 *Strom.*, 6.17 (*PG.* 9.392).

343 *Strom.*, 6.6 (*PG.* 9.265).

344 Ibid.

345 Ibid.

346 Cf. Bardy, *Clément d'Alexandrie*, 49: 'l'histoire de l'humanité se divise en deux périodes: avant et après l'Incarnation'. Mondésert, op. cit., 188, n. 3, quotes Westcott, *Dict. of Christ. Biog.*, I, 556: 'This thought of the Incarnation as the crown and the consummation of the whole history of the world is perhaps that which is most characteristic of Clement's office as interpreter of the faith ... '.

347 Cf. Harnack, op. cit., I, 248f: 'The religious philosophy of history set forth by Clement of Alexandria rests entirely upon the view that those two nations, Greeks and Jews, were alike trained by God, but that they are now ... to be raised into the higher unity of a third nation.'

348 *Strom.*, 1.18 (*PG.* 8.805). See Tit 2:14.

349 See Heb 8:8–10.

> For what belonged to the Greeks and Jews is old. But we who worship Him in a new way, in the third form, are Christians. For clearly... He showed that the one and only God was known by the Greeks in a Gentile way, by the Jews in a Jewish way, and in a new and spiritual way by us ... Accordingly then, from the Hellenic training, and also from that of the Law, are gathered into the one race of the saved people those who accept faith: not that the three peoples are separated by time, so that one might suppose three natures, but trained in different Covenants of the one Lord. For ... as God wished to save the Jews by giving them prophets, so also by raising up prophets of their own in their own tongue ... He distinguished the most excellent of the Greeks from the common herd ...[350]

The ultimate significance of Hellenism then is in relation to its historical context. A return to it now – no less than in the case of a return to Judaism – would be a return to the στοιχεῖα τοῦ κόσμου,[351] to set up permanent spiritual residence in what was intended as a stage on the road to truth – στοιχειωτικήν τινα οὖσαν καὶ προπαιδείαν τῆς ἀληθείας.[352] It would be a refusal to move with the process of history, a standing still with an anachronism.[353]

But there are no ruins in the divine economy of history. There is nothing that fades. Its progress is not through abandonment but evolution. It is the husk, not the seed, that is left behind. Christianity transcends and supersedes, but not by rejecting anything that was once significant. To Hellenism as to Judaism the Christian revelation means fulfilment, not destruction. 'Though the wild olive be wild it crowns the Olympic victors'.[354] The wild plant has more nutriment but less 'power of secretion'. The cultivated olive 'receives more nutriment from its growing in the wild one', which in turn 'gets accustomed, as it were, to secrete the nutriment, becoming thus assimilated to the fatness of the cultivated tree'.[355] So too the philosopher, 'resembling the wild olive in having much that is

---

350 *Strom.*, 6.5 (*PG.* 9.261).

351 Col 2:8 (*Strom.*, 6.8, *PG.* 9.284). Cf. *Strom.*, 6.15 (*PG.* 9.341), on the same text. Cf. also *Strom.*, 6.8 (*PG.* 9.289): στοιχειωτική τίς ἐστιν ἡ μερικὴ αὕτη φιλοσοφία ...

352 *Strom.*, 6.8 (*PG.* 9.284).

353 See *Strom.*, 6.8 (*PG.* 9.288): Providence gave philosophy to the Greeks οἷον διαθήκην οἰκείαν ... ὑποβάθραν οὖσαν τῆς κατὰ Χριστὸν φιλοσοφίας. Cf. *Strom.*, 1.2 (*PG.* 8.709): οὐ κατὰ προηγούμενον λόγον ... διὰ δὲ τὸν ἀπὸ τῆς γνώσεως καρπόν ἡμῶν. 'Aussi nous apparaît-il que le critérium quand il s'agit de juger des réalités historiques est avant tout un critérium chronologique. Une religion est fausse du fait, qu'elle est anachronique, qu'elle représente une étape révolue du plan de Dieu qui se réalise en étapes successives' (Daniélou, *Origine*, 157).

354 *Strom.*, 6.15 (*PG.* 9.341) – an image from Rom 11:17.

355 The Greek text has συνεξομοιουμένη τῇ πιότητι.

undigested,[356] on account of his devotion to the search, his propensity to follow, and his eagerness to seize the fatness of the truth; if he gets besides the divine power, through faith, by being transplanted into the good and mild knowledge, like the wild olive, engrafted in the truly fair and merciful *Logos*, he both assimilates the nutriment that is supplied, and becomes a fair and good olive tree.' So far from there being a conflict between Hellenic and Christian, it is in Christianity that Hellenism comes to fulfilment: 'For engrafting makes worthless shoots noble, and compels the barren to be fruitful by the art of culture and by gnostic skill.'[357]

The point on which all history converges is the Incarnation. Seen from the *nunc stans* of eternity, the Incarnation is the seed of temporal development. 'There took place ... a universal movement and translation through the economy of the Saviour.'[358] Such universal and cosmic consequences flow from the coming of the *Logos* that Clement takes 1 Pet 3:19 according to the letter of a descent by Christ and the Apostles to preach the Gospel in Hades – He to the Hebrews, they to the Gentiles, 'that is, those who had lived in righteousness according to the Law and philosophy'.[359] It was not fitting that those 'whose life had been pre-eminent' in either economy should want salvation, 'though found in another place'.[360] 'One righteous man ... differs not as righteous, from another righteous man, whether he be of the Law or a Greek. For God is not only Lord of the Jews, but of all men ... '.[361] 'En tout cas il ne faut pas perdre de vue les grandes idées qui l'entraînent à cet excès: d'abord le Nouveau Testament, inauguré par L'lncarnation, est l'accomplissement de l'Ancien ... Ce role, d'ailleurs, il le joue, également et toutes proportions gardées, à l'égard de la philosophie.'[362]

Despite the diversity of its forms then, history is one. The source of its unity is the *Logos*. The purpose of its progress is the Incarnation of the *Logos*.

> ... The covenant of salvation, reaching down to us from the foundation of the world ... is one, though conceived as different in respect of gift. For ... there is one unchangeable gift of salvation given by one God, through one Lord, benefiting in many ways. For which cause the middle wall which

356 ἄπεπτον (*Strom.*, 6.15, *PG.* 9.341).

357 Ibid.

358 *Strom.*, 6.6 (*PG.* 9.269): γέγονεν ἄρα τις καθολικὴ κίνησις καὶ μετάθεσις κατὰ τὴν οἰκονομίαν τοῦ σωτῆρος. Cf. O. Cullmann, *Christ and Time*, 19–20: 'From this mid-point all history is to be understood and judged ... this fact ... is the final meaning and the criterion of all history before and after it.'

359 *Strom.*, 6.6 (*PG.* 9.268).

360 Ibid.

361 Ibid. (*PG.* 9.269).

362 Mondésert, *Clém. d'Alex.*, 214.

separated the Greek from the Jew is taken away[363] in order that there might be a peculiar people. And so both meet in the unity of one faith;[364] and the selection out of both is one.

THE *LOGOS*: PRINCIPLE OF THE PRE-CHRISTIAN PAST

Hellenism by the terms of its own existence leads on to Christianity. Christianity is heir to the past – but in a sense even more profound than is indicated by the figure of grafting. The past is Christian not only in direction and purpose but in the inner principle of its movement. The Christian *Logos* Incarnate is the pre-Christian soul of history, and the Revealer of truth.[365] 'Since the unoriginated Being is one, the Omnipotent God, one too is the First-Begotten "by whom all things were made, and without whom not one thing was made .. .",[366] known as Wisdom to the prophets ... teacher of all men, Fellow-counsellor of God, who from the first foundation of the world, "in many ways and many times",[367] educates and perfects ... '. From Him the true philosophy has its origin. From Him the Greeks too have received 'certain scintillations'.[368] There is but one husbandman of the soil of humanity, who 'from the beginning, from the foundation of the world, sowed nutritious seeds; He who in each age rained down the Lord, the *Logos*.'[369] It was the times and places of the recipients that 'created the differences which exist'.[370] The *Logos* is at the beginning and the end of the divine transactions with men. It was He who appeared to Moses in the Burning Bush, 'when the almighty Lord of the universe began to legislate by the *Logos*'.[371] The Bush was a symbol of the thorns with which the *Logos* was to be crowned on His second coming. 'On His

363 Eph 2:14.

364 Eph 4:13 (*Strom.*, 6.13, *PG.* 9.328).

365 'In this fruitful, plastic and extremely valuable conception, Clement found a means of combining all that Hellenism, Hebraism, and Christianity could contribute to true religion ...' (Tollington, op. cit., I, 334).

366 John 1:3.

367 Heb 1:1 (*Strom.*, 6.7, *PG.* 9.280).

368 *Prot.*, 7 (*PG.* 8.814): ἐναύσματά τινα τοῦ λόγου τοῦ θείου λαβόντες Ἕλληνες ὀλίγα ἄττα τῆς ἀληθείας ἐφθέγξαντο.

369 *Strom.*, 1.7 (*PG.* 8.732). 'C'est par le Verbe que toute révélation nous vient: cette thèse est sans cesse exposée par Clément' (Fliche & Martin, op. cit., II, 244). Lebreton, quoted in Fliche & Martin, loc. cit., finds in this an echo of Justin and of Irenaeus: 'Il faut avouer toutefois que c'est Justin plus qu'Irénée qu'on reconnait ici, un Justin dont les vues se seraient élargies, et dont la philosophie serait plus mystique et plus ardente'. Cf. Tollington, op. cit., I, 338: 'No one had seen the full measure of the potentialities of this doctrine for Christianity until Clement taught and wrote'.

370 *Strom.*, 1.7 (*PG.* 8.732); See Mt 13:3ff.

371 *Paid.*, 2.8 (*PG.* 8.488).

departure from this world to the place whence He came, he repeated the beginning of his old descent, in order that the *Logos*, beheld at first in the bush, and afterwards taken up crowned by the thorns, might show the whole to be the work of one power. He himself being one, the Son of the Father, who is truly one, the beginning and the end of time'.[372]

The unification of all history and all truth in the *Logos* is not inconsistent with the diversity of Clement's attempts to explain the medium through which the *Logos* communicates. One of Clement's principles is that God works through secondary causes,[373] and even accidents are the ordinance of Providence.[374] As the agent of Providence, the universe is penetrated by the power of the *Logos* – 'the true athlete crowned in the theatre of the whole universe'.[375] The Son is 'The power of God, as being the Father's most ancient *Logos* before the production of all things, and His Wisdom. He is then properly called the Teacher of the beings formed by Him. Nor does He ever abandon care for man ... '.[376] He gave philosophy to the Greeks through the lower angels.[377] He is the Saviour not of some but of all men.[378] '... In proportion to the adaptation possessed by each. He has dispensed His magnificence both to Greeks and Barbarians'.[379] Alone He rules and presides, overseeing all things.[380] 'Being the Father's power He easily prevails in what He wishes, leaving not even the minutest part of His administration[381] unattended to. For otherwise the whole would not have been well executed by Him.'[382] Nowhere did He leave unbelief to flourish. To the Jews He gave the Law, to the Greeks philosophy, preparing both by different economies for His own Advent.[383] And

372 Ibid.: ἀρχὴ καὶ τέλος αἰῶνος. Cf. the Hymn to Christ (PG. 8.681), αἰωνοχραές. On the αἰών in Christian thought, see Cullmann, op. cit., n. 45ff.

373 *Strom.*, 6.16 (*PG.* 9.380).

374 *Strom.*, 1.19 (*PG.* 8.809).

375 *Prot.*, 1 (*PG.* 8.53).

376 *Strom.*, 7.2 (*PG.* 9.412).

377 Ibid. (*PG.* 9.409).

378 Ibid.

379 Ibid.

380 Ibid. (*PG.* 9.412).

381 διοίκησις – a Stoic term. See Wis 8:1, and Farrar's note (op. cit., ad. loc.).

382 *Strom.*, 7.2 (*PG.* 9.412). On Clement's concept of Providence, see *Strom.*, 6.17 (*PG.* 9.388): 'God knows all things – not those only which exist, but those also which shall be. And foreknowing the particular movements He "surveys all things and hears all things" (*Iliad*, 3.277) ... and possesses from eternity the idea of each thing individually. And what applies to theatres, and to the parts of each object, in looking at, looking round, and taking in the whole in one view, applies also to God. For in one glance He views all things together and each thing by itself; but not all things κατὰ τὴν προηγουμένην ἐπέρεισιν.'

383 *Strom.*, 7.2 (*PG.* 9.412). Cf. the *Prayer to the Paedagogus* (*PG.* 8.861) – τῷ διδασκαλικῷ καὶ πανεπισκόπῳ λόγῳ.

finally taking flesh Himself 'He came to show man what was possible through obedience to the commandments'.[384] In a word – 'Everything ... which did not hinder a man's choice from being free, He ... rendered auxiliary to virtue, in order that there might be revealed somehow or other, even to those capable of seeing but dimly, the one ... God – from eternity to eternity saving by His Son.'[385]

So Christianity is heir to the past not simply by right of temporal succession. The past itself was an expression of that eternal *Logos* that has become incarnate in Christianity. Christ the *Logos* is the *choreutes*[386] of history, the *paidagogos* of truth. Despite the seeming divergence of Judaism and the Hellenic tradition, 'au fond il n'y a ... qu'une révélation, unique comme le Dieu qui en est l'auteur'.[387] The essential presupposition of a Christian-Hellenist rapprochement is the recognition of the universalism inherent in the Judeo-Christian tradition, the uniqueness, originality and integrality of the Christian revelation, and the consequently impermanent, subordinate, propaideutic capacity of all the other economies of history. There is one God, therefore one Providence at work in time. Therefore – 'La storia profana è nel Cristianesimo'.[388]

CHRISTIAN FULLNESS

Christianity then, coming with the fullness of time, possessing Truth in Person, supersedes the incompleteness and impermanence of Hellenism. 'The Hellenic truth is distinct from that held by us ... in ... extent of knowledge, certainty of demonstration,[389] divine power ... For we are taught of God, being instructed in the truly "sacred letters"[390] by the Son of God.' The Greeks themselves may think they have hit the truth perfectly, 'but as we understand them, only partially'.[391] Not that what they know is untrue, but that it is inadequate. Revelation has not pushed back the limiting horizons that bound their view. 'They know nothing more than this world'.[392] Lacking a window on the infinite they have not grasped truth in the round. Their vision is flat, two-dimensional, wanting perspective. 'It is just like geometry which treats of measures and magnitudes and forms by drawing on plane surfaces'; like painting which 'appears to take in the whole field

384 *Strom.*, 7.2 (*PG.* 9.412).

385 Ibid. (*PG.* 9.416).

386 *Prot.*, 9 (*PG.* 8.200). Cf. *Paid.*, 1.8 (*PG.* 8.329): ὁ τῶν ὅλων ἡγεμὼν λόγος. 'In Christ time has reached its mid-point' (Cullmann, op. cit., 93).

387 Mondésert, *Clém. d'Alex.*, 209.

388 Chiocchetta, op. cit., 87. Cf. Daniélou, 'Christianisme et histoire', *Études*, 254 (1947), 179.

389 'Vielleicht redet Clemens hier in Erinnerung an Justins. *Apol.*, I, 20 ...' (Wagner, art. cit., 224, n. 1).

390 2 Tim 3:15. In allusion to the so-called sacred books of the ancients (*Strom.*, 1.20, *PG.* 8.816).

391 *Strom.*, 6.7 (*PG.* 9.277).

392 Ibid.

of view', but really consists of an illusion induced by a skilful use of a technique of lines and angles,[393] so that 'some objects seem to appear in the foreground, and others in the background' – all on a surface which itself is smooth and level. Such is the picture of truth presented by philosophy, in comparison with the fullness of the Christian revelation.

The Christian completeness in its possession of truth is complementary to its finality in history – a necessary consequence of its possessing Him who is the 'beginning and the end of time', and the 'teacher of all created beings'. The Incarnation is the key to history. The Christian revelation is the key to truth. It is the ultimate principle of all truth, wherever found – even outside the Christian revelation κατὰ προηγούμενον. The only wisdom is that possessed by Christians – the wisdom that comes from God. On this 'depend all the sources of wisdom which make conjectures at the truth'.[394] Even though the best among the Greeks believed in the same God as the Christians, 'they had not learned by perfect knowledge that which was delivered by the Son'.[395] The philosophers 'are children, unless they have been made men by Christ'.[396] They named God but did not know Him.[397] Their speculations, in the words of Empedocles, 'as passing over the tongue of the multitude, are poured out of mouths that know little of the whole'.[398] As all animals breathe the air, in different ways and to different purposes, 'so also a considerable number of people occupy themselves with the truth, or rather with discourse concerning the truth'.[399] In reality they say nothing about God, but explain Him in terms of their own feelings.[400] They 'spend life in seeking the probable, not the true'.[401] Such truth as they have attained is a Christian spark. 'As art changes the light of the sun into fire by passing it through a glass full of water, so ... philosophy, catching a spark from the divine Scripture, is visible in a few'.[402] It is a fragment from the *Logos* in whom alone truth is integral. Only as restored in the unity of the Christian *Logos* does it become integral again. Truth, that is one where error has ten-thousand by-ways, has been torn into pieces like

393 Ibid.: ψευδογραφεῖ τὴν ὄψιν, τοῖς κατὰ προσβολὴν τῶν ὀπτικῶν γραμμῶν σημείοις χρωμένη κατὰ τὸ τεχνικόν. Cf. *Strom.*, 6.17 (*PG.* 9.381): 'Philosophers have names and words, τὰ πράγματα δὲ παρ' ἡμῖν, ibid., 6.8 (*PG.* 9.289), on the philosophy which teaches 'the things of this world ... alone ... this fragmentary philosophy is very elementary ... '.

394 *Strom.*, 6.18 (*PG.* 9.400).

395 *Strom.*, 6.5 (*PG.* 9.260).

396 *Strom.*, 1.11 (*PG.* 8.752).

397 *Strom.*, 6.17 (*PG.* 9.380).

398 Ibid.

399 Ibid.

400 Ibid.

401 Ibid.: τὸ πιθανὸν ... οὐ τὸ ἀληθές.

402 Ibid.

the limbs of Pentheus. Only in Christ is it possible to see the mutual relations of the fragments which, 'though appearing unlike one another correspond in their origin and with the truth as a whole'.[403] The truth of Greek philosophy being partial, 'the real truth, like the sun glancing on the colours both black and white, shows what like each of them is'.[404] Truth, one, and comprehensive as eternity, collects its seeds from wherever they have fallen.[405] The *Logos* is the Truth,[406] by whose light the particles are illuminated.[407] Only in Him is there finality.[408] 'One speaks in one way of the truth, in another way the truth interprets itself. The guessing at truth is one thing, and truth itself is another. Resemblance is one thing, the thing itself is another.'[409]

403 *Strom.*, 1.13 (*PG.* 8.756). This is the basis of Clement's eclecticism: 'Not. ... the Stoic, or the Platonic, or the Epicurean, or the Aristotelian, but whatever has been well said by each of those sects ... this eclectic whole I call philosophy. But such conclusions of human reasonings as men have cut away and falsified I would never call divine'. Cf. *Strom.*, 1.1 (*PG.* 8.693), on Hellenic philosophy – 'the whole of which, like nuts, is not eatable'. See de Faye, op. cit., pp 161ff.

404 *Strom.*, 6.10 (*PG.* 9.304).

405 *Strom.*, 1.13 (*PG.* 8.756).

406 John 14:6.

407 *Strom.*, 1.13 (*PG.* 8.756).

408 Despite Clement's sympathy with Hellenism, 'tout ce passé est bien loin de lui; il a été saisi par une force nouvelle, qui le port plus loin, plus haut' (Fliche & Martin, op. cit., II, 243).

409 *Strom.*, 1.7 (*PG.* 8.733). Cf. Justin, 2 *Apol.*, 12. 'And already the apostle, by saying , "After the rudiments of this world, and not after Christ" (Col 2:8), makes the asseveration that the Hellenic teaching is elementary, and that of Christ perfect ...' (*Strom.*, 6.15, *PG.* 9.341).

TOTAL TRAGEDY AND HOMER'S *ILIAD*[410]

By common agreement a central element in the tragic pattern is *conflict*. For reasons close enough to the surface. The individual's action is asserted in the context of a wider supra-individual order with its correlative supra-individual laws, laws that react on his action, reveal the *hamartia* of that action, wittingly or unwittingly performed, and its potential for destruction when it is worked out in assertion to the end, to its *telos* as *completed* action, completed in the organic unfolding of its intrinsic implications and of its extrinsic consequences by reaction of the order within which it was asserted.

This gives us one (more!) hypothetical model of the tragic process: man at grips with what is greater than man. It also enables us to accommodate within a single concept a variety of tragedies that are otherwise difficult to accommodate or sometimes even to accept as tragedy at all when compared with those of the high classic tradition. How for instance does the *Oresteia* belong with the *Death of a Salesman* or a hysterical woman in Ibsen? It is hard to see how if we consider themes and substance only. But if we look at the *structure* of themes and substance we find they have in common the deep-structure theme of man versus the greater than man. For the greater-than-man can have its ceiling, so to speak, at any level, from the lowest to the highest, from the psychological laws within the self or the laws of the social order just beyond the self, through the laws of mass movement in history, all the way up to the ultimate and supreme greater-than-man, the laws of God – or Fate or Necessity or whatever name is given to the absolute Orderer, always mysterious and often appearing to be cruelly careless of mankind, but within and under whose order all finite individual man's actions are asserted.

As with all models in relation to the facts so with this one there is the problem of the commonly asserted metaphysical dimension of true tragedy. We can

410 A paper based on a first-level reading of the *Iliad* in translation with students of Epic in Classical Civilization. The version used was (and is) that by Richmond Lattimore (Abingdon-on-Thames: Routledge and Kegan Paul, 1951) – because available, at least to the lecturer.

Due acknowledgement to the students who in part suggested the idea and in part liked the result, i.e. in spots. There is progress on all sides on this point if the present writer is as wise as was C. M. Bowra in 1930 while they are already as wise as he was forty years later. With his *Tradition and Design in the Iliad*, where the concept of the *Iliad* as tragedy is used *passim*, compare his posthumous *Homer*, Ch. 6, where the same idea is relegated to the final paragraph and apparently damned with faint praise.

see that dimension in the classic tragedies at the higher levels of our model. But where is it under the lower 'ceilings' of modern bourgeois tragedies? Present by implication? Or not necessary at all?

Passons – most of the great classic tragedies do have that metaphysical dimension. And the present paper looks at tragedy under that metaphysical aspect, at the top level of our model scale. And from a feeling that our traditional and conventional conceptualization of tragedy has prevented us approaching tragedy from that higher point of view as often as we might. And with the consequence that we may not have noticed the tragic mode in places where it exists, or have realized that it is possibly a more primordial and permanent mode than we thought. It will be argued that European literature actually begins with tragedy, at the highest level on the scale of problems – in Homer's *Iliad.*

Aristotle does put Homer at the start of the historical genesis and evolution of tragedy, and his theory of epic is worked out in terms of modifications to his theory of tragedy.[411] Apart from the metre in which they are respectively written, 'Epic poetry differs from tragedy in the *scale* on which it is constructed... Epic poetry has ... a great, special capacity for *enlarging its dimensions* (Megethos) ... '[412] This last shall be of some relevance in a moment. And of course we must not make Aristotle *confuse* two different genres, epic and tragedy. The point is that in the only exemplary literature available to him he saw certain similarities as well as differences between the great examples of the one and the other.

Now despite the widely reported death of tragedy some such wider and more primordial conception of it has been growing on its theorists in recent times. Nietzsche is in, even if Aristotle is not. And broader concepts have helped to resolve the paradox that at a time when tragedy was never more abundant in life it should seem to be dead in literature. Broader concepts and a new awareness of what the finally important questions are have revealed tragedy where minds too classically tidy saw it not – from the 'infra-tragedy' of Beckett back to the epic tragedy of Homer. Most splendidly but not exclusively in Homer. He is but the supreme example of something common to all primary heroic and epic poetry. Namely that the central figure 'is always the radiant hero and conquerer ... but he appears against the sombre background of inevitable death, a death which will lead him away from his joys and plunge him into nothingness; or, a fate no better, into a mouldering world of shadows ... '.[413]

As we shall see, it is a perfect description of the terrible *lucidité* that governs the *Iliad,* in its central character Achilles. And significantly, as Lesky further points out – although we must not build too much on the fact without exact

411 *Poet.* ch. 4.7ff, chs. 23–24.

412 *Poet.* ch. 24.3ff.

413 Albin Lesky, *Greek Tragedy,* Translated by H. A. Frankfort (London-New York: Barnes & Noble, 1965), 2 .

analysis of the precise point of the comparison – the Greeks themselves seem to have looked on Homer as in some sense the father of tragedy. Lesky refers e.g. to Plato, *Rep.* 10.595 b–c, 598 d. There is a much more explicit reference, in *Theaet.* 152 e, to Homer as the 'Master' in tragedy.

We can see in what line Aristotle was when he too saw some link between Homer and later Greek tragedy. But whether he made the wrong connection, or understood better than he wrote in the *Poetics* as it survives, Lesky (clearly in a deep line running from Nietzsche to Jaspers et al.) would say that while there is in the *Poetics* 'a genuine theoretical approach to tragedy'[414] it is not much developed 'beyond a technical analysis of works of art ... '. More precisely to the point of this paper – 'though the Greeks created tragedy ... they never developed a theory of the tragic which, reaching beyond the *phenomenon of drama*, might touch on man's *spiritual attitude towards the world as a whole*'.[415]

We cannot, and need not, go into that argument here. Two general points might be made. Firstly, Aristotle's concepts for the nature of tragedy, derived inductively, as we know and as we can see, from his observation of the phenomena of the tragic experience, naturally have the richness that comes of being close to the facts, and in consequence have often a kind of inspired adaptability to interpretations more profound than he may always have consciously intended. On the other hand, despite the richness accruing from his awareness of the historical dimension of even literary forms, Aristotle saw the final form as the essential form because teleologically completed. In tragedy this for him was in the body of Greek tragedy that we know. Although here too, he has the remarkable elasticity of mind which enables him to say that we cannot be sure whether tragedy has even yet reached the term of its formal development.[416] But he had no choice but to take the most evolved form known to him as the observed basis of his inductive theory. And this it was that provided him with such core elements as strict organic unity of action, the importance of character as the radical source of action, and of the famous flaw or *hamartia* in character as the source of tragic action.

Our point is that the canonicity of Aristotle and of the Greek tragedy that provided his data has determined our whole hermeneutic of tragedy through a particular *form* of tragedy which may well be too limited. We need at least to distinguish *genre* and *form* and to bear in mind the possibility which we do accept for such genres as comedy or pastoral or even epic, namely that the genre is not necessarily confined to the forms with which it is conventionally associated. What do we mean by genre? A mode for looking at an element or aspect of

414 Ibid., 18.

415 Ibid., 4 – italics mine.

416 *Poet.* ch. 4.11.

reality, or a mode for looking at reality as *if* it were such and such – because of course the *same material* can be looked at in *different modes*, the interpretation ranging from epic significance to satiric nihilism.

The *genre* therefore is the filter for *reality* (the *object* of mimesis, as Aristotle put it) or for a particular view of reality. Should we not so regard the tragic genre? And to get a three-dimensional understanding of it should we not walk *all* around it and approach its structure less exclusively and autonomously from the side of the tragic action and the tragic character and 'flaw' and more from the side of the *universe*? It could be that the flaw is occasionally in the universe and not in the character – or thought to be. Certainly there are some great tragedies where it seems artificial to look for the triggering flaw in the tragic hero while there is every indication that it is the order of the world the author regards as booby-trapped. In any case it is only *within* and in *relation to* the *greater* structure of the universe that the *lesser* structures of the tragic process can have any meaning – as we suggested in our basic model of tragic conflict as man at grips with the greater-than-man.

Both poles are of course essential but one of them is not always given due attention. With the consequence that the tragic genre, as distinct from a certain tragic form, has not always been recognized in works where it undoubtedly exists, and that with an exemplary clarity and power. The *Iliad*, for instance, is certainly in the tragic *genre*, and at the top of our model scale of conflicts, metaphysical, turning on the ultimate problem, the problem of the final meaning and value of human existence and effort measured by the ultimate *Grenzsituation* – the inevitability of death and the pall of futility which, if it is final, it spreads over the most heroic achievements. The real root of the anger and withdrawal of Achilles is in the fact that

> a man dies still if he has done nothing, as one who has done much.[417]

And Achilles is but one – though this one equals a few – in a line which runs from Gilgamesh who raged at the death of Enkidu (as Achilles did at the death of Patroclus) to Camus' *Myth of Sisyphus*, in which, for the same reason – the 'discovery' of death – 'the fundamental question of philosophy is to decide whether life is or is not worth being lived'.

In other words here we have a tragic experience born not of this or that local and limited conflict between man and his circumstances, but of a conflict between man and the totality of things. And it *is* tragic in the strict sense, not just in any free emotive sense of the word. Because it is a conflict, and within man himself,

417 *Il.* 9.320.

an emotional psychological conflict, between his native drive to action and the sicklying over of all final value by the pale cast of death, an intellectual metaphysical conflict, between his native drive for meaning in things and the apparent absence of any such final sense. Camus (op. cit.) describes this quest for absolute meaning, this 'desperate nostalgia' for unity, as 'the essential movement of the human drama'. It is – or was – very contemporary, even fashionable. But it is a pain as old as Gilgamesh. 'If this enterprise is not to be accomplished, why did you move me, Shamash, with the restless desire to perform it?' Achilles at Troy, a man born under prophetic sentence to be 'of all men one of swiftest doom' (okumorotatos allón),[418] is torn between the drive to glory within the heroic code and the desire to return home to an inglorious but longer portion of life. If he stays,

> my return home is gone but my glory shall be everlasting.

If he leaves,

> the excellence of my glory is gone, but there will be a long life left for me,
> and my end in death will not come to me quickly.[419]

This is where we see that the 'anger of Achilles' is at the metaphysical level. And Homer makes it present from the start. His anger in the original quarrel with Agamemnon is not just a matter of primitive pique at being robbed of the spoils of war in the person of Briseis. It is an affair of heroic honour. Since he is a man born to have a short life, Zeus ... should grant him

> Honour at least. But none he has given me, not even a little.[420]

It is the genre that develops in depth and grandeur through the *Iliad* and is carried through to the *Odyssey*, where in the vision of the dead he is the irreconcilable 'révolté' who would rather 'break sod as a farmhand ... than lord it over all the exhausted dead'.[421]

In discussions of tragedy it is conventionally pointed out that mere awareness and acceptance of such a view of man's situation, with inactive, however noble, resignation does not constitute a tragedy. The prisoner, if such he be, must resist and be seen to resist. There is no obvious inconsistency with our original model or

418 *Il.* 1.505

419 *Il.* 9.412ff.

420 *Il.* 1.352ff.

421 *Od.* 11.489ff, Fitzgerald version.

with the *Iliad* and Achilles viewed as tragic genre and tragic character. In the model the *conflict* of man with greater-than-man exists at the level of life and it drives to action.[422] The *Iliad* has its hero, action and unity of action, and even the mode is dramatic rather than narrative, as Aristotle again recognised and admired.[423]

In fact when we consider the story as sheer arrangement of events ('plot'), we find at its nodal points something like the three classic moments of the tragic process: the initial passionate spring or trigger of action, the climactic 'reversal' and 'recognition' of the catastrophic consequences of that action, the *dénouement* in calm of mind, all passion spent. Those points in the *Iliad* are Books 1 and 9, 18, 24.

That story overall of course is of how the withdrawal of Achilles in anger from the fighting before Troy permits the Trojans, spear-headed by Hector, to inflict defeat after defeat on the Greeks to the point of crisis. The understanding of why the actions of Achilles and Hector, a single individual on either side, should be of such consequence, depends on the knowledge that while Achilles is the greatest, Hector is next, and both embody superhuman power and quality. The point of which in the poem is not just the primitive myth of primary heroism – their characters are far too humanly complex for that – but to write large in two individuals 'the tragic which, reaching beyond the phenomenon of drama, [touches] on man's spiritual attitude to the world as a whole'.[424] Demonic[425] man at grips with the greater-than-man. And there can be few better 'plots' in narrative dramatic literature that the one that brings them face to face in the final struggle of *Il.* 22, few more splendid expressions of the tragic sense than the 'moment of truth' which that book embodies. Which is not to say that it 'has all been said' in the *Iliad.* Only that this is archetypal, this is the 'idea' of tragedy.

To come to the concrete contents of these nodal points in the story, Achilles first withdraws to his tent in Book 1 after the quarrel with Agamemnon over Briseis. The subsequent books immediately work out the consequences in Greek retreat and Trojan advance. Which is why an embassy of Greek leaders tries to change his mind in Book 9. He only hardens, deepens and elaborates his refusal – there is development here in that the original anger has not become an overtly metaphysical 'revolt'. There is further development in the subsequent books, and specifically on the lines of tragedy, in that Achilles' continued withdrawal brings not only further catastrophe to the Greeks but personal tragic catastrophe to Achilles himself – the 'good companion' Patroclus is killed because he was moved

422 'Life consists in action and its *telos* (end) is a mode of action, not a quality' – Aristotle. *Poet.* ch. 6.9

423 *Poet.*, 4.9.

424 Lesky, op.cit., p.4.

425 This is literally true of Achilles – and Gilgamesh – who are part human and part divine by origin. A fact which does not invalidate the argument about man, but symbolically reinforces it.

to go out (in Achilles' armour) and do the battle that Achilles would not. (Here too there is *hamartia* within *hamartia*, because Hector who slays Patroclus and takes his armour thereby sets in motion the process that will lead to his own death.)

The death of Patroclus brings the moment of tragic 'recognition' of *hamartia* by Achilles. In Books 18–19 he relents, is reconciled and goes into battle. (And here we find not only the recognizable *events* of tragic process but already some of the classical Greek technical terminology for its explanation – see esp. 19.85 ff on 'delusion' (*atê*), and compare Aeschylus, *Persians*, 821 f, and perhaps St John, 9.39. To be noted here too *hamartia* within *hamartia*. For within the heroic code of honour Achilles has no choice but to go into battle to avenge the slain companion. But thereby one of his two original elements of choice is eliminated – the choice between short life glorious and longer life inglorious – 9.412 ff. He must go into battle and thereby seal his own early death).

And in that battle from Book 20 on he rises to a paroxysm of vengeance and destruction that reverses the previous Trojan advance, drives them back behind the walls of the city – all with the exception of Hector. Books 22–23 bring their climactic and mutually tragic confrontation, the death of Hector, the carrying off and attempted mutilation of his heroic remains. It is this withholding and attempted mutilation of the body of Hector that leads to the climactic nodal point that is Book 24. Climactic and nodal in the special tragic sense. Because what we can recognize here is the phenomenon that we recognize as characteristic of the end of all great tragedy, the same phenomenon that Aristotle recognized and tried to define inductively as *catharsis*. The purification of our feeling and of our seeing in an obscure and paradoxical sense of enhancement, a sense that, as Aeschylus put it, through the 'passion' (in both senses) has come perception, and possibly redemption. The vehicle of this in the final Book of the *Iliad* is the embassy of the aged Priam to beg back the body of his son. In the event the potentially fearsome confrontation between two paroxystic men, the anger of Achilles and the anger of the Lear-like Priam, dissolves their personal and private spleen into a universal pity –

Sunt lacrimae rerum et mentem mortalia tangunt.

If the exposition we have given is just we can see this is a perfect tragedy in the conventional sense. But our original thesis was that the tragedy of the *Iliad* is something much more fundamental and comprehensive, dealing with 'man's spiritual attitude towards the world as a whole'. It has already been indicated that, in this conflict of man with the *ultimate* greater-than-man, the thematic focus is death, because the last enemy indeed is death, and the real anger of Achilles is the anger of metaphysical revolt against it. We have to show that it is indeed with this higher and 'more philosophic thing' (*philosophoteron*)[426] the 'plot' we have outlined is charged.

It is well to note first something about the character of Achilles who embodies this tragic view. Especially as it is so easy to see him as what he has been called, merely 'A magnificent barbarian', in reference to his relentless heart, his savage anger and paroxystic vengeance. Even those who perceive the *Iliad* as a tragedy then find it all too easy to fit the pieces together in the traditional moralistic pattern for interpreting the tragic character. Achilles is a great character with one big 'flaw', his 'temper', which becomes the ruination of him – until he 'purges' it. And *salva reverentia* this is what Bowra does in *Tradition and Design in the Iliad.*

This, to use our original figure, puts the ceiling of the tragedy too low. It misses the vital centre of Achilles. It mistakes existential torment for a primitive force of nature, a 'restless heart' for a glandular condition, and rage against human finitude for a violent temper and want of virtuous self-control. It explains away the character of Achilles by reducing it from metaphysical to merely moral and psychological categories. It does not notice that Achilles' angry heart is first of all 'deeply troubled'.[427] It does not notice that the anger itself is more than a detonation, however violent, on the surface of life, but rather a sulphurous smouldering from the depths of the soul, a

> gall that makes a man grow angry for all his great mind, that gall of anger that swarms like smoke inside a man's heart and becomes a thing sweeter to him by far than the dripping of honey.[428]

Achilles is an *aliéné* before becoming a *révolté.*

This is the picture we get of him from the start. In a troubled brooding that goes far beyond the immediate occasion, Achilles

> weeping went and sat in sorrow apart from his companions beside the beach of the grey sea looking out on the infinite water.

Born as he was 'to be a man with a short life' he should at least have 'honour' as his portion, but even of that he has [...] been deprived in the person of

426 *Poet.* 9.

427 See *ochthesas* in *Il.* 18,5, 97; 22.14, and the *general* significance of *Il.* 18. 107ff.

428 *Il.* 18.108ff.

Briseis.[429] And then, with the magnificent Homeric foil of his divine mother's pity for human bitterness,

> Thetis answered him – letting the tears fall: Ah me, my child, your birth was bitterness. Why did I raise you? If only you could sit by your ships untroubled, not weeping, since indeed your lifetime is to be short, of no length. Now it has befallen that your life must be brief and bitter beyond all men's. To a bad destiny I bore you in my chambers.[430]

The theme of *timor mortis conturbat me* is established and Achilles, its embodiment, as one whose *angor* and *anger* is 'hatred of the doorways of death'.[431] In the light of such explicit thematic unfolding we can see more clearly the significance of the violent opening statement of the *philosophoteron* theme underlying the 'plot' of the whole poem:

> Sing, Goddess, the anger of Peleus' son Achilleus
> and its *devastation*, which put pains thousandfold upon the Achaians,
> hurled in their multitudes *to the house of Hades*, strong souls of heroes,
> but *gave their bodies to be the delicate feasting of dogs* ... [432]

The violence of statement anticipates explicitly the climactic violence of the closing books before the repose of Book 24. To be the meat of dogs is the fate Priam foresees for himself in 22.66 ff, and the fate Achilles promises Hector in 22.330 ff, 23.179 ff. And the point is not in the violent *statement* but in the underlying protest and demand for meaning – 'What god was it then set them together in bitter collision?'[433] Is life but a meaningless flux, a tale told by idiots ... ? It must be lived and yet it is Hell – as Goethe saw in his often-quoted reaction to the reading of Homer: 'The lesson of the *Iliad* is that on this earth we must enact Hell.'[434] 'Longinus' of course had already recognized essentially the same quality.[435]

It is in Book 9 (on the nodal significance of which in the 'plot', see above) that this *totally* tragic root of Achilles' anger is most fully expressed. In organic connection with the plot, for it is elicited by Phoenix as envoy from the Greeks in crisis to persuade him to relent. He will not relent – no longer merely because

429 *Il.* 1.349ff.

430 *Il.* 1.413ff.

431 *Il.* 9.312.

432 *Il.* 1.1ff.

433 *Il.* 1.8.

434 Quoted in C.S. Lewis, *A Preface to Paradise Lost,* Oxford Paperbacks ed., 31.

435 *On the Sublime,* 9.7.

the return of Briseis is still unlisted in the promised rewards but because even the concept of 'honour' has now lost its meaning. The [finality] of death has revealed all human striving as 'absurd' – a Sisyphean futility.

> We are all held in a single honour, the brave with the weaklings.
> A man dies still if he has done nothing, as one who has done much.
> Nothing is won for me, now that my heart has gone through its afflictions,
> in forever setting my life on the hazard of battle.[436]

All the fabled spoils of war do not equal the preciousness of one's own brief span of life.[437] Material possessions can always be had by one means or another,

> but a man's life cannot come back again, it cannot be lifted
> nor captured again by force, once it has crossed the teeth's barrier.[438]

And he enunciates the choice quoted earlier which destiny has imposed on him, death in glory or life inglorious.[439]

And in this same episode[440] something is subtly suggested about the *character* of Achilles which at one level provides some *psychological human* motivation for his torment, and at another gives him something like a symbolic dimension that makes him a more adequate representative of all men's condition. Since childhood he has been like an adopted son to this Phoenix who pleads with him now. They have a common background of experience – in what we might call – an unhappy childhood! Phoenix is a runaway from the father he tried to murder for loving his mistress more than his wife (mother of Phoenix). Achilles is the only son of the separated Thetis and Peleus, and Achilles certainly has a complex about his old father alone and neglected while his son is far away.[441] We cannot go into details here.

Suffice it to say that Achilles appears as a homeless *déraciné* at every level of his being, a *blasted*[442] tragic figure of the kind described precisely in 24.532 ff (quoted earlier) as *driven* over the earth by an 'evil hunger' (*boubróstis*), a *wanderer* respected neither by God nor man.

We have already referred to the *doubly* tragic structure of the 'plot' at the stage it reaches for Achilles in Book 18. Achilles 'recognizes' the loss of Patroclus

436 *Il.* 9.319ff.

437 *Il.* 9.401ff.

438 *Il.* 9.406ff.

439 *Il.* 9.410ff.

440 *Il.* 9.432ff.

441 See 24.534ff.

442 See in fact 24.39 on Achilles as 'cursed' (*oloói*).

as the *consequence* of his own anger and the *cause* of his now imposed choice and sealed personal doom.

> I must die soon, then, since I was not to stand by my companion
> When he was killed.[443]

Recognition of this truth brings reconciliation not only with the Greeks but with his own fate which is quickly to follow his vengeance on Hector.[444] (18.95f).

> So I likewise, if such is the fate that has been wrought for me,
> Shall lie still when I am dead ... [445]

And the core theme of death *structured* in action by tragic 'plot' is given the equivalent of choral amplification in the wild grief of Achilles for the dead Patroclus[446] and of Thetis for Achilles now doomed as well.[447] A lament completed later at the funeral of Patroclus whose ghost provides a chilling glimpse into the hollow abode of the dead.[448]

> Oh, wonder, even in the house of Hades, there is left something,
> a soul and an image, but there is no real heart of life in it.[449]

Achilles' reconciliation with his fate does not mean resignation to it. His terrible return to the field is with anger at a new pitch that will lead heaven itself to protest that Achilles is 'cursed' and has 'murdered pity'.[450] The final goal of vengeance on Hector passes through a paroxysm of nihilistic violence against the forces of nature itself. This dimension of the 'revolt' of Achilles is symbolized in his fight with the corpse-choked River Scamander[451] – in which the whole plain of Troy takes fire.[452] Inevitably one recalls Yeats' Cuchulain (*On Baile's Strand*)

443 *Il.* 18.98f.

444 *Il.* 18.95f.

445 *Il.* 18.120f.

446 *Il.* 18.22ff.

447 *Il.* 18.54ff.

448 *Il.* 23.65ff.

449 *Il.* 23,103f. Vision and lament recall terrible parallel episodes in the Epic of Gilgamesh, in which shorter work the theme of death and its tragic structuring are more elementally obvious than in the much longer *Iliad.*

450 *Il.* 24.39, 44.

451 *Il.* 21.240ff.

452 As on the same occasion, through the intervention of the gods on either side, 'all things – Heaven and Hell, things mortal and things immortal – war together and are at risk together in that ancient battle' (Longinus, 9.6 on *Il.* 21.385ff etc.).

who 'fought with the ungovernable tide' (*Cuchulain's Fight with the Sea*). The point of the parallel is well brought out in the comment of Unterecker,[453] 'Yeats made instinctively of Cuchulain's battle with the sea a structure designed to express man's anguish when, maddened by the complexities of warring emotions no violence can unravel, he takes arms against not only a sea of troubles but the sea itself, emblematic image of fecund destructive life'. And Camus gave a similar motivation to his murderous Caligula; ... *il n'y a qu'une façon de s'égaler aux dieux: il suffit d'être aussi cruel qu'eux.*[454]

We have earlier seen how, in *Il.* 22, *two* trains of tragic *action* meet in the final confrontation of Achilles and Hector:

I must take you now, or I must be taken.[455]

Our business at this point is not to 'plot' that action but to show here too the orchestrating of the constant high theme of the action, the *ultimate*, fundamental tragedy of man born to die ... But in this supreme Book at this supreme moment of truth the theme is elaborated in a kind of mini-action which, at a point of final concentration of the total action, re-enacts the whole as the spool of memory is said to do with life in the moments before death. The action is strictly and organically *dramatic*, i.e. expressive of the tragic theme. And, what is artistically the most marvellous, the action is both inward and outward, in the soul of Hector and around the walls of Troy – even at the transcendent level of the divine interventions. And the forward movement is organized into successive moments in which layer after layer of hope is stripped from Hector until he 'knows' and stands in the desolation of the truth concentrated to a point of light on the tip of Achilles' spear, shining like the evening star in the dark sky.[456] And through the whole the theme is sounded in bell-toll variations on 'death that lays men prostrate' (210, *tanēlegeos thanatoio* – cf. 297, 361, 436, and the climactic hammerblows in 364 ff, the moment after Hector's death:

> Now though he was a *dead* man brilliant Achilles spoke to him:
> *Die*: and I will take my own fate at whatever time Zeus and the rest of the *undying* Gods choose to accomplish it.

There is much in this inward and outward action which suggests the net, a frequent metaphor in and for tragedy. In the *Iliad* too at this point there is precisely

453 *A Reader's Guide to W.B. Yeats*, 78.

454 *Caligula* 3.2.

455 *Il.* 22.253.

456 *Il.* 22.317ff.

'this sense of the symmetrical tightening of the plot-ropes, the narrowing of the circles in the final stages ... '.[457] And Hector is indeed a man trapped in two dimensions. Outside the gate, when all the others have escaped inside,

> his deadly fate held Hector shackled, so that he stood fast
> In front of Ilion and the Skaian gates.[458]

It is the image and consequence of a psychological shackling. For the movingly human Hector has upon him the weight of earlier mistakes and reproaches for his weakness.[459] He feels

> ... shame before the Trojans ...
> ... that someone who is less of a man than I will say of me:
> 'Hector believed in his own strength and ruined his people'.[460]

Therefore it is better now to stand and fight, and 'see to which one the Olympian grants the glory'.[461]

The first stripping of Hector towards the truth occurs when at this very point of resolution his heroic courage fails him and he flees, pursued by Achilles, round and round the walls and the closed gates of the city – 'It was a great man who fled, but far better he who pursued him'.[462] And it is the moment of truth in the ultimate contest, for the race is for none of the conventional prizes –

> No, they ran for the life of Hector, breaker of horses.[463]

In a surrealist nightmare of steady-state motion in which the hunter does not catch and the hunted is not caught –

> As in a dream a man is not able to follow one who runs from him, nor can the runner escape, nor the other pursue him.[464]

---

457 T.R.Henn, *The Harvest of Tragedy*, 37, in a chapter on 'The Nature of the Net'.

458 *Il.* 22.5f.

459 See *Il.* 17.125ff.

460 *Il.* 22.105ff.

461 *Il.* 22.108ff. In the bitter event it is one of the Olympians who cruelly sets him up for the kill – 22.222ff and 293ff.

462 *Il.* 22.158.

463 *Il.* 22.161.

464 *Il.* 22.199f.

While Zeus looks down indifferently, balancing two 'fateful portions of death' in his golden scales, and registers that 'Hector's death day [is] heavier'.[465] Zeus, who earlier had looked down in pity on the divine horses weeping for Patroclus and wondered why they, immortal and ageless, have been given by the gods to a mortal man –

> Only so that among unhappy men you also might be grieved?
> Since among all creatures that breathe on the earth and crawl on it
> there is not anywhere a thing more dismal than man is.[466]

At sight of the tipped scales Hector is further stripped by heaven's withdrawal. Apollo abandons him and Athena plays the supreme and divinely 'dirty trick'. Taking the human form of Hector's dearest brother Deiphobus she joins Hector and urges that they stand and face Achilles together. When they do and Hector loses his spear in a vain cast,

> He stood discouraged, and had no other ash spear:
> but lifting his voice he called aloud on Deiphobus of the pale shield
> and asked him for a long spear, but Deiphobus was not near him.
> And Hector knew the truth inside his heart ... [467]

The catharsis begins when even the gods have pity on the remains of the fair Hector dragged in the dust behind the chariot of Achilles and outraged for twelve days around the tomb of Patroclus. For twelve days the gods protected his body from all ugliness, incorrupt and dew-fresh with 'rosy immortal oil'.[468] There descends an aura of grace akin to that with which the Christian Latin poet Prudentius envelops the remains of man, still sacred and 'noble even in its ruin', and calling up the cry for immortality: 'never, even should the wandering winds blow his flesh like dust through the void, never can we believe that a man has wholly perished'.[469]

> So it is that the blessed immortals care for your son, though he is nothing but a dead man, because in their hearts they loved him.[470]

465 *Il.* 22.212.

466 *Il.* 17.441ff.

467 *Il.* 22.293ff.

468 *Il.* 23.184ff, 24.18ff.

469 Prudentius, *Hymn for the Burial of the Dead.*

470 *Il.* 22.422f.

Words that the aged Priam hears on coming to beg for the body of his son. Priam whose anger and 'revolt' against the nature of things has become as violent as that of the enemy who has slain his son. Priam who had sat in his courtyard like Job on his dunghill,[471] surrounded by his surviving sons,[472] Job's comforters too that he drives from his sight,[473] and useless sons that he blasts as Lear does his daughters in a paroxysm of revolt.[474]

Priam embraces the knees of Achilles and kisses the hands 'that were dangerous and manslaughtering and had killed so many of his sons'.[475] Achilles looks in wonder at the king as wonder seizes the beholder of a murderer fled from his own land to another country.[476] But in the ensuing scene private and particular rages are dissolved in a calm of universal tragic pity. The theme, and with it our thoughts, are raised 'above the fierce passions of the moment, and even above the strife of Greek and Trojan. The bereavement of Priam, the loss of Patroclus, the impending fate of Achilles himself, are seen in their profound tragic meaning, as examples of the infinite sadness of human things'.[477] The plea of Priam

> stirred in the other a passion of grieving
> For his own father. He took the old man's hand and pushed him gently away. And the two remembered ... [478]

And both wept in tragic recognition ... But not for long, as part of a favourite Homeric formula might have put it. For sorrows remain, and there is nothing to be gained from 'grim lamentation'.[479]

> Such is the way the gods have spun life for unfortunate mortals, that we live in unhappiness but the gods themselves have no sorrows.[480]

The *best* we can hope for is a *mixture* from *each* of Jove's twin urns of good and evil. When the *worst* happens we receive from the urn of evil alone.[481] And

471 *Il.* 24.163ff.
472 *Il.* 24.161ff.
473 *Il.* 24.239ff.
474 *Il.* 24.252ff.
475 *Il.* 24.478ff.
476 *Il.* 24.480ff.
477 Monro, ed., to Book 24.
478 *Il.* 24.507ff.
479 *Il.* 24.524.
480 *Il.* 24.525f.
481 *Il.* 24.527ff.

that 'makes a failure of man, and the *evil hunger drives* him over the shining earth, and he *wanders* respected neither by god nor mortals'.[482] A *demonic* hunger ... of the kind that drove Achilles himself, and Gilgamesh before him.

There is nothing to be gained from grieving for Hector. He too is dead and can never be brought back – 'sooner you must go through yet another sorrow'.[483] And in this knowledge Achilles releases and Priam receives the remains of 'horse-breaking Hector', and they are taken back to the city in solemn procession on a smooth-rolling wagon to ritual lamentation. The body is placed atop the high pyre for burning, the white bones are gathered in a casket, and a barrow is piled above the grave. And thereafter all the Trojans

> Assembled in a fair gathering and held a glorious feast within the house of Priam ... [484]

So that the people might quickly 'return to what they must do ... ' was the comment at the corresponding moment in the funeral rites of Patroclus.[485] That comment is not added here at the end, but we know that the war for Troy resumed when the ritual mourning for the dead was over.

482 *Il.* 24.531ff.

483 *Il.* 24.549ff.

484 *Il.* 24.802f.

485 *Il.* 23.53.

TOTAL TRAGEDY AND THE EPIC OF GILGAMESH

I

The background to this essay is an earlier one on *Total Tragedy and Homer's Iliad*.[486] The theme of that essay was a certain concept of tragedy, as exemplified in European literature at its very beginning, in the *Iliad* of Homer. A concept born of a tragic outlook of a peculiarly radical and total kind. An outlook based on a terrible *lucidité* about man's condition in face of certain ultimates, especially death. Death realized not just with the intensity of the individual's anguish, concerned with the desire for survival and the fear of extinction. Death considered rather in a more objective and metaphysically questioning way as generating a problem of *meaning*. The meaning of all human striving (and it is the striving which makes tragedy), since death not only finally defeats it but apparently invests it with a pall of futility.

Achilles would fight no more because the man who has striven dies no less than the man who has done nothing. 'The fundamental question of philosophy is to decide whether life is or is not worth being lived' (Camus, *The Myth of Sisyphus*). The theme is in fact much older than Homer, nearly as much older than Homer as Homer is older than Camus. Gilgamesh already pleads in the third millennium BC: 'If this enterprise is not to be accomplished, why did you move me, Shamash, with the restless desire to perform it?' It is the Epic of Gilgamesh in this light, and some of its Homeric parallels that I would like to pursue in this essay.[487] Before taking up my two specific themes, the Homeric parallels and the tragic view of life, let us look at some broader reasons for an interest in the Epic of Gilgamesh. They have to do with the beginnings of civilization as we know it in the West (and I speak of civilization here in the high, developed sense, material and spiritual). Those of us concerned with the Classics tend to suggest, if not ourselves to think, that our civilization began in Greece and our literature with

486 *The Maynooth Review*, Vol. 5, No. 1 (May 1979), 71–83.

487 There are scholarly editions of the text in translation by J. B. Pritchard in *Ancient Near Eastern Texts Relating to the Bible*, and by Alexander Heidel in *The Gilgamesh Epic and Old Testament Parallels*. For the purpose of this article I use the version by N. K. Sandars, *The Epic of Gilgamesh* (Penguin Books, Harmondsworth), revised edition of 1972.

Homer. We know now that before Homer there was not only Mycenae but Crete. And Gilgamesh serves to remind us that before them all there was the millennial civilization of the Near East.

It is common to speak of the 'Greek Miracle', but we know that there are factors in the genesis of civilization other than the miracle of genius. The author of Genesis already had some awareness of the fact. It may not be possible to identify the precise location of Eden and its garden. But when he names the Tigris and the Euphrates among the four rivers that flowed from the garden, the author reveals his sense of the conditions in which civilization might begin, from something like an absolute beginning. We have heard of the Fertile Crescent and we know that the earliest great civilizations emerged in the great alluvial river valleys. The greatest of these was indeed the civilization that developed, from the fourth millennium BC in the land-between-the-rivers, Mesopotamia. It may even be also chronologically the earliest. For apparently it remains a possibility that the other great river-valley civilizations did not arise independently, but by diffusion from a single primordial beginning. That is the civilization known historically as Babylonian, from the famous capital of the ancient empire that most extensively enveloped it. It is a civilization that is connected with both of the main strands in our own. For apart from the general fact that it gravitated naturally towards the cultural vat of the Mediterranean, it is the civilization from which Abraham came and, as is now generally accepted, certain elements in Greek civilization as well. It is the civilization that produces the extraordinary Epic of Gilgamesh, in the third millennium BC.

Gilgamesh, it would now appear, was an historical king, who reigned at Uruk early in that third millennium. The poem that turns on his achievements and experience came into existence by a process like that which has given us the epics of Homer. That is to say, a cycle of originally separate poems about his life was transmitted by oral tradition and finally written down and fused into the unity of a single great poem. Its original language was Sumerian, the language of the extraordinarily gifted people who founded the Mesopotamian civilization, before being conquered by Semitic peoples. But from the original Sumerian it seems to have been translated into most of the important languages of the Near East. This fact indicates how widely known must have been the story of Gilgamesh in the Near East. He must have had a status and an influence analogous to that of Achilles and Odysseus in the Hellenic world.[488] And given that fact, plus the possible contacts between Greece and the Near East (the

488 On p. 3 Sandars refers to one piece of evidence from the eighth century BC indicating that Gilgamesh was so much a household word that his name could be used as the anchor for literary jokes and travesties. We may compare Lucian's use of the adventures of Odysseus.

Iliad and the *Odyssey* were themselves composed in Asia Minor), it is easy to understand how possible parallels between Gilgamesh and the Homeric poems might have come about. It is further due to the wide translation and diffusion of the poem that we now have it at all in a fairly complete recension, by collation of portions from different Near Eastern languages. The fullest recension is in seventh-century BC Akkadian, from the Niniveh palace library of Assurbanipal, the last king of Assyria. In 612, the Persians rolled over Niniveh, 'And all who look on you will turn their backs on you and say *Niniveh is a ruin*' (Nahum 3:7). In those ruins lay the Epic of Gilgamesh, until its rediscovery in the last century became one of the romances of archaeology.

One is at risk in talking about its quality without having access to it in its original language (or languages). But one can perceive that one element precisely in its quality, like much of Homer, is that elemental power of technique and pressure of content that can survive in translation. It would be a great poem to come even from much later and more sophisticated ages, but it is an extraordinary poem to come from the very beginnings of our civilization. Extraordinary in the range and scale encompassed within a length of story that is short by epic standards. Range and scale of action in space and time, indeed, but more importantly range and scale of consciousness of the dimensions of human existence. A consciousness that is already explicit and almost entirely free of any element of the mythical or so-called pre-logical mentality. And a consciousness that is essentially and profoundly tragic, as I have tried to define that term.

There is no point in attempting to put all this in words better than those of Sandars, and one cannot resist quoting them at some length. 'These poems [the cycle] have a right to a place in the world's literature not only because they antedate Homeric epic by at least one and a half thousand years, but mainly because of the quality and character of the story that they tell. Through the action we are shown a very human concern with mortality, the search for knowledge, and for an escape from the common lot of man ... If Gilgamesh is not the first human hero, he is the first tragic hero of whom anything is known. He is at once the most sympathetic to us, and most typical of individual man in his search for life and understanding ...' (op. cit., p. 7).[489]

II

The 'plot' or 'mythos' that carries this 'more philosophic meaning' (to use Aristotle's categories) is of the simplest, though rich with humanity and archetypal symbols (like the forest) and motifs (like the temptation and scorning of Ishtar). The poem itself sums up the plot formulaically at the beginning and the end, in context conveying the final overall tone of tragic defeat and

489 Cf. Heidel, op. cit., 19: 'The Gilgamesh Epic is a meditation on death in the form of a Tragedy'.

resignation. 'He went on a long journey, was weary, worn out with labour, returning he rested, he engraved on a stone the whole story' (Sandars, 61, 117). Two journeys in fact. The first being the journey to the forest and the Cedar Mountain to slay the evil giant guardian Humbaba. The second being, like that of Odysseus in *Od.* 11, beyond the Ocean to Dilmun, the land of the living, in quest of the secret of everlasting life. This [he will get] from Utnapishtim, the Noah of the story, the one man to whom the jealous gods had granted this gift, after preserving him alone from the flood, by which the angry gods had destroyed a sinful race. In the end of course it is not the lot of Gilgamesh, or of mankind, to have eternal life. 'The father of the gods has given you kingship, such is your destiny; everlasting life is not your destiny. Because of this do not be sad at heart ... ' (pp. 70, 118).

The connection between the two journeys is important. The second is a consequence of the first, in a way which makes the poem tragic in the strictest Greek sense. *Hubris* is committed in the slaying of Humbaba despite his pleas for mercy; as later on when in the pride of victory Gilgamesh scorns the advances of Ishtar. The penalty for those actions comes in the sickness and death of the Patroclus of the poem, the hero's good companion Enkidu. With this there emerges the deep heart of the poem, the 'discovery' by Gilgamesh of the agonizing existential reality of death and the light it casts on the heroic endeavour of the preceding half of the poem. Hence the second journey.

Important too is the motivation for the first journey. It leads us into the heart of the poem from the start. Gilgamesh is an Achilles, for whom restless heroic action is a *succedaneum* to calm the *angst* and fill the void in his 'stormy heart'. He has built Uruk. He has gone abroad and found none to withstand his arms. His arrogance lords it in the *ius primae noctis.* He is given a soul-friend in his specially created equal, Enkidu, 'like him as his own reflection, his second self ...' (p. 62). Yet the worm is still in his heart. 'Here in the city man dies oppressed at heart, man perishes with despair in his heart. I have looked over the wall and I see the bodies floating in the river, and that will be my lot also' (p. 72). And so the first journey is undertaken, so that at least he can die without rancour, because surviving in the monument of his achievements, with his name at least stamped on brick.

But that journey leads only to the full tragic awakening, to the discovery that the void in his own heart is a void at the heart of the world, that there is in fact 'no permanence' (pp. 106f).

III

Homeric parallels have often been noted in the details and motifs of the story. I have briefly referred earlier to some general reasons for believing that they are not accidental but have a foundation in some actual link between the two cycles of poems, however immediate or remote. This is not the place to attempt to argue the case in more detail, even if one had the kind of qualifications it would demand. Perhaps the really surprising thing would be not a connection but the absence of one, given what we know of historical connections, if only by trade,[490] between the Aegean and the Near East, and given further what we know of the pre-historic connection between the various Indo-European[491] peoples who moved South, into Asia Minor as well as Greece. Suffice it to say that, while details are uncertain and hard to prove, there is a consensus among scholars that there is a connection between the myths and poetry of Greece and the Near East. So G. S. Kirk: 'I remain convinced that narrative and poetical trends in second-millennium Greece, like mythological and religious ones, were strongly affected by the ancient Near East and in particular by Mesopotamia'.[492]

In cursory glances at the possible Homeric parallels, it is perhaps the *Odyssey* and its hero that are noticed first, rather than the *Iliad* and Achilles.[493] And indeed the parallels with the *Odyssey* are there, right from the start of both poems. The ritualistic characterization of Gilgamesh, at the beginning and the end of the poem, has already been quoted in part: 'this was the man to whom all things were known; this was the king who knew the countries of the world. He was wise ... He went on a long journey ... returning he rested'. It calls to mind the opening characterization of Odysseus, the 'man of many wanderings' who 'saw many men's cities and knew their ways'. The thematic statement in Gilgamesh points to the end of his story. And that end, like the Odyssean *nostos*, is a journey back home. And that home-coming is invested with a mood like that of the *Odyssey*. A recognition that the original outward journey ended in *hubris*, hence a sense of regret for having gone out in the first place, reinforced by a sense of the futility of much that the adventure entailed in mistakes, arrogance and wastage of life. All crystallizing into an *aperçu* of other values, or at least resignation in face of the unattainable, and a final sense that while from one point of view the world is too narrow for the desires of man's heart, from another point of view there comes a moment when the heart realizes that the world is in fact too wide for it and desires to turn round and retrace its steps to its island Ithaca, there, when all the trials

490 Cf. the old thesis of V. Bérard in *Les Phéniciens et l'Odysée.*

491 E.g. the Hittites.

492 *Homer and the Oral Tradition*, 106; cf. the same author's *Myth, Its Meaning and Functions*, 223 ff. Cf. also M.L. West, *Hesiod's Theogony*, 18 ff; *Greek Philosophy and the Orient*, 203 ff; P. Walcott, *Hesiod and the Near East*. Basic is chapter III in T. B. L. Webster's *From Mycenae to Homer*.

493 So Sandars, 45f., and M. Grant, *Myths of the Greeks and the Romans*, 94f. The emphasis is different in Webster, loc. cit.

have ended in peace, to await the final sleep wafted on the wind from the sea.[494] 'Because of this do not be sad at heart.'[495]

Within the second journey of Gilgamesh there are particular characters and episodes for which one may point to parallels in the *Odyssey*. His quest is for Utnapishtim because he alone was preserved by the gods from the deluge and given the gift of everlasting life, set to live at his ease far away, at the 'mouth of the rivers', in the land of Dilmun, the garden of the sun (Sandars, pp 97, 105, 107, 113). A comparison is sometimes drawn with the destiny of Menelaus in the *Odyssey*. We know the grim and negative Homeric picture of the afterlife from *Odyssey* 11. Yet a brighter kind of survival, without death, is possible for some chosen souls, such as Menelaus in Elysium, at the world's end 'where all existence is a dream of ease'.[496]

There is the strange veiled, Circe-like figure of Siduri, the wine-worker of the gods. 'Beside the sea she lives ... Siduri sits in the garden at the edge of the sea, with the golden bowl and the golden vats that the gods gave her' (Sandars, p. 100). Like Circe, she would deflect Gilgamesh from his quest to a philosophy of sensual pleasure: 'Dance and be merry, feast and rejoice, make your wife happy in your embrace: for this too is the lot of man'.[497] (Sandars, p. 102). But again, like Circe to Odysseus, it is she who consents to give Gilgamesh the instructions without which he cannot reach his goal. Odysseus may not find his way home till he sails to the bourne of Ocean and there follows her instructions to glimpse the cold halls of death and their shadowy hosts.[498] Gilgamesh has to *cross* the river of Ocean. It is the instructions of Siduri that direct him to Urshanabi, the ferryman[499] of Utnapishtim.

Mention of Circe reminds us of the magic herb *moly*, by which, on the instruction of Hermes, Odysseus is preserved from the fate of his comrades, turned into swine by the potion of Circe.[500] The parallel is not complete, but the motif of the magic plant is also in Gilgamesh (Sandars, pp. 116ff). It is the elixir that will restore to Gilgamesh his lost youth, the *pis aller* which out of pity Utnapishtim

494 See *Od.* 23.281ff.

495 Sandars, 118.

496 *Od.* 4.565 (tr. Fitzgerald). To the famous lines that follow: 'Where falls not hail, or rain, or any snow' etc. (to use the Tennyson version). Sandars (p. 39) quotes an old description of Dilmun, as the place where 'the croak of the raven was not heard, the bird of death did not utter the cry of death, the lion did not devour ... ' etc.

497 Cf. Eccles 9:9.

498 *Od.* 11.487ff.

499 And of course the grim ferryman himself, even if not found in Homer, is an archetypal figure in Western literature.

500 *Od.* 10.277ff.

reveals to him.[501] And it may be a detail worth noting that, when Circe restores the companions of Odysseus to their human shape with the touch of another *pharmakon*, they are younger as well as taller and more handsome than before.[502]

Nor must we lose sight of the master-idea for the details. The motif at the heart of the second journey of Gilgamesh is that archetypal one in Western literature,[503] the descent or crossing to the other world and the way to guidance, illumination, wisdom, *nel mezzo del cammin di nostra vita*. 'I wish to question you concerning the living and the dead ... ', says Gilgamesh to Utnapishtim in explanation of his crossing of 'the waters of death'.[504] One is liable to miss this precise rationale of Odysseus' journey to the shades,[505] as also of the descent of Aeneas in *Aeneid* 6.[506] A variation on the motif occurs in fact a second time in the *Odyssey* (4.351ff), in the capture and questioning of Proteus, the 'ancient of the deep', when Menelaus, becalmed off Egypt by the anger of the gods on his *nostos* from Troy, is enlightened on the reasons, on the various fates of his lost companions, and on all the fearful things that have happened at home in his long absence. Odysseus' vision reveals a particularly bleak picture of the nature of the limited survival after death. It pervades the whole vision, but it is most explicitly expressed by Achilles (fittingly, as he was so tragically preoccupied with it in life). How did Odysseus find his way hither

> down to the dark
> where these dim-witted dead are camped forever,
> the after-images of used-up men?[507]

Achilles himself would rather be a serf in life than lord it, as he now does, 'over all the exhausted dead'.[508]

This vision is surpassed in bleakness and an extra dimension of awesomeness by one in Gilgamesh, though it occurs not in the second journey but in the

501 It is part of the tragedy of Gilgamesh that even this he loses, stolen from him by a serpent, a motif of which, like the flood, Scripture scholars take note.

502 *Od.* 10.395f.

503 Arthur Koestler, in *Insight and Outlook*, goes as far as to assert 'authors from whose main works this motif is entirely absent suffer, despite technical virtuosity and other merits, from a lack of depth, emotional impact or significance (in the chapter entitled 'The Night Journey').

504 Sandars, 116.

505 To hear prophecy from blind Tiresias (*Od.* 10.492ff.).

506 See *Aen.* 5.731ff – to hear his people's destiny and where their city was to be – this at a critical point of discouragement in mid-voyage.

507 *Od.* 11.475 (tr. Fitzgerald).

508 *Od.* 11.488–91.

climax to the first, in the dream vision by Enkidu that precedes his death: 'there is the house whose people sit in darkness; dust is their food and clay their meat ... I entered the house of dust and I saw the kings of the earth, their crowns put away for ever ... Then I awoke like a man drained of blood who wanders alone in a waste of rushes; like one whom the bailiff has seized and his heart pounds with terror'.[509]

Although we may not be able to point to quite as many individual parallels with the *Iliad* as with the *Odyssey*, there is perhaps a more important fact: it is with the *Iliad* that there is the organic parallel, deeper, more diffused, more pervasive. Gilgamesh *is* an Achilles, or vice versa, and the first journey in particular is his *Iliad*. And the second journey is his *Odyssey*, and depends very organically on the first, as Homer's *Odyssey* does on the *Iliad*. The action of the first journey, the Forest Journey, flows entirely from his character, as does the Iliad[510] from the character of Achilles. And without that Forest Journey there is no second journey in quest of the secret of everlasting life. And his character, like that of Achilles, is not just a psychological motor to the action: it is driven by a metaphysical anxiety.[511]

'The central theme of the Gilgamesh epic ... is the problem of death'.[512] Gilgamesh, like Achilles, is an 'angry' man in a sense deeper than the psychological. He is a metaphysical *révolté*. And like Achilles this leads him into a train of action that becomes tragic at two levels: at the first level in the conventional (Greek) sense of hubristic *hamartia* and its consequences (particularly the death of the faithful companion, Enkidu, as of Patroclus in the *Iliad*); at the deeper, or more transcendent, level in what I have called[513] the 'total' tragedy of the human situation. Tragic defeat is not partial or provisional. It is total, final, absolute. 'You will never find that life for which you are looking. When the gods created man they allotted to him death.'[514]

Before tracing in more detail these two strands, which are so parallel to the chemistry of the *Iliad*, let us notice a couple of more specific parallels (which are also very germane to the unfolding of the tragedy). As already implied, Gilgamesh has his faithful companion Enkidu as the heroic Achilles has his Patroclus. The parallel extends to the fact that in both poems it is the tragic death of the

509 Sandars, 92f.

510 The *moral* dependence of the *Odyssey* on the *Iliad* is not quite as explicit as the Greek tragedians later made it, who saw in the sufferings of the returning Greeks a punishment for their *hubris* at Troy. But for Homer too the Odyssey is something more than just *post hoc*. See pp. 95f. above, and the glimpses we get in *Od.* 11.435ff., 558–60, and especially 3.130ff.

511 See my earlier article cited in footnote 1.

512 Heidel, op. cit., 137.

513 In the earlier article (after Lesky, *Greek Tragedy*, 2, 4, 8, 13 etc.).

514 Sandars, 102 and *passim*.

companion that is the occasion of the existential discovery of death and sends the respective heroes into paroxysms of grief and 'Rage, rage ... ': 'Gilgamesh laid a veil, as one veils the bride, over his friend. He began to rage like a lion, like a lioness robbed of her whelps.'[515]

Achilles and Gilgamesh have also in common the fact that both are the offspring of the union of a mortal man and an immortal goddess, Achilles of Thetis and Gilgamesh of Ninsun. 'Two thirds they made him god and one third man.'[516] The relevant implications of this semi-divine origin of the heroes are not made explicit in the poems, but we may interpret along the lines of Plato's explanatory use of the Orphic myth of man's nature as being a mixture of the divine and a fallen rebellious element. For Plato it explains man's Titanic nature. 'The spectacle of the Titanic nature of which our old legends speak is re-enacted; man returns to the old tradition of a hell of unending misery.'[517]

We are entitled to suggest that not just the 'heroic' level of their humanity, but this more-than-human divine-demonic ingredient in their natures explains the manic emotional range of a Gilgamesh and an Achilles, their capacity for depression and despair,[518] for 'that gall of anger that swarms like smoke inside a man's heart'.[519] The key to their emotions is deeper than the purely psychological or moral. It is to be found in the depths of the existential heart (in the Augustinian and Pascalian sense), the 'stormy heart', the 'restless desire', the 'restless heart'.[520] In mythic terms Gilgamesh and Achilles are part-human, part-divine. But for an Augustine, for a Pascal, indeed for a Lucretius,[521] they are Everyman in the abyss of his consciousness. As another author of the Near East put it (in one possible version), the Creator 'has put eternity in man's heart, but not the capacity to comprehend the work of God from its beginning to its end'.[522]

Interpreted in the light of these ideas the figure of Enkidu, far from being merely secondary to Gilgamesh as the hero's companion, takes on an extraordinary central significance. Indeed, in the first journey and its consequence, the first tragedy is his and only secondarily that of Gilgamesh (through his loss of

515 Sandars, 95. For Achilles see *Il.* 18.22ff.

516 Sandars, 61 etc. In both poems too we see the divine mother play the role of *consolatrix* to her tragic son: Sandars, 66f., 74f.; *Il.* 1.352ff. etc.

517 *Laws*, 3.701 c.

518 Sandars, 72.

519 *Il.* 18.109 (tr. Lattimore).

520 Sandars, 62, 72, 74.

521 See, for example, such a burning phrase as 3.1084:

sitis aequa tenet vitai semper hiantis,

'the same unquenchable thirst for life keeps us always on the gasp' (tr. Graves).

522 Eccles 3:11.

Enkidu). Through a 'fall' in reverse he becomes a kind of choral symbol of what it means to become a man in the tragically awakened sense of the poem.

The Enkidu who is specially created to be the equal and the companion of Gilgamesh is at first a man of the wilderness, at one with nature and the creatures of the wild, before being lured to the sophistication of the city and the palace. Woman, a harlot, is the conscious instrument of his 'fall'. For seven days and seven nights Enkidu forgot his home in the hills. When he returned, the wild creatures bolted at his sight. 'Enkidu would have followed, but his body was bound as though with a cord, his knees gave way ... his swiftness was gone ... Enkidu was grown weak, for wisdom was in him, and the thoughts of a man were in his heart'; and now he too, like Gilgamesh, 'longed for a comrade, for one who would understand his heart'.[523] On his death-bed he curses the agent of his fall, and the choral warnings to Gilgamesh from the start of the Forest Journey are his.

IV

It remains but to trace the essentially tragic structure[524] of that first journey, and of the second one, at the two levels indicated earlier.

The project of Gilgamesh is to destroy 'the evil that is in the land' (p. 71), in the person of Humbaba, the giant watchman of the Cedar Forest. And the purpose of this is to 'set up my home in the place where the names of famous men are written' (p. 70). The warnings of Enkidu about the tragic potential of the project only serve to bring out more intensely the *hubris* of Gilgamesh and its nihilistic roots. 'Where is the man who can clamber to heaven? Only the gods live for ever ... as for us men, our days are numbered, our occupations are a breath of wind ... If I fall, I leave behind me a name that endures' (p. 71).[525] There is a Sartrian sense of the futility of man as a useless passion in the further cry to Shamash (the Sun-god): 'If this enterprise is not to be accomplished, why did you move me with the restless desire to perform it?' (pp. 72, 74).

All wiser counsels notwithstanding, against the depth of the forest and the ferocity of its divinely appointed guardian Gilgamesh and Enkidu set out. In three days they walked as much as a journey of six weeks. They crossed seven mountains before they came to the gate of the forest. And there comes the first evil omen with the punishment of the first *hamartia*. Because Enkidu opens the gate with his hand, it is paralysed (p. 76). Gilgamesh will not heed his plea to

523 Sandars, 65; cf. 67, 70.

524 It is not strictly to the purpose of this already long paper to go into stylistic matters that are necessary for a full appreciation of the power of the poem (the hieratic language, the parallelism, anaphora etc. by which mood and atmosphere, epic scale in space and time, are powerfully produced).

525 Cf. the choice of Achilles between a short life with 'glory' or a long life without, at *Il.* 18.115ff.

turn back. They come to the mountain of cedars, 'the dwelling-place of the gods and the throne of Ishtar' (p. 77). They encamp on its slopes. Ominous dreams are dreamed by Gilgamesh, in one of which 'we stood in a deep gorge of the mountain, and beside it we two were like the smallest of camp flies; and suddenly the mountain fell, it struck me and caught my feet from under me' (p. 78). Enkidu is worried but finally interprets all these dreams as presaging the fall of Humbaba. He quickly changes his mind when Humbaba appears and fastens on Gilgamesh his 'eye of death' in answer to their provocative felling of a cedar (p. 81). Enkidu wants to return to the city. But Gilgamesh will go on. 'All living creatures born of the flesh shall sit at last in the boat of the West, and when it sinks, when the boat of Magilum sinks, they are gone; but we shall go forward and fix our eyes on this monster' (p. 81).

It should have been an unequal contest but, with the help of Shamash, Humbaba is brought to bay and pleads for his life. And now comes the moment characteristic of epic grandeur and tragic choice, the moment when man's rational judgement and man's blind passions are put in the scales over a fateful action, the moment when the victor may or may not spare his victim, and seals thereby his own later fate. It is the choice of Achilles over the fallen Hector,[526] of the pious Aeneas over the pleading Turnus.[527]

A dramatic dialogue decides the issue. Gilgamesh is indeed moved to mercy. 'If we touch him, the blaze and the glory of light will be put out in confusion, the glory and glamour will vanish ... ' (p. 83). But for Enkidu they are already 'stepp'd in too far': the strongest man wil fall to fate 'if he has no judgement (p.82). The bird must be trapped to avoid trouble from the chicks. 'Afterwards we can search out the glory and the glamour, when the chicks run distracted through the grass' (p. 83). Humbaba must be slain. And they struck him in turn. And at the third stroke Humbaba fell. 'Then there followed confusion, for this was the guardian of the forest whom they had felled to the ground' (p. 83).

The elation of victory both facilitates and is compounded by the episode of the scorning of one of the archetypal hero's rewards, the advances of Ishtar, goddess of love, and by the slaying of the Bull of Heaven[528] that she sends in revenge. But compounded also is the tragic *hubris*: for to scorn Ishtar is also *hamartia*.[529] The heroes ride in triumph through the streets of Uruk, but that night Enkidu has a dream. In his dream he sees the gods in council, and Anu says to Enlil: 'Because

526 *Il.* 22.337ff.

527 *Aen.* 12.930ff.

528 Cf. the boar sent by Artemis, at *Il.* 9.529ff.

529 An archetypal motif, which again we find in Greece, e.g. in Theocritus, *Idyll* 1.

they have killed the Bull of Heaven, and because they have killed Humbaba[530] who guarded the Cedar Mountain, one of the two must die' (p. 89). And Enkidu falls ill, and to cursing the harlot, the forest gate, and all that has brought him from original pastoral innocence to this. He has his terrible dream-vision of the 'house from which none who enters ever returns' (p. 92). The 'thoughts of a man' indeed are now mature in his heart. For (in the words of Gilgamesh) 'the dream has shown that ... the end of life is sorrow' (p. 93). When he dies, Gilgamesh mourns seven days and seven nights over his body, 'until the worm fastened on him. Only then did he give him up to the earth' (p. 96).[531]

It is the individual death of Enkidu that awakens Gilgamesh to its universal inevitability and finality. 'Wherever my foot rests, there I find death' (p. 115). The discovery involves both tragic 'recognition' and classic 'conversion': 'What my brother is now, that shall I be when I am dead' (p. 97). Tragic 'recognition' because it is now clear that it is not enough to set up one's name 'where the names of famous men are written' (p. 72). Heroic achievement has not filled the void in his heart. It has but opened up a deeper abyss. The original *Angst* in his heart has now become despair (p. 97). Action and achievement are not enough. They demand a ground and condition of their meaning. It is already the Augustinian discovery, that 'our hearts are restless' until they rest in permanence (and Augustine also discovered this in great part through the 'discovery' of death); hence the classic 'conversion' to the higher quest. 'Because I am afraid of death I will go to find Utnapishtim whom they call the Faraway, for he has entered the assembly of the gods' (p. 97).

It is an essential part of our interpretation of the meaning of the whole poem that this second journey too is tragic. Not that we can trace there the conventional tragic structures in the familiar stricter sense, as we could in the first journey. But that is part of its very meaning. Gilgamesh is looking for the answer to an individual tragedy, and he finds 'total' tragedy. Behind all particular and partial defeats there is universal and final defeat. There is *no* permanence (p. 107). And the structure of tragedy is there too, in its elemental form. For Gilgamesh is a man driven by a passion, a passion to obtain what appears, and turns out to be, greater-than-human. And his quest entails a struggle against fate and the gods. But the gods are jealous. They have allotted death to man and kept everlasting life to themselves (p. 102).

530 Cf. one of the reasons for the wanderings of Odysseus, namely the anger of Poseidon at his blinding of Polyphemus, Poseidon's son (*Od.*1.19ff, 74f; 9.528ff).

531 Cf. *Il.* 18.334ff. for Achilles over Patroclus. With the preceding dirge of Gilgamesh (94f) compare *Il.* 18.28 ff. But, more specifically, in the lament of *universal nature* in *Gilgamesh* we surely have the remote origins of that other Greek genre, the pastoral elegy (Enkidu had also been a watchman with the shepherds).

That it is impossible to transcend this limitation is the ritual refrain of the journey. That to try to transcend it is *hubris* is the point of the pathetic and failed ordeal of sleep-resistance to which Utnapishtim submits Gilgamesh (p. 114f).[532] This is tragedy in the very structure of existence, the same kind of larger, total tragic view as we find in early Greece, in the *Iliad*, in Herodotus, and in a good deal of Greek tragedy. It is tragedy with a range of *spoudaion* not encompassed by the more narrowly moral and humanist theory of Aristotle that has so influenced our understanding.

The journey itself is an archetypal sequence of dangerous *passages* through mythic geography into another world, through the mountain passes, and the lions, through Mashu the mountain of the sun, through the Garden of the Gods, over Ocean and the 'waters of death', to Dilmun the Land of the Living, into the presence of Utnapishtim. As action this is splendidly epic, but not specifically tragic in the same way as the action in the Forest Journey, unless in one or two episodes we get a glimpse of tragic rage against nature itself, like that of Achilles in his fight with the River Scamander.[533] There is the violent slaying of the lions that Gilgamesh saw around him 'glorying in life': 'he fell upon them like an arrow from the string, and struck, and destroyed and scattered them' (p. 97). There is the unexplained smashing of the unidentified 'holy things, the things of stone' belonging to the ferryman (p. 102f).

For the rest, the tragic values are in what Aristotle calls the *dianoia* (thought), thought which here is particularly reinforced by the style and technique, hieratic, formulaic, anaphoric, thought carried rather as it is carried by the Greek tragic chorus. Again and again at the moments of *passage* there is the same question to and reply from Gilgamesh on the cause and the goal of his quest, and the same comment on its feasibility: 'you will never find that life for which you are searching' (pp. 100, 102). The thought and the effect of its style can only be conveyed in an extended sample, such as the exchange with Siduri (p. 101f):

> 'I am Gilgamesh who seized and killed the Bull of Heaven. I killed the watchman of the cedar forest, I overthrew Humbaba who lived in the forest, and I killed the lions in the passes of the mountain'.
> Then Siduri said to him, 'If you are that Gilgamesh who seized and killed (etc.), why are your cheeks so starved and why is your face so drawn? Why is despair in your heart, and your face like the face of one who has made a long journey?'

532 And cf. the banishment of the ferryman for having dared to take him across the waters of death (115).

533 *Il.* 21.211ff. See my article, 'Total Tragedy and Homer's Illiad', in: *The Maynooth Review* 5 (1979), 80 [= previous chapter, p. 86]

> Gilgamesh answered her, 'And why should not my cheeks be starved and my face drawn? Despair is in my heart, and my face is the face of one who has made a long journey ... Enkidu my brother, whom I loved, the end of mortality has overtaken him ... Because of my brother I am afraid of death, because of my brother I stray through the wilderness and cannot rest ... Do not let me see the face of death which I dread so much'.
> She answered, 'Gilgamesh, where are you hurrying to? You will never find that life for which you are looking'.

And Utnapishtim confirms it. He has no secret way to disclose. He owes his own immortality to the fact that he was first preserved, like Noah, from the deluge sent by the gods to exterminate insufferable mankind, and then invited by the gods to live with them. This privilege he appears to owe to no higher reason that that (if one may so put it) he had a Deep Throat among the gods who forewarned him, and once he had surfaced from the waters they did not quite know what else to do with him (we might, though, also see this more favourable god as a kind of Prometheus towards wretched mankind). But Gilgamesh can expect no such council of the gods in his case (p. 114). The tragic truth is that 'there is no permanence ... It is only the nymph of the dragonfly who sheds her larva and sees the sun in his glory' (p. 107).

Nothing remains except to retrace his journey, to return to Uruk, with nothing gained except tragic wisdom, and a new companion in the excommunicate ferryman. But the poem shows a fine sense of an ending by taking us to that point of return through two final episodes. They are the failed ordeal of sleep and the lost magic herb of youth, doubtless both motifs with high archetypal origins. But as processed to this ending they produce a note of bitter pathos, deep humanity and final simplicity. Pathos-bitter too in the insistence on reducing the great king and epic hero to the final nakedness of a Lear, of a mortal so frail he cannot even stay awake: 'Look at him now, the strong man who would have everlasting life' (p. 114). Pathos bitter too is the thought that the serpent who stole the plant can slough his skin, while man cannot. Deep humanity in the cry it evokes: 'Was it for this that I toiled with my hands, is it for this I have wrung out my heart's blood?' (p. 117). Resignation and final simplicity[534] in the decision: 'Let us leave the boat on the bank and go' (p. 117).

534 While making such aesthetic judgements we have to recall again that we are seeing through the dark glass of translation. But the more scientific rendering in Heidel (op. cit.) does not belie it (Tablet XI, lines 299f). In any case we have to crave some indulgence towards our own search for an ending!

EXODOS

In due time 'the destiny was fulfilled which the father of the gods ... had decreed for Gilgamesh' (p. 118). The Sandars version ends with his death. Apparently this fragment exists only in the Sumerian and it is not certain that it belongs here in the final recension of the poem. The least that can be said is that it deserves to be here, providing as it does an end like the choral *exodos* of a Greek tragedy:

> *The King has laid himself down and will not rise again,*
> *The Lord of Kullab will not rise again;*
> *He overcame evil, he will not come again;*
> *Though he was strong of arm he will not rise again.*

THE MYTH OF THE INNOCENT SUFFERER: SOME GREEK PARADIGMS

For this question of the innocent sufferer in Greek literature I shall be concentrating on its presence at the very beginning of Greek literature, in Homer's Iliad – *ab Jove incipiendum.* But before coming to Homer I would like to indicate its setting and *suite* in Greek literature down to the end of the Classical period by giving some references which show the constant presence of the question of man's suffering and the justice of Zeus.

First there is Hesiod. Nearly half of the *Works and Days* is concerned with setting the labours of man in the context of the total cosmic order of Justice under Zeus, its guarantor. And that already in the technical terminology of tragic theory as we meet it frequently in Aeschylus – δίκη, ὕβρις, ἄτη, and wisdom from suffering: παθὼν δέ τε νήπιος ἔγνω 213ff; cf. Aeschylus, *Persae* 807ff, and *Agam.* 177: πάθει μάθος. The eye of Zeus sees all (*W. D.* 267). And in a striking parallel to the Yahweh of Job he even has his *agents* who keep watch upon the earth:

> For upon the bounteous earth Zeus has thrice ten thousand spirits, watchers of mortal men, and these keep watch on judgements and deeds of wrong as they roam φοιτῶντες clothed in mist, all over the earth.[535]
> One day the Sons of God came to attend on Yahweh, and among them was Satan. So Yahweh said to Satan, 'Where have you been?' 'Round the earth' he answered 'roaming about'. So Yahweh asked him, 'Did you notice my servant Job ... ?'[536]

But Hesiod is working with more elements than he can quite fuse together into a systematic theodicy. And one of them is the anfractuous fact that the ways of Zeus with man are hard and jealous, and that *la condition humaine* is unexplainable except by positing a primordial 'fall' of man, in the two myths of Prometheus and the five ages of the human race. At the end of this present age

535 *W. D.* 252–5.

536 Job 1:6ff, to which see the note in M. H. Pope, *Job*.

man will be entirely abandoned by the gods, and nothing left him but bitter pain and no defence against evil.[537]

Next there are the lyric poets:

Archilochus (680–640):

> To the gods all things are easy. Many times from circumstance of disaster they set upright those who have been sprawled at length on the ground, but often again when men stand planted on firm feet, these same gods will knock them on their backs and then the evils come, so that a man wanders homeless, destitute, at his wits' end.[538]

Semonides of Amorgos (fl. mid-7th century):

> My child, Zeus the deep-thundering holds the ends of all things in his hands, disposes as he will of everything. We who are human have no minds, but live from day to day, like beasts, and nothing know of what god plans to make happen to each of us.[539]

Mimnermus (fl. 2nd half of 7th c.) concludes a bleak meditation on life with the summary that 'no man on earth eludes the net of unending sorrows sent us by Zeus'.[540]

Theognis (6th c.) asks the fundamental question of theodicy:

> I am surprised at you, dear Zeus! You're lord
> Everywhere, hold all honour and great power;
> You know the mind and heart of every man;
> Your rule's supreme, my king, in all the world.
> How then, O son of Kronos, can your mind
> Bear to see criminals and honest men –
> Both thoughtful men whose minds are moderate,
> And sinful weaklings – share the selfsame fate?[541]

537 *W. D.* 197–201.

538 J. M. Edmonds, *Elegy and Iambus*, Loeb (II), 126 (tr. Lattimore). Cf. *Iliad* 24, 527–33; *Works and Days*, 3ff.

539 Edmonds, op. cit. (II), 212ff, tr. Lattimore.

540 Edmonds, op. cit. (I), 90.

541 373ff, tr. Wender.

Again, and consequently:

> For man the best thing is never to be born,
> Never to look upon the hot sun's rays,
> Next best, to speed at once through Hades' gates
> And lie beneath a piled-up heap of earth.[542]

Next there is the age of the great tragedians. Here we find not just the question but great Gilgamesh- and Job-like figures that embody the question. Reference to the *Prometheus* of Aeschylus is commonplace. But there is not only Prometheus. There is the figure of Hercules in Sophocles (*Trachiniae*) and Euripides (*Heracles*). There is the Ajax of Sophocles. Above all there is the Oedipus of Sophocles, especially as we see him in *Oedipus at Colonus*. With the persistent refusal of Job to accept the imputation of guilt we may compare the similar refusal of Oedipus in *Oed. Col.* 538–541:

> Chor.: Thou hast endured –
> Oed.: Intolerable woe.
> Chor.: And sinned –
> Oed.: I sinned not.
> Chor.: How so?
> Oed.: I served the State: would I had never won
> That graceless grace by which I was undone.[543]

The theme is still present in the post-Classical disillusionment of Aristophanes' *Ploutos* (388 BC):

> Chremylus: And this your sad affliction, how this?
> (to the old, blind, disguised god Ploutos)
>
> Ploutos: It was Zeus did this to me, out of spite against mankind. In my youth I used to say I would visit only the upright and wise and modest. So he made me blind so I couldn't know who they were. That just shows how much ill-will he bears against decent people.
>
> Chremylus: And yet it's only the good and the upright who pay Zeus himself due honour.[544]

542 425–8, tr. Wender. Cf. Sophocles, *Oed. Col.* 1225–8.

543 Cf. 545–8.

544 *Ploutos* 86ff.

Lastly we note that our question is given by Plato as the reason for the practical atheism of those who believe that even if the gods exist they are indifferent to human affairs: 'What drives you to impiety is the good fortune of scoundrels and criminals in public and private life ...'.[545]

To revert to Homer's *Iliad*, then, in the context outlined, our problem is present at the very beginning of Greek literature in two ways.

Firstly – and most interestingly – at the level of the conscious, explicitly reflective level of the *question*:

> Ah me, I am full of sorrow for great-hearted Aeneas
> who must presently go down to death, overpowered by Achilles,
> because he believed the words of Apollo, the far-ranging;
> poor fool, since Apollo will do nothing to keep grim death from him.
> But why does this man, who is guiltless,[546] suffer his sorrows
> for no reason, for the sake of others' unhappiness, and always
> he gives gifts that please them to the gods who hold the wide heaven.[547]

In this passage we see implied already the quest for that moral order of the world which the Greeks were soon to concentrate into the formal term *dikē*.[548] It is not named here and *dikē* is not a prominent term in the *Iliad*, but equivalents are common – or what I take to be equivalents or on the way to it. Thus Ares knows nothing of Justice – οὔ τινα οἶδε θέμιστα (5.761). Neither does the warrior Athena, 'whose mind is forever fixed on unjust action', ἀήσυλα ἔργα μέμηλεν (5.876). In the breast of the 'cursed Achilles' ὀλοῷ Ἀχιλῆϊ there are no feelings of justice, οὔτ' ἄρ φρένες εἰσὶν ἐναίσιμοι (24.39f).

And the guarantor of sanctions against Injustice is Zeus – 6.384ff, where the term *dikē* is used. The passage is a simile, describing the hurtling of the horses of Patroclus against Hector:

> As underneath the hurricane all the black earth is burdened on an autumn day, when Zeus sends down the most violent waters in deep rage against mortals after they stir him to anger because in violent assembly they pass decrees that are crooked and drive righteousness δίκην from among them and care nothing for what the gods think ...

545 *Laws*, 899.

546 ἀναίτιος.

547 Poseidon in *Il.* 20.293ff, tr. Lattimore.

548 And of course justice, the moral order of the world, is Job's quest too – see explicitly 8:3; 27:2, and the pervasive imagery of Yahweh on trial on the one hand and Job on the other.

This last passage is a veritable résumé of the moral order, the *dikē*, between man and Zeus, the exposition of which we have noted in the first half of Hesiod's *Works and Days*.

Secondly, our problem is present from the start in the *mythic* mode. I refer to myth here of course in its more elastic sense of paradigmatic character or situation. A character or situation that was originally historical may become mythic in that sense. So we see the Greek tragedians constantly handling and re-handling inherited characters and situations as paradigmatic of contemporary and perennial problems. So the Job-like characters I mentioned from Greek tragedy are mythic. So Gilgamesh and Job from the Near East are mythic. So Achilles from the Aegean is mythic. And whatever about Job there can be little doubt that the figure of Achilles owes something to the older Gilgamesh.

That the *Iliad* does embody our problem could not be made clearer than it is made in the opening thematic statement of the poem itself:

> Sing, goddess, the anger of Peleus' son Achilles and its devastation, which put pains thousandfold upon the Achaeans, hurled in their multitudes to the house of Hades strong souls of heroes, but gave their bodies to be the delicate feasting of dogs, and of all birds, *and the will of Zeus was accomplished.*

And this theme, this human cry and its implicit, sometimes explicit, questioning of 'the father of gods of men', this theme runs through the whole poem, from this opening to its marvellous provisional resolution with the meeting of Achilles and Priam over the body of Hector.

In what ways the *question* is given *mythic* embodiment and expression I have already partially anticipated. Homer is a sophisticated poet and treats his material far beyond the level of the sagas he may have used. His interest goes beyond the heroic code of glory or the anger of Achilles for its own intrinsic sake. As I have argued in a little article elsewhere the anger of Achilles is ultimately metaphysical.[549] Achilles is a type, a representative, of *l'homme révolté.* And his mythic, universalizing, representative status is reinforced by the scarcely dubitable fact that into his making has gone not only whatever the Greek tradition may have known or imagined about the Trojan War but also elements from the as-old-again *Near Eastern* tradition of Gilgamesh. Gilgamesh too, like Job, represents *l'homme révolté* – against *la condition humaine* at its most ultimately tragic, faced not just with innocent suffering but with the final unredeemed futility of death.

549 'Total Tragedy and Homer's *Iliad'*, *Maynooth Review* 5 (1979), 71–83 [above pp. xxxx].

I have looked over the wall and I see the bodies floating on the river,
and that will be my lot too.[550]

Let me hear no smooth talk
of death from you, Odysseus ...
Better, I say, to break sod as a farmhand
for some poor countryman, on iron rations,
than lord it over all the exhausted dead.[551]

Similarly Job intensifies the pathos and the problem of his *immediate* situation in the light of the *ultimate* human situation:

The days of my life are few enough:
turn your eyes away, leave me a little joy,
before I go to the place of no return,
the land of murk and deep shadow,
where dimness and disorder hold sway,
and light itself is like the dead of night (10.20ff).[552]

It is in the light of this supreme tragic awareness of the *Iliad* that the frequently quoted words of Goethe have their validity: 'From Homer I learn every day more clearly that in our life here above ground we have, properly speaking, to enact Hell'.[553] But the perception is already in a great ancient critic. Longinus, in the course of his fine excursus on Homer, remarks apropos of the vision of life in the *Iliad* that 'when we men are unhappy there is always death as a haven from our troubles' (9.7).

That precise sentiment we find explicit at the heart both of the *Iliad* and of Job.

Now I shall go, to overtake that killer of a dear life,
Hector; then I will accept my own death, at whatever
time Zeus wishes to bring it about, and the other immortals.
For not even the strength of Hercules fled away from destruction ...
but his fate beat him under, and the wearisome anger of Hera.
So I likewise, if such is the fate which has been wrought for me,
Shall *lie still* when I am *dead*. Now I must win excellent glory ...
(IL. 18.117FF).

550 *Gilgamesh*, tr. Sandars, 72.

551 Achilles in *Od.* 11.488ff.

552 Cf. 7:1ff; 14:1ff.

553 Quoted in Abercrombie, *The Epic*, 58; cf. Lewis, *Preface to Paradise Lost*, 31. With more concentration, perhaps, in *Il.* 17 than in any other place in literature, and quintessentially around the figure of Ajax (415ff) – who becomes a Job-like figure in Sophocles.

And of course behind this the more explicit and positive wish for death is commonplace, e.g. at points of supreme crisis, *Il.* 21.279ff, 24.244ff.

> Down there bad men bustle no more,
> there the weary rest.
> Down there high and low are all one,
> and the slave is free of his master.
> (Job 3:17ff. Cf.6:9; 17:12–14).

Within the material limits of this paper it is not possible to be more than schematic and indicative of directions and areas. I have not exhausted the analysis of the figure of Achilles. But he is not the only representative figure in the *Iliad* for our purposes. It would be unlikely that he *should* be in a poem that constitutes a world, and a world contemplated under the aspect thematically stated in the opening lines of the poem. There are figures that come closer to Job (though not to Gilgamesh) in that, unlike the ferocious Achilles, they do not resist their fate, or are too helpless to be able to resist it.

In one instance those figures are a group, representative of *collective* innocent suffering. That instance is the women – and children – of Troy.[554] Whether Homer intended it as such or not, we know from the examples of Stesichorus (*Ilioupersis*), Euripides (*Troades* and *Hecuba*), Virgil (*Aen.* 2) and Seneca (*Troades*), that this ingredient of the calamity most familiar to the imagination of the early Mediterranean world became the archetypal myth or symbol of such collective and innocent suffering in every age. It provoked the same ultimate questions as did the suffering of the innocent *individual* about the moral order of the world – or even, more nihilistically, whether there be any such order at all. There is no afterlife, says Andromache in Euripides' *Troades*, and therefore the dead are happier than the living – they remember nothing of all they suffered in life (634ff):

> Therefore we ask. Monarch of all that lives,
> Firm on your heavenly throne,
> While the destroying Fury gives
> Our homes to ashes and our flesh to worms –
> We ask, and ask: What does this mean to You?[555]

At the climax of the *Iliad* we contemplate all this collective suffering through the eyes of the patriarchal Priam. And in many ways he is closely parallel to Job. In his

554 See *Il.* 22.430ff, 24.692ff.

555 *Troades* 1077–80, tr. Vellacott; cf. *Aen.* 2.601–3.

age and helplessness and innocence of the causes of what has happened, in his loss of his sons, and daughters,[556] in his impotent grief and anger against Heaven,[557] in his revulsion against his own equivalent of Job's useless counsellors, in his isolation and affliction (as Simone Weil would call it), sitting like Job in the dust and the dung.[558]

This picture of Priam is linked especially to the narrative of the loss of Hector, the most heroic and glorious of all his sons, the *Iliad's* Trojan foil to the Greek Achilles. We meet him in *Il.* 22 looking out from behind the city walls on Hector, alone of all the Trojans isolated outside the closed city gates, there on the windy plain to come face to face with his fate in the person of Achilles, a fate described in poetry that must surely be the unsurpassed depiction of a man in the ultimate *Grenzsituation*. Out of this situation the cry of Priam goes up to Zeus:

> Oh, take
> pity on me, the unfortunate still alive, still sentient
> but ill-starred, whom the Father, Kronos' son, on the threshold of old age
> will blast with hard fate, after I have looked upon evils
> and seen my sons destroyed and my daughters dragged away captive
> and the chambers of marriage wrecked and the innocent children taken
> and dashed to the ground in the hatefulness of war, and the wives
> of my sons dragged off by the accursed hands of the Achaians.
> And myself last of all, my dogs in front of my doorway
> will rip me raw, after some man with stroke of the sharp bronze
> spear, or with spear cast, has torn the life out of my body;
> those dogs I raised in my halls to be at my table, to guard my
> gates, who will lap my blood in the savagery of their anger
> and then lie down in my courts. For a young man all decorous is
> when he is cut down in battle and torn with the sharp bronze, and lies there
> dead, and though dead still all that shows about him is beautiful;
> but when the old man is dead and down, and the dogs mutilate
> the grey head and the grey beard and the parts that are secret,
> this, for all sad mortality, is the sight most pitiful.[559]

When the message comes from Zeus to Priam bidding him go to the tent of Achilles and ransom the body of Hector, Priam has at least one counsellor against such a seemingly dangerous mission, and, by implication, against trusting such a

556 Cf. *Il.* 22.62ff, 422 f, 24.493ff, with Job 1:18f.

557 Cf. *Il.* 22.412ff, 24.237ff, with Job 3:1ff; 16:1ff.

558 Cf. *Il.* 22.414, 24.163ff, 639f, and Job 2:8.

559 *Il.* 22.59–76.

message. As in the first instance with Job, so here it is Priam's wife who counsels against (cf. Job 1:9f; *Il.* 24.200ff). From 240 and 263f it would appear that, like Job. he has other counsellors against him as well – palace hangers-on and his nine surviving but worthless sons. All these, like Job, he reviles in his anger:

> Get out, you failures, you disgraces. Have you not also mourning of your own at home that you come to me to annoy me ... ?[560]

> What sorry comforters you are!
> Is there never to be an end of airy words?
> What a plague is your need to have the final word.[561]

We have not the space to go into the question in detail, but as Yahweh is present in Job so is Zeus in the *Iliad*, and we cannot omit a glance at the question of how our problem appears from his side. We have noted how the poet brings him harshly into the equation in his opening statement of theme – in all the murderous happenings 'the will of Zeus was accomplished'.

And the first thing we can say is that, despite many complicating factors, this remains the bleak truth that pervades the poem and remains at the end. There is a most poignant moment in the most tragic Book, 22. It is a cameo of man's isolation under the vault of relentless Heaven. Hector is alone on the plain running for his life around the walls pursued by Achilles. Zeus and all the gods look down and observe. Zeus has a moment of pity because Hector has honoured him.[562] But for all that, on the fourth circuit of the walls in this fearsome race:

> the Father balanced his golden scales, and in them
> he set two fateful portions of death, which lays men prostrate,
> one for Achilles, and one for Hector, breaker of horses,
> and balanced it by the middle; and Hector's death-day was heavier
> and dragged downward towards death, and Phoibos Apollo forsook him.[563]

Achilles' turn will come later:

> There is only one life in him, and people say he is mortal.
> It is only that Zeus, the son of Kronos, is granting him glory.[564]

560 *Il.* 24.239f.

561 Job 16:2f.

562 *Il.* 22.158ff.

563 *Il.* 22.209ff.

564 *Il.* 21.569f.

Zeus is often represented as sitting apart and looking down on the clash of 'ignorant armies' from a remote and sublime indifference:

> Rejoicing in the pride of his strength he sat apart from the others
> looking out over the city of Troy and the ships of the Achaeans,
> watching the flash of the bronze, and men killing and being killed.[565]

And in his eyes

> among all creatures that breathe on earth and crawl on it
> there is not anywhere a thing more dismal than man is.[566]

That is not the whole of his attitude, as we shall see when we come to the *dénouement*, but provisionally at least it is the bottom line. And Zeus is omnipotent and the *primum movens* of the evils that happen to man. Agamemnon holds him responsible for his quarrel with Achilles as Job does Yahweh:

> I am not responsible
> but Zeus is, and Destiny, and Erinys the mist-walking
> Who in assembly caught my heart in the savage delusion ... [567]

> Is there a drought? He (Yahweh) has checked the waters.
> Do these play havoc with the earth? He has let them loose.
> In him is strength, in him resourcefulness,
> beguiler and beguiled are both alike his slave.
> He robs the country's counsellors of their wits,
> turns judges into fools. (Job 12:15ff)

The mention of 'beguiler and beguiled', and robber of 'wits' and maker of 'fools', is striking. For, quite apart from the allegation of Agamemnon, Zeus in the *Iliad* is again and again explicitly shown being precisely all those things! The whole sequence starts in Book 2 with the deceiving dream that

565 *Il.* 11.81ff – partly formulaic, cf. 8.51f.

566 *Il.* 17.446f – contrast 24.525ff on the life of the gods.

567 *Il.* 19.86ff . And in 'delusion' (ἄτη) we see already one of the key concepts of the later tragic pattern, as Aeschylus for instance understood it, in e.g. *Persae* 821ff., with this important difference, that, whereas in Aeschylus ἄτη is the consequence of a prior moral fault in man, here in Homer Ἄτη, 'the elder daughter of Zeus', is an active unprovoked *agent provocateur* of deception and consequent tragic suffering, indeed of the very ὕβρις that releases the tragic pattern (*Il.* 1.202–5, 212–4).

left Agamemnon
there, believing things in his heart that were not to be accomplished.
For he thought that on that very day he would take Priam's city;
fool, who knew nothing of all the things that Zeus planned to accomplish.[568]

'None of this would the son of Kronos accomplish' is a stock formula.[569]

Some of course would question whether Homer's God and gods deserve to be taken so seriously. He did not take them seriously himself, it would be suggested. They are merely conventional epic machinery to facilitate the psychological motivation of heroic action that is essentially human. They are themselves projections of heroic humanity, 'mainly immortal men and women'.[570] The point is already made by Longinus, himself, in the line of an already long tradition of such critical reduction: 'Homer, as it seems to me, has done his best to make the Trojan men gods, and the gods men' (9.7).

As a universal judgement that is mistaken – and must lead to an erroneously reductive interpretation of the *Iliad's* range of questioning. One might also similarly criticize the anthropomorphism of Yahweh and his court in the first two chapters of Job (a court, by the way, which provides a point of parallel with that of Zeus in the *Iliad*). But we do not therefore similarly reduce the transcendent Yahweh of Job 4:12ff. or 38ff. Similar distinctions must be made for the *Iliad*. 'Uncontrollable laughter' does break out in Heaven in one remarkable scene, as the immortals watch the lame Hephaestus hobbling about (1.599f). But *grosso modo* Zeus above all represents the pole of the transcendent, however anthropomorphic or mythic the language, the omega point without which the poem itself is diminished, because without it there is nothing and nobody against whom to measure the charge of *la condition humaine* which is at the heart of the poem.

Zeus is the constant, final and absolute point of reference for *la condition humaine*.[571] In relation to Zeus, *la condition humaine* is put, as it were, *sub specie aeternitatis* – consistently with what we have said earlier about Zeus as the *primum movens* of that condition. One good example occurs already in Book I, 493ff, where the *mise-en-scène* of the whole poem is being given. A powerful passage because it brings together the tragic condition of Achilles, ὠκυμορώτατος ἄλλων, short-lived beyond all other mortals (505), and the numinous omnipotence of Zeus who, when petitioned on behalf of Achilles, has only to nod his head in assent 'and all Olympus was shaken' (530).

568 *Il.* 2.35ff.

569 *Il.* 2.419.

570 Lattimore tr. 54.

571 Cf. Jaeger, *Paideia* (tr. Highet, ed. 1939) vol. I, 50–52.

Indeed in this last detail we get a first glimpse of a feature of Zeus that parallels him to Yahweh in Job. That feature is his omnipotence revealed in theophany through the numinous violence of cosmic disturbance. As Yahweh speaks 'from the heart of the tempest' (Job 38:1) so also does Zeus. An example is 16.384ff (and compare 12.277ff):

> As underneath the hurricane all the black earth is burdened
> on an autumn day, when Zeus sends down the most violent waters
> in deep rage against mortals after they stir him to anger
> because in violent assembly they pass decrees that are crooked,
> and drive righteousness from among them and care nothing for what the
> gods think,
> and all the rivers of these men swell current to full spate
> and in the ravines of their water-courses rip all the hillsides
> and dash whirling in huge noise down to the blue sea, out of
> the mountains headlong, so that the works of men are diminished;
> (so huge rose the noise from the horses of Troy in their running).

Authors of the kind we have been considering had to find a resolution of their questioning. It is time I turned to a resolution of my paper. What is Homer's answer – or Zeus's answer – to the questioning embodied in Achilles and Priam and the women of Troy?

Let us preface our answer with the observation that it is characteristic of even the most explicitly philosophical and rigorous theodicies arising from the problem of innocent suffering to have to admit finally that there is no answer without residue of mystery. An example is the *Consolatio* of Boethius. It has been praised for its beauty. Less often remarked is its sinewy dialectical strength, the tenacity with which Boethius (like Job) tests the metal of all abstract answers in relation to his own irreducible concrete situation, relentlessly probing the wound in existence constituted by the fact that despite a proven supreme and good all-governing Providence, he, the individual innocent Boethius, is still suffering. Till even the lady Philosophy admits:

> It is too much toil for me to speak of all this as if I were God.[572]
> For it is not permitted to a man either by his natural powers (*ingenio*) to comprehend, or in words to express, all the plans (*machinas*) of God's operation.[573]

572 *Consol.* 12.176.

573 *Consol.* 4.6.196ff, ed. Loeb.

The parallel with Job's concluding words is obvious:

> I have been holding forth on matters I cannot understand,
> on marvels beyond me and my knowledge (42:3).

And the *Iliad*? There cannot be the same explicit sense of mystery in this more humanist poem, with its more anthropomorphic Zeus. But the conclusion is only all the bleaker for that. For there is no answer, not even the residue of mystery in which hope, if not understanding, might repose. Nothing but the registering of the brute facts, between Achilles and Priam, in a moment of the meeting of common humanity in shared suffering.

> Such is the way the gods spun life for unfortunate mortals,
> that we live in unhappiness, but the gods themselves have no sorrows.
>
> ...
>
> Therefore
>
> ... bear up, nor mourn endlessly in your heart, for there is not anything to be gained from grief for your son; you will never bring him back; sooner you must go through another sorrow.
>
> (24.525FF).

There is no answer, I have said ... And yet we cannot stop there, taking no notice of other ingredients and other effects upon us, from one of the most magnificent endings in all literature – *Iliad* 24.

What I have in mind can be identified in the most general way as pathos. But then more precisely as pathos focusing into that less diffuse and more positive thing that Aristotle was to call pity, and into the mysterious catharsis that went with it. Which catharsis is more than Stoic resignation. As we all know from our own reading of the end of great tragedies, it is based on *some* kind of perception of *meaning* emerging from the very process of suffering itself – πάθει μάθος as Aeschylus put it.[574]

We find this at the end of Job. He does more than accept mystery in resigned and beaten faith. He has *perceived* something, 'having seen you with my own eyes'. He has perceived something through the very process he has undergone, something he does not just accept but bows down before. This interpretation is confirmed if we accept a translation of 42:6 which I know Dr O'Connor would argue for:[575]

574 *Agam.* 177.

575 See D. O'Connor, 'Job's Final Word – "I am consoled" (42:6b)', in *Irish Theological Quarterly* 50 (1983–4), 181–97.

I faint away (in the quasi-mystical sense)
  and (even) in dust and ashes I am consoled.

It is a thought and an experience magnificently paralleled by one of the great mythic embodiments of our topic, Hercules at the end of what we may call his 'passion', in Sophocles' *Trachiniae*:

O patience muzzle my lips
With iron, lock them in stone,
Stifle the cry,
The way is hard, but the end
Is consolation (1260–3).

More finely balanced, in a Job-like sense of mystery and paradox, are the final lines there by Hercules' son Hyllus:

Women of Trachis, you have leave to go,
You have seen strange things,
The awful hand of death, new shapes of woe,
Uncounted sufferings;
And all that you have seen is God (Zeus).

I have said that the *Iliad* provides no answer, but this is not to say it provides no resolution. The whole of its conclusion (Book 24) might be read as an unfolding and development to Homeric scale of this nucleus of themes – pathos, pity, catharsis, reconcilement, opening on to at least the possibility of final consolation. This is so because the ferocious Achilles, *l'homme révolté* against the human condition, this Achilles effectively undergoes a conversion, a conversion expressly to Aristotelian pity, ἔλεος. I have earlier attributed this conversion to the awakening of common humanity in shared suffering with Priam. But this is not the ultimate reason. The ultimate reason is that Zeus and the gods first have pity, and pour it into his heart as it were, like *agape* in the Pauline phrase (Rom. 5:5).[576]

Achilles has been mutilating the body of Hector – at the sight of which 'the blessed gods ... were filled with compassion' ἐλεαίρεσκον (24.23). In their eyes therefore Achilles is a man 'cursed' ὀλοῷ (24.39), without feelings of justice ἐναίσιμοι (24.40):

576 In a context interestingly like our own! Gloriamur in tribulationibus, scientes quod tribulatio (θλῖψις) patientiam (ὑπομονήν) operatur, patientia autem probationem (δοκιμήν) probatio vero spem; spes autem non confundit, quia caritas Dei diffusa est in cordibus nostris ... (5:3–5).

So Achilles has destroyed pity, and there is not in him
Any shame, which does much harm to men but profits them also.
For a man must some day lose one who was even closer
than this; a brother from the same womb, or a son. And yet
he weeps for him, and sorrows for him, and then it is over,
for the Destinies put in mortal man the heart of endurance.[577]
...
Great as he is, let him take care not to make us angry;
for see, he does dishonour to the dumb earth in his fury.[578]

'So be it', says Achilles,

'if the Olympian himself so urgently bids it.'

And the rest is the dissolving and resolving ἔλεος we know, in the meeting of Achilles and Priam, and the funeral cortège, and the ritual mourning and burial of Hector.

As I said, there is no explicit answer. But we could not just leave it at that, in an ending already so bathed in the atmosphere that Newman found in Virgil – 'that pain and weariness, yet hope of better things, which is the experience of (Nature's) children in every time.'[579]

577 *Il.* 24.139.

578 *Il.* 24.44ff.

579 On *pathos* one might refer to two deeply meditated chapters in N. D. O'Donoghue, *Heaven in Ordinarie* (Edinburgh, 1979).

THE DESIRED OF ALL NATIONS

My title is from the prophet Haggai 2:7. The Latin of the Vulgate says: *Veniet desideratus cunctis gentibus* – the desired [one] of all the nations will come. For obvious reasons the text has been understood as a Messianic prophecy, and is used as such especially in the liturgy of Advent. The revised Vulgate, however, reads: *Venient thesauri cunctarum gentium* – the *treasures* of all the nations will come [to Jerusalem and its Temple]. But the change is not as serious for a Messianic meaning as might appear at first sight. Firstly, the second rendering is also susceptible of a Messianic prophetic sense – we may compare Is 60:7–11. Secondly, the Hebrew means literally *that which is precious*, and therefore, by an easy extension, *that which is desirable.*

But even if it does not have that prophetic meaning it still serves the purpose for which I use it here – a purpose in which the emphasis is on the word *all, cunctis, cunctarum*, in the phrase *desired* (or better, *longed for*) *of all the nations.* For my theme will be one particular famous example of what has now long since been noticed and studied, the parallels between the founding events and rites of Christianity and the patterns of myth and ritual found world-wide in the study of comparative religion. The evidence of the parallels can be expressed in the statement attributed to Caiaphas in Jn 11:50: 'You do not understand that it is expedient for you that one man should die for the people, and that the whole nation should not perish.' And John goes on to explain this remark as unconscious prophecy: 'He did not say this of his own accord, but being High Priest that year he prophesied that Jesus should die for the nation.'

Fr Victor White quotes that passage as the opening of a chapter on 'The Dying God' in his book on *God and the Unconscious.*[580] His summary account of the parallel theme in Frazer's *Golden Bough* provides a convenient statement of its universality:

> Slowly there emerges the hint of a world-wide pattern of belief and practice according to which it is expedient that *one* should die for the people [so] that the whole nation perish not; that the slayer and the slain should alike be some embodiment of divinity, a divine king or priest, or perhaps his son or some representative or substitute or effigy, whose death and

580 Fontana Books edition, London and Glasgow, 1960, 227ff.

torment is somehow necessary if the life or power which he embodies, and on which the people depend, is to survive or revive.

White, of course, is careful to draw attention to the differences as well as the parallels between this pattern and the events referred to in John, and even to the limitation on the extent to which those phenomena make a pattern at all. Nevertheless the phenomena are common enough to justify 'patterns' as the best available word to describe their clustering. In fact, as we know, in its Hellenic and Near Eastern versions the pattern was striking enough for the liberal schools of comparative religion to purport to derive the 'mysteries' of Christianity from those of the pagan mystery cults – common to most of which was the cult of the dying and rising God.[581]

What has happened in more recent times is not just that the Christian dependence has been disproved, rather, in the light of a deeper psychology and a longer, more meaningful understanding of mankind's religious history, the dependence has been reversed. It is the myths and mysteries that have been the foreshadowings, and Christian reality their historical fulfilment. 'Where has religion reached its true maturity?', C. S. Lewis asked himself in the final stages of his conversion. 'Where, if anywhere, have the hints of all Paganism been fulfilled?'[582] 'Here and here only in all time the myth must have become fact; the Word, flesh; God, Man ...'. It is 'the summing up and actuality of all the historical hints that have gone before'.[583]

'It was not cleverly devised myths that we followed', writes the author of 2 Peter, 'when we made known to you the power and coming of our Lord Jesus Christ, but we were eye-witnesses of his majesty' (1:16). 'Pagan literature', Newman writes, 'philosophy, and mythology, properly understood, were but a preparation for the Gospel. The Greek poets and sages were in a certain sense prophets. [...] There had been a divine dispensation granted to the Jews; there had been in some sense a dispensation carried on in favour of the Gentiles'.[584] The same understanding of history unifies the panoramic surveys of Hans Urs von Balthasar. His summary comment on the tragedies of Sophocles is that 'from him the path leads directly to Gethsemane and Golgotha'.[585] Still more compre-

581 For an account, see Hugo Rahner, S.J., *Greek Myths and Christian Mystery* (London, 1963), Ch. I on 'Christian Mysteries and Pagan Mysteries'.

582 *Surprised by Joy* (Glasgow: Collins, Fount Paperbacks, 1982), 188.

583 Ibid, 189.

584 *Apologia Pro Vita Sua* (Glasgow: Collins, Fontana Books, 1959), 115.

585 *The Glory of the Lord*, vol. IV (Edinburgh: T.&T. Clark, 1989), 133; cf. 101: 'It is Greek tragedy and not Greek philosophy, with which the Christians primarily entered into dialogue, that forms the great, valid cypher of the Christ event, central to human history, by enclosing and transcending

hensively, a certain theory of 'the fundamental manner ... in which all ancient peoples experienced existence, ... conjointly mythical, religious, and political',[586] provides 'an ethnological system of categories for the appearance of every possible redeemer and salvation-bearer [...] This would allow Christ to appear as the fulfiller not only of Israel's longings but of the longings of all nations'.[587] More explicitly, the Old Testament 'is a foreshadowing of Christian existence, but at the same time it is the reality whereby all human existence assumes a form oriented towards Christ'.[588]

* * *

What we have been saying so far is meant to provide a context, or a universe of discourse, for the more particular matter on which I want to focus. That is Socrates as a possible 'Christ-figure' in his life and death, especially in the light of a famous passage in Plato concerning the fate that awaits the 'just man': 'Such being his disposition [to value justice at all costs above injustice], the just man will be scourged, tortured, chained up, have his eyes put out, and, after enduring every extremity of suffering, he will be crucified [or "impaled"]' (*Republic* 361e).

The resemblance to the life and death of Christ is remarkable, as has often been noted. It is all the more remarkable for the fact that, although obviously alluding *post eventum* to the fate of Socrates ['the best and wisest and most just of all the men of his time we have known'[589]], the details are not those of Socrates' own death. And to realise the full force of the passage we need to remember that the Greek *dikê* or *dikaiosunê* is a much stronger and more comprehensive term than the English *just* and *justice*. It is much closer to the range of the Hebrew concept of *righteousness*, or the *Just One*, especially as we see it exemplified in the figure of Christ, or in the 'type' of him in Isaiah's Suffering Servant.

It is not surprising then that Socrates became the 'type' of the 'martyr', the 'witness', the witness unto death. He became this type already in the Greco-Roman world itself. For Socrates was the archetype of the *philosopher* who lived the 'philosophic life',[590] the *bios philosophikos*, and died for it. The nearest analogue to the

---

all previous cyphers within itself'.

586 Op. cit., vol. I, 628.

587 Ibid, 633.

588 Ibid, 654. We might wonder if this says any more than St Paul said already to the Athenians, in Acts 17:23ff: 'The God whom I proclaim is in fact the one you already worship without knowing it ... '.

589 *Phaedo*, 118.

590 See e.g. the *Apology*, 28e, and the *Symposium*, 218ab. Cf., still today, the chapter on 'The Philosophical Life in Karl Jaspers', *Way to Wisdom* (Yale University Press edition, 1960).

bios philosophikos is the 'religious life' in its conventional Christian connotation.[591] Plato describes it in the *Phaedo* (61ff). It is a life of *ascesis* of the senses, the better to recollect[592] and liberate the faculties of the spirit for the contemplation of truth. And since the full liberation of the spirit into the contemplation of supreme Reality and Truth comes only with death, 'those who pursue philosophy aright devote themselves to nothing other than dying and being dead' (64a). The turning to the *bios philosophikos* could even be the result of a 'conversion'[593] – in the most radical and existential sense of that word. We have an example in St Augustine's first conversion, precisely to 'philosophy', as he describes it in the *Confessions* (III 4).

Inevitably such principled practitioners of the *meletê thanatou*,[594] the life devoted to learning to die, often found themselves in situations which demanded that they die in reality. This was often the case especially when the 'witness' to truth became a witness to liberty against totalitarianism, as he often had to do under the more tyrannical Roman emperors. Hence ideal types of the philosophical 'resistance' – especially Stoic – figure prominently in Tacitus' accounts[595] of the reign of terror under Nero and Domitian. His account[596] of the slow dying of Seneca, at the command of Nero, is one of the great death scenes in literature. The influence of the archetypal model in the *Phaedo* is obvious in many of the details. To his friends he leaves his one remaining possession, the pattern of his life (*imaginem vitae suae*).[597] Like Socrates[598] he checks their tears: 'where had the principles of their philosophy gone, and that resolution practised (*meditata ratio*) against impending misfortunes over so many years?'[599] Another victim is more pointedly Socratic in a final Stoic gesture. Not a cock to Asclepius but – 'A libation, he said, to Jupiter the Liberator!', as he sprinkled the ground with the first blood flowing from his veins.[600]

The early Christian Apologists, especially Justin Martyr and Clement of Alexandria, carried on this Socratic typology into a parallelism between Socrates and Christ – between the pagan 'philosopher', and the founder of what they

591 The Fathers of the Church already imply the analogy when, as they constantly do, they refer to Christianity as 'the true philosophy'. Clement of Alexandria, in his work entitled *Protreptic*, even took over the name of the literary genre in which the Greeks urged 'conversion' to philosophy – see n. 593, and Augustine, *Confessions*, III 4.

592 See *Phaedo* 67c.

593 Cf. the chapter on 'Conversion to Philosophy' in A. D. Nock, *Conversion* (Oxford Paperbacks edition, 1961).

594 *Phaedo* 81e; cf. Seneca, Letter XXVI 8 ff on 'meditatio mortis'.

595 See his *Agricola*, 2, and *Annals* XV 48 ff.

596 *Annals* XV 62ff.

597 Ibid, XV 62.

598 *Phaedo* 117d.

599 *Annals* XV 62.

600 Id. XVI 35.

called 'the true philosophy'. An interesting link between the pagan and the Christian use of the same motif – and a vivid insight into just how common and well known the motif was – is provided by the second-century satirical essayist, Lucian of Samosata, in his essay *On the Death of Peregrinus.* Peregrinus was a type well-known and often satirized at the time, an itinerant philosopher, of the Cynic school in Peregrinus' case, and therefore all the closer (for being a kind of 'mendicant') to the analogy between the 'philosophic life' and the Christian 'religious life'. Lucian regarded him as a charlatan. Lucian would do that in any case, but he was probably right about Peregrinus, for he imposed himself on simple Christians in Palestine, and finally came to a bad end by cremating himself in AD 165.

In Palestine the Christians revered him, and 'adopted him as their patron, next after that other, to be sure, whom they still worship, the man who was crucified in Palestine because he introduced this new cult into the world'.[601] The Christians regarded it as a calamity when Peregrinus was arrested and imprisoned. They brought him elaborate meals, and their own sacred books for reading. 'And excellent Peregrinus ... was called by them "a new Socrates".'[602] He was finally released by the governor of Syria, 'a man who was devoted to philosophy'.[603]

It is in the Christian Apologists that we find the Socratic parallel most explicitly and precisely drawn, now between Socrates and Christ.[604] There are two explicit passages in Justin Martyr: *Apology* I 5,[605] and Apology II 10.[606] In both passages the particular point of the parallel is in the fate suffered by all philosophical and religious thinkers who question older beliefs about God with a view to purifying and perfecting them. In Greece by far the greatest of all such thinkers was Socrates, and therefore 'he was called to answer the same charges as we [Christians] are. For they said he introduced new gods, and considered those regarded by the state as gods to be no gods at all'.[607] 'They bring the same accusations against us.'[608]

It is in Clement of Alexandria that we find the focus concentrated explicitly on the theme of the *Just Man's* fate, with a quotation of *Republic* 361e, and the focusing

601 *Peregrinus* 11, as translated in J. Stevenson (ed.), *A New Eusebius* (London, SPCK, 1957), 135.

602 Op. cit., 12, loc. cit.

603 Op. cit., 14, loc. cit.

604 Our treatment of the matter here can only be selective and summary; it has been the subject of two long articles by Ernst Benz: 'Der gekreuzigte Gerechte bei Plato, im Neuen Testament und in der alten Kirche', in *Abhandlungen der Geistes- und Sozialwissenschaftlichen Klasse* (Verlag der Akademie der Wissenschaften und der Literatur in Mainz, 1950), Nr. 12, 3–46; and 'Christus und Sokrates in der alten Kirche', in *Zeitschrift für die Neutestamentliche Wissenschaft*, Band 43 (1950/51), 195–224.

605 Migne *PG* 6, col. 336.

606 Ibid, col. 460–461.

607 *Apol.* II 10; cf. Plato, *Apology*, 23d.

608 *Apol.* I 5.

of the parallel on Socrates and Christ. The two relevant *loci* are in *Stromata* IV 7 and V 14.[609] The first of these passages gives little context and only an abbreviated quotation of *Republic* 361e. The second passage introduces the theme of the *Just Man* with a quotation from Scripture itself, Wis 2:12: 'Let us lie in wait for [or "eliminate"] the just man, for he is an inconvenience to us [and opposes our actions]'.[610] The *Republic* passage is then subjoined, with an introductory statement that 'Plato speaks as follows, in his prophecy (*prophêteuôn*) missing only the [Christian] economy of salvation ... '. A reference to 'the Socratic Antisthenes' immediately after the *Republic* 361e quotation makes it clear that it is understood as referring to Socrates, and in the total context the comparison is obviously with Christ.

Remarkable here is the attribution of *prophecy* to the Plato passage, and its linking to the 'economy of salvation (*tên sôtêrion oikonomian*)'. But the earlier Justin Martyr had already said as much, and more explicitly, in one of the passages from which we have quoted earlier. In *Apol.* II 10 Justin says that Socrates 'in part *knew* Christ'. The explanation lies in that profound concept which builds a bridge between Greek philosophy and Judeo-Christian revelation, the Word, the *Logos*, the ultimate principle of the reality and the intelligibility of the universe, and the ultimate source of the light by which reason understands it – the Greek *logos* also means reason. Christians know that Christ is that '*Logos* pervading all things'.[611] That being so, He enlightened not only the prophets of Israel but in some measure also the philosophers of Greece. Therefore while Christian revelation is loftier than all merely human doctrine, nevertheless, 'everything of truth and beauty that Greek philosophers and lawgivers have thought, they have elaborated and expressed only because to some degree they have profited from the light of the *Logos*'.[612]

Before we leave such texts there is one more which deserves mention. It is less well known than those of Justin and Clement, but it has the extra vividness of occurring in the *Acts* of a Roman martyr, one Apollonius, in his exchanges with the judge, Perennius, during his trial. The affair is mentioned by Eusebius,[613] as having taken place during the reign of the Emperor Commodus (180–192):

> In the city of the Romans he brought before the court Apollonius, a man famous among the Christians of the time for his learning and philosophy, having induced one of his servants ... to accuse him ... But

609 Respectively Migne, *PG* 8, col. 1263, and *PG* 9, col. 163.

610 In a context to which we shall return, and one always understood as prophetic of Christ.

611 *Apol.* II 10; cf., of course, John 1:1ff.

612 *Apol.* II 10; cf. *Apol.* II 13, on Plato and others – Stoics, poets, and historians: 'Each one of them spoke well and truly in the measure in which he had discernment from some connatural portion of the divine generative *Logos* (*spermatikou theiou Logou*).'

613 *Ecclesiastical History*, V 21.

> God's beloved martyr, when the judge pleaded with him long and earnestly, and pressed him to speak up for himself before the Senate, made before them all a most learned defence (*apologian*) of the faith to which he was witnessing, and by decree of the Senate he was 'consummated' (*teleioutai*) by decapitation.

Part of that *apologia* was a comparison of the fate of Socrates with that of 'our Master and Redeemer', supported by quotations of what both the Book of Wisdom (2:12) and 'one of the wise men of Greece' (Plato, *Rep.* 361e) have said about the fate of the Just Man.[614]

* * *

The Socratic-Christic parallel turns out to be even more striking when we look beyond the *text* to the *context* of both Wis 2:12 and *Rep.* 361e on the fate of the Just Man, itself, of course, a recurring scriptural term.[615] The whole theme of the *Republic* is also justice, justice in society, but first in the individual. But since the superiority of virtue over vice, of right over might, is likely to bring few rewards in *Realpolitik*, it is necessary that the *authenticity* of the Just Man be *tested*, tested, as it were, to destruction – the destruction described in 361e. It must be *proved* that the Just Man not only *appears* just but *is* just. Without that testing:

> we cannot be sure whether he is just for justice's sake or for the sake of the gifts and honours [which even the appearance of justice does sometimes bring!]. So we must strip him bare of everything but justice ... Though doing no wrong he must have the reputation of the greatest injustice, so that he may be put to the test as regards justice through not weakening because of ill repute and its consequences. But let him hold on his course unchangeable, even unto death ... (361c).

Wisdom 2:17–20 is an exact parallel to this – so close that we may wonder if the author, a first-century BC Alexandrian Jew imbued with Greek culture, is not echoing Plato in this passage:

614 Page 120 ff, section 38 ff, in the only text to hand: E. Theodor Klette, *Der Process und die Acta S. Apollonii* (Leipzig, 1897. *Texte und Untersuchungen zur Geschichte der Altchristlichen Literatur*, Band XV, Heft 2). Cf. Benz, *Der gekreuzigte Gerechte*, 1065ff.

615 For its application to Christ in the New Testament see e.g. Matthew 27:19, 24 (in one reading). Acts 3:14, 7:52, 22:14, James 5:6, 1 Peter 3:18.

> Let us see if his words are true, and let us test what will happen at the end of his life; for if the just man is God's son, God will help him, and deliver him from the hands of his adversaries. Let us test him with insult and torture ... and make trial of his forbearance. Let us condemn him to a shameful death, for, according to what he says, he will be protected.

Not only Plato is here, but the crucifixion too: 'He trusts in God; let God deliver him now; for he said, "I am the Son of God".'[616] Here too is another anticipatory Christ-figure, the Job of 1:8–12:

> The Lord said to Satan, 'Have you considered my servant Job, that there is none like him on the earth, a blameless and upright man ... ?' Then Satan answered the Lord, 'Does Job fear God for nothing?! ... You have blessed the work of his hands, and his possessions have increased in the land. But just put forth your hand now, and lay a finger on his possessions, and he will curse you to your face!'

* * *

Isolated excerpted texts about the Just Man, however compelling in their implications, command only 'notional' rather than 'real' assent (in Newman's sense), until we can see them as the utterances of, or utterances about, the living breathing character of the real man. What manner of man was this Socrates? How far does a living, breathing image of him confirm, or reinforce, the status given him in the texts as a Christ-figure?

There is ample material in Plato's *Dialogues* for a literary portrait of Socrates, or, more exactly to our purpose, a psychological portrait. And, as it happens, apart from the portrait by Socrates' friend Alcibiades in the *Symposium* (214e ff), the best of the material is in the *Dialogues* which are associated with the trial, imprisonment, and death of Socrates,[617] the *Apology*, the *Crito*[618] and the *Phaedo*.

It is beyond the requirements of our present purposes to elaborate all the data of this material. The *Phaedo* is too well known to need elaboration, presenting the last night of Socrates with his friends before execution, discussing the 'boundary

616 Matthew 27:43; cf. also Matthew 26:67, and the Messianic Suffering Servant in Isaiah 50:6 : 'I offered my back to those who struck me,/my cheeks to those who tore at my beard;/I did not cover my face/ against insult and spittle'.

617 They are the *Dialogues* drawn on by Romano Guardini in one of his numerous studies of seminal historical figures, perennially fruitful and essentially mysterious: *Der Tod des Sokrates* (Bern, 1947).

618 Its theme by itself provides a Christic parallel – Socrates' refusal to escape from prison and death, out of reverence for the law.

questions' that arise in such a situation, and ending with one of the most beautiful, if not *the* most beautiful, of death scenes in all literature. 'Such was the end, Echecrates, of our friend, who was, as we may say, of all those of his time whom we have known, the best and wisest and most just of men' (118, the end).

If anywhere, it is in his own final address to his judges that such a man will utter the essence of what he is. Speeches from the dock come from a concentrated mind, especially, as has been said with gallows humour, after the ultimate sentence has been passed. Socrates' final address, as we have it in the *Apology*, and with the literary and dramatic art of Plato, is the archetype of many other great instances in later history.[619] It is in two parts. The first is his defence to the jury before they retire: 'I trust that what I say is just, and let none of you expect anything else' (17c). 'I entrust my case to you and to God to decide it as shall be best for me and for you' (35d). The second part is his final address to the jury after hearing their sentence of death. 'I am not grieved, men of Athens, at this vote of condemnation you have cast against me ... ' (36a). At the end, 'the time has come to go away. I go to die, and you to live; but which of us goes to the better lot is known to none but God' (42). Surely, we might comment, this was a Just Man, adapting the Roman centurion's remark about Another.[620]

And the remarkable fact is that throughout the *Apology* we find details that have striking parallels in the life and the trial of that Other. Indeed there is a correspondence in a basic *question* that arises in both trials, that is, why they should be taking place at all. Socrates does not *understand the reason* for the reputation that has brought him to trial for his life. But, he imagines his judges rejoining, that is the very problem about him, just why have those prejudices arisen against him?

> For certainly this great report and talk has not arisen while you were doing nothing more out of the way than everybody else, unless you were doing something other than what most people do, so do tell us what it is, so that we do not act unadvisedly in your case (20c).

'The chief priests brought many accusations against Him. Pilate questioned Him again, "Have you no reply at all? See how many accusations they are bringing against you!"' (Mk 15:3–4). And eventually Pilate has to ask the crowd who

619 St Thomas More provides one such instance – see e.g. R. W. Chambers, *Thomas More* (London: Jonathan Cape, 1938), 340f of the Bedford Historical Series edition. More himself, of course, was to be described as 'our noble new Christian Socrates' by his first formal biographer, Nicholas Harpsfield, already in the sixteenth century – see Chambers, op. cit., 16ff, 168, 351 ('both are figures in world history'), 385, 398ff.

620 See Mt 27:54, Mk 15:39, Lk 23:47.

are calling for the death of 'this Just Man'.[621] 'Why? What harm has this man done? I have found no case against him that deserves death ... ' (Lk 23:22).

Socrates does promise to answer his judges' request, but he anticipates that 'perhaps I shall appear to some of you to be joking! For the fact is, men of Athens, that I have acquired this reputation for no other reason than a certain kind of wisdom (*sophian tina*), possibly 'some wisdom greater than human ...for I do not fully understand it ... ' (20de). One is reminded of the comment sometimes made on Christ's assertions about himself, that to make such claims he must really *be* the Son of God, or else a lunatic! (And indeed, according to Mk 3:21, some did think He was the latter.)

But Socrates is not to be regarded as a joker, or be interrupted by noisy protests, 'even if I seem to you to be boasting' (20e). For 'the word which I speak is not my own' (23a), it is ultimately the word of the God of Delphi (20c). It is the God who is 'really wise', and when he declared that Socrates was the wisest of men (21a),[622] what he really meant was that '*human* wisdom is of little or no value' (21b).

Parallels in the words of Christ come to mind. 'My word is not my own ... ' (Jn 14:24). 'The Father who sent me bears witness to me Himself' (Jn 5:37). 'You judge by human standards' (Jn 3:34). He 'bears witness to the things He has seen and heard, even if his testimony is not accepted' (Jn 3:32). In neither case – of Socrates or of Christ – will the testimony be accepted. 'You want to kill me because nothing I say has penetrated into you' (Jn 8:37). Socrates will be freed on condition that he give up his 'philosophy'. If not 'you shall die' (29b). But since he is following God's 'command' (30a),[623] 'I shall obey God rather than you ... ' (29d). Similarly Peter and John before the Sanhedrin: 'You must judge whether in God's eyes it is right to listen to you rather than to God. We cannot stop proclaiming what we have seen and heard' (Acts 4:19-20).[624]

The consequences are predictable, all the more so for being in the archetypal tradition[625] of what happens to the Just Man and his prophetic witness:

621 Mt 27:24, in one reading.

622 Cf. 21c ff: the reference is to Socrates' dialectical skill, shown in all the Platonic Dialogues in which he has a central role, in reducing opponents' opinions to their latent inadequacy, contradiction, or absurdity. We see something parallel in Christ's exchanges with his opponents in John's Gospel, e.g. 8:3 ff, 10:22ff. In the case of Socrates there is also the Socratic irony of professed ignorance.

623 For 'when God gave me a station, [it was], as I believed and understood, with orders to devote my life to "philosophy" ... ' (28e).

624 With the second sentence cf. *Apol.* 37e on 'disobedience to the God'.

625 Cf. Boethius' anguished problem in theodicy – precisely the fate of 'philosophers'– in *The Consolation of Philosophy*, Bk.1, chs. 3–4.

> This it is which will cause my condemnation ... not [individual accusers such as] Meletus or Anytus, but the prejudice and hatred of the multitude (*hoi polloi*). This has condemned many other good men ... , and there is no danger that it will stop with me (*Apol.* 28a).

'Is there a single one of the prophets your ancestors did not persecute?', Stephen cries out to his stoners (Acts 7:52). 'In the past they foretold the coming of the Just One, and now you have become his betrayers, his murderers.'[626]

The crime is all the greater because, like the Son of Man,[627] Socrates too has been 'sent', sent 'as a kind of gift from God to the city' (31a). The consequences of rejecting the One who has been thus sent are correspondingly ominous. Socrates warns his judges and fellow citizens that 'if you kill me, being such a man as I say I am, you will not injure me so much as yourselves' (30c). 'And so, men of Athens, I am now making my defence not for my own sake, as one might imagine, but far more for yours, that you may not, by condemning me, make a mistake in your treatment of the gift God has given you' (30d).[628] A mistake all the more serious because the gift may not be repeated – 'such another is not likely to come to you ... unless God, in his care for you, should send someone else ...' (31a). So did Christ admonish Jerusalem:

> Jerusalem, Jerusalem, you that kill the prophets and stone those who are sent to you![629] How often have I longed to gather your children, as a hen gathers her chicks under her wing, but you refused! So be it! Your house will be left to you desolate ... (Mt 23:37–39).

A contrast to such an occasional access of passionate eloquence from figures like Socrates and Christ is their more usual reserve and simplicity, simplicity of life as well as of style. 'The Son of Man has nowhere to lay his head' (Mt 8:20). Socrates has one 'sufficient witness that I speak the truth, namely my poverty' (31c). Even at his trial he will indulge in no forensic eloquence, but make his defence 'through the same words in which I have been accustomed to speak ... in the market-place ... , where many of you have heard me ... ' (I7c). We are familiar with Christ's reserve at his trial. There is no need to question Him insistently, 'ask my hearers what I taught – I have spoken openly for all the world to hear ... in the synagogue and in the Temple where all the Jews meet together ... ' (Jn 18:20).

626 Cf. Matthew 23:33ff. Apollonius joins this motif to the Socratic one – see n. 614, p. 125 above.

627 E.g. Jn 17:8.

628 The warning is much more explicit in 39c.

629 Recall Wisdom 2:12ff above; cf. Jeremiah 11:18–19.

This reserve is part of the troubling and troublesome mystery of both Socrates and Christ. 'Who do people say the Son of Man is?' (Mt 16:13). 'They were filled with awe, and said to one another, "Who then is this ... ?"' (Mk 4:41). An analogous question underlies Alcibiades' evocation of the spell-casting influence of Socrates in the *Symposium* (214e ff). Socrates can be compared only to Silenus (215b), the type of the ironic and uncouth exterior from behind which issue words of such strange power that, even when few and simple, or heard only in an indifferent second-hand account of them, they 'stir us to the depths and cast a spell on us ...' (215cd). Alcibiades can compare the effect only to (what we would call) a charismatic religious experience (215de). No other speaker has such an effect, not even the great Pericles (215d). 'No man ever spoke like this man' (Jn 7:46).

Such effects of simple words from a special speaker of them provide the appropriately numinous context in which to mention one last strange parallel between the last night of Socrates and the last night of Jesus, a parallel in which two simple phrases become instinct with that quality which literary theory calls the 'grand' or the 'sublime'.

In the *Phaedo* (116ff), as the time approaches when Socrates must at last drink the cup (of hemlock), he leaves the company and goes to another room to have a bath. While he is out his friends talk over the long discussion they have had with him, and about the great misfortune to them that his imminent death will be: 'for we felt that he was like a father to us, and that bereft of him we would pass the rest of our lives as orphans' (116a). When Socrates returns the women and children of his family are brought to him. He gives them his last directions, bids them farewell, and sends them away. There remains only the taking of the cup, and the last exchanges with his little company as the effect of the hemlock advances.

'And it was now close to sunset' (116d).

That concluding phrase reminds us of Jn 13:30: 'And it was night' (ên de nux). The parallel with the *Phaedo* is not only in the phrase itself, but also in its setting, the Last Supper, and in the particular moment of that setting which builds up to the concluding phrase, 13:21ff. It is the critical moment when Jesus grows troubled in spirit, and troubles the disciples: one of them is going to betray Him. That one, being identified, is sent away; only then could Jesus continue his last discourse to the chosen group He now calls his friends (Jn 15:14–15). Judas therefore took the dipped morsel and went out at once. 'And it was night' – in his soul as well.

As indicated already, the parallel here between Plato and John is not only in the two sentences and their setting, but also in the literary art which makes those two climactic sentences 'sublime' or 'grand' in that setting. One is reminded of the single-sentence examples – one of them from Scripture – given by Longinus in his first-century Greek treatise *On the Sublime.*[630] He defines sublimity as 'a certain elevation and distinction in the writing' (I 3), due not to the externals of style but to the interior intensity of great *thought* and strong *emotion*, the two natural *sources* of the sublime.[631] In the appropriate setting then 'sublimity often resides in just a single thought' (XII 1). Just such is the thought in our two simple concluding sentences. They move from the light into the darkness and the night. There is no need to spell out the range of significance with which that movement resonates within the symbolism of John. Neither is it necessary to spell it out in the case of Plato, for whom the sun is a metaphor for the ultimate Really Real, the Form of the Good, in effect God, source not only of the *being* of all that exists but also of its luminous intelligibility.[632]

* * *

So far have we been taken by the theme of the Just Man and his fate, as focused in the parallels between Socrates and Christ, and more narrowly still in the seemingly prophetic quality of that remarkable passage in Plato's *Republic*, 361e. We must not leave the theme without addressing, if only in a summary coda, the question of whether it is right to regard that passage, and the many other detailed parallels we have noted, as being in some valid sense prophetic, as assumed by Justin Martyr and Clement of Alexandria.

Already at the start we noted some of the grounds on which the prophetic interpretation has been based. The earliest ground, and perhaps still the most profoundly metaphysical and theological, we saw in the Greek Christian Apologists' interpretation of the *Logos* as being active in universal history, secular as well as sacred. In modern times also it is on a unified view of universal history that Newman and von Balthasar have based their interpretation of all pre-Christian religion as in some sense preparatory to its fulfilment in the *vera religio* in which myth and symbol became historical fact and event 'Where has religion reached its true maturity? ... Where, if anywhere, have the hints of all Paganism been

630 In IX 9 he quotes Genesis 1:3: 'God said, "Let there be light", and there was light', to illustrate the profound insight that even a single sentence can be sublime, or grand, by reason of the range of its implications, in this instance the immensity of God's power implied in the fact that He only has to 'say' and it is 'done'. Cf. St Augustine in *De Doctrina Christiana,* IV 18,37, on the implications of the 'cup of cold water' in Matthew 20:42.

631 Ch. VIII; cf. St Augustine, op. cit., IV 20, 42: 'The grand style (*grande*) differs from the temperate style (*temperato*) above all in this, that it is not so much decked out in stylistic ornament as given intensity by the emotions of the soul'.

632 *Rep.* 509b, in the context of the Simile of the Sun, 507a ff, and of the Cave, 514a ff.

fulfilled?'[633] It is Newman's theme in his comparing and contrasting of natural religion and revealed religion in the *Grammar of Assent.* There is a recurring system of 'natural beliefs and sentiments, which, though true and divine, is still possible to us independently of revelation, and is the preparation for it'.[634] Von Balthasar accepts Socrates into this system, as 'an intimation of Christ', with the natural qualification that one should do this only if at the same time one realizes the differences as well as the similarities between the two.[635]

In attempting to answer our question about the possible prophetic or 'typical' status of Socrates, it is precisely that religious dimension of him which it is important to note first.[636] It is a dimension of his life and character that is obvious in the *Symposium* and in all the *Dialogues* concerned with his trial and death. And it exists not only at the level of thought but also at the level of experience, even of mystical experience. Many passages already cited bear this out, for instance the many references in the *Apology* to 'the God', and, in the *Symposium*, Alcibiades' description of the strange entrancing effect of Socrates on his hearers. In fact Alcibiades' whole account in *Symposium* 214e ff uses the terminology[637] of that ecstatic religious experience mentioned in 215e. Socrates' own account, in 201d ff, of the nature of love, as he purports to have heard it from the mysterious Diotima, is an account of the steps in the ascent to union with the transcendent summit, source, and ground of religious experience, the 'vast ocean of beauty' (210d), which is also 'divine' (211e), and which makes the beholder 'immortal' and 'beloved of God' (212a).[638]

The importance of such religious experience is that it provides context and background for Socrates' frequent mention of *prophecy* (*mantikê*, Latin *divinatio*). He is well acquainted with the phenomena of that 'enthusiasm' or divine

633 See nn. 582 and 583, p.120 above.

634 Longmans, Green and Co. edition (1909), 408.

635 *The Glory of the Lord,* Vol. I, e.

636 It is noted by Romano Guardini in the work already cited (n. 617, p. 126 above); see 93ff and 314ff of the Italian translation, *La Morte di Socrate* (Brescia, 1984).

637 I.e. recurring references to *thaumaston, ekplêxis, mania,* etc., sacral terms that express the 'aweful' experience of the *mysterium tremendum.*

638 The most worthwhile comment on that 'ascent' is a page by a classical scholar, A. E. Taylor, *Plato. The Man and His Work* (London, 1960 [1st ed. 1926]), 225: 'In spite of all the differences of precise outlook, the best comment on the whole narrative is furnished by the great writers who, in verse or prose, have described the "mystic way" by which the soul "goes out of herself" to find herself again in finding God.' The passage is too long to quote in full, but among those 'great writers' it goes on to name St John of the Cross (*En una noche oscura*), Richard Crashaw (*The Flaming Heart*), and St Bonaventure (*Itinerarium mentis in Deum*). We can, of course, think of many others, as the author of the passage indicates that he also could – combining, as he does, a wide-ranging scholarship with a profoundly religious, and specifically Christian, awareness.

inspiration that issues not only in poetry but also in prophecy.[639] And in the *Apology* he himself not only uses the word 'prophecy', he speaks in its solemn tone, to introduce his strongest prediction of the fate that awaits his judges. 'I now wish to prophesy (*chrêsmôidêsai*) to you, to you who have condemned me. For I am now come to that time when men most do prophesy, the time when they are going to die. And I say to you, O you who have slain me ... ' (39c). One of the most lyrical passages in the *Phaedo* is 84e ff where he compares his own situation to that of the swans,[640] the birds of Apollo, who sing before death, from joy of the prophetic vision they have of the life to come. Socrates regards himself as a fellow-servant with the swans: 'I am consecrated to the same God [Apollo],[641] and I have received a gift of prophecy (*mantikên*) in no way inferior to theirs, and I go out from life with as little sorrow as they' (85f).

In the *Phaedrus* Socrates goes beyond those *personal* professions to a general statement: the charism (*mania*) of prophecy is ancient, well known, and source of 'the greatest blessings ... when given by divine gift' (244a). He goes on to give as examples the Delphic prophetess (*prophêtis*), the priestesses at Dodona, the Sibyl, 'and all the others who by divine inspiration (*mantikêi entheôi*) have foretold (*prolegontes*) many things to many persons ...' (244b).

The *fact* of prophecy is deepened into *theory* and *principle* by Plato himself[642] in the *Timaeus*, a work of his old age which becomes his equivalent to the creation narrative in the Book of Genesis, because in it he tries to bridge the gap between metaphysics and facts by telling a 'likely story'[643] about how, in the concrete, the world and humanity were brought into existence. In the account of the making of human beings, they are given a specific faculty of prophecy, located in the liver. 'For the authors of our being, remembering the command of their Father to make mortal creatures as perfect as possible, in order to elevate even our inferior parts and make them attain some measure of truth, placed in the liver the faculty of prophecy' (*to manteion*, 71d).

In Plato such a faculty is not just an optional extra. It is a positive requirement if human reason is to transcend the limitations of its capacity to answer ultimate questions. 'Human wisdom is of little or no value', we have heard the

639 See *Apol*, 22bc, *Ion* 533cff, *Phaedrus* 244f.

640 *Phaedo* 85b: the swans have 'foreknowledge' (*proeidotes*).

641 In the pages referred to in n. 636, p. 132 above Guardini emphasises the significance of Apollo's presence in the *Apology* and the *Phaedo*, because Apollo was the god of light; but he does not note, for the religious dimension of Socrates, that Apollo was also the god of prophecy.

642 Even if it is through a long discourse, without dialogue, by the character who gives his name to the *Timaeus*.

643 29a: 'because we must remember that I who am the speaker and you who are the judges are only mortal men' in regard to questions 'about the Gods and the generation of the universe' (29c).

God of Delphi indicate to Socrates.[644] Halfway through the arguments for the immortality of the soul it has to be admitted that 'it is either impossible or very difficult to acquire clear knowledge about these matters in this life'.[645] Hence 'some stronger vehicle' may be necessary for life's journey, 'some divine revelation' (*logou theiou tinos*).[646] The case is the same for the 'likely story' of the *Timaeus*: 'if God should confirm that we have spoken the truth, then, and only then, can we be confident' (72d).[647]

In that section of the *Timaeus* (71a ff) Plato does not confine himself to stating that a faculty of prophecy is part of the human psyche. He also gives an exceptionally clear summary answer to two very relevant questions about it: how it knows what it purports to know, and how the expression of that knowledge is to be interpreted. In brief, the answer to the first question is: through the 'irrational' levels of the psyche, in the sense, that is, of the supra-rational, and, at the opposite pole, the sub-rational or sub-conscious.[648] The answer to the second question takes account of this 'irrationality': *reason* must *interpret* the irrational, and this is the function, not of the irrational prophet himself, but of a separate and distinct interpreter.[649] This distinction anticipates St Paul on the charisms – including prophecy – in 1 Cor 14! And the recognition of the 'irrational' mode of knowledge gives us a glimpse on the one hand of the surprising awareness the Greeks had of that mode, both 'supra' and 'sub',[650] and on the other hand it is at the head of a stream of data on prophecy and the irrational which will flow down through Cicero[651] and others to St Augustine[652] and on to Thomas Aquinas[653] on the nature of prophecy.

644 *Apol.* 23a.

645 *Phaedo* 85c.

646 Ibid. 85d.

647 We have quoted Newman's *Apologia* on prophecy, n. 584, p. 120 above; those comments of Plato on reason and revelation anticipate what Newman says on the same subject, op. cit., ed. cit., 275 ff (opening pages of 'General Answer to Mr. Kingsley').

648 'No man, in his wits, attains prophetic truth and inspiration (*mantikês entheou*), but when he receives the inspired word either his intelligence is inhibited in sleep, or he is in an abnormal condition owing to disease or some divine possession' (*enthousiasmou*, 71e).

649 'For this reason it is customary to appoint interpreters to be judges of the inspired prophecies (*entheois manteiais*). Some persons call these prophets, being blind to the fact that they are only expositors of dark sayings and visions, and are not to be called prophets at all but only interpreters of prophecy' (72ab).

650 See e.g. E. R. Dodds, *The Greeks and the Irrational* (University of California Press, 1961).

651 *De divinatione.*

652 *De Genesi ad litteram*, XII 9, 20ff.

653 *De Veritate* q. XII, and *Summa Theol.*, IIa IIae q. 171ff; see V. White, op. cit. (n. 580, p. 119 above), chs. VI and VII, on 'Aristotle, Aquinas and Man', and 'Revelation and the Unconscious'.

To pursue our subject through Augustine and Aquinas would take us far beyond the limits of our present space.[654] But they do each raise one question which is of particular relevance to our own: whether 'the human spirit has some faculty of prophecy (*divinationis*) *in itself*' (Augustine);[655] 'whether prophecy can be *natural*' (Aquinas).[656]

Augustine, as often in Book XII, refuses to be pressed into a definite answer, and therefore in effect leaves the question open. Not entirely surprising, given the combination of his Platonist understanding of the wide and deep *a priori* contents of the vast recesses of *memoria*,[657] and his own native sense of the *abyssus humanae conscientiae*.[658] He therefore lists a number of possibilities, including one obviously tinged with that Platonism, with corresponding possible objections, and concludes that 'which of those explanations be the right one should not be hastily asserted'.

This section of Augustine is at the heart of Aquinas' answer to the same question. His answer is inevitably much more decisive and clear, because based on Scholastic method and a clearer definition of prophecy, with a clearer distinction of the *natural* from the *supernatural*. Prophetic knowledge is of 'those things which by nature are beyond (*naturaliter excedunt*) human knowledge.' And therefore the answer must be that prophecy *simpliciter dicta* cannot be from nature but solely from divine revelation.

Yet, an important qualification to this clear conclusion is implicit in the second argument that Aquinas uses, an argument from the theory of knowledge that he finds underpinning one of Augustine's suggestions in favour of natural prophecy. In this theory, the soul has knowledge of all things by participation in the Platonic *ideas*. Consequently it can know the future 'according to its own proper knowledge' (*secundum propriam scientiam*). But Aquinas prefers Aristotle's theory of knowledge: 'it seems more true that the soul acquires knowledge from sensible things (*ex sensibilibus*)'. Therefore *natural* knowledge of the future cannot extend to things which by definition 'are of their nature beyond human knowledge'. It can extend only to what can be foretold from knowledge of natural causes and effects acquired by experiment and experience. The principles are summed up again in

654 Hans Urs von Balthasar has done it in two works: M. E. Korger und Hans Urs von Balthasar, *Aurelias Augustinus. Psychologie und Mystik* (De Gen. ad litt. XII), (Einsiedeln: Johannes Verlag, 1960); Hans Urs von Balthasar, *Thomas von Aquin. Besondere Gnadengaben und die zwei Wege menschlichen Lebens. Kommentar zur Summa Theologica II– II 171–182.* (Deutsche Thomas-Ausgabe Bd. 23) (Heidelberg und Graz-Wien-Salzburg: F.H. Kerle/A. Pustet, 1954), 252–464.

655 Op. cit., XII 13, 27.

656 IIa–IIae q, 172, art. 1.

657 See e.g. *Conf.* X 8ff.

658 Id. X 2, 2.

Art. 3. Prophecy *vere et simpliciter* so called is from divine inspiration; that which is from natural causality is called prophecy only in a manner of speaking (*secundum quid*). And yet, he has only said of Aristotle's theory that 'it *seems* (*videtur*) more true'. But, supposing it were not?

We need not worry about that question, if only we avoid a confusion about it. The exclusion of *natural* prophecy does not exclude the natural from being enlightened by the *supernatural*, even outside the Judeo-Christian canon of revelation. And in the requirement of divine inspiration we have seen that Socrates and Plato, within their lights, are as clear-thinking as Aquinas. The primary, and etymological, meaning of *enthousiasmos* is not the secondary psychological phenomena of the trance and the 'frenzy',[659] but the being filled with, possessed by, the God who 'inspires', breathes into, the prophet. Aristotle himself makes the same distinction as Aquinas, between the prediction or the 'seeing' that is based purely on reason (*logos*) and experience, and that which comes from divine inspiration in *enthousiasmos*. The very starting-point of reason itself 'is not reason but something superior to reason'.[660] This can only be God. And those who are 'unreasonable', 'irrational' (*alogoi*), through contact with Him, 'have within them a principle of a kind that is superior to mind and deliberation ..., they have inspiration (*enthousiasmos*) ... For, although irrational, they attain even what belongs to the prudent and the wise – swiftness of divination (*mantikê*)'.

Cicero preserves the same distinction between predictions that are the result of divine inspiration (*divini impetus*) and those that are the result of merely human reason (*rationis humanae*).[661] There are those who are capable of the latter, whom we may call 'men of foresight' (*prudentes*), that is, 'able to see ahead' (*providentes*). But we would no more apply the term 'divine' (*divinus*) to them than we would to Thales for having had the market acumen to buy up the whole Milesian olive crop before it had yet even blossomed![662] Divination properly so called is due to the contact of the human spirit with the omnipresent eternal intelligence of the divine mind.[663] In Stoic terms, the human soul itself 'is in some de-

659 For descriptions see Cassandra in Aeschylus' *Agamemnon*, 1072ff, and the Sibyl in Virgil's *Aeneid*, VI 42ff.

660 *Eudemian Ethics*, VIII 2, 1248a 25ff.

661 *De divinatione*, I 49, 111. The importance of the subject for Cicero is indicated by the fact that he writes his treatise as a complement to his work on the existence and attributes of the gods (*De natura deorum*), so that all *related* questions may be treated (II 1, 3: cf. I 5, 9). A principal argument in favour of divination is that the divine attribute of *providence* positively requires it. If the gods exist and they give mankind no guidance about the future, then 'either they do not love mankind or they are themselves ignorant of that future' (I 38, 82; cf. I 51, 117; II 49, 101ff).

662 Ibid. I 38, 82.

663 Ibid. I 49, 110.

gree derived and drawn from a source exterior to itself', namely 'a divine soul'.[664] In the human spirit therefore, there is a divinely infused potential of foreknowing. It is by a divine impulsion (*divino instinctu*) that this potential is awakened to prophetic inspiration, and in extreme cases to the secondary phenomena of trance and 'frenzy' (*furor*).[665]

* * *

We referred earlier (n. 659, p. 136) to Virgil's description of the prophetic state and its accompanying phenomena in the case of the Cumaean Sibyl. There were several Sibyls in Greco-Roman antiquity, and several collections of their prophecies. The fact that a number of the Church Fathers read some of them as prophecies of Christ[666] gives us another light on the possibility of 'Gentile' prophecy, a light with a wider focus than the technical texts we have cited from Augustine and Aquinas. In fact it is Augustine himself who provides us with one example.

In Book XVIII of the *City of God* Augustine traces the history of the *earthly* city, aligning it with *sacred* history from Abraham down to the coming of Christ, and inevitably therefore dealing with prophecy along the way. In Chapter 23 he quotes, in Latin translation, twenty-seven verses of a Greek prophetic poem by the Erythraean Sibyl, dated by some to the time of Romulus and the founding of Rome. Its theme is the future coming of a King to judge mankind, bring the world to an end, and reign forever after. The parallels with Christ and the Last Judgement are obvious.[667] But, more striking still, the initial letters of the twenty-seven verses form an acrostic which reads (in both the original Greek and the Latin translation): 'Jesus Christ Son of God Saviour'. Nor is that all. The initial letters of the five Greek words in that expression make the Greek word for *fish* (*ichthus*), one of the earliest and most common Christian symbols.[668] What we are to make of all this is not our concern here,[669] rather what Augustine makes of it. He has no trouble in accepting it as an extra-biblical prophecy of Christ.

664 Ibid. I 32, 70.

665 Ibid. I 31, 66.

666 As they also interpreted Virgil's fourth 'Messianic' *Eclogue*; for von Balthasar on Virgil, see op.cit., Vol IV, 249ff. For a theologically 'literate' literary critic's approach to the fourth *Eclogue* see C. S. Lewis, *Reflections on the Psalms* (Fontana Books edition, 1961), 84ff on 'Second Meanings'.

667 Hence the 'witness' of 'David cum Sibylla' in the *Dies Irae!*

668 Iêsus CHreistos THeou Uios Sôtêr = ichthus.

669 See G. Bardy and G. Combès, *La Cité de Dieu, Livres XV-XVIII* (Oeuvres de Saint Augustin, t. 36), (Paris: Desclée de Brouwer, 1960), note 50, 755–9.

> Now this Sibyl – whether the Sibyl of Erythraea or, as some are inclined to believe, of Cumae – has nothing in her whole poem, of which this is but a tiny fragment, relating to the worship of false or created gods. In fact, she attacks them and their worshippers so strongly that she is evidently to be counted among those who belong to the City of God.[670]

And he goes on to gather into one consecutive passage a series of separate quotations from the Sibyls by Lactantius, who also reads them as prophecies of Christ.[671]

We must not leave this text without noting the wider dimension of significance it acquires from its *context*. The Roman Sibyl is cited in the context of a theory of universal history, especially the history of the world empire of Rome in relation to the history of Judeo-Christian revelation. In the preceding chapter (XVIII 22), Augustine has enunciated the common early Christian interpretation of Rome as a providential preparation for the coming of Christ – through its unification and civilizing of the world and its establishing of universal peace.[672] Augustine sees this providence at work in history not just at its culmination, but also in certain significant stages that lead up to it. In Chapter 27 he aligns the date of Rome's founding, by Romulus and Numa, with the beginning of the particular kind of prophecy that bore a message for the *Gentile* nations, in Amos and Hosea. 'The appropriate time for that beginning was when this city of Rome was being founded, which was to have dominion over the nations'. Hence 'those men [Amos and Hosea], two springs, as it were, of prophecy, gushed out together, at the time when the Assyrian Empire failed and the Roman Empire started'.

As in Newman and von Balthasar, Augustine's framework is a view of the direction of history as a whole. Within such a framework it is not surprising that he should accept the possibility of prophecy in secular history too, as do Newman and von Balthasar. From a global view of providence directing history *in general* it is a short step to the prophetic *particularities* which point it up more specifically, in 'some divine word', such as Plato *hoped* for,[673] and Cicero even *required* as a condition of believing in gods and providence at all.[674] It is the Apostle of the Gentiles himself who directs the Athenians to that universal providence of the Creator of the whole human race by which He has arranged that 'all nations should seek God, and feel their way towards Him ...' (Acts 17:27). To his reader

670 Translation by Henry Bettenson, in Augustine: *City of God*, ed. David Knowles (Pelican Books, 1972).

671 Augustine himself also uses the Sibylline prophecies elsewhere in his works – references loc. cit. n. 669 above.

672 Cf. XVIII 46; cf. the 'prophecies' about Rome in *Aeneid* I 278f and VI 847f.

673 *Phaedo* 85d.

674 See n. 611, p. 136 above.

in the world capital of the Empire that *united* 'all nations', the Apostle is, appropriately, even more universalist: 'from the beginning until now' not only the human race but 'the entire creation has been in the travail of one great act of giving birth ...' (Rom 8:22).

That statement is not merely a Judeo-Christian *interpretation* of profane history. Its truth is illustrated in profane history itself, not just in its religion but in its metaphysics – from its beginnings in Parmenides' quest for the transcendent *One* that is the ground of all, down to St Augustine on the heart that is restless until it rests in that One.[675] Aristotle, as so often, pithily expresses it in the opening sentence of his *Metaphysics*: 'All men by their nature are driven by a desire for understanding', a desire that is unsatisfied short of ultimate understanding. And throughout that tradition the desire goes beyond mere understanding to contemplation, vision, union – even in Aristotle.[676]

As we have seen,[677] it is the same Aristotle who recognized that reason by itself did not suffice for that goal – something superior to reason is needed. In effect what is needed is a light from that goal itself, as we saw at the end of the 'ascent' in Plato's *Symposium*,[678] and as he lays down as a principle in his *Seventh Letter* (341 bc). 'Let no man write my philosophy', he says there. He has not even done so himself, nor ever will: 'for there is no way of putting it into words like other studies'. Acquaintance with it comes not at the end of syllogism or sorites, but at the end of the long *ascesis* of the *bios philosophikos*, at which point, 'suddenly,[679] like a blaze enkindled by a leaping spark, it is generated in the soul and becomes self-sustaining'.

We may bring all those data to a point in brief and contemporary terms: they express not just man's *need* of the divine Transcendent but also his *openness* to it. And in so doing they provide one of the elements from which to define not only man's *condition* but his very *nature*. What is man if he is not more than man?, Augustine exclaims somewhere. In the terms of a modern philosopher,[680] man exists in the *metaxu*, the middle region between the immanent and the Transcendent. And the correlative to man's openness to the divine Transcendent is the nearness, the omnipresence, of that divine Transcendent. 'He is not far from any of us', says St Paul to the Athenian philosophers, 'for it is in Him that we live

675 *Conf.* I 1, 1.

676 See *Nicomachean Ethics*, X 7–8.

677 See n. 660, p.136 above.

678 See n. 638, p. 132 above.

679 Referring to one well-known feature of the onset of *enthousiasmos*, vision, revelation.

680 Eric Voegelin – see e.g. his *Anamnesis*, translated and edited by G. Niemeyer (University of Notre Dame, 1978), passim. Cf. Karl Jaspers, op. cit., Chapter VIII on Faith and Enlightenment.

and move and exist, as indeed some of your own writers have said ... '.[681] One out of many such writers was Aristotle: 'The divine pervades all that exists.'[682]

In view of this universal complementarity of human *openness* to the divine Transcendent and the guiding omnipresence of that Transcendent itself, it would be surprising if Cicero's *requirement* and Plato's *hope* for 'some divine word'[683] were entirely frustrated in profane history, if no light from the *Logos* were diffused beyond the single beam of Judeo-Christian revelation. If *universal* history has a direction and meaning, with Christ as its focus, we can hardly exclude profane history from the *praeparatio evangelica*. Even modern philosophers of history see it as punctuated by 'axial ages', ages, that is, when diverse high civilizations make parallel spiritual progress. Karl Jaspers[684] sees the period beginning in 800 BC as one such age, a climactic one, in fact, for Greco-Roman and Judeo-Christian history. That is the age not only of Just Men like Job and Isaiah's Suffering Servant but also of Socrates, and not only of Socrates but of all the longings of all the suffering ones in Greek tragedy.[685] St Augustine puzzled over the paradox involved in how tragedy speaks to our condition.[686] He also found – or thought he found – the equivalent of St John's *Prologue* in the books of the Platonists.[687] Yet 'it is one thing to see the land of peace from a wooded mountain-top ... and quite another to hold to the way that leads there ... '.[688] What he did not find in the Platonists was that the *Logos* had in person come down to us, to be our Way, to show us the face of love, and to teach us the tears of confession.[689] Only through St Paul did he discover that historical event, after which he 'looked on [God's] works and trembled'.[690]

* * *

Augustine's 'way', through Plato to Christ, leaves Israel still unique, axial, and essential, without, for all that, snuffing the light emanating from the Gentile sage. To return to one of the 'supporters' we cited from the start, von Balthasar is

681 Acts 17:28.

682 *Met.* XII 8, 1074 b.

683 See n. 661, p.136 and n.673, p.138 above.

684 Op. cit., 98; cf. the volumes of Eric Voegelin on *Order and History*.

685 On Greek Tragedy in relation to our theme, in addition to n. 585, p. 120 above, see Martin Hengel, *The Atonement* (London: SCM Press, 1981), 9ff.

686 *Conf.* III 2.

687 Ibid. VII 9; he has in mind the Neoplatonists, especially the *Enneads* of the great Plotinus, *mystic* as well as metaphysician, and who therefore showed Augustine the 'way' to his own first mystical experience, described in *Confessions* VII 10.

688 Ibid VII 21, 27.

689 Ibid.

690 Ibid.

definitively positive about that possibility. In the second work of his great trilogy, *Theo-Drama*, vol. III,[691] he confronts expressly the problem of 'The Nations' in their relation to the centrality of Israel in sacred history. To cut a long story short we may give him the last word on the questions we have asked about the significance of the strange figure of Socrates, and others along the way:

> It is part of the living God's freedom ... to reveal himself among the pagans according to his good pleasure; he can raise up individual sages and prophets from among them, to whom Israel has to listen and from whom it must learn.[692]

691 (San Francisco: Ignatius Press,1992),401ff.

692 Ibid., 415.

AUGUSTINE

ST AUGUSTINE

I

In this season sixteen hundred years ago Aurelius Augustinus was baptized by Bishop Ambrose in his cathedral church in Milan, at the Easter ceremonies of 24–25 April 387. Together with Augustine his life-long friend Alypius, future Bishop of Thagaste, Augustine's birthplace. With them also Augustine's natural son, Adeodatus, 'carnally begotten by me in my sin'.

The event was the end of a long search by a man who was born into the Faith, became a troubled questioning adolescent, a disaffected university intellectual, joined the more 'scientific'-seeming sect of the Manicheans, eventually saw through them too, dallied then with sceptical despair of ever finding philosophic and religious truth, returned to the Catholic Church as a provisional catechumen – 'until some certain light should appear by which I might steer my course' – became a reborn Christian in August, and presented himself as a candidate for baptism in the following March at the beginning of Lent.

'In my beginning is my end.' This was the man who, no matter how unhappy with orthodoxy, could never be happy with any 'doxa' that excluded Christ. 'Any book that lacked his name, no matter how learned and excellently written, could never win me completely' (*Conf.* 3.4). The baptism he now received he had already begged when he once fell gravely ill as a child. But when he suddenly got well again, his mother postponed it to adult years, after a custom of the time. 'I was then a believer, as was my mother, and all our household except my father' (*Conf.* 1.11).

In retrospect Augustine was critical of his mother's decision. Baptism, he believed, would have saved him from 'the many mighty waves of temptation' that were about to break over him as he grew out of boyhood. If he had been so saved, we should now know a lot less about the *grande profundum*, the great deep that is man. We should lack one of the great books of the world, Augustine's *Confessions*. We should be without all the spoils of 'wisdom' that the exile brought back from 'Egypt'. In a word we should be without one of the great exemplars of man's spiritual Odyssey.

Now at last 'we were baptized, and all anxiety about our past fled away. The days were not long enough as I meditated ... on the depth of your design for the salvation of the human race. I wept at the beauty of your hymns and canticles...

Those sounds flowed into my ears, and the truth streamed into my heart: so that my feeling of devotion overflowed, and the tears ran from my eyes, and I was happy in them' (*Conf.* 9.6).

No baptism since that of St Paul was more momentous for the history of Christianity. And not for Christianity only but also for the civilization it leavened, or created. For the teeming heart and mind of this Church Father made him also one of a few ever-fruitful fathers of philosophic thought and its search for truth.

II

Who is this man and what can he say to us sixteen centuries on? By birth a North African. Southern shore of the age-old Mediterranean gravitational centre of the movement of races and civilizations. Of Roman settler stock. A stock that could discipline but not suppress the indigenous influence of geography, climate and race, aboriginal Berber race and colonizing Semitic Phoenician before the Roman came. The influence that produced the characteristic African temper, the *furor Africanus* that we know from its Latin writers, pagan and Christian. Born at Thagaste, Souk Ahras in modern Algeria. Into a small-town 'ascendancy' family of limited means in hard times. Of a pious, pushful mother, Monica, and an earthy pagan father, Patricius. Provincial circumstances from which it will be the first ambition of the young and upwardly mobile Augustine to escape – to Carthage and imperial Rome and Milan. To return reborn into a new world-view. The greatest of many representatives of an age in which a world was passing away, and another being painfully born.

Son then of an ancient flourishing province of Rome – as Empire and Church. A man of the ancient civilization – who yet has earned the cliché of 'the first modern man'. His life (354–430) coincided with the last stages of the decline and fall of Rome. If that be 'ancient history', to know it is to realize about much of our own experience: that we have been there before. He knew the inflation, taxation, economic decay, and restrictions on personal freedom that were the internal symptoms of Roman decline. He knew the sack of the 'eternal city' in 410, an event that, even to Christians, looked like the end of the world. As he lay on his death-bed the Vandal fleet was blockading his episcopal city of Hippo. He prayed for one or other of two favours. To be called away before they got in, otherwise for the strength to endure what men must. He was granted the former. In those last days his 'dialogue of comfort against tribulation' was with certain of the Psalms of David hung on the wall in front of him, and with a thought from Plotinus, Greek philosopher and mystic: 'He will be no great man who thinks it a matter of great importance that timber and stone should collapse and mortal men should die.'

III

But Augustine saw that the soul had left the ancient body politic long before its physical collapse. And, far from that collapse being due to the triumph of religion and barbarism (in Gibbon's gibe), he saw religion as the soul of the true City. And even then ... all civilizations are mortal. Only the City of God is 'eternal'. His work of that title was occasioned by the need to reflect on the cataclysm of 410. It is one of the 'great books' of civilization. It is the first philosophy, or more correctly theology, of history. History no longer interpreted from the limited viewpoint of Rome or Athens but from the viewpoint of the heavenly Jerusalem, *sub specie aeternitatis.* A viewpoint that could only be given from beyond history, from the Alpha and Omega given in the Judeo-Christian revelation.

From this glimpse of the world of Augustine and the holistic range of the questions for which Christianity was to be the 'true philosophy' (as the early Christians called their religion), it is easy to see how far beyond the individual and personal were the implications of Augustine's conversion. He is the most voluminous as well as the most powerful intellectual and spiritual force among the Latin Fathers. His range is the range of truth, revealed truth and the truth of philosophical reason in so far as it is necessary to understand as well as believe.

This range is also the range of his own searching genius.

It is the range of the vertical drive of his metaphysical temperament. Augustine is one of those peak representatives of man's condition who have been called pilgrims of the absolute. Because their spirits are restless until they rest in an absolute, some final insight into the origin and purpose of existence. Augustine's first 'conversion' was an intellectual conversion. In his nineteenth year, to the philosophical search for 'deathless wisdom' (i.e. the old high sapiential quest for *sophia*, common to Jew and Greek). Wisdom not in the confused cackle of competing philosophical schools, but 'Wisdom itself, wherever it might be' (*Conf.* 3.4).

The drive of such pilgrims usually has a religious dimension. In such men it is the heart as well as the reason that is in search of satisfaction. After the Bible and Plato, and anticipating Pascal, Augustine is also a philosopher of the heart. He anticipates Newman in 'the thought of two and two only supreme and luminously self-evident beings, myself and my creator' (*Apologia*). 'My longing is to know God and to know my soul' (*Soliloquies*). He anticipates Pascal on the 'fire' and the 'joy' of knowing the 'God of Abraham, God of Isaac, God of Jacob, not of the philosophers and savants'. The leitmotiv of the *Confessions* is that 'thou hast made us towards thyself and our hearts are restless until they rest in thee' (1.1). The *grande profundum*, the 'great deep' of man, is his longing and capacity for the infinity of God. Augustine was always a God-tormented man. Long before he could resolve his intellectual difficulties about God's nature,

God's existence was a haunting 'interior melody', towards which he strained the ears of his heart.

The eventual finding of God is not the finding of one compartmental truth among others in the general search for truth. God is the source both of reality and the light by which it is understood. He is the *principium*, the 'beginning', the One Truth on which all partial truths depend. The metaphysical 'convert' of nineteen did not know it at the time, but 'I had begun that journey upwards by which I was to return to you' (*Conf.* 3.4).

Augustine is a philosophic mind, driven by the need to understand as well as believe. Yet one of his favourite texts and fundamental principles is that 'unless you believe you will not understand' (Isaiah 7:9 LXX). (No cheap principle, but one with its own philosophic validity, as Augustine knew.) God's word then became the 'true philosophy'. 'Marvellous is the profundity of thy scriptures. Their surface lies open to us, charming us as we charm children. But marvellous is their profundity, O my God, marvellous is their profundity. To gaze into it is a shuddering, the shudder of awe, the shudder of love' (*Conf.* 11.14). And when the historical and philological exegetes objected that the sacred writers could not have been conscious of all that Augustine found in their words, the principle of his answer was that, 'if I myself had to write with such vast authority, I should prefer so to write that my words should mean whatever truth anyone could find in them rather than express one true meaning so clearly as to exclude all others ...' (*Conf.* 12.31).

And if the word of God be indeed the word of God, should not Augustine have the rights of the matter? Centuries of the spiritual exercise of *lectio divina* might seem to confirm it. St Teresa of Avila describes a state in which 'a truth was revealed to me which is the fulfilment of all truths. I cannot tell how this was, for I saw nothing. I was told, without seeing by whom, but I clearly understood that it was the Truth itself: " ... All the harm that befalls the world comes from a failure to understand the truths of scripture in all their true clarity ... "' (*Life*, c. 40). And a great contemporary theologian includes St Augustine in a long line of spiritual exegetes who have 'realized how the infinite shines directly through the fearful intensity of the prophets, of Jesus, of Paul and of John: how the human word and gesture are but a thin veil before it ... '.

Hence it is that, at the point in the *Confessions* where he projects his spiritual Odyssey from the past and the present into the future, the thirst of Augustine is that of the Psalmist – to 'meditate on the wonders of thy law' (*Conf.* 10.43). Law understood here not as a merely ritual or moral code but as the all-comprehending uttered word of subsistent Truth, the 'Way' of other great traditions, the Source of reality and truth ('I am the way and the truth ...'). In this light the range of the meditation has to be co-extensive with existence and its history, from the first beginning to the last end of things, 'from the first *beginning*, when you *made heaven and earth* (Gen.1:1), until our everlasting reign with you in your holy city' (*Conf.* 11.2). (Hence the at first sight strange appendage of a commentary on the Genesis creation account in the last three Books of the *Confessions*. It was the classical Patristic focus for cosmogony and eschatology.)

IV

Obviously in a few pages we cannot follow the detailed steps of that 'way' in this most voluminous of early Christian writers. But it is important to see him whole. And glancing forward to his influence in history I don't know if it is relevant any longer to mention what used to be called the 'perennial philosophy'. Some of us were reared – *in illis diebus* – on the Aristotelian Aquinas, at least in vitamin tablet form. We did not know that there was another scholastic *summa*, in St Bonaventure's Platonist Augustinianism. The pity of it is obvious, if it be true, as has been said, that everyone is born either a Platonist or an Aristotelian. (But by now both may have fallen into the pit!)

Of course the Thomist of strict observance denied that Augustine was a 'philosopher' at all (*sit venia verbo* from Lisnagoola[1]). He was not technical, systematic or complete. He did not distinguish departments and levels of thinking. He mixed up philosophy with theology, and both with something called Christian wisdom. Since then of course handmaid and mistress alike have lost their stays and look a great deal less neat and tidily 'scientific'. Augustine sought the whole truth, not the compartmental kind (hence 'wisdom'). He sought it where and how he could find it – including the path of 'driest' dialectic. But his thinking with the heart as well as the head makes him congenial to the 'existential' and religious sensibility.

This congeniality is due also to the deep and varied human needs that he requires truth to satisfy. Truth for the intellect alone is notional and abstract. It is 'real' only as possessing and possessed by the heart. And the Augustinian quest is two-fold, not for truth alone but for *beatitudo* as well, two facets of the same reality. The search can come to rest only in God. All lesser truths, all lower kinds of happiness, are incomplete and frustrating. Man's search cannot rest short of their ground in the Absolute. His whole being is magnetized towards what is his own ground too. 'Thou hast made us towards thyself, and our hearts are restless until they rest in thee.'

This drive towards rest only in God is also rooted in a deep metaphysical insight – the contingence of all that exists outside its ground in God. He had the

1 Lisnagoola was the title under which Fr Brendan Hoban wrote a series of articles in the 1980s. He subsequently collected them and published a book under the title of *Lisnagoola Chronicle*.

insight by nature, but, like the conversion to philosophy, there was a moment of particularly forceful awakening to its truth. That was when a friend of his youth died and he 'discovered' death and the contingence of frail, individual human existence. 'I became a great enigma to myself, and I was forever asking my soul why it was so sad and why it disquieted me so sorely' (*Conf.* 4.4). Hence the search for the ground in which we may stand and be established forever. God is the life of this transient life that is ours – 'should I call it dying life or living death?' (*Conf.* 1.6). God alone 'stands and abides forever'. In him alone can our transience be established in stability forever (*Conf.* 4.11).

Only hereafter will this stability be permanent. But Augustine knew that it begins in this life. He had an occasional experience of its reality. And he longed for the occasional experience to become a permanent state. A constant motif after conversion is the longing not, as he puts it, to be made more intellectually certain of God's existence but 'to be established more firmly *in* him'. Could the passing moment of experience be made permanent that would be, in a way, to abide in what abides forever, to 'enter into the joy of the Lord'. But, as classically, the moment always passed, leaving only a memory, a fragrance and a longing. 'I can remain in my ordinary state though unwilling. I would remain in that other state but I am unable. In both states I know my misery' (*Conf.* 10.40).

V

Saints alive! Have we already pitched Augustine out of sight? Not, I should hope, for the many who still experience their existence as that of 'a particle adrift in the universe' (Teilhard). Nor for the many who would like the 'spiritual life' to be really a life. In prayer, for instance, that reaches beyond the clichés and the formulae to some sense of the reality of God. Nor again for all who have to start where Augustine starts:

> where all the ladders start,
> In the foul rag-and-bone shop of the heart.[2]

For this transcendentalist also insisted that it is only from where a man has fallen that he can start to get up. (As regards his often alleged over-emphasis on that fallenness ... I don't know if we have the right to be too bland about that in the century of Freud and Jung and Treblinka.)

It is at this ground-floor level that Augustine first comes 'alive'. He travels far and ascends high but his starting point is experience. The journey is experience. Even the metaphysics along the way are experience, not so much abstract

2 W. B. Yeats, 'The Circus Animal's Desertion'.

excogitation as a key discovered to unlock experience. The farthest point of arrival is experience, in those 'higher' moments already mentioned. Experience deep enough does not date. So Augustine can be a contemporary across the centuries. Even the ground-floor experience is a sounding of the depths, a descent into the basement, into the 'abyss of human consciousness'. 'Great is the power of *memoria*, a thing, O my God, to be in awe of, a profound and immeasurable multiplicity. And this thing is my mind, this thing am I. What then am I, O my God? Of what kind is my being? A life powerfully various, manifold, immeasurable' (*Conf.* 10.17).

VI

There is no conveying that life without reading Augustine's own *Confessions*. There we savour it in all its inexhaustible density, as a lived experience and a meditated question. At all its levels from nature to supernature. In all its extension between its two infinities, from its origins *ex nihilo* to its destiny in eternity. The *Confessions* end, as indicated earlier, with the end of journeying in the repose of the eternal Sabbath. They begin with exploration backwards into the darkness of unremembered infancy. Before that again a question about the nature of pre-natal existence in the mother's womb. 'And before that again, O God of my joy? Was I anywhere? Was I anyone? There is no one to tell me – neither my parents nor any man's experience, nor any memory of my own' (*Conf.* 1.6).

Confession in fact is a new literary *genre* generated by such meditations. It is deeper and more comprehensive than the autobiography which the *Confessions* also are at one level (and the first fully developed example of it). Confession is the *genre* appropriate to the relation between *me* and *thee*, the individual soul and its creator, the two luminous poles of reality we referred to earlier. Confession at a depth which has its taproot in the Bible – although glimpsed by Plotinus too – as the spontaneous avowal of what comes home to the creature on glimpsing its condition in relation to its creator. Confession of sin and praise, of man's guilt and of God's glory, and of the gulf that divides creator from created. 'I was shaken with love and with dread, and I knew that I was far from thee in a region of unlikeness' (*Conf.* 7.10).

At their core then, the *Confessions* are an extended spiritual exercise. Augustine himself tells us (in 10.3) how the first instalments already stirred up the hearts of the readers. Written in his mid-forties, they stirred up his own heart in old age, when he re-read them in the course of revising all his works (*oeuvre*-conscious writer that he was). And a distinguished, if little-known, woman in the history of spirituality recorded in the seventeenth century how she was liberated (into prayer) by the *Confessions* of her 'glorious St Augustine' (after long misery with 'methods' and 'idiot's devotions' of every kind).

We have not the space to go in detail through all the stages of human experience, outer and inner and higher, through which the reader of the *Confessions* is led. But we must trace an outline.

We can get a quick line and part of the way with Shakespeare's seven ages of man. Augustine was there before him, through the symbolism of the seven days of the creation narrative in Genesis. We have already noted the framing of the *Confessions* between 'their exits and their entrances'. Within that framework Augustine too follows

first the infant
Mewling and puking in the nurse's arms.
Then the whining schoolboy ...
... creeping like snail
Unwillingly to school. And then the lover
Sighing like furnace ...

But already the northern sequence is not quite right for the man of the south. Reading his Virgil as a precocious secondary student Augustine sighed over the love of Dido for Aeneas. 'And if I were kept from reading I grieved at not reading the tales that caused me such grief' (*Conf.* 1.13). The 'love' proper began in the steaming adolescence of his sixteenth year. (Another 'first' for Augustine – his anticipation of so many 'portraits of the artist as a young man'.) Not much romantic sighing there – except in frustration with his inability to 'distinguish the white light of love from the fog of lust' (*Conf.* 2.2). With this conflict the 'lover' would dally for another sixteen years. ('Give me chastity ... but not just yet, *Conf.* 8.7). It would be resolved only in the *Walpurgisnacht* of the garden scene in Milan (*Conf.* 8.11–12). Meanwhile ... 'I became to myself a waste land' (*Conf.* 1.10).

'To Carthage then I came.' Teen-and-twenty university years of continued emotional tides but also of intellectual awakening. A Stephen Dedalus, moody and brooding, alternately gregarious and solitary, in need of companions and contemptuous of their crude ways. Hungry before 'the gates of all the ways of error and glory'. Hungry above all for love, the love given and returned in which, transposed, he will eventually locate the whole gravitational field of man. ('You have made us towards yourself ... ') But love still divided by the fissure between the limpid commerce of soul with soul and the pitch of instinctual desire. 'O my God ... with what gall did you sprinkle the sweets of that time ... ' (*Conf.* 1.3).

Conflicting emotions however that in those years already settled on one woman, 'not joined to me in lawful marriage, but one whom wandering desire and no particular judgement brought my way. Yet I had but that woman, and I was faithful to her' (*Conf.* 4.2). A union that 'needed only the honourable name of marriage' but was broken after many years by the career-conscious Monica. Augustine's heart, 'which had held that woman very dear, was broken and wounded and bleeding' (*Conf.* 6.15). Like Stephen, an image 'had passed into his soul for ever'.

University years of emotional tides that brought the equally tidal intellectual awakening that set the course of his life. The 'conversion' to philosophy – as philosophy was then understood, in the high, serious existential sense of the search for the meaning of existence. 'Suddenly all the vanity I had hoped in I saw as worthless, and with an incredible intensity of desire I longed for deathless wisdom ...' (*Conf.* 3.4).

The search took all the years into his thirties. Years of which he often took stock in despair at the little progress made since his turning round in his nineteenth year. Years made more burdensome by the conflict between the search for meaning and the necessary futility of careerist advancement. 'Perish all this. Let me dismiss this vanity and emptiness and give myself wholly to the search for truth' (*Conf.* 6.11).

The problems that held him back are still pertinent, and even at times reassuring for those still on the road. Problems with the anthropomorphism of scripture. Problems with the nature and meaning of Christ. Problems of the intense intellectual, unable to take on faith what he wanted to understand. And, for such an intellectual, the strangest – and for our little positivistic minds the most consoling – problem of all: his inability to conceive how God, or any spiritual being, could be anything other than nothing without matter and spatial extension. And all the time the endless problem of evil, no academic problem for him but felt in the marrow of the bone in his own dividedness against himself. Hence the long sojourn with Manicheanism, a system elaborate in the details but simple in principle – the age-old cutting of the Gordian knot by dualism.

Barriers broken down by the combined light of the Christian bishop and the pagan philosopher, Ambrose and Plotinus. And the barriers being down, the streaming in of the transcendent light, in a flash of higher seeing. He had long sought truth. Now 'he who knows that light knows Truth ... And I said "Is Truth then nothing at all, merely because it is not extended either through finite spaces or infinite?" And thou didst cry to me from afar "I am who am" And I heard thee as one hears in the heart; and from that moment there was no ground of doubt in me' (*Conf.* 7.10).

That was intellectual light. Moral light was needed before the practical step could be taken. The reason was Augustine's option for the absolute Christianity of the evangelical counsels. Very bothersome here was the single state for the sake of the Kingdom. The struggle, slip and slide of the final release into that is,

I suppose, the most dramatic scene in the history of religious experience. When the moment came 'it was as though a light of utter confidence shone in my heart, and all the darkness of uncertainty vanished away' (*Conf.* 8.12).

There remained but a couple of weeks to the end of the teaching year. Augustine had long wanted to withdraw, a disenchanted academic in an age of leafmeal words, words, words. To avoid public attention he would stick it out to the end. Eight months to Easter and baptism. To prepare for it – and to restore his physical health and jangled nerves – he retired to a friend's house in the country, somewhere in the plain of Lombardy, in a 'quiet watered land' in sight of the Alpine peaks.

With the candidate for baptism we have come round to where we began. To us it looks like an ending. For Augustine it was more like the real beginning. In Augustine, after the Bible, Plotinus, and earlier Fathers, 'conversion' is one of the directing ideas of the complete spiritual life. It is not a once-for-all event but a life-long process. After the initial *epistrophê, conversio, turning* round and towards, there is the sustained *moving* towards the source and the term of our being. That is the axis of our orientation. 'Thou has made us towards thyself ... '. Consequently a recurring motif in the *Confessions* after conversion is the prayer to God to *complete* the conversion he then began. A completion to be accomplished only at the point where the *Confessions* end, echoing their opening theme, in the anticipated repose of the eternal Sabbath, symbolized in that seventh day when God rested after all his works.

That is the range of the life's project Augustine had set himself as he retraced his steps in the autumn of 387, from Milan to Rome and Ostia to take ship again for Africa. A project to be lived at first within the formal structures of a contemplative life. Later to be reconciled with the pastoral cares to which he was quickly called. It was not a narrow project. Like much in Augustine, and others of the age, it combined the highest ideals of Greek philosophy with the highest of Christianity. Throughout his life Augustine remained what he was as a questioning youth, the man of 'faith seeking understanding'.

And beyond theoretic understanding some experiential foretaste of the supreme Reality, its joy, its repose, and something we get only from spirits as great as Augustine's – an adequate notion of the grandeur of God. 'All heaven and earth cannot contain you. For you made them, and me in them' (*Conf.* 1.2).

It was in Ostia that he had his most famous foretaste of that Reality. Resting before the voyage, mother and son talked together in peace as they leaned out of a window looking on to the garden of the house they were staying in. 'With the mouth of our heart we panted for the high waters of your fountain, the fountain of the life that is with you: that being sprinkled from that fountain according to our capacity we might in some sense meditate upon so great a matter. (...) Higher and higher we soared ... to come at last to that region of richness unending where you feed Israel forever with the food of truth, and where life is that Wisdom by which all things are made ... And while we were thus talking of his Wisdom, and panting after it, with all the effort of our heart we did for one instant attain to touch it. Then sighing, and leaving the first fruits of our spirit bound to it, we returned to the sound of our own voices ... ' (*Conf.* 9.10).

A MYSTIC IN MILAN
'REVERBERASTI' REVISITED

Among the most discussed passages of St Augustine's *Confessions*[3*] have been 7.10.16 and 7.17.23, with their echoes in 7.18.24 and 7.20.26. The reason is that, while they appear to recount pre-conversion mystical experiences in Milan in the wake of St Augustine's discovery of Plotinus and Platonism, the 'success' or genuinely mystical nature of these experiences has been questioned – notably by Pierre Courcelle, in a chapter with a title that came to enjoy a kind of provocative *succès de scandale*: '*Les vaines tentatives d'extases Plotiniennes*'.[4] Some of the reactions were vivid, but Courcelle returned to the charge in 1963.[5] It could be said that some of those who defended the authenticity of the experiences in question did so in ways that, when analyzed, were not all that much more positive than the criticism of Courcelle himself.[6] This imbalance was corrected in 1968 by André Mandouze at the end of a magisterial *opus* on St Augustine's intellectual and spiritual development.[7] He interprets the Milan experiences not as failed or inauthentic, and not even as isolated events, but rather as one decisive moment in a series of positive points on a rising line of true mystical experiences. Of these experiences the most famous and universally accepted as genuine is the Vision at Ostia.[8] But then, 'si celle d'Ostie peut être considérée comme mystique, celle de Milan ne l'est pas moins'.[9]

3* Where the *Confessions* of St Augustine are quoted in translation, the version used is that by Frank Sheed (London, 1944), except for occasional minor modifications. For the *Enneads* of Plotinus the honour is still left to Stephen McKenna (second edition, revised by B. S. Page, London, 1956).

4 P. Courcelle, *Recherches sur les Confessions de Saint Augustin* (Paris, 1950), 157–67.

5 P. Courcelle, *Les Confessions de Saint Augustin dans la tradition littéraire* (Paris, 1963), 43–58.

6 For a summary see Courcelle, *Les Confessions*, 43f.

7 A. Mandouze, *Saint Augustin. L'Aventure de la raison et de la grâce* (Paris, 1968), ch. 12, 'Rencontres avec Dieu.' On the fundamental question of whether St Augustine was a mystic at all, Mandouze had given an exhaustive *rapport* in 1954 to the Paris *Congrès International Augustinien*; see *Augustinus Magister* (Paris, 1954), 103–63: 'Où en est la question de la mystique augustinienne?' As is well known, the great divide on this question was between F. Cayré, *La contemplation augustinienne* (Paris, 1929; revised ed., 1954), and E. Hendrikx, *Augustins Verhältnis zur Mystik* (Würzburg, 1936). It is of course possible to see now that the 'quarrel', as then stated, arose from mutually exclusive doctrinaire starting points on the meaning of mysticism. For a recent short overview see M. T. Clark, *Augustine of Hippo. Selected Writings*, The Classics of Western Spirituality (London, 1984), 35ff.

8 *Conf.* 9.10.23ff.

9 Mandouze, *L'Aventure*, 697.

What gave rise to the suggestion of failure, of *vaines tentatives*, was one recurring element in the accounts of the Milan experiences, an element concentrated in variations on the verbs *reverberare, repercutere, repellere,* etc. 'Et reverberasti infirmitatem aspectus mei radians in me vehementer, ... et inueni longe me esse a te in regione dissimilitudinis...'.[10] 'Sed aciem figere non eualui et repercussa infirmitate redditus solitis non mecum ferebam nisi amantem memoriam et quasi olefacta desiderantem, quae comedere nondum possem.'[11] With these two principal texts we may compare their closely following echoes: 'Et quarebam uiam comparandi roboris quod esset idoneum ad fruendum te, nec inueniebam ... '.[12] 'Repulsus sensi quid per tenebras animae meae contemplari non sinerer ... nimis ... infirmus ad fruendum te.'[13]

The topic contained in these passages deserves closer attention than it seems yet to have been given. As regards the scholars quoted, two brief comments may be made. Courcelle took the topic too quickly at its face value, despite the abundance of its occurrence in the background tradition – which he found principally in Philo. Mandouze scarcely considered its significance at all, and defended the genuinely mystical nature of the experiences in spite of these passages. 'Il est trop faible (*infirmitas*) pour pouvoir persister (*figere non evalui*) dans la contemplation (*contemplari non sinerer*) de L'Être dont l'evidence lui est pourtant apparue en un instant.'[14] That is true, as far as it goes. But there is more to be said.

> The substance of what remains to be said is:
> 1. The motif goes much further back into tradition, both Greek and Judeo-Christian, than Courcelle recognized;
> 2. It recurs throughout the *corpus* of St Augustine;[15]
> 3. It is a constant in the later mystical tradition, and to a degree that cannot all be accounted for by the influence of St Augustine on personal experience in that tradition;
> 4. Throughout the tradition of that experience, including the experience of St Augustine, it occurs in many contexts of which the genuinely mystical nature can hardly be doubted.[16]

10 *Conf.* 7.10.16.

11 *Conf.* 7.17.23.

12 *Conf.* 7.18.24.

13 *Conf.* 7.20.26.

14 Mandouze, *L'Aventure*, 696.

15 Courcelle did recognize this – see *Les Confessions*, 53. It is, perhaps, most sustained in that other great 'quest' for God, the *De Trin.* 8ff.

16 Suffice it here to refer to the sections on 'the transiency of the experience' in Dom C. Butler, *Western Mysticism* (London, 1922 and 1927), 66–68, 115–16, 154–57.

In examining the tradition one could in fact 'begin with Jove,' i.e. Homer! But within the confines of a brief contribution it is obviously not possible to explore the topic in detail on a scale as large as that. I propose to take soundings in a defined area of St Augustine himself, with such references to tradition, before him and after him, as shed light on his meaning. And the focus of our interest is the association of light and dazzlement with the experience of 'theophany,' or the radiant unveiling of ultimate, supreme Being. That is the focus of the Augustinian experience, 'Vidi ... supra mentem meam lucem incommutabilem ... Tu es Deus meus, tibi suspiro die ac nocte.'[17] And we can quote at once even the un-mystical Aristotle for the essence of the tradition of experience to which Augustine's statement belongs. Concerning the ultimate realities – which are also the 'truest' and intrinsically clearest – our human, finite *noûs* is like the eyes of bats to daylight.[18] A passage cited centuries later by Dante *à propos* of a supreme moment of personal vision is recounted in the *Vita Nuova*.[19] And if we mention Dante, in whose *Commedia* so many strands of the mystical as well as other traditions are given supreme expression, it is apposite to refer to *Paradiso* 25.118ff. The passage describes the experience of trying to gaze on the splendour of the glorified soul of St John:

> Qual è colui ch'adocchia, e s'argomenta
> di vedere eclissar lo sole un poco,
> che, per veder, non vedente diventa;
> tal mi fec'io a quell' ultimo foco ...
>
> [As who doth gaze and strain
> to see the sun eclipsed a space,
> who by seeing is deprived of sight,
> so did I become to this final flame ...]

It is natural to look first into Plotinus, whose 'discovery' produced the impulse to these *tentatives*,[20] and whose language is echoed in St Augustine's own description of them.[21] It is strange that Courcelle should not have seen our topic in Plotinus.[22] We find it there again and again.

17 *Conf.* 7.10.16; cf. 10.6.8: 'Quid autem amo cum te amo? ... Non candorem lucis ecce istis amicum oculis ... Et tamen amo quandam lucem ... ubi fulget animae meae quod non capit locus ...'.

18 *Met.* 2.1.993b7ff.

19 Ch. 41.

20 *Inde admonitus...* (*Conf.* 7.10.16).

21 For an *aperçu* of the parallels see the Bibliothèque Augustinienne edition of the *Confessions* (Paris, 1962), vol. 13, 682ff.

22 See Courcelle, *Les Confessions*, 46: 'Rien de tel, que je sache, dans les sources néo-platoniciennes: Plotin écrit seulement que l'oeil mal nettoyé ne voit rien' – and he quotes from *Enn.* 1.6.9.

That Plotinus personally had authentic mystical experiences we know from himself[23] and from Porphyry's *Life*.[24] Yet he is keenly aware that it is always transient, and often only momentary, a flash of vision, because that is all the soul can bear of transcendent light. Always 'there comes the moment of descent from intellection to reasoning, and after that sojourn in the divine I ask myself how it happens that I can now be descending ...'.[25] About that highest light, which the soul 'sees sometimes in a momentary flash',[26] we are left wondering whence it came, from within or without; and when it has gone, we say, 'It was here. Yet no; it was beyond!'[27] 'It is clear that we cannot possess ourselves of the power of this principle [the Good] in its concentrated fullness ... but some partial attainment is within our reach.'[28] 'The state is painful, often it [the soul] seeks relief by retreating from all this vagueness to the region of sense, there to rest as on solid ground ...'.[29] 'How comes the soul not to keep that ground? Because it has not yet escaped wholly: but there will be the time of vision unbroken ...'.[30] 'And this inner vision, what is its operation? Newly awakened it is all too feeble to bear the ultimate splendour ... '.[31]

Plato, naturally, is one aboriginal source of the Plotinian metaphysic and mysticism of light. According to the *Seventh Letter* there is no way of putting the ultimate knowledge into words. 'Acquaintance with it must come rather after a long period of attendance on instruction in the subject itself and of close companionship, when, suddenly, like a blaze kindled by a leaping spark, it is generated in the soul ... '.[32] Suddenly, after long discipline, 'understanding ... blazes up, and the mind, as it exerts all its powers to the limit of human capacity, is flooded with light.'[33]

Elsewhere in Plato we learn that the vision of this light of ultimate reality is hard to sustain. 'The philosopher, whose thoughts constantly dwell upon the nature of reality, is difficult to see because his region is so bright, for the eye of the vulgar soul cannot endure to keep its gaze fixed on the divine.'[34]

---

23 *Enn.* 4.8.1.

24 Ch. 23.

25 *Enn.* 4.8.1.7ff.

26 *Enn.* 5.5.7.9.

27 *Enn.* 5.5.7.34ff.

28 *Enn.* 5.5.10.1ff.

29 *Enn.* 6.9.3.4ff.

30 *Enn.* 6.9.10.1ff.

31 *Enn.* 1.6.9.1ff.

32 341c.

33 344b.

34 *Sophist*, 254a.

On such a topic one thinks naturally of the Allegory of the Cave in *Rep.* 514ff,[35] to see what parallels it might contain in its imagery of the human condition as an ascent from shadows and darkness to reality and light. The imagery all turns precisely on the successive stages of painful adjustment and turning round, 'conversion',[36] whereby vision accustomed only to darkness can endure to look on successively higher and truer levels of reality in successively brighter intensities of light, 'until the soul is able to endure the contemplation of the really real and the brightest region of Being, which is what we call the Good'.[37] In the process of 'turning round' and ascending there is hurt and dazzlement and the temptation to turn back and retreat to the more accustomed level of reality that can more properly be seen.[38] 'Suppose one were freed from his bonds and compelled to stand up suddenly and turn his head around and walk and to lift up his eyes to the light – in doing so he would feel pain, and because of the dazzle and glitter of the light he would be unable to see properly the objects whose shadows he formerly saw.'[39]

As regards the last passage, R.P. Festugière[40] provides a reference that reveals the unfolding of the full mystical implications of this passage in the Platonist tradition. He discovers a clear reminiscence of this passage in Celsus.[41] If God is ineffable, 'how then are we to know God? How are we to learn the way which leads to Him?' In the event, 'those who have been led from the darkness to the light cannot endure the dazzle of its rays. Their vision is so dulled and impaired that they think they are blind.'

Festugière[42] further draws attention to a passage in Xenophon's *Memorabilia*,[43] which is the ultimate source of Stobaeus II.15.5.[44] These two passages are particularly to the point in that they turn on the distinction between the partial visibility of God in His works and His absolute invisibility in His form or essence. We shall see in a moment how that enables us to give a profounder interpretation of Augustine, *Conf.* 7.10.16.

35 Known to Augustine from the Platonist tradition, as we see from *Solil.* 1.13.23 and *Civ. Dei.* 10.2.

36 The terminology of 'conversion' occurs in *Rep.* 514b, 515cde, 518cd. This concept was to become fundamental to the philosophy as well as to the spirituality of the Fathers – and nowhere more than in Augustine – from the twin sources consisting of Neoplatonism and the Septuagint (ἐπιστροφή/ἀποστροφή, *conversio/aversio*). See e.g. Plotinus, *Enn.* 1.3.1, 1.6.8, 5.2.1, 6.9.7–8; Augustine, *Conf.* 12.9–13, 13.2ff.

37 *Rep.* 518c.

38 *Rep.* 515e.

39 *Rep.* 515c.

40 In *La révélation d'Hermès Trismégiste*, t. iv, *Le Dieu inconnu et la gnose* (Paris, 1954), 116.

41 *Alēthēs Logos*, vi.66 (ed. Glöckner).

42 Op. cit., 13.

43 4.3.13–14 (quoted also by Clement of Alexandria in *Protr.* 6.71.3).

44 Ed. Wachsmuth.

According to the passage in Xenophon the gods bestow their gifts on us, but in so doing never themselves appear. The supreme God is disclosed in His works and yet remains unseen in His ordering of them. 'Mark that even the sun, who seems to reveal himself to all, permits not man to behold him clearly, but if anyone attempts to gaze recklessly upon him, his vision is blinded?' Stobaeus has this same comparison with the sun,[45] after a statement that is even more technically explicit than Xenophon's. 'The gods are all that is least perceptible to man,[46] for all their accomplishing of works that are the mightiest. He who gives to all things movement and repose is clearly revealed[47] as great and powerful: but as to what He is in His form[48] He remains hidden.'[49]

What is particularly valuable in these two passages, beyond their illustration of the background to *reverberatio*, is that they say explicitly what is left implicit elsewhere. Namely, that the *reverberatio* itself is not due to human failure or *vaines tentatives* but rather to the intrinsic limitations of human vision and to the infinite transcendence of its Object. The highest Reality, even to the highest 'seeing', is so transcendent to human modes that it is finally invisible in its essence. It is the same question as is discussed by Dom Butler,[50] *à propos* of St Augustine precisely, whether in this life any man can see the divine Essence. Dom Butler's answer, from Scripture, tradition, and theology, is negative, despite certain things at first sight to the contrary in St Augustine. I have quoted Dante to illustrate this tradition. Gregory the Great has some forceful statements of the same facts and their reasons. 'Because we are weighed down by the corruptible flesh we cannot possibly look at the brightness of the divine power in the mode in which in itself it stands immutably. The reason is that the weak eyes of our seeing cannot sustain the light that shines unbearably upon us from the ray of its own eternity.'[51] And this is a statement of principle, not just of a passing experience of 'failure', from one of the *experti* in the Western mystical tradition.

I have indicated that this principle would enable us to suggest a profounder interpretation[52] of Augustine, *Conf.* 7.10.16. That interpretation turns on how we

45 Used also in Cicero, *Tusc. Disp.* 1.30.73; Minucius Felix, *Octavius* 32:5; the *Epistle of Barnabas* 5.10; St Augustine, *Solil.* 1.10.17: 'Nonne vides hos corporis oculos etiam sanos, luce solis istius saepe repercuti et averti, atque ad illa sua obscura confugere?' The image would seem to be in fact a commonplace in the Fathers.

46 ἥκιστα ἀνθρώποισιν ἐπιφαίνονται.

47 φάνερος.

48 μορφήν.

49 ἀφανή.

50 Op. cit., 78ff.

51 *Libri Moralium* 5.29.52.

52 What follows is suggested by a note in the edition of the *Confessions* already cited, vol. 13, 616f.

translate one sentence in the passage. It is this: 'et cum primum cognovi tu assumpsisti me, ut viderem esse quod viderem, et nondum me esse qui viderem.' (*Et reverberasti* ... follows immediately.)

The first 'unexamined' interpretation one tends to give of this sentence is to take *nondum me esse qui viderem* as referring to a present, temporary, merely *moral* unworthiness and a consequent incapacity to see the Reality he knew was there to be seen – *viderem esse quod viderem.*[53] But it is possible to put the emphasis of the meaning elsewhere – on the twice-used verb *esse.* The contrast is then not just moral and temporary but ontological and permanent, the constant Augustinian contrast between the uncreated, eternal, plenary, immutable Being of God and the created, temporal, contingent, participated being of man.[54] The reason then for the *infirmitas reverberata* is correspondingly ontological,[55] not merely moral. An ontological interpretation considerably reinforced by the immediately following reference to the Plotinian *regio dissimilitudinis* – 'I found that I was far from You in a region of unlikeness.'

This interpretation is reinforced by a couple of *Sermon* passages, where Augustine, though he uses language closely parallel to *Conf.* 7.10.16, is stating principle and theory rather than personal experience – although it may of course be based on personal experience. One such passage is in *Sermon* 7.7. The context is an exposition of the ontology of transcendent and eternal Being implied in Exodus 3:14 ('I am who I am ... He who is has sent me to you'). He who understands that the 'name' of God is this 'Being,' transcendent, eternal, beyond the loss and gain of becoming, such a person realizes that between the being of finite, contingent man and such a Reality there is a vast dimensional distance.[56] 'For he who has adequately understood that which is and truly is, he who in any way has been breathed on by the light of authentic Being, even in passing, as in a flash – such a person sees that he is far down below, at a far, far remove, far, far dissimilar ... '.[57]

The parallels with *Conf.* 7.10.16 are obvious. It is all the more significant, then, that this *Sermon* passage allows for the reality, however transient, of the same kind of vision that in *Conf.* 7.10.16 has been read as a *vaine tentative.*

53 Ultimate provenance from Plato? ὅτι ... τοιοῦτόν τι ἰδεῖν, ἰσχυριστέον (*Rep.* 533a).

54 Cf. *Conf.* 7.10.16f.: 'And You cried to me from afar: "Yes, truly, I am who I am." ... And I inspected all the other things that are less than You, and I saw that they neither absolutely are nor yet totally are not. I saw that they are since they are from You, but are not in as much as they are not what You are. For that truly is which abides unchangeably'.

55 That is, of course, until either man's nature is raised up, or the divine nature condescends to it. On the former we have *assumpsisti me* in *Conf.* 7.10.16, and *assumpta mente* in *Serm.* 7.7. On the latter we have in *Serm.* 7.7 a distinction between what God is *in se* (*Ego sum qui sum*) and what He makes Himself *ad nos* (*Ego sum Deus Abraham et Deus Isaac et Deus Jacob*).

56 ' ... multum ... distare ab hominibus'.

57 ' ... longe se videt infra, longe remotissimum, longe dissimillimum'.

The same terminology, the same Scripture texts, and the same assertions of fact and principle, emerge in *Sermon* 52.6.16. 'For I saw something in my ecstasy[58] which I could not long sustain. And, returned to my mortal members and to the many mortal thoughts from the body that weighs down the soul, I said, Why? *I am cast out from the sight of your eyes.*[59] You are far above, I am far below.'[60] And there follows one of the great Augustinian statements of the incomprehensible transcendence of God.

It is clear from the preceding that for his ideas on divine transcendence and the corresponding essential disproportion between the divine light and the human capacity for seeing, Augustine is indebted to the biblical as well as the Greek tradition. We have noted in particular his use of core statements from the theophany in Exodus 3. Very prominent in him also is that other theophany described in Exodus 33:18–23. It is an essential complement to Exodus 3 in as much as it is a *locus classicus* for the constant Old Testament motif that man cannot look on God and live.[61] As such it became a *locus classicus* in the Judaeo-Christian mystical tradition.[62]

The context is that after previous experiences in which he saw God not as He is in himself but in His awesome *effects* Moses finally asks God to 'show me your *glory*'.[63] But he is permitted only to see that glory veiled. 'You cannot see my face ... for man cannot see me and live.' Moses is to stand in the cleft of a rock and be shielded by God's hand while His glory passes by. 'Then I will take my hand away and you shall see my back; but my face is not to be seen.'[64]

In *Sermon* 7.7 Augustine links this request of Moses to the passage on divine transcendence already quoted from that sermon. 'Because I said, "I am who am," and, "He who is has sent me," you have understood what Being is, and you have despaired of understanding it: but raise your hopes.' The hope here however is not the hope of seeing God's Essence – whatever Augustine may seem to suggest

58 Referring to Ps 30:23.

59 Ps 30:23.

60 'Longe sursum es, longe deorsum sum'; cf. *Conf.* 7.10.16: 'superior [lux] quia ipsa fecit me, et ego inferior quia factus ab ea.'

61 Exodus 33:20; cf. 19:21, Leviticus 16:2, Numbers 4:20, Isaiah 6:2, 5.

62 See e.g. Philo, *De Fuga* 29.164f; *De Mut. Nom.* 2.7–9; *De Spec. Leg.* 1.8.41–44; Gregory of Nyssa, *De Vita Moysis, PG* 44.398D-404B; St Augustine, *De Gen. ad Litt.* 12 27.55, *Letters* 147 (*De Videndo Deo*), ch. 5.13, 8.20, 13.31; Ps.-Dionysius, *De Mystica Theologia* 1.3; Gregory the Great, *Libri Moralium* 18.54.88.

63 The radiance of God's 'glory' (*gloria, claritas, doxa, kabod*) is of course a major motif of Scripture, and very relevant to our present theme – behind Augustine there is more than just the Platonist metaphysics and symbolism of the 'sun' and its light; cf. 1 John 1:5: 'Deus lux est'.

64 Cf. Exodus 34:29f. on the numinous radiance from the face of Moses himself after his speaking with God on Sinai: 'When Aaron and all the sons of Israel saw Moses, the skin on his face shone so much that they would not venture near him.'

elsewhere.[65] The hope turns on a distinction Augustine has indicated earlier, between God *in se* and God *ad nos*, between the God 'who is' and the God who takes the initiative in historical modes of presence to Abraham, Isaac, and Jacob. 'I am the God of Abraham, Isaac and Jacob.[66] I am what I am, I am Being Itself, I am with Being Itself, but I am all these things in such a way as not to deny my presence to man.' And Augustine quotes Acts 17:27–28 on the *omnipresent* God in whom we live and move and have our being, and who is therefore not far from any of us. Let us therefore ineffably praise His transcendent *essentia in se* and love the *misericordia* in which He reveals His face in history *ad nos*.

It is to this scriptural tradition of theophany that we find an allusion in what looks like Augustine's earliest reference to the experience of *Conf.* 7.10.16. It is in *Con. Acad.* 1.1.3. The context is the introductory 'protreptic' to Romanianus, urging his conversion to the life of the true contemplative, 'philosophy'. Philosophy it is that rightly teaches us to abandon the cult of any reality accessible to the eyes of the body or to any other corporeal sense. 'She it is who promises that the most true and hidden God will reveal Himself in all clarity, and even now she deigns to give glimpses of Him, as through translucent clouds [*quasi per lucidas nubes*].'[67]

Now, consistent with what has been said about seeing the face of God, the cloud is an accompaniment of theophanies in Scripture. In Exodus 19:16ff a dense cloud (*nubes densissima*) is one of the elements in the theophany on Sinai.[68] A bright cloud (*nubes lucida*) covers the mountain of the Transfiguration in Matthew 17:5. And from within it there came the voice of God.[69]

One further point about the passage from *Con. Acad.* 1.1.3. Its apparent optimism that the 'hidden God will reveal Himself ... ' is already balanced by 1.8.22. Only 'rarely perhaps does the intellect, the senses never, attain to the touching of the most true and hidden God.' And it is to be noted that Augustine, while asserting the rarity, does not deny the possibility. A note to this passage in the Bibliothèque Augustinienne edition sees an allusion to the supposed rarity of the experience according to Plotinus, and especially according to Porphyry's *Life*.[70]

65 See Butler, op. cit., 78ff.

66 Exodus 3:6, which Augustine, as already noted, counterposes to the transcendent God of Exodus 3:14: 'Ego sum qui sum.'

67 Cf. *In Joann. Ev. tract.* 19.5: 'subtexit ... nubilo lucem suam; et difficile est aquilae more volare supra omnem nebulam qua tegitur omnis terra (Sir 24:6), et videre in verbis Domini sincerissimam lucem'.

68 From there we also learn that Scripture as well as Plotinus (*Enn.* 1.6.7.13ff.) is behind the *contremui amore et horrore* of *Conf.* 7.10.16: 'Inside the camp all the people *trembled*.'

69 Followed here too by numinous fear, as in *Conf.* 7.10.16; 'When they heard this, the disciples fell on their faces, overcome with fear.'

70 Ch. 23.

Apart from the fact that there is no such emphasis in Porphyry, why should the reference not be to Augustine's own experience in Milan, or concurrently in Cassiciacum? Book I of the *Soliloquies* is a yearning for and a meditation on the way of ascent to this light. There is the occasional allusion there to perceptions already attained.[71] There is a similar allusion in a letter[72] to Nebridius from Cassiciacum. 'When after calling God to my aid I begin to be raised to Him and to the realities most truly real, I am occasionally filled with such a sense of the things that abide as to be surprised I should ever require [any] process of reasoning to believe in the reality of Realities that are as really present to me as I am to myself.' And finally, the Cassiciacum writings again and again use the Milanese terminology of *reverberatio*, etc.[73]

It would be a logical development of our present theme to follow the use and development of that terminology in Augustine's writings from Cassiciacum to the moment of his describing the Milanese experiences in *Conf.* 7.10.16ff. But that would exceed our present space. Instead we shall look at its use in the period immediately *following* the Milanese experiences, and see how far it confirms our interpretation of those experiences as authentically mystical, even though transient. And even here there are more stages and material than we have space to examine. These stages consist of the period from the Milanese experiences to the conversion at the end of *Conf.* 8, the Cassiciacum experiences as described especially in *Conf.* 9.4, the retrospective analysis of the quest for and finding of God in *Conf.* 10.6ff., and the higher levels of the spiritual life analyzed in Books 11–13. The sum of what we find in all this is, firstly, that the Milanese experiences remain a point of reference, secondly, that in such references Augustine seems to speak of positive mystical experiences rather than of *vaines tentatives*, and thirdly, that the goal of his spiritual striving is to make more stable and permanent what in Milan was real but transient.

Taking up the first of these stages we get the key at once in 7.18.24. 'I set about finding a way to acquire the strength that was necessary for *enjoying* You (*ad fruendum te*).' In 7.20.26 he was indeed *repulsus*, but he had 'seen' (*conspexi*). Still he was 'too weak to *enjoy* You (*ad fruendum te*).' In 8.5.10 his new will, which is still too weak to overcome the old, is a will to 'worship you freely and to *enjoy* You (*fruique te*)' (italics mine). It is of course unnecessary to elaborate the force

71 E.g. 1.12.20: '... si quid forte percepi ... quod iam teneo ...'; cf. 1.14.26 on 'vicinitate nonnulla lucis illius, quam, si quid profeci, tolerare iam possum ... '; and *Con. Acad.* 2.2.6: '... quantulocumque iam lumine asperso ... '.

72 *Letters* 4:2; cf. *Conf.* 3.6.11: 'tu autem eras interior intimo meo'; 7.10.16: 'audivi sicut auditur in corde ... '; 9.4.10: 'o si viderent internum aeternum, quod ego ... gustaveram.'

73 In addition to passages already cited, see e.g. *Solil.* 1.13.23; *De Quant. Animae* 15.25, 33.75; *De Beata Vita* 33, 35; *De Ordine* 2.19.51: ' ... audebit iam Deum videre'.

and centrality of the drive and goal of *fruitio* in Augustinian thought. It is man's fundamental *intentio* or orientation, and its object is the supreme and absolute Reality.[74] It is in fact the deepest key to the *Confessions*, their 'story line', direction, and eschatological range – from the opening thematic *fecisti nos ad te* ...[75] to the concluding repose in the Eternal Sabbath.[76]

Augustine's striving for *fruitio* does not mean however that he has never hitherto attained it. The terms he uses make a clear distinction between *transient* seeing and *holding* in *stability*. 'Of Your eternal life I was certain, although I had seen it (*videram*) in a dark manner and as through a glass ... My desire now was not now to be more sure (*certior*) of You but more steadfast (*stabilior*) in You.'[77] The terms already occur in one of the Milanese accounts.[78] 'I could not stably (*non stabam*)[79] enjoy my God.' And again, 'Then indeed I saw (*conspexi*) ... but I lacked the strength to fix (*figere*) my gaze.'

It was Augustine's discovery of St Paul on the Incarnation, with its gift of grace and truth, that brought the theoretical solution to this problem. 'I found that whatever truth I had read in the Platonists was said here with the additional commendation of Your grace ... so that he [who sees] is not only reminded (*admoneatur*)[80] to see You (*videat*) ... but is also healed to enable him to hold You (*teneat*),[81] and that he who is unable to see You because he is far away can still walk the way by which he may arrive and see and hold (*veniat et videat et teneat*).'[82] Through all the eloquence of Paul he discerned 'one face', the face of the divine Mediator. There was no such help in the Platonists. 'It is one thing to discern the land of peace from a wooded mountain-top ... quite another to hold (*tenere*) to the road that brings us there ... '[83]

74 'Res igitur quibus fruendum est, Pater et Filius et Spiritus sanctus, eademque Trinitas, una quaedam summa res' (*De Doct. Chr.* 1.5.5).

75 *Conf.* 1.1.1.

76 *Conf.* 13.35ff.

77 *Conf.* 8.1.1.

78 *Conf.* 7.17.23.

79 Cf. 4.12.18: 'state cum eo et stabitis'; 7.11.17: 'si non manebo in illo nec in me potero'; 11.11.13: 'quis tenebit cor hominis, ut stet et videat ... ?'; 11.30.40: 'stabo atque solidabor in te'; 13.20.28: 'genus humanum ... instabiliter fluidum'. Also worth noticing in the background are Wisdom 7:27: 'in se permanens omnia innovat'; John 8:44: 'in veritate non stabat'; and μονή in the Neoplatonist triad of μονή, πρόοδος and ἐπιστροφή (e.g. Plotinus, *Enn.* 3.8.10, 5.2.2).

80 In Augustine this is a word with Platonist overtones – 'reminding' unto *anamnesis*; cf. *Conf.* 7.10.16: 'inde admonitus ... '; *De Lib. Arb.* 2.14.38: 'foris admonet, intus docet'; *Solil.* 1.13.23: 'nec doctore indigent, sed sola fortasse admonitione.'

81 Cf. *De Lib. Arb.* 2.9.26: 'num aliam putas esse sapientiam nisi veritatem, in qua cernitur et tenetur summum bonum?'

82 *Conf.* 7.21.27.

83 Ibid.

St Paul solved the theoretical problem. But in practice Augustine was to discover that, even with grace, higher *experiences*, though real, are still transient. For the retrospection of *Conf.* 10, the Milanese experiences are clearly a high point of reference. For present introspection, there are parallel experiences at the time of writing.[84] Though the later experiences may be more profound and sustained (as already at Ostia),[85] the pattern of events and language is essentially the same – transcendent experiences, transience, longing, divine discontent. 'Because I am not filled with Thee I am a burden to myself.'[86]

At the culmination of the analysis of *memoria* and the search for the 'place' where God is found in it, in 10.24.35ff, there is clear reference back to 7.10.16ff. as a high point in the positive discovery of God. 'From the moment I "learned" You (*ex quo didici te*)[87] I have not forgotten You. For where I found Truth there I found my God, Truth itself, which from the moment I learned it I have not forgotten.' Again in 10.25.36, 'from the moment I "learned" You, You have deigned to dwell in my memory.' Which raises the still more a priori question of transcendence – 'where then did I find You, to "learn" You?' i.e. so that God should be hence in the memory. 'Where ... but in Yourself above me (*in te supra me*).'[88]

The phrase *ex quo didici te* is parallel to *cum te primum cognovi* in 7.10.16. Parallel also is the identification of God with absolute subsistent *Veritas* – 'he who knows Truth knows that light'.[89] And finally in 7.10.16 that Truth is not *in* the beholder but '*above* the eye of my soul, an unchangeable light *above* my mind'.

This is the sequence into which comes the climactic apostrophe: *sero te amavi* ... .[90] 'You lightened, Your splendour shone, and You scattered my blindness' (*coruscasti, splenduisti et fugasti caecitatem meam*).[91] To what can this refer if not to the radiance under which in 7.10.16 he 'trembled with love and with dread'? And in this retrospective view, far from being a *vaine tentative*, it is the very light of all his later seeing, and of all his straining for ever-higher seeing.

Of course the Milanese experiences were transient. But transient too are his unquestionably positive mystical experiences at the time he is writing. Well known is the passage in 10.40.65 on his occasional extraordinary states, which, if they could be made permanent, would be hard to distinguish from

84 E.g. *Conf.* 10.40.65.

85 *Conf.* 9.10.23ff.

86 *Conf.* 10.28.39; cf. *De Beata Vita* 35: 'quamdiu quaerimus, nondum ipso fonte, atque ut illo verbo utar, plenitudine saturati, nondum ad nostrum modum nos pervenisse fateamur'.

87 I.e. as a transcendent 'a priori' of reality and thought; cf. *De Trin.*, 12.14.23.

88 *Conf.* 10.26.37.

89 *Conf.* 7.10.16. *De Trin.* 8.2.3 also identifies *Veritas* with the *lux* of *Deus lux est* (1 John 1:5).

90 *Conf.* 10.27.38.

91 Ibid.

the life to come. 'But I fall back into actuality with its crushing weight, and I am swallowed up by the ordinary, and I am bound down, and I weep bitterly, but I stay bitterly bound.' To speak of it at all is to be reminded at once of the original paradigmatic experience. 'For in my wounded heart I saw Your radiance, but beaten back (*repercussus*) I said: Who can attain thither? I am cast away from the sight of Your eyes.'[92]

Only 'when I shall cleave to Thee with all my being shall there be no more grief and toil, and my life shall live wholly filled with Thee'.[93] A growing characteristic of Augustine's spirituality will be the darkening realization that such permanent transcending of the self into the absolute Being is not realizable in this earthly *regio dissimilitudinis*. The Milanese experiences were paradigmatic of this truth too. Even the vision at Ostia was not an exception.[94] This moment of understanding (*hoc momentum intellegentiae*), if it could be made permanent (*si continuetur*), would that not be to *enter into the* [eternal] *joy of thy Lord*? But even at that high moment it could not be so – 'We came back to the noise of our own speech', back to temporality, in which the condition of words, in a favourite figure of Augustine's, is that they sound and then die away, in their ever-dying fall.

And yet to stop there would be to stop short of the final truth. From all that we read on such experiences it is clear that even one such moment suffices to enlighten and orient a lifetime. From the sapiential level of his thought, from his constant striving toward vision, from the constancy of the terminology of *Conf.* 7.10.16, etc., it is clear that the Milanese experience was such a moment of illumination and orientation in the life of St Augustine. The original pattern is always present.

> What is the source of the light that shines upon me at times and beats on my heart, though with no wounding?[95] It sets me trembling with awe and burning with desire: with awe to the degree of my difference from it, with desire to the degree of my likeness to it. It is Wisdom, Wisdom itself, that at

92 *Conf.* 10.41.66; Ps. 30:23.

93 *Conf.* 10.28.39.

94 *Conf.* 9.10.23ff.

95 '... percutit cor meum sine laesione'; cf. Plotinus, *Enn.* 1.6.7.17, ἐκπλήττεσθαι ἀβλαβῶς,, and St John of the Cross:

¡Oh cauterio suave!
¡Oh regalada llaga!

Oh cautery most tender!
Oh gash that is my guerdon!
(*Canciones del alma*, Roy Campbell, tr.)

> those moments shines upon me, cleaving through my cloud. And the cloud closes over again, to wrap me round once more, as my strength fails from the light, through the darkness and the weight of my sin and its penalty.[96]

If this be not the real thing, *alors,* as one interlocutor interjected in Paris in 1954, *je me demande ce que c'est que la mystique.*[97]

96 *Conf.* 11.9.11. 'That was a way of putting it', as the man said. But if we could feel a gusto for a more up-to-the-hour prose to describe the same old phenomenon, how about this: 'In all mystical union from first to last there are two different ways of experience, that I call "light off" and "light on"' (Ruth Burrows, *Guidelines for Mystical Prayer*, London, 1976, 45).

97 Ch. Boyer, in *Augustinus Magister*, 168.

THOMAS FINAN

MODES OF VISION IN ST AUGUSTINE: *DE GENESI AD LITTERAM* XII

I

The present paper is the first part of an enquiry into what has been called 'the way of images' as a way of spiritual 'ascent'. In both the Platonist and the Christian world-view one would expect it to be at least an important *part* of the 'way', since we know the importance of image in both of them, and especially in incarnational Christianity. Yet, in the Christian tradition, the way of images seems to have been largely distrusted.[98] In the present age, with its discovery[99] of the 'new continent' of depth-psychology and the importance of the image therein, it is appropriate to try to see whether this distrust is justified, in itself or as an interpretation of the sources of tradition.

Book XII of St Augustine's *De Genesi ad litteram* is a fundamental source. It is there we first find the systematic triple classification of modes of vision which the tradition used ever afterwards. That is the classification of visions into *corporalis*, *spiritualis* and *intellectualis*. The second of these will be our principal concern, for reasons that will emerge. But to explore the whole question I have set out would take us beyond the limits of one paper. Certain technical questions have to be addressed first. And this paper is about them.

II

The twelve Books of the *De Gen. ad litt.*, composed over the years from 401 to 414, constitute Augustine's definitive and most extensive commentary on Genesis. It is also one of his major works as a source for his thought in general. That is due not only to its size but also to the fact that in it he finally succeeded in completing a commentary on the literal, historical and 'scientific' meaning of Genesis.

It was preceded by three earlier commentaries – all of them less extensive and one of them abandoned as a failure. The *De Genesi contra Manichaeos* (389) is an

98 See e.g. Karl Rahner, *Visions and Prophecies* (London, 1963), for a balanced analysis.

99 Or rediscovery, in the light of such ancient soundings as Augustine's of the *abyssus humanae conscientiae*, of the *magna vis memoriae, nescio quid horrendum ... profunda et infinita multiplicitas ... varies, multimoda vita et immensa vehementer* (*Conf.* X 2, 2 and 17, 26); see Ann and Barry Ulanov, *Religion and the Unconscious* (Philadelphia, 1975).

allegorical or figurative interpretation. The *De Genesi ad litteram liber imperfectus* (393) is an abandoned attempt at a complementary literal interpretation. Books XI–XIII of the *Confessiones* (c. 400) combine both in a dense, poetic, spiritual, climactic effusion meant to complete the *Confessiones* by a survey of the totality of human existence, from its hidden origins in 'the dark backward and abysm of time'[100] to its hidden destiny beyond time in the eternal Sabbath.

These commentaries, of course, are only on the first three chapters of Genesis. But that fact gives an inadequate idea of the range of their reflection. For these are the chapters which give us the *origins* of all things and, by implication at least, their meaning and destiny. They give us the creation story, of the cosmos and of mankind within it, the story

> Of man's first disobedience and the fruit
> Of that forbidden tree whose mortal taste
> Brought death into the world, and all our woe,
> With loss of Eden ...

The range of meaning glimpsed in *Conf.* XI–XIII is not surprising then. Ever since Philo the creation narrative in Genesis had become the framework for Judeo-Christian reflection on the 'boundary questions' about the origin, meaning and destiny of man and the universe. Even as late as Eriugena it is still the framework of his massive metaphysical and theological *De divisione naturae.*

Given that range of the search for total meaning, it is not surprising either that we find those commentaries drawing on all the intellectual resources available in the ambient classical civilization. Throughout the centuries in which the Genesis framework was used those intellectual resources would be heavily Platonist. From *Conf.* VII 9, 13–15 we know the weight of the Platonist influence on the intellectual liberation and the Christian conversion of St. Augustine. We know too what a 'pilgrim of the Absolute' he was by temperament. It is easy to understand, then, how to him particularly the 'totalizing' cadre of Genesis would appeal – especially when its dimensions were further enlarged by Augustine's own innate sense of symbolism. And we find him particularly fond of the symbolic dimension of the seventh day of the creation narrative, the Sabbath, on which God rested after all his works were completed. Augustine's two great surveys of human existence end with its extrapolation into the *eternal* Sabbath. Those are the surveys of *individual* human existence in the *Confessiones*, and of *collective*

100 'Behold, my infancy is long since dead, yet myself ... I am living. But you, Lord, who live forever ... tell me whether my infancy was preceded by some earlier now dead age of mine. Or is that the one I spent in my mother's womb? ... And before that again ... ? Was I anywhere or anyone?' (*Conf.* I 6, 9.).

human existence in universal *history* as surveyed in the *De civitate Dei*. 'Likewise the voice of your book tells us that we also, after our works ... will rest in you in the Sabbath of life everlasting' (*Conf.* XIII 36, 51).

We know too of course that the Augustinian drive to 'the Absolute' was not only intellectual but also mystical, meant to attain not only conceptual understanding but also unmediated vision – and that not only in the eternal Sabbath but already in foretaste here on earth. This we know from his account of his first mystical experience in Milan (*Conf.* VII 10, 16). We know it also from the vision at Ostia (*Conf.* IX 10, 24f). It is no surprise then to find that it is an important dimension of the 'totalization' striven for in the commentaries on Genesis. And in Book XIII of the *Confessiones*, one of the important sources for Augustine's spirituality, a symbolic dimension of the sequence of days in the creation narrative is the sequence of stages in the spiritual ascent to experience and vision. *De Gen. ad litt.* XII provides a systematic and definitive analysis of the epistemological and psychological modes of that vision.

III

Now Scripture is replete with visionary experiences, again making the later distrust of them all the more surprising at first sight. But in this domain, as in so many others, it will not surprise us to find Augustine systematizing scriptural data with the aid of Platonist concepts.

Throughout its history Platonism had a religious, even a mystical, orientation. It aimed beyond mediated conceptual understanding to immediate contemplative vision of ultimate, supreme reality. As is well known, it had an incalculable influence on the goals and methods of the Christian tradition of higher spirituality. In the West at least, Augustine provides the first and most striking illustration of this fact – becoming in turn himself a mediator of that influence to the tradition. His own first directed impulse on that way was from his 'discovery' of Plotinus – Plotinus being the example *par excellence* of a tightly systematic conceptual philosopher tipped with the arrow of the mystic whose flight is 'the passing of solitary to solitary' (*Enn.* VI 9, 11). Equivalently, when transposed, this is Newman's 'thought of two and two only supreme and luminously self-evident beings, myself and my Creator'.[101] *Deum et animam scire cupio* is Augustine's transposition.[102]

'Being reminded by all this to return to my own self I entered into my own inner depths, with you [God] as my guide ... I entered within, and with the eye of my soul – of whatever kind it was – I saw the unchangeable Light above that eye

101 *Apologia Pro Vita Sua* (London, Everyman Edition, 1966), 31.

102 *Soliloquia* I 2, 7.

of my soul ... ' (*Conf.* VII 10, 16). This is perhaps the most personal and dramatic moment in the tradition of the way known as the 'journey inward', and its paradox – that by turning away from the multiple external 'all' we rediscover it in the unique transcendent 'All' within and above us.

In addition to Augustine's own undoubted interest in the question, and the fact already mentioned, that the Genesis creation narrative was a universalizing framework, the immediate occasion of his rounding off the *De Gen. ad litt.* with such an extensive treatment of visions was the need to complete the treatment of the paradise of Eden by reference to the famous mention of paradise in St Paul, 2 Cor 12:2–4. The concluding Book then 'will treat the question of paradise more freely and fully, lest we be thought to have avoided the fact that St. Paul seems to suggest a paradise in the third heaven; when he says: "I know a man in Christ who, fourteen years ago, was caught up – whether still in the body or out of the body I do not know, God knows ... – was caught up into paradise and heard things which must not and cannot be put into human language".'[103]

It might seem to us that the connection between Paul's paradise and the paradise of Eden is a tenuous one, based only on the ambiguity of words. But it was not necessarily so for Augustine. In the *De Gen. con. Man.* he could find only a non-literal, symbolic meaning for the paradise of Eden. Its nature is still a matter of argument in *De Gen. ad litt.* (VIII 1, 1ff). But while Augustine now insists on its literal, historical reality, he also emphasizes its 'allegorical' dimension as a symbol of a *spiritual* reality – of the kind adumbrated in the Pauline experience – temporally future, but transcendently omnipresent.

Two main questions arise then from the Pauline passage. 'Firstly ... the question of what the "third heaven" *means*: then, whether Paul intended paradise to be understood as being *in* that third heaven, or meant rather that *after* he was caught up into the third heaven he was [then] also caught up into paradise, *wherever* that paradise may be; implying not that to be caught up into the third heaven is the *same* as to be caught up into paradise, but first into the third heaven and then from there into paradise' (*De Gen. ad litt.* XII 1, 2).

We need not here go into the lateral questions and the dizzying permutations and combinations of possibilities into which Augustine is led by that already nodulous setting out of the problem. In the end Augustine himself has no option but to return to basics and start from a fundamental analysis of visions, their nature and their possible epistemological modes (XII 6, 15ff). Even then the matter is complex – and Augustine is not given to brevity in exposition. In the space of the present paper then one can focus only on the interest of the question and the schematic lines of its exploration. That interest and those lines have been

103 *De Gen. ad litt.* XII I, 1.

indicated earlier – in relation to psychology and symbolism, and to the triple classification of modes of vision into *corporalis*, *spiritualis*, and *intellectualis*.

IV

It is the *visio spiritualis* which will be the final focus of our attention – as being a surprising *terminology* and as providing the main evidence for Neoplatonist influence. But we cannot understand it without a prior understanding of its place in the triple classification, and of the triple classification in relation to general epistemological theory.

At their first level of meaning the three modes are immediately intelligible in terms of the classical three stages and levels in the process of knowing – the same terms in which Augustine explains them here and which he uses extensively elsewhere, in his early problem with the nature of knowledge and frequent later continued concern with it. Those stages are: the *percept* of sense perception (*visio corporalis*), the interior image or *phantasm* formed and retained in the 'imaginative' faculty, the *phantasia* (*visio spiritualis* as explained in *De Gen. ad litt.* XII), and finally the *concept* formed by the abstracting, conceptualizing *intellect* (*visio intellectualis*). Augustine illustrates all this with the written Scripture commandment of love: 'Thou shalt love thy neighbour as thyself' (Mt 22:39). The seeing of the written letters with the eyes is corporeal vision. The inner visualizing of the *neighbour* even when absent is spiritual vision – *per spiritum hominis*. Intellectual vision is illustrated by that insight of the *mind* through which the *love itself* is conceptually grasped and understood.

To avoid later confusion something else needs to be explained about this terminology. It concerns *visio intellectualis* as Augustine explains it in *De Gen. ad litt.* XII 6, 15. We have no problem with the term *visio* used of the *percept* and the *phantasm*. But can it properly be used of the intellectual *concept* – in the special context of *mystical* vision?

The first is simple. It is a natural, spontaneous use of analogy to speak of abstract conceptual knowing as *seeing* – as in Augustine's own illustration, *per contuitum mentis quo ipsa dilectio intellecta conspicitur.*[104] The second point is the essential. As emerges from *De Gen. ad litt.* XII 10, 21, behind Augustine's terminology of *intellectus* and *intellectualis* there lies the Neoplatonist terminology of νοῦς – epistemological and ontological – with *two* corresponding adjectives, νοερός and νοητός.[105] Now the point about the Greek terminology of

104 Cf. XII 3, 6: *sed alia quadam visione, alia luce, alia rerum evidentia, et ex longe caeteris praestantiore atque certiore.*

105 Cf. the use of those terms in Iamblichus, *De mysteriis Aegyptiorum* I 15, 46, with the note *ad loc.* by Édouard des Places in his edition, *Jamblique, Les mystères d'Égypte* (Paris, 1966); also the note by P.

νοῦς, νοερός, and νοητός is that its range of meaning extends above and beyond the epistemological connotations of *intellectualis* and *intellectual* in Latin and English, beyond, that is, the abstract, discursive, conceptual mode of knowing, into a transcendent *transconceptual* level that is properly mystical and properly described as *visio*, visionary, a kind of seeing – *really* a kind of seeing, even though it transcends all modes of seeing known to the mind in its normal state. It transcends all material *forms* known to sense perception and the imagination, all conceptual forms or categories known to the rational discursive mind in its normal state. Consequently it is very hard to describe it to those who have not had the *vision* – who have not been 'there', as Plotinus puts it. And yet it is a kind of seeing, a seeing of the *transcendent* realities, a seeing of the singular, unique, supreme Reality that is the Ground of all particular realities. And the fact that it is a kind of seeing, *visio*, is reflected in the fact that classically it is an experience of a supreme light – from Plato to e.g. Augustine, *Conf.* VII 10, 16.

A fine incisive statement of this distinction between the two levels of *intellectus* is provided by Plotinus in *Enn.* I 3, 4 on the highest final attainment of the mind through the ascent of dialectic:

> Now it rests: instructed and satisfied as to the Being in that sphere, it is no longer busy about many things: it has arrived at Unity and it contemplates: it leaves to another science all that coil of premises and conclusions called the art of reasoning, much as it leaves the art of writing: some of the matter of logic, no doubt, it considers necessary – to clear the ground – but it makes itself the judge, here as in everything else .... (MacKenna tr.)

At this point it would both clear the ground for ourselves and economize on exposition if we used a couple of extended quotations, from Augustine and a Neoplatonist, to *show* this transconceptual meaning of *visio intellectualis* at work in an explicitly visionary context. Two such passages come to mind, one from Augustine, *De Gen. ad litt.* XII 26, 54, and one from Iamblichus, *De myst.* X 6.

> But if in the same way as he was ravished from the bodily senses into the midst of those images of bodies seen by the spirit he were ravished from those images into the region of *intellectualia* and *intelligibilia*, where *perspicua veritas* itself is perceived with no clouds of false opinion – in that region the powers of the Soul will not be laborious and painful ... There the one and only power is to love what you see, and the highest felicity is to possess what you love. For

Agaësse and A. Solignac in their two-volume edition of the *De Genesi ad litteram. La Genèse au sens littéral* (Bruges, 1966), 566–8 of Vol. 29 in the series *Oeuvres de Saint Augustin.*

> there the *beata vita* is drunk at its source, the source from which some drops are sprinkled on this human life of ours ... It is to attain this goal, where there will be *secura quies* and the ineffable vision of Truth, that we undertake the labour of the containing of pleasure and the sustaining of adversity and the maintaining of poverty and the resisting of deceivers. There the glory of the Lord is seen not by a symbolic vision, whether corporeal like that of Moses on Mount Sinai (Exod 19:18), or *spiritual* like that of Isaiah (6:1) or of John in the Apocalypse ... Rather the vision is face to face and not in enigmas – as far, that is, as the human soul can bear it – lifted up by the favour of God to be spoken to by God mouth to mouth – not with the mouth of the body but with the mouth of the soul .... (St Augustine, *loc. cit.*)[106]

In *De myst.* X 6 Iamblichus describes the summit of the soul's ascent, through the rites of theurgy and those of related *mantikê* or prophetic vision:

> After having united the Soul successfully to the diverse departments of the All, and to all the divine powers that compenetrate them, those rites conduct the soul to the universal Demiurge and seat her beside him and, outside of all matter (ὕλης), unite her to the eternal *Logos* and to it alone. That is, I repeat, they attach her to the power that is self-engendered, self-moved and sustainer of all things, to the intellectual power (νοερᾷ) that orders the universe and raises up to intellectual Truth (ἀλήθειαν τὴν νοητὴν), the power that creates and has its end in itself; likewise successively up to the other demiurgic powers of God (δημιουργικαῖς δυνάμεσι τοῦ θεοῦ), so that the soul is established in perfection (τελέως) in their life and operations (ἐνεργείαις), in their activities of creation (δημιουργίαις) and in their intellections (νοήσεσι).

V

We come to the question of the meaning of *visio spiritualis* in more analytic detail. In the light of our earlier situating of it in the double context of Augustine's triple classification of *visiones* and of classical theory of knowledge, the problem is not so much the significance of the mode itself[107] as of the term Augustine uses to describe it – *spiritualis*.

106 It is worth noting that there are many linguistic parallels between this passage and the account of the vision at Ostia in *Conf.* IX 10, 23ff – which is known to be coloured by the language of Plotinus on spiritual experience; see Paul Henry, *La Vision d'Ostie* (Paris, 1938).

107 At least not for our present purposes; in their note on *spiritus* in *De Gen. ad litt.* XII, pp. 559ff in the second vol. of the edition cited, Agaësse and Solignac argue for a distinction between the faculty of *visio spiritualis* and the imagination or phantasia of classical epistemology.

In all the many places[108] where Augustine has occasion to speak of the mode and faculty of this level of knowing in general epistemology, the recurring terms are *imago, imaginatio, phantasia, phantasma*, with such corresponding adjectives as *imaginaria* and *imaginalis* (with *imaginaliter*).[109] Why does he opt for the term *spiritualis* here?

That question is the more pressing in view of the fact that precisely in the context of spirituality – even in Augustine himself – *spiritualis* as used in *De Gen. ad litt.* XII is at first sight a positively misleading term. When we recall St. Paul's use of *spiritualis* (translating πνευματικός) in such passages as 1 Corinthians 2:6–8, 13ff; Romans 7:14 etc., and, based on these passages, Augustine's corresponding use of the term in e.g. *Conf.* XIII 12, 13ff, we would expect Augustine's ordering of *visiones* to place *visio spiritualis* above *visio intellectualis* rather than below it. In both Paul and *Conf.* XIII *spiritualis* describes the *highest* level of the spiritual life. Yet in *De Gen. ad litt.* XII 9, 20 Augustine defines *spiritus* as *vis animae quaedam mente inferior, ubi corporalium rerum similitudines exprimuntur.*

The solution to the crux provides us with an object-lesson in what is so often St Augustine's method of systematic Christian thinking. That is to say, he takes his matter from Scripture but systematizes it through the mediation of Neoplatonist categories and terminology. He tells us explicitly in *De Gen. ad litt.* XII 8, 19 that his technical use of *spiritus* and *spiritualis* is based on one particular technical usage in Scripture. He has first cleared the ground in XII 7, 18 by going through the whole gamut of the ordinary meanings of the term,[110] all of them also found in Scripture, all the way from air and wind up to the Spirit that is God, for 'God is Spirit, and those who worship him must worship him in spirit and in truth' (Jn 4:24). In fact 'whatever is not body, and yet is something, is rightly called spirit' (XII 7, 16). But ... 'it is not from all those meanings ... that we have taken this term in which we have called spiritual this class of visions which we are now discussing. Rather from that one meaning which we find in the Epistle to the Corinthians, where spirit is distinguished from mind (*mente*) on the clearest evidence'. And he quotes 1 Corinthians 14:4, 'If I pray in tongues ... my spirit is praying but my *mind* has no fruit from it' (XII 8, 19).

This he explains as implying that to speak in tongues is to utter 'obscure and mystical meanings, by which nobody is enlightened if you take away the understanding of the mind (*intellectum mentis*)'. Which statement he further elaborates by quoting 1 Corinthians 14:2, 'Anybody with the gift of tongues speaks to God

108 E.g. *De musica* VI 11, 32; *De vera rel.* XXXIV 64, XXXIX 73; *Conf.* VII 1, 1, VII 7, 11, X 8, 12ff; *De Trin.* VIII 6, 9, XI 5, 8.

109 Even in *De Gen. ad litt.* XII 2, 3, XII 4, 11–12, XII 5, 14 etc.

110 Cf. *De Trin.* XIV 16, 22.

but not to other people; because nobody understands him when he speaks in the spirit about mysterious things (*spiritus... loquitur mysteria*).' And he goes on to explain this last quotation as meaning that to speak in tongues is to utter 'meanings in terms of images and likenesses of things (*imagines et similitudines rerum*), images and likenesses which for understanding need the insight of the mind'. For when they are not understood they are only *in spiritu* ... not *in mente*.

So far so clear on the scriptural connection. Before we go on to identify a Neoplatonist connection we may take a parenthetic moment to point to some further far-reaching implications of the language we have just seen Augustine using. The implications concern that modern interest to which I linked this paper from the start, although we cannot develop it here, that is depth-psychology and symbolism.

A little earlier we quoted Augustine's explanation of speaking in tongues as the utterance of 'obscure and mystical meanings' (*obscuras et mysticas significationes*) which demand interpretation by the *mind* (XII 8, 19). He goes on to interpret Paul as expanding the meaning of *tongues* to a transferred sense which subsumes '*any* production of *signs* before they are understood' (*quamlibet signorum prolationem priusquam intelligantur*). This takes us into the domain of visions proper. And it takes us into the domain of psychology: for even though the *signa* be corporeal they are seen *within*, by interior *visio spiritualis*. And finally it takes us into the domain of symbolism. For the reference is to *signa* that are not *understood*, to *obscuras et mysticas significationes* that demand interpretation by the *mind*. And, quite apart from the fact that transcendent, formless realities cannot be 'seen' at the level of *spiritus* except by 'translation' into symbolic corporeal forms,[111] Augustine is clearly distinguishing the seen *signa* from their *obscuras et mysticas significationes*. Furthermore he introduces this extended, *visionary* meaning of 'tongues' with the statement that it is the *signa rerum* which are produced, not the *res ipsae* (XII 8, 19). And lastly the whole context is of *signa* produced from within the *spiritus* itself, not from an impact on the senses by objective, external *corporalia*.

VI

To return to the terminology of *spiritus* and *spiritualis*, we have identified its scriptural provenance for the specialized context of visions. But a question still remains. Why does Augustine extend that terminology to the wider context of general epistemology? For that is the implication of the fact that, as we have seen, he explains it in the very terms of that general epistemology. It is explicit in certain summary statements. One we have referred to already. 'There are three kinds of vision: one is through the eyes, by which

111 On this, Augustine has a lot to say in *De Trin.* II 10, 17ff.

the [written] letters themselves are seen: a second kind is through man's spirit (*per spiritum hominis*), by which one's neighbour is imagined even when absent ... when, though we see nothing with the eyes of the body, we still contemplate corporeal images in the mind (*animo*) ... ' (XII 6, 15). To this we may add the definitive statement in XII 9, 20, already quoted, which defines *spiritus* as 'a certain power of the soul, lower than the mind, in which the images of corporeal things are expressed' (*vis animae quaedam mente inferior, ubi corporalium rerum similitudines exprimuntur*).

The answer to our present question gives us one of the clearest illustrations of the Augustinian method already mentioned. Namely that while taking his 'matter' from Scripture (and in the case of *spiritus* his technical term as well) he gives it 'form', and thinks it through into system, theory and formulation with the conceptual apparatus and terminology of Greco-Roman thought. In the case of our present topic the terms are those of Neoplatonist epistemology and *genera visionum*.

That is not surprising, given the intense and all-pervading religious *finalité* of Neoplatonism. But the connection is more specific – as the religious orientation of Platonism was more specific. Augustine takes the term and the theory of *spiritus* from precisely that level of Neoplatonist thought that was as absolutist in its quest, as contemplative, visionary, and mystical in its orientation as was Augustine himself. And in that domain the key to Augustine's usage of *spiritus* is the Neoplatonist usage of *pneuma*. And behind the Neoplatonist usage stretch the centuries of the historical development of the meaning of *pneuma*, as traced in the classic survey by Verbeke.[112] It was one of those aboriginal and permanently rich core concepts of Greek thought – and well suited to an eventual marriage with its equally perennial and fecund Judeo-Christian analogue (*ruach*). Within the limits of this paper it is impossible to do more than briefly indicate the results of that development of *pneuma*, as the background to Augustine and his *spiritus*. The following indications derive from Verbeke.

In Stoicism *pneuma* was not distinguished from *psukhê*, soul. It *was* the soul. And, naturally, in Stoicism it was a *material* principle. Neoplatonism reacted strongly against Stoic materialism, and consequently emphasized the non-material nature of soul. But it nevertheless preserved the term and notion of *pneuma* as a real psychic entity in man. One of the principles of Neoplatonism demanded such an entity – the requirement of an intermediate element mediating between the material and the non-material, and so between body and soul in the human composite. And that is what *pneuma* becomes. That is why in epistemology it becomes the locus of the image or phantasm, intermediate between the sense

112 G. Verbeke, *L'Évolution de la doctrine du pneuma du stoïcisme à S. Augustin* (Paris, 1945); see also the article on πνεῦμα etc., by various authors, in Kittel, *Theological Dictionary of the New Testament*, vol. VI.

percept and the intellectual concept. In Iamblichus' *De mysteriis*, for instance, we find *pneuma* and *phantasia* being used more or less interchangeably.

There does not seem to be much development of *pneuma* in Plotinus. But we do glimpse it there, and with the meaning we have outlined. An instance is in *Enn.* II 2, 2, where we find a reference to τὸ πνεῦμα τὸ περὶ τὴν ψυχὴν (the *pneuma* that surrounds the soul). The notion is much more developed in Plotinus' successor, Porphyry. We will confine ourselves here to one piece of supporting evidence. Conveniently enough we can find it in St. Augustine, *De civ. Dei* X 9, 2. And, still more conveniently, the context is precisely the domain of contemplative ascent, to vision of God, and even union with Him. That is clear not only from the context in Augustine but also from the title of the work by Porphyry from which Augustine is quoting, the *De regressu animae*.[113]

Augustine's particular theme at this point is Porphyry's apparent inconsistency in regard to *theurgy*, or *mystagogy*, those 'sacramental' rites by which the soul's ascent to the light was thought to be aided – or not, in as much as Augustine accuses Porphyry of saying both yes and no. For at one moment he is warning us to beware of such practices as fraudulent ... and the next minute ... he is saying that they are effective for the purification of a part of the soul. Not however the 'intellectual' part (*intellectuali*) which perceives the truth of 'intelligible' realities (*rerum intelligibilium*) which have no likeness to things corporeal (*similitudines corporum*). Rather it is the 'spiritual' part of the soul (*spiritali*), by which it apprehends the images of corporeal things (*corporalium ... imagines*). For Porphyry declares that by certain theurgic rites called *teletae* this part of the soul is disposed and prepared to receive spirits and angels and to see the gods (*ad videndos deos*). He admits however that those theurgic rites do not effect any purification of the intellectual soul (*intellectuali animae*) which would fit it to see its God and to look on the ultimate really real existents (*ea quae vere sunt*).

Porphyry seems to have made up his mind (or to have shown better sense, as Augustine puts it)[114] about the efficacy of theurgy in a letter to a certain Anebo, an Egyptian priest. The letter was an attack on theurgy. It is known from Iamblichus' quotations from it in his *De mysteriis*.[115] For Porphyry's letter was the occasion of that work, in which Iamblichus counters with an *apologia* for the efficacy of theurgic ritual.

The *De mysteriis* is a rich source for the notion of *pneuma*. Indeed it is a rich source for a high Neoplatonist spirituality, as already seen in the passage we

113 On the possible identity and nature of this non-extant work, see John O'Meara, *Porphyry's Philosophy from Oracles in Augustine* (Paris, 1959).

114 *De civ. Dei* X 11, 1.

115 Augustine gives an outline of the contents of the letter in *De civ. Dei* X 11; and there are extended quotations from it in Eusebius of Caesarea, *Praepar. Evang.*, III 4 and V 8–10.

juxtaposed with St Augustine on transconceptual *visio intellectualis*. But it also provides a good understanding of Augustine's *visio spiritualis* – and of why he so called it – vision that is, in the normal sense of imaged visions, produced within, and *from* within, the *phantasia*. An extract from III 14, 133 provides a good illustration. In the context Iamblichus is explaining – and defending – the induction of visions by the ritual of light known as *photagogia*.

> In this rite, he says, the ethereal and luminous vehicle surrounding the soul[116] is shone upon by a divine light; in consequence of which divine representations (φαντασίαι θείαι), called up by the will of the gods, take hold of our imaginative faculty (φανταστικὴν δύναμιν) ... The attention and intelligence of the soul (προσοχὴ καὶ διάνοια τῆς ψυχῆς) stay conscious of what is taking place because they are not touched by the divine light. Rather the imaginative faculty (τὸ φανταστικόν) works under a divine influence (ἐπιθειάζει). And therefore it is not by its own power but by the action of the gods that the imaginative faculty is awakened to the play of forms in the imagination (ἐγείρεται εἰς τρόπους φαντασιῶν), once the normal modes of human perception have been suppressed.

All this Neoplatonist theory of knowledge, and of spiritual enlightenment, is clearly in the background to Augustine's hierarchy of *visio spiritualis* and *visio intellectualis*. The connection is clinched at one point when Augustine assigns to *spiritus* the same intermediate status between the material and the totally spiritual which it has in Neoplatonism:

> I do not think it unreasonable or discordant to regard spiritual vision as holding an intermediate position (*medietatem obtinere*) between the intellectual and the corporeal. For I do not think it incongruous to call that entity intermediate (*medium*) which is not in fact a corporeal substance (*corpus*) but *resembles* a corporeal substance, intermediate between what is truly corporeal and what neither is nor resembles corporeal substance. (*De Gen. ad litt.* XII 24, 51).

Another extract from the *De mysteriis* reveals succinctly in what detailed ways the highest Neoplatonist spirituality helped to systematize that of Christianity. Speaking of the effects of the *eudaimonia*[117] attained at the summit of the spiritual ascent Iamblichus tells us that:

116 τὸ περικείμενον τῇ ψυχῇ αἰθερῶδες; cf. the phrase already quoted from Plotinus, *Enn.* II 2, 2.

117 Cf. Augustine, *De civ. Dei* X 11, 2, on Porphyry's *Letter to Anebo*: 'Finally, towards the end of the letter, he asks Anebo to teach him what is the way to beatitude according to the wisdom of Egypt'(*quae sit ad beatitudinem via ex Aegyptia sapientia*).

It brings the intellectual fulfilment of souls (νοερὰν ... ἀνοπλήρωσιν) in the union with God. It is the door of access to the God who is the Demiurge of all things, the place and the palace of the Good. It brings as its first effect a purification (ἁγνείαν) of the soul more perfect (τελειοτέραν) than that of the body. Next it trains the faculty of intellect (διανοίας) to the participation and contemplation of the Good, with liberation from all that is opposed to it. And beyond all that, it brings union (ἕνωσιν) with the divine dispensers of good. (*De myst.* X 5).

ST AUGUSTINE ON THE *MIRA PROFUNDITAS* OF SCRIPTURE: TEXTS AND CONTEXTS

> What we call the City of God is the one witnessed to by that Scripture which, manifested by no choice impulses of human minds but by the guiding power of God's supreme providence, surpasses all the writings of all mankind, and in consequence of its supreme divine authority has subordinated to itself every genre of human genius.[118]

> It is in point to notice also the structure and style of Scripture, a structure so unsystematic and various and a style so figurative and indirect that no one would presume at first to say what is in it and what is not. It cannot, as it were, be mapped or its contents catalogued; but after all our diligence, to the end of our lives and to the end of the Church, it must be an unexplored and unsubdued land, with heights and valleys, forests and streams on the right and left of our path and close about us, full of concealed wonders and choice treasures.[119]

> The Bible's claim to truth ... excludes all other claims ... The world of the Scripture stories is not satisfied with claiming to be an historically true reality – it insists that it is the only real world... let no one object that this goes too far, that not the stories but the religious doctrine raises the claim to absolute authority; because the stories are not ... simply narrated 'reality.' Doctrine and promise are incarnate in them and inseparable from them; for that very reason they are fraught with background, and mysterious, containing a second, concealed meaning.[120]

I have used these three extended quotations as an overture to my theme. One of the authors is ancient, two are modern. Two of the authors are religious and theological writers. The third is a secular scholar of European literature from

118 St Augustine, *De civ. Dei*, XI 1; cf. his *De doctrina Christiana*, II 42, 63.

119 John Henry Newman, *An Essay on the Development of Christian Doctrine* (New York: Image Books, 1960), 90f.

120 Erich Auerbach, *Mimesis* (New York: Anchor Books, 1957), 12.

its earliest beginnings down to modern times – under the rubric of 'the representation of reality in western literature'. The significance of that rubric is in the underlying question: What *is* reality?, and consequently, what is an adequate 'representation' of it in literature? And consequently further, what is an adequate 'interpretation' of the representation? To use St Augustine's terms[121] is a *res* (thing), or the *verbum* (word) representing it, *merely* a thing or a fact, and the word merely a nominalist naming of it? Or is the thing or the fact something more than its mere facticity? Is it in some sense also a *signum* (sign) pointing to a reality beyond itself, or even, in the stricter sense of symbol, embodying, incarnating, revealing while concealing another reality beyond itself? The same question obviously arises about the dimensions of meaning of the *verbum* itself as *signum* to the *res* represented.

The terms of the distinction are ancient, but the distinction itself is familiar to us in the terminology of contemporary literary criticism and theory. It is the distinction between the literature of two-dimensional factual realism and the literature of multi-dimensional levels of reality and the corresponding multivalent levels of meaning in the medium of its representation. That is a distinction first formally made by Aristotle, in his perennially canonical *Poetics*. In Chapter 9 he makes a famous distinction between history and poetry. 'The poet and the historian differ not by writing in verse or in prose ... The true difference is that one relates what has happened (the facts – *ta genomena*), the other what could potentially happen. Poetry, therefore, is a more philosophical thing and of weightier import than history; for poetry tends to express universal truths, but history particular facts and events.'

To realize the full import of this statement we need to attend to some of its terms. 'History' in classical antiquity was a 'literary' as well a 'scientific' genre, and Aristotle was not unaware of its search for causes and meaning as well as facts and events. The distinction he is pointing to is in the mode in which causes and meaning are sought and set out in history – by explicit 'scientific' analysis of the facts rather than by multivalent poetic embodiment of 'universal' meaning in what is sometimes called the 'concrete universal' of the facts themselves. And 'concrete universal' is an apt term to bring out what Aristotle meant by poetry expressing 'universal truths' (*ta katholou*). He did not mean abstract general 'concepts' ungrounded in concrete particular percepts. His aesthetic theory is a particular application of his general metaphysical system, and in that system it is well known that he transferred Plato's universal 'ideas' from the transcendent world of 'forms' to the immanent world of concrete particulars.

That Aristotelian principle provides a close analogy to the exegetical principle which insists that the 'fuller' meaning of Scripture be rooted in the literal and

121 *De doctrina Christiana*, I 2, 2f.

historical truth of word and event. And Aristotle also links up with Auerbach on that theme. Auerbach's title, *Mimesis*, is borrowed from Aristotle's generic definition of poetry and art as *mimêsis*, conventionally translated as *imitation*, with its attendant connotation of merely realist fidelity to the surface appearance of phenomena, instead of what is really meant, namely 're-presentation' of phenomena in such a way as to 'interpret' them, to express their *inner* nature and meaning. Aristotle has often been misunderstood in the former of these two senses. And, of course, without the benefit of Aristotle at all, it is now a commonplace of literary history that in the tradition there is a classification of literature corresponding to each of the two meanings – to use contemporary terms: 'realism,' and 'symbolism' (multi-layeredness), in the largest and loosest sense of that word.

The general relevance of Auerbach to our theme is twofold. First he finds this division into realist and symbolic or multivalent present in a line of critical classification that runs through the representation of reality in western literature from its very beginnings. Western literature of course is a river flowing from the confluence of two earlier streams, the Judeo-Christian and the Greco-Roman. Secondly, he finds this dividing line of critical classification already most incisively in the very earliest literature of the two originating streams, the Bible and Homer. And, interestingly, he finds it through purely *literary* analysis of texts, without benefit yet of the later technical classification of scriptural meanings into literal and figurative and the famous four levels of significance – literal, allegorical, tropological and anagogical.

We cannot here go into the details of the literary analysis of his sample texts. The main results of the detailed analysis may be stated in two very important points. There is, firstly, in Old Testament narrative, as compared with Homer, the awesome penumbra of implied but unexpressed 'background' and 'mystery' against which characters and events are presented, and out of which they are seen to emerge. And, secondly, there is the corresponding penumbra of 'background' and 'mysterious' significance which the narrative is made to imply, and not just imply but demand – the demand of a claim to universal and absolute Truth.

'The decisive points of the narrative alone are emphasized, what lies between is non-existent: time and place are undefined and call for interpretation; thoughts and feelings remain unexpressed, are only suggested by the silence and the fragmentary speeches; the whole... remains mysterious and "fraught with background."'[122] 'The Bible's claim to Truth is not only far more urgent than Homer's – it excludes all other claims.'[123] 'The Old Testament ... presents universal history: it begins with the beginning of time ... and will end with the Last Days ... Everything else that

122 Auerbach, op.cit., 9, commenting on the command to Abraham to sacrifice in Gen 22:1ff.

123 Ibid., 12.

happens in the world can only be conceived as an element in this sequence; into it everything that is known about the world ... must be fitted as an ingredient of the divine plan ...', and this, he goes on to say, is possible only by 'interpretation.'[124] St Augustine hardly expressed similar ideas more powerfully, as we shall see.

In comparison with such Old Testament narratives of events and characters, 'whose depth of background is veritably abysmal'[125], the world depicted by Homer has of course its own depths, even to the tragic dimension. And even though 'he does not need to base his story on historical reality, his reality is powerful enough in itself; it ensnares us, weaving its web around us ... '. But 'this "real" world into which we are lured, exists only for itself, contains nothing but itself; the Homeric poems conceal nothing, they contain no teaching and no secret second meaning. Homer can be analyzed ... but he cannot be interpreted. Later allegorizing trends have tried their arts of interpretation upon him, but to no avail'.[126]

In sum, and as a starting point for an investigation into the literary representation of reality in European culture, we have two styles representing two basic types. 'On the one hand fully externalized description ... all events in the foreground, displaying unmistakable meaning, few elements of historical development and of psychological perspective; on the other, certain parts brought into high relief, others left obscure ... suggestive influence of the unexpressed, "background" quality, multiplicity of meanings and the need for interpretation, universal-historical claims, development of the concept of the historically becoming ... '.[127]

Auerbach carries forward this 'concept of the historically becoming' from the Old Testament to its culmination in the New Testament. And there – still by purely literary analysis – he finds the same dimension of dark penumbral 'background' and 'mystery', and the corresponding dimension of abyssal depths of suggested meaning, and the same absolute demands of its truth. The same, but more finally absolute than the Old Testament could ever be, based as it was on the sense of 'promise' and 'historical becoming' as unfulfilled. That fulfilment was in the Incarnation, the embodiment of the Infinite itself in one unique concrete individual Being, one unique 'concrete universal' – 'harshly dramatized through God's incarnation in a human being of the humblest social station, through his existence on earth amid humble everyday people and conditions, and through his Passion which, judged by earthly standards, was ignominious ... '.[128]

124 Ibid.,13.

125 Ibid.,10.

126 Ibid.,11.

127 Ibid.,19.

128 Ibid., 36.

Auerbach chooses the dramatic scene of St Peter's denial (in Mark's version) to illustrate the agonizing and even tragic implications of confrontation with such an embodiment of unsoundable 'background' and 'mysterious' depths of meaning. (He might also have chosen many confrontational scenes in John's Gospel ...). 'Peter is called to the most tremendous role ... how tremendous it is, viewed in relation to the life a fisherman from the Sea of Galilee normally lives, and what enormous "pendulation" [Harnack's word – *Pendelausschlag*] is going on in him!'[129] And Peter's experience is itself a universal – it applies to every other occurrence in the New Testament. 'Every one of them is concerned with the same question, the same conflict with which every human being is basically confronted and which therefore remains *infinite* and eternally pending.'[130] By the Incarnation of the Timeless in time, in 'Christ the power of God and the wisdom of God',[131] a transformation of earthly reality and historical existence has taken place whose full meaning and development 'progresses to somewhere outside of history, to the end of time or to the coincidence of all times, in other words upwards, and does not, like the scientific concepts of evolutionary history, remain on the horizontal plane of historical [i.e. merely *intra*-historical] events'.[132]

It is within that incarnational context, with its transvaluation of the values of the concrete real, that Augustine broke the Greco-Roman connection between levels of literary style and the corresponding levels of reality as they understood them – the high or grand, the middle, and the low. In Christianity even the 'low' is 'high' or 'grand' because it has an eternal, and therefore infinite, dimension and implication. 'When we are speaking of the eloquence of those men whom we wish to be teachers of things which will liberate us from eternal evil or lead us to eternal good ... whether in extended speech or in conversation, whether in treatises or in books, whether in long letters or in short, they are great things. Unless, perhaps, because a cup of cold water is a small and most insignificant thing, we should also regard as small and most insignificant the promise of the Lord that he who gives such a cup to one of his disciples "shall not lose his reward".'[133]

This was what Augustine could not yet understand when he turned to the Scripture after his first 'conversion' – to the quest for 'immortal wisdom'. 'They

129 Ibid.

130 Ibid., 37 – italics mine.

131 1 Corinthians1:24, a recurring text in Augustine.

132 Auerbach, op.cit., 39.

133 *De doctrina Christiana*, IV 8,37; Matthew 10:42; cf. the famous quotation by Longinus, *On the Sublime*, Ch. 9, from the Genesis Creation narrative, to illustrate the capacity of a single sentence to express the sublime: 'The lawgiver of the Jews, no ordinary man – for he understood and expressed God's power in accordance with its worth – writes at the beginning of his Laws: "God said" – now what? – "Let there be light", and there was light: "Let there be earth", and there was earth.'

seemed to me unworthy to be compared with the majesty of Cicero. My conceit was repelled by their simplicity, and I had not the mind to penetrate into their depths.'[134] Looking back even on his own earliest philosophical writings, the Cassiciacum *Dialogues*, he sees that 'the writing was now in your [God's] service, but during this breathing-space still smacked of the pride of the schools'.[135] Even his friend and fellow convert thought at first 'it would be in some sense lowering to put into my writings the name of Jesus Christ'[136] – the name without which not even a philosophical work could ever wholly satisfy Augustine,[137] and in whom alone, doubly revealed, in the flesh and in the Scriptures, his first conversion to the quest for 'immortal wisdom'[138] was to be ultimately fulfilled. For 'philosophy' means love of wisdom, but wisdom is with God,[139] and it is in Christ there indwells corporeally the whole plenitude of divinity.[140] Even the secular book that 'converted' him to the quest of 'immortal wisdom', Cicero's now lost exhortation to the philosophic quest, the *Hortensius*, by its critique of all the innumerable schools which used the 'great and fair and honourable name' of philosophy to lead men's minds astray, 'illustrates the wholesome advice given by the Spirit through your good and loving servant: "Make sure that no one traps you and deprives you of your freedom by some secondhand, empty, rational philosophy based on the principles of this world instead of on Christ".'[141]

Christ being the central and total meaning of Scripture in Augustine's exegesis of its fuller sense,[142] the foregoing illuminates our opening quotation from *The*

134 *Conf.* III 5,9; on Augustine's initiation into Scripture, see Anne-Marie la Bonnardière, 'L'initiation biblique de Augustin', in *Saint Augustin et la Bible*, edited by same author (Paris, 1986).

135 Ibid. IX 4,7.

136 Ibid.

137 *Conf.* III 4,8.

138 Ibid. III 4,7.

139 Ibid. III 4,8; Job 12:13.

140 Ibid. III 4,8; Colossians 2:9.

141 Ibid. III 4,8; Colossians 2:8, in *Jerusalem Bible* version.

142 See e.g. *Contra Faustum*, XII 27: *Christus mihi ubique illorum librorum* ... (I find Christ everywhere in those Books ...); cf. the even more forceful remarks in XII 39 on the futile ingenuity of 'a certain Philo', attempting to interpret Scripture without Christ, 'in whom he did not believe', and thereby only succeeding in showing 'what a difference it makes whether you refer everything to Christ, with reference to whom everything was truly said in this way, or, ignoring Him, you hunt after no-matter-what conjecture with no-matter-what ingenuity of mind ... '. In other – and very contemporary – words, the whole of Scripture is meaningless without its fulfilment in Christ; see Hans Urs von Balthasar, *The Glory of the Lord* (Edinburgh: T & T Clarke, 1982), vol. I, 658: 'For the eyes of faith, the "riddle of Israel" does not exist ... The figure is legible, but only on Christian presuppositions. Israel and Christianity form one single figure, carved in bold relief from the block of world-history – a figure whose higher centre is the God-Man ... '; this in a context where much of profound interest is said about the true meaning and permanent validity – even necessity – of the

City of God, and anticipates *in nuce* so much that we shall find Augustine asserting about Scripture as inexhaustible in its potential meaning. This potential inexhaustibility is in fact anticipated in one of the Cassiciacum *Dialogues*. 'What is it that we ought to call by the name of Wisdom except the Wisdom that is God's? But we have also learned on divine authority that the Son of God is none other than the Wisdom of God [1 Cor 1:25] ... But what do you suppose Wisdom to be except Truth? For this too has been said: "I am the Truth" [Jn 14:6].' It is Christ then who is Wisdom and Truth, and if He is the whole meaning of Scripture we can once more see the ground of the absolute claim made for Scripture in our opening quotation from *The City of God*. But we can see it fully only if we understand the full significance of the terms wisdom (*sapientia*) and truth (*veritas*). They do not resonate much in English but they are high metaphysical concepts, as fundamental to Augustine's philosophical and theological thinking as they are to his personal existential drive towards absolutes.

Truth is the eternal, immutable, absolute, infinite subsistent Reality, a Truth which is the Ground and the Condition of all other realities and of all other truths, and is also the source of the light by which we know reality and its truth. Plato had already said as much in his simile of the sun for the Supreme Reality that is the Form of the Good. 'What gives the objects of knowledge their truth and the knower's mind the power of knowing them is the Form of the Good... The Good therefore may be said to be the source not only of the intelligibility of the objects of knowledge, but also of their being and reality...'[143] 'He who knows the Truth knows that Light, says Augustine of his first mystical experience (Plotinus-influenced, but 'with [God] as my guide'), and he who knows that Light knows eternity.'[144] 'This mysterious Sun radiates its light into our inner eyes. By its light is true every truth we utter, even when, with still ailing or only half-opened eyes, we tremble to turn boldly towards it and look upon it wholly face to face.'[145]

We have Augustine's theory of knowledge already in germ, as elaborated for instance in the *De magistro*. There it is established by what one might call strict 'phenomenological' analysis, proving that all perception of truth is in the light of, conditional upon – by 'consulting', to use his own recurrent term – an unconditioned, absolute *a priori* Truth. This principle itself takes even

---

traditional figural exegesis of Scripture: 'We have no choice ... but to characterize all Old Testament existence ... as an existence *in typo*. Thus, it is a foreshadowing of Christian existence, but at the same time it is a *reality* whereby all human existence assumes a form oriented towards Christ'(ibid., 654).

143 *Rep.* 508e and 509b.

144 *Conf.* VII 10,16.

145 *De beata vita*, 35 – the concluding phrase clearly alluding to the experience of *Conf.* VII 10,16, where in the dazzle of the Light 'you beat back the weakness of my gaze by the intensity of its radiance upon me, making me tremble with love and with dread'.

philosophical analysis to the point where 'faith' too is necessary, for the ultimate *a priori* cannot itself be 'proved'![146] This gives the rationale for Augustine's much-quoted principle from Isaiah 7:9 (in the version he knew): 'Unless you believe you will not understand.'[147]

But in whom or what are we to believe in the quest for Truth? Whose shall be the teaching, who the teacher-master who will initiate us? What is 'written with divine authority' provides the answer: 'You must not allow yourselves to be called teachers, for you have only one Teacher, the Christ' (Mt 23:10).[148] What is meant is not extrinsic teaching but interior enlightenment by the indwelling Christ of Eph 3:16f, that is, the Christ of 1 Cor 1:24, 'the immutable Power and sempiternal Wisdom of God'.[149] This epistemology will underpin not just his philosophical thought but his scriptural exegesis as well, with its vast assertions of the inexhaustible meanings of Scripture. And concerning that range of meaning, the whole passage of Eph 3:16f. is significant, for it provides an ontological as well as an epistemological basis for that range. Through the indwelling Christ 'you will ... have strength to grasp the breadth and the length, the height and the depth, until, knowing the love of Christ, which is beyond all knowing (*gnôseôs*), you are filled with the total plenitude (*pan to plêrôma*) of God'.[150] As commentators point out, the relevant terms here, 'grasp', 'breadth' etc, and *plêrôma*, are technical terms borrowed from Greek philosophy, evoking both the *cosmic* dimension of Christ and the ungraspable range of what is to be known about Him.

When to that cosmic dimension of Christ we add Augustine's already noted sense of Christ's omnipresence in Scripture, and when to those dimensions we add his epistemological significance as the Light, so to speak, in whose light we shall see light,[151] we glimpse again the vast background to our opening quotation from *The City of God*, with its categorical assertion that Scripture 'surpasses all the writings of all mankind, and in consequence of its divine authority has subordinated to itself every genre of human genius'.

146 Elaborated in *De utilitate credendi* – written specifically against the Manichean 'intellectual' insistence on accepting truth, even Christian truth, only as rationally demonstrated and not as based merely on the faith of orthodox Christianity.

147 *De mag.* XI 37.

148 See *De mag.* XIV 46; cf. *Conf.* V 6,10: 'You, O my God, had taught me in secret and marvellous ways. That it was You who taught me, I believe: for it is the truth and there is no teacher of truth (*doctor veri*) save You, no matter where or when it may happen to shine.'

149 *De mag.* XI 38.

150 Cf. Eph 1:23 on 'the plenitude (*plêrôma*) of Him who fills the whole creation'.

151 Ratified in any case already by Jn 1:9: 'The Word was the true light that enlightens every man, and He was coming into the world' – or any other way we choose to read it.

That is but one of many such statements, which are found in greatest concentration and in their most developed form in the *Confessions* and in the *De doctrina Christiana*. They are statements that attribute to Scripture a certain *mira profunditas*,[152] an awesome[153] profundity. They are statements that attribute to Scripture not just two senses, a literal and a figurative, not just the four senses of the traditional classification (although of course he does use that classification), nor yet even a 'plurality' of senses in some definable and delimited sense. They are statements which entirely transcend such classification, and attribute to Scripture an unlimited, inexhaustible, indeed infinite, potential of meaning. They recur throughout the *Confessions* from the moment of his 'conversion' to philosophy and its quest of 'immortal wisdom'.

At that point 'I resolved to make some study of the Sacred Scriptures and find out what kind of books they were. But what I came upon was something not grasped by the proud, nor revealed to children either, rather something lowly in access but, once entered, sublime and enveloped in mysteries (*excelsam et velatam mysteriis*).'[154] As we noted earlier from the context, he was not yet of a mentality capable of entering or bending his proud neck to take the necessary steps.[155]

It was the preaching of Ambrose in Milan that enabled him to enter, by revealing the fuller, figurative sense of Scripture and so unblocking also the Manichean objections to the apparent anthropomorphisms and other problems of Scripture. Augustine's reaction expresses the same ideas as before, but now in more elaborate and enthusiastic terms.

> Now that I heard them expounded so convincingly, I saw that many passages in those books, which had at one time struck me as absurdities, must be referred to the profundity of mystery.[156] Indeed the authority of Scripture seemed more to be revered and more worthy of devoted faith in that it was at once a book that all could read, and read easily, while yet it preserved the majesty of its mystery (*secreti sui dignitatem*) in a more profound interpretation (*in intellectu profundiore*): for it offers itself to all in

152 *Conf.* XII 14,17.

153 This rendering is not too strong, as we shall see.

154 *Conf.* III 5,9; Augustine likes the metaphor of veiling/unveiling – ultimately from 2 Cor 3:16ff – see *De utilitate credendi* III 9; *Contra Faustum* XII 11.

155 *Conf.* III 5,9.

156 *Sacramentorum altitudinem*: see C. Couturier, '"Sacramentum" et "mysterium" dans l'oeuvre de Saint Augustin', in H. Rondet et al., Études Augustiniennes (Paris, 1953), 161-274; cf. von Balthasar, op. cit., vol. I, 548: 'Even if we would not attribute to Scripture a sacramental and eucharistic structure in the strict sense, as Origen usually seems to do, we must still maintain the closest kind of connection between Scripture and Sacrament.'

> the plainest words and the simplest expressions, yet demands the closest attention of the most serious minds.[157]

Augustine's confessional analysis of the meaning and the quest of his life from the past to the present is completed by a quest into the future, through a meditation on Scripture, on 'the wondrous things of thy Law' [Ps 118:18], for the analysis and the quest are in the light of Him 'in whom [the mystery of God the Father, *mysterium Dei Patris*] are hidden all the treasures of wisdom and knowledge'.[158] This projection into the future through Scripture implies by itself the totalizing range of meaning he attributes to Scripture. For the range of the *Confessions* themselves, with their quest for 'immortal wisdom', is a 'totalizing' range – from the mystery of his origins in the dark backward and abysm of time,[159] forward into the abysm of futurity in destined eternity.[160] The same totalizing range is implicit in the part of Scripture chosen to be meditated on in the three concluding books of the *Confessions* – the creation narrative in the opening chapter of Genesis. Ever since Philo, down even to Eriugena in the *Periphyseôn*, that narrative provides the framework for exposition of the total order, origin and destiny of creation and of human existence under the Creator. And that is precisely the range of Augustine's opening prayer in *Confessions* XI 2,3; 'O Lord complete thy work in me, and open these pages to me ... Let me confess to Thee whatever I shall find in your Books ... from the first "beginning" in which You made "the heavens and the earth", up to our everlasting reign with Thee in thy Holy City.'

And again Christ is the source and the ground[161] of this totality, and the light by which it is understood. He is the Word 'by which You made all things[162] ... It is through Him that I beseech you ... through Him "in whom are hidden all the treasures of wisdom and knowledge". It is those treasures [or, variant, Him] that I

157 *Conf.* VI 5,8.

158 *Conf.* X 43,70; Colossians 2:3.

159 See the questioning in *Conf.* I 6,9: 'And before that again [existence in his mother's womb] ... my God? Was I somewhere or someone?'

160 See *Conf.* XIII 36,51: 'You rested on the seventh day, to let us know in advance by the word of your Book that we too, at the end of our works ... will rest in You in the Sabbath of eternal life'; cf. the conclusion of *The City of God.*

161 See *Conf.* XI 3ff on the question of what is meant by the statement that 'in the beginning' (*in principio*) God made heaven and earth (Gen 1:1); the explanation culminates in the interpretation of *principium* not as a temporal beginning but as an ultimate metaphysical principle, an eternal reason or *logos* (*ratio aeterna*) identified with the eternal *Logos* that is Christ, on the basis of a reading of Jn 8:25: 'They said therefore to Him: Who are you? Jesus said to them: The *principium* (*arkhên*), O God, in which You made heaven and earth, in your Word ... ' (*Conf.* XI 9,11).

162 Cf. John 1:3.

seek in your Books. It is of Him that Moses wrote[163]: this He himself says, this He says who is Truth[164] itself.'[165]

It is in the account of his sojourn at Cassiciacum in preparation for Baptism in *Conf.* IX 4 that we find Augustine's first full 'discovery' of Scripture and the depth of the meaning he found in it. The account is a rhapsody on the Psalms, composed around a meditation on Psalm 4 in particular. The tone is intensified by the realization of how wrong the Manicheans had been about Scripture – the Manicheans with whom he had himself been 'a blind bitter barker against Writings all honeyed with the honey of heaven and all luminous with your light ... ' (IX 4,11). The language is at times that of the higher states of prayer, or even of mystical experience. 'I was speaking with myself and to myself in your presence out of the intimate feeling of my spirit. I was in awe and dread ... I heard and trembled ... *inhorrui timendo ... audivi et contremui'* (IX 4,8f). 'Oh if they could but see the internal eternal (*internum aeternum*) which ... I had tasted ... I cried out as I read these things aloud and recognized their truth within me. And I no longer wanted to fragment myself in earthly goods, devouring time and devoured by time, since in the simplicity of the eternal (*aeterna simplicitate*) I now had other corn and wine and oil' (IX 4,10; Ps 4:7).

'Behold, O Lord my God, how much I have written on those few words, how much, I ask You! What stamina, what time, would be required to study all your Books at such a rate!'[166] The few words in question are the first two verses of Genesis – they have taken up two whole Books of the *Confessions* (XI–XII). Those few words have raised, and Augustine has found answers to, all the ultimate metaphysical questions about the nature of reality. Creator and creation, the transcendent spiritual world and the material phenomenal universe, the nature of eternity and of time, of being and of the nothingness from which being is created, of 'form' and that almost ungraspable entity, the 'primal matter' which is the substrate of 'form'. 'If one could call it "a nothing which is something" and "a being which is non-being", that is what I would call it. And yet it *was* in some way, in order to receive those visible and organized forms.'[167] His heart indeed 'is hard wrought in the poverty of my present life when the words of your Scripture knock on its door', and the poverty of human understanding uses more words in asking questions than in finding the answers.[168]

It is out of this sense of mystery and unsoundable depths of meaning that Augustine breaks into one of his lyrical, even mystical, apostrophes to Scripture.

163 Cf. John 5:46.

164 Cf. John 14:6.

165 *Conf.* XI 2,4.

166 *Conf.* XII 32,43.

167 Id. XII 6,6.

168 Id. XII 1,1.

'Wondrous is the profundity (*mira profunditas*) of your oracles. We see their surface before us enticing us as children. But wondrous is their profundity, my God, wondrous their profundity! To look into them is to experience a shudder, the shudder of awe and the trembling of love – *horror honoris et tremor amoris*.'[169] This is the language of the sacred, the holy, the *mysterium tremendum*.[170] The fact that Augustine could have borrowed the terminology from Plotinus[171] does not invalidate the experience. We have seen him use the same terms about the mystical experience in Milan.[172] He uses that language in an even more explicit and extended passage in *Conf.* XI 9, 11, meditating on the realization that Christ, the *Logos*, is the *Principium* in whom God created heaven and earth.

> Who will understand this? Who will explain it? What is that which shines upon me intermittently and strikes my heart without wounding it?[173] I am on fire and draw back in dread (*inhorresco et inardesco*) ... It is Wisdom, Wisdom itself, that in those moments shines upon me, cleaving through my cloud ...

In case we be tempted to regard such language as unique and excessive, or just rhetoric, let us put beside it a summary statement from a modern theologian.

> It is a pity that both orthodox Protestant and Catholic biblical scholars often speak as if the human, historical and philological content of Scripture formed a closed world, and that the divine or 'spiritual' sense begins only beyond it. The saints realized how the infinite shines directly through the fearful intensity of the prophets, of Jesus, of Paul and of John; how the human word and gesture are but a thin film before it ... '.[174]

169 Id. XII 14,17.

170 See e.g. Rudolf Ott, *The Idea of the Holy* (Oxford, 1923, repr. 1973).

171 E.g. *Enn* I 6,4.

172 *Conf.* VII 10,16: *contremui amore et horrore.*

173 Cf. St John of the Cross, *Canciones del Alma* ... (Song of the Soul ...),
O cautery most tender!
O gash that is my guerdon! (tr. Roy Campbell).
¡Oh cauterio suavei¡
¡Oh regalada llaga¡

174 Hans Urs von Balthasar, *Science, Religion and Christianity* (London, 1958), 102; cf. 112 on 'the abyss of silence from which springs the Word of God ... All the words ... all the gestures and deeds of Jesus Christ are not only surrounded by silence, they are steeped in the ineffable, drawn from silence ... '; also p. 99 on the same idea: 'The Fathers worked on this golden background [symbol of the infinite in iconic art]. They had the feeling for the dialectic of that which is always greater ... '; cf. also, by the same author, *First Glance at Adrienne von Speyr* (San Francisco: Ignatius Press, 1981), 101: 'Every single sentence which seen from without has a finite meaning, to

It is to be noted too that Augustine's sense of the inexhaustible potential of the meaning of Scripture, though perhaps more powerful, explicit and frequent in his expression of it, is but a link in a millennial tradition, based both on professional exegesis and on contemplative study in the spirituality of *lectio divina.*[175] Henri de Lubac's vast explorations[176] save us the labour of hacking our own way through those woods with all their thickets and undergrowth. We can cull our own *florilegium* from one section of his research in particular – headed precisely with Augustine's phrase, *mira profunditas.*[177] Scripture is 'an infinite forest of meanings' – *infinita sensuum silva.* It is a treasury of the Holy Spirit, with riches as infinite as He is. It is 'an unplumbed abyss', 'an ocean immeasurable, wide and deep',[178] and so on. It is of interest to an Irish reader to get the flavour of the tradition as expressed in a *résumé* of Scotus Eriugena. He works with the concept of a double divine revelation – in Scripture and creation. Both are 'sacrament and symbol' for us. Each of them is 'a letter, a visible and sensible aspect', which however, must be transcended to attain to the 'spirit' (*intellectus*) of the one and the 'reason' (*ratio*) which runs through the other. 'Starting from the "simplicity of the letter and of the visible creation" we must let ourselves be led thus by degrees "right to the summit of contemplation",' – 'to the pure and invisible beauty of Truth itself, *ipsius Veritatis.*'[179] This is the frame and the scale of ascent for Augustine too in the study of Scripture.[180]

It is important to note that it is not only in the descants of 'enthusiasm' in the *Confessions* that we find Augustine's assertions of the all-encompassing meaning of Scripture. He had already stated the principle in the earlier *De doctrina Christiana,* written as a systematic handbook to professional exegesis. 'The knowledge collected from the pagans, although some of it is useful, is also little as compared with that derived from the divine Scriptures. For whatever one has learned outside them is censured there if it is harmful, and if it is useful it is found there. And ... moreover he will find there in much greater abundance what can be

be precisely differentiated from other sentences, partakes ... of an infinity always inherent in divine Truth. Without ceasing to have a *definite* meaning, every sentence shares as the word of God in the divine quality of the ever-more, ever-greater, and consequently ever-inexhaustible.' That amounts not just to a parallel with Augustine, but to a magisterial summary of Augustine's scattered but connected assertions, and of his ultimate reasons for them.

175 See e.g. von Balthasar, *The Glory of the Lord,* I, 659; also Jean Leclerq, *The Love of Learning and the Desire for God* (New York: Mentor Omega, 1962).

176 In *Exégèse Médiévale,* Paris, 1959.

177 Op. cit., Première Partie, vol. I, 119f.

178 Ibid., 119f.

179 Ibid., 121f.

180 See *De doct. Chr.,* II 7,9–11.

learned nowhere else at all, but only in the wondrous sublimity and the wondrous humility (*mirabili altitudine et mirabili humilitate*) of those Scriptures.'[181]

Another passage in the same work (III 27,38) comes close even to the expressions we find in the *Confessions*. It has the additional interest of being late, written in Augustine's old age in 427 or 428, more than a quarter of a century after the *Confessions* and the greater part of the *De doctrina Christiana*, which was left unfinished in 396 at III 25,35. It thus shows the permanence of Augustine's exegetical principles. And more than that, it confirms his conviction about their validity For at the time of completing the *De doctrina Christiana* he was writing the *Retractationes*, a rereading, and revision where necessary, of his *opera omnia*.[182]

The section in III 27,38 is concerned with passages of Scripture where 'from the same words not one but two or even several meanings can be understood', without the exegete being able to decide 'what meaning was intended by the author'. The exegete may take any or all of those possible meanings provided they are not invalidated by some other passage in Scripture, and provided also that he who is scrutinizing the divine utterances does make an effort to arrive at the intention of the author, 'through whom the Holy Spirit composed that Scripture'. But even if he fails and takes a meaning different from that intended by the author his interpretation is valid if compatible with any other passage in Scripture.

> For in fact the author himself may well have seen that same additional meaning in those same words that we are trying to understand. And certainly the Spirit of God, who worked through that author, foresaw without any doubt that that particular meaning too would occur to the reader or the hearer. Nay, more, He *provided* for its occurring to him, for that meaning too is grounded in Truth – *veritate subnixa*. In fact, what more rich and generous provision could have been divinely made in the divine words than that the same words be interpretable in several ways made acceptable by the witness of other no less divinely inspired passages?[183]

* * *

That passage takes us to an important question, the same question asked by opponents of Augustine's exegesis:[184] how do we know that Scripture has this range of

181 Op. cit., II 42,63; note the recurring motif of Scripture's combination of *altitudo* and *humilitas*; on *De doctrina Christiana* see Madeleine Moreau, 'Lecture du *De Doctrina Christiana*' in Anne Marie la Bonnardière, op. cit.

182 *Retractationes* II 4,30.

183 Cf. the same idea in *Conf.* XIII 24,37.

184 See *Conf.* XII 14,17.

meaning? What is the rationale of such interpretation? We have touched on some elements of the answer earlier, but the question demands to be examined more closely. It occupies Augustine at great length in *Conf.* XII 14,17ff, but he poses the question already at the start[185] of the three Books of reflection on the creation narrative. How are we to know what Moses really meant by 'In the beginning (*principium*) God made heaven and earth?' The answer is, by consulting that supreme Truth, *Veritas*, as in *De doct. Chr.* III 27,38, the full transcendent dimensions of which we have explained already, dimensions epistemological and ontological, as identified with Christ the *Logos* and the ultimate metaphysical *principium*. But here Augustine himself sketches the epistemology that leads up to that *principium*. Moses is gone and we cannot ask him what he meant. If he were here we could ask him, but if he answered in Hebrew we would understand nothing. If he spoke Latin then? We would know what he *said*, 'but whence should I know whether what he said was *true*? And if I did know it, would it be from him that I knew it? No, it would be from within myself, in the inner retreat of my own thought, where the Truth which speaks neither Hebrew nor Greek nor Barbarian would say to me without lips or tongue or sound of syllables: "he speaks truth".'[186] It is the epistemology elaborated in the *De magistro*, in which the teacher does not teach the student in the sense of conveying knowledge from one mind to another. Rather, as in the Socratic-Platonic maieutic,[187] he helps the student to *see* truth by himself, by 'recalling' to him, 'reminding him' of, that transcendent, subsistent Truth which is the ultimate presupposition of all truths, and without which their truth could not be recognized.[188] 'These [truths] we know, thanks to You, and our knowledge compared with your knowledge is ignorance.'[189] 'Let him hear You speaking within who can ... "You have made all things in your Wisdom",[190] and that is the *Principium*, and it is "in" *that* "Principium" [i.e. the *Logos*, Christ], that You have made heaven and earth.'[191] 'For it is true, Lord, that You made heaven and earth. It is true that the *Principium* is your Wisdom *in* which You "made all things".'[192] That is, in the transcendent but also immanent and omnipresent 'cosmic' (as we have called him earlier) *Logos*-Christ.[193]

185 *Conf.* XI 3,5

186 Ibid.

187 See e.g. Plato's *Meno*, 81bf. on 'teaching' Pythagoras' theorem!

188 See the concluding summary in *De Mag.* XIV 45f.

189 *Conf.* XI 4,6.

190 Psalm 103:24.

191 *Conf.* XI 9,11.

192 *Conf.* XII 19,28; Psalm 103:24.

193 Cf. the poetry of G.M. Hopkins – on which see von Balthasar, *The Glory of the Lord*, vol. III (Edinburgh, 1986), 353–99; there is of course an analogy between the sensibility that can recognize

That is the basis of his sustained and detailed argument in *Conf.* XII 14,17ff against those opposed to his totalizing interpretation of Gen 1:1, 'In the beginning God made heaven and earth,' as meaning that 'in his Word, co-eternal with Himself, God made both the intelligible and the sensible worlds, or in other words, both the spiritual and the material creation', that is, the total universe of being, transcendent and phenomenal.[194] Whether Moses did mean that or not, it is still *true*, as is clear to all whom God has enabled to see such matters with an interior eye, 'and who believe unshakeably that Moses, the servant of God, spoke in "the Spirit of Truth".'[195] And in any case, 'even if Moses himself were to appear and say; "This is what I meant", even then we would not see its truth but would have to take his word and *believe* it'.[196] That statement is based on Augustine's theory of knowledge, already explained. 'If therefore we are in no disagreement about the Light itself of the Lord our God, why should we dispute about the thought of our neighbour, which we cannot see in the same way as we see the immutable Truth [which is above our minds, i.e. as their Light]?'[197]

Augustine carries this criterion of truth even further in *Conf.* XIII 29,44 and XIII 31,46. There, in the context of the truth of judgements about the goodness of creation (Genesis 1:31, and with the Manicheans in mind), he says that when the

---

the inexhaustible or even transcendent significance of the aesthetic experience and that of understanding the Scriptures in their transcendent height and depth – see von Balthasar, *The Glory of the Lord*, passim, also George Steiner, *Real Presences* (London, 1989), passim; Augustine of course was a professor and lover of literature, and himself a poet in prose, and he too points up the analogy in *De utilitate credendi*, VI 13; it is an analogy of current contemporary interest – see e.g. Paul S. Fiddes, *Freedom and Limit: A Dialogue Between Literature and Christian Doctrine* (London, 1991); one point of the analogy is well made in a sentence by Jean Leclercq, op. cit., 265: 'The extreme frontiers of literature ... open into the whole realm of the ineffable'; cf. Karl Rahner, 'Poetry and the Christian', in his *Theological Investigations*, vol. IV (Baltimore and London, 1966), 357–67. And despite the appearances of his theoretical anti-art Puritanism, in 'the long-standing quarrel between philosophy and literature', Plato recognized the point in his practice – resorting to his literary 'myths' when dialectical reasoning reached its own frontiers – see e.g. J. A. Stewart, *The Myths of Plato* (New York, 1905). In fact Plato himself anticipated Augustine's assertions about Plato and the Platonists, that 'there are none who have come closer to us than they have' (*De civ. Dei* VIII 5), and, if they were alive today, 'with the change of only a few words and ideas they would become Christians, as so many more recent Platonists of our own times have done' (*De ver. rel.* IV 7): the anticipation is in the fact that Plato too, when reason's raft had taken him as far as it could, hoped for 'some stronger vessel, some divine revelation (*logou theiou tinos*) on which to voyage with less risk and in greater security' (*Phaedo* 85d); cf. J. Pieper, 'Gottgeschenkte Mania. Eine Platon-Interpretation', in *IKZ Communio* 23 (1994), 260–70.

194 *Conf.* XII 20,29.

195 Ibid.; John 14:17.

196 *Conf.* XII 25,35.

197 Ibid.

human mind judges truth and value under the light of the Word and the inspiration of the Holy Spirit it is God himself who judges in us.[198] 'You say to me, for You are my God and You speak with strong voice to the inner ear of your servant ... : "O Man, it is clear that what my Scripture says it is I who say ... Thus, what *you* see through my Spirit I see, just as what *you* say through my Spirit I say".'[199]

The Manicheans are wrong about Scripture and the goodness of creation, 'because they do not see your works through your Spirit, nor recognize You in them'.[200] 'But as for those who see those things through your Spirit, it is You who see in them ... And I am moved to add: Assuredly "no one knows the things of God except the Spirit of God".[201] How then do we know, we too, "the gifts given us by God"?[202] The answer is given me: when we know things through his Spirit, even then "no one knows them except the Spirit of God". For just as it has been rightly said to those who would *speak* in the Spirit of God, "It is not you who speak",[203] similarly to those who *know* in the Spirit of God it is rightly said: "It is not you who know".'[204]

In the course of the argument that begins in *Conf.* XII 14,17ff Augustine eventually prefers the higher Truth of charity to contentious argument – '"which is to no profit except to the subverting of the listeners"[205] ... And our Teacher knows well on what two precepts He hung "the whole law and the prophets".'[206] And Scripture itself 'prescribes nothing but charity' and proscribes nothing but its opposite, 'cupidity.'[207]

But Augustine brings in another remarkable supporting argument, one that is also more easily graspable – despite the fact that it is so far-reaching, and even anticipatory of some powerfully stated contemporary exegetical principles.[208] The gist of the argument is that a book like the Bible, composed in a particular time and place but, as the Word of God, intended to be not only authoritative but universally meaningful over space and time to all men in all ages and situations, such a book must have an ever-inexhaustible potential of meaning. That is the simple

198 See the note to III 31,46 in *Les Confessions de Saint Augustin, Livres VIII–XIII* (Bruges, 1962), and its reference to Franz Koerner, 'Deus in homine videt', in *Phil. Jahrb.* 64 (1956), 166–217.

199 *Conf.* XIII 29,40.

200 *Conf.* XIII 30,45.

201 1 Corinthians 2:11, but see the whole context for the full implications in Augustine as well as Paul.

202 1 Corinthians 2:12.

203 Matthew10:20.

204 *Conf.* XIII 31,48.

205 2 Timothy 2:14.

206 *Conf.* XII 18,27; Matt. 22:40.

207 *De doct. Chr.* III 10,15.

208 See n. 174, p. 194 and n. 335, p. 219.

summary, but without quotation *in extenso* we miss the power of the argument – as indeed we miss also Augustine's own trained and practised sense of literary and semiotic complexity.

> I cannot think that Moses your most faithful servant was given lesser gifts by You than I should have wished and longed to have for myself if I had been born at the same time as he, and You had settled me in the same place, to dispense by the service of my heart and my language those Writings which for so long after, from such a summit of authority, were to benefit all nations and throughout the whole world to overtop the words of all the doctrines produced by falsehood and pride.[209] If I had been Moses at that time, I would wish therefore, had I been then what he was and You had enjoined on me the writing of the Book of Genesis, I would wish to be granted such a skill in writing and such a way with weaving words that those who cannot yet understand how God creates would still not reject my words as beyond their capacity; and again that those who do already understand would find in the few words of your servant any truth they had already attained by their own thinking; and if in the light of Truth some other person saw some other truth I would wish that it too could be seen in those same words of mine.[210]

That wish he expresses again in *Conf.* XII 31,42, in terms more explicit about the inexhaustible meaning of Scripture. 'For myself – and I say this without fear and from my heart – had I to write something of supreme authority I would prefer so to write that my words should resonate with any truth that anyone could find on these matters – I would prefer that to having my words express one true meaning so clearly that they excluded all others ... ' And at this point he cannot believe that a man as great as Moses was not thus gifted. 'Yes, of course, when he was writing those words he did discern and think of all the truth we have been able to find in them, as also all that we have not – or not yet – been able to find in them, and yet is in there to be found.'

Augustine the artist has an innate sense of the complexity and the depths of reality and thought, and of the polysemy of language that tries to express them – and often is unable to express them.[211] 'I know that the corporeal

209 Recall *Conf.* III 4,8 on the debasing of the noble name of 'philosophy' by the discordant schools.

210 *Conf.* XII 26,36.

211 See *De catechizandis rudibus* X 14ff on the various kinds of writer's block and their remedies! And in II 3 a glimpse of his own labour pains: 'Myself too, I am nearly always dissatisfied with what I compose ... I want the hearer to understand what I understand myself, and I feel that I do not so express myself as to succeed. The main reason is that the intuitive conception floods my

signifies in multiple ways what the spirit understands in one way only, and conversely, that the spirit understands in multiple ways what the corporeal signifies in one way only.'[212] The statement is made in the course of a long reflection on something he finds very strange, why it is only the *human* and *animal* creation that is bidden to 'increase and multiply' in Gen 1:28. 'What can this mean? What kind of mystery is this? ... It cannot be that you imply nothing particular by it ... '[213] 'What then am I to say, O Truth, my light? That the fact means nothing, that the expression was used without any particular meaning? Never! ... Far be it from the servant of your Word to say such a thing.'[214] If we consider the nature of things in their literal sense the phrase 'increase and multiply' applies to all things born of seed. But if we take the phrase in a figurative sense (*figurate*) – 'which in my opinion was rather what Scripture intended' – then we find the hermeneutics of the *multiple* meaning in the *one* and of the *one* meaning in the *multiple*.

> What is in question is that kind of increasing and multiplying in which one meaning is expressed in multiple ways and one expression is understood in multiple meanings; and that kind of increasing and multiplying we find only in signs made corporeally and in things conceived intellectually ... In that blessing then [Increase and multiply] I understand that You have granted us the faculty and the power both to express in multiple ways what we have conceived intellectually in the mode of a single idea, and to understand in multiple ways what we have read darkly expressed in a single mode.[215]

We do not necessarily have to accept the reasoning that led up to this insight in order to accept its validity. The polysemy of great literature, the inexhaustibility of the 'classic', is a commonplace of modern[216] literary theory and

soul with the rapidity of a lightning flash, while the expression is slow, long and very unlike the original intuition; and while the expression is unfolding the intuition has already disappeared into a hidden retreat ... '.

212 *Conf.* XIII 24,36.

213 *Conf.* XIII 24,35; Augustine insists on the significance even of details; in *Con. Faustum* XII 37 he asks: 'What are we to believe about so many things done outside any usage of nature and without any necessity of the business in hand?'; he goes on to list examples in 38f, the creation of Eve from the side of the sleeping Adam, the details of the construction of the ark, the order to Abraham to sacrifice his son, etc. The answer to his question he finds in 1 Cor 10:6: 'All these things were done as figures, types and symbols for ourselves.'

214 *Conf.* XIII 24,36.

215 *Conf.* XIII 24,37.

216 Even though the insight itself is as ancient as Longinus; one of the marks of the authentic 'sublime'

criticism[217] – even before its excesses of 'interpretation' outdo those of the maligned allegorizers of Scripture!

It is in the light of such principles that the more flowery passages are to be understood. In XII 27,37 he compares Scripture to a spring – though enclosed in a confined space it is more abundant, and from its many streams waters a wider territory, than any one of those streams on its own however far they flow. Likewise, 'the narrative of the dispenser of your Word, meant to serve many who would later discourse upon it, from brevity of utterance sets flowing streams of limpid truth from which everyone can draw for himself such truth as he can find therein, one person this, another that, but in the exposition of it demanding much longer windings of words'.

Or again, expressing once more his constant motif of the combined simplicity and depth of Scripture, it is a nest for 'the poor unfeathered nestling' (XII 27,37), while for others its words are no longer a nest, but rather a leafy orchard in which they find hidden fruits and flutter joyfully around them, gazing, chattering and picking. 'For when they read or hear these words of yours, O God eternal, they see that all times past and all times to come are over-arched by your changeless abiding ... Those things they see, and they rejoice in the light of your Truth, to what little extent they are able to see it here below' (XII 28,38).

* * *

We have been analysing at some length the concept of Truth in Augustine, and the epistemology, ontology, and hermeneutics through which he finds it 'totally' in Scripture – to the extent, as we saw at the beginning, of subordinating to itself every other product of human genius.[218] To understand more fully these assertions of all-inclusive and absolute Truth in Scripture we need to look at them in a larger context and in a less dialectical, more 'existential' or experiential mode.

---

is that it 'disposes the mind of the reader to high thoughts (*megalophrosunên*), and leaves his intellect with more to think on than is contained in the mere words', op. cit., 7,3; cf. 35,2ff: 'What then was the vision that inspired these godlike writers ... ? ... The universe itself... is not wide enough for the range of human speculation and intellect... Other literary qualities show their authors to be merely human, but the sublime lifts us close to the high thoughts of a god'; it has been suggested that Augustine knew this work: see L. J. van der Lof, 'Verbricht Augustin das Schweigen des Klassischen Altertums um Ps-Longinus?', *Vigiliae Christianae*, 16 (1962), 21–33.

217 Of the many references that could be given see William F. Lynch, *Christ and Apollo: The Dimensions of the Literary Imagination* (New York, 1960). Its particular interest is that it constructs a theory of the levels of meaning in literature on the double basis of the philosophical doctrine of the analogy of being and the traditional four senses of Scripture; and of the latter he makes solid sense – see e.g. 165 and 187ff, with which pages cf. de Lubac, op. cit., Première Partie, II, 630ff, 643ff.

218 See n. 118, p. 183 above.

To take the latter first, we have already glimpsed it in the phenomenon of Augustine's 'conversion' to 'philosophy' with its quest for immortal wisdom in *Conf.* III 4,8 – 'not this or that philosophical sect but Wisdom *itself* whatever it might be', and not just in an abstract intellectual mode, but to be 'loved, sought, attained, seized and passionately embraced'.[219] The Manicheans cried 'Truth, truth!' and spoke much of it, 'but it was nowhere in them'.[220] 'O Truth, Truth, from how deep within me did I sigh for You from the very marrow of my soul.'[221] Ten years later, in the throes of philosophical scepticism, he is tormented[222] by the realization of how little progress he has made since that nineteenth year of his life when he first 'began to burn with a passion for the pursuit of Wisdom'.[223] Perish all else, all the vain distractions and empty ambitions of life! 'Let us devote ourselves to the sole pursuit of truth. Life is a poor unhappy business, death is uncertain, and suppose it crept up on us suddenly – in what state will we go hence, and where then shall we learn what we neglected to learn in life?' – if death itself be not the end of everything.[224]

At this stage he is speaking from among a group of like-minded friends, all troubled by the same problems as Augustine, and detesting the distractions of the cares and troubles of life in the world. It was in that situation that they discussed the project of pooling their resources to withdraw from the world and live the common life in a community devoted to the pursuit of truth in a life of philosophical thinking and contemplation.[225] The project and the terms may sound strangely parallel to the Christian contemplative religious life.[226] And so in fact the project was, and is. For such philosophical communities were well known in the ancient world, from the Pythagorean communities down to, for instance, that of Plotinus in Rome.[227] There are two reasons for the parallel, the

219 Language which anticipates the ultimately mystical dimension of Augustine's quest – cf. VII 10,16; X 7,11.

220 *Conf.* III 6,10.

221 Ibid.

222 Although now with a dawning hope in Christianity, after hearing Ambrose on Scripture: 'I shall plant my foot on that step where my parents set me as a child until I find the clear light of Truth (*perspicua Veritas*); but where am I to look for it?' – *Conf.* VI 11,18.

223 Ibid.

224 *Conf.* VI 11,19.

225 *Conf.* VI 14,24.

226 Which in fact was Augustine's own final project on returning to Africa after conversion and Baptism – *Conf.* IX 8,17.

227 See Porphyry's *Life of Plotinus*; cf. Pierre Courcelle, *Recherches sur les Confessions de Saint Augustin* (Paris, 1950), 178f.; relevant too of course is Augustine's own sojourn with his group in Cassiciacum, from which issued his first philosophical Dialogues in the months between his Christian conversion and Baptism.

nature and goal of philosophy as understood in the Greco-Roman world, and the process by which its truth and goal were understood to be attained, especially in the Platonist tradition. In that tradition the finality of philosophy was religious, in a sense of philosophy we are no longer familiar with: the Absolute, not only as the ultimate cause and ground of being but as the source of the light of truth about it – in a Supreme Being, the Form of the Good, the One, God. And that not in a merely abstract conceptual mode of knowledge, but ultimately in unmediated vision and experience. Understood in that demanding sense,[228] it is not surprising that the ultimate Reality, and the ultimate Truth of philosophy, was not thought to be found at the end of a syllogism but only at the end of the *askêsis* of a 'way', a way of life, the 'philosophic life,' the *bios philosophikos.*[229] In that sense early Christian writers could refer to Christianity as the 'true philosophy'.[230] It is in that sense that there could be the experience of conversion to philosophy. It is out of that sense there could develop the philosophical *genre* known as the *protreptic*, an 'exhortation' to such conversion. That was the genre of Cicero's *Hortensius*, which 'converted' Augustine.

Thirteen years later, after conversion to Christianity, it is still to 'philosophy' that he sees himself called in the Cassiciacum *Dialogues*, and it is to 'philosophy' that he 'exhorts' their dedicatees. 'Wake up, wake up!', he cries to his friend Romanianus (whom he had himself inducted into Manicheanism), inviting him to give up worldly pursuits and falsehoods for the life of true philosophy.[231] He has just done that himself, withdrawn into the bosom of philosophy, *in gremium philosophiae.* It is she that has delivered him wholly from 'that abyss of irreligion (*superstitione*) into which I had precipitated you along with myself ... It is she who promises to show us the most true (*verissimum*) and invisible God, and already has begun to do so in stages, as it were through luminous clouds'.[232] This 'showing' is 'promised from the philosophy to which I invite you, the truth proclaimed to those who love it, and far removed from the profane, in the richest of all the oracles of knowledge'[233]

228 Implicit in *Conf.* III 4.

229 See e.g. the account of the 'ascent' in Plato's *Symposium*, 209ef; cf. his *Seventh Letter*, 344b, on the long way to the moment when 'at last in a flash understanding ... blazes up, and the mind ... is flooded with light'; cf. Augustine, *De civ. Dei* IX 16, quoting Apuleius to the same effect; Plato describes the *bios philosophikos* and its rationale in the *Phaedo*, 62dff, and cf. *Rep.* 474bff.

230 A term the lost understanding of which brought suspicion on Erasmus when he revived it! In an earlier age, Clement of Alexandria could call one of his works the *Protrepticus* – to the 'true philosophy'.

231 See A. D. Nock, *Conversion* (Oxford, pb. ed. 1961), Ch. XI on Conversion to Philosophy; Paul Aubin, *Le Problème de la 'Conversion'* (Paris, 1963).

232 *Contra Academicos* I 7, 3; cf. *De beata vita*, I 1 ff.

233 Ibid. I 1, 1.

– obviously the Scriptures. And for that enlightenment of Romanianus Augustine prays daily to 'the Power and the Wisdom itself of the Supreme God, revealed by the Christian mysteries as none other than the Son of God'.[234]

Five years later, in 391, the quest, the problem, and its scriptural solution are set out much more systematically in the *De utilitate credendi*, written to one Honoratus to win him back from the Manichean heresy into which Augustine himself had led him. The quest is the quest for Truth, *Veritas*, 'for which as you know, we burned with a passionate love from earliest adolescence'.[235] The problem is to prove that the Manicheans are wrong in attacking 'those who follow the *authority* of Catholic *faith*' rather than *reason* in the quest for truth, to prove that believers, before they are capable of perceiving 'that truth which is seen only by the purified mind ... are strengthened precisely by *believing*, and prepared for the God who alone will enlighten them'.[236] That was the only reason that kept Augustine himself with the Manicheans for nearly nine years – their promise to 'compel' no one to *believe* before truth was investigated by, and made accessible to, the light of reason:[237] And 'who would not be seduced by such a prospect, especially the soul of an adolescent hungry for truth, even to the point of pride and garrulity in argument with learned men in the schools?!'[238] The solution is twofold – to establish the necessity of *believing*, and to establish that it is Scripture which is to be believed.

The necessity of believing does not mean eliminating reason, but establishing the *priority* of believing – Augustine always conjoins both ways to the truth, 'authority' and reason, *auctoritas* and *ratio*.[239] The priority of believing exists at different levels, from the *moral* inability of reason to attain supreme Truth, up to that *philosophical* necessity of believing which emerges from the implications of epistemology – namely that reason itself depends on belief in its ultimate unproven and unprovable presuppositions.[240] The same argument is used in *De utilitate credendi*, at different levels of its application. Firstly at the highest philosophical level, in XIII 28f. The search for Truth and Wisdom implies the a priori *belief* that despite the variety and the dissensions of philosophical schools, it does exist. 'For what, I ask you, is it that we are in search of with such effort and desire?

234 Ibid. II 1, 1.

235 *De util. cred.* I 1.

236 Ibid, I 2; cf. *Con. Faustum* XIII 46.

237 Ibid.

238 Ibid.

239 E.g. *De ordine* II 98, 26 ff, *De vera religione* XXIV 43 ff; in the former, loc. cit., he is explicit: 'Of necessity we are led to knowledge in two ways, by authority and by reason. Temporally, authority comes first, but in logic reason has priority.'

240 See n. 147, p. 190.

What is it that we want to attain? Where is it that we want to arrive? Is it to somewhere we do not even believe to exist or concern us? There is nothing more self-contradictory and preposterous than such a state of mind!'[241] And in any case, given the drive of 'philosophy', both in Platonism and in Augustine's own Christian Platonism, towards the visionary and experiential level of knowledge already noted, a higher illumination is necessary. It is belief, faith, that provides the *askêsis* towards that 'illumination'.[242]

Lower down the scale, faith is implied even in the choice among the options of where to look for the answer to the quest.[243] And on the lowest and broadest plane of all Augustine demonstrates at length the extent to which all human life, individual and social, is based on knowledge not known as proven but accepted on trust, belief, in other words faith'.[244]

When it comes to making a choice of the 'authority' (*auctoritas*) in which to put one's faith, Augustine is fond of the argument from the authority that accrues to Scripture and Christianity from the fact of their universal diffusion throughout the world – that fact cannot be without providential significance. This argument is made more explicit in *De utilitate credendi.* In view of man's need of an 'authority', 'what more indulgent and generous could be done by God than that the very Wisdom of God himself, authentic, eternal and immutable ... should deign to become man?'[245] 'This, believe me, is the soundest *auctoritas* ... this is the *conversion* to the true God from the fate of this world. It is the sole *auctoritas* which moves those who lack wisdom (*sapientiam*) to hasten towards it.'[246] And its claims are doubly supported, 'in part by miracles, in part by the multitude of its followers'.[247] Moreover, whatever is in its Scriptures, 'believe me, is lofty and from God: in them is truth entirely, together with a discipline (*disciplina*) finely adapted to the renewing and restoring of souls: so well regulated in fact that nobody can fail to draw from it to the measure that answers his own needs, provided only that he comes to draw from its well with devotion and reverence, as true religion demands.'[248]

241 Loc. cit., 29; cf. XIV 30, and the occasional modern argument that 'rational' science presupposes 'faith' in the 'rationality' of its object, i.e. the universe, in general and in its particulars.

242 See n. 236, p. 205; cf. *De util. cred.* XVI 24: 'It is therefore perverse and preposterous to want to *see* Truth in order to purify your spirit, when in fact it is the other way round – you purify your spirit in order to see.' Cf. also e.g. *De util. cred.* VII 14ff.

243 Ibid. X 23–VII 26.

244 See e.g. *De vera religione* III 3–5, *Conf.* VI 5,8 and 11,19; XI 2,3: 'No, it is not for nothing that You have willed so many umbral and mysterious pages to be written ... '.

245 *De util. cred.* XV 33.

246 Ibid. XVI 34.

247 Ibid.

248 Ibid. VI 13.

* * *

We have been sketching the larger and wider context of Augustine's quest, within which his truth-claims for Scripture are better understood. We now come to a more systematic setting out of the exact measure of that 'truth entirely' which is the measure both of his own quest and of the context of Scripture.

To set that out as briefly and succinctly as possible, we can draw upon a multi-volume work by a contemporary philosopher, Karl Jaspers on *The Great Philosophers*.[249] Among the 'greats' – great because they are the great founders and perennially fertilizing fountains of thought – along with Parmenides, Socrates, Plato, Plotinus et al., he includes St Augustine.[250] But what more exactly constitutes their greatness – including, necessarily, that of Augustine? *Qu'est-ce que la grandeur*? Jaspers asks.[251]

The answer is in a certain totality and universality of range. 'The great man is like a reflection of the *whole* of being, *infinitely interpretable*. He is its mirror or its representative ... He lets himself be guided by the all-inclusive (*l'englobant*)... greatness is there where the real ... becomes by this distant reflection a symbol of the *whole* ... greatness is that which has something of the *universal* in it ... '[252] 'From the great thinkers there emanates an energy which makes ourselves grow by our own freedom: they fill us with the world of the invisible, whose *figures* they unveil and make visible, the world and its figures whose language they enable us to read.'[253] 'The existence of the Greats is like a guarantee against nothingness (*le néant*). To see them is itself a satisfaction beyond compare.'[254]

In such passages we already find expressions which we have found in, or ourselves used about, St Augustine on Scripture, e.g. 'infinitely interpretable', *interprétable à l'infini*. And to develop his idea he quotes *in extenso* the great passage in the first-century Longinus' *On the Sublime* which we have already referred to and quoted from.[255] The passage not only expresses that 'wholeness', 'all-inclusiveness', and sense of the 'infinite' that are Jaspers' criteria of greatness. It is also expressed in language characteristic of Longinus' work as a whole, the language

249 *Die Grossen Philosophen*, in the original German; I refer to it in the French translation, *Les Grands Philosophes* (Paris, 1972).

250 In Vol. 2 – to the full dimensions of Augustine's thought, reason and 'authority', philosophy and revelation in Scripture.

251 Vol. I, 20.

252 Ibid. (italics mine).

253 Ibid. 22 (italics mine).

254 Ibid. 23.

255 Ibid. 24; see n. 216, p. 202.

of the transconceptual drive to unmediated *vision* of the 'whole'. 'For greatness produces *ecstasy* rather than mere persuasion in the hearer; and the combination of wonder (*thaumasion*) and astonishment (*ekplêxis*) always proves superior to the merely persuasive and graceful.'[256] We have already noted this dimension in the 'philosophy' of Platonism and of Augustine.

The relevance of the above to the wider context of St Augustine's sense of the ever-inexhaustible meaning of Scripture is that nobody provides better expressions of Jaspers' criteria of greatness – 'wholeness' or totality, 'all-inclusiveness', 'universality'. There is no need to cite again all the passages that imply precisely *interprétable à l'infini*. We can now draw attention to more precise philosophical statements of them.

One of the Cassiciacum *Dialogues* is the *De ordine*. Its theme is stated in the opening sentence: 'to seek out the order of the universe (*ordinem rerum*), and to conform ourselves to it, as befits all existents, to seek out the order of the *whole* (*universitatis*) which contains and governs this world ... '. It has been remarked that all is not orderly in Augustine's book about order, but only the holistic range of the question concerns us here. And towards the end he gives us a *résumé*, 'lest anyone think we have embraced too vast a subject'.[257] The ultimate principle of order is in 'that supreme law and supreme principle of order in the universe'.[258] That supreme law and supreme principle is one of the transcendentals of all being, unity. Every existent is an ordered unity, a one. That metaphysical fact can be explained only by ascending to an ultimate all-ordering, transcendent One. And the ascent is through – again – an *askêsis* of study leading to the wisdom (*sapientia*) 'by which one becomes capable of understanding the universal order, that is, of discerning the two worlds [the material and the spiritual] and the Father himself of the universe, whom the soul knows only in knowing how far it knows Him not'.[259]

Some four years later, in 390, all this is expressed in a much more analytic and systematic way in what amounts to Augustine's first ordered *summa* of his thought to date, the *De vera religione*, written to convert Romanianus, on foot of a promise made to him in the course of his 'protreptic' to him in *Con. acad.* II 3,8.[260] Here, from the opening sentence, the dimensions of 'true philosophy' and of 'true religion' are equivalently defined as identical. 'The way of every good and blessed (*beatae*) life is established in the true religion, in which the one God

256 Longinus, op. cit., I 4.

257 *De Ord.* II 18.

258 Ibid.

259 Ibid.

260 Cf, *De vera rel.* VII 12.

is worshipped, and in which, by reverent purification of spirit, we come to know the Ground and Principle (*principium*) of all existents, the *principium* by which the universe (*universitas*) begins, is completed, and contained.'[261] In Greek 'philosophy' only the Platonists came to that realization,[262] that 'there is one God, superior to our minds, by whom all life and the whole universe was made'[263] – through his Truth, *per ejus Veritatem.*[264] But Platonism failed to achieve the *auctoritas* and the universality of Christianity and its Scriptures.[265] If Plato were asked today how the soul could be purified for the seeing of 'the immutable form of [all] things ... he would reply, I believe, that this can be achieved by no man, or by no human teaching, but only by interior illumination from the Power itself and the Wisdom of God'.[266] The only *Principium* and the only light to it is the One declared in St John's Prologue – the *Principium* through whom 'all things were made, and without whom nothing was made'.[267] It is in this holistic sense that he interprets the Trinity itself as the *Principium* (*arkhê*) of all things. For ... 'we need to know the following three things about every created being: who made it, by what means, and why?'[268] The pre-eminence of Plato and the Platonists is due to the fact that they 'seem to have had a conception of God that enabled them to find in Him the Cause of existence, the Principle of understanding it, and the Order according to which life should be lived'.[269] And that is the rationale of their triple division of philosophy into metaphysics, logic and ethics. All other philosophical systems must yield to the Platonists, who 'recognize the *true* God as the Author of being, the Source of the light of truth about it, and the Dispenser of the beatitude [that is its purpose]'.[270] But do not these three questions (Who? How? Why?) and their answers intimate the revealed Trinity?[271] They do – their very necessity

---

261 Ibid. I 1; *principium* of course translates not only Gen 1:1 and Jn 1:1, but also the age-old Greek term for the ultimate metaphysical ground of reality, '*arkhê* of all things', e.g. Plotinus in *Enn.* I 3, 1; VI 9, 3; VI 9, 5; in its triadic nature of One, Nous and Soul it is replaced by the Christian Trinity, see *Conf.* VII 9, 13 and *De civ. Dei* VIII 4ff – with which cf. *De vera rel.* XVI 32ff.

262 They 'represent the closest approximation to our Christian position', *De civ. Dei* VIII 9.

263 *De vera rel.* II 2.

264 Ibid. III 3.

265 Ibid. III 4ff.

266 Ibid. III 3; 1 Corinthians 1:24; cf. *Conf.* VII 21, 27, in conclusion to his reflections on what St Paul on Christ had to offer, but not the Platonists: 'In astonishing ways these truths penetrated the very core of my being as I read that least of your apostles; I had considered [or read] your works and been stricken with awe (*expaveram*)'.

267 *De vera rel.* III 4.

268 *De civ. Dei.* XI 24; cf. XI 21.

269 Ibid. VIII 4: cf. XI 24f, and *De vera rel.* XVI 32f.

270 *De civ. Dei* VIII 5.

271 See e.g. id. XI 23.

makes creation itself an image of the Trinity.[272] More specifically in the attribution of the respective roles of the Three Persons in Creation. The Father is the source, the Son-and-Word is the means and the light, the Holy Spirit is the purpose – the Good and its correlative Beatitude.[273]

'It is the Trinity, whole and entire, that is intimated in its works. And it is from the same Trinity that the Holy City, the celestial city of the holy angels, derives her origin, her form, and her beatitude. For if we ask *whence* she is, the answer is that it is God who founded her; and if we ask whence her wisdom, the answer is that it is God who illuminates her; and if we ask whence her beatitude, the answer is that it is in God she has her joy. By *subsisting* in God she has her degree of being; by *contemplating* Him she is enlightened; by *cleaving* to him she has joy. She is, she sees, she loves. She is strong in God's eternity, she shines in God's truth, she is blissful in God's goodness.'[274]

* * *

Such are the dimensions, holistic, 'totalizing', infinite indeed, of the cadre within which only, as we have said, Augustine's assertions of the inexhaustible meaning of Scripture, its *mira profunditas*, can be adequately understood. It remains to show, in conclusion, that he does explicitly situate the study of Scripture within such a comprehensive 'philosophical' framework. That can be shown from his own manual on the methodology of Scriptural exegesis, the *De doctrina Christiana*, already referred to. In a way, and within the limits of its purpose, it too is a little *summa* of Augustine's thought, in so far as the axes and outlines of that thought are expressly used here to draw the 'horizon' within which Scripture is to be studied professionally.[275]

The whole first Book is devoted to drawing that horizon – in fact an infinitely receding horizon. And once again it is coloured by Platonist 'philosophy' adapted to the purposes of the 'true philosophy', but it is not to our own purposes to dwell on that here. All learning concerns either existents (things, *res*) or their signifiers (signs, *signa*). Book I will deal with *res*.[276] It goes on to deal with them by establishing the ontological scale of *res*, the great chain of being, as it were, and the

272 Ibid. XI 24ff.

273 Ibid. XI 24.

274 Ibid.; cf. *De vera rel.* XII 26 on the destiny of fallen mankind restored: 'It will return from multiplicity and mutability to the unchanging One, reformed through the Wisdom itself unformed but through whom all things are formed and informed, and it will have joy in God through the Holy Spirit, who is the Gift of God.'

275 And for how insistent he is on 'professionalism', see the Prologue, and II 8,12ff.

276 *De doctrina Christiana* I 2, 2.

corresponding great scale of *values* in the scale of being of the existents. The scale of values is determined by Augustine's fundamental distinction between things to be 'enjoyed' (*frui*) and those to be merely 'used' (*uti*).[277] The terms are defined. 'To "enjoy" something is to cleave to it for its own sake [i.e. its own intrinsic value, as an end in itself]. But to "use" something is to employ it merely as a *means* to the obtaining of that which you love [i.e. because it has its own intrinsic value, and is an end in itself].'[278] The *res* to be enjoyed make us blessed (*beatos*), while the *res* to be merely used are such because they are only the means that keep and sustain us on the way to that blessedness (*beatitudo*), 'in order that we may attain and adhere to the *res* that make us blessed (*beatos*)'.[279]

But in Augustine *beatitudo*, blessedness, is an *absolute* value, the absolute end in itself.[280] It is logical then that only the absolute Reality has this absolute intrinsic value. 'Consequently the things to be "enjoyed" are the Father, the Son and the Holy Spirit, self-identical Trinity, the unique and supreme Reality ... if "Reality" it be and not rather the *Cause* of all realities – if even "Cause" it may be called. For it is not easy to find a name appropriate to such a transcendent Reality ... one God from whom all things, through whom all things, towards whom all things flow.'[281] That is the 'horizon' and that is the whole meaning (*summa*) of Book I, and the whole meaning of Scripture and of God's whole temporal dispensation is to enable us to know this absolute Reality and to attain to its absolute Value.[282]

Such emphasis on absolutes might seem to short-circuit *contingent* realities, with their truth and value, and the range of truth he attributes to Scripture in the passage already quoted from *De doct. Chr.* II 42, 63. We must recall a number of corrective factors. Firstly there is his constant insistence, especially against the Manicheans, that the scale of being is a scale of *degrees* of being, from the highest to the lowest, every level of which has its corresponding degree of truth, goodness and value.[283] We recall too the Trinitarian imagery already referred to in *De civ. Dei* XI 24f. Similarly the supreme creative Wisdom itself pervades all creation, 'reaches with power from end to end of the world ordering all things in beauty'.[284] Created reality is everywhere so transparent to that informing, ordering, and

277 Ibid. I 2, 3.

278 Ibid. I 4, 4.

279 Ibid. I 3, 3.

280 See e.g. earlier references to the 'eternal Sabbath' in which both the *Conf.* and the *De civ. Dei* culminate; and of course the much-quoted *Conf.* I 1,1: 'You have made us oriented to Thyself, and our heart is unquiet until it repose in Thee.'

281 I 5,5; Romans 11:36.

282 I 35, 39.

283 See e.g. *Conf.* VII 11,17; 13,19 and 15,21.

284 *De libero arbitrio*, II 11, 124; cf. Wisdom 8:1.

consequently beautifying Wisdom that it provides one of Augustine's principal proofs for the existence of God, by ascent from the image to the Reality.[285] And its aesthetic dimension is such that von Balthasar can include St Augustine among the great theologians of *glory*.[286]

Finally, in *De doct. Chr.* II 19,19 ff, Augustine sets out at length and in detail 'a matter of supreme importance' as a 'professional qualification' for the study of Scripture – the study of the complete curriculum of the Greco-Roman ideal of liberal education, in the humanities, science, and philosophy. Not of course as though those disciplines were an ultimate end in themselves, but rather as steps intrinsic to the scale of being and truth. They are a necessary propaedeutic in the ascent of the mind to the supreme Being and Truth from which they derive.[287] Understanding is not complete until the searcher understands 'on what *ground* those things are "true" which he has only "sensed" to be true, and on what ground those things are not only true but immutably true which he has understood to be immutably true'.[288] That demands turning round to see all particular and partial truths in the light of 'the ultimate immutable Truth which is *above* the human mind' as the Source of its light.[289] That is the unique God 'from whom he knows that all things have their being'.[290] He who does not know that can appear 'learned' (*doctus*), but by no manner of means 'wise' (*sapiens*)![291]

All this is Platonist-coloured, but Augustine has already been at pains to set it out systematically on a uniquely scriptural foundation in *De doct. Chr.* II 7, 9–11.[292] Its purpose there is, again, to outline the framework within which Scripture is to

285 Id. II 8 ff; and cf. Rom 1:20, also echoing Wisdom 7:22ff.

286 *The Glory of the Lord*, vol. II.

287 Cf. *De ord.* II 10, 28f.; *De musica* VI; the latter 'demonstrates how from corporeal and even spiritual but still mutable rhythms we arrive at the immutable rhythms (*numeri*) which are the attributes of the immutable Truth, so that by those mutable rhythms the invisible perfections of God are revealed to us in their stamp on created things' – *Retractationes*, I 6.

288 *De doct. Chr.* II 38, 57.

289 Ibid.; cf. *Conf.* VII 10, 16.

290 *De doct. Chr.* II 38, 57.

291 Ibid.; cf. Plato, *Rep.* 551bf, and 531f. on 'dialectic', the ascent from the hypothetical axioms of the individual sciences to the ultimate non-hypothetical precondition of truth, the axiom-of-all-axioms, and the pages on it in A. E. Taylor, *Plato* (London, 1960 ed.), 291f.; also Plotinus, *Enn.* I 3, and Augustine himself, already in *De ord.* II, 11, 30f.

292 Described as 'pièce maîtresse de la synthèse augustinienne' in an extended note on the passage in *Oeuvres de Saint Augustin*, vol. XI, Le Magistère Chrétien, text, translation and notes by G. Combès and M. Farges (Paris, 1949), 568–70; see references there to the numerous other *loci* in Augustine on the same theme – the steps of 'ascent'. It should also be observed at this point that the concepts of *veritas* and *sapientia* (Greek *sophia*), which we have used so much, are not only Greek and philosophical but also profoundly biblical, as any concordance shows.

be studied and interpreted, in particular the epistemological (and morally conditioned) levels at which its meaning is to be sought. They are on an ascending scale of seven stages, based on what we have come to know as the seven gifts of the Holy Spirit – taken from Psalm 110:10 and Isaiah 11:2–3. They are, in ascending order: the reverential fear of the Lord, piety, knowledge, fortitude, counsel, understanding, and at the summit, wisdom. Augustine sets out the framework also to make clear which level of interpretation he is going to speak about in his present work – that of *knowledge, scientia*,[293] the third stage.[294]

It is at the fourth and following stages that 'higher' insight begins. The fourth is the turning point, literally a turning, a 'conversion'[295] – away from transient things and towards the eternal, that is, towards the 'unity unchanging and self-identical that is the Trinity.'[296] 'When one has glimpsed it glowing in the distance, within the narrow limits of his capacity, and discovers that the weakness of his sight cannot endure such light',[297] he then enters on the fifth stage – one of deeper spiritual purification.[298] At the sixth stage he 'purifies that eye by which God may be seen – in so far as He can be seen by those who die to this world ... '.[299] At this stage that Light begins to appear more certain (*certior*), and more tolerable (*tolerabilior*), but still only 'through a glass darkly'.[300] The seventh and last step is the ascent to wisdom, 'which gives him the supreme joy (*perfruitur*) of peace and tranquillity',[301] in other words the *beatitudo* that is the concomitant of the supreme *Veritas* and *Sapientia*.[302] '"The fear of the Lord is the beginning of Wisdom" ... From it to transcendent subsistent Wisdom these are the steps ... '.[303]

More than twenty years later, as he approaches the completion of one of his greatest works, speculative, spiritual and psychological, the subject is still that transcendent Wisdom – and based still on Isaiah 11:2–3.[304] 'It is this contemplative wisdom that the Scriptures, in my opinion, call "wisdom" exclusively (*sapientiam proprie*), and specifically distinguished from "knowledge" (*scientia*): the wisdom of man indeed, but acquired only from the One who, by our participation

293 *De doct. Chr.* II 7, 10 and II 8, 11.

294 On the difference between *scientia* and *sapientia* see e.g. *De Trinitate* XII 14, 21ff.

295 *Se avertens convertit* ... .

296 *De doct. Chr.* II 7, 10.

297 Cf. *Conf.* VII 10, 16.

298 *De doct. Chr.* II 7, 11.

299 Ibid.

300 Ibid.; 1 Corinthians 13:12.

301 Ibid.

302 See e.g. *Conf.* X 23, 34, on *beata vita, quae non est nisi gaudium de veritate.*

303 *De doct. Chr.* II 7,11.

304 *De Trinitate* (AD399-419), Book XIV.

in Him, can make the rational and intellectual soul truly wise.'[305] And, extraordinarily in such a work and after such a span of time, he relates that wisdom to the decisive event of his reading Cicero's *Hortensius* some forty years before. The passage is worth quoting, because it gives us the savour of what a 'protreptic' was, and gives us an insight into why this particular one had such a definitive effect on Augustine.

'This is the contemplative wisdom that Cicero commends [although he does not know its source, as Augustine has noted] at the end of his dialogue *Hortensius*, when he says':

> This is our great hope as we ponder night and day, and sharpen the understanding which is the fine point of the mind (*mentis acies*) and take care it does not get blunt, that is to say as we live in philosophy; either that we will have a cheerful sunset to our days when we have completed our tasks, and an untroubled and quiet quenching of life, if this capacity of ours to perceive and be wise is mortal and fleeting; or else, if we have eternal and divine souls, as the ancient philosophers agreed, and they the greatest and by far the most brilliant, we must suppose that the more these souls keep always to their course, that is to reason and to passionate enquiry, and the less they mix themselves up in the tangled vices and errors of men, the easier will be their ascent and return to heaven.[306]

The culminating Book of the *Confessions*, XIII, is also organized in seven stages, based on the seven days of the creation narrative. In their figurative meaning[307] they also are stages of ascent, from the dark formlessness (*informitas*)[308] illumined and informed by the light to which it turned and clove on the first day,[309] up to the 'renewal of the human spirit in [God's] "image and likeness",' so that 'submitting itself to Him alone it needs no human *auctoritas*'.[310] But between those two extremes of darkness and the unmediated light of God's *auctoritas*, there is established the mediated '*auctoritas* of [God's] Book'.[311] And already in

305 Ibid. XIV 19, 26; on the distinction between *scientia* and *sapientia* see also *Conf.* XIII 18, 23.

306 Ibid.; translation, with slight modification, by Edmund Hill, O.P., in *Saint Augustine: The Trinity*, (New York, 1991).

307 Summarized in *Conf.* XIII 34,49.

308 See n. 167, p. 193 to Conf. XII 6,6 above – in the total context of XII 3,3ff, on the *informitas* referred to in Genesis 1:2: *terra erat invisibilis et incomposita*; see also XIII 3,4; 5,6; 12,13, and many other *loci* in Augustine.

309 *Conf.* XIII 3,4.

310 Ibid. XIII 34, 49.

311 Ibid.

its opening two verses the Trinity is glimpsed 'darkly'.[312] For God, who made the heavens and the earth, is the Father. And the 'Beginning' (*Principium*) in which He made them is the '*Principium* of our wisdom, the *Principium* which is your Wisdom born of You, equal to You and coeternal'.[313] And looking further, 'behold, your "Spirit was borne over the waters" ... There, my God, is your Trinity, Father, Son and Holy Spirit, Creator of every creature'.[314]

Augustine repeatedly describes the *auctoritas* of Scripture figuratively as a '*firmament* of authority,' *firmamentum auctoritatis*,[315] an analogy based on the figurative sense of Gen 1:6-8, on the dividing of the waters above the heavens from those below by a firmament or vault.[316] Augustine sees the figurative sense of the waters above and the waters below as referring to the inhabitants of the lower material world and those of the transcendent immaterial heaven. In that higher world the supercelestial hosts of the angels 'do not need to lift their eyes to this firmament [of Scripture] and to get to know your word by reading it. For they always behold your face, and in that face they read your eternal will without utterance in syllables of time'.[317] Not so those who live in the world of time and materiality, on pilgrimage through it, and seeing only in a glass darkly. They need a mediating *auctoritas*. And that is 'the firmament of your Book, the firmament of your ever concordant words, which you set over us by the ministry of mortal men'.[318] By their very mortality the *auctoritas* of the sacred writers has become all the greater and more universal. For while they lived their words were not widely known. But by their death 'the reinforcing firmament (*solidamentum*), the authority of the words You sent out through them, was stretched out sublimely and universally over everything that lies below'.[319] The preachers of this Word of God pass from this life, but 'his Scripture is stretched out over the peoples to the end of time'.[320] And we should complement the life of action in the world by rising to the delights of contemplating that Word of life ... firmly established in the firmament of Scripture, from there to shine on the world, as do the heavenly bodies from the earthly firmament.[321]

---

312 Ibid. XIII 5, 6; cf. 1 Corinthians 13:12.

313 *Conf.* XIII 5, 6.

314 Ibid.; cf. XIII 11, 12.

315 Ibid. XIII 15, 16; cf. 18, 22.

316 Ibid.

317 Ibid. XIII 15, 18.

318 Ibid. XIII 15, 16.

319 Ibid.; and once again, the characteristically personal, lyrical 'confessional' grace-note: 'I know not Lord, I know not any words of such "pure alloy" [Ps 11:6], none that could so powerfully move me to confession ... or call me to worship You for your own sake alone.'

320 *Conf.* XIII 15, 18.

321 Ibid. XIII 18, 22.

Insight into the full dimensions of Scripture's meaning depends precisely on a contemplation based on a distinction parallel to that constant motif of Augustine which we noted earlier; Scripture's fusing of surface simplicity for the simple with inexhaustible depths of meaning for the more intellectually and spiritually advanced. That is the distinction between the 'spiritual' and the 'carnal' (*spiritales et carnales*) members of the Church – for there too 'God has created a "heaven and earth"'![322] The distinction is based on a number of Pauline texts, especially 1 Cor 2:10–3:3 and Rom 7:14. We need not here go into all the complexities of that distinction in Augustine.[323] For our purposes 1 Cor 3:1f suffices – in its total context:[324] 'Brothers, I myself was unable to speak to you as people of the Spirit (*spiritalibus, pneumatikois*): I treated you as people of the senses (*carnalibus, sarkikois*), still infants in Christ. What I fed you with was milk, not solid food, for you were not yet ready for it ... '

The reference to the Spirit is to be given its full value: for, as is clear from both Paul[325] and Augustine, the reference is to a charism, a gift of the Spirit, if not even of mystical insight. 'It is no longer the voice of the Apostle that speaks, but yours in him, You who sent your Spirit upon him from on high, through Him who ascended up on high, and opened the floodgates of his gifts that the rush of the river might make your City joyous', the City for which '"the friend of the Bridegroom" sighs, having already the "first fruits of the Spirit" within himself'.[326] It is in the Pauline context of the charisms of the Spirit that Augustine speaks of the *spiritales* in *Conf.* XIII 18, and distinguishes specifically the 'word of knowledge' from 'the word of wisdom' (1 Cor 12:8). The 'word of knowledge' deals only with those sacred signs (*sacramenta*) that are subject to temporal change. It differs from 'the radiant light of wisdom' as the stars of night differ from the dawning of the day.[327]

It is the charism of the *spiritales* to speak this 'word of wisdom' about the deeper depths of Scripture. Theirs to 'shine in the firmament' that 'the heavens

322 Ibid. XIII 12, 13.

323 See the extensive note to *Conf.* XIII 12, 13f in ed. cit.

324 E.g. 1 Corinthians 2:13: 'We speak not in the learned words of human wisdom (*sapientia, sophia*), but in the way the Spirit teaches us ... '; and cf. 1:13f. on philosophical speculation contrasted with the Wisdom of God.

325 Cf. 1 Corinthians 12–14, and *Conf.* XIII 18,23.

326 *Conf.* XIII 13,14; John 3:29 and Romans 8:23; on 'the first fruits of the Spirit', *spiritus primitias*, see the use of the expression in *Conf.* IX 10,24 to evoke Augustine's and Monica's mystical experience at Ostia: 'While we were talking of these things together and longing for [the region of inexhaustible abundance where You graze Israel for ever on the pastures of Truth], for one brief instant, for one whole beat of the heart, we did come into contact with it; we sighed, and leaving the first fruits of our spirit bound to it, we returned to the time-bound sound of our own voices ... '

327 XIII 18,23.

may recount his glory', and thus 'divide the light of the perfect – though not yet the light of the angels – from the darkness of the little ones – though not the darkness of those without hope'.[328] The *spiritalis* is of the new creation of '"man renewed in the knowledge of God according to the image of Him who created him", and having become *spiritalis* he "judges all things" – all things, that is, which it is permissible to judge – and he himself "is judged by none".'[329] 'All things, that is, which it is permissible to judge!' For even the *spiritales*, even if in authority themselves, 'judge not the spiritual truths which shine "in the firmament": it is not for man to judge so sublime an *auctoritas* ... They may not judge that Book of yours, even when something in it is unclear; rather do we *submit* our understanding to it, and hold it as a certainty that even what is closed to our eyes in it is said with the rightness of Truth'.[330]

And in this matter of 'judging' there is a wider range of implication than meets the eye at once. So often in Augustine what appears to be philosophical is found to be also scriptural, and *vice versa*. Here 'judging' is a scriptural term. But it is also Augustine's technical term in epistemology – and the metaphysical implications he finds in it. We looked at Augustine's epistemology earlier, in particular the argument from the necessity and immutability inherent in any particular truth – best illustrated in mathematical truths[331] – to the requirement of a ground and precondition of that necessity and immutability in an absolute, transcendent Truth, eternal, immutable and unconditioned.[332] The argument becomes a proof of the existence of God, with whom that Truth is identified and who is the ultimate unconditioned 'axiom' of all the merely provisional though apparently 'necessary' axioms on which the various theoretical disciplines hang.[333]

This argument is more immediately intelligible in one of Augustine's favourite areas of its application, in comparative 'judgements' of *value*, as in ethics and aesthetics. To judge that something is morally better or aesthetically more beautiful than another implies immediately a non-empirical, *a priori* criterion of judgement, which by fairly simple analysis is shown to depend on an *absolute* criterion. We see the ethical argument in *De libero arbitrio* II 9,100ff, succinctly stated in II 10,113; and again in *Conf.* X 20,29ff, succinctly in X 23,33. There is a fine statement of the aesthetic argument in *Conf.* VII 17,23:

328 *Conf.* XIII 19,25; Psalm 18:2f.

329 Ibid. XIII 22,32; 1 Corinthians 2:15.

330 Ibid. XIII 23,33.

331 See e.g. *De libero arbitrio* II 8, 79ff.

332 An argument already developed in the *Soliloquia*, II 1, 1ff – *si quid verum est, veritate ubique verum est*, I 15, 27.

333 So already in *Soliloquia* I 8, 15.

> I was seeking to understand on what ground I approved the beauty of corporeal things, and on what principle I made a valid judgement ... when I said: 'This *ought* to be so, that *not* so.' Enquiring then on what *basis* I judged when I judged in this way, I had found the immutable and true eternity of Truth.

He goes on to trace the actual steps in the argument –

> to find out what light suffused the mind when, without hesitation or doubt, 'it proclaimed that the immutable was to be valued above the changing. From where in fact did it know of the immutable at all? For unless it had in some sense known it, the mind could not possibly judge it with such certainty to be valued above the mutable. And in the flash of a trembling glance my mind arrived at *That Which Is* – *id quod est* – absolutely.'

That is the penumbra to Augustine's quoting of Paul's terminology of 'judging'. That is the sense in which, by analogy, Scripture is the 'firmament', the absolute and universal *auctoritas*, under and in whose light the *spiritalis* 'judges all things' – but not Scripture itself, rather does Scripture 'judge' him. Only here below of course, for 'there are other "waters" above this "firmament", I believe, waters immortal and beyond all earthly corruption and transience. May they praise your name!'[334]

* * *

We opened these pages with an 'overture' of sample thematic texts, ancient and modern. It would be appropriate to conclude with a 'coda'. I take one from the late contemporary far-firing Apollo to whom I have already referred more than once – Hans Urs von Balthasar. It is a passage written in this twentieth century that could have been written by Augustine in the fourth.

> Thus we can risk making the general proposition that the meaning of Scripture (where it is in process of development) journeys along with history, and this journeying is attested to not merely externally but in the details of its text. Of course this raises the problem of how this journeying of the word is related to the closing of objective revelation at the end of the apostolic age and to the completeness of the canon of Scripture. The 'closing' as such arises from the definitive and unsurpassable character of the divine Word uttered in Jesus; but the fact that the word is henceforth present in

334 *Conf.* XIII 15,18.

> world history in this fullest form, capable of assimilation and interpretation, is in truth not a 'closing' at all but the widest imaginable 'opening'.[335]

The rainbow arc of which that passage is one earthing spans a space even vaster than that from Balthasar to Augustine. Its other earthing is in the Old Testament itself and in pre-Christian Jewish interpretation of it. And that in two stages. Firstly, it appears to be now accepted (*sit venia profano!*) that the Old Testament Scriptures as we have them are the end-product of a process of revising and editing that began already in the sixth-century BC post-exilic period. 'This means that the beginnings of scriptural interpretation are to be looked for within the Scriptures themselves. Scholars now recognize that the making of the Scriptures was already a hermeneutical process in which earlier biblical materials were rewritten in order to make them intelligible and applicable to later situations.'[336]

The second stage in this Jewish, and pre-Christian, hermeneutical process was its systematizing in the professional *Midrash* exegesis of the established texts of the Old Testament. Its core significance for our present purposes is that same ever-inexhaustible openness of Scripture to that ever-inexhaustible interpretability that has been our theme. And its rationale links up with much that we have been saying on that theme – even with certain contemporary approaches to metaphysics.[337] In the first place it is based on the realization that the word of revelation is the Word of God, and therefore of the Transcendent and Infinite – and therefore in the written Scriptures adapted to and 'translated' into the mode of the finite idiom of human language, which inevitably 'conceals' as much it 'reveals' of the infinity and the mystery and the inexhaustibility of the transcendent Word and Reality in the silent depths of which it originates.[338] Therefore, 'Once God has spoken; twice have I heard this'.[339]

In the second place there is the often neglected linguistic factor, in the verbal and syntactical structures of the Hebrew language in which the Old Testament

335 *Theo-Drama*, vol. II (San Francisco, 1990), 105 – italics mine, in a section on Theodramatic Hermenutics, 91f.; cf. n. 174, p. 194 above.

336 Gerald L. Bruns, 'Midrash and Allegory: The Beginnings of Scriptural Interpretation', in Robert Alter and Frank Kermode (eds.), *The Literary Guide to the Bible* (London, Fontana Press ed. 1989), 626; see 638 for remarks on St Augustine in that line.

337 I have in mind such philosophers as Jaspers and Heidegger, with their sense of 'comprehensive', enveloping (*englobant*), transcendent-immanent Being, and of man as the *locus* of 'openness' to it, as it is revealed-and-concealed in its 'cyphers'; cf. also von Balthasar again, in *The Glory of the Lord, passim.*

338 See e.g. Emmanuel Levinas, 'Revelation in the Jewish Tradition', in Seán Hand (ed.), *The Levinas Reader* (Oxford U.K. and Cambridge U.S.A., 1992 repr.), 205f; it is worth noting that Levinas, like Augustine, is a notable philosopher as well as a commentator on Scripture.

339 Psalm 62:11, quoted by Levinas, art. cit., 194.

Scriptures were written, so different from the analytic, unidimensional, linear logic of our western languages. 'We must leave the translations, however worthy of respect they may be, and return to the Hebraic text to reveal the strange and mysterious ambiguity or polysemy which the Hebraic syntax permits. In this syntax the words co-exist, rather than falling immediately into structures of co-ordination and sub-ordination, unlike the dominant tendency in the "developed" or functional languages.'[340]

Consequently –

> the specifically Jewish exegesis of the Scriptures is punctuated by these concerns: the distinction between the obvious meaning and the one which has to be deciphered, the search for this buried meaning and the one which lies deeper still, contained within the first. There is not one verse, not one word, of the Old Testament, if the reading is the religious one that takes it as Revelation, that does not open up an entire world, unsuspected at first, in which the text to be read is embedded ... These scribes and doctors ... would try to extort from the letters all the meanings they can carry or bring to our attention, just as if the letters were the folded wings of the Holy Spirit, and could be unfurled to show all the horizons which the flight of the Spirit can embrace.[341]

340 Levinas, art. cit., 193; cf. the professional qualifications laid down by Augustine in *De doct. Chr.* II 11, 16.

341 Levinas, ibid., 194; it may be noted too that in the context of this ever-inexhaustible interpretability Levinas in this article also addresses the necessary question of how to give reason its rights (like Augustine), and how to avoid subjectivity in interpretation. Cf. Josef Pieper, 'What does it mean to say "God Speaks"?', in *Problems of Modern Faith: Essays and Addresses* (Chicago, 1985), 117–48.

EARLY IRISH CHRISTIAN LITERATURE

HIBERNO-LATIN CHRISTIAN LITERATURE

CONTEXT AND BEGINNINGS

The written literature of Ireland actually begins in Latin. Despite a rich oral literary tradition, later to be written down under the influence of Latin and Christianity, there was no commodious system of writing in Ireland until in the fifth century the language of Christianity and the Empire of Rome came with St Patrick. His Latin *Confession* and *Letter to Coroticus* constitute the earliest works of Irish literature. It is not colonial to claim them as Irish, though written by a man in exile from another country. Patrick himself, from Romano-Celtic Britain, was probably of Celtic blood. He was certainly a Celt in character, fiery, religious, visionary, mystical. And like many a later Briton he became Irish of the Irish among his adopted people. His writings are steeped in that sentiment. In one pithy sentence he positively asserts it by implication. A sentence addressed to his opponents in Britain. A sentence that also utters for the first time in literature another sentiment that has often since been thought but rarely so well expressed. 'To them it is annoying and unbecoming that we should be the Irishry!'[1]

Before sampling that beginning of Irish literature it will be helpful if we sketch the historical background to it, in Celtic Ireland, Romano-Celtic Britain, and imperial Roman Europe. Two dramatic moments in history frame the picture for us.

The first is a moment in the definitive Roman conquest of Britain, in a series of campaigns by the Roman commander Agricola from 77 to 84 AD. By the fifth year of campaigning in 81 or 82, Agricola had advanced probably to the coast of Cumberland. From there he looked westwards across the narrow sea. We can leave the vivid view to the Roman historian Tacitus:[2]

> The whole side of Britain that faces Ireland was lined with his forces. But his motive was rather hope than fear. Ireland, lying between Britain and Spain, and easily accessible also from the Gallic sea, might, to great general advantage, bind in close union that powerful section of the empire. Ireland is small in extent as compared to Britain, but larger than the islands of

1 *Letter to Coroticus*, 16.

2 *Agricola*, 24 (Penguin Classics).

> the Mediterranean. In soil, in climate and in the character and civilization of its inhabitants it is much like Britain. Its approaches and harbours are tolerably well known from merchants who trade there. Agricola had given a welcome to an Irish prince, who had been driven from home by a rebellion; nominally a friend, he might be used as a pawn in the game. I have often heard Agricola say that Ireland could be reduced and held by a single legion and a few auxiliaries, and that the conquest would also pay from the point of view of Britain, if Roman arms were in evidence on every side and liberty vanished off the map.

It was not to be. As some commentator has remarked, Agricola was the first of many optimists about Ireland. The Roman legions never came across the sea to Ireland. But then neither did the language and literature of Rome, the material civilization and organization of Rome, nor the intellectual discipline of Greco-Roman Europe. Ireland remained the only surviving nation of that Celtic race and culture that was once nearly co-extensive with Western Europe – until the Romans came and overlaid it all.

That is why 'until the coming of Patrick speech was not suffered to be given in Ireland but to three: to a historian for narration and the relating of tales; to a poet for eulogy and satire; to a brehon lawyer for giving judgement according to the old tradition and precedent. But after the coming of Patrick every speech of these men is under the yoke of the white [blessed] language, that is, the Scriptures'[3] – i.e. Latin, and written.

The second of the two dramatic moments of our historical backdrop belongs to the times of Patrick's coming. For our present purposes let us accept the traditional dates of his mission in Ireland, 432–61. In 432 he would be in his late forties, born therefore about 385. His lifespan then coincides with the last stages of the fall of the Roman Empire in the West – from internal maladies and the external blows of invaders in flood-tide across the frontiers. The last western Emperor was deposed fifteen years after Patrick's death. Patrick was a young man of twenty-five in 410 when the unbelievable happened. Rome, the city they already called eternal, was put to fire and sword by Alaric and his Goths.

That was also the year in which Rome decided she could no longer defend Britain – and told them so – from invading Picts, Scots [Irish], Angles and Saxons. Bede provides a convenient and vivid picture of the consequences.[4]

3 Quoted from old Irish by Robin Flower, *The Irish Tradition* (Oxford, 1947), 4.

4 *A History of the English Church and People*, 1.12 (Penguin Classics).

> On the departure of the Romans, the Picts and Scots, learning that they would not return, were quick to attack, and becoming bolder than ever, occupied all the northern and outer part of the island up to the wall. Here a dispirited British garrison stationed on the fortifications pined in terror night and day, while from beyond the wall the enemy constantly harassed them with hooked weapons, dragging the cowardly defenders down from their wall, and dashing them to the ground.
>
> At length the Britons abandoned their cities and wall and fled in disorder. Pursued by their foes, the slaughter was more ghastly than ever before, and the wretched citizens were torn in pieces by their enemies, as lambs are torn by wild beasts. They were driven from their homes, and sought to save themselves from starvation by robbery and violence against one another, their own internal anarchy adding to the miseries caused by others, until there was no food left in the whole land except whatever could be obtained by hunting.

There we get a glimpse of the times and conditions in which the sixteen-year-old Patrick was first taken to Ireland as a slave, of the conditions in which on escaping back to Britain after six years he could walk twenty-eight days through deserted country,[5] of the conditions which, many decades later, drew from the missionary bishop the burning *Letter to Coroticus*, chieftain of the raiding Picts and Scots who slaughtered Patrick's freshly anointed Irish Christians or sold them into slavery.

Out of such dark times did Patrick write. In a world breaking down, where an ancient civilization in decline was being given the *coup de grâce* by barbarians on the march, where an already ancient Christianity was being overrun by the resurgent heathen. A world in which language itself was breaking down, the universal language of Western Europe, Latin the once stiff-jointed medium of the Seven Hills, enriched and refined into subtlety over a thousand years and forged into the *Romani sermonis maiestas*.

This matter of language is relevant to the understanding of Patrick. His often seemingly dim wrestlings with Latin are mostly not due at all to his own much-professed rusticity. His Latin is 'bad' only by the standards of a too academic classicism. His Latin is the Latin of his day, 'as she was spoke' – and often written. Broken down, of course, but clear enough once its idiom is understood. What opacity remains we may ascribe to the conditions of the text, to the quest for brevity that becomes obscure, and to that running Pauline intensity that sets thought and feeling out of synchromesh with syntax.

5 *Confession*, 19.

GENRES OF THE LITERATURE

Although the vernacular took over in Ireland as the literary medium earlier than elsewhere, Irish Christianity did leave a considerable body of writing in Latin,[6] and of a great variety. But like much of Irish civilization it has not all survived, or only in fragmentary form, much of it scattered through the ancient libraries of Europe, in the places to which it wandered with the Irish monks and scholars, or in which they actually wrote it. It is beyond our present scope to survey all of that.[7] Our business is with religion. We shall confine ourselves to that, and within that to important mainline works.

Chronologically those works will take us from the beginnings of Christianity and Latin literature in Ireland down to the twelfth century – the moment of one of the reforms in Irish Christianity. About works extending over such an extended period one thing should be noted at once, as we shall not be constantly referring to it. Our concern here is with the nature and flavour of those works as representative of *Celtic Christianity*, of 'the Celtic *fringe*', as the phrase has it. This does not mean that they are *only* 'insular'. They are European-influenced – as had to be the case, given the sources of Irish Christianity. Patrick himself was certainly trained in France. In turn they influenced Europe,[8] sometimes profoundly, as we shall note. As again had to be the case, given the *leitmotiv* of Irish Christianity and its learning for centuries – to voyage for Christ, *peregrinari pro Christo.*

In kind, those works cover most of the important genres of Christian literature. And that is the organization I propose to follow, keeping also to a chronological sequence.

In St Patrick's *Confession* we have one of the two most famous examples of a genre which owes its impulse and origins to Judeo-Christianity, rooted as it is deep down into the Old Testament sense of man before God, and deep down into the enhanced sense of man's inner life that emerged with Christianity, the sense of the abyss of the human soul, the *abyssus humanae conscientiae*, as St Augustine sounded and phrased it. And *qua* 'confession', as I have briefly explained the genre, Patrick's does bear comparison with the *Confessions* of Augustine. And indeed, quite apart from hints in the text, it is hardly conceivable that without the example of Augustine he should have so explicitly written in the genre. 'Behold, again and again I would set down the words of my confession ... This is my confession before I die.'[9]

6 For major texts, many in the course of editing and publication, with translation, by the Dublin Institute for Advanced Studies, see the series *Scriptores Latini Hiberniae* (S.L.H.).

7 See chapters VI and VII of Kenney, *Sources for the Early History of Ireland*, vol. I.

8 See e.g. Ludwig Bieler, *Ireland, Harbinger of the Middle Ages* (OUP, 1963).

9 *Confession*, 61–2.

We have lives of the Irish saints, including two of St Patrick.[10] Hagiography, of course, is a genre not of the most inspiring as learned from Europe. But even that genre occasionally took on a particular coloration in Ireland. And one particular example is positively beautiful, the most beautiful, I should think, in the genre anywhere. And, as a bonus, it must even be largely true – as true as the traditions about St Francis, however strange, that produced the *Fioretti*. No such portrait of a man could emerge, and in a very Celtic tone, except from the living form. I refer to Adamnan's *Life of Columba* of Iona.[11] Columba from 'Derry all full of white angels', who in 565, the year Justinian died in Constantinople, founded the famous community from which half of Britain was re-Christianized. And so much in Celtic colours that the somewhat self-satisfied Anglo-Saxon Bede, while not as radical as Coroticus, certainly has a superiority complex towards the Celts and their Christianity.

If we could limit ourselves to Adamnan's *Life of Columba* that alone would give us an object lesson in all that is best and beautiful and 'Celtic' in Celtic Christianity. As also an illustration of the reasons why its spirit is so often compared to the Franciscan. I have mentioned the *Fioretti*.

The spirit of St Columba is a spirit which, like that of St Francis, combines, and ranges between, the two poles of earth and Heaven, between what we might call for want of better terms, a mystique and a mysticism. A mystique of the natural world and a mysticism towards its Creator.

Like the typical Irish saint, he sought the exile and silence of the hermitage, the 'desert', the 'desert of God' as they called it, the *díseart Dé*. But never to the deadening of their Celtic sense of the beauty of nature, so prominent in indigenous Irish literature, and which produced such gems of nature poetry in Old Irish. 'Let us adore the Lord, /maker of wondrous works, /great bright heaven with its

10 By Muirchú and Tírechán, both seventh-century. Both in Ludwig Bieler, *The Patrician Texts in the Book of Armagh* (S.L.H. vol. X). Muirchú informs us that his only predecessor in the genre of Ireland was Cogitosus, who wrote a life of St Brigid of Kildare.
In both Muirchú and Tírechán we have some striking examples of one aspect of Irish hagiography, the coloration of Lives of the Saints by the indigenous sagas. Tírechán is deeply imbued with another Irish characteristic, the cultivation of the traditional lore of famous sites and ancient places. His work is not so much a Life of St Patrick as a gathering of all the traditions of places associated with him. It is the adaptation to hagiographical purposes of the indigenous genre of the *dindshenchas*. Tírechán had good reason to be interested. He came from the region around the most famous place of all, the Wood of Foclut, 'by the western sea', where Patrick must have served his six years of captivity, and whence he heard the call in a vision to come again to Ireland (*Confession*, 23).

11 Text and translation by A. O. and M. O. Anderson, *Adomnan's Life of Columba* (London and New York, 1961). Adamnan was a kinsman of Columba. Died in 704 as Abbot of Iona. Author also of a contemporary description of a visit to the Holy Land, as recounted to him by a French bishop (*De Locis Sanctis*, ed. Denis Meehan in SLH vol. III).

angels, /the white-waved sea on the earth'.[12] The aura that surrounds Columba is one of a love and tenderness and *sympathie* towards all creatures great and small, the weary stormbird or the elements of earth and sea and sky. Famous is the episode in his approaching death, (an account of a Saint's death in itself unsurpassed in hagiography), when the old white horse that used to carry the milk-pail came up and wept into his lap. Beautiful too his gesture when he told his monks of his approaching death – his blessing of the whole island. '"My sons, I know that from this day forward you will never more be able to see my face within this little plain." When he saw that they were greatly saddened by hearing this, he tried to comfort them as far as might be, and raising both his holy hands he blessed all this island of ours ... '[13]

In a word, outside the *Odyssey* I know of no piece of literature where one so inhales the tang of the earth and the wind and the sea and the islands as around Columba's isle of Iona in Adamnan's *Life*.

This mystique of the earth not just because nature is 'natural', but because it is open and translucent to the *super*natural. A trait of even the pre-Christian Celtic, as we shall explain later.

And hence the other pole of the spirit of Columba, the mystical, as I have called it, loosely but also in its strictly valid sense. He was a man of higher spiritual experiences, a man of prayer, and, as the Irish used to say, a man who had 'power'. The three Books of the Life are divided into prophecies, miracles, and phenomena of light and angelic visitations.

Now this of course is 'hagiography', but it is also a spiritual climate. A climate where we see striking parallels to the phenomena attaching to the tradition of St Francis and his early followers. And critical history has no more right to reject *all* the phenomena in the one case than it has in the other. And in any case, even if the world were not like that, even the world of the saints, would we not *like* it to be so in our dreaming?! Certainly the Celts did, and the followers of St Columba and St Francis.

There is one mystical experience recounted of Columba – authentic or borrowed?! – that bridges the two poles of his spirituality. It also makes him one of the company of a few saints of whom the same experience is told – St Benedict, the Franciscan Brother John, Julian of Norwich, and others I am sure I do not know of.

Is prophecy of the future possible? And perception of things absent? Yes, according to Adamnan, if we believe the words of St Paul, that 'he who clings to the Lord is one spirit'. 'So too, as this holy man of the Lord, Columba, himself admitted to a few brothers who once questioned him closely about this very thing,

12 From the ninth-century Irish.

13 *Life*, 2.28, ed. cit.

in some speculations made with divine favour the scope of his mind was miraculously enlarged and he saw plainly, and contemplated, even the whole world as it were caught up in one ray of the sun.'[14]

***

We have also the genre of the Sermon or Instruction. The most notable example is the series of Sermons or Instructions by Columbanus, who voyaged from Bangor to France, Germany, Switzerland and Italy, to found and end his days in the monastery at Bobbio. In them we find that blend of the Celtic and the European that I referred to earlier.

The Celtic in him is both general and particular. That is to say, it pertains both to the background and to the special temper of the man. Columbanus was not only a Celtic Christian but a 'twice-born' one as well. He underwent some profound 'conversion' experience in his youth. We can imagine what metal this produced when fused with his own intense, fiery and fearless temperament. No Irish saint was ever more consumed by 'zeal for thy house', more restlessly driven by the Celtic longing *peregrinari pro Christo.*[15]

With all that he was a man of imagination and sentiment. The imagination comes out in his image-strewn language, in his ability to paint a scene or make the abstract concretely vivid. The sentiment is seen in his affection for people and places, in the sadness of disappointments and partings.

But the imagination and the sentiment go much deeper than the surface of things. If it be true of the Celts that 'all their songs are sad', none ever felt a sadder interior melody than Columbanus. He has a Pascalian sense of the *misère* of the human condition, a Celtic as well as a metaphysical sense of the transience and relativity and ultimate unreality of the visible world.[16] 'O human life, feeble and mortal, how many have you deceived, beguiled and blinded! While you fly you are nothing, while you are seen you are like a shadow, while you arise you are but smoke ...' (*Serm.* 5.1). 'What, I ask, is the difference between what I saw yesterday and dreamt this night? Do they not seem to you today to be equally unreal?' (*Serm.* 6.1)

It is not surprising that reality for him is elsewhere. 'I shall hasten towards death that there I may see sure things and true, and all things together in one, which is impossible for me here.' (*Serm.* 6.1) So the complement to his sense of

14 Ibid., 1.1.

15 There is a vivid Life of him by Jonas, a seventh-century monk of Bobbio (ed. by Krusch in *Monumenta Germaniae Historica*). See also Tomás Ó Fiaich, *Columbanus in his own Words* (Dublin, 1974). Text and translation of his writings by G. S. M. Walker, *Sancti Columbani Opera* (S.L.H. vol. II), from which I take the quotations.

16 One of his poems is 'On the World's Impermanence'.

misère is his *Sehnsucht* for God and Heaven – as the heroes of both pre-Christian and Christianized Irish tales voyaged in search of the Island of Delights or the Land of Promise of the Saints. 'Wretched man that I am, if there I shall not see life, which I never see [here] in its truth; for it must be true there, where eternity dwells.' (*Serm.* 6.2)

Truth and reality are 'over there'... But over there too the ultimate *unreality*, the fulfilling of the unreality here in the ultimate negativity of Hell. This is the other pole of Columbanus's sense of the human condition. Both poles, as we shall see, are prominent in the Irish tradition – from the old vision literature to James Joyce's Retreat, with its famous sermon on Hell (answering, it should be noted, to his own private sense of it!) and its subsequent brief season in Heaven.[17]

Add to all this that Columbanus is an artist and a poet – in temper and performance. His poetry shows it, but also his prose. Not even Augustine in his *Confessions* rises to higher levels of sustained stylistic eloquence than does Columbanus at high points in his *Sermons*.

I said that this Celt was European too. I am not referring to his work and influence in Europe.[18] Rather to that organizing and controlling intellect, the lack of which has often left the products of Celtic imagination unstructured. In his Sermons, Columbanus shows his intellect not only in the ordering of his theme within each instruction but also in the sequence of themes from Sermon to Sermon. His favourite metaphor is the Christian life as a road and a journey. In the order of his tracing of the journey, our end is in our beginning. ' ... Our doctrine should commence from that point whence all that is arises ... ', that is from God, 'wholly invisible, inconceivable, ineffable, whose property it is ever to exist...' (*Serm.* 1.1). The final Sermon ends with a lyrically intense and longing invocation of God that constitutes one of the great mystical passages in any literature.

***

Hiberno-Latin has made a distinguished contribution to the great corpus of another specifically Christian literary genre, religious poetry born of the Christian vision of reality, and the hymnody directly related to the Christian liturgy.[19] A specifically Christian genre because we can trace its historical emergence in Greek and Latin Christianity. In the West the genre first found fitting form and style in

17 In *Portrait of the Artist as a Young Man.*

18 See e.g. M. M. Dubois, *St Columban. A Pioneer of Western Civilization* (Dublin, 1961).

19 Two important sources survive. The seventh-century *Antiphonary of Bangor* (ed. Warren in the Henry Bradshaw Society series). And the eleventh-century Irish *Liber Hymnorum* (ed. Bernard and Atkinson in the same series). See also Michael Curran, *The Antiphonary of Bangor and the Early Irish Monastic Liturgy* (Irish Academic Press, 1984).

the hymns by Ambrose of Milan. There is a precious passage in St Augustine's *Confessions*[20] describing the occasion on which Ambrose, 'after the manner of the Eastern churches', introduced 'this kind of consolation and exultation', the singing of hymns and psalms in church. 'The custom has been retained from that day to this, and has been imitated by many. Indeed in almost all congregations throughout the world.' We can also trace how the style and forms of Christian poetry and hymnody were determined by its various functions. The Sequence is the most remarkably beautiful and original example of this. And there is good reason to believe that this form first attained its marvellous verbal music and its symmetries of feeling, thought and structure under Irish influence. That is, as we see it in the Sequences of Notker of St Gall, an Irish foundation by the companion of Columbanus after whom it is named, where Notker had an Irish teacher.

For the unique formal quality of Hiberno-Latin hymns at their best is in their verbal music. The genre of course the Irish learned from Europe. Metres also, and to some extent the impulse to rhyme – which in the Latin language first emerges in Christian poetry. Of continental Christian Latin poetry it has been said that, until the Christian poets introduced rhyme and new accentual rhythms, nobody could have imagined, on the basis of classical pagan poetry, what enchanting music lay unsounded in the language. It sounded now because its strings vibrated to a new melody, the 'interior melody' of those new depths of interior life mentioned earlier. But nothing had been heard yet, so to speak, until the Irish plucked the strings of their acquired instrument. Even the best rhyming Christian Latin poetry on the Continent is a taste mechanical beside the subtleties of sound woven by the Irish in filigree patterns of alliteration, assonance and rhyme – end-rhyme and internal rhyme.

Whence did they get the impulse and the skills? We can see from very early in the Irish tradition the magic they felt in music and their magical genius for it. It is one of the few qualities of any kind, not to mention genius, for which the Irish are given credit by Gerald of Wales,[21] that outstanding medieval Anglo-Norman qualifier for the sardonic sentence quoted earlier from Patrick's *Letter to Coroticus*. And to this day a gusto for the music of language is thought to be very Celtic in general and Irish in particular. What is certainly true is that the forms and music of Hiberno-Latin poetry are closely parallel to those of poetry in the early Irish vernacular.

Further there are certain qualities of that vernacular itself, at least as the poets use it, which have clearly come across into the way the religious poets use the Latin language. It gives a uniquely Irish quality to the best of their compositions.

20 9.7.

21 In his *Topographia Hibernica* (*History and Topography of Ireland*, Penguin Classics, ch. 94).

Early Irish could be very strict and concise in structure, asyntactical, exclamatory. With that quality of the language went a parallel quality in the Celtic way of seeing and stating, an economy of details, a concentration on the simple, the essential and the vivid, a tendency to state core facts and pass on rather than elaborate and develop into drawn-out chains of argument or doctrine. Both these qualities, in the language and the users of it, are surprising given the conventional Celtic reputation for rhetoric. But they are none the less true. And the result, both in Irish and in Latin, is poetry of a very special beauty in both content and form, a poetry that outdoes the Roman in the well-known genius of Latin for conciseness and lapidarity. The result is a restrained pointillism, a grave and strong simplicity, ballasted but limpid,

Here is an example translated from the old Irish.[22]

My tidings for you: the stag bells.
Winter snows, summer is gone.
Wind high and cold, low the sun.
Short his course, sea running high.
Deep-red the bracken, its shape all gone –
The wild-goose has raised his wonted cry.
Cold has caught the wings of birds;
Season of ice – these are my tidings.

And even this is wordy by comparison with the linguistic economy of the original – and lacks its subtle rhyme and alliteration.

And here is a stanza to God from a Hiberno-Latin hymn in the *Antiphonary of Bangor.*

Universorum
Fontis jubar luminum
Aethereorum
Et orbi lucentium.

Brightness of the fount of every light
shining from heaven on the world.

For tone, mood and spirituality the Celtic background also provided a mould and world-view into which Christian Latin poetry could easily fit. The native Irish temperament had a profoundly religious view of the universe. Earlier I connected the otherworldly *Sehnsucht* of St Columbanus to something already native

22 Quoted from Kuno Meyer, *Selections from Ancient Irish Poetry* (London, 1959).

to the Celtic temper, a kind of natural Platonism in its sense of a world 'beyond' the present, 'behind' appearances. But unlike Plato that 'other' world is felt to be near at hand. A trembling of the veil and it can appear, or the one around us disappear. Native Irish literature is often characteristically unquiet with a sense of the relativity of time and space and appearances.[23] The seeming solid world is unstable. One set of appearances can metamorphose into another – as in the magical verses from *The Voyage of Bran* that I refer to later. Yeats is still a master in catching the mood. In an early poem, *The Song of Wandering Aengus*, 'a little silver trout' is caught from the stream.

> When I had laid it on the floor
> I went to blow the fire aflame.
> And something rustled on the floor,
> And someone called me by my name:
> It had become a glimmering girl
> With apple blossom in her hair
> Who called me by my name and ran
> And faded through the brightening air.

At the religious level, this cast of feeling generates a sense of sacrality in which 'all things are filled with God', or gods – in a pagan pantheism or a Christian panentheism of omnipresence. Here is a medieval example from Irish:[24]

> I am the wind which breathes upon the sea,
> I am the wave of the ocean,
> I am the murmur of the billows ...
> I am a beam of the sun ...
> I am a salmon in the water,
> I am a lake in the plain,
> I am a word of knowledge ...
> I am the God who created the fire in the head ...

And here is a stanza from the Latin of St Columba's *Altus Prosator*,[25] a long poem on creation.

23 Which in James Joyce still gives this impression. See also his theory of 'epiphany' in *Stephen Hero*. Compare too the nature of Celtic art – non-representational, non-classical and – dare we say it! – romantic. Still so in the painting of Jack B. Yeats.

24 Quoted from Patrick Murray (ed.), *The Deer's Cry. A Treasury of Irish Religious Verse* (Dublin, 1986).

25 In the *Liber Hymnorum*.

From the divine powers of the great God is suspended
the globe of the earth, and thereto is appended
the circle of the great deep,
sustained by the strong hand of almighty God;
promontories and rocks upholding that deep,
with columns like bars on solid foundations
immovable ...

It is a way of seeing the world which makes nature poetry in the Irish language the earliest and the freshest in any vernacular, fresher than anything in classical Greek or Latin lyric for that matter. Firstly because nature itself is seen with the natural eye in the concrete detail that was also a Celtic characteristic, despite the modern Celtic reputation for the mistily mystical and the vaguely twilit. Secondly because nature is also [seen] *through*, in its transparence to the Divine. As only St Francis elsewhere saw it. And with the same faculty of perception, a *spiritual* eye washed clean and clear to clarity of seeing by concentration and contemplation.[26]

But it is not only in poetry that we see this spiritualized vision of reality. I have already suggested that it irradiates the spiritual aura that envelops St Columba of Iona, Franciscan *avant la lettre*. It is also the background to a moment in the most beautiful and artistically elaborated episode in Tírechán's Life of St Patrick. 'God above heaven and in heaven and under heaven; he has his dwelling in heaven and earth and sea and in everything that is in them; he breathes in all things and makes all things live, surpasses all things, sustains all things; he illumines the light of the sun, he consolidates the light of the night and the stars ... ' (ch. 26).

***

We have reached a cosmic range in those last remarks. We noted it earlier in Columbanus, in the 'totalizing' framework of his religious instruction, a journey from the Beginning back to the Beginning, from God the source and ground of existence back to God the end and fulfilment of existence. It is an appropriate moment to introduce John Scotus Eriugena, the ninth-century Irish philosopher theologian who taught and wrote in post-Carolingian France. We shall not have

26 Compare still in modern times Joseph Mary Plunkett:

I see His blood upon the rose
    And in the stars the glory of His eyes.
His body gleams amid eternal snows,
    His tears fall from the skies.

the space to say much about him – he is too big for our scope. But it would be inappropriate not to mention him at all. We are surveying genres, and philosophical theology is an important one, even if it goes beyond the literary. And in the matter of 'totalizing' range of reflection, his range is the most elaborate and totalizing that early Christian Ireland produced. Or early Christian Europe for that matter. A barbarian from the ends of the earth was how a continental contemporary described him. But his major work has been described as the most impressive piece of philosophical writing between the ages of Augustine and Thomas Aquinas.

The major work in question is entitled *On the Division of Nature* (*De Divisione Naturae*).[27] The 'nature' in question is the whole of reality, from the Creator down to the lowest limits of the created. And the 'division' refers to the classifications and grades of reality within those 'totalizing' cadres.

'Gyring in a gyre the Spirit goes forth and [then] comes back to its own place.' We might think it is Yeats, but Eriugena is quoting Ecclesiastes 1.6.[28] It is a good motif to indicate theme and range. For the theme is all existence as seen in relation to God, the Beginning, the Middle and the End of all that exists. A way of putting it which of course he owes to Platonism as well as to Scripture. 'He is the causal Beginning of all those things, and the essential Middle which fulfils them, and the End in which they are consummated and which brings all movement to rest ... '.[29]

This of course is Neoplatonism. It echoes a pattern of movement, from source unto source, which is one of the great patterns of speculation we owe to Platonism in thought's struggle to net and order the universe. A triple movement: outgoing from Source, turning or 'conversion', return to Source.

It is, however, Christian Platonism. Eriugena learned it through reading and translating the great Greek Christian Platonist Fathers of the Eastern Church. And one of the mysteries about the achievement of Eriugena is where he learned his own Greek, almost the only man in Latin Europe at the time to have achieved such mastery of that language – in Ireland or on the Continent? The effect the Christian Platonist Greek Fathers had upon him can perhaps be explained by that kind of natural Platonism of the Celtic world-view that I mentioned earlier. Sheldon-Williams writes somewhere that 'the effect of their influence upon him was to bring him as wholly into the Greek tradition as if he had been a Byzantine writing in Greek, and to make of him the agent through whom the Western world came into this valuable inheritance'. (And in passing we might remark that as far as Christianity is concerned it has not yet come into that inheritance.)

27 In course of publication in S.L.H., the first volumes being by I. P. Sheldon-Williams.

28 Page 166 of S.L.H., vol. XI.

29 Ibid., 32.

To explain the way his own genius caught fire from the Greek Christian contact, perhaps we can point to something more precise than that natural Celtic Platonism. It has been observed that one strand in early Irish Christian writing is a fondness precisely for cosmological speculation. One of the earliest Hiberno-Latin poems is the *Altus Prosator* of Columba, quoted already. It is in fact a kind of little cosmological epic of the origin, history and destiny of creation. From its issuing from the hands of the High Creator, the *Altus Prosator*, to its consummation in destruction or transformation at the end of time, when for mankind there will remain but the two ultimates, Hell and heavenly glory. It runs the whole gamut of the cosmic epic, the creation and fall of choirs of angels, the creation of the rich harmony of the complex universe (*mundi machinam ... et harmoniam*), the heavens and the earth, the stars and the great luminaries of the sky – at the making of which the faithful angels sang to the glory of the Creator for the marvellous making of the whole immensity (*factura pro mirabili/ immensae molis*). And so on down to the end of time, at which point the concluding stanzas give us one of the great treatments of the perennial Judeo-Christian theme of the Last Judgement. And interestingly the author of all this seems also to have caught fire from a contact with the East – the Jewish-Hellenistic *farrago* of the apocryphal Book of Enoch.

One notices this 'totalizing' tendency in other ways too in Hiberno-Latin poems. For instance hymns to or poems about Christ tend to tell the *whole* story, to set him in the context of the complete cosmic epic of creation, Fall, Incarnation, redemption and consummation.

Relevant also in the Celtic background is the Irish contribution to the literature of visions, transcendent cosmic visions that is, the journey through Hell, Purgatory and Heaven that was to culminate in the cosmic epic of Dante. In Eriugena's own treatment of the 'beyond' – naturally very 'demythologizing' – there are some indications that he was familiar with this kind of material. But to it we come later.

Relevant too is that Celtic intensity of religious longing, that *desiderium* that we have noted many times already. I have referred to Eriugena as a 'philosopher theologian'. This because there is no speculative theology without philosophy, and in those days there was no compartmentalized philosophy outside a theological setting. In fact Eriugena sets the whole work in the traditional frame for 'totalizing' questions, a commentary on the creation narrative in the Book of Genesis.

But in none of these roles is Eriugena merely 'academic'. He is fired by his own drive, religious as well as metaphysical. He is one of those types called pilgrims of the absolute. And the arrow he shoots is tipped with the mystical. After St John's own Prologue to his Gospel, it is hard to find anything more inspired, more full of fire and light, than Eriugena's Homily on that Prologue.

One magnificent excursus into prayer towards the end of *The Division of Nature* makes explicit the goal of it all.[30]

> Lord Jesus, I ask no other reward of you, no other beatitude, no other joy, except clear, pure understanding... of your words, words inspired by your Holy Spirit. For this is the sum of my happiness, this is the goal of perfect contemplation. Since no rational soul, even the purest, will find anything beyond that. For beyond that there is nothing... For it is there you dwell, and thither you lead those who seek you and love you. There for your elect you prepare the spiritual banquet of true knowing, there you pass and minister to them. And what, O Lord, is that passing of yours, if not the ascent through the infinite levels of your contemplation? For ever and always you pass in the understandings of those who seek you and find you. By them you are ever sought and ever found... You are found in your theophanies, in which in multiple modes, as in a certain kind of mirror, you come to meet the minds of those who understand you. In that mode and measure in which you allow understanding of you, understanding not of *what* you are but of what you are *not*, and of the fact *that* you are. But you are not found in your superessential essence, in which you pass beyond and above any intellect desiring and climbing to grasp you. That is why to your friends you grant your presence by appearing to them in some way that cannot be expressed. But you pass away beyond them in the ungraspable sublimity and infinity of your essential nature.

***

We now come to two genres, distinct but related, about which I have suggested above that they are not unrelated to the matter and range of Eriugena. They are related at least by the fact that the voyage or journey ends in or includes a vision, and that conversely the vision is itself a journey to and through the regions of the Otherworld. Indeed Dante fused the two modes in the epic poem that is a *summa* of the Christian Middle Ages. I refer to the literature of voyages or journeys and that of visions, comprehensive visions of the Otherworld – on all three storeys, Hell, Purgatory, and Heaven. Both pre-Christian and Christian Irish literature is rich in these two genres, and in both languages, Irish and Latin.[31] And in them

30 Migne, *PL*, 122.1010.

31 See e.g. St John D. Seymour, *Irish Visions of the Other World* (London, 1930); C. S. Boswell, *An Irish Precursor of Dante* (London, 1908); A. D'Ancona, *Scritti Danteschi* (Florence, 1912), on *I Precursori di Dante*.

we can see a particularly obvious influence of the Celtic on the Christian. And the converse too, since the indigenous stories were to some extent Christianized when they came to be written down in Christian times. At this point too we can mention the fact that some of the Hiberno-Latin examples came to be widely known on the Continent. Deservedly so. Because there is no doubt but that the Irish imposed on those age-old genres (not unique to Ireland) a degree of shape and structure which they did not have before. In this way, and because some of them were well known in Europe, they represent important stages in the progress of the genre that culminated in the *Divine Comedy.* And it has been suggested, with some plausibility, that Dante may in fact have known certain of them.

The connection that I have suggested between the impulse that produced those two genres, especially the vision literature, and the impulse behind the work of Eriugena, may not at first sight be very obvious. They are in two very different modes. One might explain the connection somewhat as follows.

The anthropologists tell us of two stages in the development of man's thinking about the world, the pre-logical or mythic, and the abstract philosophical. We might easily suppose that it is only in the second stage, with the crossing of the threshold into strict philosophical thinking, that the great ultimate boundary-questions should come into consciousness. The questions about the nature of all that exists, and why, in the famous phrase, anything at all should exist and not just nothing. It is not so, however. Cosmogonies and cosmologies are as old as our written records of humanity – and indeed obviously older. As someone has put it, man had scarcely opened his eyes on the universe than he began the effort to understand it and reconstruct it in thought. So all civilizations, even the most ancient, have their cosmogonies. The 'thought' at work of course is not logical, abstract, philosophical. It is imaginative, pictured, visionary, mythic. But, as Aristotle observed, even the myth-makers are doing philosophy. And Lucretius, in his philosophical epic *On the Nature of the Universe* (*De Rerum Natura*), is in a tradition that begins with the myths in Hesiod's *Theogony* (which is in fact a *cosmogony* too).

Now, even the (at first sight) endless variety in mythic attempts to see into the nature of things tends to follow certain archetypal and recurring patterns of organization – which in turn have led to certain archetypal and recurring structures of plot in literature. The voyage or journey is one such. The *apocalypsis* or vision is another. *Odyssey* and *Aeneid* have become common nouns. And 'apocalyptic' literature is a genre more extensive than just the last book of the Bible.

The earliest journey in literature is as old again as Homer is older than us. It is the Sumerian *Epic of Gilgamesh* from the third millennium BC. It is still the most concentrated and powerful example of the metaphysical significance that I am suggesting even a mythic story can have. It turns on man's existential awakening to the reality, finality and anguish of mortality. *Timor mortis conturbat me*, as the refrain of a medieval poem puts it. ' ... Man perishes with despair in his heart. I have looked over the wall and I see the bodies floating on the river, and that will be my lot also.'[32] There are two journeys in the poem. The first is a forest journey – itself archetypal. Its purpose is to assuage mortal anguish by winning the immortality of heroic fame at least, mainly by slaying the giant Humbaba, who represents some principle of evil in the world. When that goes wrong, and the hero's own companion dies, Gilgamesh sets out on a second journey, with the purpose of wresting immortal life from the jealous gods. 'Because I am afraid of death I will go as best I can to find Utnapishtim, whom they call the Faraway, for he has entered the assembly of the gods.'[33]

The journey ends in definitive and tragic failure. But the fact that he does reach that faraway region illustrates the fact that the journey can include the vision. In the great epic journeys it nearly always does. The *Odyssey* and the *Aeneid* have their descents into the *Under*world. They are really passages to the *Other*world, motivated by the quest for a larger enlightenment, and haunted particularly by the *lacrimae rerum* of mortality. 'I had not thought death had undone so many ... ' A sentiment which, by the way, in its Dantean original (*Inf.* 3.56f) is remarkably parallel to a sentence in the twelfth-century Hiberno-Latin *Vision of Tundal*. At the pit of Hell, Satan is surrounded by 'a multitude of souls and demons so great that no one could believe the world would bring forth so many souls from its beginning'.[34]

The apocalyptic or revelational otherworldly vision on its own is equally archetypal, and often entails a journey as well. The Vision of Er at the end of Plato's *Republic* is well known. It is perhaps the first example in literature of something beginning to be *à la mode* at the moment, the so-called 'near death experience'. It is in fact a constant throughout the history of this kind of thing. And the Hiberno-Latin *Vision of Tundal* is the highest point of its development before Dante. Er dies, or appears to die, is taken on a journey in which he is shown not only the ancient equivalent of Hell, Purgatory and Heaven, but also the whole system and governance of the universe. After which his soul returns to his body, so that he can tell the whole story of the ultimate nature of the world and of human destiny.

Long before Plato, Hesiod attributes the 'wisdom' of his *Theogony* to a vision of the Muses. Either he or they were already cannier than some. 'We know how

32 Quoted from N. K. Sandars, *The Epic of Gilgamesh* (Penguin Classics, 1977), 72.

33 Sandars, 97.

34 Page 36 of Wagner, ed. given *infra* n.53.

to speak many false things as though they were true; but we also know, when we will, how to utter true things.'[35]

Mention of the Muses reminds us of the archetypal role of woman as the mediatrix of the vision and the knowledge – from the Lady Philosophy in Boethius' work of theodicy, *The Consolation of Philosophy*, down to Beatrice in the *Divine Comedy*. It is a constant in Ireland. The most magical instance in any literature is in the eighth-century Irish-language *Voyage of Bran* – a voyage which begins in vision and consists in a further quest for it. The motif continues through the Irish-language literature of the late Middle Ages, and is still alive in Yeats's *Wanderings of Oisín*, enchanted away to Tír na nÓg and back by the visionary visitant Niamh:

> A pearl-pale, high-born lady who rode
> On a horse with bridle of findrinny,
> And like a sunset were her lips;
> A stormy sunset on doomed ships ...

The tone of that may be out of fashion in these days of grit and cinders. But the genres of voyages and visions which we have been illustrating as archetypal and universal were particularly fruitful in Celtic Ireland. And they took on a uniquely Celtic coloration. It is necessary to appreciate both points of background to those genres in Hiberno-Latin. Now for obvious reasons, due to the limitations of translation, it is not easy to reproduce the qualities of the original Irish-language examples, especially the poetic parts of them. But Yeats's poem is an original composition. And he does capture that Celtic coloration of the old tales – even if perhaps he does gild the lily a bit. For these reasons an extended quotation will replace a lot of explanation:

> O Oisín, mount by me and ride
> To shores by the wash of the tremulous tide,
> Where men have heaped no burial-mounds,
> And the days pass by like a wayward tune,
> Where broken faith has never been known
> And the blushes of first love never have flown ...
> We galloped over the glossy sea;
> I know not if days passed or hours.
> We galloped; now a hornless deer
> Passed by us, chased by a phantom hound
> All pearly white, save one red ear;

35 *Theogony*, 27f.

And now a lady rode like the wind
With an apple of gold in her tossing hand;
And a beautiful young man followed behind
With quenchless gaze and fluttering hair.
'Were these two born in the Danaan land,
Or have they breathed the mortal air?'

Thus Gilgamesh's Garden of the gods, Homer's island of Calypso, his Isles of the Blessed, Virgil's Elysian Fields – all these archetypal and universal goals of the human quest for higher enlightenment, for liberation from mortality and the human lot, took on in Ireland the Celtic colours of The Land of Youth, Tír na nÓg, Islands of Delights, Lands of Promise beyond the sea, or just behind the veil of the unsteady appearances of the only relatively normal. They gave not only the impulse but often their coloration to the Hiberno-Latin Christian examples of the genres. The indigenous lands of promise or islands of delights became the lands of promise of the *saints*, or the lost Earthly Paradise, where, in this particular tradition, even the Blessed (unlike Dante's) remained until they were admitted to the Heavenly Paradise, only after the final universal judgement. (Incidentally the Earthly Paradise provides a good example of the frequently multiple sources of a highly developed theme in Christian literature. The first and most beautiful literary elaboration of it is in another 'myth' or 'story' of Plato's, in the *Phaedo*, 108ff.)

***

Of course the indigenous were not the only sources of impulse, and influence. The genres existed on the Continent too. And there they came not only from the Greco-Roman tradition but from Christianity's own tradition of apocryphal works like the *Book of Enoch* or the *Apocalypse of Paul*. (The Apocrypha in general seem to have been well known in Ireland.) But this is to say no more than what we underlined from the beginning, that Celtic Irish Latin writing underwent European influence too. But also the converse. And there is no better example of the converse than the genres of voyage and vision. I have already referred to the fact that the Hiberno-Latin examples – and indeed one in medieval Irish – prepared the way to Dante by giving order and architecture to a domain of the Judeo-Christian quest and imagination which in the tradition was a *farrago*.

We have devoted some considerable time to explaining the nature, genesis and rationale of those two genres. It has been necessary, especially as it is not easy even for the native unskilled in the field to find his way through that element in the Irish tradition. For the same reason it is time to come to some specifics about the principal works in the genres.

To take the voyage first, we are lucky to have many indigenous examples in Irish. I shall mention two – pre-Christian though somewhat 'contaminated'. And also, it must be said, somewhat incomplete and disorganized by the time they came to be written down. They are *The Voyage of Bran* (*Immram Brain*), probably written down in the eighth century, and *The Voyage of Máel Dúin* (*Immram Máele Dúin*) from the same period.[36]

Of the two, much the more sequential, elaborated and poetic is the Voyage of Bran. It shows all the motifs of the genre. The mysterious call to the hero heard in magical music, and in the magical poetry in which a mysterious woman visitant from 'The Land of Wonders' describes the Otherworld. Then the voyage over the sea – in which the Celtic theme of relativity marvellously emerges. For Bran and his shipboard companions meet one Manannán mac Lir driving over the sea in a chariot. What for Bran is the open clear bright ocean is for Manannán a flowery plain of dry land! And that is not all. In strict fact, as Manannán tells him, Bran is really rowing over a rich and blossoming forest! The inhabitants of the land below are described – without age or decay of freshness since the beginning of creation, because they have never sinned. Thus Christian elements are introduced – the Fall, and a prophecy of the coming of Christ. Bran reaches an 'Island of Joy', and eventually an 'Island of Women'. His companions go ashore, but not Bran ... Many years they stay there, though it seemed only one. But as always there is one who is overcome by nostalgia for home, by longing from the midst of Circe's delights for plainer Penelope and Rocky Ithaca! The returned sentimental jumps ashore in Ireland – and becomes a heap of ashes. Bran writes down his adventure, says farewell – and is never heard of again.

I quoted Yeats earlier to give the tone of such Celtic tales. Precisely because here we must make do with translation. But some of it should be quoted. In the prose introduction, 'one day Bran went about alone in the neighbourhood of his fort. He heard music behind him. When he would look back it was still behind him the music was. Finally he fell asleep on account of the sweetness of the music ... '.

When he wakes up his mysterious visitant is there. And this (as they say) was the song she sang:[37]

> There is an island far away
> around which sea-horses glisten;

36 Editions, with translation, in Séamus Mac Mathúna, *Immram Brain* (Tübingen, 1985); and H. P. A. Oskamp, *The Voyage of Máel Dúin* (Groningen, 1970).

37 Quoted from Mac Mathúna.

a fair course against the little white-sided wave,
four legs hold it up ...
Legs of white silver are under it;
it shines through ages of beauty;
a fair country throughout the world's age
on which the many blossoms drop.
There is an ancient tree in blossom there
on which the birds call to the Hours ...

Islands of Birds are one of the motifs in the indigenous genre. But the reference to the Hours is clearly a Christian modification. And in fact an Island of Birds, with their calls to the chanting of the Hours of the monastic Office, is one of the principal and most beautiful motifs in the Hiberno-Latin *Voyage of St Brendan.*[38]

The Voyage of Brendan is probably from the ninth century. Later than *Bran*, but clearly influenced by it and its kind. It is more than just influenced. It is clearly parallel, only adapting the idea and its motifs to the new Christian context. In addition to the rationale of the whole genre as suggested earlier, the adaptation suggested itself all the more easily to the island Irish, given the characteristic urge of its monks to 'voyage for Christ', *peregrinari pro Christo*. Whether to carry the Gospel or to find their own personal island of retreat and contemplation wheresoever they might find, in the Spirit, if not in the world, that Land of Wonders, that Land of Promise, which their own spirit longed for and their imagination bodied forth.

In *The Voyage of St Brendan* those lands fuse with the Judeo-Christian myth of the Earthly Paradise and become the Land of Promise of *the Saints*, that abode of lower-lighted bliss where, as already indicated, the blessed await the Paradise of Heaven after the General Judgement. 'From the very beginning of the world it has remained exactly as you see it now. Do you need any food, drink or clothing? You have been here a whole year already without tasting food or drink. You have never felt the need for sleep, for it has been daylight all the time. Here there is no obscuring darkness but only perpetual day, the Lord Jesus Christ being Himself our light.'[39]

Brendan's search for it takes seven years, in the course of which many other strange islands are visited, some of them as strange and primordial as episodes in Homer's *Odyssey* or in Apuleius' tale of *Cupid and Psyche*. But the atmosphere of the whole is bathed in a gentle religious light and in the pervasive Celtic world of

38 Edition and translation by Carl Selmer, *Navigatio Sancti Brendani Abbatis* (University of Notre Dame, 1959).

39 Ch. 1, quoted in the translation of F. J. Webb, *The Age of Bede* (Penguin Classics).

wonders. 'The Lord Jesus Christ did not allow you to find it immediately because first He wished to show you the richness of His wonders in the deep.'[40] The years are cycles marked by the Christian seasons and the great feasts of the liturgical year, for which the voyagers always return to the same islands. And ever investing everything, even at sea, the aura of the monastic ritual of the daily Hours, linking hours, days, seasons and years in a rosary of prayer.

In the details there are many parallels with the *Voyages* of Bran and Máel Dúin. I have already referred to the Island of Birds. Suffice it to mention further the beginning and the end of the Brendan *Voyage*. The mysterious enchanting visitant who occasions the voyage of Bran becomes in *The Voyage of Brendan* the monk Barinthus, who visits Brendan at his monastery. He is sad and weeping, because he has a story both of joy and sorrow to tell. He has been there and back – to the island Land of Promise of the Saints. Brendan is at once consumed with a desire to seek it out. 'I have resolved, if it be God's will, to seek out that Land of Promise of the Saints which our father Barinthus described.' When he does reach it after seven years it is also to be told that here below death is the end of all voyaging – as it was for Odysseus as well as for Bran and his companion. 'The day of your final journey is at hand: you shall soon be laid to rest with your fathers.'[41]

On returning to his monastery Brendan told the whole story to his enraptured community. But he also told them of the prophecy. 'Events proved him right; he put all his affairs in order, and very shortly afterwards, fortified with the Sacraments of the Church, lay back in the arms of his disciples and gave up his illustrious spirit to the Lord ... '.[42]

In telling his tale the author of *Brendan* sometimes gives us the feeling that he goes round in cycles in more ways than the liturgical. But he did have the sense of an ending.

***

We come to apocalyptic, the visionary genre in the fully developed sense of the vision of, or more fully still, the journey through, the three realms of the Otherworld, Hell, Purgatory and Heaven. Four realms in fact when we bear in mind the function of the Earthly Paradise in that tradition. A function present as far back as the Book of Enoch and the Apocalypse of Paul, but particularly elaborated in Ireland – due no doubt to the influence of the indigenous motif of the Land of Wonders, the Land of Promise and so on, that we have seen in the voyage literature.

40 Ch. 28, quoted from Webb.

41 Ibid.

42 Ibid.

The earliest Hiberno-Latin vision literature seems to have been in a work no longer extant in its original state. It was in a Life of the seventh-century Irishman Fursey. Bede cites it as his source for his own account of Fursey.[43] (He also tells us that he himself knew an old brother in Bede's own monastery who testified to the historical truth of Fursey's experience, on the evidence of an older man who professed to have been told of it by Fursey himself.) This Fursey, in the tradition of Irish pilgrims for Christ, founded a monastery in East Anglia in the mid-seventh century, and later another at Lagny on the Marne in France.

The Life of him referred to by Bede must be the basis of the later medieval Life[44] which gives a good deal of space to the experiences summarized by Bede.

Fursey's vision occurs in the context of the 'near death experience', in which the soul leaves the body, to all appearances dead, and later returns to it, often unwillingly in the light of what it has seen. To the stupefaction of the temporarily bereaved, but also to their edification, since the experience is for reporting to them. Very 'modern', as I have said. But it is as old as Plato, and is the setting for most of the Irish apocalyptic literature.

Fursey's description of the Otherworld is not elaborate. But it has the beginnings of that new precision which, as I have said, the Irish gave it. It also has the beginnings of something else that the Irish gave it more and more. About the nature of the Heavenly Paradise it has that sense of the final ineffability of it which was to reach supreme expression in Dante – 'to the high imagination here power failed'. Like Dante, after their best efforts – and they are very good – the Irish reiterate that sentiment. Doubtless both the degree of success and the admission of the impossible are related to their native imagination and its literary preoccupation with Lands of Wonders and the Otherworld.

The elements of the medium in which they paint it are often Celtic, with its marvellous sense of colour, of the ornamental, the precious, the golden. But like Dante they typically culminate in the two media *par excellence* of the ineffable, light and music – the latter also characteristic of the Celtic genius, as we saw earlier.

Thus Fursey. 'He saw a great brightness ... and hosts of angels in four choirs singing and repeating: Holy, holy, holy. Lord God of hosts.' Fursey's soul is 'filled with the sweetness of supernal song and the sound of ineffable joy'. He knows that it must come from an even loftier heaven than the one he is in. 'Then the holy Angel said to him: "Do you know where such gladness and joy is lived?" When he answered that he knew not the holy Angel replied: "Among the supernal company, in the region from which we also are come".'[45]

43 *History*, 3.19.

44 In W. W. Heist, *Vitae Sanctorum Hiberniae* (Brussels, 1965).

45 *Vita*, 1.14 (Heist, 43).

The earliest completely apocalyptic work we have is not in Latin but in medieval Irish. It is the eleventh-century *Vision of* (pseudo-)*Adamnan* (*Fís Adamnáin*).[46] All the features I mentioned *a propos* of Fursey are so wonderfully developed in it that it has been described as the best example of the genre before Dante. I would reserve that accolade for the twelfth-century *Vision of Tundal.* The vision of Adamnan, 'the High Scholar of the Western World', is set in the great tradition of Christian apocalyptic seers, since St Paul (2 Cor 12:2–4) and the apocryphal tradition that on the day of Mary's dormition 'all the apostles were brought to look upon the pains and miserable punishments of the unblest'. Yet much of that tradition is transposed into Celtic colours.

Here we have again the clear distinction of Hell, Purgatory and Heaven – and of course the Earthly Paradise, that temporary Land of the Saints. But we have the beginnings of something else, namely that gradation within each realm which *Tundal* develops further and which was given definitive form by Dante.

Here there is a more elaborate attempt to rise to the evocation of the Heavenly Paradise – and a realization of its final impossibility. 'Great and vast as are the splendour and the radiance in the Land of Saints ... , more vast, a thousand times, the splendour in the region of the Heavenly Host, around the Lord's own throne.' But in the end 'to describe the mighty Lord that is upon that throne is not for any, unless Himself should do so, or should so direct the heavenly dignitaries'.[47]

Yet the attempt is made – in the Celtic colours we have seen before. 'This throne is fashioned like unto a canopied chair, and beneath it are four columns of precious stone. Though one should have no minstrelsy at all, save the harmonious music of these four columns, yet would he have his fill of melody and delight. Three stately birds are perched upon that chair, in front of the King, their minds intent upon the Creator throughout all ages, for that is their vocation. They celebrate the Hours, praising and adoring the Lord, and the Archangels accompany them. For the birds and the Archangels lead the music and then the Heavenly Host with the Saints and Virgins make response.'[48]

We are reminded of a much later Celtic singer and seer, dreaming of his state 'once out of nature':

> Once out of nature I shall never take
> My bodily form from any natural thing,
> But such a form as Grecian goldsmiths make
> Of hammered gold and gold enamelling

46 Translation in Boswell, op. cit., from which quotations are taken.

47 Ch. 7.

48 Ibid.

To keep a drowsy Emperor awake;
Or set upon a golden bough to sing
To lords and ladies of Byzantium
Of what is past, or passing, or to come.[49]

In Hiberno-Latin there are three main successors to *The Vision of Adamnan*. Certain writings of Bishop Patrick of Dublin (1084), the *Vision of Tundal* (1149), and *St Patrick's Purgatory* (about 1180) – the last the best known, no doubt, but in fact inferior to all the others.

Bishop Patrick[50] is particularly interesting, as both a contrast and a complement to *Adamnan*. He is so close to *Adamnan* in time, possibly a generation later. Yet he is steeped in the European scholastic intellect, particularly in Augustinianism, which he acquired apparently as a Benedictine at Worcester in England. Yet for all that he is also steeped in the Irish tradition. There is no better proof of this than one of his long poems, 'On the Wonders of Ireland' (*De Mirabilibus Hiberniae*). We know how Celtic that theme is. But it seems to be an early effusion of Patrick's, and not one of his best. Some of the 'wonders' have the unfortunate effect of weakening our resolve against Gerald of Wales a century later. But then the family's private right to private yarns at its own expense does not confer the right on intruders.

Bishop Patrick reminds us in many ways of Columbanus as we have described him: intense, evangelical, pessimistic about the human lot, spiritual, mystical even, and, for our particular purposes here, preoccupied with the last things, Heaven and/or Hell. As we saw, one of Columbanus' poems is 'On the World's Impermanence' (*De Mundi Transitu*). One of Bishop Patrick's is 'On the Frailty of Life' (*De Caduca Vita*). And so to the same intense conclusion of mystical *desiderium*:

So may I seek Thee Christ, so yearn for Thee in the depth of my heart
As he who thirsts for water, as the beggar for wealth.
So may my mind, so also may my body cleave to Thee
As light to the sun in heaven, as stars to the sky.[51]

It is an easy step to the personal genesis of the inherited theme of the 'last things'.

He treats that theme in two of his writings. One is a long allegorical poem, *Versus Allegorici*. The other a prose tractate, 'On the Three Dwelling Places of the

49 Yeats, 'Sailing to Byzantium'.

50 Text and translation in Aubrey Gwynn, *The Writings of Bishop Patrick* (S.L.H. vol. I), from which quotations are taken.

51 Lines 69ff.

Soul' (*De Tribus Habitaculis Animae*). Those three places do not include Purgatory. They refer to the world and the Church here below, and Heaven and Hell beyond. The two pieces are complementary. The poem deals with the first, the prose with the other two. But the title of the prose is accurate. For the world is here again the third dwelling-place, seen with characteristic pessimism as a permanently unsatisfying composite of that good and evil which attain their separate and absolute condition only hereafter, in Heaven and Hell.

Now apart from their theme the Celtic relevance of these two pieces lies in their mode of presentation. In their matter and argument they are doctrinal, rigorously and scholastically logical. But stylistically eloquent too. At times more linkedly logical and eloquent even than the Augustine in the background. Yet the substance is presented through the make-believe form of vision, especially in the *Allegorical Verses.*

Of course the allegory owes much to Europe. But it is also clearly a forerunner of a later prolific convention in Irish poetry, the *aisling* or vision poem. The core of all the elements can be illustrated in lines towards the end of the poem which summarize what has gone before and anticipate the theme of the prose:[52]

> ... I have sung the midmost, and pass by unsung the lowest and the highest.
> Who, who could sing them? who could mark their numbers?
> [...]
> Who could sing the silent speech of people who see men's hearts?
> Who the endless abiding joy of the mind?
> Who the united choirs singing hymns and praises,
> And the love that burns in the hearts of each and all?
> Who the lyres and every apt form of melody?
> Psalter and strange harps or threefold organs?
> The golden temples, the market-place, the throne, the seated King?
> Who could tell how great, how wondrous the good? Who the hidden time
> Of the star-bearing blessed summit where all these are to be found;
> That like a citadel stands forth far above the aforesaid city?
> [...]
> As its members to the head, as the slight shadow is less
> Than that which casts the shadow, as dreams are less than real things.
> So the former city is less than this in beauty and all splendour.
> [...]

52 Lines 192ff.

With *The Vision of Tundal*[53] we advance nearly a century. But we revert from exposition, literal or thinly veiled, to the more traditional vision, from the systematic and doctrinal to the vividly imagined. Yet one of the principal points to note will be how profound the doctrine that underlies the imagined – or seen! – at its best. Thus we shall see, looking back, how far the genre has come since *Adamnan*. And, looking forward, how close the development has come to Dante. So close in some details that, unless there is another source, one is led to think that Dante must have known *The Vision of Tundal*. As he could have, since it was written on the Continent and was widely known there.

The vision is explicitly dated to 1149. The dating is further defined by reference to some contemporary events and persons in Irish ecclesiastical history, such as Malachy of Down and the account of him written by Bernard of Clairvaux. The vision purports to be written by a certain Marcus for the benefit of an unidentified Mother Abbess in Ratisbon, where there was a traditional Irish presence. The vision is presented as the narrative of Tundal himself to whom it happened. He was a noble knight of Cashel, but unruly and irreligious. Hence the elaborate lesson he was given when, after apparently dying, suddenly of a Wednesday, his soul was given a guided tour by his guardian angel. Down to Hell, up through Purgatory, into the Earthly Paradise, and beyond it through the spheres of the Heavenly Paradise to the Dantean summit where vision of the Creator of all is given. And with the vision knowledge and understanding of all. 'Not only vision ... but unparalleled knowledge, so that he no longer had any need to enquire about anything, but everything he desired to know he now knew clearly and totally.'[54] 'Within its depths I saw ingathered, bound by love in one volume, the scattered leaves of all the universe.'[55]

Four days it took. On the Saturday his soul returned to its body, and to the amazement of clergy and people who were gathered for his funeral.

'A long road lies before us', says the Angel at the start. 'The way is long and the road hard', says Virgil to Dante.[56] And so for us. We cannot walk it in detail here.

In the architecture of the whole to be noted is the great advance in the clear demarcation of the realms of the Otherworld, Hell, Purgatory, Earthly Paradise and Heaven. And an even more remarkable advance towards Dante is the grading within each realm, into circles and spheres according to the degrees of guilt or bliss. And

53 Edition in Albrecht Wagner, *Visio Tnugdali* (Erlangen, 1882).

54 Wagner, 53.

55 Dante, *Paradiso*, 33.85–87. Bishop Patrick is splendid on this supreme knowledge – what Dante calls (*Par.* 33.91) 'the universal form of this complex', *la forma universale di questo modo*. Patrick owes it to two sources – the Columbanian intensity of his own longing for the light, and the Augustinian epistemology and metaphysics of that light, subsistent *Veritas*, Truth in the absolute.

56 *Inferno*, 34.95.

in the guilt and the bliss, as in Dante, a high degree of the fitting of the punishment and the reward to the sin and the virtue. And in the degrees of bliss, as in Dante, the harmonious contentment of each with his own.[57] And, as in both Dante and the developing Irish tradition, a sense, at the appropriate points, of the unsounded depths and the unscalable heights. With the concomitant sense of the need to rise to the height of the great argument, and finally to yield before the inexpressible.

We see this sense intensifying as Tundal descends through the circles of Hell. There, as in Dante, the tormented souls 'longed for death and could not find it'.[58] 'These have no hope of death ... '[59] The way grows narrower as Tundal and his guide descend to the ultimate pit, past a Dantean frozen lake, through regions where 'all the foundations of the world seemed to shake', down to the Dantean well or cistern, at the bottom of which reigns the very principle of evil and negativity in the world, the Prince of Darkness in person. Here 'none who once enters will ever exit'.[60] 'Abandon all hope, you who enter.'[61]

The emergence from Hell into Purgatory is the emergence from darkness into light. A fresh dawn light like that in Dante at the same point.[62] There is suffering but there is hope, and even a kind of joy, and even a kind of rest. *Requies* is a thematic word here.

With the transition to the Earthly Paradise and the ascending spheres of Heaven the thematic word is glory, *gloria*. *Ascendamus*! Let us climb. And as they climb – often not knowing how, as in Dante – an ever-growing sense of the dazzle of the glory and the impossibility of expressing it. Here especially we observe Celtic details in the description. Light is everywhere, as in Dante. But above all music, as in the Irish tradition, and of course again in Dante. 'And they sang Alleluia to the Lord, with a new song and such sweet melody that for the soul who once heard it all memory of the past would sink into oblivion.'[63] *Un punto solo* ... 'A single moment brings me deeper lethargy than five-and-twenty centuries ... '[64]

The summit of the vision has already been quoted. Let us end therefore with one moment of particular glory shortly before the summit is reached. It is a

57 *Paradiso*, 3.52–54. A sentiment made explicit in *St Patrick's Purgatory*: 'Each individual rejoiced in his own felicity, but they all exulted at the joy of each of the others...' (Quoted from J.-M. Picard and Y. de Pontfarcy, *St Patrick's Purgatory*, Blackrock, 1985, 67). Cf. Bishop Patrick, *On the Three Dwelling Places*, lines 116ff.

58 Wagner, 31.

59 *Inferno*, 3.46.

60 Wagner, 38.

61 *Inferno*, 3.1ff.

62 *Purgatorio*, 1.13ff.

63 Wagner, 48.

64 *Paradiso*, 33.94f.

glimpse into one of the highest spheres, the one where the monks and the nuns abide, those 'monks and virgins for Christ', as St Patrick loved to call them.[65] There all is a radiance of light and a vibrant symphony of musical sound. The glory of that light and sound 'surpassed all the glory seen before'. The instruments played without touch. The lips of the singers sang without movement.

But more splendid still is the 'firmament' above their heads. From it 'hung chains of the purest gold, intermingled with rods of silver ... from which in turn perfumed censers were suspended, cymbals and bells, lilies and little golden spheres. And all through them a great host of angels floated, flying on golden wings, in between the golden chains, with wafting wings emitting to the hearer sounds the most pleasing and the sweetest ever'.[66]

Most of the elements in that high point of description, and certainly their combination, could come from nowhere but a Celtic climate. I wonder could Dante have known the passage? For just so, at a comparable point near the summit, just so do the flying angels minister between God above and the ranks of the Blessed ranged in the petals of the White Rose below.

> As bees ply back and forth, now in the flowers
> Busying themselves, and now intent to wend
> Where all their toil is turned to sweetest stores,
> So did the host of Angels now descend
> Amid the Flower of the countless leaves,
> Now rise to where their love dwells without end.
> Their glowing faces were as fire that gives
> Forth flame, golden their wings; the purest snow
> The whiteness of their raiment ne'er achieves.
> Down floating to the Flower, from row to row,
> Each ministered the peace and burning love
> They gathered in their waftings to and fro.
> Between the Flower and that which blazed above
> The volant concourse interposed no screen
> To dim the splendour and the sight thereof;
> For God's rays penetrate with shafts so keen
> Through all the universe, in due degree,
> There's naught can parry them or intervene.[67]

65 *Confession*, 41; *Letter to Coroticus*, 12.

66 Wagner, 50.

67 *Paradiso*, 31.7ff, in the version by Dorothy Sayers and Barbara Reynolds (Penguin Classics).

THE TRINITY IN EARLY IRISH CHRISTIAN WRITINGS

Given the context of this conference and the theme of this essay, the topic will inevitably have a theological dimension and indeed a philosophical one, philosophy being the long-standing complement to theology. But it is not my purpose to treat either discipline at a high level of conceptual abstraction. My purpose is more concrete, although at a high level of *spirituality*, including its frequent high levels of spiritual *experience*. As the title indicates, the spirituality I will deal with is early Irish, although its after-effects continued down through many centuries we cannot call early, centuries of turbulent history, of a fragmented civilization, and of a Catholic faith often hunted down but never hunted out. That spirituality has come into vogue again in recent times, under the label of 'Celtic Spirituality'.[68] There is indeed a Celtic dimension to early Irish spirituality, even if, as a relatively late-converted territory, the Irish owed much to older Christian Europe. But the 'Celtic' label, like the proverbial charity, can cover a lot. And, to my limited knowledge, some of that lot is rather soft at the centre. Or should one say soft at the *bottom*, in its *foundation*, in its ultimate transcendent spiritual *ground*, or *principium* (the Greek non-temporal *archē*), with which Genesis and the Gospel of John begin. It is that supreme non-temporal *ground*, *principium*, *archē*, that entails the philosophical and theological dimension. And nowhere has that dimension been more entailed than in the 'Augustinian/Anselmian faith seeking understanding' of the Trinity, *three* persons in *one* God. As indicated, I am not getting into the dialectics of that 'search for understanding'. But we must keep it in mind to understand the importance of the Trinity in early Irish writing, and that not only as the Ground of spirituality but also as the Ground, Creator and all-encompassing sustainer of all that exists.

I have indirectly introduced a metaphysical dimension into a theological context. It added to the cosmic significance of the Trinity when, once upon a time, I read the reverse: the introduction of the theological Trinity as the best solution to an age-old metaphysical problem. It was in a history of Greek philosophy, the author of which had the rare common sense to *explain* why abstract metaphysical

68 See James P. Mackey (ed.), *An Introduction to Celtic Christianity*, (Edinburgh: T&T Clark, 1989); see also my chapter there on 'Hiberno-Latin Christian Literature' (64–120). See also Peter O'Dwyer, O Carm, *Towards a History of Irish Spirituality* (Dublin: The Columba Press, 1995).

problems arise at all. One such problem (or is it two?) he explained, was the ancient Greek, but also perennial, problem known as that of 'the One and the Many'. The metaphysical search is for the absolute *One* entity that grounds all the others. But once that is found (or thought to be), another problem emerges. As was first *metaphysically* proved by Parmenides in the fifth century BC, that absolute One (being, *einai, esse* in this case), has to be 'one' in the strict metaphysical sense of simple, *simplex*, without parts. In light of that absolute unchanging 'oneness', the corollary problem arises, how absolute unchanging oneness can generate the multiplicity of all the other existing entities.

Our author goes through all the ancient and modern attempts to solve it – attempts too many to go through here. But in his analysis they all fail. He comes therefore to an interesting conclusion:

> Monism ... is a necessary idea in philosophy. The Absolute must be one. But an utterly abstract monism is impossible. If the Absolute is simply One, wholly excluding all process and multiplicity, out of such an abstraction the process and multiplicity of the world cannot issue. The Absolute is not simply one, or simply many. It must be a many-in-one, as correctly set forth in the Christian doctrine of the Trinity.[69]

It was not until the ninth-century Scotus Eriugena that any early Irish Christian writer so metaphysically systematized the theology of the revealed Trinity, its primacy as the absolute transcendent Being, and its immanent cosmic range as the Source of the being (*esse*) of all contingent created beings. But all the *elements* of Eriugena's systematics were already in his Irish predecessors. The difference was in their mode. They set those elements in the context of a vital spirituality, in which the abstract 'essentials' of 'systematics' are given life in an 'existential', and often 'experiential' faith. And the three persons of the Trinity remarkably recur as the vitalizing ground and beating heart of it.[70]

As far as I know, this emphasis on the Trinity is distinctive of this 'Celtic' spirituality. Distinctive too is the 'totalizing' dimension given to the Trinity in that other Irish impulsion, to the metaphysical dimension without its systematics, to

69 W. T. Stace, *A Critical History of Greek Philosophy* (London: Macmillan, 1920; many reprints, down to the 1969 from which I quote), 70–71. For a magisterial exposition of the implications of the Trinity for metaphysical, cosmic, historical and societal ordering, see Charles Norris Cochrane, *Christianity and Classical Culture; A Study of Thought from Augustus to Augustine* (New York/Oxford: University Press, 1940; revised ed. 1944, Galaxy Book repr. 1957); see especially Part 3.

70 'Thugtaí an-deabhóid don Tríonóid (there was great devotion to the Trinity)', says Seán de Fréine on p. 39 of *Croí Cine, An Clóchomhar Tta* (Dublin, 1990), an Irish-language spiritual anthology that contains many Trinitarian items.

an understanding of the universe as a whole. The triune God is not only the transcendent Creator of it; He is its transcendent 'Lord of the Universe', or 'Lord of the Elements' – recurring themes in Old and Middle Irish poetry[71] – even Eriugena uses its Latin equivalent in one of his poems.[72] But this transcendent Creator Lord is also immanent in his own creation. And this gives its cosmic dimension to early Irish 'spirituality' – spirituality being a term that, on its own, can have different levels of meaning, some high, some low. Hence the two aspects of that cosmic dimension which pervades early Irish Christian writing, especially its Gaelic poetry, but also some in Latin. The first aspect is its universalizing vision, which enables the greater poet to escape from immanence and his own subjectivity, and relate the concrete particular to its universal context – or ultimate source, as we will mention presently. The second aspect is also a vision, but at a deeper level that enriches the first. In the Christian context, the 'spiritual man' (in the Pauline sense, 1 Cor 2:10ff, or at least in the inspired poetic sense!) can see the universal not just through or beyond the concrete particular but *within* it. For he knows the transcendent Creator as also immanent in his creation.[73] This immanent presence gives the created not only the beauty that reflects its Creator, but also the stamp of the Creator's triune Being in creation's structured image of it.[74]

This fusion of the spiritual and the material worlds produces an early Irish poetry, some in Latin but most in Gaelic, of a rare lyricism, in response to a rare pre-Franciscan transparency of the visible world to the invisible, both beyond it and immanent in it. By 'poetry' here I refer not just to pure *nature* poetry. I include the spiritual poetry that is also involved with the beauty of nature.[75] I include also, but only rather economically, writings that are not poetry in the strict technical sense of form, but are infused with an intensity

71 Cf. the opening of an Old Irish tenth-century poem; 'O God, Lord of Creation, I invoke thee' (no. 15 in Gerard Murphy, *Early Irish Lyrics* [Oxford: Clarendon Press, 1956]).

72 Poem no. 2 v. 9 in Michael W. Herren (ed.), *Johannis Scotti Eriugenae Carmina* (Dublin: Institute for Advanced Studies, 1956; Volume 7 of the *Scriptores Latini Hiberniae* series, hereafter referred to as SLH). In his poems too, Eriugena maintains the Trinitarian and cosmic totalising range of his theologico-metaphysical opus, the *De Divisione Naturae* (On the Division of Nature).

73 Cf. St John of the Cross in his commentary on the 'silent music' of stanza 15 of his *Spiritual Canticle*: 'In that knowledge of the divine light the soul becomes aware of Wisdom's wonderful harmony ... in the variety of his creatures and works. Each of these is endowed with a certain likeness of God and in its own way gives voice to the Creator's immanence in his creation.' (*The Collected Works of St John of the Cross*, translated by Kieran Kavanagh, OCD. [Washington DC, 1979], 472.

74 See e.g. Augustine, *City of God*, 11, 24–25.

75 See e.g. the haiku-like ninth-century quatrain (no. 4 in Murphy, op. cit.): 'Let us adore the Lord/ Maker of wondrous works/ great bright heaven with its angels/ the white-waved sea on earth.' Cf. Patrick Kavanagh's poems: 'Ploughman'; 'To a Blackbird'; 'Beech Tree'; 'A View of God and the Devil'; 'The One'.

of feeling that we may call 'prose poetry' in liturgy, offices, litanies, prayers, even rhyming collects.[76]

The transparency of nature to invisible *super*-nature was probably natural to early Irish Christians, in view of the fact that it was a characteristic of pre-Christian Celtic civilization. From its myths, legends, sagas, lands of eternal youth, and above all, the genre of otherworld journeys and voyages, we know that the other world was not far away, just beyond the veil, to adopt Yeats's phrase. Irish Christian writers took over the genre of the otherworld journey and adapted it to the specifically Christian totalizing vision of otherworld reality, the three-storey world of hell, purgatory and heaven.[77] There was of course a long Judaeo-Christian tradition of that genre, which culminated in Dante's *Divine Comedy* and its all-encompassing fusion of poetry, philosophy, theology and mysticism, with the vision of the Trinity at its summit – as in the best of the Irish versions, well before Dante. In fact the Irish versions made an important contribution to the development of that genre. They developed its structure in the stages of the descent to the underworld and the ascent to the supreme vision of the Trinity. Since some of the Irish versions were in Latin[78], and known in Europe, Dante could well have known them. And certainly there are striking parallels between them.

76 See the seventh-century *Antiphonary of Bangor*, edited by F. E. Warren (London: 1893, Part 1; 1893, Part 2).

77 See Jonathan M. Wooding (ed.), *The Otherworld Voyage in Early Irish Literature* (Dublin: Four Courts Press, 2000).

78 E.g. the twelfth-century *Visio Tnugdali* (The Vision of Tundal), narrated and written by an Irish monk of the *Schottenkloster* of St James, Regensburg, Germany, to the abbess of a convent in Regensburg, edited by A. Wagner in his *Visio Tnugdali Lateinisch und Altdeutsch* (Erlangen, 1882).

TEXTS

ST PATRICK

From that introductory overview we turn to specific Irish texts that represent the primacy of the Trinity and its all-encompassing range. I will take them mostly in chronological order, and that enables us to start with one of the most succinct and powerful statements of them all, St Patrick's own credal profession in chapter 4 of his *Confessio*:[79]

> There is no other God, nor ever was nor ever will be, than God the Father unbegotten, without beginning (*principium*), source of every *principium*, encompassing all that exists ... ; and His son Jesus Christ whom we declare to have been always with the Father ... , begotten by the Father . . . before every *principium* ... And He has abundantly poured out upon us the Holy Spirit ... who makes obedient believers sons of God and joint heirs with Christ. That is the God we confess and adore, one God in the Holy name of the Trinity.

That Trinitarian profession is the overture to the theme that Patrick develops in depth throughout the *Confessio*. In a cyclical summary, he restates it at the end of the *Confessio*. Its final sentence shows a sure sense of an ending: 'This is my confession before I die.' It refers back, of course, to the whole of the *Confessio*, but it is more immediately preceded (in c. 60) by a final Trinitarian profession – in response to heathen worshippers of the sun: 'But we ... adore and believe in the true Sun, Christ, who [unlike the material sun] will never perish ... but will abide for ever, reigning with God the omnipotent Father and with the Holy Spirit, prior to all worlds and ages now and for ever and ever.'

Between that opening and ending Patrick recounts the individual roles of the Persons of the Trinity, especially of the Holy Spirit, in profound spiritual experiences. Chapter 20 includes all three Persons in an account of an occasion when

79 Editions Newport, J. D. White, *Libri Sancti Patricii; The Latin Writings of St Patrick*, with introduction, translation and notes (Dublin, 1905); Ludwig Bieler, *Libri Epistolarum Sancti Patricii Episcopi*, 2 vols. with introduction, text and commentary (Dublin: Stationery Office, 1952); Daniel Conneely, St *Patrick's Letters; A Study of their Theological Dimension*, edited and presented by Patrick Bastable and others: including the present writer (Maynooth: *An Sagart*, 1993).

'Satan mightily tested me'. He 'fell upon me like a huge rock', paralysing Patrick's limbs. He could not understand what made him 'call out to Helios' [Greek sun-god] in his distress, at the same moment as he saw a radiant sun rising in the heavens. Its radiance shone down on him and cast off at once all the weight that oppressed him. 'I believe that Christ the Lord came to my aid, and it was his Spirit who was already calling out for me.' He recalls Christ's own promise; 'In that day ... it is not you who speak but the Spirit of your Father speaking in you' (Mt 10:20).

In chapter 33, Patrick refers back to chapters 1–3 on his captivity in Ireland. In chapter 3, he announces a fundamental reason for writing his *Confessio*: he cannot keep silent about the favours and graces that God gave him during that captivity. The Lord opened the heart of his ignorance and unbelief (*incredulitatis meae*),[80] enabling him to turn with his whole heart 'to the Lord my God' (c. 2). He sought and found Him. And that, he believes, he owes to 'God's indwelling Spirit, who has worked in me down to this day' (c. 33).

In chapter 24, Patrick narrates a Pauline experience (2 Cor 12:2ff). One night he heard words spoken that came from the indwelling second Person of the Trinity. What they meant or whence they came he did not know: 'God knows, whether they were spoken within me or outside me', until a final voice said; 'He who gives his life for you is the one who is speaking within you' (cf. Mt 10:20, Jn 3:16).

In the following chapter (25), he relates another Pauline experience, with a possible echo of Augustine's *Confessions*. He saw [or heard] someone praying within him:

> I was, as it were, within my body, and I heard (him) above me, that is, above the inner man,[81] and there he was praying with intense and fervent groanings. While this was happening, I was stricken with awe and stunned into a stupor, and I wondered who it could be that was praying within me. But at the end of the prayer He spoke in terms which gave me to ... understand that He was the Holy Spirit.

At that point, Patrick awoke and at once recalled the words of St Paul (Rom 8:26): 'We know not how to pray as we should, but the Spirit himself prays our petitions for us, with groanings so inexpressible that they cannot be put into words.'

80 See chap. 1: *Deum verum ignorabam* (I did not know the true God).

81 On 'above the inner man' cf. Augustine's emphasis in *Conf.* VII 10,16; Patrick could have known Augustine's *Confessions* – there are many parallels. See e.g. his *Conf.* VIII 12,29 on the mysterious voice he heard in the garden during the final crisis of his conversion.

He has already told us in chapter 23 that it was in a night vision and a voice (some years after his escape from Ireland and his later return to Britain), that he heard the 'voice of the Irish'. They were calling him from the region 'beside the Wood of Foclut, close to the western sea', to return and walk among them again. That was an evangelizing call that revealed his destiny. The 'apostle of Ireland' accepted Christ's call to the first apostles: Go now therefore and teach all peoples, baptizing them in the name of the Father and of the Son and of the Holy Spirit (c. 40; Mt 28:19).

ST PATRICK'S BREASTPLATE

In light of the strong, intense, forceful and spiritual personality that emerges from the *Confessio* and his *Breastplate* hymn (see note 83), we can understand why Patrick – the 'apostle of Ireland'- impressed his memory and influence on later generations. Not all of that memory will pass with historians, but that doesn't necessarily eliminate all truth behind the memory, and especially behind Patrick's lasting influence. As even Aristotle admits,[82] the wonderful is attractive, so every teller of a story adds something of his own! The best example of that, as both a memory and a Trinitarian, spiritual, and cosmic hymn is *St Patrick's Breastplate.*[83] It is named after him because attributed to him, but we know it cannot be his, because it is composed in Old Irish of a certain date too late to be Patrick's – even supposing that he was ever familiar with the language at all. Yet the language of the hymn is indeed old, and consequently early. That is confirmed by a note in the life of Patrick by Tírechán about AD 700. The note says that he must be given a fourfold honour in every Irish monastery. The fourth of these is always to chant his Gaelic 'canticle' (*canticum ejus Scotticum semper canere),* taken to be the *Breastplate.*[84]

It is a splendid hymn, not only in its Trinitarian and cosmic range, but also in the lapidary style of the language. As a highly inflected language, Old Irish was capable of a very artistic economy of words, resulting in a concentrated density of expression and meaning that is hard for any modern 'analytic' language to achieve, or to transmit its effect in translation – only Latin can approach its lapidarity. And

82 *Poetics*, XXIV, 8

83 Text and translation in the eleventh-century Irish *Liber Hymnorum*, edited by J. H. Bernard and R. Atkinson (London, 1898), Vol. 1: text and introduction; Vol. 2: translations and notes; see N. D. O'Donoghue, 'St. Patrick's Breastplate', in Mackey, op. cit., 45–63. Patrick often echoes St Paul, in whom the metaphor of the 'breastplate', or 'armour', recurs: Eph 6:14 and 1 Thess 5:8; Rom 13:12, Eph 6:11 and 13.

84 In *The Patrician Texts of the Book of Armagh* (SLH, Vol. 10), edited, with an introduction, translation and commentary, by Ludwig Bieler, with a contribution by Fergus Kelly (Dublin: Institute for Advanced Studies, 1979), 166 and 167.

as an invocation for strength and protection against evil, the 'breastplate' (Latin *lorica*, Gaelic *lúireach*), has a long later history as a very 'Celtic' genre in both Irish and Latin, less grand in scale but still Trinitarian and artistic.[85]

Here then are some translated samples from 'Patrick's' *Breastplate*. It opens with the Trinity:

> I arise today (in)
> Vast might, invocation of the Trinity –
> Belief in a Threeness,
> Confession of Oneness,
> Meeting in the Creator. . . etc.

This Trinitarian opening motif returns in the cyclical conclusion. In between there are 'stanzas' invoking Christ specifically. Here is the opening of the one that is too long and rich, and hopefully well enough known, to need quotation *in extenso*:

> Christ for my protection today ... ;
> Christ with me, Christ before me,
> Christ behind me, Christ in me, etc.

The 'stanza' that must be quoted in full is the one that adds the grandeur and beauty of the cosmos to the hymn's Trinitarian dimension:

> I arise today (in)
> Might of heavens,
> Brightness of sun,
> Whiteness of snow,
> Splendour of fire,
> speed of light,
> swiftness of wind,
> depth of sea,
> stability of earth,
> firmness of rock.

A note on this hymn in Volume 2 of the *Liber Hymnorum* (p.210) gives a glimpse of its long remembrance in tradition. The author of the note quotes from an article written by a Celtic scholar in 1839, who says that portions of this hymn were still in use among the people, and repeated at bedtime 'as a protection against evil'. The author of the note comments; 'We do not know if that is still true ... '. He was writing in 1897. What was known in the Jubilee year 2000, we don't know either.

85 On the Irish contribution to the artistic development of rhyme and assonance in continental Latin poetry, see F. J. E. Raby, *A History of Christian Latin Poetry*, 2nd ed. (Oxford, Clarendon Press, 1953), 135ff and 181–2.

SECUNDINUS (GAELIC SECHNALL)

In addition to St Patrick's Trinitarian emphasis and intense spirituality, I have also mentioned his long-lasting influence. That influence was expressed very early (in his own lifetime?) in a long hymn of praise by Secundinus. Secundinus is said to have been Patrick's nephew and a companion in his work. If that is true, Secundinus' Latin hymn is the earliest in Ireland. And as far as I know, apart from the Acts of the Apostles, and Patrick's own *Confessio,* the hymn is a unique personal hymn in praise of a founder of Christianity in virgin territory.

The hymn is abecedarian, in ninety-two lines of twenty-three quatrains in trochaic metre. It exalts the virtues, labours, achievements, spirituality and orthodox doctrine of Patrick, for all of which he will be given his future heavenly reward. His perfect life makes him an equal of the Apostles – an apostolate that Patrick also got in a call from God himself. 'For his immense labour he will ... reign with the Apostles as a saint over Israel' (lines 91–92).

Those two last lines are preceded by a quatrain on Patrick's spirituality and missionary zeal – all based on the Holy Trinity:

> Hymns he chants, with the Apocalypse and the Psalms of God,
> And expounds them to build up the People of God,
> Whose law he believes in the holy name of the Trinity,
> Teaching it as one Substance in three Persons.[86]

COLMCILLE

From Patrick's later but greater and better known *Breastplate,* we turn back to an earlier Latin poem that also opens and cyclically closes with the Trinity, framing its universal range in even more detail than does the *Breastplate.* The poem is the *Altus Prosator* (The High Creator),[87] composed by Colmcille (a.k.a. Columba) of Iona (c. 521–597). Its title is taken from its opening words. Those words begin what we might call an *epyllion* of all creation, from its origin to its end, and of all its history in between, from the fall of the angels and mankind, through salvation history and man's redemption by the incarnate Christ, culminating in the loss or gain of the final human destiny intended by mankind's Creator, the beatific vision of the triune God, to be lost or won on the *dies irae* of the Last Judgement.

> The High Creator, the Ancient of Days and unbegotten,
> was without origin or ground of his beginning:
> He is and will be through infinite generation after generation.

86 Text in *The Oxford Book of Medieval Latin Verse,* by F. J. E. Raby (Oxford University Press, 1959).
87 Text, translation and notes in the *Liber Hymnorum.*

With Him his only-begotten Son and the Holy Spirit
are co-eternal in the everlasting glory of Godhead.
[In that] it is not three Gods but the one God we profess, preserving our faith in the three most glorious Persons.

The second stanza sets down a list of God's primordial creations – the ranks of the angels, archangels, principalities and powers ... And this He did in order that the goodness and majesty of the Trinity be not slack in all the gifts of its largesse ...

The body of the poem expands into the creation of the universe, the fall of the rebellious angels, the creation, the fall and the redemption of man. The fallen angels descend into hell. The same descent is an option open to the freedom of fallen man, even though redeemed by the incarnate second Person of the Trinity. This final human option for hell or heaven leads into a sequence of several stanzas that evoke the terrors of the Last Judgement, when 'we shall stand trembling before the tribunal of the Lord', in a *Dies Irae* that surpasses even the fear and trembling of the better known medieval one.

Conversely, those judged to have chosen the better part ascend to the glorious court of the Trinity:

With chants of hymns constantly ringing,
with numberless angels rejoicing in sacred dances,
with the four living creatures of the multiple eyes (Apoc 4:6),
and the four-and-twenty blessed elders (ibid. 4:4)
laying their crowns at the feet of the Lamb of God (ibid. 4:9, 5:6)
the Trinity is praised in three-fold turns eternal.[88]

The old Irish preface to the poem in the *Liber Hymnorum* tells an ironic story of how Colmcille came to write another trinitarian poem included there. In return for a gift from Pope Gregory the Great, Colmcille sent him a copy of the *Altus Prosator*. The pope was not impressed, commenting that it gave more praise to the created than to the Creator! So Colmcille composed another hymn, the *In te Christe*. It builds up to the glory of the Trinity via the glories of Christ as God – 'You are God for ever and ever in glory'. The cosmic dimension is there too, in God as *formator omnium*, in Christ as *creator omnium*. Finally –

88 The *Altus Prosator* must have been well known on the continent – Rabanus Maurus (780–856) borrowed from it. According to Raby (op. cit.,181), although one admirer regarded Rabanus as a poet second to none of his time, he borrowed freely from classical and Christian predecessors. 'The most conspicuous example of such plagiarism is the long rhythmical poem on the Catholic faith, which incorporates, with appropriate adaptations, the *Altus Prosator* of Columba.'

> This glory is glory to the most high unbegotten God the Father
> and honour to the supreme only-begotten Son;
> and to the noble Spirit, holy, perfect and solicitous,
> let there be a perpetual *Amen* for ever and ever.

COLUMBANUS

From Colmcille of blessed memory in Donegal, Iona, and evangelizer of northern Britain, we come to another great Colm, the Columbanus of Bangor, Brittany, Auxeuil in France and Bobbio in Italy (543–615).[89] In him we reach a new level of doctrinal elaboration, but still in a profoundly spiritual context, expressed in a Latin that is clear, insistent, and with an intensity of feeling partly driven by his natural temperament, but also by a spirituality of which the ultimate goal is the contemplative, mystical level. The richest expression of both the doctrine and the consequent spirituality is in the sequence of thirteen sermons (*Instructiones*) delivered to religious in Milan. That location gives another reason for the emphasis on the Trinity and on its cosmic as well as spiritual range – for Arianism was still abroad in the Lombard region of northern Italy. 'Who shall examine the secret depths of God? Who shall dare to treat of the eternal ground and source (*principium*) of the universe?'[90] The way to it is via the 'Fountain of Life', that is, via the incarnate second Person of the Trinity, Jesus Christ, the same 'Who with the Father and the Holy Spirit is one unto ages and ages'.[91]

Columbanus declares his programme from the start, with the principle that 'our doctrine should commence from that point whence all that is arises and what has not been begins'.[92] What that point is can be best expressed in his own words:

> Let every man therefore who wants to be saved believe first in God, the first and the last, one and three, one in substance, three in character; one in *potentia*, three in *persona*; one in nature, three in name; one in Godhead, who is Father and Son and Holy Spirit, one God, wholly invisible, inconceivable, inexpressible, in whom Being always is (*in quo est semper esse*), since God the Trinity is eternal ... [93]

89 Works edited, with translation, by G. S. M. Walker, *Sancti Colombani Opera* (SLH, Vol 2), (Dublin: Institute for Advanced Studies, 1957; repr. 1970); I use the translation with occasional modifications.

90 *Serm.* I, 3

91 *Serm.* XIII, 3; cf. John 14:6: 'I am the way and the truth and the life, nobody comes to the Father except through me.'

92 *Serm.* I, 1.

93 *Serm.* I 2; in a note to this passage Walker says that its language recalls the *Quicumque Vult* (the Athanasian Creed), and consequently suggesting an allusion to the Arian heresy. That Creed recurs in early Irish liturgy – text and translation in the *Liber Hymnorum*.

But that supreme transcendence is complemented by God's immanent omnipresence in the world He has created. Therefore God is everywhere, wholly boundless, yet everywhere near at hand ... . 'I am', he says, 'a God at hand and not a God far away'.[94] Therefore it is not from afar that we have to seek Him: 'He resides in us like soul in body, if only we be sound members of Him ... He fills all things and encompasses all things ... enters all and transcends all...'[95]

> Therefore the great Trinity is to be piously believed and not impiously questioned; for the one God, the Trinity, is an ocean that cannot be crossed over or searched out. High is the heaven, broad the earth, deep the sea and long the ages; but higher and broader and deeper and longer is our knowledge of Him ... who created all that world from nothing (*Serm.* I, 4).

As we have already indicated, that 'knowledge', based on doctrine and faith, is but the beginning of a 'way' towards the higher and (in Cardinal Newman's term) more 'real', and ultimately mystical, knowledge attained only in the ascent of the soul. So, in *Serm.* VIII, 1, Columbanus reminds his hearers that 'now, you see, we must speak of the end of the way; for as we have already said that human life is a roadway ... it is for travellers to hasten to their homeland ...'. We have already anticipated what that roadway is, the incarnate second Person of the Trinity. Hence the prayer in the concluding sermon:

> O our Jesus, inspire our hearts, we beg thee, with that breath of thy Spirit ... 'Show me Him whom my soul has loved' (Cant 1:6) ... Blessed is the soul which is wounded by love ... And with this healing wound may our God and Lord Jesus Christ ... deign to wound the inner parts of our soul ... [i.e.] He who with the Father and the Son is one for ever and ever.[96]

TÍRECHÁN

From that rarefied atmosphere, we come down to the more breathable air, but equally high Trinitarian content, of the most beautiful story ever told about St Patrick. It is the story told by Tírechán in part II, chapter 26 of the life we have mentioned earlier, written about 700, although the story may be taken from an earlier written version – for reasons we will come to. In fact, that life is not really such in the conventional sense. It is more a collection of Patrician *memorabilia* he has gathered

94 *Serm.* I, 3; Jeremiah 23:2.

95 *Serm.* I, 3.

96 *Serm.* XIII, 3 [Shades of St John of the Cross!]

from tradition. So, once again, not all of it would pass the historian. Nevertheless there are points that might be made in favour of some of its contents.

Tírechán was a native of Mayo, that western area of Ireland where it is now mostly agreed that Patrick spent his captivity, and from where he tells us himself (*Conf.* 23), that he mysteriously heard a call to return, 'the voice of the Irish ... of the people who lived beside the wood of Foclut, which is close to the western sea (*prope mare occidentale*)'. Tírechán would then be close to at least some local traditions. In chapter II, 42–5, he gives an account of a mission by Patrick to the same region. The episode in chapter II, 26 is located further east but still well west of the Shannon. Whatever we make of the historicity of the episode, one thinks of the monk's answer to Etienne Gilson's question whether the correspondence of Abelard and Héloise was really theirs: It is too beautiful not to be authentic!

The beauty of Tírechán's episode is enhanced both by its style and its setting. The Latin is so superior to Tírechán's normal style that some have argued that he is using an earlier version, more literary than anything he could himself produce,[97] in which case the episode would be earlier than Tírechán's. The beauty of the setting[98] emerges at once in the happenstance that culminates in a conversion from anthropomorphic pagan gods to the true transcendent but omnipresent God who is both One and Three. With his holy assembly of bishops, Patrick came to the Hill of Cruachain before sunrise and sat beside the well called Clébach on the hill's eastern slopes. Who should turn up at the same well but the two daughters of the High King of Ireland, 'as women are wont to do in the morning to wash'.[99] Surprised at meeting so strange a company the maidens put them a series of questions as ancient as Homer in similar sudden meetings. Who are these people? Whence do they come? From this world or the other? Or do they come from fairyland?! Patrick gives us a characteristically bluff answer: 'It would be better for you to profess our true God than to question us about our race!' The two maidens follow with a series of naive anthropomorphic questions about this God: Who is He? Where does He live? Does He have sons and daughters? And are the daughters 'dear and beautiful in the eyes of the men of the earth?'!

'Filled with the Holy Spirit', Patrick rises to the comprehensive answer. 'Our God is the God of all men, the God of heaven and earth, of the sea and the rivers, God of the sun and the moon and the stars ... [As] God above heaven and in heaven and under heaven He has his dwelling in heaven and earth and sea ... ; He breathes in all things, gives life to all things, surpasses all things, sustains all

97 See James Carney, *The Problem of St Patrick* (Dublin: Institute for Advanced Studies, 1961), 127ff; Bieler does not fully agree with Carney. Bieler's own commentary on the same episode in the ed. cit.

98 Cf. the analogous idyllic setting of Plato's *Phaedrus*, 227a, 229ab, 230bc.

99 Cf. Homer's *Odyssey*, 7, 15ff – on Odysseus and Nausicaa.

things ... '. On the question of whether He has sons and daughters, Patrick makes one ironic concession!

> He [does] have a Son, co-eternal with Him [and] con-similar to Him; the Son is not younger than the Father, nor is the Father older than the Son, and the Holy Spirit breathes in them; neither is there any separateness between the Father and the Son and the Holy Spirit.

To that faith the maidens confess and receive baptism into it. The whole episode amounts to a 'story-theology' well *avant la lettre* – with due allowance of course for the parabolic pedagogy of the incarnate second Person of the Trinity.

It would be a pity to omit the coda, with its combination of grandeur and the perennial human pathos of death and the tomb. As Scripture reminds us (Exod. 33:20), nobody can see God here below and live. The maidens had wished to see this 'true God' already before their credal profession and baptism. Shortly afterwards they died – to enable them to see that God. When the ritual days of mourning were over, the friends of the King's maiden daughters 'buried them beside the well of Clébach and made a round fosse after the manner of the [Irish] *ferta*.[100] And the *ferta* was made over to Patrick, with the bones of the holy virgins, and to his heirs after him for ever ... '.

SCOTUS ERIUGENA

From that enchanting pastoral story of Tírechán's, we climb to the rarer air of John Scotus Eriugena (c. 810–877) in his *De Divisione Naturae* (On the Division of Nature).[101] It is a systematized *summa* of our diverse preceding universalizing material, from the cosmos to its Trinitarian Creator, at all levels from scriptural exegesis via philosophy and theology to the supreme mystical vision. The range of the Latin word *natura* in the title of the work is clearer in the Greek title, *Periphyseōn*, 'about natures', in the more comprehensive and cosmic plural. Eriugena makes its meaning plain in the opening statement of his project: to 'ever more carefully investigate the fact that the first and fundamental division of all things that can either be grasped by the mind, or lie beyond its grasp, is into those that are (*sunt*), and those that are not'. The generic term that comes to his mind

100 'But we call it *relic*, that is, the remains of the maidens – *residuae puellarum*' (ibid.); *ferta* might possibly mean a grave mound or barrow, as in pre-historic burial practice – see e.g. Homer's *Iliad*, 24, 797–801.

101 Editions; Migne, *Patrologia Latina*, vol. 122; four of the five books in the SLH series, with translation; between 1996 and 1999. Books 1–3 edited by E. A. Jeauneau in six tomes, vols. 161–3 in the *Corpus Christianorum: Continuatio Mediaevalis* (Brepols). Where available, I use the SLH translation, with occasional modification.

for them all is the Greek *physis* and its Latin equivalent *natura*. The resultant work has been described as the greatest theologico-philosophical achievement from Augustine down to Thomas Aquinas. It amounts to a cosmological 'epic' of egress and regress – influenced by Greek Christian Platonists[102] – in which all creation issues from its Creator and returns to Him at the end.

How the Trinity comes into that all-encompassing epic process we need not explain again. Neither is this the occasion to get too involved in the abstract dialectics that systematize both the theology and the way of the ascent to the peaks of spirituality. One illustrative sample will suffice – under the focal term of *cause*, the quest for the ultimate Cause (*ratio*) of all things, the Cause of *all* causes.

> The theologians have correctly deduced from the things that are (*sunt*), that this Cause is (*esse*), and is wise (*sapientem*) ... and from the stable motion and moving and the mobile stability of all things, that that Cause has life (*vivere*). In this way they have also discovered the great truth that the Cause of all things is a threefold substance (*ter subsistentem*) ... Therefore the Cause and creative Nature of all things is (*est*), is wise (*sapit*) and lives (*vivit*). And from this those who search out the truth that by its Being (*essentia*) is understood the Father, by its wisdom (*sapientia*) the Son, by its life (*vitam*) the Holy Spirit.'[103]

And he goes on to assert that 'even this (truth) was discovered only through the combined light of the spirit's intuitive understanding and the reason's investigation (*spiritualis intelligentiae rationabilisque investigationis*)'.[104] For the triune God 'is not unity or trinity of such a kind as can be conceived by any human intellect, however pure'.[105]

I leave the dialectics there, and turn to Eriugena's scriptural approach in Book 2, where he finds the Trinity in the opening words of Genesis, at the start of a hexaemeron that continues to the end of Book 4. From the words of Genesis 1:1–2 we are to 'understand that the most high and unique Cause of all things, I mean the Holy Trinity, is openly revealed by these words: "In the beginning (*in principio*) God made heaven and earth", that is to say, the Father under the name God, and his Word under the name of Beginning (*principium*), and the Holy Spirit a little later where the Scripture says; "The Spirit of God hovered (*superferebatur*) over (the waters)"; for Holy Scripture did not here mean any other spirit ... '.[106]

102 In translations and commentaries he made them available in the Latin West.

103 SLH 1, 66–9; PL 455c.

104 SLH 1, 68–9; PL 456b.

105 SLH 1, 68–9; PL 456a.

106 SLH 2, 68–9; PL 555cd.

That argument might look like mere *symbolica verba*, but Augustine had already used it in his *Confessions* (VII 5, 6ff). And in both cases the argument starts from a 'beginning' (*principium*), interpreted not as merely temporal but as the metaphysical and theological uncreated Ground of all being. As explained earlier, that is the deeper meaning of the Greek term *archē*, used by Greek philosophers in analogous contexts, translated into Latin as *principium*. It is the term used in the Greek (LXX) translation of Genesis (1:1), and echoed in John's Gospel (1:1) – where John begins the Trinitarian dimension: 'Thus you have ... the ... Cause of (all) causes openly and distinctly declared in those pages from the word of God.'[107]

But this triune transcendent Cause of causes is also immanent and omnipresent in his creation. He is above all things, within all things, and 'encompasses all things because all things are within Him, and outside Him there is nothing'.[108]

That immanence 'within all things' (*intra omnia*) has a particular relevance for *human* nature, created by God with the significantly plural phrase: 'in our own image, in the likeness of ourselves' (Gen 1:26). In *Conf.* XIII 11, 12, St Augustine interprets this plural 'ourselves' as Trinitarian – and yet one. Human beings should 'meditate on three things to be found in themselves ... The three things of which I speak are existence, knowledge, will (*esse, nosse, velle*). For I *am* and I *know* and I *will*.' These three are distinct, and yet there is in them only one 'inseparable life, one life, one mind, one essence'. Eriugena takes over Augustine's analogies from these Trinitarian writings, 'where he searches by a wonderful investigation (*mirabili indagatione*) into the Trinity's image in human nature'.[109]

Well might Eriugena turn to that 'wonderful investigation' – by the thinker who thinks from the human heart, 'restless till it rests in God':[110] the thinker who sounds the 'great deep' (*grande profundum*)[111] that man is, and the 'abyss of the human psyche' (*abyssus humanae conscientiae*).[112] It was by entry into his own 'interior depths (*intima mea*)' that Augustine had his first mystical experience, in which he saw the transcendent Light that is the Light of all lights. But he is careful to add that he owed this vision not to his own human effort alone, but to the guiding light and help of God Himself. 'You called from afar: "Yes! I am who am." And I heard as one hears in the heart.'[113] On Plotinian influence see *Conf.* VII 9, 13 ff.

This effort, and its resulting experience, represents already an intense drive towards a supreme spiritual goal. Augustine's prayer in the *Soliloquia* (II 1,1) is

107 SLH 2, 68–71; PL 555d–556a.

108 SLH 2, 144–5; PL 590b.

109 *De Trinitate*, Books VIII, ff; Eriugena, SLH 2, 174–5; PL 603ab.

110 *Conf.* I 1, 1.

111 *Conf.* IV 14, 22

112 *Conf.* X 2, 2; cf. a modern Latin version of Psalm 63:7; *Profunditas est homo, et cor ejus abyssus.*

113 *Conf.* VII 10,16.

to 'know myself, to know thee' (*noverim me, noverim te*).[114] And to 'know thee' is to ascend to the contemplative knowledge of the Trinity here below, through a glass darkly, but finally in the glory of the beatific vision. The stages of that ascent Augustine outlines in the *De doctrina Christiana* (II 7, 9–10), and in the ultimate vision evoked in the prayer that concludes his *De Trinitate* (XV 28, 51). It is a prayer of thanks and praise to 'the Lord, the God who is One and unique, the God who is the Trinity', on attaining Whom our higher knowledge will put an end to all the multiple words we utter on earth without ever arriving at the Reality they try to express (ibid.).[115]

That arrival is a return, Eriugena's 'regress', to the source of our being and of our nature. And both Augustine and Eriugena find the polar pull to that return integrated into human nature itself. It is the *point de départ* of Augustine's *Confessions*, and of his way of ascent to ultimate truth. 'Thou hast made us oriented towards Thyself, and our hearts are restless until they rest in Thee' (*Conf.* I 1,1). Eriugena expresses the same principle in Book 5, the book of the ultimate regress. Human nature 'strives after nothing other than its supreme good, to which it is drawn as by a primary polar principle (*principio*)', the magnet of human attraction towards it as towards a teleological fulfilment. 'For every rational created nature, which is understood to exist specifically in the human being, even in his sins ... is ever seeking his God, from whom he has his being, and for whose contemplation he was created.'[116]

But even such a God-oriented human nature cannot by itself attain the supreme spiritual level of knowing Him. For that spiritual ascent *human* nature needs the descent of the *supernatural* graces from the Trinity itself. And here, in both Augustine and Eriugena, the Holy Spirit comes into particular prominence. The extrinsic operations of the Trinity are of course common to all.[117] But each of the three Persons has a particular individual role in the shared Trinitarian operation. For Eriugena, in that dispensation, 'it is the Holy Spirit ... who perfects all things (*perficit omnia*)'[118]. To illustrate that in the spiritual life he quotes St Paul at

114 Cf. John Henry Newman on resting 'in the thought of two and two only absolute and luminously self-evident beings, myself and my Creator ...'. *Apologia pro Vita Sua* (William Oddie's edition, Everyman's Library, 1993), 89.

115 Cf. Plotinus, *Enneads*, 1, Third Tractate, Section 3, on the level of knowledge that leaves all reasoning dialectic behind.

116 PL 919a. Eriugena is building here on three governing concepts that start in Plato and are continued in Aristotle, Cicero, Plotinus, Augustine and Boethius. They are: *supreme happiness* (*eudaimonia, beatitudo*), which is attained through the *supreme good* (*megiston agathon, summum bonum*); both of which concepts depend on *supreme wisdom* (*sophia, sapientia*).

117 Augustine *Conf.* XIII 9,10; Eriugena, SLH 2, 84–5; PL 562c.

118 SLH 2, pp. 66-67; PL 554a.

length, on the charisms in 1 Cor 12: "To one is given the speaking of wisdom, to another the knowledge according to the same Spirit. . . All these are operated by one and the same Spirit, Who dispenses to each as he decides what is appropriate to each". '[119] 'It is in your gift (the Holy Spirit) that we rest (*requiescimus*)' says Augustine, 'it is there that we enjoy (*fruimur*) you.'[120] 'And this', says Eriugena, 'is that spiritual way that stretches out into the infinite' – this after first quoting Psalm 105:4: Look for the Lord and get strength from his power.[121]

It is in his Homily on the Prologue to St John's Gospel that Eriugena, using his own wings on the 'eagle' himself, flies highest into the trinitarian infinite. John is the spiritual eagle who overflies not merely the world of the senses but, on the wings of the deepest interior theology, transcends even the vision of all philosophical theorizing, seeing, as he does, 'beyond all that is and is not, seeing with the inner eye of the clearest and highest contemplation'.[122] By virtue of unutterable wisdom (*ineffabili sapientiae virtute*), he gained ingress to the realities that transcend all others, that is, 'into the mysteries (*secreta*) of the one Essence in three Subsistents (*substantiis*), and of the three Subsistents in one Essence'.[123] But that he could not have done without the light of the Trinity itself – 'without having been made fit and worthy to participate in incomprehensible truth'. And that fitness means being to some degree '*in Deum transmutatus*'. He 'could not otherwise ascend to God *nisi prius fieret Deus*'.[124]

As I said earlier, Eriugena was a Christian Platonist. One recalls then Plato's *Theaetetus* (176ab): 'Therefore we ought to strive to escape from the earth to the world where Divinity dwells. And to make this escape is to grow into likeness to God, in the measure that that is possible (*homoiōsis theoi kata to dunaton*); and to become like God is to become righteous, holy and wise.'

OTHERWORLD JOURNEYS

In the introduction I mentioned the genre of three-storey otherworld visionary journeys among early Irish Christian writings. It is of course a primordial genre, from Homer[125] down to Plato[126] and Virgil[127] in the Greco-Roman world, and from Judaic writing down through the Christian world, where it culminated in Dante's

119 Conf. 13, 9,10.

120 *Conf.* 13, 9,10.

121 PL 919d.

122 PL 283b.

123 PL 285d.

124 PL 286a.

125 *Odyssey*, XI.

126 The myth of Er in *Republic* X 614ff.

127 *Aeneid*, VI, 236ff.

Divina Commedia. I need not repeat the distinctive features of the Irish Christian genre: the felt closeness of the other world in the pre-Christian Celtic imagination, the consequent easy Christian adaptation of the pre-Christian sagas of otherworld journeys and their Celtic coloration in details, the more architectonic Irish Christian version of a genre that hitherto lacked an ordered structure. It is this structural contribution in particular that enabled some scholars to describe the Irish versions as forerunners of Dante – there are in fact some striking parallels in the details.

There is one particular Irish example that could have been known to Dante, since it was written in Latin on the continent in 1149, and well known there. It is the *Vision of Tundal* (*Visio Tnugdali*) we mentioned earlier. It is also the most architectonically structured of the Irish versions. But since, like Dante's *Commedia,* they all culminate in the Trinity that is our concern here, I choose a single sample – for its specific details and its poetic prose – from an earlier work in Old Irish. It is the *Fís Adamnáin* (the Vision of Adamnán),[128] so called because attributed to Adamnán of Iona (c. 625–c. 704). It cannot however be his, but its author may be earlier than the manuscripts of the tenth or eleventh centuries.

Its Irish coloration and cosmic dimension emerges in its opening sentence: 'Noble and wonderful is the Lord of the Elements',[129] later named 'Lord of Creation',[130] the two terms that recur in early Gaelic religious poetry. We come to that Lord as Trinity through a highly artistic evocation of 'the splendour that is in the region of the Heavenly Host around the Lord's own throne ... ':[131]

> Over the Glorious One that sits upon the Royal throne is a great arch, like unto a wrought helmet or a regal diadem. And the eye that should behold it would forthwith melt away. Three circles are round about it, separating it from the (Heavenly) Host, and by no explanation may the nature of them (the circles) be known. Six thousand thousands ... surround the fiery throne, which burns on for ever without end or term.[132]

Since we have mentioned Dante's *Commedia* we may appropriately quote him on the trinitarian circles in the culminating vision of the *Paradiso,* XXXIII, 115ff:

128 Translation in C. S. Boswell, *An Irish Precursor of Dante* (London, 1908); cf. John D. Seymour, *Irish Visions of the Other World* (London: SPCK, 1930). See also Eileen Gardiner (ed.), *Visions of Hell and Heaven Before Dante* (New York: Italica Press, 1989).

129 Paragraph 1.

130 Par. 2.

131 Par. 7.

132 Par. 8.

> In the deep and radiant Being/of the transcendent light three circles appeared to me/ of three colours and one dimension;/and one from the other like rainbow from rainbow/appeared reflected, while the third appeared as fire that from the one and the other breathed equally ...
>
> [For human reason it is] like the geometer who sets all his effort/ to squaring the circle, but no measure finds,/for all his calculation no formula he finds.

This is a peak on which we well might rest, but here below what goes up must come down. I have highlighted the richer, loftier and more elaborated trinitarian texts. Yet beneath that level lies another rich seam that I have mostly left unmined, but which should not be forgotten. At the simplest level[133] devotion to the Trinity remained characteristic of Irish spirituality in Gaelic poems and prayers down through the centuries. That simpler devotional material is naturally less developed and often fragmentary, but in its very simplicity it is rich in the artistic beauty and deep spirituality of the 'poor in spirit' who are moved more by the heart than by the head. Good examples of that nether simpler seam, and its long survival, recur in the Gaelic dictated and published *Life* of Peig Sayers in the early twentieth century. She was born in Co. Kerry, but married into the Great Blasket Gaelic-speaking island. Her son's preface opens with the phrase: 'praised be the King of Creation'.

To conclude with a sample of that more nether seam, I turn not to a short or fragmentary instance, but to a much longer and more expansive outcrop in a prominent early Irish genre, the litany. Despite its length, the litany is simple in its repetitive mode, and can be devotional and deeply spiritual in private prayer or communal liturgy. Among the Irish examples is a tenth-century Irish-language *Litany of the Trinity*.[134] In a long and ordered sequence, it invokes each of the three Persons individually, each invoked in terms of the long list of rubrics that

133 See e.g. the Gaelic prayer before sleep in Douglas Hyde, *The Religious Songs of Connacht* (Shannon: Irish University Press, 1972), 368–9: 'I lay me down with thee, O Jesus/. . . /O Father who created me,/O Son who redeemed me,/O Holy Spirit who sanctified me,/ be you Three with me.' Cf. ibid. 396–7 (*Three Folds in My Garment*).

134 Irish text and translation in *Irish Litanies*, edited by the Rev. Charles Plummer (London, 1925), 79–85. It is attributed to one Mugrón, a late tenth-century *comharb* (successor) of Colmcille in Iona. See also the intense spirituality of the long series of invocations of the Trinity for forgiveness that opens the *Old Irish Litany of Confession* (ibid.), 3–5. It too includes the totalizing cosmic dimension: 'O World above all worlds,/ O Power above all powers/... O cause above all causes ... '. Two much later Trinitarian poems in English by Irish writers: 'A Prayer to the Trinity' by Richard Stanihurst (1545–1618), and Aubrey de Vere (1814–1902), in 'Feast of the Most Holy Trinity'. They are respectively in 56 and 113–14, Patrick Murray (ed.), *The Deer's Cry: A Treasury of Irish Religious Verse* (Dublin: Four Courts Press, 1986).

address their individual attributes and roles. Its length will prevent us doing justice to it here – we can only sample its intense devotional spirituality and the grandeur of its range.

I have already explained the connection of devotion and spirituality with the litany as a genre. But the specific grandeur of range in this particular litany is that its trinitarian spirituality combines with, and transfuses, the same cosmic, totalising range of the Trinity that we have emphasised from the start. The litany opens with an invocation of the Father:

> Have mercy on us, O God the Father Almighty:
> O God of Hosts,
> O high God,
> O Lord of the World,
> O ineffable God,
> O Creator of the elements ...

The same antiphon opens the invocation of 'Jesus Christ, Son of the Living God'. He is the 'beginning of all things', the 'completion of the world', the 'Word of God', the 'Life of all things', the 'Intelligence of the mystical world'.

After the same opening antiphon the Holy Spirit is invoked. He is the 'highest of all spirits', the 'Finger of God', the 'Septiform Spirit', the 'Spirit by whom is ordered every lofty thing', the 'Holy Spirit that rules all created things, visible and invisible'.

The conclusion invokes all three persons together:

> Have mercy upon me, O Father, O Son, O Holy Spirit. Have mercy upon me, O God, from whom and through whom is the rule of all created things for Thee, O God.
>
> To Thee be glory and honour for ever and ever.

That last prayer concludes with *Amen. Ainsi soit-il* here too – at least until the author, or *quicunque vult,* resumes.

ADDENDUM

In this paper I have emphasized the prominence of the universal range of the Trinity in Irish early Christian writing – up to my last page. I should not then omit a late mention of a possible source of influence on that Irish tradition, a source reference I owe to a scripture scholar in Maynooth, Reverend Dr. Séamus

O'Connell. He gave it to me after I had completed the paper, in answer to a casual question I asked him about that Irish tradition. He told me that the Irish tradition was influenced by the same theme in earlier *apocryphal* works from abroad, including the influence of early contacts with sources in the Holy Land and Syria. To provide me with some samples he gave me a volume edited by Máire Herbert and Martin McNamara, MSC: *Irish Biblical Apocrypha: Selected Texts in Translation*, T&T Clark, Edinburgh 1989.

At this late stage, I must confine myself to quoting one good sample from the first paragraph of 'The Evernew Tongue' (pp. 109–18 of ed. cit.).

> *In principio fecit Deus caelum et terram, et reliqua.* The High-King of the world, stronger than any King, higher than any power ... , the only Son of God the Father – he it was who gave this account of the formation and creation of the world to the many peoples on earth, because it was not known to anyone except God ... For this reason, then, ... this account came from heaven to open the mind and intellect of all, so that souls might find the way of life and salvation.

They had no knowledge 'of who made' the world. The Trinity is completed in paragraph 11 – on the role of the Holy Spirit in the creation.

In paragraphs 23 and following, an account is given of each day in the six days of creation. One very Irish theme pervades it, but much more developed. That theme is the wondrous beauty of the endless variety and complexity of design in all the elements and living creatures in that 'nature' that the triune God has created.

DANTE

DANTE AND THE RELIGIOUS IMAGINATION

I

Two preliminary questions are omitted from this essay. They are omitted because I presuppose them as asked and variously answered by other contributors. Both questions have to do with imagination: what kind of 'faculty' have we in mind? and how do we understand its cognitive mode and estimate its cognitive value – especially in comparison with logical reason? Another justification for dispensing with these questions is that they can be answered only after a 'phenomenological' study of the actual working and achievements of the imagination. After which we might work inductively towards definition and theory. Or maybe, like à Kempis in *The Imitation*, happier to feel than define, just rest content with the self-validating savour of the apple.

Something like that is the case with Dante himself. Few men's work better embodies the two poles of our problem, reason and imagination. Reason we might expect, *il ben dello intelletto,* from a man whose *corpus* is the distillation and crystallization of the great Classical and Scholastic achievements of intellect. That he is also a man of the imagination must be obvious even *a priori,* merely from the implications of the rôle played by what we may call the Beatrician experience at the heart of his perceptions and the works that embody them. Yet he seldom or never called this mode of experience and knowledge by the name of imagination in any sense coextensive with our contemporary 'imagination', 'a licentious and vagrant faculty, unsusceptible of limitations, and impatient of restraint'.[1] And, despite the status of *intelletto* in him, no more did he feel obliged to address himself to our problem, the theoretical justification and evaluation of the imaginative vis-à-vis that *intelletto.* One explanation is that he could take for granted – and confirmed in his experience – a great deal of traditional theory about modes and levels of knowing that we are less familiar with, or cannot be so naive about. Theory which puts imagination – though without calling it such – in a locatable position on the map, in a way that the moderns, for all their Romanticism (or because of it?) cannot do.

A first example and very early instance of what Dante could and did take for granted will serve also to introduce us to both radical experience and radical

1 Samuel Johnson speaking.

questions about the understanding of it. The example I take is that which occasioned the first sonnet of the *Vita Nuova* (*VN*)[2] a sonnet therefore from among the earliest that Dante wrote, the first written expressly out of the Beatrician experience, or in any case chosen as the starting-point for reflexive analysis of that experience. It represents therefore the starting-point of the imaginative and poetic process which culminated in the penetration to the heart of reality at the summit of the *Paradiso*.

The occasion of this sonnet is narrated in the prose of *VN* 3. In a dream on the night after the famous greeting by Beatrice to Dante in his eighteenth year he has a *maravigliosa visione* – of Love ('a lord of awesome aspect') and of Beatrice sleeping in his arms. Love awakens the sleeping Beatrice and forces her to eat Dante's burning heart. And now the hitherto joyous Love begins to weep, and clasping Beatrice in his arms he is seen to turn away and carry her off up to heaven. Out of this strange experience Dante writes his sonnet (*A ciascun alma presa*), addressing it to his fellow-poets, the *fedeli d'Amore*, and asking them to interpret the experience it describes.

Of course there is much here that, especially out of context, may sound naive, if not fictive. But we have the evidence of surviving replies to the request for interpretation. And there is the fact that once we start to question the historicity of *maravigliose visioni* in Dante we can hardly stop. But in any case I do not think the question of historicity affects our present point – which is the extent to which Dante accepted the imaginative as significant and susceptible of interpretation. This point is reinforced when we remember that the *VN* is a 'confessional' book written out of experience seen in retrospect. A book therefore which singles out what has already been *seen* to have significance.[3] And in fact this vision does turn out to foreshadow essential elements in the course of events to come, as they are unfolded in the *VN*. Nobody fully understood it at the time, he tells us, *ma ora è manifestissimo a li più semplici*.

And Dante's own sense that there is a meaning is reinforced by the replies of his poet friends. Even if nobody fully understood that meaning at the time there was one, Guido Cavalcanti, who, by good luck or good guidance, did divine a lot that events validated (no. 6a in FB). 'He took your heart away, seeing that your lady was sinking towards death … '. But it is not this temporally *prophetic* significance of the imaginative that shall most concern us in Dante – rather the 'vertical' significance of sign, symbol, image, as disclosing a higher plane of reality.

2 For the poems in the *VN*, I use the translations of Kenelm Foster and Patrick Boyde, *Dante's Lyric Poetry* (2 vols, Oxford, Clarendon Press, 1967), hereafter referred to as FB. References to 'Sayers' and 'Reynolds' are to their Penguin versions of the *Vita Nuova* and the *Commedia*.

3 Like St Augustine's *Confessions* – or even the Gospels?

And here Cavalcanti is much to our purposes. 'What you saw, I think, was all nobility (*valore*) and all joy and all the good (*bene*) that man can know ... '.[4] These are among the prime 'values', the sense of which, pursued, will lead Dante to the heart and fount of reality, to 'the Love that moves the sun and the other stars'. The *sense* of these values, I have said, not just the intellectual concepts and theory of them, a sense first 'felt in the blood and felt along the heart', and only then, and from there, passing into the 'purer mind'.

By way of this first example of an imaginative experience with a felt significance we have been able to come to a point where we could speak intelligibly of higher reality translated into image or symbol, and not only of the 'realities' but of a dimension of their reality that we can only designate by that poor, homeless concept of 'value'. We have been able to speak also of a special mode of awareness of those realities and values, a pre-conceptual mode, but not one which we may therefore feel free to devalue. For the pre-conceptual may very well be the condition, and provide the material, of the conceptual. Concepts without percepts, said Kant, are empty, percepts without concepts are blind.[5] Dante, as already indicated, was supremely a man of both modes.

With this minimal *mise-en-scène*, including our insistent *mise-en-valeur(s)* (as we might label it) my hope is that we have insinuated ourselves into an angle of viewing from which the role of the imagination in Dante will be intelligible without too much heavy annotation. Intelligible, that is, in its original and originating experience, in its progress, in the cadres of its interpretation, and in its supreme point of arrival.

This essay, of course, cannot hope to trace the *organic* development to that supreme point. Besides, it is a point that is long since far beyond mere imagination –

4 The taste may be doubtful but 'beautiful is the *risqué*' that makes it irresistible to give the details of another of the replies that Dante got back, from one Dante da Maiano (6c in FB). It is something of a corrective against taking either ourselves or Dante with too precious a seriousness on these necessarily ambivalent matters: 'Having considered, my rather ignorant friend, the matter you ask me about, I answer briefly and explain its true significance. With your needs in mind I say this: if you are well and in your right mind, *che lavi la tua coglia largamente*, so that the vapours that make you talk nonsense be extinguished and dispersed; but if you are suffering from a serious illness, then, believe me, the only thing I understand from your words is that you were raving. Such is my opinion, duly returned; nor will I ever alter my judgement *fin che tua acqua al medico no stendo.*' Dante was to 'put down' a lot of people in his time. I don't know if he ever gave better than he got here – who knows but he may even have deserved it at the priggish age of eighteen. And apparently the put-down was not just witty but 'scientific' as well – see FB note ad loc. cit.

5 That, however, is an exaggeration of truth. For 'touch' is indeed sightless, and so in 'touches of God'; yet shall we say that as a 'percept' and not concept, touch is blind *tout court*?

All' alta fantasia qui mancò possa,
High imagination here broke down.

We are in the domain of *mystical* experience[6] – once again whether Dante's own or at second hand does not really affect the issue of the process he describes. Neither does it matter that we are *beyond* imagination. What matters is the rôle of imagination on the way to its own transcending. For we are beyond not only *fantasia* but *intelletto* –

As the geometer his mind applies
  To square the circle, nor for all his wit
  Finds the right formula, howe'er he tries.
(PARA. 33.133–5, TRANS. REYNOLDS)

As is well known, it is Beatrice who has been the inspiration first and then the guide of the ascent to this supreme point. And if we are to understand in organic detail the process of the imagination in Dante, we must return to the Beatrician experience, and starting from there follow its development through the three great stages of its unfolding. The first of those three stages is the *Vita Nuova*, a retrospective, systematizing, 'confessional' work, composed about 1295, five years after the death of Beatrice, ending with visions of Beatrice in glory, and supremely, in a *mirabile visione* in which Dante 'sees things' that determined him to write no more of 'this blessed lady' until by study he was qualified to 'say of her such things as have never been said of any woman' (*VN* 42).

The *Convivio*, composed about ten years later, is unfinished, but it gives us a glimpse of what that projected study was. It represents in fact nothing less than another profound experience, a kind of 'conversion'[7] to philosophy; philosophy, that is, in the old high, sapiential, contemplative, and cosmic sense of Greece and the Wisdom literature of the Bible. In this *filosofia-sapienza* drive, passion fuses with intellect, the earthly Beatrice with the visionary Lady Philosophy of Boethius, and, still more sublimely, with *la bellissima e onestissima figlia de lo Imperadore de lo universo* (*Conv.* 2.15.12). She is the hypostatized, feminine Sophia of the Creator. *Ego ex ore Altissimi prodivi primogenita ante omnem creaturam* (Sir 24:5 – and cf. *Conv.* 3.12.14).

The *Commedia* ... how shall it abide our question? It is the fruit of the projected studies and the fulfilment of the idealizing promise. But of course no such work could ever come out of study alone. It needed what for shorthand we are

6 We shall consider this in the second part of this essay.

7 As an instance of what I mean see St Augustine, *Confessions* 3.4.

calling imagination. It could not even come out of imagination alone. It needed those higher states of spiritual awareness, in which, as we have indicated, imagination is transcended. And this is precisely what it purports to be written out of, a visionary experience in Holy Week of 1300. It is the fruit of another, or other, 'conversion' experiences – sudden light from out the dark wood of crisis,

Nel mezzo del cammin di nostra vita.

But what is strange, and more to our purposes, is that it needed Beatrice too – in Dante's case, that is, for of course we do not make a rule out of such an exceptional instance. The strange thing is that this journey to the heart and fount of reality, this succession of revealings of glory within glory, is also a deeper and deeper perception of the reality of Beatrice, a revelation of glory after glory in her fully realized and glorified state. And it is essential to understand that her function as guide in the *Paradiso* is not only through didactic instruction – and even that only because she has a light of higher knowledge that Dante had not. She is in her own self the guide, through being the reflecting image of what she reveals. In the luminous phrase of *Purg.* 6.45, she is the light between Truth and intellect, *lume ... tra 'l vero e lo intelletto.* She reflects the rays of the eternal (*Para.* 31.72).

Of all that I have looked upon with these eyes
  Thy goodness and thy power have fitted me
  The holiness and grace to recognize.
(Para. 31.82–4, trans. Reynolds)

And there is something still stranger and more wonderful. The supreme point of the *Paradiso* is the supreme integration of reality, in one universal 'form', *la forma universal di questo nodo* (*Para.* 33.91), the scattered leaves of all the universe bound into one volume within the abyss of light (Para. 33.85–7). And yet, paradoxically, in this abyssal in-one-ing of all reality in its ground, the reality of concrete, individual, historical being and experience is preserved. As with the human features of Christ, mysteriously limned in the Trinity (*Para.* 33.131), so with the Florentine girl and Dante's earthly experience of her. From the summit of the Earthly Paradise where Beatrice is first glimpsed again, an arc is thrown back over space and time to the original moment of his earthly vision of her. So that the whole original complex of experience is reactivated, resurrected we might say.

And instantly, for all the years between
  Since her mere presence with a kind of fright
  Could awe me and make my spirit faint within,

There came on me, needing no further sight,
Just by that strange, outflowing power of hers,
The old, old love in all its mastering might.
(PURG. 30.34–39, TRANS. SAYERS)

Guardami ben! Ben son, ben son Beatrice.
Look, look at me well! I really am the real Beatrice.
(PURG. 30.73)

And when, in Paradise, she finally ascends to her place in the Sempiternal Rose, thus putting between the mortal Dante and herself a distance greater in earthly terms than that from the heights of the heavens to the deeps of the ocean, her image still comes down to him distinct (*Para.* 31.73ff). And in answer to his parting prayer to her, she still, though ascended so high, could be seen to smile and look on him once more (*Para.* 31.91–2).

***

In order to provide an overall understanding of the Dantean pattern I have been giving a synoptic view of the three main stages of its development. It is time to return to the experience from which it started and try to trace in detail the logic of its unfolding within the single stage we shall have space to deal with, that is the stage unfolded in the *VN.* If there is a logic and rationale of the imagination, the only illuminating place to start investigating it is in the place where imagination itself works, along the pulse of life. To *start*, I say, for I have not forgotten what we said about *il ben dello intelletto*, the organizing, systematizing, validating intellect. And behind the pattern I have already sketched there lies (as suggested earlier) not only experience but a strong intellectual structure of epistemology and ontology, and even specialized epistemological questions like the relative priority of will and intellect, love and knowledge, i.e. whether love depends on knowledge or vice versa. The answers to such questions did not just validate experience *post eventum*. They facilitated the *a priori* acceptance of experience *in eventu*. But for us these questions must wait till after we have studied the experience. As indeed they did for Dante, initially untutored in *filosofia*. They are among the questions we can watch him working out in the *Convivio*.

The Beatrician experience began in a kind of epiphany, with all the force of a revelation, and the immediate effect of a kind of 'conversion', with all the power over heart and intellect that 'conversion' implies. The event took place when the nine-year-old Dante first laid eyes on the eight-year-old Beatrice Portinari. What he saw and felt at that miraculous moment has to be described in his own words:

> She was dressed in a very noble colour, a decorous and delicate crimson, tied with a girdle and trimmed in a manner suited to her tender age. The moment I saw her I say in all truth that the vital spirit, which dwells in the innermost depths of the heart, began to tremble (*tremare*) so violently that I felt the vibration alarmingly in all my pulses, even the weakest of them. As it trembled it uttered these words: *Ecce deus fortior me, qui veniens dominabitur michi* [Behold a god stronger than I, who in his coming will rule over me – i.e. Love] (*VN* 2, trans. Reynolds).

This is the effect upon the *heart* – let us say on the *imagination*. The account goes on to describe how the effect was carried from the heart to the intellect, which 'began to be greatly wonder-stricken' (*maravigliare*) and pronounced to the image-bearing senses its conviction that *apparuit iam beatitudo vestra* – the source of your blessedness has now appeared.

The lasting consequence must also be quoted *in extenso.*

> From that time onwards I declare that Love ruled my soul, which was wedded to him thus early in my life. And he began to exert such assurance and mastery over me through the power my imagination (*imaginazione*) gave him that I was obliged to fulfill all his wishes absolutely. Many a time he ordered me to seek out and see[8] this young angel ... And in all her ways I saw her as so noble and praiseworthy that one could apply to her that verse of the poet Homer: She did not look like the daughter of a mortal man but of a god.(*VN* 2).

I have quoted those passages *in extenso* to enable us to identify more easily the essential elements of what happens in them. Let us see what those five elements are.

At the most comprehensive level Dante discovers that his being and his faculties are in the power of a force beyond himself and his control – a power personified here in the conventional god of Love but later (*VN* 25) philosophically analyzed and 'demythologized'. (And the deepening understanding of Love as a metaphysical, and ultimately theological and personal power in man and the universe will go on through the *Convivio* and the *Commedia.*)

What that most comprehensive power subsumes in the experience of it may be organized along two lines already mentioned, ontological levels in reality and epistemological levels in knowing. As regards levels of reality, Beatrice in the experience is the perfect example of an 'image' or 'symbol' in e.g. the Coleridgean

8 Cf. Plato's *Phaedrus*, 251E, in view of the mention we shall later make of that work.

sense. That is to say, a concrete, individual object, existing *in itself* but also *deriving* from something greater than itself, and *embodying* in itself that *nescio quid maius*, that greater something from which it derives. I mention Coleridge as being a familiar source of useful ideas. But of course well before Coleridge, Dante was heir to all the underpinning available in the medieval heritage of Platonist exemplarism, the Christian concept of incarnation, and the Scholastic theory of analogy. Whatever theory we use to validate it, the experience itself adds up to the sense that Beatrice, as the *VN* later puts it, was a *miracolo*. A *miracolo*, moreover, in which has 'appeared' the beholder's highest fulfilment, *beatitudo*, that concept central to the ethical, philosophical and theological thought of the Greco-Roman-Christian tradition. (And in this respect what begins here in the *VN* is what culminated in the *Paradiso*.)

As regards modes and levels of knowing it is obvious *de iure* and *de facto* that this understanding of Beatrice could not and did not come from mere rational, conceptual analysis. The experience came first. And the experience was a given, an overwhelming given, given to the *whole* being of Dante at all levels, to the heart, to the intellect, and (in a passage of *VN* 2 not quoted) to the instincts. Even Dante himself seems to use the word *imaginazione* in something like our own ill-defined but inclusive sense to cover this complex of cognitive experience.[9]

Unique, of course, as this experience of Dante's may appear to be – or perhaps *because* of its apparent uniqueness and the consequently possible questions about the authenticity of the experience – it is usual to indicate how much it owes to the tradition of courtly love within which he writes, though eventually far transcending it. I should like briefly to indicate some elements in Dante's experience that belong to a tradition much older than courtly love à la lettre. Not for the purpose of reducing Dante to a convention. On the contrary, to confirm his experience by relating it to age-old, permanent possibilities.

The 'epiphany' that Dante saw in Beatrice he sums up in a quotation from Homer. Dante scarcely knew Homer, and this verse, *Iliad* 24.258f (referring in fact to Hector), he probably borrows and adapts from an Aristotelian quotation of it. The point I wish to make is that had Dante known Homer he could have found *passim* the idea of the Lady as an epiphany of the divine. And most notably of all in the remarkable evocation of Nausicaa as she appeared to Odysseus in *Odyssey*, 6.149ff. 'Are you divine or mortal?' he asks her. 'Never have I laid eyes on such a mortal ...'. And he goes on to speak of the *reverence*, the *awe* he feels in her presence, and even of the *beatitudo* of those who experience her grace and presence

9 It cannot be our business here to go into the question of how far the prose of the *VN* retrospectively modifies the original experience. But as a gesture it is worth remarking that the essentials are already in an earlier canzone not included in the *VN* – see FB 32.57ff.

now – thrice-blessed they, but most blessed of all the man who shall enjoy her presence as his bride.

Later (c.620–550 BC) there is the famous love-lyric of Sappho that begins: 'Like to the gods he appears ...' Sappho is early, but the felt relevance of her experience is confirmed centuries later by the fact that the Roman poet Catullus[10] translated her lyric to address it to his own Lesbia. Sappho's lyric starts from the same two basic elements as Homer, *beatitudo* in the presence of a quasi-divine epiphany. But then it moves into details of the 'pathology' of the experience which are remarkably parallel to those in Dante. Those parallels include specifically Dante's *tremare*, and in general a 'seizure' of the whole being and its faculties, up to the climactic experience of being 'all but dead'. This last item is not in the passages we quoted from the *VN* but it is implied in the early *canzone* I referred to (FB 32.57ff). And it does occur at later moments in the *VN* when the original experience was – as often – repeated, e.g. *VN* 14 and the sonnet of *VN* 15 (... Moia, moia! Die! die!).

Lastly there is Plato. Platonism, as everyone knows, is a whole metaphysic of *eros*, at the heart and summit of reality and in the heart of man. And the stages in its progress are the rungs on a ladder of ascent of the one to the other. Its diffused influence on later ages is incalculable, even in ages to which the Platonist *corpus* was not available. When we see the wood for the trees we have to see in it the far

10 Forerunner of that unusual and important moment in the literature of love, the Augustan Elegists, in whose experience there is much of courtly love *avant la lettre*. Lattimore's translation of Catullus' Sappho lyric tries to render the rhythm of the original:

Like[1] the very gods in my sight is he who
sits where he can look in your eyes, who listens
close to you, to hear the soft voice, its sweetness
        murmur in love and
laughter, all for him. But it breaks my spirit;
underneath my breast all the heart is shaken.
Let me only glance where you are, the voice dies
        I can say nothing,
But my lips are stricken to silence,[2] underneath my skin the tenuous flame suffuses;
nothing shows in front of my eyes,[3] my ears are
        muted in thunder.[4]
And the sweat breaks running upon me, fever
shakes my body,[5] paler I turn than grass is;
I can feel that I have been changed, I feel that
        Death has come near me.[6]

1. Literally *the equal of...* 2. Literally *my tongue is frozen*, or *paralyzed*. 3. Literally *I cannot see with my eyes*. 4. Literally *have a whirring* or *thunderous noise in them*. 5. Literally *a trembling* (tromos) *seizes me totally*. 6. Literally *I seem to be all but dead*.

forerunner of the Dantean pattern. But what I am concerned with at this point is nothing as large as that. I wish merely to draw attention to a section of the *Phaedrus* (250Eff), in which analysis of experience reveals more or less exactly the same phenomena as in the Sapphic and Dantean moments. It will suffice to quote and leave those details to be recognized for what they are.

'He who is newly initiated [observe the mystagogical term], who beheld many of those realities [i.e. transcendent realities, 'imaged' in those of this world], when he sees a god-like face or form which is a good image of beauty, trembles at first, and something of the old awe comes over him,[11] then, as he gazes, he reveres the beautiful one as a god ... ' (251A, trans. Loeb). Further, as separation is pain (passim in *VN*) so presence is *beatitudo*. 'Therefore the soul will not, if it can help it, be left alone by the beautiful one, but ... it is ready to be a slave ... as near as possible to the beloved; for it not only feels reverence for the one who has beauty, but finds in that one the only healer of its suffering' (252A).[12]

It will be noticed that with Plato we have introduced a notion that is wider than what we conventionally call romantic love. That notion is the love provoked by beauty in general. And in point of fact in the Platonist metaphysic as a whole it is this more universal occasion of eros that is operative. 'Surely we love only what is beautiful?' remarks St Augustine, steeped in this same Platonism (*Conf.* 4,13). The beauty that occasions romantic sexual love is only a particular instance of the more universal phenomenon. In Plato this can be seen to some extent even in the *Phaedrus* (e.g. 248D), but most obviously in the *Symposium* (especially 204ff).

What I wanted to do in this brief *excursus* was to set the 'way' of the Dantean imagination in a context. The Beatrician experience, and the consequent way, is but *one* of a whole *genre* which provides many other *analogous* possibilities. *Any* passionate, personal experience – in the domain of beauty or even beyond – could be the 'trigger'. St Augustine, for instance, is an example of a man for whom the aesthetic experience was an important starting-point – by temperament as well as Platonist influence (see e.g. *Conf.* 4.13, 15; 7.17; *De Musica* 6). This is a point made by Charles Williams, who is fond of the example of Wordsworth's experience of 'Nature'. Retaining the term 'Romantic', Williams insists that it 'includes other loves besides the 'sexual' (*The Figure of Beatrice*, 14).

11 Cf. *Purg.* 30.39 (quoted earlier), and Virgil, *Aen.* 4.23.

12 This line of the 'epiphany' is sometimes continued by reference to Joyce, with whom in fact it was an early theme – 'the supreme quality of beauty being a light from some other world' (*Portrait of the Artist*, p. 219 of Penguin *The Essential James Joyce*). See the episode of the girl on Dollymount strand. 'Her image had passed into his soul for ever ...A wild angel had appeared to him ... an envoy from the fair courts of life, to throw open before him in an instant of ecstasy the gates of all the ways of error and glory' (op. cit., 186f.).

Now as a matter of fact this is exactly what we find Dante himself saying, in a striking passage in *Conv.* 4.25 – by then, as we recall, he was complementing experience by *filosofia* and its quest for *sapienza. Conv.* 4 is devoted to ethical and moral matters,[13] in the course of which Dante, discussing the *vertudi* appropriate to each of the four ages of life, comes to consider those appropriate to the first age, *adolescenza.* Also necessary to this age is *la passione de la vergogna* – a quality actually shown by nature itself at this age in *la buona e nobile natura.* In fact in *adolescenza* it is 'the clearest mark ... of *nobilitade*' (*Conv.* 4.25.3).

The first thing worth noting here is that Dante describes *la vergogna* as a 'passion' – worthy of noting because, unless things have changed (since my time, as it were), both our sense of 'virtue' and the pallid word itself have long since lost any connotation remotely approaching *la passione.* Of course Dante is translating the technical Scholastic term *passio,* but, as will presently appear, he is giving it a more positive meaning than his sources did.

The next question is the precise meaning of *vergogna.* It is clear from the sequel that no single English term will render it. The Latin *verecundia* in its Classical sense comes near it, combining 'modesty' with at least a suggestion of the more radical sense of 'reverence' and 'awe'. Dante goes on to explain that in his intention it subsumes three *passioni* that are the foundation of the moral life. These are *stupore, pudore* and *verecundia.* As he defines them *pudore* is the sense of *pudor,* modesty, that *preveniently* restrains from the dishonourable, *verecundia* is the sense of shame after the event. There remains *stupore,* which is the focus of our interest.

Dante goes on to define it as 'a stunning (*stordimento*) of the soul through hearing, seeing or in any other way becoming aware of things sublime and wondrous (*grandi e maravigliose cose*). Things which in so far as they appear sublime generate reverence in him who perceives them, and in so far as they appear wondrous generate the desire to understand them'. It is clear that what is being described here is an emotional and imaginative capacity for wonder, awe, *admiratio, thaumazein.* An emotion not existing in a subjective void but generated by an objective reality – and therefore, we may add, positing the possibility of a pre-conceptual mode of perception. An emotion not static either, or destined to remain purely an emotion, but generating the desire for and the process of conceptual understanding of the reality that produced it. We are reminded of how

13 Specifically the quality of *nobilitade* – the sun-like source of all the other moral qualities, itself put by God in the soul, and being the 'seed of *beatitudo*' (see e.g. 4.20.9). The feeling for it is very Dantean, and after understanding it we might expect *a priori* to find it among the qualities that actuate the Beatrician experience. We are not surprised to find that is the case again and again. From the very first moment in fact, when Beatrice appeared *vestita di nobilissimo colore* (*VN* 2.3).

Plato and Aristotle saw the condition of philosophy in the capacity for wonder. And indeed since we have used the term 'sublime' we are reminded of the two natural capacities in which Longinus placed its condition. Namely the capacity for grand *emotions* and the capacity for grand *conceptions* (*On the Sublime*, ch. 8).

Patently in *stupore* we have Dante's own 'theory' of his Beatrician experience and of the imagination. And it is also a theory original to himself – precisely, no doubt, because it is indebted to his own experience. We discover this originality when we check his Thomist and Aristotelian sources.[14] Dante's generic term *vergogna* derives from their *verecundia*. But in the sources this remains merely a negative virtue – in fact Aquinas will not allow that it is technically a virtue at all (*Summa Theologiae*, II.IIae, Q. 144, art. I). It relates only to the avoidance or repentance of evil – at the level of Dante's *pudore* and *verecundia*. It does not include the positive element of *stupore*. And a striking thing is that in making *vergogna* include it Dante restored an early, original sense of both the Latin *verecundia* and its Greek equivalent, *aidōs*.

Further, in *stupore* we have not only the theory of Dante's initial experience. We have also the theory of its development. The experiences that produce *stupore* produce, as we saw, the desire to understand its occasion. This is the project announced at the end of the *VN*. It runs through the *Convivio* and comes to fulfillment in the *Commedia*. But observe that understanding is not a purely intellectual operation on the data of a once-for-all experience of *stupore*. Experience and the intellect continue together. In the *Convivio* there is a connection between love and understanding. The *Commedia*, as we know, is based on further and deeper experiences. And these often involve *stupore*, sometimes explicitly mentioned – e.g. *Purg.* 31.127, *Para.* 31.31–40. And, at the base of the whole ascent, the initial and initiating *stupore* is repeated and deepened throughout the *VN*, in ways we shall not have space to detail. One of the marked stages in that work is when those experiences already generate the desire to understand (*VN* 13). And, as already noted, the work is itself composed at a stage of retrospective understanding.

Thus does *stupore* become 'the beginning of wisdom'.[15] And we might venture the opinion that this is imagination (if we may so identify it) of a precious kind, and a corrective to some undesirable connotations of the word. It starts 'where all the ladders start' – in the concrete and individual, which then becomes the concrete universal. For the 'sublime and wondrous things' are at first perceived

14 See references ad loc. in G. Busnelli and G. Vandelli, *Il Convivio* (2 vols, Florence, Felice Le Monier, 1934 and 1937).

15 C. Williams, *The Figure of Beatrice* (Faber and Faber, London, successive impressions from 1st Ed 1943), 80.

not above and beyond the particular but in and through it. At least this is the way of the imagination in Dante. To adapt the remark of Coleridge, he elevates our thoughts by first sending them down deeper.

II

In the preceding pages we have got little further than a kind of 'notes and commentary' to the single, initial experience of the *VN*. At such a pace through the Dante *corpus* we would be headed for a volume rather than an essay. And although we have occasionally looked towards higher dimensions we have concentrated on the first storey of the Dantean imagination in its sense of the transcendent, the *grandi e maravigliose cose*, in and behind the concrete and particular *cose*. We might call it the natural, or secular, dimension – *salva reverentia* to Dante in comparison with the more usual returns from this dimension in literature. That storey is a necessary foundation for the second storey that is the ultimate subject of this essay, the *religious* imagination. And even if it were not the subject, any treatment of the imagination that omitted it – even in a consideration of the *VN* – would be truncated. To that religious dimension we shall now turn.

It is necessary to anticipate that here too we shall get little further than notes and commentary to the same core material to which we have limited ourselves in the first part. That is indeed a limitation, but within our space it will also serve the interests of simplicity and clarity (such clarity, that is, as the subject permits!). Such concentration will also serve an ideal I mentioned early on, coming down from the 'high priori' to the close weave of the phenomena.

I anticipate also that in this paper I shall not, except incidentally, take up the epistemology of how the cognitive awareness of Dante's imagination gets from what I have called the natural, or secular, dimension to the *praeter-* or *super*natural religious dimension. *Can* it be explained? Or is it a kind of quantum leap? I have indeed indicated directions in the tradition along which we might look for a theory. But here we shall concentrate on showing the ways and the extent of the presence of that dimension.

Another necessary anticipation concerns mysticism. As I said earlier, mysticism is not the same as imagination. But I said on the same occasion that in Dante it would also seem to be in some sort of continuity with imagination, and of course with *intelletto*. It will figure in the following pages because much of what I say concerning the religious dimension of Dante's imagination will turn on the phenomena of mystical experience. They will be derived from the phenomena of authentic mysticism, or descriptions of it. But for shorthand's sake I shall be obliged to commit the (common) fault of using the term *mystical* in an elastic way to describe the religious dimension in Dante – without, however, begging the question of whether some things in the *VN* imply mystical experience in the strict sense or not. A question on which the most positive arguments are in C. S. Singleton.[16] Rejected, however, by Domenico de Robertis.[17]

I do not propose to pursue the argument on this question. It is the same question, at a different level, and as finally soluble or insoluble, as the old one of whether *any* experience of 'higher consciousness' can be authenticated as really being what it appears to be. One could also get distracted by failing to distinguish between the question of the nature and implications of Dante's *language* and the question of whether it is based on *personal* experience. It does not matter whether it is or not. What matters is that the *language* of the religious dimension, including the mystical, is there. And this is established by Singleton, and not denied by de Robertis.[18] At the very least, therefore, it represents Dante's *interpretation* of the meaning, or logical potential, of the experience he did have.[19]

The moment in the *VN* where the religious dimension is most explicitly present is at its culmination in chapters 41 and 42 where there is recounted, first a vision of Beatrice in glory,[20] and then the *mirabile visione* in which things were beheld which determined Dante to be silent until he could speak worthily of her. As we have seen, this was probably the moment of perception which begot the retrospective *VN* and the project which eventually became the *Commedia*. But here I wish to attend not to what is explicitly present at the climax but to what is implicitly present along the way to that climax. And along that way I do not wish to cover again such ground as has been covered by Singleton, e.g. the Christological dimension (in chapter 1) and the parallel to the stages of the mystical ascent in the stages of Dante's ascent from love to *caritas* (chapters 3–4). I have already indicated that I would stay with the same core material we considered in the first section. And that means looking again at the 'pathology' of Dante's experience to see what further dimension of significance it might

16 C. S. Singleton, *An Essay on the Vita Nuova* (John Hopkins University Press, Baltimore and London, 1949, reprint 1977), especially chs. 3 and 4.

17 D. de Robertis, *Il libro della 'Vita Nuova'* (G. C. Sansoni, Florence, 1961). 'Ma la *Vita Nuova* testo di esperienza mistica non è ...', 121. See also p. 123.

18 On the contrary, in chapter V (*La Nuova Materia*) he brings in a greater wealth of background material.

19 As de Robertis also seems to admit on p. 121. That is if I read him correctly and if he is not rather engaged in the reductionism of interpreting Dante's language as the mere hyperbole (una capacità d'entusiasmo) of an introverted and 'modernist' concern with the status and development of his 'art'. With that possibility I do not wish to have an argument here.

20 Both Singleton (102) and de Robertis (123) rightly deny the term 'mystical' to this experience, in as much as it is an experience not of God but only of Beatrice. But de Robertis sounds more radically reductionist – 'in realtà è *solo* un "sospiro", un "pensero" ...' (italics mine). In any case, what are we to make of chapter 41 of the *VN*? (i.e. the penultimate chapter – numberings vary).

have, this time at the religious level. The 'pathology' I have in mind is that contained in all the phenomena of *tremare*, *beatitudo*, etc. which we analyzed from the initial experience of them in *VN* 2 but which recur at many later stages in the presence of Beatrice.

Before turning to them we might give ourselves some contextual room by glancing at some passages where we can see the presence of the religious dimension without the need for much analysis. Thus in *VN* 3 there is the famous greeting from Beatrice in her eighteenth year. Under its influence (itself *ineffabile*) Dante's experience is no longer merely of *beatitudo* but of the heights and extremes of it, *absolute* blessedness – *tutti li termini de la beatitudine.*

In *VN* 11, the blessed influence of this greeting is further elaborated. It produces an *intollerabile beatitudine*, which is often beyond the capacity of nature to endure – *molte volte passava e redundava la mia capacitade.* It further generates the Christian virtues of humility and the flame of charity. 'Whenever and wherever she appeared, in the hope of receiving her miraculous salutation (*mirabile salute*) I felt I had not an enemy in the world. Indeed I glowed with a flame of charity (*una fiamma di caritade*) which moved me to forgive all who had ever injured me; and if at that moment someone had asked me a question, about anything, my only reply would have been: "Love", with a countenance clothed in humility'[21] (trans. Reynolds – cf. *VN* 26–8).

All this crystallizes into the feeling that she is a 'miracle'[22] (*uno miracolo*, 30.3). A miracle come down from heaven to earth (26, sonnet), a miracle whose effect on the beholder 'can neither be described nor held before the mind' (21, sonnet – recall *ineffabile* in 3.1). Of course this notion of her heavenly origin owes something to the courtly tradition of the *donna angelicata*. But there is a difference in what it means for Dante. One of the differences is quite simply the sensed difference between literary convention and intensely realized experience. An example of that particular difference is provided by the early canzone (FB 32) already cited as containing the germ of *VN* 2 although not included in the *VN*. 'The day that this lady came into the world ... my childish body felt a strange emotion (*una passion nova*) so that I was filled with fear (*di paura pieno*); and suddenly a check was placed on all my faculties, so that I fell to the

21 Charles Williams would probably compare the Wordsworthian

eye made quiet by the power
Of harmony and the deep power of joy,
which see(s) into the life of things.

Possibly also *Measure for Measure* – see his essay on 'Forgiveness in Shakespeare', in the collection *He Came Down from Heaven* (Faber & Faber, London, 1950).

22 On this theme see also *Conv.* 3.7.16f.

ground, from a light that struck me through to the heart (*sì ch'io caddi in terra,/ per una luce che nel cuor percosse*).'

As regards the concluding phrases I do not know if anybody has noticed the echo of St Paul's conversion, in his meeting with Christ on the road to Damascus. *Subito circumfulsit eum lux de caelo. Et cadens in terram audivit vocem* ... (Acts 9:3–4, cf. 22:7, 26:13–14). And with Dante 'filled with fear'[23] we may compare Paul *tremens ac stupens* (Acts 9:5). We recall our earlier discussion of *tremare* and *stupore*. But here we see the 'other' dimension of their meaning, the experientially religious, the sacral fear and trembling in the presence of the numinous. That anticipates the essence of what we shall argue about the religious dimension implied in the initial Dantean experience. This phrase of an early canzone, then, contains *in nuce* not only the *VN* but its completion in the *Commedia* to the summit of the *Paradiso*.

As is indeed made clearer by another difference between Dante and the tradition of the *donna angelicata*. The logical complement of her descent from heaven is her eventual ascent whence she came. This of course is at the heart of the actual experience from the moment of her death in the *VN* through the subsequent studies, and into the *Commedia*. But the experience is anticipated from the start, in puzzling signs (*VN* 3), in logical implication (*VN* 19, canzone), and finally in the prevision of her death (*VN* 23).

But, after all, we are concerned not with what logic can *deduce* from experience, and not with 'signs and visions' which go *beyond* experience into the 'extraordinary'. We are concerned rather with dimensions of meaning, in object and event, felt in a way intrinsic to the actual experience of the object or event. So in the prevision of the death of Beatrice a detail is to be noticed which implies a felt analogy between the nature and 'ascension' of Beatrice and the nature and Ascension of the incarnate Christ. 'I thought I was looking up into the heavens, where I seemed to see a multitude of angels returning to their realm, and before them floated a little cloud of purest white' (*VN* 23, trans. Reynolds). To the Christological parallels noted by Singleton I think it is relevant here to add Acts 1:9: ' ... While they looked on he was lifted up, and a cloud received him out of their sight'. In Scripture the cloud goes with theophanies. And we recall that already in the experience of *VN* 3, which anticipates all this, a flame-coloured cloud is seen.

In this general *aperçu* we have found a fusion of levels of meaning, the religious dimension explicitly perceived in and through, as well as beyond, what we have called the natural or secular dimension of transcendence. Turning from the

23 Fear (*era molto pauroso*) is also part of Dante's experience of her greeting in his eighteenth year, on the ninth anniversary of their first meeting (*VN* 3). Again in the vision of Love in *VN* 4 he is a lord of fearsome appearance, *uno segnore di pauroso aspetto*.

religious dimension in general to the particular dimension of the mystical we find the same fusion of levels of experience, through an analysis of the *tremare* complex of phenomena. We have already touched on a connection in Dante's echo of the Pauline experience, *tremens ac stupens*, of Acts 9:5.

The overall situation is that in the mystical tradition there is a 'pathology' which is closely parallel, in the phenomena and in the language used to describe them, between the mystical tradition and Dante's repeated experience in the presence of Beatrice. And this is true of *two* mystical traditions, the Judeo-Christian and the ancient Greek – we shall have another look not only at Dante's language but also at the background of the lyric of Sappho that I cited earlier.

The general parallel lies in the phenomena of fear, awe, trembling, pain, suspension of the faculties, even to a point resembling a kind of death, a sense of being 'blasted with ecstasy'. In a word, all the phenomena that Dante sums up in the expression: *distrutti ... spiriti* (*VN* 14.5).[24] In the Judeo-Christian mystical tradition these phenomena are summed up in the 'fear and trembling' of biblical theophanies. 'My whole being trembles before you' (Psalm 119:120). A striking example is Job 4:14ff:

> A shiver of horror ran through me,
>   and my bones quaked with fear.
> A breath slid over my face,
>   the hairs of my body bristled.
> Someone stood there ...

Early in the Christian mystical tradition there is St Augustine, describing his first such experience. 'You beat back the weakness of my gaze with the beating of your radiance upon me, and I trembled with love and with dread – *contremui amore et horrore*' (*Conf.* 7.10.16).[25] 'At times', says St John of the Cross, 'the torture felt in such visits of rapture is so great that there is no torture which so wrenches asunder the bones and straitens the physical nature – so much so that unless God provided for the soul its life would come to an end' (*Spiritual Canticle*, Stanza XII.3, First Recension, trans. Peers).

Within this phenomenological complex certain specifics keep recurring. Numinous *fear* and *trembling* we have seen more than once already. Gregory the

24 The first appearance of the phrase (constant in Cavalcanti), as distinct from the experience. See further on the loss of faculties, to the point of quasi-death, *VN* 15, 16, 22 (canzone, 37f.). On death see also *VN* 19 (canzone), 22 (canzone, 42).

25 Behind this passage there is Plotinus, 'flooded with awe ... stricken by a salutary terror' (*Enneads*, 1.6.7). With *horrore* compare *orrore* in *VN* 3 (sonnet, 11). Cf. the *Life* of St Teresa of Avila, in a section of ch. 29.

Great has this to say: 'The higher the realities glimpsed by the human soul when lifted up by the engine, as it were, of contemplation, the more it trembles with awe within itself (*eo in semetipso terribilius contremiscit*)'.[26] He is commenting on the theophany on Sinai (Ex 19:16ff), in particular the statement there that 'inside the camp all the people trembled'.

Not only is there fear and trembling but what is beheld cannot long be endured by untransformed human nature. We have already seen Augustine to this effect. Later in the tradition there is Gregory once again. 'Because we are weighted down by the corruptible flesh we cannot possibly look at the brightness of the divine power in the mode in which in itself it stays immutably. The reason is that the weak eyes of our seeing cannot sustain the light that shines unbearably upon us from the ray of its eternity.'[27]

We may compare *VN* 14–16. And lines 35f and 55f of the canzone in *VN* 19: 'Were any ... person to stay and regard her, he would either become noble[28] or die ... You see Love depicted in her face, there where no one can fix his gaze.' We find a transcendent, unmediated version of the experience in, e.g. *Paradiso* 25.118ff. There, looking into the depths of the brightness of the soul of St John, Dante compares himself to

> one who squinnies and strains
> to look a while at the sun in eclipse,
> but by looking is bereft of sight,
> Such did I become in face of this final flame.

And the dichotomy of death-or-transfiguration reminds us of the motif in Scriptural theophanies, that no one can look on God and live. *Loci* are too numerous to list. But one, Exodus 33:18–23, became a *locus classicus* in the mystical tradition. The occasion comes as the climax to a series of theophanies in which God has been seen by Moses not as he is in himself but only with his glory veiled or in his awesome *effects*. Moses now makes bold to ask, 'Show me your glory' (*doxan, gloriam*). God agrees to let his splendour pass in front of Moses. But Moses must stand in the cleft of a rock and be shielded by God's hand until God has passed by and only his back may be looked upon. 'You cannot see my face', he said, 'for man cannot see me and live.'

Interestingly enough, something like this motif is found also in Greek mythology. The story of Actaeon is well known.[29] He looked on Artemis in her undraped beauty.

26 *Moralia*, 5.31.55; cf. 5.30.53 (*PL* 75.710 and 707).

27 Ibid., 5.29.52.

28 I.e. be transformed, transfigured, in view of both the meaning of *nobilitade* and the repeated experience of Dante in the *VN*, described as *trasfiguramento* and *trasfigurazione* in 14.10 and 15.1.

29 Told in Ovid, *Metam*. 3.

He was turned into a stag, filled with panic and fear and torn to pieces by the dogs of the huntress deity. There is also the story of Anchises, who became the father of Aeneas with Aphrodite. But on realizing her identity he was filled with fear and numinous awe. 'For he who lies with an immortal goddess is no hale man afterwards.'[30]

The last motif I shall illustrate is that of the *ineffability*[31] of what is felt and seen in mystical experience. It is, of course, a commonplace that it so far transcends normal experience and conceptual thinking as to be inexpressible in normal language and conceptual categories. Augustine again provides us with an instance. 'In the lightning-flash of a trembling glance the innermost intellect arrived at *That Which Is* ... But I lacked the strength to fix my gaze, my weakness was beaten back and I came back down to my ordinary modes, bearing with me nothing but a memory of love and longing as for something of which I had caught the fragrance but had not yet the strength to eat' (*Conf.* 7.17.23).

There is, in fact, no better statement of the matter than in Dante himself.

> Henceforth my vision mounted to a height
>   Where speech is vanquished and must lag behind.
>   And memory surrenders in such plight.
>
> (Para. 33.55–7, trans. Reynolds)

A passage in the *Letter to Can Grande* gives the rationale. 'One must realize that because of the connaturality and affinity it has with separate intellectual substance, when the human intellect is raised in this life it is so far raised that on its return memory fails, because the measure of the human has been transcended' (28.78), And in support he goes on to cite instances from the whole tradition – beginning with the experience of St Paul (2 Cor 12:1ff).

***

We have been looking at the Judeo-Christian mystical tradition. There was also an ancient Greek one. And I said we would look again at Sappho's lyric, to see whether it too might not have a dimension of meaning beyond what meets the eye, and thus show that Dante's religious imagination is not absolutely unique, and therefore is that much more possible and credible. What that dimension

30 *Homeric Hymns*, 5 (*To Aphrodite*), 182ff.

31 For the motif in the *VN*, in addition to 3 and 21 (sonnet), already cited, see 26.3, 32 (canzone, 35f), 41.6. The last is climactic and anticipates the importance of the theme in the *Conv.* – 3.3.12 into 3.4, 3.8.14ff. In *VN* 41 (sonnet) note also the mention of *intelligenza nova*, given by Love and drawing upwards.

would be is of course already obvious from the parallels in the poem to the complex of motifs we have been looking at in the Judeo-Christian tradition. What I wish to do is to confirm it from within its own Greek tradition. We can do it briefly with the aid of two or three pieces of evidence, taken from the domain of mystery religion and mystical experience, at least in the elastic sense in which I have permitted myself to use that term.

The first piece of evidence is from Plato's *Phaedrus*. In the first part of this essay I drew attention to the parallel between Sappho's 'pathology' of love and that of *Phaedrus* 250E ff. We left it at that level then. But of course context, process and language in the *Phaedrus* are those of 'enthusiasm', 'mystery', mystical initiation, divine possession, 'ascent' (244ff). Love is one form of that divinely-sent *mania* which is wiser than the wisdom of reason. To prove it we must learn the truth about soul, divine and human, by observing how it acts and is acted upon (245C). It is not necessary to labour the details.[32]

However, while this may be persuasive we cannot argue backwards in time, from Plato to Sappho. We need evidence from her own time, or earlier if possible. That is provided by the *Homeric Hymn to Demeter*, not later than the seventh century BC according to one estimate. It tells the story – the myth – of the origins of the Eleusinian Mysteries, from an episode in the wanderings of the goddess Demeter in search of her lost daughter Persephone.

She comes to Eleusis and the house of one Keleus – in the guise of an old woman. A theophany takes place as her divinity is revealed. And the details of that theophany parallel those of Sappho's poem.

> The goddess walked to the threshold: and her head reached the roof and she filled the doorway with a heavenly radiance. Then awe and reverence[33] and pale fear[34] took hold of Metaneira ...
> (188-90, TRANS. LOEB)

> The goddess changed her stature and her looks, thrusting old age away from her: beauty spread round about her and a lovely fragrance was wafted from her sweet-smelling robes, and from the divine body of the goddess a light shone afar ... And straightway Metaneira's knees were loosed[35] and she remained speechless[36] for a long while ... (275ff)

32 We find the same 'enthusiastic' language at the end of the *Symposium* (215ff), in Alcibiades' description of the strange effect of Socrates upon him.

33 Recall *Odyssey* 6.149ff on Odysseus in face of Nausicaa.

34 Detail paralleled in Sappho.

35 Detail paralleled in Sappho.

36 Detail paralleled in Sappho.

Plutarch (c.46–120 AD) was right then to read Sappho's poem in the way I have been arguing towards. And his is our final and best statement of it. At one point in his Platonising Dialogue on Love (*Eroticos* or *Amatorius*) someone is asked to quote the verses in which 'the fair Sappho tells how at the epiphany of the beloved her voice fails and her body flames, and she is seized by pallor, derangement and swooning'. This being done,

> Then my father commenting said; By Zeus, is it not a clear case of divine possession? Is this not a supernatural agitation of the soul? The transport of the Pythian priestess, when she touches her tripod, is it anything like this? Are any of those who are divinely possessed in the rites of Cybele so put beside themselves by the flute and tympanum and the chants to the Great Mother? (763A).

And so say we of Dante's Beatrician experience. *Quod erat demonstrandum*, or at least *tentandum*.

***

I have examined in any detail only the *VN* – and indeed only focal points even of it. I have omitted the epistemological question – what structure of knowing, and specifically of imaginative knowing, permits such perceptions? I have omitted the ontological question – what structure of reality permits the ascription of such dimensions to the reality of Beatrice? 'If, we are told, Beatrice was only a woman, Dante could not, "without blasphemy", have written about her what he did. To which we have to answer that we must resign ourselves to the facts: if that be the case Dante *was* a blasphemer.'[37]

Gilson does not accept that that *is* the case. But to enter into that question would take us into another essay. Let us conclude, however, with one point, inspired by some of Gilson's. It is this, that the author of Genesis 1:26 was the first 'blasphemer'! For it is he who tells us that 'God said, "Let us make man in our own image ... ".' *Man* here, we are told, is a common and collective noun. So it includes *woman* too – God bless her again.

At the other end of history we may quote a humble modern Irish poet – though not with all that much to be humble about. Without benefit of *più latinamente vedere* he lighted on the essential insights, or was lightened by them, out of the 'stony grey soil of Monaghan'.

37 E. Gilson, *Dante et la philosophie* (Paris, Vrin, 1939), 74.

Now I must search till I have found my God –
...
Surely my God is feminine, for Heaven
Is the generous impulse, is contented
With feeding praise to the good. And all
Of these that I have known have come from women.
While men the poet's tragic light resented.
The spirit that is Woman caressed his soul.[38]

In other words ... *la sua ineffabile cortesia* (*VN* 3.1).

38 Patrick Kavanagh, 'God in Woman', in *Collected Poems*, MacGibbon & Kee, 1964.

DANTE AND THE POETIC IMAGINATION[39]

Chose essentielle se passe entre l'Etre et moi,
dont le poème est le theâtre
PIERRE EMMANUEL

My topic is the poetic imagination. And by way of a poetic and imaginative introduction to it let me say that, when I sat down to think about these two nebulous and indefinable words, I had an imagination of myself and Polonius being had on by Hamlet about the exact shape of 'yonder cloud'. You know the passage:

Ham. Do you see yonder cloud that's almost in shape of a camel?
Pol. By the mass, and 'tis like a camel indeed.
Ham. Methinks it is like a weasel.
Pol. It is backed like a weasel.
Ham. Or like a whale?
Pol. Very like a whale.
(HAMLET, 3.2)

That image reminds us that we need some preliminary delimitations to indicate what I am doing in this paper and what I am not doing, or, more radically, what I am capable of doing and what not ...

(1) 'In my end is my beginning ... '. If an attempt to understand and validate the 'poetic imagination' is to be anything more than itself a piece of poetic imagination, it has to be pretty radically and sustainedly analytic. But in my own attempts to be just that, I found that I would need several multiples of my allotted time. So what I have to say will be more indicative of directions than rigorous in demonstration and illustration.

(2) A second delimitation to this paper arises from the delimitations of its author. I am not qualified to be a theorist of the poetic imagination to the extent that I might be if I were a professional philosopher or theologian or student of modern literature and critical theory. My own world is that of the Ancient Classics. And

39 ITQ 52 (1986), 66–80.

whether because or in spite of their classical status, the Classics did not, by and large, have a profound understanding or a very high estimate of imagination in some of its manifold modern senses.

So to whatever extent there is a modern literature on the nature of the poetic imagination I am not widely or deeply acquainted with it in any professional way. And therefore such arguments as I make in defence of the imagination – and I do intend to make them – will be based on more traditional, or, in the large sense, 'classical', understandings of the nature of the human spirit and its faculties.

(3) Thirdly, having mentioned that matter of the faculties of the human spirit, perhaps I should take this moment to indicate one of my main directions about them in this paper. It has a negative and a positive side.

The negative side would be to get rid of the term 'imagination' altogether. It has so many meanings – some of them so misleading, others of them so 'morbid' – as to be worthless in rigorous discussion.

> Imagination – here the Power so called
> Through sad incompetence of human speech ...
> (Wordsworth, 'The Prelude', 6.592f)

Or in the more forthright language of Samuel Johnson: 'Imagination, a licentious and vagrant faculty, unsusceptible of limitations, and impatient of restraint ... '. We might compare the statement of the problem in Wordsworth, *The Excursion*, 4.763 ff.

On the positive side, what should I put in place of imagination ... ? There's the rub. As terminological shorthand, imagination has the advantage of being in possession. From the point of view of meaning, both denotation and connotation, I should like a term of less subjectivist associations, a term which would convey the idea of *presence*, presence of the subject to reality and of reality to the subject. The reason for this is that it seems to me we can only validate the poetic imagination by validating some modes of knowledge other than the rational, discursive, conceptualising mode.

> And I have felt
> A presence that disturbs me with the joy
> Of elevated thoughts; a sense sublime
> Of something far more deeply interfused ...
> ('Tintern Abbey', 93ff)

(4) Fourthly, from these last remarks it is clear by implication under what aspect I wish to consider this topic of the poetic imagination. That aspect is the question of its cognitive value.

Clearly there are many 'uses of poetry' (in T. S. Eliot's phrase). They range from the lowest and most obvious one of entertainment, pleasure, *hedoné* (Aristotle's term), up to rare peaks of the experience of what purports to be ecstasy and ultimate vision of the transcendent abyss where

> love holds bound
> Into one volume all the leaves whose flight
> Is scattered through the universe around.
> (DANTE, PARA., 33.85–7, TR. REYNOLDS)

And concomitant to this range of the uses of poetry in our subjective reaction to it, there is the corresponding range of the objective depth and authenticity of poetry in itself – from the Parnassian peaks of the truly 'inspired' (whatever that may mean) down to the mere craft and flat plains of mere verse – and worse. (I have in mind a certain scale outlined in a letter of G. M. Hopkins.)

Now corresponding to those two scales, subjective and objective, our problem is twofold. Firstly, if we want to validate poetry we are concerned with validating what it *can* be (but may not necessarily *often* be), in its essence and its highest best. Secondly, if we want to validate poetry at a level which is finally serious and worth the trouble of our concern with it, we cannot be content with any merely psychological level of *hedoné*, pleasure, even when the pleasure is that special kind called aesthetic. I do not see how we can finally take 'great' poetry seriously, as we do, without looking into it for that particular value that consists in its *truth*. Our problem therefore is to validate poetic imagination by giving it a cognitive function. And that, as I wanted to make clear, is the particular aspect under which I wish to consider the topic of poetic imagination.

Now such a project poses, indeed arises from, a problem that goes deeper than appears at first sight. The first level of the problem is one we are familiar enough with, at least once we remind ourselves of it. That is the fact that, putting it crudely, truth is one thing and the products of the imagination are something else. And, conventionally, the adequate *organ* of truth is the rigorous, logical, conceptual, scientific reason. Imagination may give us fine feelings in ourselves and something called beauty in the object. But it is subjective, emotional, inexact. Feelings are not intellect. And beauty, even if it is not just in the eye of the beholder, beauty is not necessarily truth, *pace* what the poet *ipse dixit*.

But the problem goes deeper – into a real antinomy in fact. That antinomy lies in the fact that whereas the conceptual reason is in quest of truth, the greatest products of the poetic imagination are almost by definition fiction, i.e. *inventions*, *constructs* – precisely of the imagination. Its statements are not of literal or factual truth. And its 'arguments' are not controlled by logic. This is the deepest ground of what Plato called the longstanding quarrel between poetry and philosophy. And his great originality is to have isolated the problem once and for all. And that in spite of his own poetic imagination – 'for we are well aware of being ourselves enchanted by ... poetry' (*Rep.* 607c).

I have already used up some of the time which would be necessary for resolving the antinomy I have tried to state. But I see no way of saving on the time needed to identify what is the precise question one is trying to answer.

And when I say 'answer' I use the word with the limitations of space and competence that I indicated earlier. For I think an adequate answer requires knowledge in a number of disparate areas. And not just knowledge but familiarity, and an ability to move without getting one's feet in a knot. A variety of competence, needless to say, I do not possess. I have in mind psychology – including that of the subconscious these days. I have in mind sociology and anthropology, with their predetermining 'structures'. I have in mind epistemology, the metaphysics of Being (*sit venia verbo*), the philosophy of the symbol. I have in mind even the modes and experiences of the traditional interior or spiritual life – it is commonplace to observe analogies between the experiences of mysticism and those of the highest levels of poetic imagination. Perhaps I should even have theology in mind. Theology is based on revelation and inspiration, revelation that is itself to a large extent even expressed in poetry and symbol. So that perhaps we should call on theology to provide us with an understanding of poetry, and not the other way round!

And as a constant point of reference for *all* these abstractions one needs familiarity with what we may call the phenomenology of the poetic imagination itself. That is the rope which must keep our balloon from floating off into the empyrean. For here, if anywhere in the domain of poetry, concepts without percepts are indeed empty. As George Steiner recently expressed it, we need 'a scrupulous alertness to the irreducibility of the poetic ... '.

Clearly in the space available here it is not possible to explore all these 'regional' disciplines, much less relate them to one another and synthesize their data into a theory of the cognitive value of the poetic imagination. And there is the additional difficulty, especially in the domains of epistemology and metaphysics, of deciding *which* of the variety of available systems to use as a hermeneutic. For of course I need hardly mention that the sequence of systems in the history of philosophy itself does not sit easily to its truth-claims over against mere imagination! Yet if poetry was devalued by Plato for philosophical reasons, we can only revalue it by the same means. (And this of course implies an important truth in any revaluation of the cognitive value of the poetic imagination; we can only revalue it to the status of *complementing* conceptual thought, not *replacing* it.)

I mention this *embarras de choix* for the additional reason that I feel a certain kind of modern philosophy provides very suggestive insights into ways of validating a cognitive dimension to the poetic imagination ... But for my present purposes I think it might be at once more useful for others, and more prudent for myself, to see what can be derived from more traditional material. If then we concentrate on our mutton, at last our problem can be broken down into three questions:

(1) How can *fiction* be *true*?
(2) To what ontological order, so to speak, does this truth belong, *if* it exists?
(3) What is the nature and the epistemological mode of the 'faculty', if any, by which such truth, if any, is perceived?

I have just said that, for 'lines towards' an answer to these questions within the limits of this paper, I would draw on traditional rather than modern material. If one were to put in summary and schematic form the categories one can derive from this tradition for our present purposes, they would be something like this:

(1) an *ontological* scale of levels of Being;
(2) A corresponding *epistemological* scale of *adequatio* to Being in levels of knowledge of it.

One may compare, as late as Pascal, his 'orders' of reality and the corresponding appropriate *vues* of them.

I take up the first of these three questions – or rather the first and the second rolled into one. There could hardly be a more classical and traditional source of an answer than Aristotle. And he is the more relevant to our purposes for looking over his shoulder at Plato, who, as I said, first enucleated our problem. Among the indications he provides us with are two undeveloped but very significant statements in the *Poetics* – statements that are an obvious riposte to Plato. 'We must remember ... [says Aristotle] that the standard of correctness [say 'truth'] is not the same in poetry as in political theory or any other discipline [say 'the domain of natural fact or scientific theory']' (*Poet.*, 25.3). This statement I suppose, though left magisterially undeveloped, is the first explicit recognition in literary theory of a distinction between scientific or factual truth and some other kind of truth in art.

Aristotle's second statement is the well-known one in *Poet.* 9, to the effect that 'Poetry is something more philosophical and of deeper import than history; for poetry expresses universal truths, history particular facts'. Although again Aristotle does not develop this statement, we can see expressed here also, for the first time in literary theory, one essential basis for the validation of a truth-content in poetry. And that basis is a theory of what we would now call the image or the symbol, i.e. the *particular* object or event seen as not only existing in its own concrete individuality but as also deriving from and embodying something *more than* itself, the *transcendent* in fact. This is a doctrine of the image or symbol as what has been called the concrete universal. It is in fact Platonism, with its theory of universal, transcendent forms, participated in by particulars, that best provides a philosophy for this. Yet Plato himself did not work this out for poetry – perhaps because of the well-known unbridged gap or *chorismos* between his transcendent forms and the concrete existents of the material world. Perhaps a doctrine of the concrete universal could occur more easily to the less poetic and transcendental Aristotle because he saw the universal form existing only as immanent in the particular. (Much later, of course, the Neoplatonist Plotinus, in his philosophy of art, did explicitly bridge the *chorismos* left by Plato between the transcendent universal forms and the concrete material particulars – see e.g. *Enneads*, 5.8.1.)

But there we must leave that matter of the truth expressed by the poetic image, even when it is a 'fictional' image. Except perhaps to add that, although I have expressed it in terms of Plato and Aristotle, it is not dependent on their particular philosophies. Any serious metaphysic of the relation between Being and beings, between *das Sein* and *das Seiende*, to use the Heideggerian jargon, entails some kind of coinherence of the universal or transcendent and the particular.

And yet perhaps we will not leave the matter just yet. For it occurs to me that it is appropriate to link on to it an element in the phenomenology of poetry that I had planned to introduce at a different point.

This notion of the poetic 'image' as concrete universal, as particular, individual existent issuing from, grounded in and embodying, 'disclosing' what transcends it – what other notion can better do justice to our actual *experience* of poetry at its most intense? Fundamental to that experience is the sense of a strange richness, an over-plus of reality and meaning in the aesthetic object, an *abundantia* of significance as from inexhaustible deeps, a foreground *splendor* that seems to emerge from infinite background distances, silent distances yet vibrant with silent music and sounding solitude:

La musica callada.
La soledad sonora.

One must verify this for oneself, but there are some great written witnesses to the experience. Longinus *On the Sublime* is steeped in it. Proust's excursus on the *petite phrase* in the *Vinteuil Sonata* is famous. More easily quotable is one Sir Thomas Browne. 'There is something in it [music] of divinity more than the ear discovers: it is an Hieroglyphical and shadowed lesson of the whole world and creatures of God: such a melody to the ear as the whole world, well understood, would afford the understanding. In brief, it is a sensible fit of that harmony which intellectually sounds in the ears of God!'

And since my acquaintance with Sir Thomas Browne is limited to that quotation, I hasten to add that I use it only as a fine and concise expression of what I find less quotably in authors I have looked at, from Plotinus (1.3.1) to Proust on the *petite phrase*, passing on the way through even the puritan Augustine. 'I observe ... that all the diverse movements of my spirit [in a mystical context] have modes proper to them in voice and song, whereby, through some secret affinity, they are brought alive' (*Conf.* 10.33).

And our own experience of the poem has its parallel in that of the poet before the object or event that generates the poem. Naturally enough, since our experience is the communication and participation of his. (And it is the moment to remind ourselves again of my earlier delimitation, namely that there are many kinds and levels of poetry, and I am trying to speak of the most obviously authentic and 'enthusiastic' as my test case.) I cannot spend much time illustrating this easily enough illustratable phenomenon. The essential phenomenon – simplifying greatly perhaps, but unavoidably – the essential phenomenon is that the poet too, more 'visionary' than the rest of us in face of particulars, can see the heavenly spheres reflected in a globule of dew:

The greater Heaven in an Heaven less.
(A. MARVELL, 'ON A DROP OF DEW')

He can

... see a world in a grain of sand.
And a heaven in a wild flower,
Hold infinity in the palm of [his] hand,
And eternity in an hour.
(BLAKE, 'AUGURIES OF INNOCENCE')

So often the poets are natural Platonists in their sense of the transcendence in and behind phenomena.

La nature est un temple où de vivants piliers
Laissent parfois sortir de confuses paroles . . .
L'homme y passe à travers des forêts de symboles ...
(BAUDELAIRE, 'CORRESPONDANCES')

If I had time to dilate on this, I would base myself on two great examples and accounts that we have of the actual experience and development of a poet's mind. One would be Dante, for whom a Florentine girl became in literal truth the bearer of

The Greater heaven in an Heaven less.

The other would be Wordsworth of 'The Prelude' for his confessional exploration of the awakening and growth of

a dim and undetermined sense
Of unknown modes of being

in and behind the face of nature. But all that would take us too long.

It would also take too long to develop, but it is important to mention, how significant all this should be for Christian theology. Where image and Incarnation are central, the transcendent embodied and made visible, the *Logos* made *sarx* and tented among us. And indeed that is the theme of a great work that is strangely little known in our Celtic-Anglo-Saxon world, von Balthasar's *Herrlichkeit.* We know the centrality and frequency of glory, *gloria, claritas, doxa, kabod,* in the Scriptures. It would be interesting to chart the occurrence of that word, or its equivalent, among the poets. As things are re-presented to us in the words of great poets, they are, as Wordsworth put it,

cirumfused
By that transparent veil with light divine,
And, through the turnings intricate of verse,
Present themselves as objects recognized,
In flashes, and with glory not their own.
('THE PRELUDE', 5.601–5)

The poet has experienced something analogous to the Transfiguration .... .

We come to the third of the three basic questions into which we broke down our problem, namely the epistemological *mode* of such deeper and higher ontological perceptions as I have just been ascribing to the 'poetic imagination'. In a way the fact itself of such perception should suffice without the how. But in view of the 'ancient quarrel' already mentioned, it is necessary to try and show the epistemological *possibility* of such perceptions of truth as the poet may claim. Philosophers, scientists and theologians regard reason, discursive, dialectical intellect, as the organ of knowledge and truth. It is not easy for that kind of reason to understand the *different* mode of what we conventionally call imagination. It is easy to 'unsoul' imagination 'by syllogistic words' ('The Prelude', 12.83f), and reduce it to the subjective, emotive, fictive, illusionist. And without an appeal to self-validating immediate experience, there is indeed a difficulty involved in justifying it. For it is by reason that we have to validate a possible cognitive mode that is different from reason, and is indeed 'irreducible' to the conventional categories of reason. And yet there is nothing *un*reasonable in reason recognizing a point, either in levels of knowledge or levels of reality, beyond which the categories of reason fail. Traditional philosophy at its highest points always came to the inexpressible mystery – there is the well-known example of Plato. *A fortiori,* theology came to mystery – beyond theology lay contemplation and ineffable vision. And, if I am not mistaken, even science today is deep into regions full of paradoxes for conventional reason.

To take up this question in detail would be to get into an area of endless tangle. Only someone closely familiar with both the ways of the spirit and the ways of technical philosophy could hope to find an Ariadne thread through the maze. And I am not Ariadne – who in any case came to a pathetic end. And so I recall what I mentioned earlier, that our possible validation of the imagination mode depends on something traditional philosophy and theology were more familiar with than we are. I mean levels of reality and levels of knowledge that go much deeper than those surfaces of things which are most real for our more positivist mentality.

I have related this to a tradition of higher spiritual experience. But in fact that experience is itself grounded in a tradition of philosophical and epistemological analysis. This tradition begins in one of the great similes of Plato's *Republic,* the Simile of the Sun (507–9) – complemented by those of the Divided Line and the Cave. The point of the simile is that ultimate Reality, the Supreme Form, is the final ground and source *both* of the *reality* of all that exists *and* of the light of *knowledge* by which reality is *known.* As reality is scaled so is the knowledge by which it is known. And as corporeal seeing requires an organ adapted to the reception of the light, so knowing requires an appropriate spiritual organ adapted to another kind of light. 'To any vision [says Plotinus] there must be brought an eye adapted to what is to be seen, and having some likeness to it. Never did eye see the sun unless it had first become sunlike, and never can the soul have vision of the First Beauty unless itself be beautiful' (*Enn.* 1.6.9. – cf. Plato, *Rep.* 518 c). And from this Platonist ontology and epistemology a strand runs through early Christian and medieval philosophy that has an 'illuminative' theory of knowledge and an 'ontological' theory of truth. We can see that such an epistemology is more richly 'poetic' and cognitive than the supposedly more 'scientific' (but equally gratuitous?!) Aristotelian machinery of the abstracting, concept-producing intellect – 'active', 'passive' etc. And as regards truth, the Aristotelian strand emphasizes not the 'vertical' ontological truth of reality in relation to its ground and source, but merely the 'horizontal' truth of the correspondence between concept or proposition in the mind and the extra-mental reality in the world of phenomena.

But few of us, I should think, find it easy to manipulate all this complex machinery of epistemology and ontology. Let us come back therefore to the *phenomena* of the *genesis* of poetry itself. The data are rich, if not always very precise, from Plato's *Phaedrus* down through Longinus' *On the Sublime* to Wordsworth's 'Prelude', and T. S. Eliot on the origin and uses of poetry. It would be tedious, and space does not allow us, to quote or analyse even this selection – Plato's divinely inspired *mania*, Longinus' Platonist-derived *enthousiamos*, Wordsworth's *imagination*, Eliot's 'disturbance of our quotidian character which results in an incantation, an outburst of words which we hardly recognize as our own ... '.

There are two recurring elements in these data. One is obvious – feeling, emotion. Less obvious, but none the less present, is the sense – however justified, that is the question – that the experience has a cognitive dimension, though in a mode very different from the discursive, conceptual mode. The most explicit statement of this is, I suppose, Wordsworth's 'feeling intellect' ('The Prelude', 14.226).

... Imagination, which, in truth,
Is but another name for absolute power
And clearest insight, amplitude of mind,
And Reason in her most exalted mood.
('THE PRELUDE', 14.189FF)

The same two elements are present in Longinus' two 'natural' sources of the sublime – the double capacity for (1) grand conceptions and (2) strong and inspired emotion (*On the Sublime*, 8.1). We find them also in Coleridge's 'more than usual state of emotion, with more than usual order' (*Biog. Lit.* 14). The 'order' I take to refer to an order felt to be in *rerum natura*, a feeling consequent on a higher state of awareness, awareness of a higher unity in things, an awareness that often has analogies with mystical experience. And I take it that it is some similar state of expanded consciousness that Eliot is touching on, though rather more gingerly, when he identifies certain concomitants of the 'incantation'. These are 'moments, which are characterised by the sudden lifting of the burden of anxiety and fear which presses upon our daily life ... the breaking down of strong habitual barriers ... Some obstruction is momentarily whisked away ... ' (*Selected Prose*, ed. Kermode, 89f. Cf. 'Burnt Norton', 70ff).

I have been discussing the third of our three originally stated questions. To this third question two 'supplementaries' remain. (1) Can we more precisely identify and more rigorously explain the nature of the 'faculty' of this possible cognition in the poetic experience? (2) What value do we assign such possible knowledge in comparison with that of the more 'scientific' conceptual mode?

On the first of these two questions I do not have the time – or the desire – to go into the details of epistemology beyond the general directions suggested earlier from within a certain spiritual and philosophical tradition. Except perhaps to add that here again one may refer to Aristotle. This rigorously systematic and scientific thinker, anti-Platonist, un-'poetic' and un-'enthusiastic', nevertheless allows for the Platonist *mania* and 'ecstatic' states among the possible explanations of poetic perception – which for him, as we saw, is 'philosophic' (*Poet.*, 17.2). For the rest, let us rather take the larger view of an epistemological map, as it were, and consider whereabouts upon it we might locate the poetic 'faculty'.

The oldest and most conventional location of all, 'inspiration', is excluded in so far as it suggests the influence of a higher power on the knowing subject. Which is not to deny, in a theological context, that there is any poetry at all written under such external influence. One thinks of the poetry in the Bible, St John of the Cross, the peak moments in Dante. But they are hardly normal or normative. Yet the term inspiration does identify a feature of poetic cognition which does distinguish it from the conceptual mode. That feature is the sense that is something *given*, from a region *beyond* the active, seizing, conscious reason. The analogy with the mystical or mystery-religion experience comes to mind again. And again one recalls a fragment of Aristotle, according to which the 'initiate' does not so much actively learn something as dispose himself for submission to a higher experience.

On imagination as a 'faculty' I commented at the start. Too briefly and brusquely, no doubt. There is, of course, a stage in the process of knowing to which the term properly applies. But as a term for what we are after in 'the poetic imagination' it is more a label than an explanation.

More exact and more easily locatable on our map are various attempts by more strictly philosophical thinkers to define some kind of *complement* of the conceptual reason. There is Maritain's '*intuition poétique*'. There is Newman's 'illative sense' as distinct from mere 'logic'. There is his 'real' as distinct from 'notional' knowledge and assent. There is the Jungian (and Claudelian) *animus* and *anima*. Most familiar of all, and perhaps most profound and valuable, coming as it does from such a rigorous conceptual thinker – there is Pascal's *esprit de finesse* as distinct from the *esprit de géométrie* (cf. Wordsworth, 'The Prelude', 5.65ff on 'poetry and geometric truth'). There is *le coeur* as distinct from *la raison. Le coeur a ses raisons que la raison ne connaît point: on le sait en mille choses* (*Pensées*, 277, ed. Brunschvicg). The same Pascal, by the way, who dismantled 'imagination – *cette partie dominante dans l'homme, cette maîtresse d'erreur et défausseté* ... (ibid. 82).

I think this hypothetical cognitive organ of the *heart* is particularly worth the attention of theologians on our problem. For it throws a bridge between poetic and philosophic *reflection* and a long, rich tradition of Judeo-Christian *spiritual* experience. I find it perfectly expressed in an excerpt from De Quincey on *The Poetry of Pope*: 'The Scriptures themselves never condescended to deal by suggestion or co-operation with the mere discursive understanding; when speaking of man in his intellectual capacity, the Scriptures speak not of the understanding, but of "the understanding heart" – making the heart, i.e. the great intuitive (or non-discursive) organ, to be the interchangeable formula for man in his highest state of capacity for the infinite'(quoted in Maritain, *L'intuition créatrice*, 136). And in the words of Wordsworth:

> *our being's heart and home*
> *Is with infinitude ...*
> ('THE PRELUDE', 6.604F)

Inquietum est cor nostrum donec requiescat in Te . . . (Augustine, *Conf.*, 1.1). We may compare Longinus, 35.

I will not try to go into the mechanics of such a non-conceptual cognitive faculty. I have already referred more than once to a philosophical and spiritual tradition of degrees and modes of knowledge beyond the conceptual. One should also take note of the cognitive dimension of the whole affective side of man's nature:

> *We live by Admiration, Hope and Love;*
> *And, even as these are well and wisely fixed,*
> *In dignity of being we ascend ...*
> (WORDSWORTH, 'THE EXCURSION', 4.763FF)

According to Plato and Aristotle, philosophy itself begins in wonder, *thaumazein* – a word which it is important to remember does express an emotion, often even the emotion of the numinous – 'a presence that disturbs me ... '.

Personally I like this notion of presence, opened out into that of man to reality and of reality to man. We can then play with the Claudelian *jeu* of poetic knowledge as *connaissance* by *co-naissance* and *con-naturalité*. Or, ploughing deeper, we can try the Heideggerian categories of man's openness to Being and Being's self-disclosure to man. And it has been noted how much these categories of Heidegger look like theological categories secularized.

The foundation to any of these categories is the obvious enough truth that man's soul is more than that little outcrop of it that is the discursive reason, more even than that outcrop of it that is consciousness. It is with his *whole* soul, indeed with his whole being, that man auscultates reality. And, in Coleridge's words, 'the poet, described in *ideal* perfection, brings the whole soul of man into activity ... ' (*Biog*. Lit., 14) – with the 'habitual barriers' broken down, as we saw Eliot put it. Put another way, poetry is born at various levels of spiritual experience. And in his capacity for spiritual experience ... *grande profundum est ipse homo ... capilli ejus magis numerabiles quam affectus ejus et motus cordis ejus* (*Conf.* 4.14). About all of which *affectus spiritus nostri* this Christian-Platonist puritan critic of poetry was compelled, as we saw, by the phenomenology of experience, to admit that they found in music both their expression and, conversely, their occasion – *nescio qua occulta familiaritate*, by I know not what secret affinity (*Conf.* 10.33).

The second of our two supplementaries still remains. Even if we succeed along such lines in validating a cognitive dimension of the poetic imagination, how do we estimate its worth compared with that of the conceptual mode? Precisely because it is non-conceptual is it not inchoative, volatile, vague, in a word 'unscientific'?

There is more than one approach one can take to answering this question – though perhaps one can relate them all to that frame of reference I have mentioned more than once: the levels of reality and the corresponding *adaequatio* of levels of knowledge. And speaking generally, there should be little difficulty for theologians in seeing an answer, at least by analogy. Theologians, before ever we reach the mystics, have always been *apophatic* as well as *kataphatic*. They have recognised the *inadaequatio* of their concepts to the reality of God. Higher states of spiritual experience transcend this limitation by experiential knowledge. It is a commonplace that what is 'known' in such higher states of awareness is inexpressible conceptually. To the extent that it is expressible at all it is expressible only through 'poetic' images and patterns of form.

Only by the form, the pattern,
Can words or music reach
The stillness ...
('Burnt Norton', 140ff)

The possible analogy with the function of poetry in the experience of reality at lower levels is obvious.

The premise to such an argument is the obvious one that reality is more than our concepts of it – that life is larger than logic. Yeats speaks of the error it is 'to continually mistake a philosophical idea for a spiritual experience' (*Autob.*, 467). Which is not to suggest that poetry should or could replace concepts and logical argument. At the very least they must provide the armature without which no experience can even be organized for expression, much less interpreted in depth.

And precisely in this matter of the relation of concepts and logic to 'percepts' and lived experience there is another question it would be interesting to pursue. And that is to what extent experience, at every level, including the poetic, is in fact the prior condition of the concepts, and provides the material on which logic does but operate and to which it must constantly return. Was it Kant who said that concepts without percepts are empty, percepts without concepts are blind?

Again theology provides an analogy in its relation to religious experience. *Tu ne me chercherais pas, si tu na m'avais trouvé*, says Pascal (echoing Augustine) in *Le Mystère de Jésus.* 'Grant me O Lord', prays Augustine, 'to know, and to understand ... which comes first, to know you or to call upon you' (*Conf.* 1.1). A long time *before* he could articulate belief intellectually he was striving to grasp a certain interior melody – *interiorem melodiam tuam*, heard with the ears of the heart, *cordis mei auribus* (*Conf.*, 4.15).

We might ask of just how much philosophical systematizing the same is true. It should be true of the modern philosophies known as existential. But there is existentialism *avant la lettre* – back through Pascal to St Augustine. And a philosophy like Platonism, where the awareness of beauty and *eros* is so central, surely owes much to reflection on deep, prior spiritual experience of these dimensions of existence. And again, at a higher metaphysical level, it must owe much to the experience of dimensions of reality that could only emerge in that higher consciousness which the Platonists and all tradition after them called *theoria*, contemplation.

It is in poetry at its deepest and most authentic that we get the most sustained resonance of this

dim and undetermined sense
Of unknown modes of being ...
('THE PRELUDE', 1.392F)

A sense that should commend itself above all to the theologian. It is born not from a world-fleeing leap into the transcendent but from within 'spots of time', 'points of intersection of the timeless/With time ... ', moments in the rose-garden, moments at which the *visibilia* of creation become epiphanies, translucent, *valde bona* once more as they were to the original *Poietes.* 'I doubt', says Yeats, 'that love itself would be more than an animal hunger but for the poet and his shadow the priest ... ' (*Essays and Interpretations*, 158). The most famous of such epiphanies, the Beatrician one, generated one of the greatest and most comprehensive of all poems. 'After this sonnet', says Dante at the end of the *Vita Nuova*, 'a marvellous vision appeared to me, in which I saw things that made me decide to write no more of this blessed lady until I could do it more adequately. And to this end I study as hard as I can ... '. What he studied was philosophy and theology. But these he did not 'discover' until *after* the Beatrician experience. And conversely only in poetry again could he integrate the experience with the thought that made sense of it.

To conclude, if in all this I seem to have concentrated on poetic imagination of a very pure water, drawn from springs very high on Parnassus, well ... that is what I said I would do. Clearly, as I said at the start, not all poetry is from that level. But *non omnes possumus omnia*, not within one paper anyway. I have tried to focus on essences, ideas in a quasi-Platonic sense, ideal possibilities. It is in any case a fact that since poetry began its recorded history one of its constant drives has been a

> *yearning toward some philosophic song*
> *Of Truth ...*

And it is under the rubric of such great overarching ideas as Truth, Being, the Holy etc., that Heidegger has reconnected poet and philosopher, dwelling on mountains apart yet looking towards one another. Pseudo-mystical, maybe, at times, but at least rising above the dusty bric-à-brac of much busy activity in both domains.

And if at the end of all that we still have the problem of deciding which poetry embodies what truth – witness the recurring preoccupation of Eliot – the *argumentum ad hominem*, if nothing better, is to hand. The range of variety in 'philosophic song', from the atheistic materialism of a Lucretius to the mystical theology of a Dante, puts it in no worse case than the history of philosophical systems – or of theological systems for that matter! And poetry may well have this advantage, namely that, if genuine, it will always at least express some truth about the 'unchristened heart'. In poetic and religious experience alike the *regio egestatis*, the 'waste land', is as authentic as the final fulfilment in *la forma universal.*

POSTSCRIPT

As it stands this paper is really no more than the record of the author's own journey up-river – undertaken at relatively short notice. Not therefore the definitive mapping of the whole territory. It follows a particular question about the poetic imagination at a particular level. The exploration was done with some ancient and hence possibly shabby equipment. But even an Ancient Classicist registers modern rumours of more up-to-date theoretical technology (the metaphor is mixed but buried, and therefore harmless). Technology reported to be so finely programmed for self-criticism that it self-destructs at the appropriately critical moment of self-awareness ('Know thyself'). It will be natural enough then, that much of what the more ancient equipment has registered should sound like news from nowhere. That will not have made the journey entirely worthless. There is much that can be seen and heard and recorded without any special equipment at all. But for the rest it would not be sensible of the author to maintain that everything up the river is exactly as he has tried to describe it.

PPS

There may be those who will note that frequent use has been made of Wordsworth. Really and truly only for the convenience of striking example and quotation. So in case it matters, it will not do to hang out the label of 'Romanticism', and the accusation of being hooked on it, without further definition of terms. The first Romantic poet in Western literature as I understand it was the composer of the *Odyssey*. And the first Romantic critic was Longinus – although he didn't quite know it himself and down-rated the *Odyssey* accordingly in comparison with the more naturalistic *Iliad*. But the dreaming in the *Odyssey* was still for him the dreaming of Zeus (Longinus 9.14).

RENAISSANCE

SOME MORE COMFORTS: MORE AND THE CONSOLATORY TRADITION

PART I

The following pages do not pretend to add to the sum of professional knowledge about St Thomas More. Those in search of that will have to 'fetch the counsel at some wiser man'. Such men grow more numerous as the study of St Thomas More expands. Many of them have been seen or read in the last two years at one or other of the many quincentenary commemorations of his birth. One such commemoration was the Summer Colloquium in University College Dublin, one session of which Maynooth had the honour of hosting. These pages are the result of some reflections provoked by that occasion. They turn particularly on More's *Dialogue of Comfort against Tribulation*, but in that one work it is possible to taste much of the seasoning and seasonableness of the man for all seasons – and all humours too.

The quincentenary drew some striking statements of that seasonableness. It rated a leader in *The Times* of 7 February 1978, and, on another page, tributes from both sides of the divide that made him a martyr, 'because he accepted martyrdom rather than swear the oath accepting King Henry VIII as head of the Church of England. The dedication of his life to the principle of a man's duty to his own conscience makes him, however, a martyr as much valued by members of the Church of England as by Roman Catholics ... he is a reassurance to us in a world almost as difficult and disordered as his.' As *The Tablet* put it (11 February 1978), 'More has become the saint, par excellence, of the modern world's totalitarian seasons.'

But *vixere fortes ante Agamemnona*: there have been martyrs in the same cause before More and since. One of the things that distinguished More is that his mind was as scrupulous as his conscience. 'His great statement in Westminster Hall during his trial asserts that duty to conscience while it distinguishes between the rights of conscience and of order in society: *ye must understand that, in things touching conscience, every true and good subject is more bound to have respect to his said conscience and to his soul than to any other thing in all the world beside; namely when his conscience is in such sort of mine is, that is to say, where the person giveth no occasion of slander, of tumult and sedition against his prince as it is with me*' (quoted in *The Times*). In his better known and pithier phrase – 'the king's good servant, but God's first'.

But this is a high cold climate, and there is another unique and attractive equilibrium in More – a declining to walk there earlier and longer than necessary. No doubt he was made of tougher stuff than Montaigne, but he would have agreed conditionally that *les humeurs transcendantes m'effraient.* In one special sense they did, in the doubt and fear and desolation that he knew as he prepared for the final witness. But that is psychological and human, and the point is not there. The point is in the temperament of the man. It too was scrupulous – to avoid the challenge of the final witness by all legitimate means for as long as legitimate, and when the choice might no longer be evaded, by self-analysis to avoid still doing the right thing for the wrong reason. And the point is yet not wholly there. Montaigne's *humeurs transcendantes* refer to the rabid theory of would-be disembodied spirit. But the attractiveness of More as man, Christian and saint, is that he was an *incarnate* spirit. He was humanist as well as saint, and not as scholar only but as a man of the world in the best sense, a civilized man who loved life, his home, family and friends, and the converse of that 'proper pleasant talking which is called *eutrapelia*' (out of Aristotle by Aquinas, but let that not put us off!). And when spirit had to have its priority – as it must for sanctity and martyrdom – it was the spirit of the spiritual man who was also *l'homme spirituel.* For More's wit and humour is one of the most unusual characteristics of his sanctity. From many a merry tale in life it accompanied him right to the pathos of the scaffold, as some well-known *mots* illustrate. 'I pray thee see me safe up, and for my coming down let me shift for myself ... Pluck up thy spirits man, and be not afraid to do thy office. My neck is very short: take heed therefore thou strike not awry for saving of thine honesty.'[1]

A concretion of characteristics which led *The Times* to suggest that 'More's character is the English character, but brought to a level of virtue which cannot otherwise be found'. *Stet* for Chaucer's England. He may also have had a little of Renaissance Mediterranean Europe – the joking martyr was the erstwhile translator of Lucian. There might even be an Irish connection, as his family at one stage thought – More reveals an unusual knowledge of the more manic sources of the humours that flow below the springing humour.

One of the events that coincided with the quincentenary was the appearance of *A Dialogue of Comfort against Tribulation.*[2] This is More's spiritual testament, his facing of the ultimate questions and the last things, written during his fifteen months in the Tower awaiting trial and eventual execution. What the end would be, he was not yet certain, but that only meant that More must decide what it *should* be. What Henry would decide More decided ten years earlier, in his garden at Chelsea, in the high sun of his favour – 'if my head could win him a castle in France, it would not fail to go'.

1 Quoted in Bridgett, *Blessed Thomas More*, 434.

2 Martz & Manley (eds), in the Yale series of *The Complete Works of Saint Thomas More.*

I suppose no other work of More's so welds greatness of theme and treatment to the incarnation of the man in his style. The theme is as great and as old as Job, the problem of the just man's tribulation and his quest for comforting – in a comfort derived not from moral poultices but from theoretical understanding, from a complete theodicy, a justification of the ways of God to man. The treatment, as in Job, is in the mode of art, fictional, dramatic and universalizing. So powerfully and sustainedly universalizing that even More's contemporary reader without knowledge of the context would not recognize it as written out of the author's own situation. 'His references to Henry's cruelty, to the disturbances in England, to the fear and expectation of the spread of heresy, to what comfort the good may have in view of such evils, present or to come, are all devised cleverly and naturally ... so that we would be convinced that a Hungarian is speaking of his own land and not More of England.'[3] The dialogue is set in Christian Hungary on the eve of a Turkish invasion. This situation was real enough at the time, and so the setting is no mere disguise for More's personal situation in England. It is part of the total frame of reference and could easily be read on that level. For the contemporary reader 'the literary surface would be perfectly intelligible and completely efficient within itself. More never departs from the fictional scene, and in Europe at the time, with its entire civilization threatened for almost a century by the increasing military power of the Turks, it would have great emotional reverberation.'[4] So should it still perhaps, and ever since

> the banks of oars that swam upon
> The many-headed foam at Salamis.

Yet all this can be read at another level in the particularity of More's own immediate situation, in England, now, in the Tower. And that not just by the decoding key of allegorical interpretation but by reading all the levels of More's layered and ironic art which often processes material barely disguised in its address to his family and friends, and barely processed in its derivation from the episodes of shared experience in the anecdotes of a shared world of discourse. We cannot be introduced to such a world without its furniture telling us a great deal about its chief inhabitant – as it does in all sorts of ways, from More's justification of property in the presence of poverty ('Who might live by the tailor's craft if no man were able to put a gown to make?' – 2.17), down to Dame Alice's unsophisticated sulks when her husband's talkative dalliance

3 Stapleton, *The Life and Illustrious Martyrdom of Sir Thomas More*, quoted in Martz and Manley (eds), cxxi.

4 Martz and Manley, ibid., xxxii.

with learned friends kept him out late for what she had in the pot for dinner (2 Pref.). Indeed the global problem of tribulation cannot be treated as More treats it without becoming a revelation of the man. For the theodicy at a certain point ceases to be an abstract attempt to 'justify', and becomes instead an analysis of the great psychological temptations that threaten to deflect understanding from the solution and the resolution provided by faith, hope and charity. But it is in the style that the man is everywhere, bathing and bounding the contents like atmosphere in a painting. There is the atmosphere as well as the theory of the theological virtues. And there is the atmosphere of the human as well as the infused virtues, a grace of a human kind which does not argue on the high argument but moves forward in dialogue of 'proper, pleasant talking'. And advances not by the straight geometric line but by the vital serpentining of many a winding divagation – with the logic of the organic line curved to the contours of empirical reality. And flavoured ever with irony and many a merry tale told to illustrate the argument simply because, even while he talks of Heaven, a man must 'take now and then some honest worldly mirth' (2.1), and because, however high the argument, we must regularly 'leave talking and assay how our dinner shall like us and how fair we can fall to feeding ... ' (2.17).

PART II

Yet this very personal work is also an impersonal work because composed in a classical tradition of such works written out of an archetypal situation in a tradition of civilized thought and spirituality.

The situation might be summed up in Chaucer's much-quoted definition of tragedy, as the Middle Ages understood it – the story

> Of him that stood in great prosperitie
> And is fallen out of high degree
> Into myserie, and endeth wrecchedlie.
> (PROLOGUE TO THE MONK'S TALE)

The situation is obviously parallel to tragedy, yet in one important respect it is different from tragedy in the stricter Aristotelian conception. In the Aristotelian analysis of the tragic pattern, there is identifiable in the tragic character, if not always some positive moral flaw, then some miscalculation or some wilful human self-assertion, whereby the victim can be identified as also in part the agent of his own destruction. The tragic pattern is therefore to that extent *intelligible*. And here is an essential difference from the kind of situation with which More and his tradition deal. In that situation, to all outward appearances, it is a just man who has fallen – and often – to make it more paradoxical, at the hands of the evil man.

It clashes with our sense of a moral order in the universe – and indeed for that very reason Aristotle excluded it from tragedy properly so called.

For that Aristotle has been criticized as too restrictive in his concept of tragedy – and in complementary fashion Job has been criticized for failing to be tragedy. But situations and their problems are what they are – and Aristotle's method was precisely to look at them closely before inductively defining their natures and their specific differences. For in fact the tribulation of the just man is much more problematical than that of the tragic hero – precisely because it is harder to explain and make significant within the moral order of the universe. It seems, as we have said, to conflict with our sense of that order. Works therefore that address themselves to that problem have to be more comprehensive than tragedy, and more explicitly metaphysical or theological. They cannot just focus on the pattern and process of downfall as embodied in the central character – since the problem is precisely that it is not there [that] sense can be found. We need a theodicy, not a catharsis. It is the total moral order of the universe that must be examined – first to find out whether there is such an order of justice at all, and then to try to understand its working. The choice ranges from the nihilism of the absurd to a recognition of the limitations of human reason in face of mystery. 'Evil therefore is nothing ... ', exclaims Philosophy to Boethius at a climactic moment (*Consol. Philos.*, 3.12). In other words God is *not* dead, everything is *not* permitted – 'A great obligation is upon you ... to be good, since you do act before the eyes of an all-seeing Judge' (ibid., 5.6). With less rationality but equal confidence and greater sense of mystery, the Hebrew Job transcends his comforters and his own revolt:

> I know that you are all-powerful:
> what you conceive you can perform.
> I am the man who obscured your designs
> with my empty-headed words.
> I have been holding forth on matters I cannot understand,
> on marvels beyond me and my knowledge.
> (Job 42.2ff)

This situation is archetypal in life before becoming classic in the great books it has occasioned. We might even suggest it is more 'true to life' than the situations of classical tragedy. In tragedy the plot is an 'ordering of the Events' (Aristotle, *Poetics*). In the tribulation of the just man no such ordering is needed, events are as they are, and we know that they can happen and have, in a way that is less easy to imagine for the heroics of high tragedy. A serious critic has estimated that 'the bad luck of Oedipus calls for as much suspension of disbelief as the good luck of Monte Cristo'. The least that can be said is that few real dyings are as splendid as his. That is certainly to mistake the point of tragedy. But we cannot mistake the point about Job, about Socrates in prison awaiting the hemlock, about Seneca in his bath struggling to hasten the sluggish flow of his slow veins on a word from Nero's KGB, about Boethius consigned by the rude Theodoric to his cell in Pavia – to win release only by accepting exile and martyrdom into *questa pace* in which Dante saw him glorious. And so on down to More in the Tower, and many another of whom there is no memorial.

The problem posed by this classic situation – to justify the ways of God – is ground enough by itself to produce grand works of theodicy. But they would not thereby be works in grand style. It is the relation of the problem to life that gives their special quality to the outstanding works in this 'consolatory' tradition. They have the quality of works of literary art, products of the imagination over and above the mode of discursive argumentation. We may not see how the artistic dimension has any importance beyond the rhetorically persuasive. An exclusive rationality has left no *truth* value to the imagination as a faculty or to art as its medium of communication. The coinage of the vocabulary itself has been devalued. We have no words which without further gloss will convey the sense of the imagination as the whole soul processing the world to meaning, and of the artefact as the patterned precipitate of that meaning. Yet even Aristotle granted that the myth-makers were also philosophers. And Thomas Aquinas declared that poetry no less than philosophy begins in wonder.

Now there is a kind of wonder less blandly and magisterially objective than Aristotle seems to have known – or at least has left much evidence of – a wonder more personal, violent and shaking than the purely speculative. He was at pains to assert the permanence of the material universe but has left no evidence that he lost much sleep over the permanence of the soul of individual man. We are most familiar now with the kind of philosophy which takes its point of departure from the reverse order of priorities in its wondering. It is born of an anguished sense of what bothered Aristotle so little, the *im*permanence of things, their terrible contingency, in particular; the contingency of human existence. We call it existentialist dread, Angst, angoisse etc., and think that it was born in Paris during the war, or if not in Paris then only a little earlier in Copenhagen.

In fact of course, like M. Jourdain's prose, the thing itself as distinct from the vocabulary has been there at least since the time of Pythagoras. And a good deal of the vocabulary occurs in Lucretius, for instance, so inadequately understood as the didactic port of philosophic materialism, when the system is but the projection of the 'dread and darkness in his soul' (*terrorem animi tenebrasque* – 1.146), the *anxius angor* of existence (3.993) and the absurd of the unquenchable but useless passion for life in the face of extinction (*sitis ... tenet vitai semper hiantis* – 3.1084).

> And then you endowed me with life,
>   watched each breath of mine with tender care.
> Yet, after all, you were dissembling:
>   biding your time ...
> Why did you bring me out of the womb? ...
> (Job 10.13ff)

Now whether by grace or a wonderful economy of nature or the slumbers of unawakened stolidity, most men get through life without getting into quite such a spin. Or do they? And if they do, is it necessarily a grace? 'Tribulation ... a thing whereof the contrary long continued is perilous ... '? (*Dialogue*, 1.20). What of the unexamined life? What of the once-born man? For our existence is contingent, ex-sisting out of, and over, the abyss. And if one beginning of wisdom is to 'know thyself', it entails knowing this too. Many people fear death by earthquake most of all, wrote Seneca in the wake of the Campanian cataclysm that preceded Pompeii and Herculaneum, the death in which they go down into the pit along with their residential seats (*N.Q.*, 6.1.8). But it makes no difference whether I give up the ghost in the bright light of day or engulfed in the gaping earth (6.1.9). No difference whether I am carried off by a tidal wave or by a drop of water gone down the wrong passage (6.2.5). Every death comes to the same end (6.1.8). Every ground is finally as flawed as Campania (6.1.15). And every man is flawed with death. We are all in prison, More will argue, all under sentence of death, and in the charge of a cruel gaoler while we wait (*Dialogue*, 2.20).

There is no essential difference between the drop of water and the tidal wave, none between the local and the total flaw in the earth, none between the personal and the global prison. But there is a vast qualitative, existential difference. It is only through the experiential shock of the local, particular and intensely personal that most men are woken from their unwondering slumber. It is only when the ground opens under our feet that we realise the void is everywhere. And from the vision of the *Abgrund* we are converted to the search for the *Grund* of all things.

Qui cecidit, stabili non erat ille gradu (Boethius, *Consol.*, 1.M.1.23). We now call such a situation a *Grenzsituation*. But we can see that those situations existed long before their name. 'Depend upon it, Sir, when a man knows he is to be hanged in a fortnight, it concentrates his mind wonderfully ...' It concentrates it still more intensely, if he is to be hanged in the wrong. But some such experience is the existential root of all the great works in the consolatory tradition of theodicy.

And, to close the circle of this excursus, only the theodicy which is also in the imaginative and artistic mode can both communicate the fullness of the human experience which generates the question, and provide an answer which will be an answer to the whole man, to his heart as well as to his head. 'You are playing with me, aren't you?', Boethius protests to Philosophy on her pat conclusion that 'evil then is nothing', 'you are playing with me by weaving a labyrinth of arguments from which I can't find the way out' (*Consol.*, 3.12). And that is why in this 'golden book' of the consolatory tradition, poetic meditation alternates with prose dialectic, like action and Chorus in a Greek tragedy, to 'bring to bear the persuasory powers of sweet-voiced 'Rhetoric' ... and 'Music' in modes alternately grave and gay ...' (2.1).

PART III

The present connotation of the terms comfort and consolation falls short of the tone and the range we have been describing. They suggest pain-soothers rather than pain-curers, coated with the mould of the moralistic and the anodyne. 'But Comfort ... is properly taken by them that take it right rather for the consolation of good hope, that men take in their heart of some good growing toward them, than for a present pleasure with which the body is delighted and tickled for the while ...' (*Dialogue,* 1.19). To this end 'comfort' must be understood in its derivation from the Latin *confortare* and in relation to the promised divine agent of such comforting, the Paraclete, the Comforter. The range of consolation is analogous. Its consolation is of the understanding by philosophic argument. But it understood Philosophy in an older and more comprehensive sense, the philosophic 'life' or 'way'. The validity of the argument is not confined to what may be seen at the end of the syllogism. It extends to what may be seen at the end of the way, the way of ascent through interior transformation to a higher light and a higher capacity to see by it. And in this problem, as we have seen, the final seeing is always of the residue that goes beyond seeing except as mystery, in the irreducible crux of the Cross or in the transcendence of divine seeing to ours. 'I have been holding forth', concludes Job, 'on matters I cannot understand' (42.3). 'The point of greatest importance is this', says Boethius as he begins the last climb to God's way of seeing: 'The superior manner of knowledge includes the inferior, but it is quite impossible for the inferior to rise to the superior' (5.4).

Now St Thomas More's method is to start from, in order to pass beyond, the achievements of natural reason in the consolatory tradition. 'Some drugs have they yet in their shops ... ', because 'this thing laboured the philosophers very much about, and many goodly sayings have they toward the strength of comfort against tribulation ... Howbeit ... I never yet could find that ever these natural reasons were able to give sufficient comfort of themself, for they never stretch so far ... but that they leave untouched, for want of necessary knowledge, that special point which is not only the chief comfort of all, but without which also all other comforts are nothing, that is to wit the referring the final end of their comfort unto God ... ' (1.1). Specifically the essential 'ground and foundation' is faith (1.2). To this the 'good drugs' of the tradition of natural reason become auxiliary, preambulary – to faith 'without which ... all the spiritual comfort that any man may speak of can never avail a fly' (ibid.). And the pattern of what at first seems an excessively discursive book is a Dantean ascent beyond natural reason, though with its aid, via faith, through hope, to that summit of charity in which the mystery of tribulation and human trepidation before it are consumed in a positive passion to be dissolved and to be with Christ by the same way that he went. *Non sunt condigne passiones huius temporis futuram gloriam que revelabitur in nobis* (3.27).

Once More has put the problem on to the platform of the theological virtues, which the unaided reason of the Greco-Roman tradition could not reach, faith, hope and charity become the successive *foci* of the three books of the *Dialogue*. By faith we know what is the meaning and value of tribulation. By hope we trust in divine help to endure it, sustained by future glory not worthy to be compared with present sufferings. By charity we do endure it, since charity is a yearning for and an absorption into God by which we are raised beyond ourselves and our own resources, above all in union with Christ's Passion.

If we lay first for a sure ground a very fast faith ... then shall we consider tribulation as a gracious gift of God: a gift that he specially gave his special friends ... a thing whereof the contrary long continued is perilous ... the thing without which no man can get to Heaven. (1.20)

A great comfort may this be in all kinds of temptation, that God hath His hand upon him that is willing to stand and will trust in Him and call up to Him, that He hath made him sure by many faithful promises in Holy Scripture, that either he shall not fall or... his fall shall be no sore bruising. (2.10)

Would God we would hear to the shame of our cold affection ... Would God we would I say but consider what hot affection many of us fleshly lovers have borne and daily do, to those upon whom they dote ... Men would be willing to die many times over for human affections ... How cold lovers be we then unto God if, rather than die for Him once, we will refuse Him and forsake Him forever, that hath both died for us before and hath also provided that if we die here for Him, we shall everlastingly both live and also reign with Him ... (3.27)

But we do not leap on to such a platform, we climb up to it – the business of theodicy is to justify the ways of God. And, true to the relation between reason and faith, and consistently with his own acceptance of the 'good drugs' still in their shops, More uses the rational arguments of the Greco-Roman consolatory tradition as a ladder to climb beyond them. So it is that we find the pattern of the theological virtues subsuming another with which we are familiar from Boethius' *Consolatio*. Thus in 3.3 ff we find a traditional inventory of the external goods of Fortune that a man loses in his fall from prosperity, and a traditional evaluation of what it is he really loses, and what pain he suffers in the process – 'money, plate, and other moveable substance, then offices, authority, and finally all the lands of his inheritance forever, that himself and his heirs perpetually might else enjoy'.[5]

More unfolds this 'high argument' with a complex literary art. Or rather for reasons in the nature of the genre which we have seen, the argument *becomes* a work of literary art and persuasion that leads the spirit up to a point of seeing and acceptance by all the techniques which art employs. Indeed the procedure is particularly valid in a Christian context, where it is inbuilt that all is 'exercise', propaedeutic, 'ascent' to the point where a higher Spirit than ours will enlighten us. The penultimate sentence of the whole work beseeches Our Lord 'to breathe of his Holy Spirit into the reader's breast, which inwardly may teach him in heart, without whom little availeth all that all the mouths of the world were able to teach in men's ears'. Within this framework More's art and meaning are as complex, – or more so – indirect and layered as a Socratic dialogue such as Plato's *Symposium*. (There comes to mind the comparison used there to describe the strange power of Socratic discourse – the Chinese-box figures of Silenus holding pipes or flutes, hollow inside but when opened found to contain little figures of gods – 215.) The *Dialogue* 'carries with it More's whole manner and mode of thought -- complexity of the dialogue form, the artistic structure and design, the various levels of audience address, and the strange, Menippean combination of more tales and anecdotes side by side with the grim realities of mental and physical torture.'[6]

An art of *spoudaiogeloion* in fact, in which 'talk of as earnest sad matter as man can devise' is ever and again 'refreshed with a foolish merry tale' (2.1.), and the one desire of a foolish old man's life – 'to sit well and warm with a cup and a roasted crab and drivel and drink and talk' (2 Pref.) – is the accompaniment to the sombre theme of a meditation on Ps.90 and four great trials to which all tribulation comes down:

> Scuto circumdabit te veritas eius; non timebis
> a timore nocturno;
> A sagitta volante in die, a negotio perambulante
> in tenebris, ab incursu et daemonio meridiano.' (2.11ff)

5 Cf. Boethius, *Consolatio*, 2.5ff, 3.3ff.

6 Martz and Manley, op.cit., cxix.

The legitimate role of the *geloion* is expressly established at the start of Book 2. It was an essential part of his own character – 'of truth Cousin, as you know very well, myself am of nature even half a giglot and more – I would I could mend my fault ... ' (2.1). But he didn't want to mend it, because he instinctively knew what the greatest humour illustrates – that the comic vision transcends tragedy. Humour ... empirical and temperamental and ... divine – divine because 'it had to do with his relationship with God, which allowed him to see the world with sufficient detachment to be aware of its insignificance in the face of eternity'.[7] A sense of divine proportion, in other words.

This divine sense of humour is seen at its most human, rich and deep, in his analysis of the first kind of temptation – the 'night's fear' (2.12–16). There are reasons why it should be so – the work itself is richest and deepest at this point. The 'consolatory' becomes also the 'confessional' – through the psychological exploration of motives in depth. In the very principle of focusing on 'temptation' as the essential tribulation, we recognise at once an existential depth which the classical *consolatio* did not reach. The Socrates of the *Crito* anticipates the temptation *situation* but not this Christian interiority *de profundis* ... And the deepest *profundum* is in the exploration of the 'night's fear'. That is the fear of human weakness in the hour against which we pray – 'lead us not into temptation ... ' . It is the fear of despair in the hour of darkness, and conversely the fear of surmounting fear only by pride and presumption.

> The last temptation is the greatest treason.
> To do the right deed for the wrong reason.

And so More descends into the depths before ascending to the heights – in the archetypal pattern, we might note – 'exploring by degrees the intensity of the various manifestations of despair, from pusillanimity to scrupulosity to suicide and death by demonic illusion ... Anecdotes of paradoxical self-destruction – suicide for revenge and martyrdom for pride – appear side by side with astute psychological observation ... while underneath it all runs a strong subcurrent of autobiographical revelation, as More probes the question of his own fears and motives in the Tower'.[8] It is well called 'the night's fear ... for that many times the cause of tribulation is unto him that suffereth dark and unknown' (2.12).

Not a region where we might think humour is much in order. But laughter too is cathartic of terror. It is more fun to joke past the graveyard than to whistle, as illustrated in one of More's anecdotes to immunise the 'night's fear'. 'I remember ...

7 Ibid., xcviii.

8 Ibid., cii.

when I was a young man ... in the war with the Turks and camped in Turkish territory ... many a mile beyond Belgrade.' At midnight there was a red alert because an excited scout reported that he had spied the Turkish host advancing under cover of the night. But in the morning when nothing had happened 'they found that the great fearful army of the Turks so soberly coming on, turned (God be thanked) into a fair long hedge standing even stone still' (2.12). There is a long tradition behind this mood – since Socrates went out with a cock to Asclepius. And Socrates it was who argued that the man who could write a comedy could also write a tragedy, and vice versa (*Sympos.* 223). It would be a truth well-known to More. For his humour is the other side of his sense of *lacrimae rerum* – 'to prove that this life is no laughing time but rather a time of weeping, we find that Our Saviour himself wept twice or thrice but never find we that he laughed so much as once. I will not swear that he never did, but at the least wise he left us no samples of it' (1.13).

The laughter and the tears together go into that perception in which he puts his own imprisonment and prospective suffering and death into divine perspective. For is not the whole world a prison – 'wander we never so far about therein' – with God as its chief gaoler, every inmate under sentence of death, and while he waits for its carrying out 'as sore handled and as hardly, as wrenched and wronged and (broken) in such painful wise' that if we only thought about it we would have as good cause to feel the horror of the one as of the other (3.20).

It is a perfect example of More's art as well as of his humanity when he gets the same tragi-comic cosmic view into the cameo of the anecdote identifiably at the affectionate expense of poor Dame Alice, whose perspectives were – and perhaps had to be – shorter than her husband's. She was naturally concerned about the conditions of his life in prison, but she was also fussy by nature. She got particularly excited and claustrophobic about her husband's unopenable cell doors locked nightly from the outside, 'For by my troth, quoth she ... if the door should be shut upon me I ... ween it would stop my breath. At that word of hers the prisoner laughed in his mind, but he durst not laugh aloud ... for something indeed he stood in awe of her ... But he could not but laugh inwardly while he wist well enough that she used on the inside to shut every night full surely her own both door and windows too, and used not to open them all the night. And what difference then to the stopping of the breath, whether they were shut up within or without?!' (3.20).

There is also the blacker humour of the 'tragical tales' arising out of the black theme of that first temptation of the night's fear. There is the story of the suicidal monk whose delusions of spiritual grandeur persuaded him it was God's will he should hang himself, 'and that thereby he should go straight to Heaven' (2.16).

From which folly if Counsel cannot wake him but he must take his dream for reality More can see no other treatment but that either he be strait-jacketed in his bed, or else he be given the assistance the carver's wife offered her husband in a similar 'frantic fantasy'. He, on a Good Friday, would kill himself for Christ's sake – as Christ died for him. Whereupon she put him in remembrance that it were meet he should die in the same manner as Christ did. Christ was killed by others – in definite fashion and in particular stages. All of which offices the wife offered to perform for her husband. At the Crowning with Thorns he would leave the rest till Good Friday came again – 'but when it came again the next year then was his lust past; he longed to follow Christ no further' (2.16).

And there is the tale of the fiendish carpenter's wife, whose ploy to punish her husband was to provoke him into decapitating her with his axe so that he should then hang for her. And there is the rich widow who paid a friend to slay her and deposit the axe in the house of the neighbour with whom she was in dispute – 'in some such manner ... as it might be thought he had murdered her for malice, and then she thought she should be taken for a martyr'. Consequent on which notion 'she further devised that another sum of money should after be sent to Rome and there should be means made to the Pope that she might in all haste be canonised' (2.15).

Lastly there is the simplest rationale of all for humour, namely that so we can best accommodate 'the diversity of divers men's minds' (2.1). This however is but the outcrop of the deepest of all, the comic contradiction of man's nature and condition, a spirit tied to a body which obliges him to hear of heaven only through things of the earth earthly. And More recounts Cassian's anecdote about the holy father who in his sermon 'Spake of heavenly things so celestially that much of his audience with the sound thereof began to forget all the world and fall asleep ... '; suddenly he said to them, 'I shall tell you a merry tale', at which they lifted up their heads and hearkened unto that ... ! If such earthly stimulant be the condition of sustained interest in heaven ... you must let them have it, More concludes. 'Better would I wish it but I cannot help it' (2.1). A fact which we must assume St Thomas More found as sad as did Chaucer when he prayed that Christ would have mercy and forgive him his sins, especially his 'translations and enditings of worldly vanities', such as, inter alia, *The Tales of Canterbury* just told – 'those', that is, 'that tend towards sin'.

THOMAS MORE IN HIS TIME: RENAISSANCE HUMANISM AND RENAISSANCE LAW[9]

PART ONE: INTRODUCTION TO CALL FOR PAPERS

INTERNATIONAL THOMAS MORE CONFERENCE,
MAYNOOTH COLLEGE, 9-16 AUGUST 1998

Abstract
A consideration of the full dimensions of *humanism* and of the humanist dimension of *law* invites two questions: is 'humanism' compatible with theocentric religion, and therefore, is the Renaissance compatible with the 'otherworldly' Middle Ages, and, has law any humanist dimension at all? The answer to the first question provides the insights that answer the second. Fully integrated humanism includes both the Classical immanence of humanity in the world and the value accorded to the human being by the declaration in Genesis that all creation is 'very good', a principle [rein]forced by the Incarnation of the *Logos* as a man. Understood in the full range of its human relevance, from the quotidian to the transcendent, law too has a humanist dimension.[10]

I HUMANISM

The principal topic in our conference theme is humanism, Renaissance humanism. In the present company, so to speak, it would be otiose to introduce the call for papers on humanism by an explanation of its meaning. At worst we are only in the situation of Augustine on the meaning of time; we know its meaning until we are asked to explain it. Yet, when the focus of the topic is *Thomas More in his time*, some particular remarks are in order.

They turn especially on the fact that Thomas More is both saint and humanist, indeed a theologian as well as a humanist, and also – in the interpretation of Chambers' biography – a man of the Middle Ages as well as a man of the Renaissance. In one of the summary and simplistic explanations of humanism

9 In connection with the *International Thomas More Conference* held at Maynooth College, 9–16 August 1998.

10 Key words: *humanitas, grande profundum, virtù*, prison literature, conscience, human interest.

and the Renaissance, those combinations may seem improbable, if not contradictory. Is not humanism a 'discovery' of the human and the ideal of its perfection, and consequently anthropocentric as distinct from the so-called theocentrism of the Middle Ages? Is not the Renaissance a 'discovery' and rebirth of pre-Christian Classical antiquity, and consequently a 'discovery' of, and a turning towards, the autonomous reality and beauty of this world as distinct from the so-called otherworldly orientation of the Christian Middle Ages? How could Thomas More combine those opposites, as a man of this world and a man certainly of the other world? Or is there a Christian humanism? Is there a humanism which integrates the Classical and the Judeo-Christian?

Doubtless, that question too is otiose, as is also the positive answer that has often been given to it. But in a conference on Thomas More it may not be otiose to recall briefly the rationale of the answer. And in sum the rationale is in the fact that western humanism has not one but two taproots, not only Greco-Roman civilization but also Judeo-Christian religion. Not that Greco-Roman humanism was merely anthropocentric, or lacked the religious dimension of complete *humanitas*. But Judeo-Christian revelation gave a new clarity and a more certain foundation to the meaning of both *deitas* and *humanitas*.

At the end of the account of creation in Genesis, 'God saw all that he had made, and it was very good' (1:31). This text is foundational for the positive value of the phenomenal world. Foundational too for the values of the human and the 'humanist' is the text on the creation of human beings: 'Let us make man in our own image and likeness ... ' (Gen 1:26). Those terrestrial values are confirmed by Christianity, which is founded on the Incarnation. 'The Word (*Logos*) became flesh (*sarx*), and dwelt among us, and we have seen his glory ... ' (Jn 1:14). Christianity is thus a religion not only of the Book, but also of the incarnational, i.e. of the invisible and transcendent embodied in the visible and material, of the ideal embodied in the real.

This is a truth and a value which Christianity had to defend from the start – and precisely against certain excessively spiritualizing tendencies of Platonism – and more outlandish versions of dualism, for which the Incarnation was a scandal. It was in this context that the first systematic Christian theologian, the second-century Irenaeus of Lyons, wrote the often quoted sentence: 'The glory of God is the human being fully alive' (*Adversus haereses*, IV 20, 7). It is a perennial theme of the great Christian poets and artists. Dante is instinct with it. So is Péguy:

> Il [le Christ] allait hériter d'un monde déjà fait.
> Et pourtant il allait tout jeune le refaire.
> Il allait procéder de la cause à l'effet
> Comme le Fils procède en descendant du Père. ('Ève')

Yeats also has this *humanisme intégral* (as Maritain called it) which integrates the natural and the supernatural orders. 'That civilization may not sink', he writes in one of his poems,

> Shut the door of the Pope's chapel,
> Keep those children out.
> There on the scaffolding reclines
> Michael Angelo. ('Long-legged Fly')

It was the medieval Aquinas who, with the aid of Aristotle, provided the philosophical and theological articulation of the distinction and the relation between those two orders. And that was the fruit of an earlier 'Renaissance', that of the twelfth and thirteenth centuries. There were Renaissances before '*the* Renaissance'.

Given that range of 'integral humanism' – all things human and divine, to borrow Cicero's humanist definition of the range of philosophy – there is little need to elaborate the range suggested by our covering title: *Thomas More in his time.* For that is also the range both of More and of his time: the Renaissance. The 'rebirth' was not only of humanism in any narrow anthropocentric sense. It was a 'rebirth' of religion too – and that in an intense, profound and far-reaching degree, as we know from both the Catholic and Protestant Reformations. In both cases the 'rebirth' was by a discovery of, and a return to, antiquity – for a revitalization through a *ressourcement* from the springing pristine sources. And the journey back was not along two roads running merely parallel to each other. The study of the divine in theology cannot be dissociated from the study of the human in humanism. For both studies are concerned with great and. mysterious deeps – a *grande profundum* as Augustine says of man (*Conf.* IV 14,22). Indeed it is religious experience which has revealed just how *grande* is the *profundum* of man, of Augustine's *abyssus humanae conscientiae* (*Conf.* X 2,2). 'What are human beings', exclaims the Psalmist, 'that you spare a thought for them ... ? Yet you have made them little less than gods ... ' (Ps 8). *Grandeur et misère de l'homme ...*, reflects Pascal. Theology too is a humanist discipline in so far as it is concerned with the mystery of man. And we know how schools of theology have differed on that mystery – more than ever during the Renaissance and the Reformation.

'Thomas More in his time' then ranges over the whole republic of learning that was the Renaissance, humanism not in a confined literary sense, but as extending to history, philosophy, biblica, patristics, theology, the visual arts, political theory – even law which, as we shall show, has a humanist dimension too, and not merely because there were two schools of interpretation at the time: the Humanists and the Glossators.

The range is geographical as well as intellectual. For the universe of Thomas More extends beyond England to the Continent and its great European figures and centres of humanism. And that universe is composed of both sexes. Women's contribution to humanism is an area to be explored for papers – contributions personal and direct, or indirect through women's influence in humanist circles. Here we can start from the instance of the education and role of the women in More's own household. In *Utopia*, women as well as men attend the lectures delivered daily before daybreak (CW4 128/3ff). In his colloquy on *The Abbot and the Learned Lady*, Erasmus provides an example of a woman educated far beyond her male interlocutor.

Such a liberal attitude is not as totally new as it is sometimes thought to be, as the humanists themselves would be aware. For already in classical antiquity the role of accomplished women is quite prominent, especially in Rome – and in spite of the authority of the Roman *paterfamilias*. The most striking evidence is provided by that group of poets known as the Augustan Love Elegists – who in so many ways anticipate the courtly ideal and code of the *Dolce Stil Nuovisti*. They are principally Catullus, Tibullus, and, above all, Propertius. Propertius' Cynthia is the type *par excellence* of the 'liberated' lady who becomes the poet's muse principally because of her own literary and artistic accomplishments. We know the long history of that motif – down to Dante's Beatrice, and the Laura of that 'Father of the Renaissance', Petrarch. And to that company belongs the visionary Lady Philosophy, in the book that Thomas More as well as Dante read in his troubles, Boethius' *Consolation of Philosophy*. And Dante himself continued the motif in the status accorded to Beatrice.

Even Augustine had already praised the contributions of his mother Monica, present at some of the philosophical discussions reported in the Cassiciacum *Dialogues* of the autumn of 386 after his conversion. More surprising still, the stern St Jerome cultivated the spirituality and the Christian intelligence of distinguished Roman women like Eustochium and Paula. In the Middle Ages they had successors in the creative talents, not only religious but literary and humanist, of women like St Hildegarde of Bingen (named in More's *Supplication of Souls*, CW7, 209/24), Marie de France and Christine de Pizan. The list continues in the Renaissance in the contributions of Marguerite de Navarre, Margaret Roper, Mary Roper Basset, Mary Queen of Scots, Aemilia Lanyer, Caritas Pirckheimer – to name only a very few. In the seventeenth century, there is Katherine Philips ('the matchless Orinda'), poet and translator of poets, including Horace and Corneille (*Pompée*), for which latter she won acclaim in Dublin and London, There is also the late seventeenth- into eighteenth-century Irish woman poet and friend of Jonathan Swift, Mary Barber.

***

The Renaissance has both antecedents and an afterlife, a *Nachleben*, which are still relevant today, and therefore provide subjects for exploration. We mentioned earlier that it was the medieval Aquinas whose metaphysics corrected the other-worldly Platonist Augustinianism in favour of the relative autonomy and validity of the secular world and its values so characteristic of the Renaissance.

Aquinas was followed by Dante in his distinguishing of the domains of Church and state, of secular and sacral, in the political theory of his *De monarchia*. Etienne Gilson found an analagous anticipation in the story of Abelard – especially in that profound interest in the individual life and experience which emerges from the confessional, autobiographical self-analysis in Abelard's *Historia Calamitatum*. This is in direct continuity with a double source in antiquity. Firstly, there is the growing Greco-Roman interest in biography and autobiography consequent on a growing interest in the individual life and experience – exterior and interior. Secondly, there is the related but much profounder early Christian genre of the confession – culminating in the *Confessions* of St Augustine but having a long history ahead of it, through e.g. Abelard's *Historia Calamitatum*, DuBelley's *Regrets* (inspired by Ovid's *Tristia*), the literary 'portraits' of the humanists, down to such modern *confessions* as Rousseau's, Joyce's *Portrait of the Artist as a Young Man* and George Moore's *Confessions of a Young Man*.

The Renaissance was an age of heroic exploration and the discovery of new worlds far beyond the confines of Europe. Its humanism consequently encompassed also the cult of the *virtù* of the heroic individual. Often cited as an anticipation of this type of 'Renaissance man' is the famous passage in Dante's *Inferno* where Ulysses narrates his last voyage with his companions in quest of the ultimate 'experience of the unpeopled world behind the sun' (*Canto* XXVI, 91ff). 'Consider your origin', he addresses his companions, 'you were not formed to live like brutes but to pursue *virtute* and knowledge.' Not even the faithful Penelope could overcome his ardour to sail away again to 'gain experience of the world and of human vice and value'. And the end of the voyage remarkably anticipates the end of *Moby Dick*. Three times the sudden storm spun the ship. At the fourth the poop rose up and the prow went down, 'as pleased Another (*altrui*), till the sea closed over above us' (139ff).

We have been emphasizing a concluding point about Renaissance humanism, and its dimensions, that they have both antecedents and a *Nachleben* – scarcely surprising, come to think of it, given the continuity of the two sources of what we call Western civilization, the Greco-Roman and the Judeo-Christian. The Odyssean episode in Dante embodies a good illustration of both antecedents and

Nachleben. An antecedent of Renaissance *virtù* in general and of Renaissance epics of explorers (such as *Os Lusíadas* of Camões), it also embodies the *Nachleben* of Homer's *Odyssey*. And how well it does that, despite the fact that Dante did not have the *Odyssey* in Greek, and only the *disiecta membra* in Latin. For Odysseus/ Ulysses is introduced at the opening of the *Odyssey* as the much-travelled hero who knew many cities of men. And at the conclusion, after the homecoming from ten years of sailing the seas, he is fated to set out once more. More recalls him in *Utopia*, in the person of Hythlodaeus, whose 'sailing has not been like that of Palinurus but that of Ulysses ... '. Hence, like Ulysses, he surpassed all living mortals in his knowledge of 'unknown peoples and lands' (CW4, 49/30ff).

This would be only a *fait divers* of literary history were it not for the fact that, firstly, the *journey* is one of the archetypal plots in literature, and, secondly, that the *Odyssey* is the archetypal embodiment of it in Western literature – except in so far as the biblical *exodus* is another archetype. Virgil's *Aeneid* continues it, and Dante continues the *Aeneid*, not only as journey but as incorporating Aeneas as guide. For T. S. Eliot the *Aeneid* is the *European* 'classic', and the *Commedia* is the 'classic' of *Christendom*. And the motif continues down to Joyce's *Ulysses*, Ezra Pound's *Cantos*, and most recently Derek Walcott's *Omeros*.

But what Dante embodies too in the Ulysses episode is the dark side of humanist *virtù*, its hubristic and consequently tragic dimension. Promethean man is still finite, and the elemental waters swallow the ships of both Dante's Ulysses and Melville's Captain Ahab. This dénouement is not an innovation to the tradition. All the heroes of Troy are sad shades in the underworld when Odysseus meets them in *Odyssey* XI. And the greatest of them all, Achilles, confesses that he would rather be a serf in the world than be king of all the shades in the afterlife. The *lacrimae rerum* of Virgil's *Aeneid* are well known. *Tantae molis erat Romanam condere gentem* (I. 33) – so mighty a task it was to found the Roman race. But the constant question *en sourdine* is whether the results justified the sacrifices involved in the effort – and what deities directed it all. Tragedy *avant la lettre* begins in the great archetypal epics. Their overtures always announce not just an epic story to be told but also a metahistorical question about it. *Tantaene animis caelestibus irae*? (I. 11) asks Virgil – is there such resentment in the hearts of the gods? And the *Aeneid* ends with the *pius* Aeneas running his sword through the fallen Turnus – who expires with a protesting suspiration. *Sunt lacrimae rerum et mentem mortalia tangunt* (I. 462) – there are tears at the heart of things, and the human spirit is touched by mortality.

There may be something here for our own Promethean times. In the film *Space Odyssey 2001* the space-travelling hero comes back to his island Ithaca, to be welcomed home – as in Homer – by his old but still remembering house-dog.

II LAW AND HUMANISM

Humanism, as we have said, needs little explanation to cognoscenti, only the highlighting of aspects relevant to a context. The same can hardly be said for the juxtaposition of law with humanism. Humanism is the exploration and cultivation of all that constitutes *humanitas* in its full range, from the delimiting definition of essence and individual personhood to the limitless variety of its creative expression in culture and high civilization, and beyond that again to the 'ever more' of the drive to transcendence expressive of the *animal metaphysicum* and his capacity for the infinite. It was as a Platonist as well as a Christian that Augustine could exclaim: 'Our hearts are restless until they rest in Thee' (*Conf.* I 1,1). Humanism is concerned with man in his full range, from his littleness, even his *misère*, to his *grandeur*. That is the range of man in all his great humanist definitions from the classical Sophocles to the Renaissance Shakespeare. 'Many awesome things (*deina*) there are, but none more awesome than man (...) yet death he cannot overcome' (*Antigone*, 330ff). 'What a piece of work is a man! How noble in reason, how infinite in faculty (...). Yet what to me is this quintessence of dust ... ' (*Hamlet* II 2,2, 305ff).

That is the range of the 'human interest' of humanism, of so-called humane studies, the human interest which they must in fact defend against all ancient or modern critical methodologies which may tend precisely to *dehumanize* them, and thus to eliminate the very values in the name of which they are pursued. More specifically it is the 'human interest' that a conference should have whose focus is Thomas More, that most human of humanists and saints, acquainted with the depths and ascended to the heights.

How does law sit to that human and humanist range? On first acquaintance is it not, on the contrary, a bloodless abstraction in its principles? In their interpretation is it not a spinner of tenuous webs that make confining nets for human freedom and humanist transcendence? In their application is it not time and again *inhuman* and *anti-humanist*? – witness the archetypal instances of Socrates, More, and many others in our own time.

And yet, it was Socrates who awaited his death in prison rather than offend against the reverence due to the law by escaping. And it was More, a lawyer himself as well as a humanist, who would give even the Devil his rights under the law, and faced his own fate only when he had exhausted all the possibilities afforded by the law to avoid it. And in the Renaissance – and already in its medieval antecedents – law itself was one of the disciplines recovered and 'reborn' from Classical antiquity, to the extent even that there was a specifically 'humanist' school of juridical interpretation.

The solution to those paradoxes is simple, but just as far-reaching as the range of humanism. For law touches human existence at every level from the lowest to the highest, from the empirical regulations that keep *anomie* at bay in even the simplest society, up to the cosmic 'natural' law and the 'supernatural' divine law that determines the final meaning, order, and destiny of human existence. And ultimately law touches human existence not in a merely extrinsic way, but in the very core of one's being, in the interior castle of one's conscience, the ultimate court of appeal from all merely extrinsic codes. There is the higher law written in the heart – for Antigone, Socrates, St Paul, and Thomas More.

It is understandable then that codes of law should have been a feature of all high civilizations since their emergence millennia ago. In fact, as we know most familiarly from classical Rome, law itself has been one of the signal creations of high civilization. And characteristically, it was the Roman Virgil who gave majestic expression to the fact:

> *Tu regere imperio populos, Romane, memento.* (AENEID VI, 851)

Rome will let others excel in the conventional arts and sciences. The Roman discipline *par excellence* – *hae tibi erunt artes* – will be to rule and govern, by the authority of universal *imperium*, and thus to impose the custom of peace, to be kind to the conquered, and to bring down the pride of the *haughty* (*Aeneid* VI, 851–3). That destiny was fulfilled through the single greatest expression of the Roman genius, the corpus of Roman law that developed over a millennium, from its beginnings with the *Twelve Tables* in the fifth century BC to its codification in the *Corpus* of Justinian in the sixth century AD. And one of the many earlier renaissances, one of the defining moments in Western civilization, was when the heritage of Roman law resumed its long history with the re-emergence of its study in the eleventh century in the University of Bologna.

That is the range of law in time and space – from the earliest high civilizations, down through Rome to the Middle Ages, the Renaissance, and the modern West. Its intellectual range we noted earlier. Law relates to human existence in all its variety, and at all its levels from the empirical and practical to the theoretical and the transcendent. It is one of the central intellectual disciplines by which the human mind has tried to understand, order, direct, and fulfill the nature and potentialities of human existence. How then could it fail to have not merely 'human interest' but a humanist dimension, so closely linked as it is with *humanitas*?

The status of law as an intellectual discipline brought it into relation with all the other disciplines that make up the curriculum of humanist studies and culture from its beginnings in Greco-Roman civilization. Law was neither studied nor practised in isolation from the liberal arts. On the contrary, it presupposed them, as the propaedeutic which imparted that training of the mind and that broad culture without which the law would be indeed a lifeless abstraction in its principles and a system of barren autonomous techniques in its interpretation. In *A Dialogue Concerning Heresies*, More adds law and philosophy to the liberal arts curriculum as quickeners and sharpeners of the mind.[11] The result was that law itself became a specific ingredient in the humanist formation of the Roman mind – as it did again in the formation of the European mind after the revival of legal studies through the *Corpus* of Justinian. And in the universities it became again what it had been in ancient Rome – one of the core subjects of liberal education.

The Dimensions: The range of law's concerns extends, as we have said, from the practical quotidian to the theoretical transcendent. The reason for the latter pole is that law is ultimately concerned with the totality of human existence – its meaning and destiny within the total order of the world, and consequently within what order of earthly society that meaning can be realized and that destiny attained. That is what we see in the very beginning of political theory – in Plato, through Aristotle and Cicero to St Augustine. Plato and Aristotle approach the subject on two levels: the empirical and the theoretical. The empirical level deals with the kind of social organization that is necessary to provide for the survival and the amenities of physical and material human existence. But once that is assured, what is life lived *for*? What is the *ideal* life – the *good* life, as they called it? We are immediately into the realm of philosophical thinking, into metaphysics, even theology, into ethics – and consequently into the question of what social order law should articulate. This logical sequence of thought is reflected in the order of the two fundamental works in which both Plato and Cicero treated of political theory. Each wrote a *Republic* and a *Laws*. In each case the *Republic* speculates on the fundamental question of what values the ideal society should embody. In each case the *Laws* then treats of the particular system of laws that will ensure that embodiment. An ideal pyramid indeed – or a ladder, like Jacob's, linking the earthly to the 'heavenly' order.

But suppose there is no such universal ideal Platonic order in the cosmos by which to determine the ideal earthly order ... ? Suppose there is only matter and its laws – as already in the atheistic materialism of Epicurus and the cosmic epic of Lucretius. It is the age-old and ever-present fundamental option between a materialist and an idealist metaphysics. Its consequent question for law is whether there are or are not absolute transcendent norms of the good and the just by which man-made law should be determined. If there are no such norms, then there are no criteria distinguishing good from evil, justice from injustice. Everything is permitted – unless for utilitarian reasons of self-preservation. The only law is the law of the strongest. Might is right. Plato had to deal with

11 CW6, 132/3ff – cf. *Moreana* 111–112/45.

proponents – even practitioners – of that option. And so again have had thinkers to do in this twentieth century.

On the choice between those fundamental options will depend the answers to some very important particular questions that arise in law: the relation of the free individual to the laws of collective society, the relation of the private conscience – the law written in the heart – to the public law of the state, the relation of the laws of the state to the laws of other institutions within the state, religious, educational, cultural.

Such questions are as relevant to our own time as they were to Thomas More's time and to Plato's time, as Elizabeth McCutcheon has pointed out in the current number of the *Thomas More Gazette*. Indeed Thomas More's biographers have seen him from the start as another Socrates. How many more such exemplars there have been since those two, most of them with no memorial, and most of all in our own century, with its monstrous 'legal' perversions of the law!

And, to keep in mind the humanist dimension of our theme, what literature those questions and experiences have generated! A whole literary genre in fact, 'prison literature' – and often more than a merely *literary* genre, a philosophical genre as well: theodicy. The list from the Socratic *Apology*, *Crito* and *Phaedo*, through Boethius' *Consolation of Philosophy*, down to More's *Dialogue of Comfort*, and on to such works as those of Solzhenitsyn and Bonhoeffer in our own century.

An Irish Dimension: The ultimate principles of law are universal, but their interpretation is in particular historical times and situations. The great figures who stand to the death for law's ultimate principles are also universal types. More was himself a universalist not only in the understanding of law but also, for instance, in his understanding of the universal unity of Christendom. But particularly he is an embodiment in his own situation of the universal types we have referred to. Ever since Cardinal Pole and Nicholas Harpsfield he has been seen as another Socrates. It would be fitting then to give him some local habitation in a conference held in Ireland.

Given that the experience that began for England under Henry VIII began also for Ireland, Ireland must have many such local habitations and names. Only scholars of Irish history will know quite how many. It suffices to mention just some possibilities here. As it happens, Maynooth College stands on such a local habitation, the former demesne of the Norman-Irish FitzGeralds, the Earls of Kildare. Their great castle stands just outside the College gates. At their high point in Tudor times they were practically kings of Ireland. It was natural then that one of their great stands should have been against Henry VIII's attempt to reconquer Ireland for the English Crown. They stood again in 1798, the 'Year of the French' and their ill-fated expedition to Ireland – the bicentenary commemoration of which will coincide with the year of the More conference.

The FitzGeralds were acquainted with the Renaissance, and their library included some of More's works. They were also acquainted with the law – through that larger and long-standing Irish dimension of it: the colonial conflict between the imposed English law and the indigenous Irish system – Brehon Law as it is commonly called. The poet Spenser refers to that conflict in his *View of the Present State of Ireland.* The question is discussed in greater detail by Sir John Davies, Attorney General for Ireland under James I, for whom he wrote a report on the problem in 1612.

There are also some Irish lawyer statesmen who, whether influenced by More or not, certainly stood for similar ideas. Daniel O'Connell is one possibility. O'Connell's *floruit* was in the first half of the nineteenth century. His main struggle was for Catholic Emancipation. The nineteenth century was the period of a revival of interest in More in England, and in the cause of tolerance, *inter alia.* Like More, O'Connell was a student of Lincoln's Inn. And we know of O'Connell's knowledge and estimation of More from a remark of his in a letter of 1831 concerning the Lord Chancellor of the day (Lord Brougham): 'Such a man has not been in high office since the days of the martyr Sir Thomas More'. Edmund Burke is certainly another possibility – Chambers expressly puts him in the company of More in his biography (pp.364ff).

And of course there is Jonathan Swift (mentioned also by Chambers), whose *Gulliver* is in the line of Rabelais but also of More's *Utopia.* Across two centuries, the 'gloomy Dean' of St Patrick's pays high tribute to More, as one of 'a sextumvirate [including Socrates] to which all the ages of the world cannot add a seventh'.[12]

The Humanist Dimension: We have already indicated how the humanist dimension is intrinsic to law ... Law is a marriage of the abstract and the concrete, of the universal and the particular, in as much as it is addressed to the human condition, in all its particularities, variables, and existential concerns. Humanism therefore, in this large and perennial sense, is an inevitable dimension of a conference that is concerned with something broader than the internal technicalities of law understood as an autonomous discipline. Above all should this be the case in a conference on Thomas More, humanist scholar and man of the law, a man of the law indeed to the ultimate point where he put his life and conscience on the line – but only when, as we said earlier, he had exhausted all the possibilities

12 In *Gulliver's Travels,* Part III, 205 of *Prose Works,* vol. VIII of Temple Scott ed. (London, 1897–1908). See also Dorothy F. Donnelly, '*Utopia* and *Gulliver's Travels*: Another Perspective', in *Moreana* 97/115–124.

offered by the law to enable him to do otherwise. It was the act of the ultimate integral theocentric humanism, of putting the law written in the heart before the law made by man. And as we have said, out of such humanism some of the greatest literature has been written – from the *Antigone* of Sophocles down through the examples already mentioned.

But of More ... more later. In the late Middle Ages and the Renaissance the *Corpus* of Justinian was studied and interpreted in two different ways by two opposing schools: the Glossators and the Humanists. The Glossators were the earlier, and still in the medieval tradition. Lacking consequently a historical sense, they saw Roman law as timeless and universal, perennially and unchangeably valid. The Humanists reacted against that understanding of the great texts of the law in the same way as they reacted against the scholastic theologians' understanding of the texts of Scripture. They saw both as belonging to a particular period in history, and to be adequately understood only in that context. As in theology so in law, this understanding could be attained only by a return to the sources, and to their interpretation with the aid of the light that could be shed upon them by all the other disciplines of classical antiquity and the Renaissance. It is obvious how this sense of the time-conditioned combines the double necessity of change within permanence. The opposing views of the two schools can be seen in the *De iuris interpretibus* of the Anglo-Italian jurist Alberico Gentili.

As already indicated, this humanist dimension of the study of law is not a mere grace-note or applied ornament. It is of the essence, for a reason that has been pithily expressed: 'Law is the place where life and logic meet.'[13] Consequently, 'the sparks of all the sciences in the world are raked up in the ashes of the law'![14] And their range is from the temporal banal quotidian to the high transcendent theoretical – which will also have its quotidian consequences. What shall be the difference, asks an ancient Sumerian Code, between the fines to be imposed on a man who strikes an ox and damages its eye ... or injures its flesh at the nose ring ... or breaks its horn?! Later ages were to ask what is the ultimate *a priori* basis of just law. What is the relation between the law of God and the law of the land, the law of the Church and the law of the state, the law written in the heart and the law written in the statutes? And as already remarked, those questions are even more alive in the twentieth century than in any century of the past.

It is not surprising that they have found some of their finest expressions in literature and art, from a Solomon or a Daniel come to judgment, from Aeschylus' *Oresteia* or Sophocles' *Antigone*, through Shakespeare's *Merchant of Venice* or *Sir*

13 Richard O'Sullivan in *The Spirit of the Common Law*, ed. B.A. Wortley (Tenbury Wells, England, 1965), 67.

14 Op. cit., 68.

Thomas More, down to the oeuvre of Alexander Solzhenitsyn. Much of that literature is tragic but, like all things human, the law too has its comedy – 'the law is a idiot', says Mr Bumble in Dickens' *Oliver Twist*. Consequently much of that literature is also comic or satirical.

> 'Let the jury consider their verdict', the king said...
> 'No, no!' said the queen. 'Sentence first – verdict afterward.'
> (*Alice in Wonderland*)

And artists like Hogarth, Goya, Daumier, Rouault and many others provide us with visuals in the same tone – and worse.

Thomas More: That tone provides an appropriate moment to introduce – and conclude with – Thomas More himself. For he resembles that comprehensive artist described by Socrates at the end of the *Symposium*, who can write both tragedy and comedy – or, as is rather the case with More, combine them in the double vision of tragicomedy. He expressly follows the Horatian motto of telling the hard truth with the sauce of wit, humour, and irony – of bringing in 'among the most earnest matters, fancies and sports and merry tales. For as Horace sayth, a man may sometime say sooth [truth] in game. And one that is but a lay man as I am, it may better haply become him merrily to tell his mind than seriously and solemnly to preach' (*Apology*, CW9, 170/34ff). He had that double vision of the law too.

> Pleading the lawe,
> For every strawe,
> Shall prove a thrifty man,
> With bate and strife,
> But by my life,
> I cannot tell you whan.[15]

The Utopians 'absolutely banish from their country all lawyers, who cleverly manipulate cases and cunningly argue legal points' (CW4, 195/15ff). It is the kind of thing More has no time for against St German in *The Debellation* – it merely amuses him. 'For I was waxen with the readyng of his answer very merry, and waxen me thought a young man again and seemed set at a vacation moot with him in some Inne of the chancery, because of his entendment [of common law], and his proper casys of lawe' (CW10, 37/32ff). It is an attitude that emerges already in one of his epigrams – on the thief and his lawyer: 'While Snatch feared

15 *A Mery Jest*, in *The English Works of Sir Thomas More*, vol. 1, ed. W.E. Campbell (London/New York, 1931), 327.

that he would be convicted of theft he consulted a lawyer – at a considerable fee. When the lawyer had pondered his mighty tomes, often and long, "Snatch", says he, "you will get off, I hope, were you to take off"' (*effugies ... si fugias* – CW3, Part II, No. 117).

And as with the rest of his humour, so with his legal humour – that too stayed with him on his way to the block. Harpsfield records his reply to the woman who called out to him at the Tower Gate to have back certain legal documents of hers given to him while he was still in office. '"Good woman", sayth he, "content thyself, and take patience a little while, for the king is so good and gratious to me, that even within this half hour he will disburden me of all worldly business, and help thee himself".'[16]

Humanism means the cultivation of all that perfects the human as human – the ideal *humanitas*, as Cicero first called it. *Homo sum, nihil humani a me alienum puto*, said the earlier Roman humanist Terence, and adapted by More in CW14, 349. And that reminds us that the human being can be defined not only as a rational animal but also as a humorous animal. Which is why all the Greek and Roman treatises on rhetoric – leading principally to the practice of law – discuss humour as one of the essential modes of proving a point. Even St Paul recommended it: 'Always speak pleasantly and with a flavour of wit ... ' (Col 4:6).

***

All of this explains why a modern jurist, Roscoe Pound, on the question of what constitutes a good legal education, put first 'a solid all round cultural training' – i.e. a humanist one, as it was in the beginning with Cicero and still with Thomas More. We can hardly leave out that dimension in discussing him. It will be a bonus if we are able to include his wit as well as his wisdom. Apparently that was one of the lecturing qualities of that great lawyer and patron of the cause of Thomas More, Richard O'Sullivan. In the introduction to the volume by Wortley already cited, Douglas Woodruff quotes the report of a member of O'Sullivan's audience: 'He laughed his way through his course and took his fortunate students with him ... This was real education in the sense that it drew out of the bare words *contract* and *tort* a subtle and at times moving philosophy.' And Woodruff adds his own comment, to the effect that O'Sullivan made 'conceptions that are generally thought of as the tools of a dry profession come alive with human significance'.[17]

16 Harpsfield's *Life*, Hitchcock and Chambers ed. (1932), 203.

17 Op. cit., 14.

THOMAS MORE IN HIS TIME: RENAISSANCE HUMANISM AND RENAISSANCE LAW

PART TWO: INTRODUCTION TO THE PROGRAMME

International Thomas More Conference,
Maynooth College, 9–16 August 2018

'All things have their season', saith Ecclesiastes (3:1). He was anxious particularly about how seasons come and pass. I grow conscious of the phenomenon myself – the season fast approaches for our Conference on the 'man for all seasons'. We planted the seeds of it in winter in the Call for Papers of *Moreana* 127–128, December 1996. We present its fruits in this spring of already 1998 – best consumed by August. A short time hence for directors of conferences, but adequate for the seasonal ripening of fruit into early autumn. In Ireland too that is a season not only of the mists that everyone knows about, but also of mellow fruitfulness. And nowhere is that mellowness better savoured than in the afterglow of summer in Maynooth's gardens and apple orchard, and in the vibrant autumnal tints of crimson, gold, and darkening green of the creeper on the walls around St Joseph's Square.

***

That Call for Papers, many will have noticed, did not err on the side of brevity – if, like Thomas More, I may indulge in a little litotes.[18] There were two sets of reasons for that.

There was first the very range of the Conference theme. 'Renaissance Humanism and Renaissance Law' casts a wide trawl, even when centred on 'Thomas More in his Time'. Humanism, Law, and the Renaissance are each large and complex subjects in themselves. Their largeness and complexity are increased by their European range in space, with all of Europe's regional differences. Add to that the range in time and history entailed by the return of humanists, lawyers, and Christian reformers to the ancient sources. Even of Thomas More in person that also is the range; for

18 I have just been re-reading Elizabeth McCutcheon's illuminating *Moreana* 31–32 article on that figure, reprinted in *Essential Articles for the Study of Thomas More*.

in addition to being a 'European' he too was a humanist, a lawyer, and a Catholic Christian reformer. Indeed his range was even wider than that. As a Christian, his range was not just Europe but *universal* Christendom. His range, in fact, was even wider still. For, as we see especially in *Utopia* and in *A Dialogue of Comfort*, his field of vision extended far beyond Europe and Christendom to the non-Christian East and West: to the East from the shadow of its ancient menace to Europe and Christendom, to the West towards the light brightening from its new-found lands and their rumour of a natural virtue whose simplicity might have something to say to the complexities of old Europe, its humanism, its law, its Christianity, its political and religious divisions, its ancient hatreds.

And then there was Ireland! For from the wide horizons of East and West, from Europe and its regions, it is right that we should zoom back home and in on our own island Ithaca! The reason is that humanism, like all generalizing and abstract 'isms', inevitably and rightly takes specifically concrete form and colour in a 'local habitation'. Hence it is right that the local habitation of the Conference should make what relevant contribution it can to the Conference theme. And in any case, the 'man for all seasons' speaks to the condition of diverse locations as well as to diverse times and seasons – witness the diverse international range of his *Amici*.

Such are the various factors we had to consider in setting out the Conference theme, and in light of them to tease out possible topics, select specific suggestions from them, and hope to have something like a meaningful whole in the outcome.

But a 'meaningful whole' entails more than the unities of merely space and time. It entails the intrinsic, organic unity of a theme or themes. In our Call for Papers we had to devote some time to showing that the combination of humanism and law has the potential for such an intrinsic organic thematic unity. It was necessary to address the question especially concerning law. It is not exactly a subject which most of us immediately connect with humanism. On the contrary, considered as a discipline, its fine-spun abstract techniques suggest at first sight that it is the very antithesis of *humanitas*. The case is worse still when we consider the reputation won by law – in all ages – not only from the abuse of its techniques by sophistical practitioners but also from the perennial pharisaism that judges every human situation in terms of the law and nothing but the law, without consideration of humanity or equity. That reputation is well illustrated by the fact that at one point Thomas More excludes the whole useless tribe of lawyers from his ideal commonwealth of Utopia! (CW4, 194/12ff). Yet More himself was a lawyer and a venerator of the law, so there must be much more than that to be said about law in relation to humanism. And we start by recognizing that both terms are problematic, for neither is univocal in meaning.

'Humanism' is already an ambivalent concept, in itself and in its history.[19] Here we need only indicate the two extreme poles of that ambivalence, and the resultant tensions between them, the human pole and the divine. As the term itself implies, humanism centres on human beings, their *humanitas* and its full realization. But in a theocentric understanding of the world not man but God is the centre, the centre of all centres. In such an order of things the problem for humanism is how to balance the tensions between the two poles, the human and the divine. The two extreme solutions are absolutist theocracy on the one hand, and on the other the real or effective atheism – and Prometheanism – of a 'humanism' qui substitue l'homme à Dieu sinon comme centre et maître de l'univers, du moins comme créateur de sa propre humanité.[20]

We are familiar with periods of history in which that latter has been the solution – did the late Renaissance itself already verge towards it? But it was not the solution of the model humanism of Greco-Roman Classicism or of the Judeo-Christian humanism that followed it and subsumed it. They were able to effect an equilibrium between the pulls of the two extreme poles of reality, the divine transcendent and the immanent human. Aristotle bridged Plato's fracture between the two worlds by making the transcendent forms immanent to the existents of the phenomenal world, thus giving to that world, and to humanity within it, its own degree of ontological autonomy and value. Judeo-Christianity would confirm that autonomy and value from its own revealed resources. All the created world was 'very good' (Gen 1:31). Humanity, the culmination of that creation, was made in the very 'image and likeness' of the Creator himself (Gen 1:26). And finally, at the Incarnation, the Second Person of the creative Trinity itself – through whom 'all things were made' (Jn 1:3) – took the form of a man within his own created world.[21]

***

We come to the problem of how we relate law to this humanism, in a way that makes their combination an integration and synthesis and not a merely extrinsic juxtaposition. We have earlier indicated some of the usual obstacles. Here we can add to them an obstacle arising from a particular feature of our own time. That is a pervasive *alienation* from, and a consequent *resistance* to, law as having

19 See e.g. Jacques Chomarat, 'Faut-il donner un sens philosophique au mot humanisme?', in *Renaissance and Reformation/Renaissance et Réforme*, 21, I (1997), 49–64.

20 Chomarat, 50f.

21 The second-century Irenaeus of Lyon is already the emphatic and systematic defender of this humanist dimension of Christianity against all Gnostic 'spiritualizing'.

any controlling or formative role in the living of the personal life. It is an attitude that extends to religious as well as to secular life. In a 'liberated' age the old antinomy of liberty and law is intensified. In relation to 'humanism', law is seen as a constraint on that personal freedom of choice and action which is seen as the condition of personal expression and development. By all accounts it is an attitude not unknown even in sections of academia! – in the questioning of whatever 'laws' established the traditional literary and artistic canon on which *traditional* humanism has itself been based. For whatever reasons, we are in an ambience that is far from the reverence accorded to the law by a Socrates, Jesus, or Thomas More, rejecting the option of freedom even when they were prisoners of the law's injustice.

Their reason was of course that, like Plato in his ideal *Republic* and *Laws*, they saw that total individual freedom leads to total *anomia*, the total absence of any law, and the resulting total *disorder*, first within the individual and then consequently in the collective that is society – which is why those projects of the ideal society and its ideal laws include also the project of the ideal humanist education. The result is the realization that law, even when misapplied, is still the condition of a larger liberty and a larger order. It is through this concept of order, ultimately a universal and transcendent order, that we find a fundamental connection between humanism and law. At a deep level, order and law are correlative concepts. And they have implications for humanism once we understand them not as extrinsically imposed constraints but as an order and law ontologically intrinsic to existents, defining therefore their nature and the teleological completion and fulfilment of that nature. Greek philosophy first developed these concepts. Christianity had them already, for that is the ultimate meaning of 'the law' in Scripture,[22] but what it knew in an unreflected mode from revelation it rationally systematized in the Greek categories.

***

In relation to humanism this intrinsic ontological order and law has two aspects, the human and the cosmic – the Greek word *kosmos* itself means order, harmony, beauty.

An understanding of humanism depends on an understanding of human beings and their *humanitas*. Greek philosophy – and subsequent Christian thought – understood human nature as intrinsically incomplete in itself, and therefore determined by a teleological drive to its ultimate fulfilment. This fulfilment was understood as the attaining to an ultimate supreme *beatitudo*, *eudaimonia* – very

22 In his commentary on the Genesis account of Creation (*De opificio mundi*) Philo praises the wisdom of Moses for first setting out the order of the world, and only then the laws that order life within it.

inadequately translated as mere 'happiness'. This *beatitudo/eudaimonia* is consequent on the attaining to union with a *summum bonum*, or a supreme 'good'. That is the intrinsic 'order' and 'law' of *humanitas*, and necessarily therefore of its 'humanism'.

It is the nature and location of this *sunmum bonum*, and of its consequent *beatitudo/eudaimonia* that links it to the universal cosmic order and its intrinsic law – and beyond the cosmic to the divine, for in a theocentric world view, order and law imply a supreme divine ground of them. Within that total divine/cosmic order, the human *summum bonum* can only be transcendent, for two reasons. Firstly, because that order is a *total* order, a *kosmos*, and the human being is within it. Secondly, and more profoundly for humanism, after Plato the drive of Greek philosophy was *beyond* philosophy to religion, to vision of and union with the supreme Reality that is the ultimate Cause and Ground of the cosmos – God, the One, the Form of Forms that is the Supreme 'Good'. As the Supreme Good, that ultimate Reality is not only the Ground but the polar point that pulls all things towards it.

In that context, Greek philosophy anticipated what Judeo-Christian revelation confirmed, namely that the ultimate 'law' of all things is an order of *erôs*. That *erôs* has two *foci*, in the Supreme Being and in the human being's unquiet heart. Plotinus as well as revelation and personal experience is behind Augustine's confession that 'You have made us oriented towards Yourself, and our hearts are restless until they rest in You' (*Confessions* I 1). Even the austerely technical Aristotle understood the Prime Mover as moving all things 'by the attraction of love' (*Metaphysics* XII 7). That remains the supreme point of Dante's epic of Christendom – the vision of 'the Love that moves the sun and the other stars'. That transcendent point does not devalue the human being's *humanitas* and its drive towards the ideals of humanism. Rather does it provide those ideals with their classical and Judeo-Christian ground, in that 'law' whose rationale is not extrinsic constraint but liberation into harmony with the intrinsic 'order' and teleology of human beings and their world. Irenaeus of Lyon already provides the formula for that integral humanism: *gloria Dei homo vivens, vita hominis visio Dei* – the glory of God is man fully alive, the life of man is the vision of God. Pascal's 'order of charity' is in the same tradition. From Pascal also we have the best known formula for the consequences to *humanitas* of a fracture in that order: *Grandeur de l'homme* indeed but, *misère de l'homme sans Dieu* (*Pensées* 255 [165] and 73 [25], ed. Pléiade). That, of course, was already a principal theme of Greek tragedy.

[...]

HOMAGE TO W. J. KINSELLA: WITH EVOCATIONS OF IRISH MOREAN LAWYERS

The article recalls some notable Irish contributors to the modern revival and continuation of interest in Thomas More. It begins with a commemoration of William J. Kinsella, late president of the Thomas More Society of Ireland. It goes on to recall briefly the contributions of a number of distinguished Irish-born lawyers since the nineteenth century. All those students of More had one thing in common: they saw in him a man of special interest for modern times – as a witness to unchanging values in an age of change. The article gives particular notice to Richard O'Sullivan – for the range and depth of his legal learning, and his sense of the importance of More in the history of law.

It is with a great sense of loss that we commemorate the passing of one of the long-standing *amici* of Thomas More, William J. Kinsella. For some thirty years he was Honorary President of the Thomas More Society of Ireland. He died unexpectedly and quietly, in the presence of his wife and extended family, at the end of the day he had spent with them in seasonal joy and celebration. That was last Christmas Day. Naturally that sense of loss at his passing is greatest for his widow Teresa and their family, but it will be felt by the many around the world who knew this intensely devoted friend of Thomas More. Our sense of loss is compensated by the obverse of which I have little doubt – the significant fact that it was on Christmas Day he entered into another dimension of joy and celebration, 'merrily in heaven' with his great patron!

There are countless Morean friends of William in Ireland and around the world who are better qualified than I am to pen these words to his memory – they have known him longer, and more personally than I have. For although I knew him by repute, I met him only once. But that one time was to be so precious in memory, when it turned out to be the last time as well as the first. I met a man for whom Thomas More was not only an intense intellectual enthusiasm, but also a profound spiritual influence in his own life.

I had, naturally, intended to contact him with a view to a wider consultation about the forthcoming International Thomas More Conference in Maynooth, the first to be held in Ireland. But, with characteristic alacrity about all things Morean, William anticipated me. Early on a November morning *he* rang *me*, to arrange to meet and to talk. Within a week he came to Maynooth, and talk we did, through lunch and into late afternoon. It was clear that he enjoyed the occasion and was in no undue haste to take leave. It was obvious that Thomas More was the passionate focus of his interests – as consequently was his anticipation of the Maynooth Conference. It was clear too, though left not quite spoken, that certain personal reasons intensified his dedication to More. Reasons one glimpsed not through a solemn piety, but through his geniality and humour – such as his anecdote about the 'sign' (this one *was* spoken) that determined him, against initial hesitations, to buy his house in Dalkey – eventually named 'Moreana'! Among the items he had brought with him to show me was his handwritten and updated catalogue of the collection of books by and about Thomas More that he had assiduously acquired over the years. (One of his desires was to have such a collection available for students of More.) If one thing more than another made his eyes shine even brighter, it was that, before we left my rooms, he was able to look over my own Thomas More corner – not quite as big as his but, happily, not overlapping too much, and therefore complementary!

We parted, intending to keep in touch. He went home to his beautiful 'Moreana' south of Dublin. I went to 'Moreanum' in Angers. The sojourn I intended for December turned out to take in January too. In the mail that awaited me on my return was a telephone message from William's good friend, Brendan Fitzgerald, LL.B. William J. Kinsella had passed away on the previous Christmas Day. It was a shock and a loss. But I counted myself privileged to have known him for that one long afternoon, and to have had the enthusiastic letter he wrote me by return after we parted.

William Kinsella, though passionate about Thomas More, declined any suggestion of being a More scholar in the conventional sense. Yet, as a professional man (auditor and accountant), he could be, and in fact was, more learned about More than he admitted to being. He pursued every work by and about More that came to his notice over the years. He had a Russian biography of More[23] translated into English, with the possibility of eventual publication, after modifications to the text and content. A lecture he gave to his Thomas More Society he elaborated into a little volume of his own on More.[24]

In preparation for 1978 he was working towards a quincentenary seminar on More, until, as President of what he called his 'still embryo' Society, he understood

23 By I.N. Osinovsky, of the Moscow Academy of General History, published in 1985.

24 *Thomas More: A Man for our Time.* With a Foreword by Mr Justice Thomas A. Finlay. Privately published in a limited edition by the Saint Thomas More Society, Dublin, 1984.

that his idea was to be more adequately realised in the Quincentenary Conference held under the auspices of the Irish Catholic Historical Committee and the Board of Medieval Studies, University College, Dublin. (One session was held in Maynooth.) William did, in fact, have his own large, long-term scholarly ideals for his society – to promote the study of the life and times of Thomas More, an ideal that included acquiring a library with the resources necessary for research.

William's immediate concerns, however, were more practical. He put the emphasis on the relevance and application of More studies to our own times. Like many another he saw Thomas More as the ideal type of the witness to unchanging principle amid the flux and flow of the tides in changing times. For William, like many, was troubled by the tides of our time – a time like More's, as someone expressed it for him, a time of transition, of critical changes, of the breakdown and restructuring of social institutions. Those tides of change are global, of course, but William's first concern was with the effect of their wash on the shores of Ireland. Would 'modern' Ireland lose her ancient soul? Hence as President of his Thomas More Society he was sensitive to every suggested change to law and constitution.[25] He was aware of the ambivalence of the honourable term 'liberal', and of the valid distinction between the laws of the state and the laws of the Church. He was concerned, in an expression of his own, to ensure that God and the affairs of God be not gradually enclosed and confined to the closet. And that is not an 'illiberal' concern. It has been the concern of large and liberal minds, like those of Hans Urs von Balthasar in our own time,[26] and John Henry Newman in one of his Dublin lectures on *The Idea of a University*.[27] Very much to the point, and in the same ironic mode as these two, is an excerpt that Kinsella, on page 28 of his little volume, quotes from a 1968 lecture on More by Professor Howard Root of the University of Southampton. Thomas More ... 'a noble spirit', of course, but one 'who, as it happens took certain religious matters rather too seriously. You know, just a little bit unbalanced ... '. And the lecturer goes on to recall Kant on the need to be constantly reminded that there was once a man called Socrates:

> What he [Kant] meant was that when everybody is saying 'After all I've got to live', remember that Socrates said 'No, I haven't got to live; not if the price is too high'. Thomas More's answer is the same ... [28]

25 Essentially the same concerns motivated the London Thomas More Society, as stated by its founder, Richard O'Sullivan: 'The object of the Society was to study and discuss intellectual and moral problems touching law and legislation' (*The King's Good Servant*, edited by Richard O'Sullivan, Oxford: Basil Blackwell, 1948, 23).

26 *Heart of the World* (San Francisco: Ignatius Press, 1979), e.g. 122ff.

27 'A Form of Infidelity of the Day', *The Idea of a University* (New York: Image Books, 1959), 353ff.

28 For the complete text of Professor Root's lecture, see *Thomas More Through Many Eyes*, ed. Leighton Thomson (London: Chelsea Old Church, 1978), 100–4.

And hence for William Kinsella More was 'a man for our time' too.

He was not himself a lawyer by profession, but, as we have seen, his concerns kept him in touch with legal matters.[29] And, as in Thomas More Societies around the world (with whom he was an indefatigable correspondent), many of his friends in his society were – and are – men of the law. Since law is a theme of the 1998 Thomas More Conference in Maynooth, it will not be out of place here to recall the contribution to the contemporary renewal of interest in More made by Irish lawyers, notably by a number whose careers were at the English Bar.

***

The Cork-born Richard O'Sullivan is of course *facile princeps* in his association with the name and fame of Thomas More. He died on his seventy-fifth birthday in 1963 – the very first number of *Moreana* carried an *In Memoriam* to him. As we have mentioned, he had founded the Thomas More Society of London in 1928. In 1934, he was the principal layman of those who brought the petition to Rome for More's canonization. Concerning that petition he is credited with a very Irish – indeed native Corkonian – quip in response to the devil's advocate's allegation that candidate More had worked no miracle, and to a curious question, why an Irishman should be so enthusiastically supporting the cause of an Englishman: 'That is the miracle ... !'

But the influence of his enthusiasm radiated far beyond the confines of England and Ireland. His London society was the prototype for others around the world. To mention but two, there is the Guild of Catholic Lawyers in Bridgeport, Connecticut, and the Thomas More Society of Sydney, Australia – which in 1995 celebrated the fiftieth anniversary of its foundation.[30] His influence flowed from the radiation of his own interest in Thomas More and his time into the history, philosophy, and theology of law – and its concomitant humanist studies. In papers of his own, and of others that he elicited through his society, he opened up the wide perspectives of the splendid panorama of jurisprudence, from its classical beginnings in Greece and Rome, into the contribution of theologians and canonists in the Christian centuries, down to the various philosophical and social influences of modern times.[31]

But O'Sullivan had Irish predecessors and early contemporaries in his cause.

29 An interesting section on More as lawyer and Lord Chancellor in his own little volume (10ff) raises the still moot question of his contribution to the development of equity during his tenure in Chancery and the Star Chamber (1ff).

30 See its Golden Jubilee collection of papers in *Thomas More: The Saint and the Society*, edited by John McCarthy QC, and Anthony Reynolds KHS (Sydney: Saint Thomas More Society), 1995.

31 See e.g. the survey by Abbé Marc'hadour in McCarthy and Reynolds, op. cit. 122–4.

The earliest was Judge John O'Hagan (1822–1890). An address he gave to the Catholic Union of Ireland provided the introduction to the Everyman edition of More's *Utopia* with the *Dialogue of Comfort* (J. M. Dent, 1910). In the course of that introduction he draws attention to the fact that

> strange as it may seem to our modern notions ... our system of jurisprudence is, in the main, owing to the succession of great churchmen [as Lord Chancellors], versed in the Roman and civil law, and the canon law, by which, as Burke truly says, the jejuneness and barrenness of our municipal law was enriched and strengthened (xxiv).

Noting that More was familiar with all that tradition, he tells us that 'he even attempted, three centuries before the time, to effect that fusion of law and *equity* so loudly demanded and partly accomplished at the present day' (ibid.). More was resisted in that attempt, but how far he applied equity in his own judements is a question not yet exhaustively investigated.[32]

O'Hagan concludes his Introduction with a portion of Wordsworth's sonnet ('Apology') on those two blocks in the ageless 'arch of Christendom ... , saintly Fisher and unbending More'.

> ... More's gay genius played
> With the inoffensive sword of native wit,
> Than the bare axe more luminous and keen.

***

Starting from a contemporary of Judge O'Hagan three successive generations of Lords Russell of Killowen, father, son, and grandson, rose to distinction at the English Bar. The Russells took their title from their native region in the North of Ireland, in an area of County Down remarkable for the number of distinguished men – including Judge O'Hagan – that it produced in the early nineteenth century.'[33] They included diplomats, Prime Ministers (in Australia and Canada), Lord

32 See e.g. the articles by Richard Schoeck, 'Common Law and Canon Law in their Relation to Thomas More', and Margaret Hastings. 'Sir Thomas More: Maker of English Law?' both articles in R. S. Sylvester and G. P. Marc'hadour (eds), *Essential Articles for the Study of Thomas More* (Hamden, CT: Archon Books), 1977. See also John A. Guy, 'Law, Equity, and Conscience in Henrician Juristic Thought', in Gordon J. Schochet (ed.), *Reformation, Humanism, and 'Revolution'* (Washington, DC: The Folger Institute, 1990), 1–15.

33 In the twentieth century it has produced that romantic about the Latin Middle Ages, Helen Waddell; and the no less classically and medievally learned Professor of English literature and lay theologian,

Chancellors (of England and Ireland) – and withal, firm patriots and Catholics. The first Lord Russell of Killowen (1832–1900) used to insist on calling himself 'a Celt'. Doubtless, by that stage he had enough Celtic blood in his veins to warrant the appellation – even if, as apparently he was fond of saying himself, he was not exactly descended from Brian Boru (famous in Irish history as the King who finally defeated the Vikings in 1014). The Russells in fact were only a little less ancient than that, but they were Norman. Their line in Ireland – and in County Down – went back unbroken to a companion of Strongbow in the twelfth-century Anglo-Norman invasion of Ireland. Their later history illustrates the often-quoted dictum about those Normans – that they became more Irish than the Irish themselves. (Which is why the Tudors had to undertake a reconquest of Ireland.) An uncle of the first Lord Russell was the Dr Charles Russell (1812–1880) who became President of Maynooth College, and was that friend about whom Newman recorded in his *Apologia* that he 'had, perhaps, more to do with my conversion than anyone else ... he was always gentle, mild, unobtrusive, uncontroversial. He let me alone'.

The last Lord Russell died in 1986 at the age of seventy-eight. He had been called to the Bar by Lincoln's Inn in 1931, and reached the climax of his career with his appointment as a Law Lord. His grandfather (1832–1900) was Lord Chief Justice of England. His father (1867–1946), was called to the Bar by Lincoln's Inn in 1893. He became a Chancery judge, a lord of appeal, and a member of the Privy Council. In his article on him in the *Dictionary of National Biography*, Richard O'Sullivan makes special mention of one of his most notable achievements, for an appellant in the House of Lords. In a famous case in 1919, he 'succeeded in persuading their lordships ... "to take the greatest liberty the House of Lords has ever taken with established legal principles" and to declare that a bequest for Masses for the dead is a valid charitable bequest, and no longer void as a gift to superstitious uses'.[34]

This second Lord Russell was President of the London Thomas More Society from its inception in 1928 until his death in 1946. The opening paragraph of his foreword to the published version[35] of one the many learned lectures delivered

C. S. Lewis – author of 'Thomas More' in *Essential Articles*. (Both were romantics about County Down as well.) *Sit venia verbo* if we also mention the recently elected President of Ireland Mary McAleese – a Professor of Law to boot!

34 Further to this case see O'Sullivan in *The King's Good Servant*: 'In this case, at the instance of the Crown, a statement of the theology of the Mass, made by an Irish Catholic Bishop for the purposes of an Irish case in 1875, was accepted by all the parties and by the Court and thus integrated into the English Law' (23f). For a magisterial article occasioned by an analogous case see 'The Catholic Concept of the Church' by Hilary Carpenter O.P., in Richard O'Sullivan (ed.), *Under God and the Law* (Oxford: Basil Blackwell, 1949).

35 R. W. Chambers, *The Place of St Thomas More in English Literature and History* (London/New York/Toronto: Longmans Green, 1937).

to it evokes with witty understatement the genial ambience in which they were heard. The members met for a *dîner maigre* about twice a term on a Friday.

> As an aid to digestion they secure the kind attendance of some eminent authority, who, after dinner, addresses them, or reads a paper on a subject of which he is a master. When he sits down, the members in turn say exactly what they think about him and his views, to the general satisfaction of all concerned.

He could have registered little lack of satisfaction after Chambers' paper. The published version contains a classic summary statement of the permanent meaning of More:

> More's death was one of those mighty events, for their own sakes infinitely valuable, in which a great man has given proof of 'man's unconquerable mind', by facing death rather than say what he believes to be untrue (id. 87f).

In the late 1930s, that 'infinitely valuable' was due to be tested by other 'mighty events' much more imminently than the hundred years that G. K. Chesterton foresaw:

> Blessed Thomas More is more important at this moment than at any moment since his death, even perhaps the great moment of his dying; but he is not quite so important as he will be in about a hundred years time. He may come to be counted the greatest Englishman, or at least the greatest historical character in English history. For he was above all things historic; he represented at once a type, a turning point and an ultimate destiny. If there had not happened to be that particular man at that particular moment, the whole of history would have been different.[36]

The modern significance of More's death is foreshadowed in the concluding sentence of Chambers' lecture:

> Upon that difference – whether or no we place Divine Law in the last resort above the Law of the State – depends the whole future of the world (118).[37]

36 In *The Fame of Blessed Thomas More.* Addresses Delivered in his Honour in Chelsea, July 1929. With an Introductory Essay by Professor R.W. Chambers (London: Sheed and Ward, 1929), 63. Reprinted in *Essential Articles*, 501.

37 Cf. 38, and *Under God and the Law*, 44f and 169f.

***

At that point enter Richard O'Sullivan. For among Irish legal eagles it was he above all who opened up – or provided the forum for others to open up – those larger questions. It would be otiose to repeat here what has been written already about him in *Moreana* and elsewhere, or to survey again what he has written or edited himself.[38] The relevance of commemorating him here is to recall briefly in our present context what qualities made his contribution to the cause of Thomas More so distinguished – a contribution not only to More's memory but through him to law in general.

In the first place it was the quality of his mind that distinguished his writings on law. It was clear in analysis, limpid, succinct in exposition. It was also a historical,[39] philosophical, and theological mind which looked for the transcendent ground of jurisprudence in an understanding of man 'under God and the Law' and traced the critical stages of its origins and development in the classical and Christian tradition. He saw this development embodied above all in the Common Law of England, so profoundly influenced by Christianity and the Canon Law of the Church. Two important consequences followed for him from this combination of a philosophy and a theology of man and of law. The first consequence is that law is intrinsically related to humanism, since both are concerned with the realisation of the complete nature and destiny of man.[40] Hence he noted that liberal studies too were an ingredient in the tradition of legal education.[41] The second consequence is that the resultant humanism – of *humanitas* under God and the law – is incompatible with the decline into positivism and secularism that O'Sullivan saw as a tendency of jurisprudence in his own and early modern times.[42]

It is perhaps in *The Inheritance of the Common Law* that we discern most immediately and clearly the classical and Christian framework of O'Sullivan's philosophy of law. The work is the published version of The Hamlyn Lectures of 1950, and is essentially about the law in relation to human beings in *society*. A sentence on page 33 gives us the key to it: 'In the classical and Christian tradition

38 In addition to references already given see especially his *The Inheritance of the Common Law* (London: Stevens & Sons, 1950); and a representative selection of his papers is *The Spirit of the Common Law*, edited by B. A. Wortley (Tenbury Wells, England: Fowler Wright Books, 1965).

39 In *The Spirit of the Common Law*, 69ff, he glances at the great names and their contributions, and quotes (69, n.2) Pollock and Maitland (*History of English Law*) on the period 1154–1272 – 'the critical moment in English legal history and therefore in the innermost history of our land and race'.

40 See e.g. *The Spirit of the Common Law*, 75ff.

41 Ibid. 45f and 67ff; cf. O'Sullivan's 'St. Thomas More and Lincoln's Inn', in *Essential Articles*, 161-163.

42 See his 'Changing Tides in English Law and History', in *The King's Good Servant.*

which animates the Common Law, the political community consists in the last analysis of three elements: the individual, the family, the City or State (or Polis).' Hence the titles of the first three out of its four chapters: 'The Concept of Man in the Common Law', 'The Family', and 'The Political Community'.

This triple classification goes back to the very beginnings of political philosophy in Plato, Aristotle, Cicero and St Augustine.[43] The concluding chapter is on 'Law and Conscience'. That too begins in Greek, Roman, and Christian thinking about the rights of the individual vis-à-vis the state, about positive law vis-à-vis that higher law written in the heart and in the universal divine and cosmic order of things. The problem is of course most famously illustrated in Sophocles' *Antigone* (from which O'Sullivan quotes). But St Augustine can argue from Cicero and Seneca for his blunt statement that without justice (already for Greek and Roman under God and the higher law) kingdoms are only bands of brigands on a larger scale.[44]

For O'Sullivan the rights of the individual conscience against the collective accrue not just extrinsically from the individual's status under God and the higher Law. They are also rooted intrinsically in the metaphysical constitution of the individual himself, in that ultimate impenetrable level of his being by which he is constituted not merely a nature or essence as a human being, but a particular unique, free, autonomous *self*, an unsoundable well of interiority, a *subject*, in the technical language of Christian philosophy and theology, a *persona*, a person. It designates the second of what Newman refers to in the *Apologia*[45] as 'the two only supreme and luminously self-evident beings, myself and my Creator'. Boethius' definition of it became classical for the Scholastics: 'The individual substance of a rational nature'.[46]

This concept was unknown to the Classical world, as therefore was its profundity and its consequences for the 'dignity' of the individual. The concept and its dimensions emerged only in Christianity, especially in the technical context of Christological and Trinitarian problems, but reinforced by the keener Christian sense of the deeps of human subjectivity. O'Sullivan – and his sources – introduces the concept of person and personality again and again. He quotes[47] Aquinas' statement about it: '*Person* signifies that which is most perfect in the whole of creation (*in tota natura*).'[48]

43 See Plato's *Laws*. III 676ff; Aristotle's *Politics*, Book 1, ch. 2–3; Cicero's *Republic*, I 24, 38ff and III 2, 3ff; Augustine's *City of God*, XIX 3.

44 *Magna latrocinia*, *City of God*, IV 4.

45 Page 98 of the Fontana Books edition (London/Glasgow, 1959). Cf. St Augustine on *me* and *Te* at the beginning of his *Soliloquia*.

46 *Naturae rationalis individua substantia*, in *Contra Eutychen*, chapter III.

47 *The Inheritance of the Common Law*, 66; *The Spirit of the Common Law*, 77.

48 For a philosophical exposition of the concept of the person see the chapter on 'The Existent', in Jacques Maritain, Existence and the Existent (New York: Image Books, 1956).

With man 'under God' then, man understood as a free autonomous *person* is the second pole of the traditional philosophy which O'Sullivan elucidates. In his Introduction to *Under God and the Law*, speaking of the separate organization of Church and state, he writes[49] that behind it

> we have to recognize the appearance, in the consciousness of the civilized world, of principles new and immensely significant. The first of these is the principle of the autonomy of the spiritual life, a development of the conception of individuality or personality that was unknown to the ancient world. The soul of man has an individual relation with God that goes beyond the control of society ... The moral and spiritual life of man must be outside the power and reach of the political officers of the community ...

Needless to say, this 'conception of individuality or personality' does not mean that there is *only* the *individual* (as currently understood) and no need of society and its laws – a degree of individualist autonomy for which, according to Aristotle,[50] only a beast or a god would be qualified! And the reasons for the necessity of society, with its institutions and laws, go beyond the merely functional necessity of organization – whether to keep order or to provide for the material needs of society by the division of labour. Man is a political animal, Aristotle also said.[51] By which he meant not what the expression now connotes, rather that man is by nature a social being. By which he meant that only in relation to 'the other', in society, can man realise the full potential of his nature and its teleology. That links law and humanism once more, as all the great theorists of both have done since Plato. Recovering that great tradition, O'Sullivan links them too.[52]

He does it magnificently in a quotation from the seventeenth-century Sir Henry Finch[53] which concludes with the statement that 'the sparks of all the sciences of the world are raked up in the ashes of the law.'[54] That statement gives us the opportunity to juxtapose one of the many parallels between the ideas of O'Sullivan and those of Edmund Burke, to whom he occasionally refers. For Burke 'the science of jurisprudence [is] the pride of the human intellect, which, with all

49 Page xi, based on Carlyle's *Medieval Political Theory in the West.*

50 *Politics* I 2.

51 Ibid.

52 See nn. 40 and 41 above, p. 356; for a Catholic exposition of 'the full potential of [human] nature and its teleology', see the paper by Hilary Carpenter O.P., mentioned in n.34, p. 354 above.

53 *Description of the Common Law.*

54 *Essential Articles*, 163.

its defects, redundancies, and errors, is the collected wisdom of ages, combining the principles of original justice with infinite variety of human concerns … '.[55]

But it was from Thomas More that O'Sullivan entered into that great inheritance. He sums up the centrality of More in one splendid paragraph:

> At the turning-point of English history one who had held office as Speaker of the House of Commons and as Lord Chancellor stood forth as the incarnation of English law and equity, and of the Christian philosophy and theology that gave it energy and character. The life and writings of the most illustrious of the Common lawyers show that he held in all [its] fullness the Christian sense of human personality … , and that he, who as a stripling had lectured on the *City of God* of St Augustine … and who had been twice named Reader in Law at Lincoln's Inn, had always before his mind the wide perspectives of Christian jurisprudence, with its threefold vision of the law of God, the law of Nature (or of Reason), and the law of the land.[56]

To return to William J. Kinsella, he will of course be blinking at the dazzle of the company into which he has diverted us. But their ideas were his too, even if he could never have elaborated them as magnificently as they did. Their meeting must be going right merrily in Heaven. Each in his degree, they were all faithful servants of *the* King, and therefore, in the second place, of Thomas More.

55 *Reflections on the Revolution in France*, Penguin Classics edition (edited by Conor Cruise O'Brien, 1986), 193.

56 *Under God and the Law*, xvii .

ERASMUS: LETTERS OF 1525[57]

INTRODUCTION

From many points of view the year 1525 was an *annus criticus* for Erasmus.

1. In September of 1524 he had finally yielded to long persuasion and much criticism, come off the fence and into the arena, and thrown down the gauntlet to Luther in *De libero arbitrio*. 'The die is cast', he writes to Henry VIII on 6 September 1524 (CWE10, 1493): 'a short book on the freedom of the will has seen the light of day – a desperate step, believe me, in the present state of Germany. I await a shower of stones, and several raving pamphlets have already taken wing, aimed at my head.' The result for himself was indeed not less but more of what he had already endured from his opponents before he declared his hand, namely the intensifying of the Reformers' attacks on him without diminishing of those from the conservative orthodox side.

2. He was 'tethered' in Basel (1554/21), and as it turned out, for eight years in all, from 1521 to 1529. The reason was a combination of the surrounding German Peasant War and the fact that he had few other places of escape that were not infested by his enemies. This hemmed-in citizen of the world felt himself in physical as well as politico-religious danger. Basel looked as though it was going Lutheran. And apart from his Catholic arch-opponent Noël Béda in Paris, his two principal Protestant critics had their seat in Basel. They were Johannes Oecolampadius and Conradus Pellicanus.

3. Consequently, under the aspect of religious controversy, the core of this volume is in the exchanges with those three. The exchanges are polemical of course, but on questions of profound and far-reaching significance, and that not only for theology and the Reformation but also for humanism and the Renaissance. A significance, further, that is pertinent not only to the age of Renaissance and Reformation but also to the succeeding ages that have been so profoundly influenced by them.

57 Review of *The Collected Works of Erasmus*, Volume 11, *The Correspondence: Letters 1535 to 1657*: January-December 1525. Translated by Alexander Dalzell; annotated by Charles G. Nauert Jr. (Toronto: University Press, 1994), xxiv + 476 pp., 17 illustrations.

4. In his handling of those questions Erasmus shows that breadth of view that can see the conflicts in a context larger – and more truly tragic – than the mere blind clashing of ignorant armies by night.

That context turns out to be a recurring one in European history and its more philosophical historians. It is the recurring 'crisis' of 'civilization' against 'barbarism'. European historiography begins with that framework, in Herodotus' presentation of the wars between Greeks and Persians as the latest phase in the age-old conflict between 'East' and 'West', and by implication, between 'barbarism' and 'civilization'. That is the framework also of Aeschylus' *The Persians.* We see it again in the great Funeral Speech of Pericles in Thucydides' history of the first European 'thirty-years war' – between 'civilized' Athens and 'totalitarian' Sparta. Finally, the theme is carved in marble by Phidias in the symbolic motifs of the Parthenon sculptures – imperial Pericles' visual version of Thucydides' literary 'possession for ever'.

The theme did not end there. It became the theme of 'Christendom' against 'the Turk'. That was a theme actual enough in real history, but it could be made resonant with powerful symbolism – as we see it used, for instance, by Thomas More in the imaginary setting of his *Dialogue of Comfort against Tribulation.* Erasmus has the same historical awareness. 'I wish his victory had been over the Turks', he writes to Margaret of Angoulême after the defeat of her brother, Francis I of France, by the imperial army at Pavia in February 1525. 'What rejoicing there would have been throughout the world if the two greatest monarchs on the earth had made peace and joined their arms to repel the assaults of the enemy on Christ's kingdom' (1615/37–40). And More writes: 'That is a right heavy thing, to see such variance in our belief rise and grow among ourselves to the great encouraging of the common enemies of us all, whereby they have our faith in derision and catch hope to overwhelm us all' (Leland Miles ed., Indiana UP, 1965, 36; CW12, 37–38).

The deeper – and potentially symbolic – implication of that historical awareness is that the 'barbarian' can be *within.* 'What I see at present', writes Erasmus, 'is a depressing and general collapse, with the whole of Christendom sinking into a state of Turkish barbarism' (1581/366–8; cf. 1584/24–5). Both More and Erasmus saw the internal divisions of Christendom indicating the lack of a deeper and broader historical awareness, a classical failure to 'know thyself' and a consequent classical blindness to reality. In essence that is the classical *tragic* situation. It is not surprising then that Erasmus repeatedly sees the whole unfolding situation around him precisely in terms of the tragic process. 'The different roles in this drama pass from one actor to another. In the first act we had the rumpus about the humanities. Here Reuchlin played his part and your humble servant contributed something too. Then the plot turned to the subject of faith. Here Luther had the chief part as the leading actor in a bloody drama. There were parts also for the kings to perform ... Recently nobles and peasants made their appearance on the stage. The plot was decidedly bloody ... What the *dénouement* will be I do not know' (1601/3ff).

These are all weighty public matters, *spoudaia* – of serious import, as Aristotle says of the subjects appropriate to the tragic genre. But letters too belong to a distinctive literary genre. And its distinguishing and most attractive feature is to reveal – *veluti descripta tabella* – the private individual rather than, or at least in addition to, the public *persona* in the public event. We know this from both the practice and the theory of the great letter writers. In a letter we do not talk like a book, Cicero says somewhere about his own. And it was to Cicero that Petrarch – 'father of the Renaissance' – addressed his famous public letter, in the excitement of discovery at meeting Cicero, the man as distinct from the public figure, in the newly recovered letters to Atticus. 'I have avidly read through your letters, long sought and finally found where I least expected. And, Marcus Tullius, I have heard your voice, speaking at length, complaining at length, endlessly changing your moods. Long time I knew you as the public preceptor of others: now at last I have seen you as you appeared to yourself.'[58]

Erasmus is in that tradition – in his theory as well as his practice. 'Letters which are deficient in true feeling and do not reflect a man's actual life do not deserve to be called letters.' And he goes on to take out of the canon Seneca's letters to Lucilius, along with much of Cyprian, Basil, Jerome and Augustine, on the grounds that most of their so-called letters would more appropriately be classified as pamphlets or tracts (*libros*). What is properly of the epistolary genre is 'the kind of letter that displays like a picture (*velut in tabula*) the writer's character and fortunes and sentiments, and the state of affairs both public and private – such, for example, as the letters of Cicero and Pliny ... ' (CWE8, 1206/97ff).

The present volume provides endless illustration of this principle, whether in the effect of public events on the private man or in the countless *faits divers* of private life itself. There is the passing of friends and of former opponents (advancing years and battle weariness is a strand in 1525). There is the concern with the arrears in the payment of his imperial pension, his constant and often humorous problem with 'the stone', and his concern with the provision of the good Burgundy thought to alleviate it. There is his allergy to fish and his aversion to stinking sick-making German stoves. There is the down-to-earth detail of the request to one correspondent to 'buy me a roll of Dutch linen, not too fine, but close-woven and smooth, and about eighty ells long' (1654/28–9). To what minute

58 *De rebus familiaribus*, XXIV 3.

particulars even the mighty have to attend. St Paul comes to mind, writing from prison and reminding Timothy to bring him the cloak he left behind him in Troas (2 Tim 4:13). And Erasmus would have his own reasons to appreciate Paul's addendum, warning Timothy to remember that 'Alexander the coppersmith has done me a lot of harm ... Be on your guard against him yourself, because he has been bitterly contesting everything that we say ... '!

We have been outlining the range of interest of Erasmus' letters, from the opposite but complementary poles of their great public questions and what Erasmus himself calls the character, fortunes, and sentiments of the writer. Let us look at them in more detail, and in the order in which we have outlined them.

THE GREAT QUESTIONS

We have emphasized the crucial significance of the *De libero arbitrio* for Erasmus in the *annus criticus* of 1525. As it was the result of what many had long been urging him to do, so it became the occasion of further urgings to do more in the same vein. Thus Floriano Montini in 1552/30 ff, CWE10: 'If with this little work you have relieved your dearest friends of so much worry and freed good Christian folk from the suspicions they have had about you, what will happen, I wonder, if you unfurl your banners and descend into the field of battle with all those forces which you maintain at home and marshal by lamplight?' Similarly Duke George of Saxony in 1550/31–2: 'If you turn your pen against Luther now you may be able to make good what has been lost by your procrastination ... '.

Over a period of two years prior to the *De libero arbitrio* no correspondent had been more urgent and plain-spoken than Duke George in pushing Erasmus to come off the fence of his moderation. Thus in May 1524, 1448/42ff, CWE10: 'How much easier it would have been to extinguish a fire that just then was breaking into flame, instead of trying to put it out now when it has grown into such a vast conflagration. The blame for this, to speak my mind freely, falls in the first place on you. If only ... you had adopted the attitude to Luther that you now display, and had descended into the arena and there played the part of a serious and committed combatant, there would be no reason for our present troubles.' But such plain language and simple understanding of the situation were not in the Erasmian mode, and we have to read his own more subtle and lengthy *apologia* to Duke George in December of 1524. Quoting two sentences will suffice. 'The more I tried to persuade Luther to moderate his conduct, the more savage was his rage. And when I attempted to persuade the other side, all I got for my pains was to be branded as a Lutheran sympathizer' (1526/48–50; cf. 1576/13ff, and the long *apologia* already in 1342/650ff, CWE 9; also 1523 to Melanchthon in December 1524, CWE 10).

Plus ça change ... Despite – or because of – his descent into the arena, precisely the same hostility from opposite sides was to be his experience throughout 1525. It runs like a refrain through the letters of that year – 'the intolerable burden of hostility which I now suffer' (1538/25–6). 'It seems to be my fate that, whenever I try to do my best for both parties, I have stones thrown at me from both sides. In [Italy] and Brabant I am taken for a Lutheran, while here in Germany where I live I am considered so anti-Lutheran that there is no one whom Luther's supporters attack so savagely' (1576/13ff; cf. 1624/41ff). And yet, all the while, there were those on the Catholic side who continued to reproach him for his silence, and to appeal to him to enter the lists and end the schism – 'as if that conflagration had not been out of control for a long time now' (1616/17–8). Such insistence exasperates him. 'Can I accomplish by myself what the emperor, the pope, and whole multitudes of theologians cannot accomplish? Will the world accept me as its sole authority when even the theologians' dogs ... ' – but let us translate it into the more elegant Yeatsian ferocity: when he has become a post that every passing theologian's dog defiles! (1616/14ff).

And in this climate of universal hostility the most dangerous place of all is Basel – where he is nevertheless 'tethered' as we have seen, 'stuck, as the saying goes, between the altar and the sacrificial knife' (1586/26ff). The Peasant War is raging, and all around the region the monasteries are being plundered and burned, the monks are being scattered and the nuns ravished – or, in more chivalrous fashion, wedded. In a word, as Thucydides saw, a classic case of the destructiveness of civil strife, in which the ultimate destruction is the destruction of all distinction between good and evil (1585/99ff). The city of Basel itself was in a state of only knife-edge equilibrium, still officially Catholic but under pressure from the two leading Reformers we have already mentioned, Pellicanus and Oecolampadius. No surprise then to see Erasmus perform a careful balancing act between accepting and declining to get involved when he answered the City Council's request for suggestions on some religious regulations in that delicate setting. 'You are not asking me, I think [read *hope*!], to pass a general judgement on the merits of Luther's case, nor have I the learning or the authority for such a task, to say nothing of my age or my health or the demands of the studies on which I am now engaged.' In any case, 'neither side is acting prudently. So if I offer a moderate opinion, I shall offend both; and yet I would offend both rather than give unqualified support to either.' But he has to be politic, being 'deeply conscious of the extraordinary kindness you have shown me and ... eager to prove my gratitude should an opportunity arise to serve your interests'. So to show his 'devotion to your city' he will offer some advice, but 'confine myself to the problem of maintaining the peace, which is your proper function' (1539/6ff).

De veritate corporis: But the peace he wanted was to be shattered all the same, and precisely in Basel, when the Eucharistic controversy blew up with Pellicanus and Oecolampadius (1636–40 and 1620/94ff). The controversy turns on the 'real presence' of Christ in the Eucharist. Is it indeed real, really real? Or is it 'symbolic'? That is to say, *merely* symbolic – an indication, as we shall see, that the linguistic and conceptual currency itself has already been debased. The second interpretation became known as the Sacramentarian view (another coinage of ambiguous value), first excogitated by Karlstadt and Zwingli. Pellicanus and Oecolampadius took it up and falsely credited Erasmus with holding the same view – whereas not even Luther could accept it![59] A paragraph in Erasmus to Pellicanus (1637/77ff) brings out not only the theory but its far-reaching implications with admirable force and clarity.

> What reasons do these friends of yours adduce that I should accept so unorthodox and subversive a doctrine? Their arguments are nothing but straw ... We are told to be spiritual, as if the presence of his body were an offence to the spirit. It is indeed flesh, though perceived by none of our senses; and yet it is also a pledge of God's love towards us ... The word of God is on my side. We are told: 'This is my body which is given for you, this is my blood which will be shed for you.' Where do these people read: 'This is not my body, but a symbol of my body, this is not my blood, but a symbol of my blood?'[60]

As the CWE 11 introduction to this letter observes, Erasmus' reply to this theory is 'a prime example of his willingness to defer to the tradition and authority of the church.' It is in fact something more than mere willingness. It is a positive *professio fidei*:

> I have always said that nothing could induce me to accept the position you have taken, especially since the Gospels and the apostolic Epistles speak

59 On the whole controversy, see the Introduction to Thomas More's *The Answer to a Poisoned Book* (CW11). For a modern ecumenical approach to the question, see Brian Byron, *Sacrifice and Symbol* (Catholic Institute of Sydney, 1991), Part II: 'The Eucharist – Truly the Body and Blood of Christ?'

60 Cf. the comment of More in *The Answer to a Poisoned Book*, CW11, 98/20–27, with its inimitably Morean blend of the witty and the concrete. Because faith is the way to the eucharistic food, therefore Master Masker calls faith itself the food, with as much wisdom as if he called the king's street Westminster church – because that is the way to it if you are coming from Charing Cross! 'And because men must spiritually eat this meat [i.e. food] with faith: therefore he calleth the faith the meat, as wisely as if he would, because he eateth his meat with his mouth, therefore call his mouth his meat. What wit hath this man?'

> so clearly of the 'body which is given' and the 'blood which is shed', and since it accords wonderfully well with the ineffable love of God for all mankind that he should have wished those whom he redeemed with the body and blood of his Son to be nourished in some ineffable way by that same flesh and blood and to receive as a pledge the comfort of his mysterious presence, till he returns in glory to be seen by all (1637/36ff).

And further on:

> I know what little respect you and your friends have for the councils of the church ... Hitherto, along with all the other Christians, I have always worshipped in the Eucharist the Christ who suffered for me, and I see no reason now to change my views. No argument could make me abandon what is the universal teaching of Christendom.

And since it has been alleged that by this time a 'coolness' had come between Erasmus and Thomas More, it is worth noting how the reference to 'the universal teaching of Christendom' concurs with – anticipates by ten years – the core argument of More's own final *professio fidei* before those who had condemned him:

> I am not bounden, my Lord, to conform my conscience to the Council of one realm against the general Council of Christendom ... For one Council or Parliament of yours (God knoweth what manner of one), I have all the Councils made these thousand years. And for this one kingdom, I have all Christian realms.[61]

We have suggested more than once that some of the theological controversies of the Reformation had far-reaching and long-lasting implications not only for theology but also for the ideals of humanism and the Renaissance. The Eucharistic controversy about 'real' and 'symbolic' presence is a focal example. Erasmus implies as much in the passage quoted above from 1637/77ff. One sentence in particular is striking: 'We are told to be spiritual, as if the presence of his body were an offence to the spirit.' The theological issue here is really the whole historical and incarnational character of Christianity, with its 'redemption' of matter and material reality as well as of spirit and the spiritual world. It is at that point that theology has implications for the ideals of humanism. For it is the incarnational above all that bridges the ancient Platonist or Gnostic dualism and its *chôrismos* or separation between the two worlds of spirit and matter. For

61 Quoted in R.W. Chambers, *Thomas More* (London: Jonathan Cape, 1936), 341.

transcendent invisible spirit is *embodied* in the incarnational, and visible matter is given an invisible transcendent dimension – made truly 'sacramental' in fact, made truly 'symbol' indeed as distinct from 'sign', by *embodying* a reality beyond itself as distinct from merely *pointing* to it. It is obvious that which of these two views of the material world one takes has weighty consequences for literature and art and all that goes to make up the ideals of humanism – consequences indeed for the extent to which the phenomenal world can be made 'meaningful' at all, a 'meaning' of things without which there can be no greatly meaningful literature and art and human endeavour.

It is striking then, all those centuries later, to find the modem literary critic and theorist Erich Heller, with an historical awareness and a philosophical mind, focusing on the Eucharistic controversy as the *point de départ* for what he calls the 'disinherited mind', in a world that has a horizontal axis only, two-dimensional, flattened out, emptied out, bereft of immanent-transcendent meaning – as also is the literature and art that such a condition must produce.[62]

Heller presents his case and comment dramatically, through an imagined scene in Marburg. A theological dispute is in progress there, between Luther and Zwingli. The dispute is about the nature of the Eucharist, the sacrament of the Lord's Supper. 'The bread and wine – are they the body and blood of Christ, or are they "mere symbols"?' Even for Luther, with all his deviations from tradition, the word and the sign are 'not merely "pictures of the thought", but the thing itself. Yet for Zwingli, steeped in the enlightened thought of the Italian Renaissance, this is a barbarous absurdity. The sacrament is "merely" a symbol, that is, it symbolically represents what in itself it is not.' The author's comment on the scene is succinct:

> To the modern lay-mind their debate may seem like mere scholastic hair-splitting, but history would suggest that it was more like Samson's hair-cut. Its consequences most certainly unsteadied the pillars on which a great house stood.

The 'hair-cut' consisted in the reduction of the symbol to 'the *merely* symbolic. Thus it deprived the language of religion as well as of art of an essential degree of reality. (...) What was first felt to be a liberation appeared more and more as a robbery. Robbed of its real significance, what did the symbol signify? Robbed of its symbolic meaning, what did reality mean?'

62 *The Disinherited Mind* (Edinburgh, Penguin Books, 1961), 228ff. See also the significantly titled *Real Presences* by George Steiner (Chicago: University Press, 1989), *passim*, but especially 87ff on 'fundamental breaks in the history of human perception', and specifically on the breaking of 'the covenant between word and object' (90).

Theology and humanism: Those demonstrated implications of the Eucharistic question provide the wider context in which we can understand the full import of another theme in the letters of 1525, the ideal of Christian humanism – see 1581, 1586, 1593, 1634. The concept has become vacuous and vague in an age that has lost scholastic precision of thought, and in which the term *humanism* itself has been appropriated to signify the very exclusion of Christian. But Christian humanism has a precise meaning for Erasmus – as also for Thomas More in his *Letter to Dorp*. It means both a subject matter and a methodology for the study of it. The study of the humanities is the propaedeutic to both. The subject matter is positive theology, that is, a return to the scriptural and patristic sources in order to get back behind, and to water the roots of, an autonomously speculative conceptualising scholasticism. (Kant was to say that concepts without percepts are empty, and percepts without concepts are blind!) And in so far as positive theology is a study of the *written* sources (*sacrae litterae*) it entails a literary methodology, with all that that implies for a sense of the meaning of words and sentences in a *context* rather than as isolated units to be plucked out as instantly probative plums by the sciolists of manuals and *summulae*. It entails also a faculty for the *sensus plenior* of language when, not only in Scripture but in poetry and artistic prose, language becomes multivalent, polysemous, symbolic – in the sense of that word already explained, in which the concrete particular, while remaining its concrete self, becomes a concrete universal. The loss of this faculty may have been aggravated in late and decadent scholasticism, but its loss did not begin there. Henri de Lubac points out in one of his works that this loss is already on the 'loss' side of the 'gain' in high scholasticism, through its emphasis on the linear logic of conceptual reasoning – on *l'esprit de géométrie* to the detriment of 'imagination' and *l'esprit de finesse*. The heart does indeed have its reasons, and not only the reasons but the prior perceptions on which the reasons are based.

And besides, even for Erasmus who confesses to having kept away as far as possible from the scholastics, conscious as he was of his 'modest abilities' in the 'difficult field of dogmatic theology' (1581/134ff), even for him the choice is not either/or but both/and. The teachings of the schoolmen 'I have never rejected *in toto* ... It is not my view that we should reject the teachings of the schoolmen, especially when they have won conciliar approval ... ' (1581/601ff). His ideal is a marriage between theology and humanist studies. That is also the position of More in the *Letter to Dorp*. More cites the Aristotelian dictum that 'dialectic' and 'rhetoric' are related as the closed fist to the open palm, 'since dialectic infers more concisely what rhetoric sets out more elaborately' (CW15, 17/8–9). 'For what else are the very precepts of dialectic but a particular product of intelligence, that is, the particular formulas of rational conjecture – which reason perceives to be useful in learning about the real world? So unlikely it is that Erasmus ... should prove less skilled at disputing than every dialectician, mere schoolboys included' (17, last lines).

Erasmus gives his own reasons for his ideal of a 'marriage' between the liberal arts and theological studies. He wants to 'combine the sacred with the profane' (1593/183). He wishes to make languages and literature 'serve Christ's glory – I did not want to bring the old paganism back to the modern world' (1634/102ff). He wishes 'to give literary studies a Christian voice, for ... humanists in Italy concentrated on pagan themes' (1581/124–6). And 'up to the present time those ... who are interested in literature, although excellent in [their] own field, have contributed little to the understanding of theology' (1586/12–14). And, one may remark in passing, so it was to remain. Literature became 'autonomous', the sciences became 'autonomous', and theology became one more 'science' among them – aiming of course to be 'exact' like the others, but forgetting Aristotle's qualification to the demand for 'scientific' exactness, that it is a mark of the educated mind not to demand more clarity than the subject permits. Like Newman in *The Idea of a University*, he knew the necessity of understanding the *parts* as parts of a *holon*, a whole.[63]

Free or slave will? We have been showing how the Eucharistic controversy is a focal example of a theological problem that turns out to have implications and consequences far beyond theology. It is not the only such example in 1525. There is the even deeper and more far-reaching problem of free will, denied by Luther, forcing Erasmus into the arena with *De libero arbitrio*, occasioning the numerous references to that work and to attacks on it in the letters of 1525, attacks culminating at the end of that year in the counterblast by Luther in the bluntly titled *De servo arbitrio*.

The freedom of the will is of course a primordial and perennial problem. It was a problem for Greek philosophy long before it became a problem for Christian theology – where it was intensified by those dark words of St Paul about the respective rights of the potter and his clay in Rom 9:14ff. Cicero had to deal with

63 I have in mind Newman's ideal of the 'perfecting of the intellect' by what he calls 'philosophic knowledge', based on the classical and medieval understanding of all knowledge – like reality itself – as ultimately one, and leading therefore to the integrating and unifying role he assigns to theology in *The Idea*. Of course *idea* here has Platonic overtones, and like Plato on his ideal city, Newman was aware of the gap between the 'ideas' laid up in heaven and the imitations of them realisable in the sublunary world! Cf. Brian Byron, *Loyalty in the Spirituality of St Thomas More* (Nieuwkoop: B. De Graaf, 1972), 21: 'The programme of religious renewal envisaged by the Christian humanists was interrupted by the Reformation.' That was already the conclusion of Louis Bouyer in (Eng. tr. of *Autour d'Erasme*) *Erasmus and the Humanist Experiment* (London: Geoffrey Chapman, 1959): 'The opportunity for an intellectual and cultural synthesis had by then been lost' (218, referring to the example of Thomas More's life and ending – 'the finest [figure] in the whole Catholic Renaissance').

the problem, in *De fato* and *De divinatione.* Those two works are the focus of St Augustine's treatment of the question in *De civ. Dei* V 8ff. Augustine had already written his own early treatise *De libero arbitrio* – free will was one of a number of fundamental *philosophical* problems he had to get out of the way immediately after his conversion to Christianity. And naturally the problem emerges in any *theodicy*, any attempt to justify the ways of God to man, and so it emerges in a work like Boethius' *De consolatione philosophiae.*

It is in a passage of that work that we find the most concentrated and anguished statement of just how deep and complex the problem of free will is. It is not merely one problem but a Hydra of interrelated problems:

> You invite me to a question which is among the most difficult of all to enquire into, and one which is hardly ever exhaustively solved. For the matter is such that one doubt being cut away countless others spring up in its place like the Hydra's heads ... For in this area questions arise about the singleness of Providence, about the way in which Fate runs its course, about sudden Chance, about God's knowledge and predestination, and about the freedom of the will. And how weighty these questions are you can weigh up for yourself. (IV 6)

We are not concerned here with the cause or the solution of the problem, only with the dark consequences of the elimination of free will. Perhaps no other elimination so darkens the sky of the human condition, with drastic results not only for theology but for all that goes by the name of humanism.[64]

It is not surprising then – or at least it is surprising only in the generosity shown – that Luther in his *De servo arbitrio* thanks Erasmus for the very work to which his own is a violent riposte. He pays Erasmus the compliment of having identified and concentrated on the core question, the freedom of the human will, and thus of having seen beyond and behind such *marginalia* as the papacy, purgatory, indulgences, and other such irrelevant matters! Erasmus, and only Erasmus, had 'aimed for the jugular'![65] An apt figure indeed when we see the consequences of the *denial* of free will, as expressed again in the *cri de coeur* of Boethius (op. cit., V 3). Free will being once denied –

64 That condition has recently been analysed, and depicted in very dark colours, by John Carroll in *Humanism: the Wreck of Western Culture* (London: Fontana Press, 1993).

65 Solus prae omnibus rem ipsam es agressus, hoc est summum causae ... Unus tu et solus cardinem rerum vidisti, et ipsum jugulum petisti ... .

> it is evident what ruin of human affairs will follow. For in vain are rewards and punishments proposed to good and evil, which no free and voluntary motion of their minds has merited ... Virtues and vices shall be meaningless, rather shall there follow a mingled and undiscriminating confusion of all deserts. And – most unholy of all – since the whole order of things proceeds from Providence, and human counsels can achieve nothing, it follows that our vices also shall be referred to the Author of goodness. Wherefore there is no reason left to hope or pray for anything. For why hope or pray for anything when all is determined by an unbreakable causal chain? Hope and prayer, the one and only means of communication between God and man, shall have been taken away ... The result must be that humankind ... , thus severed and disjoined from its Source, must crumble, disintegrate and collapse.

St Augustine, in *De civ. Dei*, V 9, quotes Cicero's *De fato* to the same effect. And that is no more or less than the prospect that Carroll[66] sees – or dreams he sees – actually realised in the centuries after the failed promise of renaissance and reformation.

THE EPISTOLARY PERSONAL

But let us escape from such brooding thoughts and briefly sample the more attractive personal revelations that distinguish the epistolary genre. The present volume abounds in them. They are often laced with a sardonic humour in adversity, as when Erasmus refers to the passing of the stone as a 'bringing forth'. Or when he sympathizes with a friend who has been visited by the same trouble (1558/117ff): 'Doctors tell us that gout and stone are sisters. It was enough to have this wretched bond between us of being wedded to two sisters, but I resent my wife rushing off to you every now and then without at the same time deserting me!' His 'wretched body' reminds him of some of Pliny's reported wonders of nature – the capacity of certain lakes, streams and springs to turn everything into stone. His body 'has this further remarkable quality that, while women become sterile with advancing years, old age makes me more fertile. For I bring forth with ever increasing frequency, though with greater danger to myself; it is like the birth of vipers' (1558/124ff).[67]

But there is pathos too. In the death of friends – often former opponents, as in the epitaph on the death of Dorp (1646; cf. 1603/121ff). In the loneliness of the

66 Op. cit. in n. 64, p. 370 above.

67 One cannot help recalling an earlier cry of pain from Erasmus, in 1342/540f, CWE9: 'Why, I would rather settle in an Irish bog than face even one attack of stone.' Wondering what the Latin for *bog* might be, I could only find *ad luuernos usque migrare* (Allen, t. V, 494f). Fe, fi, fo – and fum!

solitary man when friends must leave – as in the correspondence with Jan Lasky, the young Polish humanist who was a house guest of Erasmus for some months in Basel (1622/6ff; cf. 1624/59ff). In the occasional glimpse of this 'hard man' reaching out by indirections for a certain *je ne sais quoi de plus humain* – as in the letter of condolence to the recently widowed Margaret of Angoulême (1615), whose sweet portrait here bears a remarkable resemblance to that of Dame Gertrude More, the martyr's great-great-granddaughter!

But the most radical and life-determining personal revelation in the present volume is in 1581A. The letter is incomplete and lacks the name of the addressee, and is reproduced here from 1436 in CWE10 because newly dated from 1524 to 1525. It amounts to a kind of Abelardian *historia calamitatum* – how he was blackmailed into becoming a monk when 'I was a child scarcely out of my sixteenth year (...), an adolescent shy by nature and without experience, deprived of support of every kind and betrayed even by [my] own brother'. Once the halter was around his neck 'the mysteries of that life began to be revealed'. He endured it to avoid scandal, took refuge in study from a life 'to which I had the greatest possible aversion', until a chance occasion enabled him to escape to Brabant, to the Bishop of Cambrai, to Paris, and into the wide world of learning that was his real vocation.

The occasion of the letter is the accusation that he was an 'apostate' for having left his monastery and discarded his canonical habit. The word 'apostate' is of course misused. But 'if one wants to distort the word apostate and apply it to monks, it would be better to apply it to those who pile up money, the fornicators and adulterers, the gluttons and greedyguts, who vilify their bishops and attack their own official superiors not only with scandal but with fisticuffs and poison; these are the men who break their vows'. After that the least one can say is that the author was no longer either 'shy' or 'without experience'.

'But enough of this nonsense', he rings off abruptly.

ERASMUS AND MORE

A review of Erasmus in *Moreana* would be incomplete if it did not attend to his *dimidium animae*, Thomas More. We have already done so more than once, but there remains the question that calls for special attention in the period to which the present volume belongs – the alleged 'cooling' of the later relations between More and Erasmus.

There is no evidence of that cooling in this volume, unless we regard the *argumentum ex silentio* as evidence, what has been described as 'the perfunctory exchanges between them after 1520'.[68] What kind of evidence *do* we find in the

68 James J. McConica, 'The Recusant Reputation of Thomas More', in Sylvester and Marc'hadour, *Essential Articles for the Study of Thomas More*, 136–49, 145.

present volume? We find Erasmus expressing the warm desire that his friends will get acquainted with Thomas More. Thus to Maximilianus Transsilvanus in 1585/120ff: 'I wish you and More would get acquainted. Cranevelt will tell you the sort of man he is. I have already written and told him something about you. True friends are a rarity in these times; so good men must tighten the ties of friendship that bind them together.' Again in 1606/12ff to Polidoro Virgilio: 'It is not his way to dwell on insults, even insults that are serious. I have written to him, however, not to reconcile the two of you, but to strengthen your mutual friendship ... It is only fair that we should share our friends in common ... '. The fact that neither of these letters of Erasmus is extant suggests the possibility that we may not have all the evidence, and that the exchanges may not have been quite so perfunctory after all. The loss of letters was a hazard of the time. As was also the hazard of their being intercepted by enemy agents, thus making oral communication often more prudent on delicate matters. Both hazards are as old as the correspondence of Cicero. And we do have other instances of the known loss of letters between More and Erasmus. In April 1522, Vives writes to Erasmus in 1271/126ff (CWE9): 'I think you will get a letter from More by the hands of Clement [More's adoptive son-in-law], who has set off these last few days for Italy and means to pass through Basel ... '. In August of the same year Vives to Erasmus, again in 1306/25f: 'Your letters to More and to the Archbishop of Canterbury I sent off to England today ... '. None of these letters is extant.

In the present volume there is a letter from 1656 to Robert Aldridge requesting him to look up a manuscript of Seneca in King's College, Cambridge, with a view to noting textual variants for Erasmus' Froben edition: 'Then send the volume with the annotations to Thomas More, who will see that it is passed on to me.' Such easy presuming on the services of More suggests anything but coolness, or even their being in any way out of contact.

As is well known, the suggestion is first made by Stapleton in his *Life* of More (Frankfurt ed., 17; Hallett/Reynolds ed., 36f). It is not our intention here to go over that ground again,[69] only to make some further possible suggestions. According

69 See McConica, art. cit., and especially Germain Marc'hadour et Roland Galibois, *Érasme de Rotterdam et Thomas More: Correspondance* (Éditions de l'Université de Sherbrooke, 1985), 185–95. To the ample evidence provided there for continuous contact between Erasmus and More in those years one may add the evidence of the Holbein drawing for the More family portrait, done in 1527 or 1528. We find the following note on it in J. B. Trapp and Hubertus Schulte Herbrüggen, *The King's Good Servant: Sir Thomas More 1477/8–1535* (London: National Portrait Gallery, 1977), 85–6: 'Commissioned by Thomas More, perhaps at request of Erasmus; perhaps taken to Erasmus in Basel by Holbein ... . It was certainly in Erasmus's hands in Basel by 3 September 1529, when he wrote to More, as well as to Margaret Roper on 6 September (Allen 2211, 2212), expressing admiration for Holbein's skill.' Richard Marius in his *Thomas More* simply takes it for granted that 'Stapleton was entirely correct' (331). Marius of course is working with a wider thesis, developed in chapter

to Stapleton, both More and Fisher wrote to Erasmus suggesting he do like St Augustine and issue a volume of *retractationes* correcting what needed correcting in his works. 'But Erasmus, who was as unlike Augustine in humility as he was in doctrine, refused and destroyed More's letter so that it should not be inserted in his correspondence.'

Once again there is no surviving evidence of the letters by More and Fisher, or of the letter that Erasmus, according to Stapleton, wrote to Fisher in reply. But the Stapleton passage, as a whole and in the details, is strikingly parallel to a passage in 1579/82ff of the present volume (Allen t. VI, lines 71ff). The letter is a long patronising communication from Erasmus' bitter opponent Noël Béda:

> Unless I am misled by some human weakness, you would find no small profit both for your soul and for the church, if you followed the example of your mentor St Augustine and, beginning with the earliest of your many and varied writings, subjected them to critical examination, and after considering them in the light of experience and with the help of the criticisms of others, rejected completely and utterly anything which you found at odds with faith or morals. To strengthen your mind for such a task, I suggest you read the letter to Marcellinus by this same Augustine whom you admire ...

A few lines earlier Béda has made a point about humility – to which the reference to 'strengthening your mind' may be an allusion: 'You will not be on sure ground on theological matters until you unlearn many things, humbling your spirit in the eyes of God, and trusting no more in your own judgment.' The point is taken up by Erasmus in the course of his long riposte in 1581/96ff. It is indeed 'far from the humility of' ... not Augustine but Béda.

Could the Stapleton passage be a wrongly attributed echo of Béda?[70] We have to remember the climate of suspicion that surrounded Erasmus from the beginning,

---

6, that More and Erasmus were *never* all that close. Part of the evidence brought forward for this is that 'More and Erasmus seldom communicated' (93). Apart from the fact that More was a very busy man, it is worth quoting from his very first surviving letter to Erasmus, in the year 1516: 'Since you left us, dearest Erasmus, I have received three letters from you in all. If I were to say I had sent you three answers, you will perhaps not believe me, even if I lie in the most sanctimonious manner, especially as you know me for a very idle correspondent (...). Farewell once more. You must make do with this one letter for many months, for I am like a miser: he rarely invites anyone to dinner, and if he ever does he gives the man a prolonged meal, in order for the price of one dinner to escape the expense of having to invite him every day' (388/1ff and 188ff, CWE3).

70 Or a wrongly attributed echo of Bishop Tunstall's letter to Erasmus in the year 1529 and Erasmus' reply (2226 and 2263 in Allen t. VIII)? Tunstall too urges Erasmus to follow the example of Augustine, *inter alios*, in the matter of revision. But any such interpretation as Stapleton's would be a complete distortion of its tone and Erasmus' reply.

and which could only be worse in the fixed battle lines of the age of Stapleton. Stapleton's now classic but already circulating quip about Erasmus laying the eggs that Luther hatched we find equivalently already in Erasmus' own correspondents. Erasmus complains bitterly to Alberto Pio about his giving legs to slanderous rumours emanating from influential figures in the Roman Curia. 'Every time the cardinals give a dinner-party or the scholars have a meeting' it is repeated that 'all our troubles began with Erasmus', that '"Luther drew his inspiration from my books"' (1634/44ff and 78). The atmosphere could only be thickened when Paul IV condemned all the writings of Erasmus in 1559. McConica[71] quotes a clinching passage from the Jesuit Robert Parsons: 'Wheresoever Erasmus did but point with his finger, Luther rushed upon it, where Erasmus did but doubt, Luther affirmed. So as upon Erasmus' dubitations, Luther framed assertions and asseverations.' A statement, come to think of it, not very different from one by Erasmus himself, in a complaint to Pellicanus about his broadcasting insinuations that in private Erasmus agreed with Pellicanus' Sacramentarian theory of the Eucharist:

> I always thought that you at least were the sort of person to whom I could safely entrust a secret, and it was you I chose to hear the secrets of my inmost thoughts. So I cannot understand what made you broadcast about me things I never said or thought. (...) When I am with my learned friends, especially if the weaker brethren are not present, I am accustomed to speak freely whatever the subject of discussion may be; I do this to raise a question, sometimes to try out a new idea, occasionally just for the fun of it. Perhaps I am more naïve about that than I ought to be' (1637/8ff and 48ff).

Indeed and indeed! Who would not sympathize with that? It is easy to understand how by the time of Stapleton it could have become a *topos*, if not a veritable index of orthodoxy, to make Erasmus the scapegoat for a time of troubles.

How does that climate relate to the temperature between More and Erasmus in the 1520s? Irreconcilably, it would seem. Over and above the contacts between them already quoted, that climate is a world away from the atmosphere in which, as late as 1524, Margaret More is made the model for the 'learned lady' in Erasmus' colloquy *The Abbot and the Learned Lady*. It is a world away from the atmosphere in which in December 1523 Erasmus writes to John and Margaret More with commentaries on Ovid's *Nux* and two seasonal hymns of Prudentius, and refers also to 'all those loving letters' of which he had been the prior recipient from them (1402 and 1404, CWE10). 'I have been put on my mettle so often lately, my dearest Margaret, by letters from you and your sisters – such sensible,

71 Art. cit., 147f.

well-written, modest, forthright, friendly letters – that even if someone were to cut off the headings I should be able to recognize the "offspring true-born" of Thomas More' (1404/3–6).

TRANSLATION

A reviewer must come to the invidious task of gleaning where the harvesters have reaped. He will have 'had his reward' if he can light on the occasional cockle in the corn or knot in the bulrush. It would be perfection indeed, if, in a field as big as the CWE, he were to find no 'reward' at all. But let it be said at once that the present volume of translation is admirably accurate, limpid and elegant, and constantly finds the *mot juste* or the *phrase juste* to put the distant Latin idiom into the crisp modem vernacular. A task in which *noblesse oblige* when the subject is Erasmus. Few could handle the Latin *gravitas* with as crisp a grace as he. And few can approach the task of translating him adequately without some trepidation after reading his own critiques of some translators from the Greek in his own day – see e.g. 1558/185ff and 1572/49ff. It would be best not to know such a passage as his answer to Béda's recommendation that he 'read Gerson and other unpretentious writers of the same kind as a way of humbling his pride ... ': 'Now it is not my habit to despise any writer, but with regard to those so-called scholastics of yours I find nothing unpretentious about them except the quality of their style' (1581/90ff).

As it happens, it is in a passage in this same letter (lines 4ff) that I seem to find a 'knot'. It is useless to comment without giving the Latin and the English.

> *Suspitiones nihil moror ... Negligo, dissimulo, excuso, suspendo sententiam, donec manifesta pravitas saepius deprehensa compellat me dicere 'Non putaram'. Neque quicquam arbitror magis indecorum homini Christiano quam quum post temere susceptam diuque fotam de proximo suspitionem, post impetitam multis conuiciis innoxii famam, tandem expertus eum longe alium esse quam imaginatio finxerat, dicit 'Non putaram.'*
>
> Suspicions do not bother me at all ... These things I disregard and ignore; I find excuses for them or suspend judgement until there is repeated evidence of obvious malice and I am forced to say 'I never thought it possible'. Nothing, in my opinion, is more unbecoming to a Christian man than to cling to a hastily formed suspicion of a neighbour and after attacking the reputation of an innocent man with repeated abuse, to discover in the end that he was very different from the picture one had formed of him – and then to say, 'I never thought it possible'.

The long final sentence in the English version is confusing, and inconsistent with its context. In the context it is obviously Erasmus who is forced to the conclusion that he never thought possible. And it is obviously Béda who attacked the reputation of an innocent man etc., but the syntactical sequence suggests it is Erasmus. The same is true of the *suspicions* – as the first sentence makes clear, they are on the part of Béda about Erasmus, and not the other way round. This is clear also from a sentence a little later than the present passage. Erasmus had not been offended by certain remarks in previous letters from Béda – although they hinted at a less than favourable opinion of him ... . 'I was quite sure that your purpose in writing was sincere and honest' – until, that is, his eyes were opened by experience to what he never thought possible.

The passage then should perhaps be rendered somewhat as follows:

> I consider that nothing is more dishonouring to a Christian man than when, after the rashly conceived and long nurtured suspicion of a neighbour, after the reputation of an innocent man has been attacked by repeated abuse, after learning by experience that the neighbour is very different from the picture he had formed of him, he is finally forced to say, 'I had never thought it possible'.

In accord with this interpretation the word translated as *sophistries* (*strophis*) in line 32 of this letter would be more accurately rendered by the idea of veiled insinuations. It should be said however that if Toronto has wobbled here it does so in good company. Brussels is wobbly too in the French version of the same passage – always assuming that the wobble is not in the reviewer.

In the many references to Erasmus' *Diatribe sive collatio libero arbitrio* the word *diatribe* is occasionally used without capital or italics. This can be misleading for the uninitiated. The Greek *diatribe* did not have the abusive connotations of the English word – as the Latin *collatio* indicates, it meant discussion or treatise. And in any case Erasmus is careful to tell us that he wrote the work not as a 'diatribe' but in a tone of moderation, *evangelica mansuetudine*. And while we are on the word, its use in 'tragic *diatribe* against fate and fortune' in 1650/53 is not perhaps the most nuanced rendering of *tragicarum exclamationum*. In that context better perhaps *tirade*, in its technical French sense.

There is also frequent reference to Erasmus' 'paraphrases *on* ... ' e.g., in 1579/45–6, 'your paraphrase *on* Luke's Gospel'. Instead of *on* one might expect *of* or *to* – the Latin has the genitive case, the LB titles have *in* plus the accusative, the French has *de*.

In 1579/84, Béda is made to refer to Erasmus' 'mentor St Augustine'. A note comments that 'presumably Augustine is "your mentor" because Erasmus was technically still a member of the Augustinian canons regular ... '. The Latin has *beati patris tui*, and the more likely reference is to 'your holy (father) founder'.

And perhaps Augustine should also be given a reference to 1581/99f. In contrast to pretentious theologians 'there are no books which humble and mortify my pride so effectively as those of the evangelists and apostles', Erasmus writes. We may compare Augustine speaking of Scripture in *Confessions* XIII 15, 18: 'I know not ... of any other oracles so pure and simple, so apt to move me to confession to You, and to bend my stiff-necked pride to Your yoke ... '.

And in the matter of references it is worth adding one to the greatest of all the many ancient appropriations of the bitter motif quoted in 1593/8–9: 'Best never to have been born, or, once born, to perish at the earliest possible time.' That further reference is to one of the greatest of all tragedies, Sophocles' *Oedipus at Colonus*, 1225f. Not forgetting, of course, Job 3:3ff!

In 1581/98 there is one of Erasmus' recurring uncomplimentary references to 'these modern writers (*neotericos*)', i.e. 'these so-called scholastics of yours' in line 92. One might question whether the word modern is quite uncomplimentary enough either for the pejorative context or for the pejorative word *neotericos*. The reference is to those already described in 108/24f (CWE1) as 'this modern class of theologians (*neotericum hoc theologorum genus*) who spend their lives in sheer hairsplitting and sophistical quibbling ... '. Similar critical references and uses of the word occur in Thomas More, e.g. in the *Letter to Dorp*, CW15, 56/10, 62/22, 74/12. In none of these passages is the severely pejorative connotation in doubt. The use of the Greek *neotericus* in Latin with that connotation goes back at least to Cicero, e.g. *Att.* VII 2,1. It refers to dangerous revolutionary innovators, contemptuous of tradition. Perhaps it should be rendered by some such word as 'modernist', 'modernistic', 'ultra-modern', 'new-fangled'.

And still in 1581/468, should not *bolus* in *grandi bolo* be translated as *morsel* or *mouthful* rather than *haul*?

In 1557/8–9, I wonder about the rendering of *ex musico retiarius ... factus* in 'you think you have "left the band and turned gladiator"... '. In English *band* is ambiguous, and the connection between a *musicus* and a gladiator is not clear. Is the reference of *musicus* to music at all? Could it be used here in its larger sense of 'man of the Muses' – man of letters, philosopher (see Plato's *Phaedo* 62dff), theologian (see the early Christian Christ as the new Orpheus)? 'It is the music of the gospel which casts its spell upon us ... and implants within us the spirit of Christ. If Amphion could work such wonders with the sound of his lyre, and if Orpheus' lute had such power that it could move rocks and oaks, how much more powerful must be David's lyre ... And how much more effective must be the music of the gospel!' (1573/13ff; cf.1404/16ff to Margaret Roper, CWE10). And most explicitly of all, to Henry VIII in 1524: 'May it please your invincible Majesty, I knew very well that the rough-and-tumble of the gladiatorial arena (*harenae gladiatoriae*) was not for me, who have spent all my life in the delightful garden of the Muses' (*in amoenissimis Musarum ortis*, 1493, CWE10).

It is worth noting also that the word translated as *gladiator* is *retiarius*. He was the *lowest* of four grades in that base profession. He fought almost naked, and armed only with a trident and a net. Erasmus would appreciate the point as he faced his own beasts.

In 1603/119f, Shakespeare provides a beautiful phrase for one of Erasmus' preoccupations as the years pass – *abiicietur hoc syphar*: 'Soon, I am afraid, I shall *shuffle off this mortal coil* and emerge in a new form, like a cicada' (*Ham.* 3.1). It is tempting to gild the lily and go one better with Shakespeare, even at the cost of *contaminatio*: 'Soon ... I shall *shuffle off this muddy vesture of decay ...* ' (*MV* 5.1)! The Greek *syphar* denotes anything wrinkled or decrepit – skin, a fig, the skim of milk, and, more specifically, the slough of a serpent. In that last sense Erasmus would have met the word in Lucian's *Hermotimus*,[72] where, *vis-à-vis* the serpent's body coils, it is used as an image of the pursuit of shadow for substance.

FAREWELL TO MARTIN DORP

Such intimations of mortality conveniently enable us to end our gleanings with a glance at Erasmus' epitaph in verse on the untimely death of Dorp (1646). It gives us a sample of Erasmus' voluminous poetry – he 'lisped in numbers' from a very early age, as we learn from his survey in 1341A/65ff (CWE9). The present effort, he tells us, was composed *ex tempore* but not without care (*non absque cura*). The genuine – if conventionally expressed – feeling is doubtless *ex tempore*, the technique and content hardly so. Erasmus' run-on lines gives us something larger than the monotonously end-stopped verses of so much late antique, medieval and Renaissance versifying. And within its short compass it qualifies for Erasmus' praise of the subtlety of Plutarch's prose – the product of a mind 'stored with literary works of every kind' (1572/49ff).

This also corresponds with Erasmus' own requirements for poetry, as set out in his *Ecclesiastes* II (ASD V-4, 258/254ff). Poetry demands more than the capacity to make verses. It demands the capacity to think, in thoughts that have grandeur and gravity and are infused with powerful feeling, with the attraction of charm and the vividness of pictorial imagery – the whole complex inspired by 'a kind of divinity and divine possession, *enthousiasmos*'. We are back with Plato and

72 Tome I of the two-volume edition of the *Opera* of Lucian, with the Latin translation of Ioannes Benedictus (Amsterdam, 1687), 566. It is interesting to note the high praise Benedictus in his Preface to Tome II gives to Thomas More as a translator of Lucian – Benedictus himself could find hardly anything to improve on. *Proxime accedit Erasmus Roterodamus*!

Longinus, and even the more coldly analytic Aristotle. But – as also in them – perspiration must complement inspiration. 'Nature' must be 'nurtured' – by the complete intellectual formation that is the product of the complete curriculum of the traditional liberal arts and disciplines – *omni disciplinarum genere.*

No surprise then that our short poem would take more annotation than it is given in the present volume, or can be given here. It is of course edited in the complete edition of Erasmus' poems (no. 71 in CWE 85), and annotated in the accompanying CWE 86. But even there not everything relevant is mentioned. Witness the fact that the poem is in the long unbroken classical and Christian tradition of the pastoral elegy – as we see it for instance in Virgil's fifth *Eclogue* and Milton's *Lycidas*, with their central motif that *non periit ille, vivit ...*, 'he is not dead but lives' (1646/36). In the poem we also have the classic motif of Wisdom 4:14 in which the prematurely deceased is taken away only 'from the midst of iniquities'. So too Dorp

> has been rescued from this evil world.
> And all the endowments of his soul are safe.

And in the long middle time, the kindly earth will preserve the precious bodily remains, to yield them up at the resurrection call of the last trumpet – as in Prudentius' long *Hymn for the Burial of the Dead* (*Cathemerinon* X).

That hymn of Prudentius is an unmentioned influence in the epitaph on Dorp. It would be strange if it were not, given the nature of the theme and given the status of Prudentius for Erasmus as *Pindarus noster* (LB V 1340), a status reflected in the fact that Prudentius' *Preface* to his collected poems is the model for one of Erasmus' best-known poems, *On the Troubles of Old Age* (no. 2 in CWE85). We do not need Prudentius' hymn to discover the Christian attitude to the mortal remains in death, but it is splendidly expressed there, and in the light of it we may correct one note to the epitaph on Dorp in CWE 86. To *corpusculum* in line 16 it is commented that 'the diminutive is pejorative here, expressing contempt for man's mortal clay'. That is not consonant with the sentiments of either Prudentius or Erasmus. And the diminutive does not have to be pejorative. It can also express affection, affection for the dear and the precious. In Erasmus the body is to be preciously preserved in the earth until the resurrection because it has once 'lodged the pious soul' of Dorp. And in Prudentius, lines 125ff, the earth is to *cherish* the body in its bosom, because the mortal remains are the members of a *human being*, and therefore noble even in their ruin – *generosa et fragmina.*

Animae fuit haec domus olim
factoris ab ore creatae,
fervens habitavit in istis
Sapientia principe Christo.

It will not be otiose to have dwelt a little on Erasmus' poetic final tribute to Dorp. Like Augustine, Aquinas, More, and so many others who are known principally as great 'dialecticians', Erasmus had also the temperament of the artist. That emerges many times in the present volume, e.g. 1544, 1572/49ff, 1625. But nowhere is it more explicit and charming than in 1402, CWE 10, to Thomas More's young son John, with the gift of his commentary on Ovid's *Nux*. People may joke that 'here I am in my old age turned childish and gone back to play with nuts again'. But ... 'what other people say does not much worry me. I would like to convince you, my dear John, that a great artist is always himself, whether he is modelling a colossal statue or a six-inch statuette, whether he is painting a Jupiter or a Thersites ... '(lines 18ff).

And withal, Erasmus could read the signs of the times, what his particular moment in history's movement required of him, or willy-nilly was going to impose: *consideranda est temporum ratio*, he says again and again (1596/46f; cf. 1581/821f and 1620/65f). His playing with nuts could co-exist with that weighty insight, as Thomas More's prophetic wisdom could co-exist with his wit and with his drawing of goslings in the ashes.

ERASMUS: NON IN DIALECTICA?

MANFRED HOFFMAN'S RHETORIC AND THEOLOGY: THE HERMENEUTIC OF ERASMUS

Manfred Hoffmann starts from a twofold constatation. Erasmus rejected the scholastics' theological method, i.e. the deriving of cogent conclusions from metaphysical principles by syllogistic, dialectical reasoning. In his own 'theology', Erasmus reverts to the literary hermeneutics of Classical and patristic 'rhetoric'. Hoffmann examines how Erasmus thus constructs a distinct theological framework and a distinct 'rhetorical theology'. The present article discusses Hoffmann's questions about such a theology, especially whether it is theology at all, and if so, at what level of the 'systematic'. The article argues that Erasmus ignores an intrinsic and essential element in ancient rhetoric: the systematic intellectual armature of Classical and patristic metaphysics, of which dialectic is the organon or method.

***

The work on which this article is based [73]is complementary to an earlier book[74] by the same author on Erasmus' theology, a theology seen to be shaped by Erasmus' theory of knowledge, his anthropology, and his ethics. This new work follows on Hoffmann's realisation that what he calls the *rhetorical matrix* of Erasmus' thought needed a more thorough treatment than he was able to give it in his earlier work. The present treatment is thorough indeed, richly documented from texts and bibliography, clearly structured, and limpidly written.

I. RHETORIC REDEEMED

To the uninitiated the juxtaposition of rhetoric and theology may need explanation. Rhetoric had no sooner become a subject of systematic study and practice

73 Manfred Hoffman's *Rhetoric and Theology: The Hermeneutic of Erasmus* (Toronto University Press, 1994), ix + 306 pp. (Erasmus Studies 12).

74 *Erkenntnis und Verwirklichung der wahren Theologie nach Erasmus von Rotterdam* (Tübingen, 1972).

in Classical Greece than it acquired a dubious reputation. The very word came to carry a connotation which, outside technical literary contexts, perdures to this day. All the ancient treatises on rhetoric had to deal with the prior question of whether it was an 'art' at all, i.e. a *technê* or *disciplina*, or merely a natural knack, or a persuasive way with language acquired by practice alone. And if it was a legitimate *technê*, was it an honest one? What purpose did its skills and techniques serve? The cause of truth established by the rational ordering of logical argument? Or the sophist's purpose of making the false appear true, the worse cause the better, by meretricious use of the charming potential of language artistically used?[75]

The answer of course is not far to seek: *abusus non tollit usum*, the abuse does not invalidate the use. And it was no less a thinker than Aristotle who wrote the first comprehensive treatise on rhetoric – albeit elaborating and systematizing principles already laid down by Plato. In his characteristic way, he gives at one point a pithy statement of the meaning and relevance of the *technê* of rhetoric. 'It is not sufficient to have a grasp of *what* one should say: one must also say it in the *way* that one should ... ' (*Rhetoric*, III 1,2 1403 b). We have here the basic and perennially relevant artistic distinction between the *what* and the *how*, the *matter* and the *form*. We shall be returning to the *what* ... Suffice it to remark here that in the *how*, we have rhetoric legitimised, properly understood in its full range of meaning as the whole art and craft – the *technê*, the *ars* and *disciplina* of stylistics, the effective use of language as a medium of expression and communication, ex-pression and commun-ication from one interiority to another, of something illumined and understood. The illumination and understanding may have come through rational scientific enquiry or through the intuitive vision of the artist. Its matter may be the theologian's, the philosopher's, the historian's or the poet's. They all share language as their common medium of the light to be transmitted. The consequence is that rhetoric – understood as the art and craft of language – is of universal relevance. As one writer has put it, its concern is with the whole complex business of communication through the word. As such its role is analogous to that of dialectic, or logic, as the ancients understood it: an over-arching discipline of disciplines. Thus Aristotle in *Rhetoric* I 1, 1355 b, and St Augustine in *De ordine* II 13, 38.

The cultivation of the art of the word, the *logos* or *verbum*, was all the more important to the Greeks and the Romans for the reason that they saw it as a gift from the gods, a gift of the faculty that supremely distinguished humanity from all other living beings. 'There is intelligence (*noos*) and speech (*audê*) in their hearts', says Homer about the attendants of the craftsman Hephaestus in *Iliad*

75 See e.g. Plato, *Gorgias* 462–3.

XVII 419. 'Speech and wind-swift thought ... has he learned', says Sophocles in the *Antigone*, in the great choral ode that begins: 'Wonders are many, but none more wondrous than man' (11. 331ff).

As the distinctive, and even divine, gift of man then, it was natural that language should have a central place in the educational ideal that aimed not only at embracing the full round of the known sciences, but also at the full, rounded formation of human beings themselves, that is, in the programme of liberal or general education, the Greco-Roman *enkyklios paideia* and the seven liberal arts of the Christian centuries. The latter began with the *trivium* of grammar, rhetoric, and dialectic (i.e. essentially logic). We shall have something to say later on this matter of *dialectic*. Here let us conclude the background to rhetoric by noting that no less a figure than St Augustine – no mean dialectician – included rhetoric among the disciplines essential to the theologian, as outlined in *De doctrina Christiana*. The immediate purpose of that treatise is to provide a handbook on the methodology of scriptural exegesis. But in an age before the compartmentalisation of theology, scriptural exegesis was at the heart of it. Book IV of the work is devoted to rhetoric, and that for a reason which recalls Aristotle's dictum, that it is not enough to know *what* to say, it is necessary to know *how* to say it. 'There are two things necessary to the treatment of the Scriptures: a method of discovering (*inveniendi*) those things that are to be *understood* (*intelligenda*). And a method of *communicating* (*proferendi*) what we have understood. We shall speak first of discovery, and second of communication' (I 1,1).

II. ERASMUS' RETURN TO RHETORIC

The focus on Erasmus is due to the fact that he is the most systematic and developed of the Renaissance humanist reformers who returned explicitly to this tradition of concern with language. The reasons were negative as well as positive. The positive reasons included renewal of theology by returning to the sources, scriptural and patristic, and by a revivified concern with the fundamental Christian obligation to renew Christian *life* by *communicating* the founding truths of those sources. 'Go therefore and teach...' (Mt 28:19). And, as St Ambrose was to say, and equivalently already St Paul (1 Cor 1:17ff), *non in dialectica* ... , not in dialectic was salvation wrought, and *a fortiori* not by dialectic is its promised *life* communicated.[76]

Another reason for this return to the sources – the non-technical literary sources – and to the corresponding tradition of concern with the artistic dimension of language, was the urge to deepen understanding of those sources by

76 'In him was life ... ' (Jn 1:4); 'I have come that they may have life ... ' (Jn 10:10). The Ambrosian *sententia* occurs in his *De fide ad Gratianum Augustum*, I 5,42 (Migne, PL 16 537): *Non in dialectica complacuit Deo salvum facere populum suum.*

reading them in a literary critical way, and consequently interpreting them with an awareness of the multivalence of language in its historical and literary context. In itself that is a positive reason. But it has a negative aspect in that it is due also to a reaction away from the methods and achievements of scholastic philosophy and theology. That reaction, of course, was justified in part by the generally accepted sclerotic state and pseudo-filigree abstract refinements of the prevailing scholasticism. But the attendant risk is that the good will be rejected with the degenerate. In his introduction Hoffmann states his own theme plainly:

> That a coherent world view governed Erasmus' thinking had become fairly certain. Of course, his understanding of reality was neither derived from the metaphysical principles of the scholastic theologians nor arrived at, as theirs, by means of the cogent conclusions of a *syllogistic, dialectical method.* Even so, Erasmus saw all of reality, that is, nature, humanity, society, and history, ordered according to a universal plan, the parts of which he thought were arranged in a harmonious whole (...). With the main characteristics of the Erasmian world view having come to light, it was necessary to examine the way in which this concept of reality is related to language. The daunting task that lay ahead consisted in finding out how the form of Erasmus' thought is informed by an equally comprehensive awareness of speech and interpretation.

And the author goes on to assume that an examination of the hermeneutics of Erasmus' biblical interpretation will reveal the way in which he 'combined ontology and rhetoric so as to construct a distinct theological framework'.

***

Some questions come to mind at once, arising from that statement of Erasmus' method and project, some of them raised by the author himself. Can we have an ontology without metaphysical principles? What level of theology do we have if it is not systematic? And can it be made systematic by rhetoric alone without some degree of dialectical method to make its conclusions cogent? As Hoffmann observes, the question has an ancient parallel in the conflict between Socrates and the Sophists (23). A more adequate parallel is Plato's philosophical quarrel with the poets; and more precisely the quarrel between Plato's methodical and educational ideal of pure philosophy and the so-called rhetorico-literary 'philosophy' of his younger contemporary Isocrates.[77] Hoffmann raises our question

77 See Plato's *Phaedrus*, 278b ff.

and opens it with the statement that 'whether Erasmus can be called a theologian at all has not yet been settled in the mind of everyone', giving references also to some in whose minds it has been settled in the affirmative (18ff). Doubtless Erasmus, like Scripture, is large and various enough to provide texts supportive of contradictory views, even occasional bows to the scholastics – if only because, in the long tradition of Isocratean humanism, dialectic and philosophy should be part of the *enkyklios paideia* that was propaedeutic to the formation of the perfect rhetor. Yet many of Erasmus' own statements are so explicit and forceful that they can hardly be explained away. Hoffmann quotes a number of these:

> In this affair my business is not with theological subtleties but with the correction of the text. I take upon myself a schoolmaster's part; questions of truth and falsehood I leave to those master-minds (19).[78]

> To search out knowledge of the nature of God by human reasoning is recklessness; to speak of the things that cannot be set out in words is madness; to define them is sacrilege ...(68).[79]

And Hoffmann himself sums up a section of the *Ratio verae theologiae* as follows: 'Theology has to do with life rather than with the syllogistic arguments of the scholastics, who quibble over contentious questions by means of dialectics and Aristotelian philosophy' (38).

But even that admission is not the whole of the case against Erasmus as a systematic theologian. As Hoffmann admits, he is infected with a strain of philosophical scepticism. Not surprising in one steeped in that later Classical humanism where even Plato's Academy evolved into an epistemological scepticism of an extraordinary sophistication. It was the first intellectual problem St Augustine himself had to resolve – even after his conversion.[80] The infection is even less surprising in one whose thinking is steeped in the Classical tradition of rhetoric, especially Ciceronian rhetoric. For Cicero, precisely in his philosophical works, repeatedly and explicitly adopts the Academic viewpoint. And to that end he adopts the literary form that best serves it: the rhetorical dialogue that can argue both *pro* and *contra* on any question, and at the end reach at best only varying degrees of probability.[81] Hoffmann quotes to the point from Erasmus' *De libero*

78 *Letters* 1309, CWE 9, 170/54ff.

79 Paraphrase on *John*, CWE 46,13 and 15. Cf. Erasmus himself in full comic flight on that 'remarkably supercilious and touchy lot' in *The Praise of Folly* (LB IV, 463Aff ; CWE 27,126ff.

80 See *Confessions* V 10, 19, and the *Contra Academicos*.

81 See e.g. *De natura deorum* I 5, 11ff.

arbitrio 6: 'I take so little pleasure in assertions that I will gladly seek refuge in Scepticism whenever this is allowed by the inviolable authority of Holy Scripture and the Church's decrees' (21). And even more tellingly further on: 'It is more learned to be ambiguous and with the Academics to doubt than to make pronouncements' (21).[82]

Erasmus' conception of method in theology is to return to what he understands to be the theological method of an earlier age, before philosophy was applied to it and theologians 'grew old over questions meticulous, needless, and unreasonably minute ... ' (5).[83] At the beginning of that earlier age theology was a matter of faith and not of disputation. Simple piety was satisfied with charity and the oracles of Holy Scripture. 'Later, the management of theology was taken in hand by men nurtured in learning which today we commonly call rhetoric.'[84] We shall have to see later whether these statements give the full truth of the matter. For the moment, one of the things we learn from Hoffmann is that, more fundamental even than philosophical scepticism, it is the very medium of language, and, by implication, of rhetoric, that is in question for Erasmus. Language too has degenerated and has to be renewed. It is the subject of one of Hoffmann's two or three more fundamental chapters. The implications of the problem, however, extend beyond the particular case of Erasmus. We are in the presence of another Renaissance phenomenon: the beginnings of the putting into question of that connection and correspondence between language and reality, between *verbum* and *res*, between *logoi* and *Logos*, which underpinned the whole Classical and Christian intellectual tradition. A sentence in Hoffmann provides succinct terms in which to state the implications of the problem: 'While philosophers identified the *logos* primarily with *ratio*, and therefore concentrated on the human intellect in such a way that exact knowledge was declared to be a virtue in itself, the rhetoricians understood *logos* foremost as *oratio*' (23). 'Watchman, what of the night?' if *oratio* itself be put in question![85]

III. RHETORIC AND SYSTEMATIC THEOLOGY

It is important to make clear that the questions we have outlined do not by themselves put the 'orthodoxy' of Erasmus in question. A sentence quoted earlier is one example of his many professions of allegiance to 'the inviolable authority' of

82 *Ratio verae theologiae*, H 297:22–4.

83 *Letters* 1062/CWE7, 196/23ff. On the general problem in the Renaissance, see Erika Rummel, *The Humanist-Scholastic Debate in the Renaissance and Reformation* (Harvard UP, 1995), especially Chapter Seven, 'Humanist Critique of Scholastic Dialectic'.

84 Ibid.

85 On this matter, see Mary Jane Barnett, 'Erasmus and the Hermeneutics of Linguistic *Praxis*', *Renaissance Quarterly*, 49, 3 (autumn 1996), 542–72.

Scripture and Church. In fact, as Hoffmann points out, there is even a strain of Platonist idealism in him which at first sight seems at variance with his attitude to metaphysics. To take an example from Erasmus' attempts to renew the validity of language, Hoffmann refers to texts where Erasmus protects himself from subjectivist freedom of exegesis by insisting that truth is determined by the *author* of language, the ultimate authority on any text. And in the last analysis that Author is God, 'who says the first word before all human speech and speaks the last word after all is said and done' (63).[86] Indeed one element in his renewal of language, especially of scriptural language, is both ever old and ever new. Language has a transcendent dimension – inevitably, given its Author. Consequently it is to some degree symbolic, in the strict sense of that word: the embodiment of the invisible in the visible. Language contains reality in a kind of 'real presence'. And this is especially true of the word of God in Scripture – the first mode of the 'incarnation' of divinity and of the Word in person. The word of Scripture is not only symbolic in the generic sense. It is quasi-sacramental. In Hoffmann's phrase there is 'a unique inverbation of Christ in Scripture' (81). The combination of the traditional four levels of meaning in Scripture with the status of Christ as 'the power of God and the wisdom of God' (1 Cor 1:24) provides Erasmus with the light to find in Scripture not only the unsoundable riches of meaning that traditional exegesis found in it, but also that transforming power in the Christian's life which was his primary spiritual concern.

And by that route we can return to our original question, in what sense *theologia rhetorica*[87] is theology, if at all. For in Hoffmann's analysis there is a significant limitation in Erasmus' use of the four senses of Scripture, i.e. the literal (historical), the allegorical (Christological and ecclesial), the tropological (moral), and, deepest of all, the *anagogical*, the meaning that 'leads up' to transcendent and eschatological truths and realities. Erasmus prefers to stay in the middle region between history and mystery, fighting shy especially of the anagogical level of meaning. 'Since anagogy touches on [the] eschatological reality of the triune divinity itself, it remains by and large beyond the exegetical reach. This is so because the essence of divinity, God *in se*, lies beyond human comprehension and renders us speechless, and therefore must be worshipped in silence *quae supra nos nihil ad nos*' (103–4).

86 Cf. the theme of Plato's *Cratylus*.

87 The term apparently comes from Charles Trinkaus, *The Scope of Renaissance Humanism* (Michigan University Press, 1983). It is by analogy with the *theologia poetica* of the fourteenth century which interpreted the myths of pagan deities in Classical poetry as allegorical anticipations of Christian meanings (Hoffman, 25). The allegorical interpretation of pagan deities begins, of course, in Classicism itself; see e.g. Cicero, *De natura deorum*, II 23, 60ff. And Augustine takes from the Roman Varro the triple classification of pagan theology into mythic (poetic), physical (philosophical), and civil (of the people) – *De civitate Dei*, VI 5.

Of course there is a level of the search for understanding about which this comment is valid, as was admitted not only by Plato but even by Aristotle and Aquinas, not to mention Plotinus and the Christian mystics. But in the context of Erasmus there can be little doubt that what is being abandoned is the possibility of that dialectical exercise of speculative intellect by which a *systematic* theology of the data of Scripture might be constructed, as the scholastics had done, or were thought to have done.

We noted earlier Hoffmann's statement (18) that the question of whether Erasmus can be called a theologian has not yet been settled in the mind of everyone. Hoffmann's own assertion is that he was a theologian, even a 'systematic' theologian. Since the passage summarises so much that bears on the question, including the use of the term *systematic*, we quote it:

> Humanist theology does not construct from abstract first principles a metaphysical system that is an end in itself. But it does arrange theological *loci* in such a way that they form a repository from which the preacher draws the appropriate points for a sermon. In this sense, then, Erasmus was a systematic theologian. Foremost a philologist and a biblical interpreter, he derived his theological conclusions from the sacred text and collated the material according to similarity or dissimilarity in order to provide a manual for the invention and disposition of sacred oratory (58–9).

This use of the term systematic is of a lower order than its technical meaning in 'systematic theology'. The passage quoted describes rather what used to be called 'positive' theology, a technical term already used by the humanists.[88] It denotes the study, establishing, and collating of the positive facts and truths of revelation, the facts and the truths to be believed. Naturally this activity has to have system too, but ever since Augustine's *credo ut intellegam*, and the Augustinian *fides quaerens intellectum* of Anselm, this activity is, as it were, the unreflected stage that provides the data for systematic theology in its proper dialectical and 'scholastic' sense. And scholasticism itself needs to be understood not merely in its narrow time-conditioned sense, but rather as representative of a permanent instinct of the mind, to use a phrase of John Henry Newman's, who was himself no 'scholastic'! For *fides quaerens intellectum* is the search for the unifying 'theory' by which the 'facts' are comprehended.[89]

88 See e.g. Thomas More, *Letter to Dorp*, CW15, 48/3 and 140/15, with the note on p. 513.

89 A good example of the distinction between positive and systematic theology is provided by the two principal parts into which St Augustine divides his *De Trinitate*. Books I–IV establish the positive doctrine from the evidence of Scripture. Books V to the end are 'speculative', in the sense of a

Such a conclusion in no way devalues the work that Erasmus did claim to do, a claim that by and large did not include theology in the theoretical systematic sense, which, as we have seen, he 'left to the masters'. A return to the sources, biblical and patristic, and to the 'positive theology' extracted from them, is the prior condition of the renewal of 'systematic theology'. Erasmus was the first great exemplar of that return in modern times. It was Newman's way too. And that return has never been more important than in present-day theology.

Hence the value of Hoffmann's close, clear, and richly documented analysis of the methodology of Erasmus' *theologia rhetorica*. The book is focused on, but not confined to, the two works of Erasmus most explicitly on the subject, on the two aspects of the subject as we have seen them defined by Augustine: discovery and communication. The two works are the *Ratio verae theologiae* and the *Ecclesiastes* ('The Preacher'). Through them Hoffmann explores how Erasmus avails himself of the combined resources of Classical rhetorical techniques of language and the Christian hermeneutic of the literal and allegorical senses of Scripture. And all this he prefaces with two or three chapters indicating deeper questions of the kind we have already outlined.

IV. DIALECTIC AND RHETORIC

Central to those questions is the Erasmian emphasis on 'rhetoric' to the detriment of 'dialectic'. We have indicated the limitations to theology which follow from that emphasis. Given the importance of these limitations one should not perhaps conclude an outline analysis of them without finding out whether anything more definite can be said about them. In particular, are they *intrinsic* to rhetoric, or only the consequence of an incomplete understanding of it? An examination of the ancient treatises on rhetoric, both Classical and Christian, reveals that the answer is incomplete understanding of the professional requirements of rhetoric as understood in the Greco-Roman, and even Christian, treatises. Erasmus returned to the sources indeed, but he ignores[90] the fact that not just humanist studies in general but specifically philosophical dialectic is insistently required to underpin the literary techniques of rhetoric. It is implicit in the sentence we quoted earlier from Aristotle's *Rhetoric*, conjoining the double necessity of *what* to say and *how* to say it. Quite explicit is the well-known opening statement of his treatise: 'Rhetoric is the counterpart (*antistrophos*) of dialectic'.[91] And the reference is not only to

systematic attempt to *explain* the mystery – no better example of *fides quaerens intellectum* – and that by some of the most difficult concepts of *philosophy*! Newman's phrase is in the *Apologia*, 293 (Fontana Books edition, London, 1959).

90 He does not even wrestle with the *problem* of the relation of dialectic to rhetoric in the way that many humanists did, e.g. Valla, Agricola, Vives, Ramus, and others. See Erike Rummel, op. cit., chapter 7.

91 Cf. I 2, 1356a: 'Rhetoric is, as it were, a kind of offshoot (*paraphues*) of dialectic ... '.

logical argument but to that higher universal philosophical wisdom which even the lawyer and the politician should bring to bear on the particulars they have to treat of – combining convincing logic about the *matter*[92] with the persuasive rhetoric of literary *form*. We referred earlier to the quest of *intellectus* as the search for the unifying 'theory' by which the 'facts' are *comprehended*. As it happens, a passage in Plato's *Phaedrus* succinctly states the relevance of dialectic to rhetoric. Over and above mere stylistics, two controlling dialectical skills are required, 'the essence of which it would be gratifying to learn, if some *technê* could teach it'. The first is that of 'bringing together in one idea the scattered particulars, so that one may make clear by definition the particular thing one wishes to explain'. The second is that of 'dividing things again by classes, where the natural joints are, and not trying to wrench off just any part, in the manner of a bad carver!' (265de).

The importance of that passage lies in the fact that, to counter the current debasement of rhetoric, the *Phaedrus* provides the first systematic outline[93] of the valid meaning, function, and requirements of rhetoric. And, as we have just seen, an essential requirement was the intellectual armour of dialectic, the ultimate goal of which in Plato was the ascent to the supreme metaphysical understanding of reality, by transcending the axioms of all the *particular* sciences in the ultimate light of the supreme unifying principle of *all* axioms, the form of all forms, the grounding form that is the Good.[94] That requirement of arming rhetoric with dialectic survives in all the later treatises. Of course its significance in the *practice* weakened, with the weakening of philosophy itself in the period after Plato and Aristotle. But the *principle* remains, even in the eclecticism and Academic probabilism of Cicero's philosophy.[95] The early Christian theologians took over the ideal. We have already mentioned St Augustine's codification of it in his *De doctrina Christiana*. But we know already, independently of his theory, that in his practice as one of the perennially great thinkers he insists on combining the mastery of dialectic with the mastery of the literary skills of rhetoric.[96]

92 It is notable that after the opening statement just quoted Aristotle devotes the rest of his introductory chapter to emphasizing the priority of logical argument. Previous writers on rhetoric had provided only a limited part of what pertains to rhetoric as a *technê*. They said nothing about *proofs*, although 'proofs (*pisteis*) are the only things in rhetoric that are directly relevant to the *technê* – everything else is merely ancillary', especially appeals to emotion. And proof is *demonstration* (*apodeixis*, i.e. exact scientific proof). And in rhetoric the most cogent form of demonstration is the *enthymeme*. But the *enthymeme* is a form of *syllogism*. And it is the function of *dialectic* to study every form of the syllogism.

93 Especially in 258d ff.

94 *Rep.* 531d ff; cf. Plotinus, *Enneads*, I 3 on the function and ultimate goal of dialectic.

95 See his *De oratore*, II 152–61 and III 56–73; cf. Quintilian, *De institutione oratoria*, I Pref. 10ff, and XII 2, 4ff.

96 In addition to *De doct. Chr.* IV and *De Trin.* Vff already mentioned, see *De doct. Chr.* II 31, 48ff and II 40, 60, on dialectic, rhetoric, and philosophy. Cf. *Conf.* III 4 on his 'conversion' from rhetoric to the

'What then', Socrates asks Phaedrus, 'is the method of writing well or badly?' (258e). His own answer is that good writing depends on the mind of the speaker (or writer) knowing the *truth* about the matter which he is treating of. The naïve Phaedrus has heard only that persuasive exposition is achieved by what *appears* to be true, not by what is really true (259ef). Consequently 'unless the young Phaedrus devote himself sufficiently to philosophy[97] he will never be able to speak adequately about anything'. And that not only in the courts of law and the various public assemblies, but in the private domain as well (261a). If rhetoric is an art (*technê*) at all, it is 'one and the same in all domains of expression ... ' (261e).

But even Plato (or Socrates) must start from basics. And just as order is Heaven's first law, so also ordered exposition is the first law of rhetoric. 'Every discourse must be organized like a living organism (*zôion*),[98] with a body of its own, as it were, not headless or footless, having middle parts and members, arranged in fitting relation to one another and to the whole' (264c; cf. 268d).

The immediate reference here is to *artistic* order and unity. But the terminology suggests also that more conceptualised dialectical order and unity which we saw earlier in the passage quoted from 265de. The implicit reference to beginning, middle and end suggests especially the triple logical sequence of syllogistic reasoning – extended by Aristotle into its counterpart in rhetoric, the *enthymeme.*[99] And Plato repeats all that in his concluding *résumé* of what has been said in the preceding discussion. 'One must know the truth about all the subjects on which one speaks or writes, and be able to define them individually. And then when one has defined them, he must know how to divide them into classes until further division is impossible' (277b). This is the whole business of dialectic – exactly as we find it described and required again by Augustine in *De doctrina Christiana* (II 35,53).

This insistence on philosophy and logical reasoning in no way invalidates the necessity of the literary skills and the psychological awareness that are the proper domain of rhetoric. For the speaker/writer must still 'speak to' the *characters* of his audience (273d), he must adapt his style to them, he must order and adorn his styles accordingly, 'offering to the complex souls elaborate and harmonious discourses, and simple talks to the simple soul' (277c). And therein is the germ

---

quest for transcendent truth in philosophy, after reading Cicero's 'exhortation' to it – that Cicero 'whose style (*lingua*) nearly all admire, but not his philosophical mind (*pectus*)!'

97 See 269e: 'All great *technai* stand in need of keen intellect and high speculation about the origin and nature of the world; for this loftiness of mind and effectiveness in every direction seems somehow to come from such pursuits ... '. And he gives as an instance the influence of the philosopher Anaxagoras on Pericles – 'the most perfect orator in existence'.

98 Obviously the source of Aristotle's simile for artistic unity in *Poetics* XXIII 1; and cf. ch. VII on 'beginning, middle and end', etc.

99 *Rhetoric*, e.g. I 1,2 1357b.

and genesis of the extraordinary psychological analysis of the many types of characters whose condition must be 'spoken to' in Aristotle's *Rhetoric* (II 12–17).

V. DIALECTIC AND ULTIMATE TRUTH

It is not necessary here to trace the later history of this underpinning of rhetoric by dialectic. But when we come to Augustine we discover a dimension of the underpinning that must be mentioned. The briefest explanation is to say that it parallels the function of dialectic in Plato as outlined earlier: the ascent to the ultimate principle of all knowing. In Plato it is the light of the supreme form, the Form of the Good, equivalently God. In Augustine, it is the light of supreme subsistent Truth, *Veritas*, God – a light mediated by the *Logos*, Christ, the ultimate Teacher in all understanding, as we see Augustine closely argue it in the *De magistro*. It is the light of this supreme *Veritas*, which, on epistemological analysis, is found to be the ultimate light enlightening the intellect in every truth understood. It is the ultimate, necessary, *a priori* axiom – necessary because the necessity involved in all unproven but necessary truths demands an ultimate necessary ground.

So imperative is this principle in Augustine's thought that it provides his main proof of the existence of God, in *Confessions* X 6ff and *De libero arbitrio* II 8ff. The relevance of this to dialectic is that, like Plato and Plotinus, it is on the steps of the *a priori* truths, on which depend the various disciplines, that Augustine ascends to their ultimate ground in an eternal, immutable, necessary *Veritas*. We see this dialectic of ascent by degrees elsewhere also in Augustine, e.g. in *De musica* VI and *De ordine* II 12,35ff.

The axioms of mathematics are exemplary for him. He also argues from the *a priori* principles on which he finds that ethics and aesthetic evaluation depend. But in the *De doctrina Christiana* he includes precisely dialectic and rhetoric. They come into an extensive section beginning in II 19, 29, where he treats expressly of the way in which the various inherited Greco-Roman disciplines may be useful, even necessary, to the scriptural exegete. Augustine classifies them from the start into two kinds: the empirical arts invented by man, and the intellectual disciplines that have not been *invented* by man but *discovered* in the mind as *a priori*, firmly established, and divinely ordained. To that second class belong not only dialectic but also rhetoric (II 31, 48ff).

The case of dialectic is obvious – I do not know if any textbook ever explained it more clearly – in all its roles of dividing, distinguishing, defining, inferring. Nobody has more clearly explained the difference between a syllogistically *valid* conclusion and a factually *true* conclusion! 'However, the truth of valid inference was not *instituted* by men; rather it was *noticed* by men and set down, that they might either *learn* it or *teach* it. For it is divinely established in the everlasting rational order of things' (II 32,50).

But the more elaborated style of that effective writing called *eloquentia* is also governed by certain rules (*praecepta*, II 36,54). They may be used to make falsehoods persuasive, but in themselves they have an intrinsic *truth*, 'in as much as they cause things to be understood or to be believed' (ibid.). For it was not men themselves who invented such facts as that 'variety of style keeps an audience attentive and prevents them getting bored' (ibid.). The reason is that, like the rules of dialectic, such facts 'have been *discovered* to have this effect, not *invented* by men to produce it' (ibid.).

A concluding paragraph emphasizes the purely intermediate status of all such *a priori* truths. As in Plato's dialectic, their immutable necessity demands that we ascend to the *source* of their immutable truth and the *ground* of their universal validity. Whoever is unaware of that Source and that Ground may be learned indeed, but he is neither philosopher nor theologian.

Whoever delights in those intermediate truths only to parade his learning among the unlearned, instead of seeking *why* and *whence* those things are true which *he* has merely *perceived* to be true; and not only why and whence they are true, but why and whence they are *immutably* true – such a person can succeed in *appearing* possessed of learning, but no way can he *be* possessed of the supreme metaphysical wisdom (II 38,57).

To come down from those dialectical heights, we should not leave Augustine without referring to a few of his crisp psychological remarks on the actual study of rhetoric. The codification of its techniques is based on the prior *practice* of those who were by *nature* eloquent *before* they knew any rules. They fulfilled them *because* they were eloquent, not the other way round! (IV 3,4). Consequently rhetoric is a matter for youth rather than grown men to spend too much time on! And he quotes Cicero[100] to the effect that unless one can learn this art quickly one can hardly learn it at all! (ibid.). By which comments, naturally, neither Cicero nor Augustine intended any criticism of Hoffmann's admirable *opus* on rhetoric according to Erasmus.

100 *De oratore* III 23,89.

ERASMUS: POEMS 'I LISPED IN NUMBERS'

The first part of this article describes the structure and content of CWE 85 and 86 and outlines the successive stages and themes that emerge from the career of Erasmus as a poet. The second part briefly evaluates the quality of Erasmus' poetry, principally on the basis of 'On the Troubles of Old Age', as a long, mature, and representative sample. For this evaluation the reviewer comments on what is said in CWE 85 about the Classical and Renaissance background to Erasmus' poetry, especially on the techniques of rhetoric. An adequate appreciation of Erasmus' poetry requires that the meaning of rhetoric be understood in more subtle stylistic detail.

***

Here is a rich harvesting indeed, such as one would like to have for many another author in the vast and largely ungarnered acreage of Neo-Latin poetry.[101] The Introduction explains that, while the text of the present edition differs in some respects from that of the Reedijk edition, the latter is not yet superseded. For the details of the textual tradition, Reedijk's critical apparatus has still to be consulted, and also his article in *Humanistica Lovaniensia* 37 (1988), 115–74: 'Towards a

101 *Collected Works of Erasmus*, Volumes 85–6, *Poems*: (Vol. 85: Introduction, Text and Translation; Vol. 86: Notes and Indices). Translated by Clarence H. Miller; edited and annotated by Harry Vredeveld (Toronto: University Press, 1993, lix + 835 pp, 27 illustrations. Clarence Miller's translation of Erasmus' poems follows on his distinguished contributions to the Yale edition of the *Complete Works of St Thomas More*: joint editor of Volumes 7, 10 and 11 (*Letter to Bugenhagen, Supplication of Souls, Letter Against Frith, The Debellation of Salem and Bizance,* and *An Answer to a Poisoned Book*); and single editor of the two-part Volume 14 (*De tristitia Christi*); editor and translator of 'Erasmus's Poem to St Genevieve', *Moreana* 100/481–515. And the harvesting in Harry Vredeveld's fat volume of detailed notes and source references to Erasmus' poems can surely leave further gathering only for the gleaner. He also contributes the lengthy *Introduction*, and four Indices: a *general* index, and three of *references*: biblical and apocryphal; classical; patristic, medieval and Renaissance. And while we are on that subject, the volume of text and translation has indices of first lines, of metres, of medieval and Neo-Latin words, with a list of the poems in chronological order, and a table of the corresponding numbers of the poems between the present edition and the older edition by Cornelis Reedijk (Leiden: Brill, 1956).

Definitive Edition of Erasmus' Poetry'. Vredeveld is to present a new critical text of the poems in Ordo I of ASD – which will follow the organization and numbering of the present CWE edition.

The organization and numbering in question refers to one of the differences between Reedijk's earlier edition and the present one. Reedijk placed the poems in their *chronological* order, of which the disadvantage is that it takes the poems out of the *context* – manuscript or printed book – in which they originally occur. The latter is the order followed in the present edition, as explained on pp. xlix ff. Its advantage is that it provides a more *thematic* arrangement, and consequently facilitates a more thematic understanding of the corpus of Erasmus' poetry.

However, that order too turns out to have a certain overall chronological sequence. This emerges from the first section of the Introduction to the present edition, on Erasmus' career as a poet.

ERASMUS AND THE LOVE OF LETTERS

Viewed as a whole that career divides into two principal stages. The earlier one extended from Erasmus' youth up to the publication of the *Adagia* and *Epigrammata* in the winter of 1506–7. That is the period during which poetry was a conscious and 'professional' pursuit – in varying and diminishing degrees of balance with Erasmus' prose writings. In the second stage, from 1506–7 on, the balance of his interest shifts suddenly and momentously to prose. What poetry he writes from then on is mostly occasional – epitaphs, complimentary poems, records of his reactions to passing events ... . In sum, occasional poetry mostly issuing from the personal pastime of a moment or the passing request of a friend for a service.

Had we no other evidence than that kind of material, we would recognise in Erasmus no talent greater than that of the perennial *genus* of literary amateurs, competent crafters of 'verse and worse'. We would know little about the *sérieux* of his dedication to the art in the earlier period – and nothing about the *insanabile cacoethes scribendi* that was its originating drive. For we know from Erasmus' own words that he was one of those gifted and precocious talents who, as Alexander Pope puts into the mouth of Dr Arbuthnot,

> As yet a child, nor yet a fool to fame.
> ... lisped in numbers, for the numbers came.

One proof of that is in the sheer variety of the Latin metres of which he shows his mastery in the poems, a mastery inculcated by Horace in the *Ars Poetica* (vv 73ff and 251ff). In Poem 2, 'On the Troubles of Old Age', we have Erasmus' own word for his precocious enthusiasm. 'As a beardless youth I was passionately devoted to reading and writing ...I was madly in love with the figures of the rhetoricians and the beguiling fictions of mellifluous poetry ... ' (89ff). This account is from 1506, looking back from the age of forty. A much earlier account tells us the same thing, in a letter of 1489 to Cornelis Gerard. 'From boyhood I have loved literature, and still love it, so much that it seems to me rightly to be preferred to all the treasures of Arabia ... '.[102] The long dialogue, Poem 93, begun between Erasmus and Cornelis in that same year, is an apologia directed against 'the barbarous persons who scorn the eloquence (*eloquentia*) of the ancients and deride learned poetry'. New Testament and patristic authors are cited in support – St Paul, St Luke, St Jerome and Pope Leo the Great. Even when they are writing on moral themes they 'very often fit poetic rhythms into the rhetorical patterns of elegant styles' (93:58ff).

This early fascination of Erasmus with literature in general and with poetry in particular owed something to his father in the first instance. He knew Latin and Greek, had worked as a scribe in Italy, had heard humanist lectures there, and apparently even copied out for himself a small library of classical authors. This primary inspiration got a further impulse from Erasmus' years at school in Deventer and 's-Hertogenbosch (1478–87). At Deventer in particular he got instruction in the writing of Latin prose and poetry, found books to read, and even learned the basics of Greek. And above all he got his first sight and sound of a real live humanist – in the person of Rodolphus Agricola, who visited Deventer several times during the years of Erasmus' sojourn there.

The seeds thus sown first flowered and fruited in the years at Steyn (1487–92), where Erasmus joined the canons regular of St Augustine. Whatever we may think of his later account of the unpropitious circumstances in which he entered there, it did take him into a wider world – of like-minded friends among his companions, and a library well stocked with both Christian and Classical authors. There he 'greatly enjoyed the pleasant company of his contemporaries. They sang, they played games, they wrote verses in competition with one another'.[103] Those were years of intellectual ferment and literary burgeoning, in both prose and verse. But they were years also of emotional ferment. 'It is not uncommon', he confesses later, 'at [that] age to conceive passionate attachments for some of your companions'.[104] In his own case the bond could only be through a shared interest in literary and humanist studies. Many passages in the Letters[105] express that fact in terms that recall St Augustine's descant

102 Allen Ep 23:37-9; CWE1, 37/39–42.

103 Allen Ep 447:352–4; CWE4, 18/385–7.

104 Allen Ep 447:320–1; CWE4, 17/350–1.

105 References are given in n. 19 to the Introduction.

on friends and friendship in light of the trauma he experienced on the sudden death of the dearest friend of his youth:

> All kinds of things rejoiced my soul in their company, to talk and laugh and do each other kindnesses; to read pleasant books together, pass from lightest jesting to talk of the deepest things and back again; to differ without rancour, as one might differ with oneself ... ; to teach one another, to learn from one another ... ; these and such-like things, proceeding from our hearts as we gave affection and received it back, ... kindled a flame which fused our very souls and of many made one.[106]

As with Augustine so with Erasmus – this theme sheds a light on his character. But on that later – what we note here is that friendship, *amicitia*, is the first of the focal themes of Erasmus' poetry in the first of the two periods of his career as a poet. The Introduction to the present edition describes his earliest poems as 'exercises in the rhetoric of friendship' (xv f). They are *more* than 'rhetoric', but doubtless they are that too – in the less loaded and more neutrally technical sense of rhetoric. For the youthful poet is still learning his *craft*. Consequently the influence of such models as Ovid, Horace, and Virgil's *Eclogues* is omnipresent. And the influence is not just on the technique, it is on the tone and mood as well. The reason for the latter is that the course of true *amicitia* runs no more smooth than the course of true love! This is especially likely to be the case when the *amicitia* is as intense as we have to understand its potential to be in earlier ages, less exclusively programmed than ours to what we understand by romantic passion! And in the case of Erasmus, as indeed in the case of Augustine, it is necessary to bear in mind what we have already noted, namely that the bond of *amicitia* is in the shared enthusiasm for literature, especially for poetry at this stage. But Erasmus' enthusiasm could be too much even for that domain. Consequently the recipients of it change and succeed one another in the Letters and the Poems. *Hinc*, as it were, *illae lacrimae*! Hence the frequent tone and mood of the Ovidian elegiac, the Virgilian *lacrimae rerum*, and even the Horatian *carpe diem* – gather ye rosebuds while ye may!

> Therefore...while the years still allow it,
> while youth rejoices and flourishes in its own
> season, let us make use of this time in our
> lives, lest we lose it in vain through our own
> lethargy. Let us seize, sweet friend, the days of
> our youth! (104:25ff)

106 *Confessions* IV 8, 13 (tr. F. J. Sheed).

ERASMUS AND THE LOVE OF GOD

But in fact the poem that ends with those lines represents a deepening of the sense of the *carpe diem* motif, and a transition to a wider thematic range. Composed in elegiac couplets for an unnamed friend, probably in 1489, it is entitled 'On the Mutability of Time'. Although possibly modelled on a poem by the contemporary Italian humanist, Girolamo Balbi, it does not really need to be. For it is constructed, in two almost symmetrical parts, on an amplification of the ubiquitous classical use of the seasons of nature as an image of the seasons of human life. 'Summer slips away and winter follows in turn and melancholy frosts ... Just so, my sweet friend, just so the flower of our lifetime, youth, hastens away ... ' (104:11ff). Erasmus may have been only twenty-three at the time of writing, but the mood and tone already anticipate the long Poem 2, 'On the Troubles of Old Age', written in 1506 for his fortieth year. It is not surprising that Poem 104 should be followed by a number of poems on moral and philosophical themes – on patience, on false goals, satire on the follies of greed and worldly ambition – themes which, as is pointed out in the Introduction, became the core of Erasmus' prose work *De contemptu mundi* in 1491.

For a monk in his monastery – and one shortly to be ordained priest in 1492 – it is a short thematic step from moral to religious themes. And in a letter of 1491 Erasmus announces that he has taken that step – 'for the future to write nothing which does not breathe the atmosphere either of praise of holy men or of holiness itself'.[107] The decision resulted in a climactic flowering of the years in Steyn with a cluster of religious poems in the winter of 1490/91. They included a Nativity poem 'on the shed where Jesus was born ... ' (42), a hymn in praise of St Anne (1), a hymn in praise of Gregory the Great (107), a meditation on 'the four last things' (108), and an 'Ode in Praise of Michael and all the Angels' (50).

Seven or eight lean years followed this climactic blooming. From 1492 to 1495, when Erasmus was secretary to the busy bishop of Cambrai, there is nothing. It was during the years in Paris, where he went in 1495 to study theology, that he found leisure for the Muse again. But she was a frequently moody Muse, querimonious and pecuniary-minded. For Erasmus was now aiming to cut a figure in a world wider than his monastery. For that he needed money – as was so often to be the case in his life. And for money he needed patrons – hence many of the poems of this period. He was often to be a complainer about his health as well. Poem 7 combines both – the flattery of a patron with 'a lamentation about his fate, written when ill'.

Only in 1499 did he turn to poetry again with renewed enthusiasm. That was the year when his pupil, Lord Mountjoy, invited him to England. There he met Thomas More, John Colet, William Grocyn, Thomas Linacre, and of course the

107 Allen Ep 28:8–17; CWE1, 51/9–11.

child prince – the future Henry VIII. These were patrons to be impressed indeed. He did it in another cycle of religious poems, notably on the life of Christ: on the shed where he was born (42), on the preternatural signs that occurred at his death (111), on the feast of Easter and his resurrection (112). But much more obviously to Erasmus' purpose is his 'Ode in Praise of Britain and of King Henry VII and the Royal Children'. And this, by the way, is a poem of which the analytic account on p. xxix f gives us a paradigmatic glimpse of one quality of Erasmus, the *poeta doctus.* For his range of reference to earlier poetry is vast – classical, early Christian, and medieval. And here – in a poem written in some haste and embarrassment as a belated gift to his royal hosts – we see his subtle allusive use of those references. An example of 'intertextuality' *avant la lettre* ... !

Yet somewhere in the years between 1499 and 1506 Erasmus underwent some kind of 'conversion' – to Christ and to his own finally found vocation, the marrying of Christian theology and classical humanist studies. The conversion is implicit in the short poem (36) on the title-page of the *Enchiridion militis Christiani*: 'Christ alone is my Apollo, the source of my vein; his mystic words are my Helicon'. But it is in the long confessional 'Poem on the Troubles of Old Age' that the 'conversion' comes to full and final expression. The year is 1506, Erasmus' fortieth, and obviously his 'dark wood': *nel mezzo del cammin di nostra vita*! It is a turning point, a conversion in its etymological sense, a turning round of a whole life, a farewell and end to that first period of Erasmus' career in which poetry was a principal concern, or at least in some proportion to his prose.

> Farewell ... delightful Muses ...
> Now I am firmly resolved, with all
> the dedication of my heart and soul, to have
> time only for Christ. To me he alone will be
> study and sweet Muses, honour, glory,
> pleasure. He alone will be all things ... .(2:226ff)

ERASMUS AS POET

Faced with two volumes and some nine hundred pages of introduction, Latin text, English translation, and extensive notes, one must not close the account without attempting to evaluate the object of the exercise – the 144 poems of Erasmus. How does he rate as a poet? The Introduction (xxvi) refers to one of Erasmus' own rare comments on the art of poetry. It requires more than just the art of versifying. The words must also be invested with dignity, gravity, charm, attractive imagery, and, above all, flow from 'a certain divine inspiration or *enthousiasmos*'.[108] That double

108 See his *Ecclesiastes* ASD V – 4 258:256–63.

requirement of *technê* and *enthousiasmos* has of course a long classical lineage. Poets are born, not made, Horace said. But nobody knew better than Horace that once born they have to be made as well – trained in the *technê*, the *ars*, of their art. Even the dry and technical Aristotle subscribes to this double requirement. Poetry requires 'either a happy gift of nature or a strain of mania'.[109] Metre is necessary, but it is not for versifying that the name of poet is deserved.[110] We noted earlier the range of Erasmus' metrical mastery. How fares he with *enthousiasmos*?

The Introduction touches only lightly on this aspect of Erasmus' poetry. There is a reference to the 'laboured quality' of some verses in the early Poem 100 (xxviii). Again, on the same poem: 'An apprentice in the workshop of the masters, the poet is only beginning to learn his craft. Lacking a personal voice to express universal experience in a compelling way, he appears to manipulate language as an end in itself' (xxix). As against that, and as to be expected at the author's mature age of forty: 'True to its author's character, the poem 'On the Troubles of Old Age' is a deeply Christian and profoundly experienced piece of work' (xliii).

Technê: For the rest, the literary part of the Introduction concentrates on the aspects of poetic *technique* that need to be understood as background to Renaissance Latin poetry. That is done under two main headings: *Imitation and Models* and (inevitably!) *Poetry and Rhetoric*. The detailed treatment of those topics provides some very illuminating explanation, analysis and illustration. ('On the Troubles of Old Age' is analysed separately under those headings in a section all by itself.) There are however some aspects of those topics which are not included, the absence of which might seem to set the poetry of Erasmus in a more pallid light than is justified.

Depending on how it is explained and understood, *imitation* is a term which may convey the wrong connotation, especially – as indeed the Introduction points out – in our modern context, with its premium on originality and individual genius. It was not so in the classical tradition to which the Renaissance is heir. Indeed, in a certain sense, it has never been so – is not so even now. For all poets in all ages have 'imitated' models. They do so at two levels. On the first level, to get started, as it were, and to learn their craft. Then on a deeper level, because poets always write within a tradition and therefore in a dialogue with the masters of the past.[111] 'Thumb your Greek exemplars by day and by night', Horace orders his compatriots in the *Ars Poetica* (268–9). Greek and Roman theorists and practitioners alike were so aware of the role of *mimêsis* and *imitatio* that it became a technical term in their treatises on stylistics. Quintilian devotes a whole chapter

109 *Poetics* XVII 2.

110 Id. I 8.

111 See for instance T. S. Eliot's 'Tradition and the Individual Talent' (*Selected Essays, 1917–1932*).

to its necessity in his *Institutio oratoria* (*The Formation of the Orator*, X 2). But he is careful to explain that imitation by itself is not enough, 'if only for the reason that a sluggish nature is only too ready to rest content with the discoveries of others' (par. 4). It is a disgrace to owe all our achievement to imitation. No art has ever stood still in history. Artists imitate the past only to acquire the skill and the force to advance to a contribution of their own. Models enable them to do that because they are not inert objects but active inspiring forces. And in any case the qualities of the greatest of them 'are beyond all imitation' (par. 12). Longinus lifts their power to the level of *enthousiasmos*: 'The genius of the ancients acts as a kind of oracular cavern – effluences flow from them into the minds of their imitators' (*On the Sublime*, 13, 2).

On the connection of *rhetoric* with poetry, the Introduction quotes Erasmus himself on the pleasure he takes 'in rhetorical poems and in poetical rhetoric ... '.[112] An excerpt from a letter of Erasmus to Cornelis Gerard implies that only he who has mastered the art of rhetoric can be a master of the art of poetry.[113] Left without qualification that statement is liable to carry the wrong connotation – rhetoric in the pejorative sense that it has had both in classical and modern usage, and indeed in much bad poetry of both classical and modern times! But there is a meaning of *rhetoric* in which it is valid to say that mastery of the art of rhetoric is necessary for the art of poetry. That meaning is the broader and more universal one in which rhetoric extends beyond the domain of mere oratory to encompass the whole art and craft of the effective use of language – in any genre and for whatever purpose, artistic or utilitarian. In this sense rhetoric deals not just with the conventional large *structural* elements, especially of oratory – *inventio, exordium, dispositio, narratio, argumentatio*, and so on. It gets down to the fine details of literary *style*. All the ancient treatises on rhetoric come to that stage in their exposition, e.g. Aristotle in Book III of his *Rhetoric*, Cicero in Book III of his *De oratore*, Quintilian in Books VIII and IX of his *Institutio oratoria*.

The technical term in Latin for this aspect of rhetoric is *elocutio* – one of the terms used also by Erasmus in the excerpt from EP 27 referred to earlier.[114] Quintilian provides a good statement of its meaning and importance. Announcing in the preface to Book VIII (par. 13) that he 'now has to discuss the theory of style (*elocutionis*)', he goes on to cite Cicero to the effect that while *invention* and *arrangement* (*dispositio*) are within the capacity of any man of good sense, *eloquentia* is the mark of the true *orator*, and consequently it was on the rules for the cultivation of *eloquentia* that Cicero himself expended the greatest care.

112 Allen Ep 283:98–100; CWE2, 271/116–17.

113 Allen Ep 27:32–45; CWE1, 50/33–47.

114 See ibid.

> That he was justified in so doing is shown clearly by the actual name of the art about which I am speaking. For the verb *eloqui* means the expressing and communicating to the audience of all that the speaker has conceived in his mind; and without this power all the preliminary techniques of oratory [*inventio, dispositio* etc.] are as useless as a sword that is kept permanently concealed in its sheath. (QUINTILIAN VIII, PREF. 15)

In its section on 'poetry and rhetoric' the Introduction to the present volumes glances only briefly at this *elocutio* (xxxvi f), devoting most attention to those 'preliminary' *structural* elements of rhetoric. Not that these may be ignored either, for a work of literature must have its structure too, as we know ever since Aristotle's metaphor of the 'living organism'.[115] And the present Introduction applies the structures of rhetoric in an illuminating way to 'On the Troubles of Old Age' (xiii ff). The point is merely that for the purposes of critical evaluation the 'living organism' is more than the armature of its skeleton.

Enthousiasmos: And since we have not the space here for such an evaluation of the complete corpus, the poem on old age suggests itself as an appropriate experimental sample. It is Erasmus' most personal poem, one of his longest, and written in the maturity of his fortieth year – perhaps even out of some mid-life crisis.[116] It need not be born of such a specific event. The realisation of how much of life and its opportunities have passed at forty would suffice, especially in light of that earlier 'conversion' announced in 1503, in Poem 36, on the title-page of the *Enchiridion*, a conversion that is the specific climax to which the poem on old age builds up. All the more would this realisation suffice from the fact that illness, the passage of time (with its corollary, the *carpe diem* motif), the coming of death and the four last things, seem to have been an early and recurring preoccupation of Erasmus. In the Poems we glimpse them in 7, 88, 95,101, 104, 108 – not counting the particular pathos of some of his many epitaphs.

On the poem on old age we have already quoted the laudatory judgement of Vredeveld's Introduction – 'a deeply Christian and profoundly experienced piece of work' (xiii). One can agree with that. And perhaps the poem becomes all the more representative a sample of Erasmus if, as the present reader feels, that level of quality is not sustained to the end of the poem. Precisely at its culmination, in the 'conversion' to Christ, the poem lapses into the merely homiletic rhetoric of self-exhortation to a new and amended life (vv 211 to the end).

In the preceding 210 verses of the poem (out of a total of 246), there is rhetoric too. But it is the stylistic rhetoric of *elocutio* as we have explained it. And more

115 *Poetics* VII 4, from Plato's *Phaedrus*, 264c.

116 On that question there is a long introductory note ad loc. in Volume 86.

particularly it is the rhetoric of that special *eloquentia* that carries what has been called 'the poetry of statement' – the personal and confessional but public utterance of truths realised from the facts of individual experience and beaten out into definitive expression in the medium of language made resonant by the processing of form. 'This is my play's last scene, here heavens appoint/My pilgrimage's last mile', John Donne proclaims as the opening to one of his *Divine Meditations.* 'That is no country for old men', proclaims Yeats, opening his great poem, 'Sailing to Byzantium'. 'No medicines can stave off or drive away the monstrous disease that is hideous old age', Erasmus announces as his counter-statement to 'the unparalleled glory' of Guillaume Cop in the noble profession of medicine (vv 1ff and 7ff).

These are the dramatic opening statements, the *exordia*, that set down the theme to be developed and the tone to be sustained in the poems they introduce – to be developed and sustained over a distance in Erasmus' long poem. And of course while in his case a prose translation will give us the 'meaning' of the 'statement' it will not give us the poetic charge and resonance of the statement. Only the *elocutio* of the Latin will give us that. In the space available to us here we can *illustrate* but little of that *elocutio* by quotation, and only point to the rest of it.

There is one general feature of Erasmus' poetic *elocutio* which we see to fine effect again and again in this poem. It is written in couplets composed of the long hexameter followed by the short iambic dimeter catalectic – three-and-a-half iambs. In so much later Latin poetry – and indeed in classical poetry – composed in couplets, the couplet is the unit of sense, and end-stopped. This tends to monotony, and certainly spancels *eloquentia.* Erasmus is a master of the long yet limpid run-on *paragraph* unit of construction and meaning. The effect is to raise the expression of that meaning to the level of literary art – even when that meaning is 'what oft was thought', as it so often is in a poet as steeped in tradition and its *topoi* as is Erasmus, not least in a poem on the well-worn theme of old age. There are splendid examples of that construction in vv 23ff, 29ff, 46ff, 89ff (sustained over 26 lines), 126ff (with their repeated bell-tolls of the fatal *non si ...*), 156ff, 164ff, 190ff, 204ff.

Such passages of course depend on the prior mastery of the poet's craft, his 'art' in the sense of technique. But it is the transfusing and carrying wave of powerful feeling that transmutes this into *poetic* art. Those passages are the expression of something 'profoundly experienced', in the phrase of the Introduction (xliii). They are often imbued with a profound pathos – consistently with one aspect of Erasmus' own character, if we take into account all the other poems we have mentioned as dealing with themes related to old age, e.g. already the early Poem 104 'on the mutability of time'. Lines 23ff of Poem 2 provide an example, culminating in the image of the little that age leaves behind: 'a name and an empty inscription, such as we see everywhere in the epitaphs carved on marble tombs'. An ancient *topos* of course, but experienced and expressed anew in the solemnity and the economy of words in the two hexameters:

> *... nomen titulumque relinquit inanem,*
> *Cujusmodi tuemur*
> *Passim marmoreis inscalpta vocabula bustis (25-7).*

In both hexameters we note how the rhythm is affected by the coinciding of the long syllables of the quantitative metre with the stress accent of the words in the last three feet. And in the second hexameter we observe the bleak effect of the assonance in the vowel *a*. For the same assonance see also lines 65–6 and 69–70; and again the effect of the repeated dark vowel *u* in lines 63 and 77–8. In lines 77–8 we have a good example also of the use of alliteration. And throughout that whole section, beginning in line 65, we have striking examples of the effective use of the second line of the couplet to bring out the pathos of the context. After the long roll of the hexameters comes the lapse back into the sigh of the short iambic lines – the effect of which is again intensified in the rhythm by the high degree of correspondence between the long syllables of the quantitative metre and the stressed syllables of the word-accent.

> *Eheu fugaces, ohe* (70)
> *O saeculi caduci* (72)
> *Ut clanculum excidistis* [the *dulces anni*, 75–6]
> *Furtim avolastis, ohe!* (78)

***

One could go on ... But for our purposes here let these samplings suffice to show that Erasmus wrote poetry as well as verse, that he was possessed of *enthousiasmos* as well as technical mastery. Not always, of course, perhaps not even right to the end of Poem 2. Too much of his poetry is occasional to be always successful. Yet even among the occasional poems there are gems, such as the beautiful 'Salve, Regina' (118), and the exquisite sequence for the liturgy of the Virgin Mother at Loreto (133). Erasmus rarely burns with the Catullan intensity of that short-lived comet that was his own fellow countryman, Joannes Secundus (1511–1536). But he did have enough of the combined fruits of the Muse and the Matinian bee to merit the couplet in the 'Welcome to Erasmus', composed by that same countryman for an expected homecoming (that apparently never took place):

Venerunt Charites, et iuncta Sororibus octo
floribus instravit Calliopea viam.
With him came the Graces, and with her
eight Sisters Calliope strewed his
way with flowers.

Our style may be more classically restrained, but some analogous welcome is due to the joint producers of these two rich volumes of and on Erasmus' *Poems.* 'This is the way we should proceed in applying the pleasures provided by poetry', as one of his own lines (135:35) says:

Sic faciamus in his quae nutrit amoena poesis.

ADDENDUM

TEXTS WITHOUT COMMENT[1]

I

... The intolerable wrestle
With words and meanings ...
(T. S. ELIOT)

1. Genitum non factum,
consubstantialem Patri . . .
(NICENE CREED)

2. ... Unus es Deus, unus es Dominus:
non in unius singularitate personae
sed in unius Trinitate substantiae.

(...)

Et in personis proprietas
et in essentia unitas
et in majestate adoretur aequalitas.
(PREFACE OF THE TRINITY)

3. ... We have found the definition of person: the individual substance of a rational nature (naturae rationabilis individua substantia).
(BOETHIUS, CONTRA EUTYCHEN, 3)

II

Sine ipso factum est nihil quod factum est.
(JOHN 1:3)

1. It would be a hard task to discover the maker and father of this universe, and when we had found him it would be impossible to speak of him to the majority of men. ... We must be content if we can produce an account as likely

1 Translations used, with occasional modifications, are from the *Loeb Classical Library*, the *Nicene* and *Post-Nicene Fathers*, and Frank Sheed's version of St Augustine's *Confessions*.

as another, remembering that I the speaker and you the judges are no more than men, who should therefore accept the likely story on such matters and inquire no further.

(Plato, Timaeus, 28c–29c)

2. He [Symmachus] calls up Rome herself ... in plaintive tones calling for the return of her gods: 'I am free: let me live by my own traditions. Who will reproach me with my thousand years? We all breathe life from the same air under one sun ... ; but we take different roads when we inquire into the being and nature of God, and yet by roads far apart we approach the same secret. Every nation has its own traditions, and that is the road it must travel in search of the great mystery.'

(Prudentius, Contra Orat. Symmachi, 2.80–90)

3. This is our salvation, by this we live and are quickened. This is the rule we follow, never to address the Father without naming the Son, never to know God the Son without naming the Father, never to invoke the Son and the Father without naming the Holy Spirit who is one with them; while yet believing that these so exist as three that I must not make three Gods by separating them, but in these three subsists the being of one God.

(Prudentius, The Divinity of Christ, 237–44)

4. And now [in Genesis] in a dark manner I see the Trinity, which you are, O my God ... Already in the word 'God' who made these things, I recognized the Father, and in the word 'Beginning', in which he made these things, I recognized the Son; and believing that my God is a Trinity ... I searched in his sacred words, and behold I found your Spirit *moving over the waters*. Behold the Trinity, my God, Father and Son and Holy Spirit, creator of all creation.

(St Augustine, Conf. , 13.5)

5. But the 'nature' which creates the whole universe, being infinite, is enclosed by no bounds above or below. Itself it bounds all and is bounded by nothing.

(Eriugena, De Divisione Naturae, 3.1)

6. That One and Two and Three that lives and reigns
For ever and ever in Three and Two and One
Contained by nought itself the all contains,
Was hymned three times ...

(Dante, Parad., 14.28ff)

III

... The profane of every age have derided
the furious contests which the difference of
a single diphthong excited between the
Homoousians and the Homoiousians.

(Edward Gibbon)

1. Having made a careful inquiry into the origin and foundation of these differences I find the cause to be of a truly insignificant character, and quite unworthy of such fierce contention ... The cause which hinders general harmony is intrinsically trifling and of little moment. (Constantine to Alexander and Arius, in Eusebius, Life of Constantine, 2.68)

2. Who can understand the omnipotent Trinity? And yet who does not speak of it – if indeed it be truly the Trinity he speaks of? Rare is the soul that, whenever it speaks of the Trinity, knows what it is saying. Men debate and quarrel, but without peace nobody sees that vision. (St Augustine, Conf., 13.11)

3. But still we are mandated to say something about it, to think it and understand it as far as understanding can reach it, with the sacred science of God as our guide and mistress – our purpose being to provide some measure of material for our praise and blessing of it. (Eriugena, De Divisione Naturae, 2.35)

IV

... The highest Mind thinks itself, and its
thinking is a thinking of thinking.

(Aristotle, Met., 12.9)

1. For our own part we must not let our understanding of these matters be put astray by mental images (*imaginatione*); instead we must rise to the level of pure intellect, and by pure intellect approach each point – to the extent that it is accessible to intellect. (Boethius – 'the last of the Romans, the first of the scholastics'– De Trin., 6)

2. If there be any external reward we may not look for more warmth in the verdict than the subject itself arouses. For apart from yourself, wherever I turn my eyes they fall either on dull sloth or on shrewd jealousy. So that a man would seem to bring discredit on divinity by casting his thoughts before such monsters – not for recognition by them but for trampling under their feet. (Ibid., Pref.)

3. There are in all ten categories which can be universally predicated of all things. ... But when anyone turns these to predication of God all the things that can be predicated are changed ... For when we say God we seem indeed to denote a substance, but it is of a kind that is beyond substance. (IBID., 4)

4. ... The relation in the Trinity of Father to Son, and of both to Holy Spirit, is a relation of identical to identical. If no such relation can be found in all other existing things, the reason for this is the otherness connatural to existents that are transient and perishable. (IBID., 6)

5. If with the help of God's grace I have provided some apt support from philosophic reason for an article of belief that stands firm on its own foundation in Faith, then the joy of a work accomplished will redound to the source whence its accomplishment came. (IBID., 6)

6. With all due respect to the Church's official and classical formulation of the Christian doctrine of the Trinity, and taking for granted an acceptance in faith of what is meant by these formulations, we still have to admit that the assertions about the Trinity in their catechetical formulations are almost unintelligible to people today, and that they almost inevitably occasion misunderstandings. (KARL RAHNER, FOUNDATIONS OF CHRISTIAN FAITH, 134)

V

Deum et animam scire cupio.

(ST AUGUSTINE, SOLIL., 1.2)

1. But what knowledge, specific or generic, have we of that transcendent Trinity? ... The question is, from what likeness or comparison to known things do we believe, so that we may love God whom we do not yet know? (ST AUGUSTINE, DE TRIN., 8.5.8.)

2. *Socrates.* And if the soul too, my dear Alcibiades, is to know herself, she must surely look at a soul, and especially at that region of it in which occurs the aretē of a soul — *sophia*, and at any other part of a soul which resembles this?
   Alcibiades. I agree, Socrates.
   Socrates. And can we find any part of the soul that we can call more God-like than this, which is the seat of knowledge and thought?
   Alcibiades. We cannot.
   Socrates. Then this part of her resembles God, and whoever looks at this will gain thereby the best knowledge of himself.
   Alcibiades. Apparently.
   (PLATO, ALCIBIADES I, 132)

3. I became a great enigma to myself. (St Augustine, Conf., 4.4)

4. This you do not say; *Let man be made*, but *Let us make man*; nor do you say; *according to his kind*, but *to our image and likeness* ... And ... You teach him to see the Trinity of Unity or equally the Unity of Trinity. Thus to the phrase in the plural: *Let us make man*, there is added in the singular: *and God made man*; and to the phrase in the plural: *to our image*, there is added in the singular: *to the image of God*. Thus *man is renewed unto knowledge* according to the image of Him who created him.
(St Augustine, Conf., 13.11)

5. It would be good if men would meditate on three things found in themselves. These three are of course very different from the Trinity, but still I mention them that men may train their faculties on them and verify and realize just how very different they are. The three things of which I speak are being, knowledge, will. For I am, and I know, and I will ... In these three there is inseparable life, one life, one mind, one essence – so much so that it is impossible to effect separation, and yet the three are distinct. Let him see it who can. At any rate he is present to himself; let him then look within himself and see and tell me.
(St Augustine, Conf, 13.11)

6. And our exploration led us to find in the soul a still more manifest trinity, viz. in memory and intellect and will.
(St Augustine, De Trin., 15.3.5)

7. And so I come to the wide spaces and the vast palaces of memory.
(St Augustine, Conf., 10.8)

8. For the gaze of our thought does not return to something except by remembering it, and takes not the trouble to return except by loving it. In this way, in a kind of relation of parent and offspring, love conjoins the vision present in the memory and the vision of the thought formed therefrom. If love did not have knowledge of what it should seek it would not have knowledge of what is love's right object, and this knowledge is impossible without memory and intellect.
(St Augustine, De Trin., 15.21,41)

9. May I remember Thee, may I understand Thee, may I love Thee.
(St Augustine, De Trin., 15.28.51)

Part II:

OCCASIONAL ESSAYS

CONTROVERSIAL TOPICS

IRELAND AND EUROPE:

THE CULTURAL IMPLICATIONS OF UNITY[1]

In order to give some shape to such a wide subject, I should say at the beginning that this paper is like Caesar's Gaul ... it is all divided into three parts. And that, I suppose, is no bad place to start. He was a great unifier, and he had cultural as well as political ideals. He never got as far as Ireland – as was pointed out once by an Italian journalist who, after some un-Roman disorders following a football match in Belfast, reported back to his paper that it was pretty obvious Julius Caesar had never been there. The three parts will consist of something on European civilization, something on the ideal of European unity, and something on Irish culture in relation to European.

For any number of reasons what I succeed in saying will inevitably be incomplete, and possibly unbalanced. The subject is too vast. To anticipate an analogy that I shall use later, the relation between the particular and the universal, it is like setting out to write St Augustine's *Confessions* and the *City of God*. In the nature of things, I have not had time to arrive at anything like final reflection on such a complex topic. Furthermore we are dealing with the European Economic Community, and I know nothing about economics – except when a sandwich on the pavement in one EEC country costs me the equivalent of six shillings. The previous record was four shillings, achieved in Kerry. I also suspect of course that whatever economics is about, culture is not an adequate substitute for it. I have it on the authority of Aristotle (no mean influence on European civilization) that a modicum of material goods is a necessary base for those of the spirit. I should add too that my methodology is bad in that I do not start off by defining culture. My excuse is that I am not strong on definitions, and that in any case those who don't recognize culture at sight will hardly recognize it in a definition. Besides, 'culture' is not a word I like using at all. I might reach for my gun when I hear it, were it not for a suspicion I have that, when the animal has become common subject of polite enquiry, usually in capitals, he is too tame to need shooting. Culture is a *by*-product of all sorts of non-'cultural' activities. It is therefore bound up with everything that makes up a way of life. If most of what I say will concern the

1 Lecture given at a Seminar on the Common Market organized by the Western Student's Movement, Maynooth, April 1972.

'higher' reaches, it has to be understood that they begin on the ground – if not in the compost-heap.

It is necessary also to say that for professional reasons as well as some plain cultural ignorance of my own, I don't know enough about the two terms of this discussion – Irish and European – to be able to make deep judgements on either of them separately, or consequently to make closely-meshed comparisons between them, suggesting in what way integration might be to the advantage or disadvantage of one or the other. Professionally I am an *ancient* European. I refer to the Ancient Classics, so-called. Some of you will be old enough to remember what they were. They used to be the substance of an educated European's culture even among the *penitus toto divisos orbe Britannos*! Along with the Judeo-Christian tradition they are one of the two great taproots of European civilization. I presume you still want European civilization to be Christian. But I doubt if you want me to issue a manifesto on how entry into the EEC can be made to produce another classical renaissance.

Still, the return to sources has been no less characteristic of European civilisation than has been the belief in progress. That fine word renaissance means re-birth. It has been largely appropriated by one Renaissance which in many ways does not deserve the term, because under some aspects it was not a re-birth but the death of a living tradition and a sterile return to the modes of antiquity. There was a true renaissance in the twelfth and thirteenth centuries. That great European, Charlemagne, fostered an earlier one. Boethius in the sixth century sowed the seeds of one when he applied Aristotelian method to theological problems; and again when he wrote the *De Consolatione Philosophiae* which, in the Christian-philosophical outline of the *itinerarium mentis ad Deum* prepares eventually the *Divine Comedy* of Dante. St Augustine in the fourth century made the shock discovery of the analogies between the *Logos* in Platonist philosophy and the *Logos* in St John's Gospel. With that he put something into the European bloodstream which could only be removed by changing the blood. For all I know, John may have intended the analogy when he began : 'In the beginning was the *Logos* ... '. If he did not, it was a remarkable coincidence that the central Hebrew concept of Wisdom should issue in the word that expresses one of the most fruitful concepts of Greek thought, and of the European tradition: *logos* – mind, reason, order, wisdom. And if John didn't intend the parallel, later theologians like Justin and Clement soon drew it out. And even if we do not like to suggest that John was borrowing Greek terminology, it had already been done in one of the late books of the Old Testament, in the Greek-language, Greek-coloured Alexandrian Book of Wisdom.

I said I doubted whether you want me to make a paper on European civilization an apologia for things past and ancient, however classical. And yet here

I am talking about them. It is inevitable. In proof, I will use nothing more subtle than an *argumentum ad hominem*. The Irish culture, which is the occasion of your discussion (how to preserve it in the unsheltered climate of a great new European community), is a thing of tradition, of the past, which we deem it not just valuable but essential to keep with us in the present and carry forward into the future. Well, why should it be otherwise with the European cultural community which we are joining? Each member has its own traditions and its past. And if they can be a community at all, it is because they have cultural elements in common. And as a historical fact their diversity is the diversity of branches on the one great trunk with the two taproots that I have referred to – the Judeo-Christian and the Greco-Roman. And having gone so far into that past, it behoves me to complete the sketch tableau by showing that it runs in the veins of the greatest, if not perhaps the most popular, culture continuators in our day. I have in mind three of the greatest poets of our own time, Claudel, T. S. Eliot and Yeats.

Claudel was steeped in the Bible, in Aeschylus, in the great central philosophical tradition as known through Thomas Aquinas, and in the great mysteries of the Christian liturgy with its symbolic architectonic of the universe and of history and its effective bridging of the gap of transcendence between man and God, activity and meaning, time and eternity. I cannot go into all that. In a more transmissible mode, he is one of the great poets of love – you will have some knowledge of *Partage de midi* or *Le Soulier de satin*? He is both a realist and a romantic because he knows the place of both the flesh and the spirit in love. But above and beyond that conventional description, he is a love poet in a sense that has hardly been known since Dante. Because all love is one love, and love is a cosmic force. And love is a call to transcendence. And therefore its vocation here below is ultimately to death, loss and the separation that is so strong a feature of Claudel. And for that he goes back through Dante to Augustine, to Plato's Eros and the Christian revelation that God is love:

> La femme est une promesse qui ne peut être tenue ...
> Faites de lui un homme blessé
> parce qu'une fois dans cette vie il a vu la figure d'un ange.

In the case of Eliot and Yeats, one of the great themes in the theoretic background to their poetry is both a deeply thought theory of the meaning of culture and a deeply thought theory of its relation to tradition. And for both culture and tradition they insist on the particular and the general – the cultural tradition with a local habitation and a name in the region or the country to which the poet is immediately related and the general European tradition of which that should be a part. Time here permits no more than a reference to all that. As object illustration I refer to a passage from the poetry of each.

One of the themes of Eliot's *Four Quartets* is, as you know, the meaning of time and eternity and their relationship, the turning world and the still point of the turning world:

> Time present and time past
> ... both perhaps present in time future,
> And time future contained in time past.

'The plainest and commonest of words,' says St Augustine, and most of us I suppose are happy enough to leave them so, but they 'are profoundly obscure and their meaning is still to be discovered.' And their meaning is our meaning for we are creatures of time and yet need to transcend it. Do we transcend it by going through it or beyond it? Eliot's plumbing of these depths is in the great tradition of Augustine, who has behind him the *Enneads* of Plotinus. And going still further back, Eliot fuses the *logos* doctrine of Heraclitus and St John to express the transcendent still point of unity that patterns the multiplicity of time. In that abyss Dante saw

> How love held bound
> Into one volume all the leaves whose flight
> Is scattered through the universe around.

So too for Eliot

> All manner of things shall be well
> When the tongues of flame are infolded
> Into the crowned knot of fire
> And the fire and the rose are one.

Yeats's Christianity was scarcely of the Claudel or Eliot kind, and no more did his somewhat magpie philosophy have the logical incisiveness of theirs. And yet his quest was for a comprehensive wisdom and its elements were closely analogous to theirs. The local habitation of the Irish tradition, integrated with the great central European one, the Greek and the Christian. Before the Swedish Royal Academy, he thought of 'how deep down we have gone, below all that is individual, modern and restless, for an Ireland that can only come into existence in a Europe that is still but a dream.' He would have Irish children taught Irish and Greek. 'Irish can give our children love of the soil under foot; but only Greek co-ordination or intensity.' Greek intellect gave Europe form as against all Asiatic vague immensities. And Europe was born not from Salamis when the Greeks defeated the Persian hordes, but from the head of Pythagoras and his numbers, and from the workshop and chisel of Phidias. And one of Yeats's great symbols was the Greek Christian city of Byzantium where amid 'such forms as Grecian goldsmiths make' immortal soul might

> clap its hands and sing, and louder sing
> Of every tatter in its mortal dress.

The incantatory quality of the last quote and others I have used will have to take the place of a longer and more articulated statement of what European civilisation is or was, and why it is of value. If we want some vision of a Europe that is more than a common market and continues to be Europe, it is something like this tradition that is to be built upon. And I hope that I shall have enough time at the end to suggest why, if culture counts at all, Irish culture needs to get a little more inside this culture community as well as inside the economic one.

In the meantime I think I should ask: is the whole thing Utopian? What do the technocrats care about all that? Or what has this cultural past to do with the bizarre and broken cultural phenomena of modern Europe?! The second question is of course already answered by the facts of such figures as Claudel, Eliot, Yeats and others I have not mentioned. Concerning the technocrats perhaps we need not be too pessimistic. This meeting is evidence of people who want Europe to be made by others than just technocrats. And in continental writing since the acceptance of the four new members, there is plenty of evidence of that kind of desire for more than a common market of consumers. And from other sources there is the looming new frightened awareness that the production-orientated economic society has growth-limits, if life and environment are to go on. Other values may just have to be taken into account. Is man made for the market or the market for man?

But there are more immediate reasons for being optimistic. Not on bread alone does man live – otherwise we may suppose that the IRA wouldn't make a wreck of the tourist trade. And the ideal of a united Europe, a wider supra-national society, is in fact an age-old one. So much of our experience and so much of the history we have studied is taken up with the competition and the conflicts of nation-states that we can hardly visualize any other state of affairs. The Treaty of Rome is highly symbolic because of course the Roman Empire was a united Europe politically and culturally. That unity collapsed but the idea and ideal it represented haunted the Dark and Middle Ages.

The ideal did not even begin with the Romans. The Greeks arrived at it in the fourth century BC and in circumstances strikingly similar to those which have forced it again on modern Europe. Isocrates seeing Greek civilization threatened by the disunity of Greek city-states from within, and by barbarism from without, devoted his whole life to the political ideal of Pan-Hellenism which would sustain the cultural ideal to which 'the name Hellenes suggests no longer a race but an intelligence and ... is applied rather to those who share our culture than to those who share a common blood'. It was an achievement that history had reserved for the Romans as the Greek intelligence was quick to see. Witness the Greek historian, Polybius, marvelling at the convergence of the lines of universal history on Rome in the second century BC. It is not necessary to detail here the dimensions this vision took on among the Romans themselves, in Livy and Virgil. 'It was already written in the book of Fate ... that this great city of ours should arise, and the first steps to be taken towards the founding of the mightiest empire the world has known next to God's.'

His ego nec metas rerum nec tempora pono;
Imperium sine fine dedi ...

It is more important to note that the Christian historians, far from suppressing this secular dream, took it over and interpreted the preparation of the universal society and civilization as providential and parallel to the preparation of the universal religion. So, especially, Eusebius the father of Church history. Like the earlier theologians Justin and Clement, he takes up that profound concept of the *Logos*, at the heart of both the Greco-Roman and the Judeo-Christian traditions and makes it the key to a profoundly unifying interpretation of history. The Judeo-Christian and the Greco-Roman cultures were separate but parallel. The one *Logos* was at work in both. He imparted truth to both civilizations; he directed the movement of history in both. They flow providentially together into one at the Incarnation – just at the moment when the pax Romana was at its most extensive and civilized.

At one and the same kairos, from one and the same will of God, there came into being two roots of good for mankind – the Rule of Rome and the Revelation of God.

And in the universal society of the Christian Constantine he saw the reflection on earth of the universal society of God which (he) prayed would endure for all time.

Now I know of course all about recent concern with liberating ourselves from the Constantinian Age. But even though we may be less sanguine than Eusebius about particular civilizations – (*Toutes les civilisations sont mortelles*), I don't see how we can have religion and civilization without some such ideal of stability and universality ...

In any case the Barbarian invasions shattered this too neat tableau and the Urbs Aeterna itself was sacked in 410. And the Christians were as shattered as the pagan poet who saluted the *regina pulcherrima mundi* which 'made one fatherland for disparate peoples' – *Fecisti patriam diversis gentibus unam*. Out of the ruins, Augustine produced not the suppression of Rome but its extension into the greater universality of the City of God.

Charlemagne revived the imperial and the cultural ideal, and, embodied both in the New Rome of Aix-la-Chapelle, it survived the tenth century. But nostalgic elegies to *Roma Nobilis Orbis et Domina* ever and again look back from chaos to a lost unity.

Dante was born into a civilization where, culturally, Europe was one as it had not been since the days of Rome, and was not to be again. The extraordinary Renaissance of the twelfth and thirteenth centuries had one language, one religious ideal, one philosophical method, one poetry, one architecture, one continent, within which the student or the master could move from Oxford to Paris or Bologna and find the one kind of great school or university. From Athens, Rome, and Jerusalem, it produced a synthesis that has made the thirteenth century 'the most glorious of centuries' in religious and secular poetry, in the philosophical and theological *summae*, in the great cathedrals, and in the poetry of Dante, whom Eliot has described as the most universal of poets.

But the intellectual order lacked one thing if it was to last ... the same thing that the Greece of Socrates lacked: the political order of a stable, universal society. And Dante looked back to the Rome of Virgil and the ideal of a universal temporal order, to the Rome of the Popes and the ideal of a universal, spiritual order. Both powers are independent and parallel and both derive from God. Each derives historically from the development of a chosen people. And it is providential that both should have their seat at Rome. We can imagine he would have said the same thing of the Treaty of Rome. We should not allow our scepticism, no less facile perhaps in its way than medieval providentialism, to throw out the essential with the accidental. The essential is the age-old ideal he utters, and its analogy to twentieth-century attempts at a universal order like the League of Nations or the United Nations. Within that, even the European Community would be a small enough unit. But of course quantity is not our concern. The aim of the universal society is not a gigantic superstate to replace the already sufficiently oppressive nation states. A Europe united politically must still allow for its regions. Just as the idea of a unity of European culture must be understood as allowing for and even demanding the uniqueness of regional variations. The unity is to be in diversity, not uniformity. 'For the health of the culture of Europe, two conditions are required ... that the culture of each community country should be unique, and that the different cultures should recognise their relationship to each other' (T.S. Eliot).

I have not left myself with much time to suggest what the European cultural ideal should mean to Ireland, and what reasons there are for setting our faces towards it. But some of these are obvious and easily stated ... at least in a general way. And I do not intend to go beyond stating them in a general way. I am not a cultural anthropologist or theorist or whatever the term is. And my knowledge of neither modern European culture nor of Irish culture is sufficiently detailed to justify my attempting any close integration of the two.

First of all, there is the advantage accruing, from being at the centre or sources of anything. It is from the centre and the sources that we get understanding and appreciation. And on the hypothesis that there is something identifiable as European civilization and that it has a value, the closer we are to the sources, the centre, the mainstream, obviously the better our understanding and appreciation and the greater our enrichment. It is equally obvious, whether we blame history or our geographical situation or just ourselves, that we can hardly be said to have been centripetal Europeans for quite some time past. Things might have been different if Agricola had been able to follow through that thought he had in the year AD 81 when he looked across at us from the shores of Cumberland or North Wales and thought we might be brought within the Roman imperium with just one legion. The first of many optimists about Ireland, one British commentator has remarked. That, of course, would have deprived us of our Celtic heritage ... but then so did it the Britons and the Gauls and much of Central Europe. And it is what the Romans put in its place that we have unwittingly been praising. In any case we were left without our Celtic heritage.

And a couple of Barbarian peoples, the Angles and the Saxons, replaced the Romans in Britain, and Britain became an island with a non-Roman language, and we became an island behind an island, and too oppressed and unhappy for 800 years to have time for anything but to cover the shame of our misery. And then for anything but the sound of our introverted nationalism. And recently when we have begun to look out again, it has been more to what I believe is called mid-Atlantic culture than to continental Europe.

Even now, it is hardly the cultural ideal which is the immediate motive for looking towards Europe. If England goes in, can we afford to stay out? We must respect the economists for their business, but we who are looking for something higher in Europe may say, I think, that European civilization is central in an absolute sense. I mean European culture is central. That of course is dangerous talk in these sociological, anthropological, relativistic, anti-racial, egalitarian times. But if culture is worth talking about at all, it must be something more than anthropology. There must be higher and lower in the scale of values. And that combination of Greece and Rome and Jerusalem is surely unique in its material, humanist, and spiritual achievements. The emphases on one or the other of these domains may be unbalanced or in conflict at any given time. But that after all is because they are so clearly articulated in the civilization as a whole.

But we must not misinterpret the notion of the centre and seeking the centre. In 'going into Europe' economically we are not going to emigrate physically as from a declining West. After all, we want to save all these 'wests'. In going into Europe culturally no more should we understand it as a total intellectual and spiritual emigration. It used to be said that every cultured man should have two parties ... his own and France. When we speak of the centrality of European civilisation, it means that every man should have two parties ... his own and Europe. In speaking of centres, we should think perhaps not of a circle but of an ellipse, with two gravitational centres.

An individual man cannot but be himself and yet belongs by a common nature and his social dimension to a more universal order. So with individual cultures and a more universal culture. It is in the nature of what is living to diversify. And what exists is always the particular. Anything as organic as cultural values will remain particularized. And besides, this universal European culture is analogous to a universal concept – it exists only in the particular kind of civilization, but with a core of individuality. There is no greater European than Virgil in the *Aeneid*, yet he is Roman. There is no more universal poet than Dante in the *Divine Comedy*, and yet it is particularized in a personal experience, a particular city, the philosophy, theology and cosmology of an age. We don't achieve universality in art and culture by a rocket-launch into the Empyrean. It is to be found only by digging down deeper into the ground we stand on. Yeats knew it, and not only the poet but the painter, who never went the rounds of the schools, and the styles that change every decade. And that is perhaps a roundabout way of saying that this Irish Ireland, if we think it exists, not only has nothing to fear from Europe, but it had better exist, if we want to be culturally European. We will not absorb European cultural and spiritual values just by being 'in' Europe (if only because the tradition I have sketched as the European tradition is surely in no great state of spiritual health any more than our own). In the past fifty years in Ireland, we have built too many cultural illusions on what would automatically happen merely by crossing certain imaginary frontiers. It was the winning of freedom. It was the teaching of Irish. It was the setting-up of Irish television. Now it is Europe. Not free merely but Gaelic as well! Well, has it happened?

The *affaire* with Europe will be like any other *affaire*. It will be enriching to the extent that we bring to the other our own identity, our own personality, what Yeats called unity of being.

We do have *being* – there is a way of feeling and seeing the world which is Irish and Celtic. The whole corpus of Irish art from the beginning down to a Jack Yeats' painting is evidence of it. And in so far as it represents what Arnold called natural magic and a sense of mystery, it is something that we might usefully contribute to Europe – it is sometimes suggested that those qualities first came into the medieval romances of Europe from the Celts.

But we do not have unity of being. Our historical development has been too broken. And our present identity is firstly, impoverished, and, secondly, fractured along a number of lines: linguistically: Irish/English; socially: country/town; politically: nationalist/unionist; religiously: Catholic/Protestant. Plenty of other societies have these divisions, but in Ireland they are abrasive, chauvinistic, poisonous, self-consuming, resulting in the image of Joyce's old sow that eats its farrow or 'The Great Hunger' of Patrick Kavanagh. What culture can integrate with another – anymore than a person can – when its own personality is as starved, soured and vindictive as Joyce's 'Silence, exile and cunning', or Kavanagh's mother-image, 'tall hard as a Protestant spire', with 'a venemous drawl/And a wizened face like moth-eaten leatherette'?

This schizophrenia must be cured before we can integrate with Europe. But part of the cure will be the effort to make contact with that *other* that is beyond and bigger than ourselves.

And beyond the cure Europe will help us to ***grow*** in a way that for reasons, I think not just of historic but also of psychology, Irish Celtic civilization has not yet grown. In explanation I can only be brief and provocative. The Celts have a very powerful imagination and a very distinctive temperament. These are essential to great cultural achievements. But even without Longinus on the Sublime, it is obvious that intellect is necessary as well. Only intellect can analyze, order, systematize, construct. Without intellect, imagination is a formless matrix. A great culture must be more than that. It is a total order in political theory, literature, philosophy and the arts. That is what Greece was, what Rome was, what the European tradition is. Now we naturally cannot expect every civilization to produce the complete consort of an Athens, or a Rome, or a Florence, but we can expect every real culture to produce its own minor order, in which imagination and intellect complement and control each other. I see in Celtic civilization plenty of imagination but I am not so sure about the intellectual construct. Until it achieves that it will be incomplete even in its own uniqueness. When that completeness is achieved, it will still be *too* unique, particular, and provincial, until it is further controlled by integration with the European universal. 'Every literature must have some sources which are peculiarly its own, deep in its own history; but also, and at least equally important, are the sources which we share in common: that is, the literature of Rome, of Greece and of Israel' (T. S. Eliot). In the central tradition of European philosophy, the universal and the particular do not exist separately. And if you drink of the fountainhead of all European philosophy, i.e. Plato, the universal is even more real than the particular.

THE BURNING OF THE BOOKS

The following pages are in answer to a request for some comments on the results of the introduction of the vernacular into the liturgy. They are a little overdue. And they might have remained even more so were it not for a spur supplied by recent echoes of a new problem in the burning of books. Apparently old missals are slow burners. Any criticisms made concern not the fact of the introduction of the vernacular, but the kind of vernacular introduced. The remarks are summary, and themselves open to the criticism of greater expertise in the domain concerned.

The examination of texts is confined to the Order of the Mass. The gist of the criticisms arising from it might be given in the notion of reductionism. But no useful purpose is served by piecemeal criticism of texts if we do not first say what we think liturgy is, and, by implication, what qualities we think liturgical language ought to have. 'Reductionism' will then be self-explanatory.

Etymologically and, in fact, liturgy means a public action. And before ever we get to the plane of religious action, 'public' has important consequences for the *mode* of action and the speech that goes with it. What is done in public is expected to have more *form*, more style, still more if it is done *for* the public and in some sense *by* the public. Even an age like our own which has so broken down the distinction between public and private, formal and informal, and makes public display of the 'sincerity' of personal and instinctual spontaneity, even such an age, it has been observed, runs to ritual in its 'pop'.

There is a deeper reason for this 'formality' than just 'keeping up appearances'. To adapt a phrase of Aristotle's, man is the most formalizing of animals. He 'dines', when all that is really necessary is that he should eat, or just grub. He 'dresses', when all the climate requires is that he put on clothes – or a loin-cloth. He sings, when he might say. He dances, when he might walk. He pays court, when it would be more efficient to put the question and get the answer. He makes the tragic pattern out of the disorder of destruction and death. He makes ritual and ceremony out of thoughts and desires, which, if they can be expressed at all, might be thought to pass between the individual alone and God.

From what deep-seated impulse does all this 'formality' spring?

In the first place he enjoys it. He liberates himself from subjection to the material limitations of his nature by transposing its imposed activities into a new key in which they become life-enhancing. In the second place, to impose form is to organize, that is to order, to control, to reduce to unity, to give meaning. But meaning is not just *imposed* by form. Form expresses the deep-felt meaning that cannot be expressed in any other mode. Even philosophy can hardly do without some version of the matter-and-form pattern. All art is formal in this sense. It expresses meaning by re-presenting the object organized in such a way as to make visible the 'form' or the 'idea' in the matter.

Now the liturgy is also an art form of a very special kind. It expresses man's relationship with God. It is therefore an area of meaning, where, above all others, language reinforced by all the resources of form is indispensable. Mystics need symbols. Philosophy and theology need a theory of analogy to justify their talking about God at all. Hence ritual action, that is form, not formalism. Hence ceremonial action, that is not 'empty' ceremony but sacral *caerimonia*. Hence *mysteries*, that veil while they reveal what is invisible. Hence 'hieratic' liturgical language, not elevated and set apart for its own sake but so that it may the better carry the grandeur of God and the deeps of man's relationship with him. It has been so from the *Persians* of Aeschylus to *Murder in the Cathedral*.

It is against this kind of background that Christine Mohrmann, for instance, begins a series of lectures on 'Liturgical Latin' by referring to a basic distinction between language as communication and language as expression.[2] The terms are not self-explanatory. We might argue, indeed hope, that expression is also communication. For *expression* as used here is precisely the attempt to communicate *more* than is possible in the use of language described here as communication. For the distinction is the simple but basic one between *ex-pressing* and talking *about*, between the mimetic language of art and the discursive language of science, between the sign which aims somehow to re-present the object and the sign which merely points to it. The aim of the one is wholeness of evocation and totality of response, of the other selectivity of denotation and precision of understanding.

It is obvious that the clarity which is the most important virtue of 'communication' is not enough for 'expression'. Clarity depends on abstraction and selection. It has to be at the expense of what is left out of the object and out of the potential of the knower's response to it. Aristotle remarks that it is the mark of an educated man not to demand more clarity than the subject matter allows. He might add that it is also the mark of an educated man not to demand more clarity than the particular mode of knowledge allows. It was a point well understood by ancient literary critics. The expressive, says Quintilian (I translate his term, *ornatum*, into what it really means) is what goes beyond the merely clear and proved.

It is in poetry and literature that we are most familiar with the use of language that aims beyond the merely clear. In other words in the domains of deeper seeing

2 Christine Mohrmann, *Liturgical Latin: Its Origins and Character* (1957).

and higher life where the expressive medium of language must carry a higher charge of significance. There is no such domain that goes deeper than liturgical action and art. 'We are concerned with a transcendental contact between the praying individual and the divine being' (op. cit.). It is easy to see how inadequate a criterion of style a crisp, clipped clarity is in such a context:

> You use the snaffle and the curb all right,
> But where's the bloody horse?

The work I have quoted goes on to show how, from the very beginning, the language of the liturgy in Greek and in Latin, while being in the vernaculars of the time, differentiated itself from the language of everyday life. ' ... And the modern liturgists who would like to view the earliest eucharistic celebration as a "gathering round the kitchen table" certainly do not find support in the testimony of the earliest terminology.'

Of course we must be careful at this point to make clear what exactly we are defending. It is not necessary to defend archaism in order to defend the point at issue. Although in fact it seems that archaism was an element in both Classical and Christian Roman liturgical language. But it was only one element in a rich compound. Christian Latin inherited, along with the idioms and figures of the scripture, the always somewhat formalized literary language of the Classical tradition. But Christianity did what the Classical tradition mostly avoided doing. It brought in the language of the people. So much so that Christian writers of Latin created a literary revolution both in their theory and in their practice. The revolution sprang from the realization that the language of the 'sublime' was not necessarily 'sublime language' in the conventional and traditional sense. This realization was simply an extension of the significance of the incarnation. The *humile* in matter and in form was or could now be instinct with the *grande*.

The point to which such facts lead is this. To compare the present vernacular unfavourably with the Latin or with earlier English translations is not the same thing as to be an archaizing *laudator temporis acti*. On the contrary it is in some sense to carry on the meaning of so many literary revolutions. Poetry and literature ever and again try to return to the dialect of the tribe, which is the dialect of life, in which the tribe 'communicates'. But then the dialect has to be processed so that, over and above 'communication', it becomes capable of 'expression'.

Let us look at some items from the Order of the Mass in the light of those principles. There is too high an incidence of flattening out, levelling down, summarising paraphrase rather than translation – reductionism as I have called it – and sometimes just bad writing by any standards. (There is also, of course, some of the opposite kind of failure – all the more striking when it has the other as a foil – the will-to-elevation which falls into a flat 'frigidity' in the English idiom, like 'preparing ourselves to celebrate the sacred mysteries'. But in summary remarks it is as well to keep our lines simple.)

The first extensive sample to hand is in the translation of the *Confiteor*. Here one might begin by asking why the Latin itself felt it necessary to interfere with the parallelism between the first and the second halves of the prayer, in the list of those to whom confession is made and who are then asked to intercede. The first half now omits them altogether. The second half preserves a resumé. The English has an additional reduction. For whereas the Latin still keeps the emphatic triple *mea culpa*, the English compresses that forceful elaboration to a single phrase: *through my own fault*. Perhaps it is one of those things which one should not press too much. But the Irish version does manage to preserve the Latin repetition. And the English substitute is at least weak, if not banal, in comparison with the original – which has the added force of a climactic position in the centre of the prayer.

As against this reduction the Latin *fratres* is expanded to *my brothers and sisters* – the form used also in the introductory Invitation. Reactions to it run the risk of being subjective. But the translators themselves show a little uncertainty when they allow other forms 'which seem more suitable under the circumstances', including the old-fashioned 'brethren'. 'Brethren' is certainly free of the false overtones of 'brothers and sisters'. It is hard to free that phrase of the constricting suggestion of the physical relationship. At best it sounds 'familiar' in the wrong way. At worst it runs the risk of a very un-artistic and un-Roman fault – the descent into sentimentality, into the loving community of *schmalz*.

No doubt there were theological reasons for restructuring the Latin version of the old Offertory prayers – *Suscipe, sancte Pater* ... and *Suscipe, sancta Trinitas* ... But they have not been improved upon. This is in part a matter of the form. *Domine Deus universi* is not the equal of *Sancte Pater, omnipotens, aeterne Deus*. And still less so when the monumental opening imperative *Suscipe* that precedes it is suppressed and the notion of offering is relegated to a subordinate clause (*quem tibi offerimus*). This last point suggests that it is also in part a matter of content, or reductions which, it might be suggested, were not necessary. For instance, the suppression of the evocation of the power and the range of the offering – *pro omnibus circumstantibus, sed et pro omnibus fidelibus christianis vivis atque defunctis; ut mihi et illis proficiat in vitam aeternam*. And of the concept of memorial – *ob memoriam passionis ... Jesu Christi ... et illi pro nobis intercedere dignentur in coelis quorum memoriam agimus in terris ...*

Be that as it may, the English version reduces the force of the form still further. The new Latin versions, despite the suppression of *Suscipe* and the relegation of the notion of offering, still keep that notion explicit and active in a finite mood. In the English there is no explicit action of offering. 'We have this bread to offer ... We have this wine to offer ... '. I am not talking about the theological implications of the words 'to offer' – although theologians have often fought for a long time about words. And the stylistic point might seem a small one, if we were considering the English in isolation. But we are not. We are considering it in relation to two Latin originals.

In the same prayers the deliberate parallelism of *fructum terrae et operis manuum hominum* and *fructum vitis et operis manuum hominum* is somewhat modified through two different translations in the English. But that is insignificant in comparison to the figure of speech with which the second prayer ends. Whatever force may remain to *potus spiritualis* in Latin, where at least we are not distracted by the banal connotations of words in daily usage, 'spiritual drink' in English is a concoction of the flattest beer. It belongs to the worst class of tired 'spiritual' cliché.

The Prefaces are more systematically pitched at a stylistic level comparable to that of the originals, even to the extent of retaining the archaic 'thy' in the Sanctus. But in the details there are some omissions or paraphrases, which not only do less than justice to the Latin, but are inadequate even in the English taken on its own. *Domine sancte Pater* is constantly reduced to simply 'Father'. That is not only inadequate to the notion of 'Lord' and 'Holy Father'; it is also inconsistent with the hieratic intentions of the whole invocation that culminates in *omnipotens sempiterne Deus.* Further there is a structural and rhythmic parallelism between *Domine sancte Pater* and *omnipotens sempiterne Deus* that is entirely lost in the reduction to 'Father'.

The phrase 'we do well' is wishy-washy in itself, and it fits badly into its elevated context. It is very much more strikingly inadequate when we see it as a rendering of: *Vere dignum et iustum est, aequum et salutare.* The Latin has rhythm, parallelism, monumentality. The English has none of these qualities, and it is a totally slack resumé in a context where there is no need for resumé and no justification for doing it badly.

The body of the Preface for the Dead is one of the finest in this genre in the Latin:

> *In quo nobis spes beatae resurrectionis effulsit,*
> *ut, quos cortristat certa moriendi condicio,*
> *eosdem consoletur futurae immortalitatis promissio* ... etc.

There is strong stylistic structure, precision of thought, and powerful feeling that is still distanced from sentiment. In the English the structure is well enough rendered. But the precision of the thought is blurred, and with it the precision of the feeling. 'The sadness of death' is not the same, or as great a thing, as *certa moriendi condicio.* 'Your faithful people' has connotations that are not those of *tuis fidelibus.* 'The body of our earthly dwelling' is possibly ambiguous. All those phrases, as well as 'lies in death', and 'the bright hope of immortality', introduce an element of too self-conscious feeling, of the vague rhetoric of emotion, that is foreign to the powerful but precise and controlled feeling of the Latin.

It is in the translation of the Roman Canon, that 'very special and unique . . . combination of Romanitas and Christianitas ... ', [3] that the most serious inadequacies occur. They are due to a systematic process of reduction that takes account precisely of only one function of the original language – 'communication' – to the ignoring of 'expression', as these terms have been explained. In this process nuances of thought are omitted and varieties of false feelings are introduced. Thus :

> *Te igitur, clementissime Pater ...*
> *Supplices rogamus ac petimus ...*

becomes: 'We come to you. Father, with praise and thanksgiving ...'. It is perhaps a small point, but a point none the less, that the strong linking *igitur* is omitted. It is of more moment that 'Father' strikes an entirely different note from *clementissime Pater.* The hieratic is gone, replaced by the excessive intimacy of 'Father'. Excessive not because Christ did not teach us to say: 'Our Father ... ', but because that is not what the Roman Canon is about at this point. Consistently with the dominant infidelity of 'Father', 'we come to you' is at best a very watered down paraphrase of the solemn *Supplices rogamus ...* . When juxtaposed with the added 'praise and thanksgiving', it is seen to have nothing at all to do with *Supplices rogamus ...* .

In the *uti accepta habeas ...* the elevated *haec dona, haec munera, haec sancta sacrificia illibata ...* is summarized into 'these gifts'. On the score of intelligibility, clarity of 'communication', we cannot question it. It is quite accurate. But what are we after? The *perspicuum* alone, in Quintilian's phrase, or *quod perspicuo plus est*? The Latin of the Roman Canon is after both. Mention has already been made of the omission of similar elements in the new Latin Offertory Prayers. All the more reason for being at some pains to preserve them here.

In the Commemoration of the Living, *famulorum famularumque tuarum* becomes 'your people'. The expression is as colourless in feeling as it is vague in significance and unfaithful to the strong, concrete and simple original. And the reason for change is hard to see. It may well be arguable that the high biblical

3 Christine Mohrmann, op. cit.

sense of 'servant' is lost on the modern hearer. If so, it is a pity. But the notion should be preserved. And 'people' makes no attempt at all.

The rest of this balanced, rhythmic and climactic prayer is characteristically shortened and brought down to a level that is pedestrian in comparison with the original:

> You know how firmly we believe in you
> and dedicate ourselves to you.

It may be paradoxical to speak of impersonality in a prayer but it is an artistic virtue. And 'you know how ... we ... ' is too personal in the wrong sense, if not self-congratulatory, in comparison with

> *Quorum tibi fides cognita est ...*

And if there was an intention to reproduce the balance of the original, it has failed, because the simple effect of *et nota devotio* is lost in the fussy patter of the English rhythm. The parallelism and forward movement maintained by the triple anaphora of *pro quibus ... pro se ...* etc. is broken down. One of the two parallel and climactic clauses that it carried is dissolved altogether – *pro redemptione animarum suarum*. The other – *pro spe salutis et incolumitatis suae* – is displaced to the end. This displacement throws away the incomparable Latin close of sense and rhythm in *aeterno Deo, vivo et vero*. In this same phrase the English drops *aeterno*. 'Well-being' is flat for *salutis*. And *spe*, like *aeterno*, is dropped – neither of them such a negligible factor in the human or Christian scheme of things that the vernacular liturgy should not make some effort to preserve the mention of them.

In the *Hanc igitur* 'Father' as a rendering of *Domine* is subject to the same reservations as it is for *clementissime Pater* in the *Te igitur*. As is also the omission of the linking *igitur*. 'Accept' is a reductionist version of *quaesumus ... ut placatus accipias ...* . It is consistent with this tone that *servitutis nostrae* should be omitted altogether. And in this whole context, the connotations of the English 'family' are further than usual from those of the Latin *familia*.

'We pray that ...' is weak for *Supplices te rogamus ... iube ...* . Directness and force is lost by the omission of the second person *te*, and of the second person imperative *iube*. More serious is the typical omission of in *conspectu divinae maiestatis tuae* after 'your altar in heaven'.

In the Communion of the Dead *famulorum famularumque qui ...* is once again cut down to 'those who ... '. 'Those who have died' is undoubtedly the 'communicational' equivalent of *qui ... dormiunt in somno pacis*. But undoubtedly also it is not the 'expressive' equivalent, however much we might hesitate about translating that figure literally into English. This, however is what the translation goes on to do in the very next sentence: 'all those who sleep in Christ' for *omnibus in Christo quiescentibus*. Whatever about *dormiunt* in the context of Latin imagery, 'sleep' in English is a dubiously enriching evocation of the next life. But in any case the Latin here is *quiescentibus*. It suggests the much richer and more positive Christian notion of *requies*, the repose of the *cor inquietum*, the fulfilling *peace* that is mentioned in the same sentence.

In the Rite of Communion, the translation of the *Agnus Dei* provides the opportunity for a glance at the comparative merits of two possible approaches to the problem of rendering the solemnity of the Latin without doing violence to contemporary English. In accordance with the principle of breaking down complex Latin sentences into 'simple' English ones, the relative clause: *qui tollis peccata mundi* is made into a co-ordinate clause in English: 'You take away the sins of the world'. There can be no great quarrel with the result. And one would not dare to raise any question about a preference for the 'simple' sentence were it not that the translation of the *Gloria* does not follow this principle. The relative clause is let stand here, and even the archaic form of the personal pronoun: 'Thou who takest away the sins of the world.' It is of some note, because it seems superior to the 'simple' sentence of the *Agnus Dei*, and the *Gloria*, as a whole one of the most successful translations in the Mass. Such a feeling of course may be influenced by greater professional familiarity with archaisms than most of the 'faithful people' will have! However, it might also be that any of us will rise as high as a piece of writing takes us. And, when all other systems are 'go', we can ride even a subordinate clause with an archaic pronoun in its nose-cone! And with that feeling one might go for '*Behold* the lamb of God ... ' at the special moment of the raising of the Host before Communion. 'Look' (Knox and the Jerusalem) would be a bit too self-consciously breathless. And 'This is ... ' is not what either the Roman Missal or St John wrote in the first place.

But then again one would willingly tolerate a minor puff of authentic breathlessness in exchange for deliverance from the great affected gasp of it that blows in 'Happy are those who are called to his supper.' Truly 'there is no duty we so underestimate as the duty of being happy'! 'Happiness' unqualified is incapable of getting anywhere near the Latin *beati*. And as for 'supper', while it obviously passes in the defining context of the Consecration and the Last Supper, outside that it is surely flat-footed, and made doubly so by the bucolic associations of '*called* to his supper'.

These remarks have so far been deliberately confined almost exclusively to comments on the English in relation to the Latin original. The non-liturgist risks wetting his feet when he goes beyond that. Still the liturgical action as a *whole* is, or used to be, an artistic action – it used to be conceived for instance as a drama. That fact entitles the non-liturgist to venture a little beyond a critique of the language – into what Aristotle called the 'spectacle'. Any number of points suggest themselves here, at least as question marks, because in his ignorance the non-liturgist cannot always know what is happening by liturgical rule and what by whim, slippage or indifference. For instance, is a full Gregorian Mass now excluded by liturgical decree or by one of the other factors I have mentioned? Is it because a *Latin* lectionary does not exist or because it shall not be provided that, even in private, one must take the readings in the English of some committee rather than in the vital language and rhythms of St Jerome? Has the age-old music of the altar bell actually been declared offensive to pious ears, or has it merely become offensive to those ears to whose non-conformism we shall conform? It cannot be due to any preference for the *silentium mysticum*, as we shall see in a moment. And no more can it be due to the rediscovery of a classical taste for functional austerity and *dépouillement*. For then it should be visible also in the actions and the shape of the liturgy.

An artistic whole is a thing of properly proportioned parts. These days if one takes up the position of an auditor – a position that is still in practice the position of the 'people of God' – one often has the impression that it takes an unduly long time for the proceedings to come to what I assume is still the point, namely the Eucharistic Liturgy. The Introductory Rite and the Liturgy of the Word, including the Homily, can take a length of time out of all proportion to the rest. Even the Roman Canon is abbreviated, and the others are still shorter. If any of the 'dramatic actions' which the 'people of God' may have gone to on Saturday night were to take as long to come to essentials, they would be likely to have only a short run. The Liturgy of the Word is not by that fact the Liturgy of words – even if the words were of a higher order than they are often admitted to be.

Words need silence in which to sound. Real artists know how to surround them with a zone of it. The most powerful words lead inwards to silence. At the heart of them there is a still point. It is there the *Logos* is. When material words have led to the threshold of that sanctuary they should be muted. Ritual always aimed at that *silentium mysticum*. The Canon of the Mass used to be silent. It is no longer so – even if all the Ordo says is that 'the celebrant *may* say the Eucharistic Prayer in an audible voice.' It is arguable that there is now too much sound and talk in church – paradoxical importation just when so many in 'the world' want to get away from precisely that. Considered even as a spectacle there was great beauty and power in that build-up of silence towards the Consecration. At the right moment silence is more sublime than words. And this kind of silence is not created to order by self-conscious moments when 'a period of silence is observed'.

One result of the structural changes in the liturgy is that some of the finest things in the old one have not been kept even in translation. They have been simply discarded – unless again practice does not correspond with theory. The great sequences and *piae meditationes* that marked certain high points of the liturgy and of the liturgical year are gone. And nothing has been put in their place. With them more than liturgy is gone. There is gone from the general consciousness some of the highest achievements of the Christian mind and imagination. Clearly one cannot insist on the universal 'communicability' of it all to the 'people of God'. But there are some rather crude assumptions behind the discarding of it all. Is it only in the liturgy that the people have no need of what stirs the imagination? They go to the theatre for it – where they will often find experimentation that consists precisely in a return from 'naturalism' to the sense of ritual which it began. And at the highest level, art forms like opera continue to flourish – that strange baroque survival that defies all the probabilities about the 'willing suspension of disbelief', with foreign languages no bar. Yet, a Holy Thursday procession can be like a procession of shades in the underworld, because even those who should do not know the *Pange Lingua* or the *Lauda Sion*. And the opening of a retreat can depend for its traditional effect on a claque of 'elders' because they are the only members of the believing community who know the words in which the Holy Spirit has been so movingly invoked for a thousand years:

pars tollere vocem
Exiguam: inceptus clamor frustratur hiantes.

The most striking single example of this kind of loss is in the Mass for the Dead. There was nothing as moving, to the point of sublimity, as a solemn Requiem, as was appropriate for that climactic moment where art, secular and religious, has always been able to count on a concentration of the deepest and widest range of emotion. In a Requiem there was nothing greater than the Responsorium, *Libera Me*, with its 'grand and gloomy music', and the *Dies Irae*, the most majestic of medieval sequences. What has replaced it may 'communicate' more clearly, but what does it 'express'? The 'terror' of the Day of Judgement may be out of fashion as a theological emphasis. But the '*pity and* terror' of tragic meditation goes deeper than passing fashions. As Camus remarked of the 'plague', tragedy has a way of recurring in the world. Only shallow 'humanists' forget it. And 'this tremendous scene, pictured in stone above the doorway of so many churches, or in gorgeous colours in the western window, where the rays of the setting sun gave it an unearthly glamour, profoundly impressed the imagination of generations of Christian people'. No gobbledygook from 'communicators' or commentators could equal that scene as transmitted by the mass media themselves from Notre-Dame on the day of de Gaulle's funeral. An mbeidh a leithéid arís ann?

WHAT IS MORTAL SIN?

Dr [Denis] O'Callaghan's article in the [February 1972 issue of *The Furrow*] asking 'What is Mortal Sin?' sent me to some material that it would take more time to treat in depth. But it may be worth a little excursus immediately.

Mortal sin, with its correlative eternal punishment, 'is a problem' (73). At first sight it seems to contradict what we know about God's love and man's weakness, so that 'one may feel that mortal sin and an eternal penalty just do not make sense' (71). Particularly when we understand mortal sin from the 'ready reckoner' of its 'popular itemization' – suggesting a God who 'scrupulously balances the debit/credit account and punishes with implacable decisiveness ... ' (71). Dr O'Callaghan suggests that this aspect of the problem of mortal sin and eternal punishment is due to a confusion – between 'the theological concept of mortal sin' and 'the more disciplinary concept of grave sin ... '. We might say between Mortal Sin and mortal sins, as they are popularly itemized. 'Mortal sin, or better, mortal sinfulness, should be seen as a state ... in which the sinner has come to reject God ... Hell, "life" without God, is not *imposed* on him as punishment. It is the logical continuation, the *final phase* of the *choice* which he has made ...' (72, italics mine).

I am not qualified to judge the validity of the author's distinction. Or the justness of his refreshing analysis of what mortal sin and eternal punishment might be. Although, as Socrates might put it, matters must be something like this. But all that is to my purpose is to suggest that, if the confusion which the author analyses is as deep and widespread as he implies (of which again I am not competent to judge), it must mean that moral and 'eschatological' thinking has got very far from a certain great tradition. That again is a matter separate from the question of whether the tradition was right. But tradition is surely important, if only as a starting point for change. Still more important, of course, if the change should be to get back to it. What is stimulating in the analysis in question is its recall of that tradition.

It is not the place to give a long analysis of that tradition and its categories. I will refer only to some of the *loci* where it exists. Like many things in Christian civilization, the beginnings of a certain moral tradition are in pre-Christian classical civilization. As is well known, Socrates was one of the great moral witnesses of that civilization. He asked basic questions about the ultimate meaning of 'right' and 'wrong', 'good' and 'bad'. He lived, and died, by the best answers he could arrive at. He systematized the moral life as a 'tending of the soul' by the pursuit of authentic good. Put like that of course it may sound as banal as 'morality' often does. But it has to be understood in a context that cannot be gone into here – a dialectical inquiry into the ultimate presuppositions of the moral act, in which the soul and its good become the supreme business of life. Because (and this is its relevance to us here) as the soul is 'tended' in life, as it is oriented, as it chooses authentic good or not and brings itself to a certain ontological state, so will its choice and its state remain hereafter. With the attendant consequences of suffering or happiness – neither of which is a 'reward' or a 'punishment' but 'the logical continuation, the final phase of the choice' (art. cit., 72) which has already been made.

This Socratic ethic is first elaborated by Plato in the *Gorgias*. With such feeling, eloquence and close-knit thought that once upon a time at least it could be described as 'a prime favourite with all lovers of great ethical literature'. Its theme and range are best summarized in the concluding words of Socrates: 'All the other theories put forward in our long conversation have been refuted, and this conclusion alone stands firm, that one should avoid wrong-doing with more care than being wronged, and that the supreme object of a man's efforts, in public and in private life, must be the reality rather than the appearance of goodness.'

We must not get into analysis, but the gist of it, and the point for our concerns here can be conveyed as simply now as they were then by the Platonic 'myth' at the end, the 'very fine story which will, I suppose, seem fiction to you but is fact to me ... '. Ever since the days of old Cronos there had been a decree of heaven that the good went to the Isles of the Blest when they died, and the wicked to Tartarus for punishment. But even heaven was hard put to prevent the perversion of justice. In the beginning men came to their judgement alive and in their clothes before living judges on the day they knew they were going to die. This system was open to some obvious exploitation. It soon transpired that there were some surprising arrivals in one and the other place. After official complaints from the respective governors of those regions Zeus reformed the whole system of allocation – judiciary included. Men would no longer have prior knowledge of when their number was up. And they would be judged only after death – not only without their clothes but without their bodies – soul alone would be examined. And by judges in a special court, without jury who might be subject to influence. The judges too were to have their vision improved by being themselves naked and bodiless, 'viewing with bare soul the bare soul of every man as soon as he is dead'. Death is the separation of soul and body. The soul even more than the body remains in the state it has reached during life. Once stripped of the body all its qualities are seen, 'not only its natural endowments but the modifications effected in it by the various habits which its owner has formed'.

For the wicked there is some element of positive punishment. But that is additional to the suffering intrinsic to their state. Further, its purpose is not penal but either remedial or deterrent. For, lastly, there are some who are curable and go to 'purgatory'; there are others who are incurable and go to 'hell'.

Those ideas had a long history of development before and after Plato. It is not the place to go into details. But Plato himself refers to a passage in Homer's 'Book of the Dead' – in support of the possibility of eternal punishment. The passage has the further interest of showing that punishment already taking the form of some affliction related to the particular evil in their lives (*Odyssey*, 11, 568ff).

The Christian Platonist Augustine is explicit that in the case both of the good and of the bad, 'what they most love in this life will be brought to completion in them when this life is over' (*De Vera Religione*, 53, 102). 'Therefore to those who make ill use of the great good of mind, and seek the "visible" things outside it – things by which they should rather have been recalled to the vision and the love of "intelligible" (i.e. invisible and spiritual) things – to those will be given exterior darkness. For the knowledge that is by the flesh and the weakness of the bodily senses is a beginning of this darkness. And they who love strife will be estranged from peace and entangled in the ultimate troubles. For war and contentions are a beginning of that ultimate trouble.' Similarly those whose quest is for the constant experience of hunger, thirst and passion with a view to their constant satisfaction by indulgence – such people really love a state of deprivation, which is a beginning of supreme suffering. That which they love therefore will be completed in them – they will find themselves in the place where there is weeping and gnashing of teeth ... Not because they have loved that state for its own sake (who in fact could ... ?): but because the things they did love are a beginning of the other and necessarily bring those who love them to that other ... (ibid., 54, 104f).

In the sixth century another Christian Platonist, Boethius, is in the same tradition. With his sense of the importance of the great primary sources he even goes back directly to the *Gorgias*. Both as a Christian and as a Platonist he believes in two kinds of punishment after death. One is 'purifying', and therefore temporary. The other is 'penal' and, in the context, permanent (*De Consolatione Philosophiae*, 4, 4). The phrase used, 'penal harshness', suggests some element of 'vindictive' punishment, but he drops that question deliberately and goes on to prove that the essential punishment is intrinsic to the state chosen and is not imposed from outside. 'If you have conformed your soul to higher things there is no need of a judge to give a reward: you have yourself joined yourself to the more excellent things. If you have turned your interest to lower things do not look for one who punishes from without; you have yourself thrust yourself down to the baser things ... ' (ibid.). The process has already begun in life, and Boethius sums it up in the symbol of Circe, who could transform men's bodies to swine but could not touch their souls. Man's strength is in that inner citadel. More powerful than the potions of Circe are the poisons in the spirit. They can

> Drag down man from himself
> And leaving the body unharmed
> Cruelly wound the mind (ibid., 4, 3).

This line of thought culminates, I suppose, in Dante's *Inferno*. And the central place those ideas have there is an indication of the strength of the tradition and the ever-growing depth and clarity of its expression. Dante's descent into the depths of hell is also a descent into the depths of the soul. The real torments of that hell are not in the appurtenances of the 'place' but in the eternal fixity of the soul in a choice made by disordered desire through which it lost *il ben dell'intelletto*, the good of the mind, i.e. God and Truth, the supreme object of desire. So radical and final is the choice of the lost that after death they have a passion to reach their final state of suffering:

> *sì che la tema si volge in disio ...*
> They press to pass the river, for the fire
> Of heavenly justice stings and spurs them so
> That all their fear is changed into desire (CANTO, 3, 124F)

Some of the greatest episodes are great because of the way they encompass in one scene the first frail moment of yielding to a single wrong desire on earth and the final riveting of choice in an eternal bond to the object of that desire. So in the episode of Paolo and Francesca:

> *Questi, che mai da me non fia diviso,*
> *La bocca mi bacio tutto tremante ...*
> He that from me may never more be parted
> Trembling all over kissed my mouth ... (*CANTO*, 5, 135F)

The point of the vultures that attacked the liver of Tityos in Homer's underworld was that they fastened on the seat of desire. In Dante that insight into the nature of eternal punishment has been purified to a terrible logical clarity, and the punishment itself to a terrible spiritual interiority.

The question asked in the article that occasioned these remarks, still remains – to what extent and in what conditions such fixity of self-will against God is psychologically possible for a human being. By implication Plato's Socrates thought of that question too , and he would listen to 'any better or truer account of the matter ... ' (*Gorgias*, 527). In the meantime this account at least gave moral action a meaning commensurate with the traditional account of its consequences.

CATECHESIS NOW AND THEN

Reading the reports from Rome through October one realized that *aggiornamento* had caught up with the catechism too. In reality it had happened long before, but now it had become official and public; and we could see and hear what hitherto was but a rumour of squalls in the schools or the ooze of Dutch dykes leaking. The windows had been opened again. And we took more personal notice of this than of other previous and gustier occasions. Because we did not have to ask around whom the wind blew – it blew around ourselves. Biting more keenly than before because it blew around all those children that were our fathers. Not around the Synod hall and the ranked patres did it blow but around every dusty schoolroom grot of memory where ranked cubs were assembled – not to discuss the questions but to know the answers ... one Lord, one faith, one baptism ... and one questionmaster. And the wind blew through the grot and scattered the leaves of the slim volumes and they were never to be gathered into the same order again. And some:

> *Inconsulti abeunt sedemque odere Sibyllae.*

Catechism had become memory indeed.

And, like memory, catechism was no longer to be a tidy lapidary guide to life but suddenly itself a kind of living, in commitment and action, and subject to memory's lack of definition, partly interpreter and partly itself the raw material for interpretation. As in confessional autobiography like that of St Augustine, 'For a long time now I burn with the desire to meditate upon your law, and to confess to you both my knowledge of it and my ignorance of it ... '. But interpretation can be complete only when the data are complete, when life and the reel of memory is wound up. Which in strict logic takes the problem into a domain that transcends memory – both the individual and the collective. For in the very nature of things memory as we know it does not survive the life of the spool it winds it on. Catechetical memory is truly *anamnesis*, the recollection of whence we come and the way we go. It is a way of return, but the way of return is forward. Carrying the past with it, however, ontologically and in memory, what we have been as a part of what we are and are to be, a value partly interpreting and partly being interpreted as we go, interpreted and interpreter to be finally interpreted in the eternal, eschatological memory. 'Catechesis develops and at the same time interprets from within the way of life of those to whom it is addressed.'

So for many the great attic-to-cellar spring-cleaning of *aggiornamento* becomes more real, obvious, and problematical in the small maid's room of catechesis than it does in many vaster and more central chambers of the house. Or is it that the maid has suddenly grown to unprecedented stature – like the appearance of the Lady Philosophy in Boethius? 'It was difficult to be sure of her height, for sometimes she was of average human size while at other times she seemed to touch the very sky with the top of her head, and when she lifted herself still higher she pierced it and was lost to human sight.'

Hence the burden that runs through the Message to the People of God from the 1977 Synod of Bishops on *Catechesis in our Time.* A 'keen awareness of today's conditions ... in a world that is disturbed and filled with tensions ... signs of the times which call for the renewal of catechesis and which highlight its importance ... Old value systems are often no longer fully accepted and have even crumbled ... '. All adding up to a sense of 'the *complexity* of catechetical activity'. A complexity consequent on the necessity of a double adaptation of the message from transmitter to receiver – in substance and in language. But the *principle* of the adaptation is the principle central to Christianity itself – incarnation. 'The Christian message must find its roots in human cultures and also transform these cultures. A true "incarnation" of the faith through catechesis supposes not only a process of "giving" but also of "receiving".' Inseparable as matter and form are culture and the language of its expression. 'This is why there is a change in forms of expression, language and human behaviour ... Catechesis will be effective in facing these changes only in so far as it transmits its message in the language of our time.'

'Most urgent problems', in reflection on which, however, perennially vital Christian optimism sounds above the bass note of the problematical. It is recognized that one of the great cultural displacements in history has taken place, that old lines of communication have gone dead, that Christianity, which gave 'hermeneutics' to the world has to learn it back in up-dated form. It was at a different episcopal assembly that this recognition was put most incisively: 'We cannot stay by the dried-up bed of a river that has changed its course.' And in this *cannot stay* is the unique vitality of the Church, *in* every period of history but confined to none because contemporary with all. Catechesis, like the Church, is permanent, while being, like the Church, in time, and so, like the Church, *semper reformanda.* Catechesis is the constant incarnation of the transcendent mystery of God in the substance and language of contingent phenomena – 'the activity by which God's word is constantly spread in a living and effective way'. To adapt Boethius again, this maid catechesis is 'so full of years that I could hardly think of her as of my own generation, and yet she possessed a vivid colour and undiminished vigour'.

Catechesis then has arrived. But no doubt it will have to live some time yet with its dull reputation. It might therefore be an appropriate moment to draw attention again to one of the most attractive little works in patristic literature, as it must surely be in the whole history of catechesis. One had almost referred to it as the 'well-known ... ', but while that would have been accurate for fifteen centuries it is only doubtfully true any longer. I have not seen too many references to it in the recent welter .... Yet it speaks to us with extraordinary immediacy across nearly sixteen centuries – more immediately indeed and more clearly than parts of the recent message. The author was less conscious of the sociology of religion to be taken into account – although he did, and was not writing for a simple situation. And he was not a committee drafting a prose for Everyman – although he did. He wrote to one individual for a particular community. But Augustine – for it is he – seldom wrote anything, even the most personal and particular, without situating it in a universal framework. Indeed, one great interest of *First Catechetical Instruction* (*De Catechizandis Rudibus*) – for that is our work – is to see how it combines elementary simplicity with intimations of the radical rationale of belief and of the major theological themes around which Augustine systematized his thought in his greatest works. *First Catechetical Instruction* therefore became a kind of definitive work on catechesis. It drew tradition together, defined and developed it, and became a standard point of reference for the tradition to come. It is written with benefit, direct or indirect, of the principal catechetical documents of the early Church, like the *Didaché*, the *Apostolic Constitutions*, the *Demonstratio Praedicationis Apostolicae* by Irenaeus, and the filter of wider reference that came to Augustine through Ambrose. For all that it is a very personal and original work. And to this, not just to its simple availability, must be ascribed its continuous influence down to modern times – from Cassiodorus to the so-called 'Munich Method', passing via Isidore of Seville, Bede, Alcuin, Erasmus and Archbishop Gruber of Salzburg.

Even before we read it, it cannot but be an object of our curiosity, given that its author was Augustine. The most influential thinker and theologian of the West, who also reflected on the problems of breaking the bread of doctrine at the simplest level. A convert after long search for the truth, who thought about how best to present it to who have just recognized the obligation to make the same submission. (For it deals with *first* catechetical instruction – the *rudes* are such in doctrine only, they may be of any intellectual level. And the recognition of where truth is does not make catechesis easy – we know from Augustine's own case how *rudis* even the learned can be and how many obstacles there can be between the intellectual recognition and the submission in faith and practical commitment.) Augustine had also gone through the discipline of teaching in the secular domain, with its characteristic and everlasting experiences of disillusionment. Now a bishop he was a preacher of genius to all levels of the community. From the start he was a writer, with the artist's temperament about words and meaning. Throughout he was the master 'inculturator' of Christianity in the Latin world of his day. And he was an African, where, significantly, there would seem to be today a special recognition of the requirements of inculturation.

Written about AD 400, the *First Catechetical Instruction* was, like much of Augustine's writing, an 'occasional' work – a response to the needs of a particular contemporary situation. Always extremely busy, even the pastoral Augustine does not always conceal his tetchiness at the beginning of his replies to the frequent demands made on his time and genius to resolve practical or theoretical questions of the hour – which he then goes on to answer in letters often of treatise length. He shows nothing but enthusiasm – 'occupied though I am with other things' – in response to the request from the Deacon Deogratias of Carthage for some guidance on the instruction of candidates for admission to the catechumenate. The reply breaks down into two main topics: problems-and-methods of catechesis, and content – the second conveyed especially in two model catechetical addresses. In effect then the work becomes a manual of catechetical method and material.

It has already been indicated that Augustine was not writing for a simple situation that bears no relation to our own. *Catechesis in our Time* starts from a 'keen awareness of today's conditions'. So does Augustine in his model addresses. And the Carthaginian conditions were not all that different in principle – except that Christianity had then to compete with positive opponents, not just with diffused indifference. A brief indication of life in Carthage is therefore in order. It was the third city of a world empire and a millenary civilization ripe for dissolution – if it were to survive external dangers long enough to die a natural death. To look no further than the information Augustine gives us, everyone knows of his own experiences there and his sardonic play on Carthago/sartago, introductory to his account of the amenities it provided for his own dissolute life there, where a 'cauldron of disgraceful passions leapt and boiled' about him, sucking also his friend Alypius into its 'maelstrom of wicked ways'. In the *First Catechetical Instruction* this is again the explicit background to the inculcation of the Christian way – as a kaleidoscopic temptation away from it or, by the realization of its emptiness and futility, an occasion of the search for true values – away from 'the search for happiness and peace in the taverns and the houses of debauchery, in the theatres and the frivolous shows available gratis in great cities'.

Our scope here will allow us to look only at the 'problems-and-methods', but that in fact is where the first attraction of the work lies. Because beyond dull catechetics as conventionally understood, the work opens on to two permanently interesting wider areas: the workshop of Augustine, the artist with words, and through him into the 'curst hard' processes of composition that self-conscious writers have so often talked about since. The glimpse Augustine gives us is unique in the ancient world and is comparable with anything that has been vouchsafed us in modern times. In this as in other areas, Augustine joins the company for instance of Newman.

The otherwise anonymous Deogratias was clearly a special and recognizable type, with whom it is easy to imagine Augustine in rapport. For central to the document is a basic problem of Deogratias which evoked from Augustine those intimate workshop glimpses. Deogratias was recognized as a catechist 'of great ability' but he remained 'almost permanently perplexed' about how best to approach his task, and, from a sort of divine discontent with his performance of it, he fell into the double accidie of ennui with the subject and ennui with himself for the little he thought he made of it.

Augustine is consoling. Not to worry about that sense of failure, that feeling that the performance was 'flat and boring'. Your perfectionism and your over-familiarity with the subject may have made it taste that way to you, but it did not necessarily taste that way to the audience. On the contrary, being less blasé they may have found it fresh and invigorating. 'Myself too I am seldom or never satisfied with what I have written. I hunt for better ways of saying it. I gust variants on my inner palate and then I sit down to reduce my idea to a form of words. Which I have no sooner achieved that it comes home to me the gap there is between my expression and what I have thought and felt. And I am depressed that my words fall short of the perceptions of my heart. All that I perceive I want my hearer to perceive but I see that I have failed to find the words that would make it possible ... '.

And here, even in the elementary context of catechesis, Augustine the thinker of interiority plumbs the deeps of the inner world of man, that *abyssus humanae conscientiae* which is the immediate well of insight and inspiration. 'Intuition rapid as lightning floods the soul, but expression is limping and long-drawn-out and totally unlike its original. And before the expression has crystallized the intuition itself has disappeared into its hidden recesses . . .'

But this frustration is not a sophisticated agony special to the catechist or even to the writer – Augustine knew how precious the latter could be. It is no more than a particular case of the universal human condition of communication. That condition derives from a paradox in the nature of psychosomatic man, namely that his distinctive element, his lightning-quick spirit, is in this respect indeed a prisoner of his tardy, material body – on which he depends for the slow and ever inadequate signalling of the intuitions of his spirit. Long before semiology, Augustine observed this complex truth at all levels – from the speechless infant to the speechless mystic. The one fractious with the frustration of inability to externalize its small needs to its parents – 'for my wants were within me and my parents were without and they had no faculty by which to enter my mind'. The other gloomy in the dark night to think that 'even love is not strong enough to pierce the darkness of the body and break through into that eternal clarity from which even transient things derive such brightness as they have'.

For the catechist the first perfectionist and partly imagined failure leads to a second and real failure by dint of preoccupation with the first. Burning with zeal to be faithful to intuition and effective with his hearers, his failure torments him, and he wilts with distaste for an effort that seems vain, and that very distaste makes the resultant text truly flaccid and lacklustre in a way that it would not otherwise have been. The remedy is in the cultivation of a psychological climate of joy. And in this recommendation Augustine is fusing a profound pedagogical truth with a profound theological truth of the Christian life (2 Cor 9:7). Joy is in the gift of the Lord, but it is open to us to cultivate its conditions. And these Augustine analyses systematically.

So systematically that he first outlines six roots of this accidie and then in order prescribes their antidotes. Of the six the first is the one we have already seen in some detail. The second is a combination of inertia with a sense of the futility of composing our own instruction for an uncertain result when we can use the published texts of other writers so much better done than our own can hope to be. Third comes the tedium of returning to re-heated cabbage. Even when our words and thoughts are fresh to their hearers, repetition has long since made them cease to be so for ourselves. And our personal progress has taken us so far beyond this elementary material that it is profitless as well as tedious for us to plod again those well-beaten and infantile paths.

Fifth on his list is the all-too-human extrinsic obstacle that Augustine knew so well in his own life – the irritation, ill-humour and consequent psychological blockage caused by the importunity which compels us to interrupt more interesting and important personal work-in-progress and turn aside to mere catechesis. Ill-humour of another kind is sixth and last in his catalogue. It concerns the peculiarly exquisite agony of being asked to 'come and talk to so-and-so, he wants to become a Christian', and thereunto gird on our armour of Christian 'gladness' at the precise moment when from some personal blackness our own hearts are heavy and arid. Those who ask us to do this will naturally have no notion of the private problem that is draining our heart. And we cannot tell them. To their call we accede with a bad grace. And the natural consequence is that we speak from a black gloom without life or power of persuasion.

I have kept for the end what Augustine put fourth in his sequence. Not having our contemporary experience of the media business, audience-reaction measurement, TAM-ratings and the lot, he had perhaps a less climactic sense of the human animal as an object immovable even by the most irresistibly persuasive force that communication can mount. Yet to be able to speak as he does at this point he must have seen a good many Christians asleep in church. God knows, thinks Augustine, we are not in business for public plaudits. But it is a long and less acceptable step from that to the holy detachment that is not disturbed by the listener who sits unmoved in all-but-vegetable stolidity. It raises the question of course whether his immobility is due to his being in the body – totally – or out of the body, whether his spirit too is inert or only his flesh. In either case the enthusiasm of the speaker is blighted. He is collapsed in mid-flight, from the sheer doubt that he is wasting his time and his sweetness – or that he has none.

But we must not turn Augustine into a weary modern *désabusé*. From practical experience and from the accumulated tradition of 'rhetorical', i.e. stylistic theory, he knew that communication was a universe of discourse within the triangle of subject, speaker and spoken-to. Real indifference is not necessarily the fault of the audience. The conditions of its interest must be established and provided. And discussion of what those are forms the longest and most immediately interesting of his successive analyses of the antidotes to the various forms of catechetical accidie. It is the only one we shall have time to glance at here.

The prophylactics to a yawning congregation are of two kinds – physical and psychological. The one requires that they be accommodated in such material ways as will prevent physical weariness making psychological alertness impossible. The provision of seats against long standing is an obvious example. The other, the psychological, requirement is that we speak to them in a language they understand.

On the first of these conditions Augustine *en passant* gives us some rare glimpses into church mores of the fourth and fifth centuries in Africa, and, by way of comparison, glimpses into those of the overseas European churches. It is worth remarking that overall we detect that more relaxed and easy-going deportment in church which still seems to distinguish the Mediterranean congregation from the more correct and solemn attitudes of the North. In religion as in other matters due *sérieux* did not exclude that characteristic of Mediterranean civilization which the Latins translated from the Greek as *urbanitas* – 'in no way' to be re-translated as *embourgeoisée urbanity*! Be that as it may, we are to water wilting Christian flowers with the offer of a seat – where the lack of one is the established cause of the wilting. And it would be still better to provide seats from the start – 'where this can be done with propriety'. For 'things are much better done in certain overseas churches where not only does the bishop sit when he speaks to the people but seats are provided for the people too lest the physically weak be exhausted from long standing and so be distracted from the health of their souls, or worse still be obliged to leave ... I speak from experience, once while I was instructing him a man did just that ... '. (Not as drastic, we may remark, as the damage done by Paul on his last night in Troas!) And Augustine makes it a matter of Christian courtesy, citing the courtesy of the Lord who permitted a woman to be seated while he was speaking (Luke 10:39).

In his advice towards the intellectual and psychological accommodation of the audience, we find Augustine as practically aware of the 'man in the pew' as we have seen him earlier of the unsoundable sources of what he has to say to him. We discover how little of principle the ancient 'rhetoric' had to learn from the contemporary jargon of communication. (If anything the debt is in the reverse direction – as mentioned earlier, even in catechetical instruction Augustine did not shirk the deepest and most systematic nodes of the Christian message.)

In introducing his own model instruction, Augustine shows both his rigorous grasp of the theory of style in its relation to audience, and how for him theory has been verified and filled out from practical experience. And he reveals an equally important *tertium quid*, a certain on-the-spot quick intelligence and sensitivity to circumstance. Without this in the first place, theory provides only wooden 'rules', and experience remains largely fruitless. But it is experience that develops the potential of that alertness and adaptability to the immediate requirements of every new occasion. And in this domain every occasion is new and can never be completely anticipated by the a priori of theory or experience. 'I can testify from my own experience that my reactions are very different according as the person I see before me for instruction is educated or unlettered, a fellow-countryman or a foreigner, well-off or poor, a private individual or a public figure, a member of this or that family, of this or that age or sex, coming from this or that school of thought, from the background of this or that popular error. And in accordance with one or other of these varied estimates of the situation I introduce, develop and round off what I have to say.'

Prior to these particular and immediate decisions in the light of circumstances, a wide range of stylistic distinctions determines more general options to be made. The fundamental distinction is one that is still often forgotten. There is a big difference between the written and the spoken word. We are quick to be bored by one who speaks like a book, yet that is exactly what we then go on to do ourselves. Augustine distinguishes between the composition intended for a future *reader* and one that is prepared for spoken delivery to a listening audience. And even in the spoken there is a whole train of sub-distinctions to be taken account of. Ancient stylistic theory was fond of classifying and sub-classifying down to husks and chaff, but Augustine speaks from and to the *vécu*. Is the spoken instruction to be private or public; to a single individual or to a group; and if to a group is it to an intimate, informal gathering or to an assembly expecting a formal address? 'For even in dealing with a group, the approach is very different depending on whether the audience is gathered around informally for an intimate exchange of ideas or is waiting in hushed expectancy with all eyes on the person who is going to address them from the height of the tribune.'

All this of course has to do with method and technique. It has not been our present purpose to draw particular attention to something Augustine knows well – but has not always been so well known since. To wit that successful 'communication' can neither be achieved nor explained by method alone without residue, that method itself cannot be controlled by theory alone without experience, that, while we may not ignore method, one more thing at least is necessary for the Christian 'communicator' – and so available that on occasion it will supply the lack of every method. 'Someone who is without the experience of divine love and therefore without the experience of which I speak, such a one may notice that our praise is on the lips of the crowd because of some talent that gives persuasiveness to our words, and he may think that on that account we are pleased and happy. But may God, before whose sight comes the sighing of the prisoners, behold our abjection and our labour and forgive us all our sins (Ps 78:11; 24:18). And that is why, whatever in me may have attracted you enough to make you want some observations of mine for the benefit of your own preaching, you will learn them better by observing and studying my practice than you will by reading what I say about it here.'

THE FUTURE OF MAYNOOTH: IDEALS AND PRINCIPLES

In my title I see ideals and principles rear their terrible heads. I am innocent of their invitation. I am, at worst, an accessory after the fact. There is only one small part of direct responsibility to which I confess – a momentary lapse on a principle of my own, viz., that a shut mouth catches neither flies nor assignments like the present one.

The genesis of the present assignment was in the recent past, when a paper was read on the future, the future of Maynooth. The future is indeed a mysterious dimension of the mysterious element in which we all of us as well as Maynooth have our being. And it has remained mysterious despite the meditations of ancient philosophers and modern futurologists. But the mysterious is perennially appealing. And so we all came, we saw, and we were overcome. Unlike many philosophers and futurologists and ordinary crystal gazers, your seer* on that occasion performed so well that even those of us who came perhaps for a mild scoff remained if not to pray certainly to applaud, quite possessed by what we saw, or dreamed we saw, of the future and of Maynooth inside it. So transported that you decided it was good for us to be here, that the tabernacles should be left in position and that we should all come again for another revelation. And the lot fell on me, to rap the ambo – or the table. And that is how I come to be here, burdened with my apocalyptic text.[4*]

I have noticed that even theologians today speak of faith as a heavenly light of course, but also as a kind of moon among heavenly lights, shadowed by one side permanently in the dark. So, taking confidence from the lack of it in loftier domains, a poor university preacher need not lather himself into a foam of light in order to hide his darkness. So help me God – my unbelief. I do believe. But when I examine my faith or try to justify it even to other believers I am assailed by doubts. I am not sure if the belief even of the community of university believers is the same as mine. And if not, whether it is they or I who are in heresy. A serious matter in faith. And if yes, whether we do the works without which our faith is dead, or, whether the works we do are works that justify our faith.

The world, dear brethren, thinks that the towers in our towered city are of ivory. Which being interpreted means they regard our faith as vain and our works as useless. Who then has not felt his faith tested, threatened, futile, nay absurd,

4* * Dr Enda McDonagh, in 1976.

and himself a bodiless consciousness of 'ideals', a useless passion, a sickness in Being, strictly *de trop*?

> Bear with me;
> My heart is in the coffin there with Caesar,
> And I must pause till it come back to me!

It is not without method in my madness that I have slipped in the mention of 'ideals' at this point. Because, as I hope to make clearer, the university in principle is about an ideal or ideals. And ever since Plato the gap between ideal and real has been a sickness both acute and chronic in the human being. How avoid being touched by vertigo when we awake to reflexive awareness of the present gap, the great gulf, sophistic or authentic, not only between one university ideal and another but between the university ideal and the *flaque visqueuse au fond de notre temps* which is the reality of the campus that we often experience. And lucky who knows it not – or damned perhaps for having so far 'fallen' from the 'ideal' world that he no more remembers it! Even for Sartre ... 'L'ldée est toujours là, l'innommable, Elle attend, paisiblement. A présent, elle a l'air de dire: Oui? C'est *cela* que tu voulais? Eh bien, précisément c'est ce que tu n'as jamais eu ... et c'est ca que tu n'auras jamais ...

Mais pourquoi? Pourquoi?'

Do I perhaps exaggerate? Maynooth no doubt belongs to the *developing* university world, and so in that respect is living through the shortcomings which that term is devised to leave unexpressed. No Limbo indeed – to revert to our 'faith' – for there is some suffering, but a place or state thereof through which those who endure may hope to climb the Mount and in due course emerge to the beatific vision. But what then of the *developed* university world? So many have passed this way before us and have come out into the realms of what appeared to be light, have entered into the fullness of departments, faculties and schools, staffing, libraries, services and finance, all that was deemed necessary for entering into the joy of the Lord. And yet they do not seem to have entered it! At least the reports are discouraging. In the Book of Revelation the chapter headings are monotonous: THE UNIVERSITY AND THE INTELLECT; THE MIASMA AND THE MENACE; WHAT'S THE MATTER WITH HIGHER EDUCATION?; WHAT WENT WRONG WITH THE UNIVERSITY?; CAN THE UNIVERSITIES SURVIVE?; WANTED: A SURVIVAL KIT ... What *has* gone wrong? The joy of the Lord is to adore Him. Did they only adore his works? Or take means for ends, maps for destinations and arrivals?

It may be that, looked at under ordinary light, matters are not as bad as that. The 'crisis' may be due to the fact that the university is an institution which is periodically looked at under no ordinary light – but in the light of a kind of 'conversion' in which what seems not too bad to *l'homme moyen* is full of shadows, spots and wrinkles for the converted who see in the light of *absolute ideals.* I have already asserted that the university represents an ideal, an ideal of the intellect, an ideal of 'perfection' of the intellect, as it has been put by one of its highest idealists. Now the highest ideals are born of conversion, and maintained by periodic examinations of conscience and re-conversion if necessary. Conversion is associated with religion, but the intellect too has its conversions. St Augustine was converted to 'philosophy', to the quest 'for immortality of wisdom' before he was converted to religion. They are not mutually exclusive, of course, as his history shows, for philosophy led him beyond itself to mystical vision, a domain in its turn not uncontrolled by philosophy. All of which leads to deep questions about what constitutes the 'perfection' of the intellect and therefore the ideal of the university – but of that anon. For the moment let us optimistically accept that the 'crisis' of the university is in the light of perfection unattained and not of a total fall from grace.

The university then is discontent, but not with the pain of loss, only with a divine discontent on the way, or at worst with the passing pain of the 'night' of the intellect. The question persists, in the name of *what* is it discontent, desirous of being different, better? Generically it can only be in the name of ideas, ideals and principles, of a certain *ben dello intelletto.* And the crunch comes here. In a way which stated too simply will sound simplistic if not old-fashioned. And too simply is the only way it can be put within my time, but the simplistic might at least help us to cut through to the area where the essentials lie. As for being old-fashioned, well that is a matter precisely of fashion, which like fortune's wheel – or any other wheel for that matter – carried us round in circles. If we wear our coat long enough we won't need to turn it – the turn of fashion will bring its turn to fashion again. Which turn of taste, if we are serious about it, may taste of a cyclic view of history, and, if we are not serious, is of no worse consequence than a view of history as linear progress to nowhere in particular. Indeed the advantage lies with the cyclic, within which it should at least be possible to take our bearings on the wheel, to however little final purpose. But the options are not really as stark as that. And the most exhaustively documented attempt to chart the time-space parameters of civilization has concluded that it moves both ways ... cyclically forward – like the path up that Mount of some moments back or, if you prefer, any ordinary wheel-and-wagon combo! But the Mount has its axis and its fixed points, between the still centre of the earth below and the still centre of the heavens above. And the wagon wheel turns on axle, a point we may not notice if we are programmed for the plotting of forward movement only – crucial though we are told was the invention of the wheel for the forward movement of civilization. And since we are running this nag so hard, this analogical nag of movement in fixedness through circularity, let us notice how the pattern fits the oldest crux in our oldest tradition of philosophy. I referred earlier to how Plato has infected us. Parmenides and Heraclitus infected us with another virus – the dilemma of whether anything moves at all or anything does but move. In other words how reconcile the physically obvious fact of change with the metaphysically apparent fact of the impossibility of anything but unchanging permanence. As so often the best solution we have is got by tying the horns of the dilemma together – we must keep both permanence and change. Which may look like the Polonian metaphysic of keeping your cloud and metamorphosing it into a camel. But I haven't the time to argue with Aristotle. I must hurry back to the point. Which is that we have the best of good theoretical company in which to be old-fashioned. Come to think of it, the university itself is a very old-fashioned institution – in its idea much older than the dates assigned for the beginning of even the oldest of the universities conventionally so called. Yet no one as far as I know has argued that therefore the cure for what's 'wrong' with them is to abandon or dismantle them. I have heard of course about the 'de-schooling' of society. In bad moments one might think it had already happened, or would not make much difference, but I take it that the option is excluded by my text – the *future* of Maynooth. On the contrary, what we have found implicit in the criticism is a desire for a return to a lost original ideal. *Wanted: A survival kit.* Secondly, as to what that ideal is I suggest we return to the dance of the dyad in permanence and change that I introduced a moment ago. The very unquestioned institutional permanence of the university amid so much change since it first appeared provides an analogy for an ideal of the university as the wheel and axle of the wagon of civilization, in an unavoidable and desirable, and even profoundly Judeo-Christian dialectic with creative change, progress and *aggiornamento.* So much for being old-fashioned, though it may have become a little less 'simple' than I thought it would be.

But now in addition to ideals and principles we have introduced another vast imponderable – civilization. This perhaps is where really comes the crunch that I announced already, a little too early. Let us assume that within our ivory towers we ourselves are not only familiar with such invisible entities, but have kept faith in their reality and value. But what about those without the gates – and not a few already within them?

How do we get them to believe in them? Am I right in assuming that we ourselves sufficiently believe in them even to try? And in face of those who do not want them – either because they do not know them or knowing them want something more 'relevant', meaningful, or what you will, how do we set about imposing them? *Imposing* them did I say? But, if it is about academies we are talking, shall we not insist on geometry for those who would enter? I know of course about debts to society, social relevance, market demands etc., but I have tried to cover my flank on the side exposed to change without abandoning permanence. In any case that is not the kind of dogmatism that is in question at all – as we know ever since Plato set Socrates to instructing Phaedrus on the banks of the Ilissus. When we speak Greek, dogma is what has 'seemed good'. Up to its inculcators to make it seem good and *thus* impose it. Academics work by rules but they must also work by influence, even love – love of the good, *il ben dello intelletto* – a spontaneous reaction, the philosophers tell us, once the good is recognised.

Did I say love? We must watch that too! It has become as omnipresent and debilitating as a virus, a justification of too many kinds of laziness. It is a concept with a Jacob's ladder of meaning where often only putti pass up and down – as little understood at the top as it is devalued and empty at the bottom. My purpose is to avoid seeming to found the university too on a principle of *dilige et quod vis fac*, as that principle is conventionally misunderstood in theory by those who might know better, and in practice by those who for that very reason cannot be blamed for not so knowing. Love will enlighten the intelligence but it will hardly do its work. I do not know if philosophers still distinguish the faculties of intellect and will, but they did for a long time – and for experiential reasons as solid as those of St Paul or St Augustine.

It is to prejudge the issue to assert that we are again in a sophistic age, of the kind against which Plato built his Academy. But that at least is one of the questions we have to raise in thinking about our function in the university – assuming the justice of what I have been saying about the function of the university in civilization's dialectic of permanence and change. And that is a work which love alone will not do. Intellectual distinction and distinctions must come into it. I referred earlier to one of the ways in which the university ideal has been defined – perfection of the intellect. But not just our own individual intellects – the collective intellect of civilization. For our towers are not, or should not be, ivory in that sense. We do indeed owe a debt to society. But is that debt only at the level where it seems often to be put? Economies do break down – an event that affects even our ivory towers too, alas. But civilizations too break down, and for all I know it is possible that the latter is causally the prior – 'that if thinking is not kept pure and clean, and if respect for the world of the mind is no longer operative, ships and automobiles will soon cease to run right, the engineer's slide rule and the compilations of banks and stock-exchanges will forfeit validity and authority, and chaos will ensue'! In any case we must assume the minimum, that civilization matters and that it is an affair of the spirit as well as of the GNP, and that the university is not only one of its highest expressions but responsible back to it in a special way. I revert then to my reference to sophistic ages. They are potentially barbarous as well. The university's sense of its own function is particularly important at such times. Not just because the health of civilization at such times is or might appear to be critical. Also because such times may call for conscious reflection and decision by the university on what its own faith is. And this is hard not only in the deciding but in the acting thereon. When relativism and positivism are eating away at the foundations, how defend ideals and principles? When the individual is the norm, how defend the supra-individual norms that found the values of civilization? And without such universals, real or agreed, what is the future of civilization – etymologically, and in fact, a collective creation? The collective dimension of course can be supplied – like teeth on the Judgment Day. And for those who like it that way, Sparta provides a tradition as permanent as Athens. Where the immediately meaningful and relevant is the criterion of value, how defend the necessity of criteria more ultimate? When everything goes pop, how can we believe that 'no sooner were those wicked notes struck in the Royal Palace than the sky darkened, the walls trembled and collapsed, the kingdom and sovereign went to their doom'? Where elite and egalitarian have reversed their value connotations, what shall we do with the idea of the master?

This is not to say that the game cannot go on. Of course it can and does. The game of being an 'intellectual', 'interested in ideas'. But it is a game of fragments unrelated to any unity, of marginalia without a centre, of knowledge without meaning. Or worse still, a game in which ideas are mere counters without content, matterless form. A purely formal game in which nothing is at stake. But played with mandarin gravitas and without even a saving sense of the comicality of emptying out not just the substance of its own material but the values that originally justified its own occupation. I have an example in mind. A recent critical reappraisal of a classic of European literature. The reappraisal was precisely to resolve our dialectic of permanence and change. How can a work from another age continue to have meaning – or be made to have meaning – for our time? The operation was drastic indeed. Rather like the ancient Egyptian process of mummification, by drawing out the guts and brains and preserving – nay thereby the better to preserve – what was left. By removing the guts and brains of matter, substance, meaning, as the meaning was, and because it was, for a past age, thereby denying permanent meaning altogether in any substantial sense. And preserving what? The husk of 'form' – as though all that were worth preserving of a folk-tale were an anthropologist's schema of its structure. As if the human spirit through its changes in time had no memory or identity of permanence in itself or in its 'monuments of unaging intellect'. It is one thing to discover the

Emperor has nothing on. It is another and more serious matter to discover that clothes are all there is.

Omy masters, 'ideals and principles' are questionable items to have in our luggage. Have we any to declare? And shall we declare them at all? And where? Shall we declare these towers to be our symbol? Is the university the best place to declare them at all today – impersonal and mass productive as it often is, run to gigantism, monstrous growth of members and possible dislocation of the heart? We have seen Socrates leave the city to make his declaration by the banks of the llissus. A later master, Abelard, left the schools for the wilderness. Can we hope to be followed if we go into the wilderness? We can still choose our banyan tree or its local equivalent, and wait for Atman in our own soul. But things may not be as desperate as that. It is a thought worth preserving for a time of troubles that the students did follow Abelard without benefit of canteen or students' union building, 'building themselves little huts, eating wild herbs and coarse bread instead of delicate food, spreading reeds and straw in place of soft beds and using banks of turf for tables'. Thereby in the master's opinion proving themselves true philosophers. (I have rather taken the students for granted in all this, although they do have souls, and sometimes even seek music for them. In any case when we talk marketing, they are the clientele *sine qua non*. If they don't follow our piping there won't even be an academic rat race.)

I have used the apocalyptic expression 'a time of troubles'. I may seem be painting the present as such a time. As a preacher I must keep my colours primary. But I have tried to keep them from being too stark. I have taken the positive implications of questions like: What is wrong? 'Time of discontent' would be a less prejudicial phrase. And discontent, I have suggested, is divine. In the long line of existentialism *avant le mot*, it has been a principal way to wisdom. And the university ideal is certainly in some sense an ideal of wisdom. Not to be confused, need I say, with the kind of wisdom that knows the price of everything and the value of nothing. Hence Newman's university ideal of 'philosophical knowledge' – which again is not of course to be confused with knowledge of philosophy. And many contemporary experiments in university organization and teaching imply a newly felt need to return to that ideal.

Nearer home, and more relevant, for we must always dig the ground under our own feet, there is the interest of your own discontent and concern for the future of Maynooth, without which I hope you would not be listening to this. Maynooth too is going through certain discontents. They were sketched in the previous paper, at which your enthusiasm generated the present one. The enthusiasm of course was not for the discontents themselves – the point bears stating for deipnosophists in ivory towers. The enthusiasm was for the positive implications of discontents shared by the 'old' Maynooth and the 'new' Maynooth – a pool of discontent but not a slough of despond. If the shared discontents arise from shared positive ideals, there are reasons, to which I may eventually come, why Maynooth's future can be real without loss of the ideal. So far I have been banging away at ideals and principles, but without being very specific or concrete. Partly because ideals and principles are like that – in a good and in a bad sense. And it is the bad sense which makes ideals so convenient for someone like myself in an acutely embarrassing expository situation. Left like that, we are all of us as quickly and spontaneously for idealism as we are against sin. That way ideals do not hurt much. Knowing that ideals are 'out of this world' we can behold them while staying in this one, thus getting the best of both, ideal and real, dream and working reality. In using this convenience, however, I am once again in the best of company, Plato's no less, the first systematic idealist, but a realist as well. After taking us through several hard climbing books on the structure of his ideal city with its ideal education he suddenly melts our Icarus wings and lets us plummet to the ground. He whose ideals are thus, and thus 'will not enter practical politics', at least 'not in his own country, unless, some miracle happens'.

'I see what you mean, he said, you mean that he will do so in the society which we have been describing and which we have found in theory: but I doubt if it will ever exist on earth'.

In my mind's eye, Horatio ... But that is not the end of the matter or our easy dispensation from ideal effort as drawing only by illusion. The ideal pattern is 'laid up in Heaven for him who wishes to behold it, and beholding, to organize himself accordingly. And the question of its present or future existence on earth is quite unimportant. For in any case he will adopt the practices of such a city, to the exclusion of those of every other.'

So too I believe did Newman think of his Idea.

***

In my own attempt to set out some 'ideals and principles', I propose to be more Socratic than dogmatic. Part of the reason certainly is the desire to be more provocative than definitive. But there is a more positive justification. You may recall that the Socratic intent was to compel us to the point of defining our so spontaneous idealism. And its implications are that, when we so define, we are doing no more than giving birth to what we know already. Again very convenient for me if I can reverse the charges by making you show me your own ideals. And with due allowance for the difference between Plato and myself, I would like to make the process easier by dropping you down for a moment in the Platonic manner of a moment back.

One way of expressing the epistemology of Socratic pedagogy is to say that all learning is cliché. And what richer pastures for proof than the green hills of education, forested to the summit in 'ideals and principles' as mixed as the figures that follow. Once we start to talk about them are we not set fair for every cliché in the book? Is there anything new under their sun except the changing circumstances of their application? Today, if ever, are they not thicker in the air than the flocks of quail around the camps of the Israelites on their journey to the Promised Land? And how can I in my turn hope to take off in my monomotor without sucking them into my engine? What have I done from the start of this paper except pluck them out of the air and dress up the meat as best I can? How be original on such an unoriginal topic as the training of the rational and risible animal man? Behind the new *situations*, the theory of education is compact of clichés. The 'ideals and principles' are clichés. And the various ways of falling away from them are clichés. And the life-cycle of an educational idea is a cliché – from its birth in idealism to its fading and petrifaction in practice, and the attempt to climb back up to the vision lost. And that, I think, is where we came in to the present film.

Thus far, as Aristotle would say, let cynicism have been considered. More positively considered, however, those clichés do represent that pole of permanence that we tried to justify earlier. That scarcely original animal man is permanent man in the permanence of his aspirations. And certain of these it must surely be, as it always has been, the function of the university to cultivate. 'All men by nature reach out after knowledge,' asserts Aristotle as the first step of his highest climb in the *Metaphysics*. Not knowledge of this or that particular, not even encyclopedic knowledge, but total and radical knowledge in absolute causes. What Aristotle himself called *sophia*, 'wisdom', in a line from Plato to Lonergan. No more attainable perhaps in the sublunary world than in Plato's ideal City, but none the less an aspiration for all that. This is what 'philosophy' has often recognized in its very name, the *love* of sophia, an ideal quest rather than a permanent possession. Including to be sure knowledge of 'this or that particular' in the particular and autonomous sciences – of which the metaphysical Aristotle was an encyclopedic student and careful demarcator. I am not forgetting the no less traditional function of the university towards professional knowledge. But professional knowledge ideally is also architectonic knowledge, specialized knowledge in awareness of the lateral relation of science to science, and the vertical relation of science to the science of its assumed principles, and upwards to a hypothetical Principle, unconditioned Condition of all the conditions. Something like this was Newman's ideal of 'philosophical knowledge'.

In simpler terms, this is an ideal of intellectual order. And I take it that we believe in order, for ourselves and for our students. Greatly daring in comprehensiveness,

I have earlier glanced at its relevance to society and civilization. Ideally the university is the institution that in some sense embodies such order and provides its possibility for those who come to it. I say 'possibility' because, even at the risk of 'elitism', it may be that not all who come there are coming to the right place, and of those who do come not all drink equally deeply of the waters. Having already rung the changes on cliché, we can dispense our time and intelligence from a re-hash of the great classical statements of this ideal order of the university. They extend from Jaspers back to Newman, and beyond him to classical Greece and Rome where the 'idea' existed long before the technical reality of the university – as confirmed by the fact that in Newman's ideal of 'philosophical knowledge' there is a good deal of Greek, so well processed as to be invisible in the weave.

All very ideal of course and visionary, but born of human aspiration. Ideal and visionary and therefore impossible. But without a vision even the possible remains unachieved. Plato's Demiurge started from an eternal model even though it was to fabricate a world whose closest approach to the eternal could only be to go round in circles. Moses broke the tablets on seeing what he saw when he came down from the Mount, but he kept going ... He never made it to the Promised Land, but without his vision he would have perished in the desert.

To revert then to my original terms of 'faith', it is a question of what we believe. Do we believe in the idea? Or if you prefer the inductive to the deductive method (and as Aristotle remarked, it does make a difference whether we are arguing to or from first principles), do we at least believe in pushing up towards the idea? Do we believe, if not in the possibility then in the desirability of holistic knowledge and holistic organisation of the quest for it? And, turning from the object to the personal subject of knowing, do we believe in any ideal 'perfection' of the intellect? Do we believe that this holistic ideal, attainable or not, has deep roots in the human and a long history, and that therefore it is still a point by which, without star-gazing, we should take some of our compass-readings? For although I have not touched on it except under this rubric of 'perfection', educational ideals have never been solely determined by the goal of charting the objective world, no matter how architectonically. They have also been determined by the goal of an ideal development of the subject himself – *humanitas*, humanism. The word is battered. And under various guises the old idea fills the air still. But often at such a depressing level of superficiality, with such disregard both of objective knowledge and of the real depth of the *grande profundum* that is the human subject of *humanitas*. If 'all men by nature reach out after knowledge' objective and subjective goals coincide. Deep calls to deep.

In an attempt to suggest how such an ideal might be reduced from potentiality to fact, a little history might be more helpful than the high classical statements of what is ex professo only 'the idea' of the university. For instance, in his essay in *The Idea* on 'Knowledge Viewed in Relation to Professional Skill', Newman deals with a problem at the heart of the contemporary university problem but with a history going back beyond universities to Greco-Roman reflection on the problems involved in their ideals of higher education. The Greco-Roman *encyclios paideia* – *orbis ille doctrinae* -- and the related medieval system of the Seven Liberal Arts, were systematisations of the principle that professional specialization should be in the holistic context of a general education. Ideal universality had of course to accommodate itself to the demands of professional particularity. But the limitations carried a bonus. The universal was given a focus in the particular, and professional particularity was considered the more effective for being in a universal context. This higher effectiveness was not seen as a consequence merely of more knowledge as more information. It was a consequence of intellectual order, of '*philosophical* knowledge'. It was the consequence not so much of knowledge at all in the informational sense as of a certain qualitative 'perfection' of the intellect that went beyond and even survived knowledge. And such a perfection was an important element in that perfection of the *educandus* to which we have referred. And this was in fact the second main reason for the 'encyclopedic' ideal of education ever since Plato formulated the ideal of 'music for the soul'.

'Encyclopedic' and 'general' have of course now acquired connotations which make them misleading and indeed repugnant in the present context. They suggest the wrong sort of universality – the *unsystematically* general, the facile, the vaguely cultural and 'improving', top-dressing rather than cultivation. More or less the direct opposite in fact to the etymological meaning of the words themselves and to that ideal of intellectual order which was at the heart of *encyclios paideia*. It denoted the complete *circle* of knowledge, *orbis ille doctrinae*, segmented into the various *disciplinae* of which the one chosen for professional study was the point of concentrated rigour, but with a sense of its position on the map, a sense of its relation to the centre of the circle of science. We have referred earlier to the life-cycle of educational ideas. We must not assume that this one withstood fading and petrifacation through a thousand years of ancient civilization. But however diluted in practice it never disappeared as a principle. In a sense it has never disappeared since. For it can be said that this is not just one ideal among others. It is the generic ideal to which the central tradition has always kept climbing back.

The climbing back has been necessary for reasons other than the *vis inertiae* we mentioned earlier. Even in Classical civilization, matter resisted mind – Plato recognized it as a metaphysical principle that he called Necessity! Even the comparatively small *orbis doctrinae* of the ancient world was large enough to force the question of whether the ideal combination of professional and 'philosophical' knowledge was possible in practice. Even then there were only twenty-four hours in the day, and the expectancy of years in the allotted span for the general we may assume to have been less than today's mean. Plato, who was not of the general, had a span long enough to permit him to solve the problem in his head. He would organize his City in such a way that the shoemakers and the lower orders generally did the cobbling and thus provided the leisure for their guardians to do the philosophy – for as long as the subject required. (There is a lot of sociology – and maybe philosophy – hidden in *school* being Greek for leisure.) Without the benefit of Popper, we recognize that solution as pretty Utopian even for a society that had so many more servants than we have to do its living for it. So less Platonic souls had to look for less Platonic solutions.

They were principally two, and at two levels. The less profound was more a practical solution to the problem of time than a philosophic solution to the problem of knowledge. It pointed to the difference between the degree of concentration and scientific rigour required in the study of a professional discipline and that required for 'general' knowledge of the other disciplines that completed the 'circle'. Proportionately less time was needed for them, and the ideal became that much more practically feasible. Still bearing in mind that even within those limitations the goal was not just a general facility but a true initiation into the nature and the 'language' of those other disciplines. And part of the process of initiation into intellectual order was the order in the sequence of those disciplines. A sequence at once ontological and pedagogical. And a sequence in hierarchical ascent. Ontological ascent through the levels of reality, from phenomena to hypothesis and principle and cause, from the 'many' to the 'one'. A parallel pedagogical ascent through the propaedeutic sequence, in which the disciplines of successive levels of Being discipline the mind into the appropriate level of thinking, as thought ascends from concrete phenomena to successive degrees of abstracted principle. 'It is from wonder that men first began and still begin to philosophise; wonder in the first instance about the more immediate and obvious unanswered questions, and then progressively about more ultimate matters – about the moon's phases, about the sun and the stars and the origin of all things' (Aristotle, *Metaphys.*). This wondering ascent led Aristotle to the eye of his domed order of oscillating permanence-in-change, to the energizing One that unmoved moves the whole system – by the attraction of love. Only a hypothesis ... ? Still how fair is the dare of its vaulting. And without it, the concluding order of the *Paradiso* could never have been articulated. And surely *that* represents *some* kind of achieved order that 'we would not pass up'. And for the essentials is there much difference in principle between the Aristotelian hypothesis and the Teilhardian Omega Point? In any case the search is still obviously on.

The second and more philosophic solution is an application of the principle that all knowledge is ultimately one. Because the universe is one, and because the teleology of the drive to knowledge is in final unity. Therefore different disciplines are but different aspects of the one material and inter-connected in their deepest principles. Study with this organic and logical sense reduces the time and the effort involved in the pursuit of the 'encyclopedic' ideal – it is the kind of order originally meant by the word. And it is the kind of order indicated by Newman's ideal of 'philosophical knowledge'.

The modern explosion of knowledge and its implosion by specialization and consequent fragmentation into more and more about less and less must make such ideals sound like the dreams of Zeus or the editors of the *Encyclopedia Britannica*. But does not actual fragmentation make the ideal of unity more pressing than ever? We need not go into such deep sociological matters as the consequent fragmentation of the soul of the individual and of society and of disparate 'cultures' – by now two of the latter must be a conservative estimate. But how can knowledge even be used if it is not controlled? And how can it be controlled if not from some centre where there is a sense of a whole as well as of parts – if parts they even be and not atomized fragments? And where if not in the university can we hope to locate such a centre, such a co-ordinating brain of the circuity of knowledge and the civilization that depends on it? And the sense of some contemporary experiments is surely an attempt once again to provide the student with some such co-ordination. Inter-disciplinary studies come to mind, and the organization into 'schools' rather than isolated departments. One reads too of a 'European approach' – by which is meant, one hopes, not the *disiecta membra* sometimes seen under the rubric of European studies but the realization of a principle of unity, such as that, in literary studies, the various modern literatures are heirs not just each to its own national past but to a common European past, and that without this root they are truncated and are neither adequate units for the intelligence nor adequate agents for the intellectual and cultural formation it is so conventionally asserted they confer. And in that context it will become clearer that by itself, even on the European scale, literature is not a self-contained study independent of other modes of thought ... . But I must not drag in the 'ancient quarrel' between poetry and some of her neighbours!

Finally the more radical suggestion is made that the university should re-organize itself in such a way as to make the institution correspond with the 'idea'. This means organizing its disciplines around a centre in such a way as to embody and facilitate the intellectual order we have been talking about. The re-organization envisaged is one that would in fact be a return to tradition, the tradition in which the university had as its centre the disciplines traditionally regarded as central – like Arts, Philosophy, Law, Theology .... And if the central goes to the centre then the marginal must go to the ... margin. And who shall bell that cat ... ?! The tower of Babel is the cathedral of our ivory ones, and the territorial imperative is exceeding strong even as we climb to Heaven! Still the preacher's text was on 'ideals and principles' ... and the question remains. 'All knowledge as it exists has a social colouring ... But it is also based on a priori categories of the mind, and these permanent ways of grasping reality should be visible and formative in the structure of the curriculum.' Words spoken about *secondary* education ... but shall the university aim at less? Among the Platonic 'Guardian' class shall the 'Rulers' be less 'philosophical' than the 'Auxiliaries'? And who will educate the Auxiliaries? And how will they both justify their privileges to the class of cobblers? By turning the university from philosophy to a school of shoe-making? It is a contemporary philosopher, Jaspers, who has insisted that, in addition to being a 'professional school' and a 'research institute', the university should be a 'cultural centre' for the 'education of the whole man'. By 'cultural' he meant none of the more amoebic contemporary senses of that knocked-about word. He meant our intellectual order. And how much it counted for the order of civilization he was well placed to know.

Order would demand that before time runs out I say something specifically on Maynooth in the context of 'ideals and principles'. Ideals we have admitted to be clean and convenient places of refuge. The concrete is the rub. But the landing in Maynooth need not be too rough. In the first place we should expect Maynooth to justify us a little in our Platonic flights which might otherwise seem to have parted company completely with terra firma. We should expect Maynooth to be more concerned than others with 'ideals and principles'. She is a Lady of a certain age and some character and indefinable mystique who has only lately come out in secular society. And from a modest household, for all that she has been:

Magna parens frugum ...
Magna virum. . . .

Her household is still a modest one, indicating that her coming out has not been with a view to the furtherance of suddenly awakened worldly ambitions divorced from ideals and principles. We should expect her years to have given her a certain sense of permanence in change. We should expect her character to give due place to the things of the spirit. And we should be disappointed if on coming out she shed all her mystique – that she should lose some is inevitable, but no more than will confuse only such brethren as confound the hermetic with the mystic. In a word we should expect Maynooth to keep her identity.

The search for 'identity' of course is rather in vogue at the moment as a concept – if it is not perhaps more an infection than a concept, given the various symptoms such as unease, restlessness and crisis that are alleged to go with it. Maybe the case is as with 'culture' – the fact that we have grown hyper-conscious of it is indeed a symptom that something is already the matter with it. Institutions I suppose do have ethos and a kind of personality. But like personal charm or beauty in art it is less wisely cultivated directly than as a by-product of something more substantial. Let us look at Maynooth more substantially. The very modesty of our household is the basis of a certain identity. We should not wish our development to be uncontrolled so that the trees run to timber instead of fruit. We should not want mere expansion without organic growth, expansion without a centre into amorphous impersonal anonymity. If anything has 'gone wrong' with universities, this must surely be one of the deformations from which they suffer. If 'small is beautiful' anywhere, it should be in university colleges – so much so that we now sentimentalize them as 'learning communities'. (Not *too* small, however – there is a mean condition of 'golden mediocrity'.) And small not for beauty's sake but for effectiveness too. However well laid out the wares may be, the supermarket idea can hardly be the idea of the university. It is not education to give the student his trolley at the turnstile and ... *profite qui peut.* That is to take little account of the subtle process evoked by Socrates under the plane trees by the Ilissus. Minds are not made like that, and soul is not for sale.

Mention of the Ilissus brings to mind other simple but substantial elements of Maynooth's identity – its site for instance. 'What has this to do with my subject?!' With Socrates on his own, we can never be quite sure to what extent we are being had. We feel more secure when his dialectical irony is joined by the rare-veined thought of Newman. 'Why, the question of the site is the very first that comes into consideration when a *Studium Generale* is contemplated; for that site should be a liberal and a noble one ...'. And for his example he went back to the 'source of European civilization ... Athens, whose schools drew to her bosom ... the youth of the Western world for a long thousand years.' 'Bright and beautiful Athens' with air and landscape light and limpid as Attic intellect. Shall we say the anthology lines among our clichés? Not to acquaint ourselves with what we know already but to lay them as music to the soul or the balm of a prayer. 'Many a more fruitful coast or isle is washed by the blue Aegean, many is the spot more beautiful or sublime to see, many the territory more ample; but there was one charm in Attica which in the same perfection was nowhere else ... the special purity, elasticity, clearness, and salubrity of the air of Attica, fit concomitant and emblem of its genius ... '.

Now I am not quite ready to see the plains of Kildare as the equal of that ... And in our high flying we must take care even in Greece not to confuse Attica with Boeotia – just over the border but generally credited with air and brains of a much greater density than on the Attic side. No more would I see the Rye Water as having the same charm as the Ilissus. The point is the humbler one that beauty is as beauty does, and as air [...] and water go in these parts we have them, that is to say, a campus with some of the advantages that accrue to a 'learning community' from the *amoenitas* of a natural environment. And to discover not just Athens but a tradition in which such *amoenitas* clearly was important, we have only to look at the sites or the descriptions of great schools from the Vivarium of Cassiodorus to Clonmacnoise and beyond, with always their 'quiet watered land ... '. (Be it remarked in passing that we actually do have a vivarium on the campus too – or the makings of one if we can preserve it from little local environmental dangers ... .)

Our fishponds of course will be the setting for nothing more creative than the busy dartings of fish fat but ornamental, if it is not the composition of place for the identity that finally counts, an academic identity embodying our particular 'vision', our way to some kind of wisdom. And on the possibilities of this 'way' I shall confine myself to one element – that core of central and permanent disciplines talked about earlier. Here our very modesty of means has preserved for us a kind of academic identity that is an advantage to us at a time of re-thinking or re-discovering the idea of the university. We still have the centre in place, that core of central disciplines that others are trying to re-construct. If we believe in the idea, what we think of it, how we develop it, what the 'future of Maynooth' will be – the answers to all these questions depend on what we do about it. If the lines of this paper are valid, the future of Maynooth ought to be on those lines for good academic reasons, independent of the quest for identity. But it also happens to be our identity. Such an identity is something more than a quaint regional variation on the idea of the university. That is the idea of the university, older than the university technically so called, as old as Western reflection on ideals of higher education. It is Newman's idea. But he did not invent it. He only defined and elaborated the tradition magisterially. No need then to look for identity through academic gimmickry, in 'developments' and projects decided on as 'our thing', no matter how far off centre, for no better reason than that nobody else has yet staked the ground.

And why should we be speaking of these things only for 'the future' of Maynooth? How much use do we make of the possibilities we have on the ground in the present? On a compact campus, with a compact corps of teachers and students, and all the amenities of a more intimate human scale of things permitting personal and departmental contact, how much can and do we do about 'inter-disciplinary studies' without the formal fuss of theory? Consider Newman on the importance of Theology in the university – where again of course he had no need to argue from theory, only to present the evidence from the facts and the history of Classical Christian civilization. Need we wait for great constitutional changes before profiting from its presence here before our feet? What use do we make of it in criticism to illuminate literature? What use do we make of the imaginative mode of literature in our approach to the Word in Scripture and Theology? In the beginning was the Word. On matters more general, it was no very convinced believer who stood in front of Migne's *Leviathan* and thought how everything was there, *quidquid agunt homines*, 'religion, philosophy, history, biographies, arts, sciences ... gossip ... the whole range of human interest; like one of the great Middle-Age Cathedrals ... a study for life'. What provision are we making for the preservation of that vast identity at a time when even the theological student often gives the impression of believing that his subject began only with Vatican II? It is not only Theology's loss but that of so-called humanist studies as well, providers as they often are of stones instead of bread because fragmented into chaos in their 'autonomy' of any interpretative principle either historical or theoretical. And as regards specific study of Theology, in a Theological College now open to the lay student, would it not be time, a century after Newman, to take some steps towards giving the hungry sheep some theological grazing of their own?

But these are high Alps and I hurry down. I have stayed rather stubbornly high up there, in the air of 'ideals and principles'. Partly because one can be conveniently Platonic up there. But principally because 'ideals and Principles' have done civilization some service. And the university has been the great embodiment of ours. It was one order of perfection that sacred and secular agreed to join. The *Logos* was light .... The modern university is not only the heir but often stands on the site of age-old centres of light that might seem pretty dim by our standards but without which there would be no light at all.

Doubtless both physicist and philosopher are today less certain of the nature and source of light. But 'if all positions are doubtful, then the sceptical position must be doubtful, and the rest is silence'. There will always of course be history to read at the university. But that will still be in part the history, and the problem, of the 'ideals and principles' secreted by the metaphysical animal.

THE POPE AT MAYNOOTH: '... IN FRONT OF OUR FUTURE'

Arise Ierne! dry thy tears.
The shades of night are chased away;
The blissful beam of morn appears,
And long shall last the coming day.

Words taken from an ode delivered before the Lord Lieutenant of Ireland the year after the opening of the College, at the laying of the first foundation stone actually laid, on 20 April 1796, for the first addition to the Royal College of St Patrick *apud* Maynooth. The stone it was, alas, that later disappeared. Still it is handsome to have the ode and *ad rem* to recall it on the occasion of the latest, most distinguished and distinguishing visit that Maynooth has had in its history, that of Pope John Paul II on the Calends of October 1979 – when, as it happens, he blessed another foundation stone.

There was present, we are told, 'an immense crowd of people' on that day in April 1796, and 'the countenances of all manifested pleasing sensations of mind ... '. We borrow the phrases in October 1979 not for any necessary *adaequatio* they may have to the facts but to throw a span between historic moments at the extremes of Maynooth's history. If there was what could be accurately described as 'an immense crowd' in Maynooth on 20 April 1796, we need a differentiating term for the estimated 50,000 that gathered there on 1 October 1979. And 'pleasing sensations of mind ... ' would be genteel indeed for what manifested itself on their countenances, in the phenomenon of enthusiasm that broke for John Paul II at Maynooth as at every other place that he visited. In fact the College Chapel is said to have outdone all other venues – well, with one exception, perhaps. Waiting members of the household feared for the frescoes and the plaster on the roof. Never from jousting of Gael, never from any of the great waves of Ireland went there up a vocal wave like the sound that shook the Gothic vaulting from a thousand levitical throats drawn from the four seas of Erin and beyond. No wonder the Pontiff looked pale and for a while could only point mysteriously like Leonardo's John the Baptist. They were calmed with a *Pater* and a blessing. And when they wound out into view behind St Mary's, to hear there the unique address the Holy Father was to give, they came as quietly as a procession of surpliced angels with folded wings.

No odes were delivered on this occasion – though we are not without indications that Calliope stirred for a poet Pope. For one thing there would have been no time to deliver them – this visit was also one of the briskest Maynooth has had. ('The visit to Maynooth did not occupy very long; but it was very interesting ... He strode rapidly through the grounds ... ', i.e. Mr Gladstone in 1877.) Flanked by Chancellor Cardinal Ó Fiaich and President Monsignor Olden, John Paul II strode rapidly through the cloisters and his address. Little time for applause today, and none for poetry or Galway's golden flute. ('I will be visiting you soon, the Lord willing ... '.)

Address and cloisters alike asked for slow savouring, and it was no unwillingness to dally that obliged John Paul II to take them differently. But even the ten minutes that an official *ben trovato* allotted him in this place would have been a memorable moment in its history, and for the immense crowd that chose this place to see him.

As it was, when the last page of his script had been taken from him he held on to the microphone long enough to sing the Lord's Prayer – *Latine*. (And for the benefit of those who may know it only on television be it recorded that there was still enough Latin and plain chant in the Maynooth crowd to save the Pope having to do it solo – fine though his performance is.) When he grabbed the microphone again before leaving to ask us in Maynooth how many mistakes we thought the Pope had made, the present writer knew that it was definitely *not* the *Dies Irae* that had come – all previous sense for him being banged and bashed where he stood in a flying clangour of clashing trumps.

For another thing (as we were saying) the ode has gone out of fashion in an age that doubts its capacity to address the public occasion – because it doubts the public emotions, and doubting them ceases to have them. Or so we are told by the cognoscenti. But how do we identify the emotion engendered by John Paul II? Some will think they know. And none will claim that religious occasions are immune to ersatz enthusiasms. But only the ignorant or the cynical will operate on the ersatz by cutting out the genuine along with it. The false fills the void left by deprivation of the true. And however John Paul II be labelled in the conventional classifications, in a world of puff-ball emotions for tinsel occasions he brought out the depth of our need for real feelings directed to a real object. The media do a deal of business in nickel coinage and fizzed enthusiasms, but it was remarkable how often on this occasion their commentary fell back on the Christian vocabulary of joy.

And so it was at Maynooth on that chill morning. Some reporters thought the Maynooth park was strangely restrained in comparison with other venues, perhaps (they suggested) because there was no 'warm-up' in the interval before the Pope's arrival. Perhaps, indeed ... That crowd had kept all-night vigil before the

Monstrance on the papal podium, or made their way in unrestrained thousands all through the night and small hours and early morning.

If the 50,000 gathered in Maynooth made a kind of microcosm of Christianity in Ireland – past and present, College and parish, academic and pastoral, lay and religious – one might see something similar in Maynooth, College and village, throughout the preparations for the visit. Town and gown were one, and ecumenical too, in building up to a *Serdecznie Witamy* through an advent of expectation. The Pope was not due in Maynooth until Monday, but on Friday evening, the eve of his coming to the country, the village of Maynooth had the air of Christmas Eve in another clime, as the last touches were put to walls and doorposts. Saturday morning was a Sabbath again. A silent street, and commercial window wares replaced by flower arrangements draped in yellow and white. Even the waift derelict of many years' standing had been taken up by community charity and its nakedness covered. Many times one thought like the commentator on the country as a whole: would that this were for Ireland – and all the year.

All this for all that the Pope was not going to pass that way, but descend in the College with a great noise and a mighty wind from his helicopter. And in the College too that Sunday night and Monday morning made a unique eve and vigil. Especially if you allowed the long grey memory of Maynooth to brood on the scene. A memory that for one painful interval of doubt in the morning threatened to rise and take over the living. We heard of the rain and the fog in Cabra, studied the swirl around the top of the spire, watched the grey haze on Graf, and faced the grey back of St Mary's.[5] But pale pink managed to suffuse the grey East and Maynooth was not denied the consummation of this its Feast of Tabernacles.

For something like that was the mood of Maynooth through that night and morning in an unwonted combination of the genial, the expectant, and the recollected. Actual tents there were that night, set up in the best positions along Graf, to cover the vigil and the long wait for the passing of the 'popemobile' in the morning. (It never went that way, unfortunately, though it could have; but unlike the invalids at Knock the disappointed here seemed to be in the whole of their health and well able to take it.) And the setting favoured the mood. The air was mild as a Mediterranean night – a miracle some were known to have laid down as the spiritual-blackmail condition of their continued belief in the primacy of Peter and the historicity of Patrick! The Virginia creeper in its autumn flush was still unshorn from the walls of St Joseph's Square, the park trees retained their

5 The Graf (an allusion to Dublin's main shopping street, Grafton Street, then 'out of bounds') is the name given by seminarians since time immemorial to the broad path in the College Park (and playing fields) behind the west wing of the College known as St Mary's, a grey limestone building designed by Pugin the Elder.

crowning glory and the great generator lights made *chiaroscuro* of the banks of night green and the deep glades of shadow. At the apex of the scene, under St Mary's, the Monstrance radiated on the red podium where every Irish diocese took its turn to lead the vigil. In the corrals on the sward immediately in front, every variety of prayer position and mat eventually materialized. The Sisters were noticeably early in filling up theirs, combining prayer with a good eye to position for the morning. Segregated across the way the clergy were taking it more coolly, obviously content to come in a little later for the main feature. (So it was a little ungenerous, that anonymous winged word eavesdropped in the shadows, about always finding the clerics in the best places ....)

> But who was that walking towards me ... ?
> *There I saw one I knew, and stopped him ...*

Up and down Graf in the middle of this scene . . . the odd scholar, well known to be *parcus deorum cultor et infrequens* when they touched his night's rest, come to cast a humanist (Christian) eye on the scene and remaining to meditate – and lay the ghost of many a different night on Graf. Nor was it the scholar alone who was taken. In the small hours, uncomplicated visitors went in to wake their young so that they would go away on the morrow having seen this as well as the Pope. (Those young were in other tabernacles within, turned over by the residential staff given jubilee indulgence to keep such company and hospitality as in other days had dire consequences for Orders.) And all through the hours the scene filled, through the old gate and across the new bridge, dark battalions flowing back from all those Maynooth had sent out – for one morning five times the number she had sent out in two centuries.

Had the advent for which they came not taken place – and the fog this time was not in Maynooth! – the disappointment would have been cruel far beyond the moment and the numbers there. The Pope's visit to Ireland was a pastoral journey. But he is a man with a sense of history – as what Christian cannot? – and circumstances almost submerged the historical dimension of the Irish Christianity he came to visit. Maynooth is not the most ancient pile in Irish Christian history, not yet by a long shot even when the College Chapel is identified as fourteenth-century Gothic! But apart from being in modern times the principal *seminarium* from which went out the faith that brought back the loyal crowds to Maynooth – and to all other venues during those three days – Maynooth itself as a place and an institution focuses something of the history, religious, educational and political, of the Irish experience.

The gates to Maynooth are in the shadow of the great Geraldine keep, on ground where as far back as the fifteenth century there really was a 'Maynooth parliament', with plausible claim to be the political capital of Ireland. There since the thirteenth century had stood not only the Castle but the Church of St Mary. And there in the sixteenth century was founded the College of St Mary that with a bit of luck could have become the oldest university in Ireland. (Cracow was already 150 years old and had produced Copernicus.) To that ground the first modern 'Maynooth students' came in 1795, resuming the past not only of that place but of the far-flung ecclesiastical colleges in Europe to which Maynooth was to become the sole heir. From there have since gone out ten thousand ministers of Christ – not counting the carriers of *Vexilla Regis* – and three missionary movements, to every continent and to the pastorate of every parish in Ireland. It was a place that looked forward to having its hour with John Paul II.

Having spoken of Maynooth as a school of priestly holiness, an academy of theological learning, and a university of Catholic inspiration, he said to us: 'St Patrick's College is a place of rich achievement which promises a future just as great.' Time and circumstances did not permit development of that theme. But on the occasion Maynooth had assembled ecclesiastical and university students, theological and secular staff, rectors of ecclesiastical colleges and presidents of the National University of Ireland. The words heard are there to be the seeds of history. In those of Karol Wojtyla:

We stand in front of our future
which closes and opens at the same time.

And John Paul II blessed the stone for the library that will bear his name.

As we went in to lunch the big media tops were already coming down. Their revels were ended, for this time in this place. (But in their television images that night, the morning's grey haze on Graf was a purple glow, and the surrounding limes and sycamores were as solid, enclosing and venerable as rows of Roman oaks.) When we came out, so had the sun and the warmth. Yet another helicopter was banking overhead, just for the hell of it now, one felt, for the first time in weeks. Outside the sphinx gates the chrysanthemums that said *Serdecznie Witamy* had all been snatched away. In the evening a handful of purple flowers lay on a bench in the side-chapel of St Columba. A trickle of late pilgrims made their way from the late papal podium to the West Door and up the aisle to the High Altar. They asked for Communion from late celebrants who had not made it to the concelebrated Mass that still kept clergy and the great crowd together in the park behind St Mary's after the Pope had left us.

BLOOD-DIMMED TIDE? THOUGHTS ON THE APOCALYPSE

A book that provides no quotations, someone has said, is no book – it is a plaything. Well, the Apocalypse is no plaything. It is as full of [quotable quotes] as *Hamlet.* I propose to get into it simply by giving out a few of them. The Apocalypse is no joke either. Most people know that much – the very word has acquired dire connotations. Yet we discover from those quotations that we have been speaking its strange prose all our life.

'I am the Alpha and the Omega ... ' (1:8). 'If anyone has ears to hear, let him listen to what the Spirit is saying to the Churches' (2:7 – and to every one of the Churches of Asia Minor). '. . . You are neither cold nor hot. I wish you were one or the other, but since you are neither, but only lukewarm, I will spit you out of my mouth' (3:15f). 'Behold, I stand at the door and knock . . . ' (3:20). 'And day and night they never stopped singing: Holy, Holy, Holy is the Lord God, the Almighty' (4:8). 'They will never hunger or thirst again; neither the sun nor scorching wind will ever plague them ('Fear no more the heat o' the sun . . . ') . . . and God will wipe away all tears from their eyes' (7:16f). 'And a great sign appeared in heaven: a woman adorned with the sun, standing on the moon and crowned with twelve stars ... ' (12:1). 'Babylon has fallen, Babylon the great has fallen ... ' (14:8). 'And there I saw a woman riding a scarlet beast ... ' (17:3 – and the beast then was scarlet too!). 'Then I saw a new heaven and a new earth . . . I saw the holy city, the new Jerusalem, coming down from God out of heaven ... ' (21:1f). 'I shall indeed be with you soon. Amen; come, Lord Jesus' (22:20).

And I have not mentioned the Four Horsemen ... (6:2ff)! These are *direct* quotations. One should also draw attention to the *implicit* way in which for centuries and millennia Christian liturgy and civilization has spoken 'apocalyptic' in face of the apocalyptic moments of death and judgement. In the great meditation of the *Dies Irae.* In the great Responsorium *Libera Me*:

> Free me, O Lord, from eternal death on the fearful day
> when heaven and earth will be moved;
> Day of anger that day of ruin and misery, day of grandeur and grief,
> When heaven and earth will be moved ...

The same scene greets us in stone from the west doors of the great cathedrals. It is a vision of the 'last things' that stretches back to the Apocalypse, to Matthew 24 and to the 'Day of the Lord' in the Old Testament prophets. It is not a fashionable emphasis now. And we should indeed distinguish imagery from literal fact. But we should also distinguish fear from religious awe before the *mysterium tremendum*. The shudder of awe is mankind's highest faculty, somebody said.

***

It would be nice to be able to go on from there and write on the Apocalypse under the conditions that hold for other books of the New Testament. That is to say, an already shared understanding, as of a classic play or piece of music, of which we had to give not so much an explanation as a fresh 'interpretation'. But it is not easy to speak about a book as strange as the Apocalypse without some initial pedagoguery. And in any case we cannot pretend to the genius of a Pascal and expect our 'thoughts' to be anything more than 'pious' if they are detached from any overall view of the shape and meaning of the book they are derived from.

But that is our very first problem. It can hardly be the Classicist only who is frustrated if he cannot see how the work he is reading hangs together as a unity. A unity, said the very Classical Aristotle, is what has a beginning, a middle and an end. Now in the Apocalypse we see a beginning and an end all right. We would be in really bad case if we could not, in a work of which the central theme is precisely 'the Alpha and the Omega, the First and the Last, the Beginning and the End' (22:13). The problem is to follow the steps by which we get from the one to the other. And no wonder. We consult the experts, and, going no further than the Jerusalem Bible, we find that the Apocalypse 'presents many difficulties; repetitions, interruptions in the sequence of visions ... passages obviously divorced from their context ... '. We do some historical research and we find that this problem is as old as the book itself. For instance Dionysius, a third-century bishop of Alexandria, tells us that 'some of our predecessors rejected the book and pulled it entirely to pieces, criticizing it chapter by chapter and pronouncing it unintelligible and illogical, and the title false'.

But the obscurity of the book did not make the bishop reject it. He respected mystery, and would not condemn as valueless what could not be taken in at a glance. But what he further tells us about ancient criticisms of the *content* of the book can still be a mote to trouble the mind's eye. Especially the contemporary mind's eye, soft-focused as it is on *omnia vincit amor* (love overcomes everything). Christian love is indeed mentioned – 'you have less love now than you used to', the long-suffering Church at Ephesus is told (2:4). But what is this among so much that is written in the tone of 'Avenge, O Lord, thy slaughtered saints'? ' ... How much longer will you wait before you pass sentence and take vengeance for our death on the inhabitants of the earth?' (6:10). And the earth is harvested and its vintage trodden in the press of God's anger 'until the blood that came out of the winepress was up to the horses' bridles as far away as sixteen hundred furlongs' (14:20).

Exegetes wonder whether the John who wrote like this can be the same John as the evangelist of love. A Manichean dualist would wonder more fundamentally whether such material can be inspired by the God of the New Testament at all. And in fact Dionysius records that some critics before him attributed the book to the dreamings of the founder of a way-out heretical sect.

Need we protect the flank of our own orthodoxy as we mention such questionings? We can do no less than go along with the bishop we have been quoting. After as fine a piece of stylistic analysis as you could ask for, he concludes that the Apocalypse is not indeed by John the Evangelist, but is still from the pen of 'a holy and inspired writer'. The devil's advocate serves orthodoxy too. He highlights the initial difficulty, strangeness and obscurity of the Apocalypse. Such 'thoughts' as we arrive at will emerge from an attempt to make that strangeness more familiar and the obscurity a little more clear.

***

The first obscurity we struck was in the order and sequence of the book. One suggested explanation for this is that, in the properly apocalyptic part of the work, from chapter four on, two separate apocalypses have been run together. One way of reducing the result to some order for the understanding is to bear in mind that we are reading an 'apocalypse', to get a grip on some likely sequence of events in such a work, and then to allow for overlapping and consequent occasional disturbance of the sequence in the present 'contaminated' work. And that overall 'apocalyptic' sequence turns on times of trial and the ending of trials. Trials past and to come and to be faithfully endured in chapters one to three. And in chapter six and following, trials of which the end is first *prepared* and then *accomplished*, prior to the definitive ending of *all* persecution and evil and the establishment of a messianic age. All this starting from and contemplated under an all-inclusive vision of the transcendent Father and of Christ in glory (chapters four and five).

Trials ... and times of trial ... (for Christian believers, of course). None of us but knows something of that from history ancient or modern. So we can postpone that subject for the moment and start from another thought. From that vision of the transcendent God and of the glorified Christ, receiving 'praise, honour, glory and power for ever and ever' (5:14).

There is first the sheer fact of that vision. 'Apocalypse' *means* vision, revelation. The wilder connotations of 'apocalyptic' are secondary. 'This is the revelation', it begins, given by God through Jesus Christ. 'It was the Lord's day and the Spirit possessed me ... ' (1:10). 'I saw' he says again and again. What he sees in chapter four is the author of the universe, by whose will 'everything was made and exists' (4:11). And that vision generates the classical religious experience of the *holy*:

> Holy, Holy, Holy
> is the Lord God, the Almighty. (4:8)

John borrows the words of the great vision of Isaiah (6:3). And here as in so much else he puts himself in the line of the great prophets and their moments of mystical vision. How often do we say or hear those words of Isaiah and John without realizing that this is their original burden, the burden of the mystery, the *mysterium tremendum*, the transcendence before which we tremble with awe. And yet this experience is essential to vital religion. It is present not only in the grandeur of Isaiah but in the pastoral simplicity of the birth of Christ. 'The angel of the Lord appeared to them, and the *glory* of the Lord shone round about them, and they *feared* with a great fear' (Lk 2:9). Without that vision, moralistics and hermeneutics are empty cisterns, mills that grind without wheat.

Secondly, there is the function of that vision within the book. The book, as we have said, turns on trials and times of trial – the common connotation of 'apocalyptic' is not unjustified. And in this respect we have to be fairly innocent of history not to see the Apocalypse as a permanently relevant book, however obscure the details of its meaning. I am indebted to a colleague for the remark of a friend of his, to the effect that he thought the Apocalypse 'a barbarous book' – until he witnessed the final bombarding of Berlin. If anything, it is the kind of book without which we cannot come to terms with barbarism. And the deepest trial in such times of trial is the trial of faith and hope and meaning. The Apocalypse sets its times of trial within a vision of final order that looks to the goal of time, and a vision of transcendence that looks beyond time. It enlarges on Christ's own farewell words to his disciples. '... I have told you all this so that you may have peace in me. In the world you will have tribulation, but be brave, I have overcome the world' (Jn 16:33). Sin is behovely, but all shall be well ...

***

The Apocalypse starts from this high demanding level. And the historical trials are evoked in terms that are visionary, imagistic and of course obscure. And yet among the fascinations of the book is the fact that we do glimpse concrete historical reality through it. It borrows the imagery of the prophets on the Day of the Lord and the persecutions of the chosen people. But it gives that imagery a local habitation. The book was written out of a historical persecution, or persecutions, of Christians. The persecutor, imperial Rome, is clearly identifiable behind the symbolism of 'Babylon the Great' and the 'Scarlet Woman' who rides the 'beast' with seven heads. ' ... The seven heads are the seven hills, and the woman is sitting on them' (17:9). There is the clear intention of pointing to a particular emperor or emperors – 'there is need for shrewdness here ... ' (13:18; cf. 17:10).

One such identification seems to be of the notorious Nero (d. 68). Thoughts on the Apocalypse cannot fail to include a famous passage in the Roman historian Tacitus. It describes Nero's persecution of the Christians as political scapegoats for a great fire that devastated the centre of Rome in 64 – a fire otherwise thought to have been deliberately started by Nero himself, to facilitate his grandiose building projects. The passage fleshes out the lived reality out of which the Apocalypse could be written. 'First Nero had self-acknowledged Christians arrested. Then, on their information, large numbers of others were condemned, not so much for incendiarism as for their anti-social tendencies as haters of humanity. Their deaths were made farcical. Dressed in wild animals' skins they were torn to pieces by dogs, or crucified, or made into torches to be ignited after dark as substitutes for daylight. Nero provided his gardens for the spectacle ... ' (Tacitus, *Annals*, 15.44, tr. Grant).

It is worth noting too that it is not out of sympathy for what he calls the 'notoriously depraved Christians' that this sulphurous critic of Nero gives his report. 'Their originator, Christ, had been executed in Tiberius' reign by the governor of Judea, Pontius Pilatus. But in spite of this temporary setback the deadly superstition had broken out afresh, not only in Judea (where the mischief had started) but even in Rome. All degraded and shameful practices collect and flourish in the capital' (ibid.).

Under the same Nero, Sts Peter and Paul were to be put to death in the capital within a couple of years. They *could* be 'the two olive trees and the two lamps that stand before the Lord of the world' (11:4). If so, then the Apocalypse gives us a veiled contemporary glimpse of that momentous founding event. 'When they have completed their witnessing the beast that comes out of the Abyss is going to make war on them ... and kill them. Their corpses will lie in the main street of the Great City . . . Men out of every people, race, language and nation will stare at their corpses, not letting them be buried; and the people of the world will be glad about it ... because these two projects have been a plague to the people of the world' (11:7–10).

***

But the Apocalypse is more than a historical document about the past. Considered purely as literature it would have the permanent human value of a long tradition of great books written out of extreme situations which provoked meditation on ultimate questions, like the meaning of evil and of innocent suffering. But the Apocalypse is Scripture, with a claim to permanent meaning. And it is explicitly prophetic, having as its range the *whole* of history to its culmination. Under this latter aspect the book has an initial strangeness with which any thoughts about it must come to terms. A double strangeness, of content and form. Both are strange because they are truly 'apocalyptic' in the conventional connotation – prophetic of cataclysms that yet remain vague because presented through imagery and symbolism difficult to control, and in a time-frame without fixed perspective. An example is the 'four horsemen' of war, famine, plague and death.

A first solution is to observe that in this respect the Apocalypse is in no way different from, indeed belongs to, the same genre as the eschatological discourse of Christ in Matthew 24, which telescopes into one vision the end of Jerusalem and the end of the world. A second solution is to look at actual history, as it has so often been, and more than ever in our own century. I mentioned Berlin earlier. But Berlin is only one localized instance of all that this century has experienced of collective suffering and death. Ours is the century which has learned to speak of mega-death, man-made. The Marne, Verdun, the Kulaks, the Jews, the Poles, Auschwitz, Dresden, Hiroshima, Prague, Budapest, Vietnam, Biafra, El Salvador, Lebanon, Northern Ireland. We have known them all. Not just one 'holocaust' but many. The total of man-made death for the century has been estimated at a round hundred million. One writer has suggested that to the traditional 'two cities' we should now add a third, the City of the Dead. 'I had not thought death had undone so many ... '. Son of Man, can these bones live . . . ?

The initial strangeness of the apocalyptic form, or voice, can be overcome as easily as can that of its content. We do not even have to go back to the Old Testament *loci* on which John drew. We need only look at a certain kind of serious imaginative literature and art in any age. We might even be the better for so doing, if it helped us to decompartmentalize the sacred and the secular. Such literature and art often speaks with an apocalyptic voice. We need not go back to Virgil's 'Messianic' Eclogue. Our title is taken from Yeats's poem, 'The Second Coming':

> The blood-dimmed tide is loosed ...
> [. . . . . .]
> And what rough beast, its hour come round at last,
> Slouches towards Bethlehem to be born?

He did not live long enough to find out. There is Picasso's *Guernica*. There are Goya's *Capriccios* and *Disasters of War* (*no se puede saber por qué* – we cannot know the reason why). Certain poetry before the first world war is full of apocalyptic forebodings.

> The last age shall be worst of all
> And you and I shall see
> The sky wrapped in a guilty pall:
> Laughter on lips shall fail and fall, –
> Anguish of not-to-be ... (Alexander Blok)

The historian provides us with endless *facts* about our historical experience. The apocalyptist may seem to obscure the facts, but for all that it is he who lets in some light. Because he looks for the meaning of the facts, he looks below the surface of events into their depths and beyond the immediate happening to the eschatological. His visions and imagery may seem to put a blind between us and reality. But it is he who gives the deeper purchase on reality – by penetrating to the perception that only a mystery of iniquity is adequate to the enormity of the facts. A Great Beast is at the heart of the Apocalypse, 'I don't believe in the beast, of course,' says a character in William Golding's *Lord of the Flies*. 'As Piggy says, life's scientific, but we don't know, do we? Not certainly, I mean ... '.

But the Apocalypse does not stop with the mystery of iniquity. Precisely because its concern is with finality the end of its vision is an age when that mystery will be overcome. This is not the result of a point of view particular to John. It is the result of the centrality of Christ and the meaning of his accomplishment. As we have seen, the Apocalypse opens with a vision of Christ in glory. He has already redeemed men of every race and tongue. But this is only the beginning of the end-time that will see his reign established on earth. In this light the Apocalypse is like a great eschatological drama dealing with the end of the present age and the coming of a future world-era, and turning on a decisive struggle between God and Satan. In three acts: preparatory events ('beginning'), the struggle proper ('middle'), the *dénouement* ('end'). In this drama Christ is the 'hero' and the *dénouement* is the establishing of the Kingdom of God on a new earth with a new, heavenly Jerusalem as its capital. 'Then I heard a loud voice call from the throne, "You see this city? Here God lives among men. He will make his home among them; they shall be his people and He will be their God ... The world of the past has gone ... ' (21:3–4).

This final vision may seem as strange in its own way as the cataclysms on the way to it. But we forget that Christ already spoke of the moment when 'all is made new and the Son of Man sits on his throne of glory' (Mt 19:28). We forget too the vision at the heart of St Paul, the vision of the cosmos itself 'being freed like us from its slavery to decadence' (Rom 8:21). The Apocalypse is the last book in the collected works which launch man's history in a 'paradise'. The Apocalypse closes the epic circle as epics do – in return and restoration.

If we cannot accept that closing of the circle in its literal terms it may be that we have sound philosophical, exegetical or theological reasons. But the reason should not be that we too have minds that are purely scientific and positivist. That we cannot visualize the material world as other than it presently is, however opaque, preposterous, and pig-headed. That we are driven by no wonder about its final state and purpose. A historian who brought a philosophical mind to his researches has put the matter this way: 'Granted that civilizations are born and mature and perish, are we on earth merely to build – and then destroy – those civilizations that are but temporary structures, obsolescent machines, like a generation of termites building their galleried *termitaria* that will be destroyed and then reconstructed in the heedless permanence of the species?' It is the Judeo-Christian Scriptures that are most constantly and intensely concerned with an end-state that will not destroy but transform and preserve the world and all that man has lived in it. In that they are but the axis of the race. The race has never been able to do without this kind of vision, whether embodied in ancient myths of the Golden Age or in the various modern messianisms. Doubtless many are drunk. But not all. 'On the contrary, this is that which was spoken of by the prophet Joel: "And it shall come to pass in the last days (says the Lord). I will pour out my Spirit upon all flesh: and your sons and your daughters shall prophesy, and your young men shall see visions, and your old men shall dream dreams ... "' (Acts 2:16f; Joel 2:28).

VISIONS AND VISIONARIES: WHAT TO MAKE OF THEM?[6*]

THE TOPIC

In a large and complex matter the first important thing is to get clear what it is we are going to be talking about. The first part of my title, 'Visions and Visionaries', is self-explanatory, I should think. All the more so as I am talking about it at all only in response to what I hear is a recent development among yourselves – an 'outbreak' of interest in one particular visionary of modern times.[7] But I shall not be talking about her in particular. I shall be talking about the general phenomenon of which she is but one representative. In the light of what principles may emerge, I hope you will then have some few ideas to enable you, at least tentatively, to 'situate' and evaluate this particular – and particularly extraordinary – modern instance.

But from her too you will realize that the 'visions' of my title must cover 'hearings' as well as 'seeings'. In her case words spoken by and to *others*, in action and dialogue. But also in her case words spoken to and for herself alone – 'locutions' as they are called in the traditional technical term.

THE PROBLEM

The second part of my title is a question – 'What to make of them? ' For these phenomena do pose questions. They are problematical. And they are problematical for a reason obvious even to commonsense. We cannot straight away without question trust and believe things seen and heard in modes beyond the ordinary. Not even, should it happen, when seen and heard by oneself; not to mention when they are only reported to us as having been seen and heard by others.

This is not a new or particularly modern problem. It is as old as the whole Christian tradition of spirituality and spiritual experience. Indeed it is older. For visions and visionaries are not confined to Christianity. They are both pre-Christian and extra-Christian. We know of their frequency in the Old Testament. But the ancient Greeks and Romans also knew visions and visionaries, and they even

6* A talk given to Maynooth students, 7 December 1991.

7 Maria Valtorta (1897–1961), author of *Il Poema dell' Uomo-Dio* (English translation: *The Poem of the Man-God*). The work purports to narrate the whole life of Christ, as seen and heard by her.

gave a good deal of thought to the problem of 'what to make of them'. In fact, seeing visions, hearing voices, dreaming dreams, is a primordial and universal phenomenon. And a surprising amount of what the ancient Greeks and Romans worked out for the problem of what to make of them passed into the Christian grid for sifting analogous phenomena – for what Christianity came to call the discernment of spirits.

So, neither the phenomenon nor the problem is new. Nevertheless the problem has certain new dimensions today which make discernment more problematical than in other times.

One such new dimension is the sheer multiplicity of visions and apparitions in our time. Internationally known interpreters of these phenomena cannot keep up with the calls on their expertise. The Abbé Laurentin recently confessed to being 'amazed, overwhelmed, and dazzled by the contemporary multiplication of apparitions, communications, and extraordinary charisms. Seven years ago, I did not know any active seers. Today, I know dozens. I didn't know any stigmatics. Today, I know a dozen ... I ask myself the burning question, What does this multiplication mean ... illuminism or an outpouring of grace?'

Such multiplication always raises an extra degree of uncertainty, doubt, even suspicion. The doubts arise from what we know of the possibilities for mimetism, psychological suggestibility, fraud – not to mention plain old-fashioned interventions by Old Nick himself. The authentic core even of Lourdes drew after it precisely this kind of dark penumbra.

In addition to the doubts raised by multiplicity, another new dimension to the problem of discernment today is all that is known about the deeper depths of the human psyche, in particular about all its mechanics of deception, illusion and delusion.

But once again, when I refer to all that as a 'new dimension', maybe it is less the matter than the systematizing of it that is new. For long before Freud and Jung *et hoc genus omne*, the great spirituals of the great tradition were acquainted with those depths, and with the phantoms, and even the monsters that emerge from there. And they questioned their visions and voices accordingly. It was already St Augustine – and long before him the Psalmist from whom he borrowed a phrase – who wrote of the *abyssus humanae conscientiae*, the abyss of human interiority, and the *grande profundum*, the great deep that man is.

To avoid becoming entirely negative about visionary possibilities in face of this contemporary awareness of depth-psychology we must balance our attitude to it. While we must take account of it, we must not allow it to throw out the baby with the bathwater, to reject the capacities of the human spirit (not to mention the Holy Spirit) along with the aberrations of the human psyche. The human soul has different levels, and the psyche is not the spirit ... and psychology is not spirituality. All this was too was well known to the great spiritual voyagers of the past. A recurring pattern is precisely the journey inward. And the point at which they touched the Beyond, or were touched by it, they knew variously as the very Ground or Apex of the Soul.

The point then is that we must not take our modern awareness to the extreme of thinking that *every* visionary phenomenon can be explained, that is explained away, by merely psychological mechanisms, whether normal, paranormal or aberrant. Prudence is one thing – the *testing* of the spirits. It is another thing to carry prudence to the point where we are no different from the secular sceptics and reductionists (and indeed some religious ones as well). Their very *principle* of interpretation is that every visionary phenomenon can be explained (away) by natural psychology – and thereby they exclude all supernatural intervention, either because they don't believe there *is* any supernatural, or because, if there is, they do not believe it intervenes to produce visionary experiences.

That can hardly be the orthodox Christian attitude.

A THEOLOGICAL FRAMEWORK

After putting myself so far safely behind the wire of all those qualifications, let me move on to a more systematic evaluation of visionaries – what are we to make of them? The evaluation, of course, will be in terms of principles, not of individual cases, which always have to be examined on their individual merits.

But even in matters of principle, we must still weave a couple of *preliminary* principles into the protective wire.

The first of these principles is that we cannot expect any essentially new revelation from visions and locutions. That does not exclude the possibility of their giving us new directions in accord with new 'signs of the times'. But Revelation proper came definitively in Jesus Christ.

The second preliminary principle is that here below we live by faith. So St Paul, 1 Corinthians 13:12 (in the very context of talking about visions and other charisms): 'Now we are seeing a dim reflection in a mirror; but then we shall be seeing face to face. The knowledge that I have now is imperfect; but then I shall know as fully as I am known.' So spoke Christ himself to doubting Thomas: 'You believe because you can see me. Blessed are they who have *not* seen and yet believe'.

The whole Christian tradition of spirituality emphasizes that principle – and none more than the mystics and visionaries themselves. And they emphasized it all the more for another well-known fact, that outside exceptional cases 'higher experiences' are transient. They may influence an entire life, but leave it to be lived in the prose of faith – and sometimes, strangely, in painful doubt whether the experiences were ever more than imagined.

All that being said, however, I think it is safe to say that it is at least a trying religious life, if not a deprived one, that never has anything *more* than naked faith, faith that never has an experiential dimension to it, some experience to warm its heart as it were, to make our assent to faith '*real*' and not merely '*notional*' (to use Newman's well-known terms). We are told by St Paul to 'pray without ceasing' (1 Thess 5.17). One thinks of an analogous human activity. It is at the least off-putting to write letter after letter to a correspondent that never replies ... At best it is a frustrating one-way traffic. At worst we might begin to wonder if there is anybody at the address ... !

It is a dangerous phrase, but there *is* a sense in which 'seeing is believing', especially in our time. It is one key to the growth of interest in prayer and meditation. There is a widespread desire among people for a 'break-through', to 'get in touch', to 'make contact', to get beyond knowing *about* into simply *knowing* the invisible realities of faith. It is safe to say that the contemporary multiplicity of visions and visionaries is not unrelated to all that. Some of them will, of course, be illusory. But some will be genuine. And in answer to the need they may fulfil, it would be, at the least, very undiscriminating on the part of the minister of religion to adopt the attitude of, at worst, being cynical about them, at best keeping them all at the same safe distance of the proverbial barge pole. We can leave it to the secularizing reductionists to do our mocking for us.

It is time to get back to that 'systematic evaluation' I promised. By 'systematic evaluation' I do not mean here the working out of criteria by which to *judge* visions and apparitions, that is, to decide about any particular case whether it can be accepted as presumptively genuine or should be rejected as illusory. Such criteria do exist but there will be no space for them in the present paper.

Except, perhaps, to draw attention to the considerable margin of freedom we have when it comes to making judgements. Except in the most patent cases of the false or the fraudulent, judgements even by ecclesiastical authority are never definitive to the degree that would *oblige* an individual to accept them as final and binding. Even a papal judgement on such matters does not have the charism of infallibility. All of which of course does not mean that in making up our own minds we need never pay attention to official ecclesiastical judgements.

There are statements by the Magisterium to this effect. Thus Benedict XIV: 'Without prejudice to the integrity of Catholic faith a person may withhold his assent to such revelations [i.e. approved by the Church], provided he does this with due modesty, not without reason, and without contempt.' Again an authentic declaration of 1877, concerning apparitions like those of Lourdes and La

Salette; 'The Apostolic See has neither approved nor condemned such apparitions or revelations but merely permits Catholics to believe in them – where they have support of credible witnesses and documents – with a purely human faith.'

By 'systematic evaluation' then, I mean a more positive attempt to situate visions (and locutions, as I explained) within a total theological framework. Now that is a large undertaking in a small space. And it is a risky business for someone who is not a professional theologian. On the other hand, you might find my non-professionalism reassuring. For it means I shall have to borrow from the professionals. All the same though, I have found it reassuring myself to find some ideas of my own validated by those professionals.

Already many years ago, I used to be asked 'What do you think of the charismatics?' At that time, even the charismatics were still a new and doubtful phenomenon, at least on my native heath. And visions and apparitions were not as thick on the ground as they have since become – or at least they were not known to me. So I did not know too much about the problem of my charismatic questioners. But I knew how to kick for touch . . . And I found it in the Acts of the Apostles, where visions and the Gifts of the Holy Spirit are so prominent. And I said, 'I see no problem. . . If those phenomena were valid in those days why not in our own day too?'

We know the events of the first Pentecost Sunday – the descent of the Holy Spirit in tongues of fire and the speaking in foreign tongues by the Apostles so that every nationality of the assembled Jewish Diaspora each understood in their own native language. 'Everyone was amazed, and unable to explain it ... Some, however, laughed it off. "They have been drinking too much new wine", they said ... Then Peter stood up ... and addressed them in a loud voice: ... "These men are not drunk, as you imagine; why, it is only the third hour of the day. On the contrary, this is what the prophet spoke of:

> In the days to come – it is the Lord who speaks – I will pour out my spirit on all mankind. Their sons and daughters shall prophesy, your young men shall see visions, your old men shall dream dreams." ' (Acts 2:14ff, Joel 3:1ff)

And among the men later to see visions was Peter himself, and not even a literal but a symbolic vision, in the sheet let down from heaven with a complete menagerie of animals and birds – signalling to him that the pagans too were to be received into the Church, in the person of the Roman centurion Cornelius (Acts 10).

That is one pole of a theological framework, the *positive* pole. It is St Peter who also provides us with the *negative* pole, the more careful and circumspect pole. In 2 Peter 1:16ff, to prove that it is not any 'cleverly invented myths' that he is repeating when preaching the knowledge and power of Our Lord Jesus Christ, he emphasizes the fact that 'we had seen his majesty for ourselves – referring to Christ's Transfiguration – 'when we were with him on the holy mountain'.

This he regards as the fulfilment of what was said in prophecies .... 'And, he says, you will be right to depend on prophecy, and take it as a lamp for lighting a way through the dark until the dawn comes and the morning star rises in your minds.'

But ... at once a caveat. 'At the same time, we must be most careful to remember that the interpretation of Scriptural prophecy is never a matter for the individual. Why? Because no prophecy ever came from *man's* initiative. When men spoke for God it was the Holy Spirit that moved them.'

All this is only an extended and vivid illustration of the age-old Christian principle of the need for 'discernment of spirits', the need to 'test the Spirits to see if they come from God'.

The first phrase is from St Paul, 1 Corinthians 12:10. In the very chapter where he lists, approves and recommends the gifts of the Holy Spirit, including that of prophecy (which would often be in the mode of vision – as indeed in the Old Testament prophets), he includes also the necessity of another gift, or charism, the gift of 'discerning Spirits', i.e. of knowing whether a charism is from God, nature, or ... the Evil One.

This necessity is made more explicit in the second phrase I quoted above. It is from 1 John 4:1:

> It is not every spirit ... that you can trust; test them to see if they come from God; there are many *false* prophets now in the world.

It might seem that we are back to a very negative attitude again. Only if you forget that I presented the picture as a *diptych*, to show the negative *and* the positive. The *possibility* of authentic visions and prophecies: yes; that visions and prophecies are *always* authentic, and indemnified against any need to examine and test them: *no*. And to put in a nutshell the answer to my question, 'What to make of them?' – these two poles are the two permanent hard shoulders – or should I say soft margins? – of the strait and narrow way to an answer.

THEOLOGICAL PRINCIPLES DEEPENED

But with that fairly simple theological framework set up, I think we can go on to deepen it. That deepening involves setting out a certain number of principles and facts. Space here will not permit me to elaborate on them very much. But I hope that in a Christian context they are obvious enough and logical enough not to need much elaboration.

The first point concerns the *possibility* of visions, revelations, apparitions. Are they *possible*, as a matter of *principle*? On God's part, that is. You might think the question should not need to be asked – or only to provide the answer at once, that nothing is impossible to God. But maybe the question does need to be asked - in order to draw attention to the truth of the answer. In the general climate of today, physical science has become so real and God so remote and unreal that for many people the laws of matter have taken over the immutability and the omnipotence that were once the attributes of God. We see this most clearly perhaps in a widely diffused attitude to miracles – whether Scriptural or contemporary does need to be asked – in order to draw attention to the truth of the answer. In the general climate of today, physical science has become so real, and God so remote and unreal, that for many people the laws of matter have taken over the immutability and the omnipotence that once were the attributes of God. We see this most clearly perhaps in widely diffused attitudes to miracles – whether Scriptural or contemporary, They *couldn't* happen, ergo they didn't.

But of course it is preposterous as an a priori principle to assume that the Creator either cannot or will not ever override the laws inbuilt by himself into his own creation. 'The pot has no right to say to the potter: Why did you make me this shape? Surely a potter can do what he likes with his clay?' (Rom 9:20f).

The same principle applies to the possibility of extraordinary modes of seeing and hearing and knowing in which divine intervention over-rides the natural modes of human perception – and draws back the veils to reveal levels of reality that are beyond the ken and capacity of the natural modes of human cognition. Natural, that is, as distinct from *praeter-* and *super*natural.

In a second stage in laying a deeper theological foundation, we advance from possibilities to facts. For it is a historical fact that all through the Old Testament and the New Testament visions and apparitions have been a constant mode, or medium, in which Revelation itself has been communicated. 'At various times in the past and in various different ways God spoke to our ancestors through the prophets ... ' (Heb 1:1).

It is unnecessary to illustrate that fact in detail. We can check it out for ourselves in Scripture – all the way from Moses, faced with the Lord speaking out of the Burning Bush, down to the transcendent visions and voices and prophecies of the author of the last book of the Bible, the Apocalypse of St John on the island of Patmos. 'Do not be afraid; it is I, the First and the Last ... Now write down all that you see, of present happenings and of things that are still to come ... (Apoc 1:17).

The conclusion we can draw is this: if Revelation was conveyed in such modes in the Old Testament period and in the establishment of the new Christian dispensation, we cannot exclude a priori and in principle the possibility of God's speaking in similar ways in later Christian history. And of course Christian history provides us with much evidence that he has done so – unless we are prepared to get rid of the evidence by explaining away every single instance of such phenomena as due to normal or aberrant psychological mechanisms. In fact, such continuity of charisms is something we might even expect, in view of our contemporary rediscovery of the continuity of the working of the Holy Spirit and of the 'prophetic' element in the Church. 'I shall ask the Father and he will give you another Advocate, to abide with you for ever ... ' (Jn 14:15f). And consequently one of our principles must be 'never [to] try to quench the Spirit or treat the gift of prophecy with contempt' (1 Thess 5:19).

Some modern theologians have even suggested that the tradition of 'corporeal' or 'imaginative' modes of vision is more in accord with the historical and incarnational character of Christianity than is the higher mode of mystical imageless contemplation (known in the traditional terminology as 'intellectual', but in fact *trans*-intellectual in as much as it is a mode of 'seeing' that goes beyond even concepts). In much of the Christian tradition this mode has been heavily emphasized as superior, in part because of a profound distrust of the mode of images, with their greater possibilities of illusion as well as their greater inadequacy as representations of higher Realities. Of course, God and transcendent spiritual Reality is beyond all possible imaging and even conceptualizing. But in Revelation and tradition the higher unvisualizable spiritual Realities have also been 'translated' into visible images, signs and symbols. And this, too, some modern theologians have seen as not only in accord with human nature but even necessary to it. For man is a creature not only of the head, or of the apex of the soul, but also of the heart and the imagination. In fact he is not only an *animal rationale* but also an *animal symbolicum*, a symbolizing creature, who naturally and spontaneously translates even spiritual reality into the visible language of image and symbol. That is one positive thing that modern depth-psychology has made us more aware of, but once more the fact is witnessed to not only by the visionary tradition but also by the endless riches of iconography in the long and neglected tradition of Christian art.

Needless to say, here too, perhaps especially here, there is the necessity of testing the spirits. On the one hand there is the risk of the visible signs and symbols projecting only the subjectivity of the seer himself, and not the objective reality of something outside him. On the other hand, where the transcendent and the divine are concerned, what is made visible in sign and symbol is not the transcendent Reality as it is in itself. Those visible signs and symbols are only translations and transpositions of what is invisible to corporeal or imaginative seeing. We are glad to see them, but we realize that we must look through and beyond them to the Original. Said the Angel to the awe-struck Tobit and his son: 'You thought you saw me eating, but that was appearance and no more' (Tob 12:19). In this life we are always 'seeing [only] a dim reflection in a mirror', 'in a glass darkly' as the vivid old translation put it (1 Cor 13:12). It has to be noted too that even when a vision or apparition is *grosso modo* authentic and 'objective' it is not necessarily so in all of its details ... ! In the long tradition the writings even of genuine visionaries are full of obvious examples of such details ... unacceptable to the point of being bizarre.

I have dealt with two points in the attempt to put visionary phenomena into a more developed theological framework. The first was on the *principle* of their a priori *possibility*. The second was on the historical *fact* that such phenomena have been one of the modes of divine Revelation itself, a mode continued in the Christian tradition – a continuity for which we found reasons even to expect it.

A RADICAL THEOLOGY OF GLORY

My third and last point will use a great contemporary theologian to give a still deeper theological grounding to both the fact and the suggested reasons for it. I refer to that modern giant, Hans Urs von Balthasar. One of his monumental works, in several volumes, is entitled *Herrlichkeit* in the original German, translated into English as *The Glory of the Lord*. Here I want to draw attention only to that *aspect* of it that is relevant to our topic – because it provides the deepest and most comprehensive theological framework so far for an answer to our question.

Von Balthasar is profoundly relevant in that, as his title indicates, he takes up that constant attribute of God in Revelation – his *glory*, his *kabod*, his *doxa*. Glory is a poor, worn, flattened-out word in our debased vocabulary. But in divine Revelation and the Books that contain it, it is the word which names the supreme attribute of that Supreme Reality which no man might see and live. (See e.g. Ex 33:18–23.)

Now when *we* hear the word *Revelation* we think of God's *words*, of God *speaking* ... But we know that God's Revelation came also through *events* – including, as I said earlier, visionary events, even events 'translated' into non-literal, symbolic images. What von Balthasar does is to push the mode of revelation back to something even more fundamental – to the revelation, the unveiling, of God's *glory* as the first and fundamental revelatory event.

> It is significant that at decisive places in Scripture God's 'glory' (*kabod*) manifests itself *before* God's word is heard. This is the case with the great epiphany on Sinai, the vision in the burning bush, the visions through which Isaiah and Ezekiel received their vocations, the visions on Tabor

> and at Damascus, and finally the apparition of the Son of Man at the beginning of the Apocalypse. The fact that God's glory first appears without any words makes clear whence it is that it comes and the consequent paths that God's word will have to take. Such glory without words is, in effect, the apparition of him who, in his utter differentness, must be perceived in his reality and truth before his address can be heard
> (THE GLORY OF THE LORD, VOL. 6, P. 12).

Now the depth and comprehensiveness of von Balthasar is in his tracing of this mode of Revelation, this 'seeing' of God's glory, not only in Scripture but down through the post-biblical centuries, in secular as well as religious literature, in conceptual scientific theology as well as in the writings of mystics and visionaries. And through it all, the glory of the Lord is shown as made visible not only as it is in himself but also as it flashes out from its reflection in God's creation. 'His glory fills the whole earth', cried the Seraphim to one another in Isaiah's vision (6:3).

Now this sense of 'glory', this sense of the radiance of what has been unveiled, is a feature of all visions and visionaries. They speak of an unearthly radiance, an inexpressible, incommunicable beauty, 'what no eye has seen nor ear heard ... (1 Cor 2:9; Is 64:3). This refers to the glory of the Beyond, of the transcendent, of the Totally Other. But in some of the greatest visionaries, this glory envelops and transforms God's visible creation as well. St Francis is a well-known example. Maria Valtorta had that sensitivity by nature. But, inter alia, she was also a disciple of St Francis. And as a visionary, she had this natural sensitivity intensified from a higher source. She came to see all created things as existing in God – as did, for instance, St John of the Cross. I would like to end with a quotation from her, not the best one out of an endless choice, but poignant and brief.

I take the passage from her autobiography. She wrote it at a time when already for ten years she had been an invalid confined to her room. In all that time she had been cut off from 'the poem of creation', the sights and sounds of which she had loved so intensely as reflections of God. And never in the future either would she see or hear them. 'Now I see you no more with my mortal eyes. Never again will I see you, O fair things made by my God.' But that is not the end. She will see them again in God, with immortal eyes:

> Come, come O Kingdom of peace after so much suffering, and give back to me, Oh! then yes, give back to me all that I have given up ... Give me back the stars and the flowers, give me back the songs of birds and of moving waters and the shining of the sun, give me back everything, because all

> things are in God, and when I shall be one with God who is All I shall possess all things anew, and for eternity. Come, come, divine Beauty ... let the veils be drawn back that still hide your Perfection from me ... and after the cross give me the joy of being with You.

After all our qualifications and hesitations about visions and visionaries should not our last word be that:

> (1) we all stand in need of *some* glimpse of that glory, and
> (2) *some* certainly have glimpsed it, and to know them is to be reassured of its reality!

In the meantime a post-Epiphany Collect even permits us to pray God to fill our own interior vision with the same radiance that he streamed into the hearts of our Fathers [and Mothers!].

THE CANONIZATION OF EDITH STEIN

It was my first morning in Rome. It was 9 a.m. in St Peter's Square. It was ominously dark. The black sky was louring over the umbrella pines. I had an appointment, but the time passed and nobody turned up. Not being a familiar, I had chosen the wrong 'Bronze Door'. Instead of Raphael and the Apostolic Palace, I was to watch an outdoor Roman spectacle. The sullen clouds burst over the pines, over the Square, over the head of St Peter and over the heads of all his confrères ranged on top of Bernini's colonnade. Around St Peter's the waterspouts became photogenic waterfalls. Thunder rolled overhead. Beyond the pines, Jovian bolts flashed from heaven to earth. The spectacle lasted till noon, while the plasticated tourists dripped in and out and left lakes in the portico of St Peter's. In another time the spectacle would have been an epiphany of Yahweh, who rides upon the wind, makes the tumult of waters, and shoots lightning for the rain.

In any case, it was my personal prelude to the main event that took me to Rome, the canonization of the twentieth-century martyr, Edith Stein. As it happened my presence was linked to a recent commemoration of a sixteenth-century martyr, Thomas More. It was a happy conjuncture. The one had a successful career in the world, the other could look forward to that. Both not only gave it up for a higher cause but made the ultimate sacrifice in witness to that cause. On the morning of 11 October 1998, the rains were over and gone; we needed shelter only from the blue sky and its hot sun, and only the murmur of the multitude was heard in St Peter's Square and down Via della Conciliazione. There were sixty thousand there, an estimated two thirds of them from Germany and Poland – Edith Stein's native Breslau was then German and is now Polish. Ecclesiastical colours splashed as remote international dignitaries passed, met, and were suddenly human in their mutual recognition and greetings. Bursts of applause punctuated the air as Chancellor Kohl appeared striding to his place. It was most sustained when John Paul II rode by in his popemobile. Overlooking the panorama, a tapestry hung high on the façade of St Peter's, a portrait photo of Edith Stein, in Carmelite veil, with questioning visage and eyes looking into the distance.

As the Mass approached the rite of canonization, the words of the liturgy spoken by the Pope set the solemn tone and context of the event. Out of 'the brutal suffering visited upon so many' in this twentieth century 'we contemplate the witness of Edith Stein, Teresa Benedicta of the Cross (this daughter of Israel and daughter of Carmel ... The bow of the mighty has been broken, life is more powerful than death ... .'

When the formula of canonisation ended, enrolling Edith Stein among the saints, the Sistine Choir sang an exultant motet – *tibi laus Domine, tibi gloria* – 'Glory and praise to you, Lord. Your servant Teresa Benedicta of the Cross, Edith Stein, crowned with honour and glory, is now our radiant intercessor in her heavenly abode.' The Holy Father intoned the *Gloria in Excelsis* that then rose up from the great assembly. In his homily he reminded us that in annual commemoration of the new saint and martyr, this 'daughter of Israel', 'we must remember year after year the Shoah too, that barbarous scheme for the annihilation of a people, a scheme to which millions of Jewish brothers and sisters were sacrificed'. Among the listeners were some of Edith's relations.

The Pope returned briefly to this theme at the close of the ceremony. The noon bell tolled, and quiet fell for the Angelus. In some personal concluding words, the Pope linked Edith Stein to another victim of Auschwitz, his countryman, Maximilian Kolbe, who died in August 1941, exactly a year before Edith Stein. Recalling that he had canonized him too in this same place in 1982, the Holy Father went on to remark that:

I have always had the conviction that these two martyrs of Auschwitz lead us together towards the future ... I am conscious today that a certain cycle is being closed. I thank God for all that ...

Apart from his hopes for the new millennium and putting his seal on the martyrs to the barbarism that marked the closing century of the last one, the Pope would have more personal reasons for giving thanks on the occasion that Providence had given him. He would feel a bond with both, to Maximilian Kolbe as his countryman, but to Edith Stein as a kindred spirit.

That kinship is deep and various, and too complex to set out here in more than outline. In summary, one might say that they share the same intellectual and spiritual 'universe of discourse'. To start with the spiritual as the most immediate to the occasion, there is their common interest in Carmelite spirituality. The Pope's doctoral dissertation was on John of the Cross – whose name Edith Stein took in the Carmelite order, along with Teresa. The Teresa in question is Teresa of Avila; the accidental discovery of her autobiography, read throughout a whole night, was the final decisive occasion of her conversion. Her last (unfinished) work was on John of the Cross (*The Science Of the Cross*).

The spiritual quest, above all in the Carmel, is the mystical quest. And the mystical quest is the quest for ultimate *Veritas*, truth, in its very ground – at its highest point understood in a mode beyond the conceptualizing intellect. That is why the reading of St Teresa's Life was so decisive for Edith Stein: 'This is the truth!' she exclaimed.

After *Veritatis Splendor* and *Fides et Ratio*, not to mention his earlier academic career in philosophy, we need not delay with an account of the importance of the quest for truth in the œuvre of John Paul II – for him the quest did not have to start from Truth's initial absence.

The case was different for Edith Stein. Referring back later to her 'discovery' of St Teresa, she speaks of 'my long search for the Truth' – now at last ended. Parallels with St Augustine's quest have rightly been drawn. 'Oh! Truth, Truth, how deep within me, even then, the very marrow of my soul sighed for You ... ' (*Conf.* III 6,10). Augustine was nineteen at that stage. Edith Stein was thirteen when her problems started. That was the age at which this daughter of a believing and practising Jewish family discovered she could no longer pray or practise. She could no longer believe in a personal God.

But the truth about the meaning of existence, especially the existence of the human person, became all the more a question and a quest. ('I became for myself an immense question,' says Augustine (*Conf.* IV 4,9). It was precisely that question and quest that led her back to the supreme Person – but beyond that to the one God who is three Persons. And in her concern with the Person and personality we find a precise kinship with John Paul II. The human person is central to his thought. The kinship is not accidental. Both of them came to that focus through the influence of the contemporary philosophical school of phenomenology, especially in its founding fathers, Edmund Husserl and Max Scheler.

To put it simplistically, phenomenology addressed again (especially in the wake of Kant and his 'Copernican revolution') the age-old problem of what can we know, and how can we know it? It did this by turning from the 'object' to the 'subject' and studying the subjective Phenomena involved in knowing. By so doing it went beyond the conceptualizing intellect and brought the whole person into play in the process of cognition – sense and sensibility (to 'values' as well as 'truths'), imagination and intuition, the whole organic depth of what Augustine called the abyss of human consciousness. In fact, of course, there have been phenomenologists *avant la lettre,* and Augustine was one such. Similarly the concept of the unique person is as old as Christological and Trinitarian theology. But neither phenomenological epistemology nor the philosophy of the person have ever been developed as they might have been. They are particularly relevant today, with the centrality of the human individual, and the realization that abstract truths and a priori norms do not suffice to convert his *heart.* And that is one of the places where Edith Stein and John Paul II fit in – as well as together. But it is to be noted that they fit together in one other way too. On analysis, they both found that, while phenomenology furnished *phenomena,* they needed Aquinas to ground them in an *ontology* of the objective 'thing-in-itself'. But the objective personalism of even Aquinas leaves the person largely unanalyzed. Karol Wojtyla turned to the Augustinian tradition and the phenomenological method to explore what Augustine called the *abyssus humanae conscientiae*.

Very much to the phenomenological point are some words the Pope spoke at the end of his long day, after a splendid concert that culminated in a *Te Deum* composed in his honour. He quoted Edith Stein: 'There are circumstances in which we understand one another more easily without words.' He went on to add: 'Music, when it expresses the noble feelings of the human spirit, has no need of words to make itself understood.' St Augustine admitted the same truth – however reluctant the anti-sensuous Platonist in him. Hearing the Psalms sung he felt that 'every one of the diverse emotions of the human spirit has each its appropriate mode of expression in voice and song, evoked by I know not what secret affinity' (*Conf.* X 33,49).

From Aristotle through Plotinus to Aquinas and beyond, the nature of that secret affinity has been analyzed in a more philosophically technical tradition – albeit that even technicians must build on the 'phenomenology' of lived experience. The affinity is twofold, epistemological and ontological. The epistemological affinity is that between the perceiving subject and the object perceived. They stand to each other in a mutual relation of 'potency' to 'act'. The human spirit is *quodammodo omnia*, said Aristotle and Aquinas. The ontological affinity is the *splendor veritatis* that radiates from the transcendental 'circumincession' of the true and the beautiful.

Edith Stein was a mystic philosopher, and therefore knew those truths at a higher level than pure reflection. That is clear in her magnificent ode to the Holy Spirit – recited in the original German at the concert. We can fittingly conclude with a sample of it:

> Who are you, dulcet light that fills my soul,
> Illuminating the darkness of my heart?
>   [...]
> Are you perchance the enchanting chant of love
>   And sacral awe
> That resonates eternal around the Triune Throne
> Melding in itself the true-ring sound of all that exists?
>   The harmony
> That accords the members to the head,
>   Wherein each one
> Enraptured his being's mystery meaning finds ...

ART & LITERATURE

A POET IN GLASS[1*]

> 'She saw Our Lord more clearly than she had ever seen anybody else. She saw him look up when he had placed the crown on his mother's head; she heard him sing a few notes, and the saints began to sing. The window filled up with song and colour, and all along the window there was a continual transmutation of song and colour.'

That was little old Biddy M'Hale, in a moment of vision before her personally donated stained glass window, in the new church at 'Kilmore', in one of the nicest stories in George Moore's *The Untilled Field.*

The story pre-dates Harry Clarke, but the paragraph could be a description of his best work in stained glass. And in any case it expresses a striking insight into the external 'glories' and the interior 'exaltations' of those Christian truths incarnate, for the expression of which stained glass is the medium par excellence. For 'God is light', and he 'dwells in unapproachable light ...'.

It was natural therefore that, could the light be captured and processed, it should become the medium of a unique religious art. It was Christian art that first achieved it. Beginning in the Carolingian age and culminating in the glory of great churches like Chartres, Christianity created a new art form. In the stained glass windows of the great cathedrals, windows to admit the white light invisible, prisms to make visible the infinite variety of the invisible by resolving its simplicity into the opalescent refractions of irised colour.

O world invisible we view thee ...

Such worlds invisible were not available in Ireland to Biddy M'Hale or George Moore at the turn of the century. For stained glass, like the other arts, has its cycles of flowering and decline. And in an appendix from Harry Clarke in the present volume, we are told that the period from the sixteenth to the nineteenth century was an age of decline. And in Moore's story, accurately enough, Biddy's would-be supplier is a German salesman of stock samples from Munich.

But even as Moore was writing his story the seeds of rebirth were being sown in Ireland itself. In 1901 Moore's own friend, Edward Martyn – so important in the *general* Irish renaissance of the time – invited one Christopher Whale from London to make a set of stained glass windows for the family church at Laban

1* *The Life and Work of Harry Clarke*, Nicola Gordon Bowe. Irish Academic Press 1989.

near Martyn's home, at Tulyra Castle in Galway. Back of Whale lay the nineteenth-century investigation into medieval glass, revived interest in arts and crafts, and the theories of Ruskin and William Morris. As a result of Martyn's initiative An Túr Gloine was set up in Dublin in 1903, with the advice of Whale and the financial support of Sarah Purser.

But already a greater thing than this was being born. (One painful moment of its realization came many years later when Harry Clarke replaced Sarah Purser for the work generally regarded as his masterpiece, the Honan Chapel windows in Cork.)

Harry Clarke was born in Dublin on St Patrick's Day 1889. (The present work is his centenary commemoration.) That Ireland should be his birthplace and be such a strong ingredient in his genius is an accident of history rather than the result of a deliberate initiative like Edward Martyn's. His father had come to Dublin from Leeds when the family printing business failed. He found a job with a firm of ecclesiastical suppliers. But with the initiative he showed all his life, he had soon set up his own business as ecclesiastical supplier and church decorator. The business soon included a draughtsman and stained glass workers. He also found time to marry a Sligo girl. By 1887 they were able to take a lease on 33 North Frederick Street. The double outcome, of marriage and lease, was the stained glass studios – on those premises until 1973 – and the genius that emerged to make them famous in the person of the founding father's son, Harry. He was to become not just Ireland's greatest stained glass artist but, without much question, the greatest of his time anywhere. And that in a short life. For tuberculosis – helped by demonic application to work – took him away at only forty-one.

As told and richly illustrated by N. G. Bowe, giving the fruits of nearly two decades of research, the life and work of Harry Clarke is a revelation. For two reasons.

Firstly because in the nature of things the products of the stained glass artist are dispersed and not easily surveyed as a whole. Even the experts seldom give the 'laity' the benefit of such a survey. Hence the present volume is something of a landmark in the amount of information it makes available. And great credit is due to those listed in the special acknowledgements as sources of the grants that make its publication possible (among them the PP of Ballinrobe, one of Clarke's locations, Very Rev. Thomas Shannon).

Clarke's life belongs to the period of the Irish 'renaissance'. And the second revelation that comes from the book is the realization of how much more this renaissance was than the exclusively literary thing that we usually think of it as being. It was also a renaissance of the arts and crafts. In the famous Geneva Window, done to represent Ireland in the International Labour Organization building in Geneva, but rejected in the end and now gone to an American museum, Clarke combined both renaissances in eight panels illustrating scenes from twentieth-century Irish literature. A tribute to Clarke by Walter Starkie refers to Irish 'art and music and literature in those far-off days when Dublin in 1921–23 for an immortal instant recalled the Athens of Pericles'. It was a movement that 'carried' the talent of Clarke and of many others – An Túr Gloine has been mentioned. It carried him in a very material sense as well. For even if the artist above all does not live by bread alone, it is equally certain that he cannot live without it. The point is worth mentioning for another reason. Some of the old clichés about the Irish clergy and their lack of artistic taste inevitably get quoted in this book. But the fact of course is that almost the only outlet for the stained glass artist is a religious one. Yet the great bulk of Clarke's large output was for religious commissions in Ireland, a fact that is surprising for a couple of other reasons as well. 'Cash is of the essence of the contract for the parish priest', Harry wrote at one point. Yet his work never came cheap, despite his having to reckon with price-cutting competition. Again it was not as obvious then as now that he was the man for a religious job. For there was another strain in the man's make-up, as we shall see, one that runs through his secular glass, and through his work in textiles and book illustrations. (His gifts and much of his work extended to those media as well.)

As we know, the Irish renaissance was not Irish merely ... but Celtic as well. Clarke's stained glass is no exception. Outside literature in fact there is no better modern instance of the Celtic strain. The earliest designs in stained glass were taken from illuminated books and manuscripts. We know the unique talent and temper shown in that genre by early Irish Christian art. When one looks at the reproductions of Clarke's windows or panels, and looks for some analogy to what one sees, the analogy that comes to mind is Irish book and manuscript illumination. The analogy consists in that assortment of shared gifts of genius – for colour, fiery, subtle, radiant, for inventive fantasy of figure and form, for strong, abstract-tending, total design combined with an inexhaustible pointillist ability to fill every space with glowing points of bright detail. Useless to ask (and the author doesn't) whether the influence is external or one in the blood. Without the talent no influence would suffice anyway.

The Celtic thing is in the content as well as in the style and temper. Again and again in his religious work the universal Christian themes and scenes are complemented by or expressed in terms of representations from their 'local habitation' in the history and traditions of early Irish Celtic Christianity. As far as I know, that is a sense of roots and of the 'local Church' of which we have seen little enough since, although it is more relevant now than ever.

Doubtless one must allow for an input here from those who commissioned such work. But once the idea was there, Clarke went to the trouble of doing his research in the sources, to make his images as faithful as possible to Irish history and tradition. *The Voyage of Saint Brendan*, for instance, is a much-used text, so often that for one commission he excluded St Brendan as a theme he had used so much that he could not see it freshly any more.

Among the locations of those Irish scenes and saints, some in extensive series of windows, are Castletownshend, Cork City (Crawford Municipal Art Gallery and the Honan Chapel in UCC), Raheny (Oblate Fathers), Ballinasloe, Ballinrobe, Carrickmacross, Tullamore (windows formerly at Rathfarnham Castle), Wexford town. But his work also went to Britain, America (Bayonne, NJ), and Australia (Brisbane, Queensland).

It was the Honan Chapel series (1915–17) which above all other works established Clarke's reputation. It consists of nine windows, made up of a series of Munster saints, arranged in sequence from a great central three-light window representing the three patrons of Ireland, SS Patrick, Brigid and Columcille, and completed by two smaller windows representing St Joseph and Our Lady of Sorrows. It is generally regarded as his masterpiece. Of the whole series Clarke's friend, Thomas Bodkin, wrote that nothing like them 'had been made or seen before in Ireland. Their sustained magnificence of colour, their beautiful and most intricate drawing, their lavish and mysterious symbolism combine to produce an effect of splendour which is overpowering' (p. 51).

Such achievement in the hieratic, ecstatic and paradisal is the more surprising when we discover that there is another very different, indeed opposite strand in the work of Clarke, in his secular work, a kind of mystical *nostalgie* 'transcending downwards', complementary to the 'transcending upwards' in his religious work. There is a dual nature in his work. Nicola Gordon Bowe deals richly with that fact in her introductory chapter. And some of her statements are very straightforward indeed . 'His art displays a wilful decadence and an ambivalent religious mysticism of medieval intensity which ranges from the sublimely beautiful to the grotesquely macabre, rarely found in the work of his Celtic peers' (p. 1).

This dualism in his nature has a number of explanations – his adolescent experience of religious education, the early artistic influences he underwent, and doubtless something in his own make-up, without which the experiences and the influences would not have had such an effect.

Like James Joyce, Harry Clarke was a Belvedere boy. And like Joyce, Clarke too seems to have undergone the kind of conflict of ideals represented in *A Portrait of the Artist as a Young Man* by the polarities of the Virgin Mary and the girl beheld on Dollymount Strand. James White, in a foreword, refers to the famous sermon on Hell in the *Portrait*, and quotes from a pen portrait of Clarke by his elder son Michael. 'In one respect ... the priests did make an indelible mark on every sensitive child who listened with care: he would have a grim understanding of the quality of hell, and an idealized version of an improbable Paradise ... ' (p. xiii). All of which did not prevent him having Jesuit priests among his friends. And among the unfinished tasks left by his early death were five windows for his old school chapel.

But his resulting 'fascination with the terror of damnation' was well nurtured by the artistic influences with which he found his earliest affinity, in 'his predilection for "the poisonous honey of France" ' (p. 2). The honey in question could be found in England too, and Harry Clarke went early and often to London. But the originating bees were in Paris (to which Clarke also went).

The 'poisonous honey' in question is that of the turn-of-the-century, *fin-de-siècle*, literature and art. It is a world and an art not easily defined in a short space, except for those who are already to some extent *cognoscenti*. For the *cognoscenti* it is evoked by the labels of its pursuits – Aestheticism, Symbolism, Art for Art's Sake, and by the names of some of its practitioners – Beardsley, Baudelaire ('Flowers of Evil'), Oscar Wilde ('Dorian Gray'), etc. It is a hothouse world of hothouse blooms exotic, strange-scented, over-ripe, decadent. ... It is an artist's world evoked by the present author in many descriptive sentences, a world of 'predilection for dreamed images invested with iconic substance, deliberately ambiguous nuances, enigmatic, fatalistic, sensual and ominous figures ... ' (2). George Moore knew it well, having lived for ten years in Paris. He laughed at its eccentricities. But they were not without their effect on him, and that a demoralizing one; 'for in me they aggravated the fever of the unknown, and whetted my appetite for the strange, abnormal and unhealthy in art. Hence all pallidities of thought and desire were eagerly welcomed ... ' (*Confessions of a Young Man*).

Both style and content of Clarke's early drawings and illustrations are very obviously derivative from this *fin-de-siècle* world of fantastic dualistic concoctions and strange graphic techniques. But in his maturity, like-other Irish artists who did their apprenticeships in the same world, he transmuted all influences into a distillation unmistakably personal and Irish.

But the fascination with the vein of material represented by those influences never left him. Book illustrations (shades of the illuminated manuscripts) make up a big part of his best work, and it is notable how much of it was done for the literature of the imagination. Sometimes the romantic imagination, but very often the strange off-beat imagination of a world of dualisms, ambiguities, metamorphoses and overblown hothouse tropicalities. They include Poe's *Tales of Mystery and Imagination*, *The Fairy Tales of Perrault*, Goethe's *Faust*, *Selected Poems* of Algernon Charles Swinburne. Of the last two we are told that already 'even AE ... felt that the decadence associated with Swinburne had not "the character of gloom with which Clarke invests his creations", even though the drawings were "remarkable"' (p. 213).

The exaggeration proves the point mentioned by N. G. Bowe, that Clarke has been regarded by many critics as the ideal illustrator of such themes.

And to the same genre, if somewhat more towards the orthodox centre, we have to add two other remarkable works. The beautiful, twenty-two-panel, stained glass window illustrating Keats's *The Eve of St Agnes*, and a remarkable series called *The Queens*, nine stained glass panels intended to hang in the library of a rich Dublin patron, in a window overlooking Killiney Bay. The title is from a poem by that other haunted man, John M. Synge, a poem which takes up in Celtic colours the themes and moods of Villion and Ronsard. 'Tell me where, or in what country is Flora . . . But where are last year's snows?' 'These figures', N. G. Bowe remarks, 'carry the viewer into the secret haunted world of Clarke's vision, reminding one perhaps of the creations in a Fellini masquerade, disturbing images such as Kokoschka or Bacon might create' (p. 67).

I have mentioned the Geneva Window. It was Clarke's last major work. It too is illustration. Its fifteen scenes (with inscribed texts) in eight panels might not be quite what one would have expected as most representative of twentieth-century Irish literature, even in 1929. And its scenes perhaps do not add up to the unity, and certainly not to the monumentality, that one might expect in a commemoration of national achievement. But it is certainly 'Celtic', and it does represent most of Clarke, both in his choice of texts and in his translation of them into design and light and colour. The scenes are magical concentrations into jewelled miniature.

Religion is there, in Shaw's St Joan, and in Lady Gregory's St Brigid (*The Story Brought by Brigid*). Celtic history and dream and pathos and sentiment are there, in Robert Emmet and Deirdre and Padraic Colum's 'Cradle Song' and Yeats's *Countess Cathleen*, possibly Clarke's most splendid feminine figure. There too is Celtic rodomontade and its wild 'trips' of wordy unreality, in Synge's *Playboy* and O'Casey's Joxer. And in there too is the 'other' strand in Clarke. In the very Swinburnean nymph that unveils her unwinding way to O'Flaherty's raunchy Mr Gilhooley. And above all in that very un-Irish male partner, clad only in a bolero and ruched leggings, in Séamas O'Sullivan's pair of dancing midnight lovers. N. G. Bowe remarks that 'he seems half-goblin as he takes her hand in their dance over the crescent moon'. He looks more like Old Nick to me, and certainly born of the macabre *fin-de-siècle* imagination. I don't know how the lady can appear so dreamy and trusting in his company. And such an hour of the night to be out with him at all! (I bet some members of the Irish government thought so too in 1929.) But to obviate false impressions, and to indicate the final lyrical intensity of feeling and 'limit-situation' depth of the man (on the eve of his death), it should be noted that all this is framed between lines from Patrick Pearse's 'Wayfarer' ('The beauty of the world hath made me sad ... ') and, penultimately, 'The Weaver's Grave' (Séamus O'Kelly), and finally, a scene representing Joyce's poem, 'On Music' – a youth attired in golden boots, mauve coat, tabard and breeches playing his mandolin beside the silver waters – the River of Time, no doubt, and our ambivalent dance to its music. Harry Clarke was a poet in glass.

N. G. Bowe has written an epochal book. It is not for the present reviewer to say she has missed no work of Harry Clarke's, but I should not think she has. There are two appendices, consisting of a note on the art of stained glass from Clarke's own information, and a list of his stained glass windows. There are copious notes and an extensive bibliography. And of course there are hundreds of illustrations, in black and white and in colour plates.

A pity perhaps she did not leave herself room for a concluding chapter of retrospective analysis and evaluation. After the introductory chapter we are so busy chronologically following Clarke's busy life and work that we would like a backward glance before leaving him. The book ends abruptly with his death.

In such a fine work one notices a few misprints with the same regret as will the author after such diligence.

A couple of mis-descriptions have also got through. The Countess Cathleen is from Yeats's *play*, not the poem (plate 45). And in plate 4, the St Albert of Cashel, who is among the Munster saints in the Honan Chapel, is not 'the great Dominican theologian' (thirteenth-century teacher of Thomas Aquinas). It is at least a learned error. And one up for Cashel. And a pretty story, even if we must not call it history.

POSTSCRIPT

Somewhere in the preceding pages I mentioned one of the difficulties in studying a stained glass artist – the wide dispersal of his works. I might add the difficulty even on site of the eye-strain and the crick in the neck from peering up to the normal level of their setting.

Since that was written an easier glimpse of Harry Clark has become temporarily possible, in the *Exhibition of the Lough Derg Stations of the Cross in Stained Glass* at the Royal Hospital Kilmainham, from 25 January to 25 March 1990. Stained-glass windows have to be periodically re-leaded, or they sag, buckle and collapse. The *Lough Derg Stations*, installed in 1929, have just had their first overhaul.

They represent one of Clarke's latest and finest works – they were not finished by the time he had to leave for a sanatorium in Switzerland in 1927. The context of their making reveals also that pressure under which he often had to, could, and did work. In that year, the commissions included the Geneva Window, a set of windows for Bewley's Café, others in Scotland and England, the book of illustrations for Swinburne's *Poems*, etc. Yet the fourteen Lough Derg windows measure up to everything that has been said about his genius as a stained-glass artist – in design, colour, and miniature jewelled detail.

The concept of their design is inspired, for the breadth, depth and grandeur it makes possible. Each window portrays one of the twelve Apostles, with St Paul and Our Lady. And each figure holds a small oval mandorla panel depicting one of the Station scenes. Despite the relatively small size of the windows the enclosing figures look tall, elevated and hieratic, as they float against an unearthly backdrop of spiralling interstellar patterns and colours, each figure completed by the extra dimension of meaning accruing from the symbolism of colour and iconographical adjuncts.

The Station panels are exceptional achievements. Despite their small scale they combine clear design with the compression of crowded scenes, perspectival depth and exquisite detail – the whole given soul and spiritual unity through the pervading light, colour, and feeling.

Dare we however express a small reservation about these panels? Or is the impression due only to looking at them from too close up? In their exquisite detail do they slip a touch towards . . . genre painting? Are the scenes sometimes less 'dramatic' than we might expect in the pity and terror of the drama they represent? Are the features of the characters sometimes a little 'soft' and conventional? Is the figure of Christ sometimes a little flat? Its outline a little limp? Or do we dare ... ?!

Dr N. G. Bowe provides us with a crutch in her Introduction to the exhibition. Clarke was unable to oversee the *execution* of his designs for those panels ... . 'Any study of the designs for the inset panels and their realization in glass will reveal his absence'.

The executants who were present can abide the questions! But that is looking closely indeed at a golden gift. And in privileged conditions that are not those of the normal run of pilgrims to St Patrick's Purgatory:

> From Cavan and from Leitrim and from Mayo,
> from all the thin-faced parishes where hills
> Are perished noses running peaty water,
> They come to Lough Derg to fast and pray and beg
> With all the bitterness of nonentities, and the envy
> Of the inarticulate when dealing with the artist.
> (Patrick Kavanagh, 'Lough Derg')

ULYSSES AND THE IRISH GOD[2]

> Once upon a time and a very good time it was there was a moocow coming down along the road and this moocow that was down along the road met a nicens little boy named baby tuckoo. . . . Yes, the newspapers were right: snow was general all over Ireland. It was falling over every part of the dark central plain . . . falling softly upon the Bog of Allen and, further westwards, softly falling into the dark mutinous Shannon waves ... Stately, plump Buck Mulligan came from the stairhead, bearing a bowl of lather on which a mirror and a razor lay crossed ... He held the bowl aloft and intoned:
> – Introibo ad altare Dei

This cento is culled in chronological sequence from Joyce's three best-known works, *A Portrait of the Artist as a Young Man*[3] (revised from the earlier *Stephen Hero*), *Dubliners*, and *Ulysses*. Chronological sequence is important in Joyce, for he is in the line of a few great writers who continually and consciously moved on from the minor to the major in their works – *paulo maiora canamus*, let us attempt a rather larger theme. One thinks of Virgil, advancing from the pastoral 'ease' of the *Eclogues*, (*omnia vincit Amor: et nos cedamus Amori*), to the weightier and more realist Adamic theme of the necessity of *labor*, (*labor omnia vincit/improbus et duris urgens in rebus egestas*, toil masters everything, relentless toil/And the pressure of pinching poverty); and finally, like Wordsworth, on to the 'yearning toward some philosophic song/Of Truth', in Virgil's case the imperial search for the meaning of universal history as embodied in its apparent culmination in imperial Rome, the toga-clad people to whom Providence 'has set no bounds in space or time' – but with its unquiet meta-historical questioning too, for 'there are tears at the heart of things' – 'can Providence itself be so relentless in its anger?' (History, says Stephen Dedalus somewhere, is a nightmare from which I want to wake up – if he ever did, it was only to sleep and dream it all again on a grander scale in *Finnegans Wake*, 'past the wit of man to say what dream it was ... because it hath no bottom, only a very [*in*] commodius vicus of recirculation'.)

---

2 Review of Frederick K. Lang's *Ulysses and the Irish God* (London and Toronto: Associated University Presses, 1993).

3Quoted here from Harry Levin (ed.), *The Essential James Joyce*, Penguin Books, 1965.

One thinks too of Dante's three-stage movement, from the 'Beatrician experience' of childhood and adolescence in *La Vita Nuova*, to the 'Lady Philosophy' in the *Convivio*, and finally to the 'Beatrician recovery' of *todo y nada* under the all encompassing 'love that moves the sun and the other stars' at the summit of the *Divine Comedy*.

That may look like rather a 'noble company' of which to make Joyce a member. Yet that is the company in which he has been placed by critics like T. S. Eliot and George Steiner, the company of those like Virgil, Dante, Shakespeare and Proust, the greats of the great tradition, in whom the totalizing imagination 'circles ... around the compendium, the *summa* of European civilization,' 'taking an entire culture for their verbal canvas'.[4] It is already the company in which Joyce implicitly would place himself – by the title and the technique of Ulysses. There he goes back to Homer's *Odyssey*, with its archetypal plot – the wandering 'journey' – and its archetypal hero, the wandering Ulysses who saw the cities and knew the minds of many men in far-off regions, and at the end of his vicus of recirculation came home to his Penelope only to leave her and set out again. Thus Joyce is able to draw 'a continuous parallel between contemporaneity and antiquity',[5] in which the ancient wandering Greek becomes the modern wandering Everyman of Mr. Leopold Bloom, and the faithful Penelope becomes the rather less so – and certainly the much more 'floozy' – Molly Bloom. For Eliot the technique 'has the importance of a scientific discovery ... No one else has built a novel on such a foundation before'; and further, 'Mr. Joyce is pursuing a method which others must pursue after him.'[6]And Steiner[7] laments the fact that so few have actually done so – 'there have been no genuine successors to Joyce in English'. High praise – although we might question the originality of the 'scientific discovery': already in the second century Apuleius used the trick in his novel, the *Metamorphoses*. And in a famous passage Dante shows that he understands the archetypal and perennial human significance of the restless wandering Ulysses – in whom nothing 'Could conquer ... the restless

4 George Steiner, *Language and Silence*, New York, 1967, 79 and 211.

5 'Ulysses, Order, and Myth,' in Frank Kermode, *Selected Prose of T.S. Eliot*, London, 1975, 177; in the same collection 'What is a Classic?' – on Virgil's *Aeneid* as *the* founding classic of European civilization, through its 'maturity' and its 'universality'; also, ibid., 'Dante' – 'the most *universal* of poets in the modern languages', whose culture 'was not of one European country but of Europe' – and who, as we know, took Virgil as his guide in every sense, the *anima cortese mantoana*, the courtly soul from Mantua who was his master and his author, 'whose skill in song/Keeps green on earth a fame that shall not end/While motion rolls the turning spheres along' (*Inferno*, I 85, II 58ff).

6 Ibid.ff).

7 Op. cit., p. 32.

itch to rove/And rummage through the world exploring it,/All human worth and wickedness to prove.'[8]

So much for the framework and its dimensions. But the framework does not make the work of art – except in the pejorative sense of the didactic. It is but the loom for the weaving of words, for the warp and woof and web of 'those constructs of verbal, syntactic representation, or *mimesis,* which we find in Dante, Shakespeare, and Joyce'.[9] Our opening cento was meant to illustrate that too. It would be labouring the obvious to go into detail on Joyce as a superb 'musician' with language. But music has its chords and harmonics, its point, counterpoint, and polyphonic. So too has language. It *must* have, it must be intrinsic to the very technique, when the aim of the artist is precisely that multi-layered polysemy entailed in 'taking an entire culture for his verbal canvas', in drawing 'a continuous parallel between contemporaneity and antiquity'. Joyce is a master of that art. We glimpse it at once in the opening paragraph of *Ulysses* already quoted – in the 'bowl'/chalice, 'crossed' with a razor, 'held aloft'/elevated before the 'altar', preface to the 'intoning' of *Introibo ad altare Dei.*

There is an extended example of it, with the same 'religious' dimension, in the funeral scene in the Hades episode of *Ulysses.* There the low realism of the stream-of-consciousness is counterpointed with the high and hieratic ritual solemnity of the Latin liturgy for the dead.

> They halted by the bier and the priest began to read out of his book with a fluent croak.
>
> Father Coffey. I knew his name was like a coffin ... Muscular Christian. Woe betide anyone that looks crooked at him: priest, Thou art Peter ... Most amusing expressions that man finds ...
>
> – *Non intres in judicium cum servo tuo, Domine.*

And so on through several paragraphs.

> The priest took a stick with a knob at the end of it out of the boy's bucket and shook it over the coffin ... It's all written down: he has to do it.
>
> – *Et ne nos inducas in tentationem.*

8 *Inferno,* XXVI 97–99, tr. Dorothy L. Sayers (Penguin Classics); on the use and interpretation of Ulysses as an archetypal figure in literature from ancient to modern times see W. B. Stanford, *The Ulysses Theme.* Oxford, 1954; the first classic use of the voyaging-searching theme associated with him is of course in the voyaging-searching Trojans of Virgil's *Aeneid;* Virgil at the same time enlarges the frame of reference and significance far beyond that of Homer – he had so much more history behind him and a correspondingly greater awareness of the questions it raises.

9 Steiner, *op. cit.,* 79 and 211.

> ... All the year round he prayed the same thing over them all and shook water on top of them: sleep ...
>
> – *In paradisum.*
>
> Said he was going to paradise or is in paradise. Says that over everybody. Tiresome kind of a job. But he has to say something ...
>
> Mr. Kiernan said with solemnity:
> – I am the resurrection and the life. That touches a man's inmost heart.
> – It does, Mr. Bloom said.

***

But now our question. What *is* this 'music' that creeps in our ears? Is it in the earth or in the air? What does it *mean*? What does Mr. Joyce mean? Is he playing the *voix céleste* or . . . the strumpet Siren? Or both together? Is he in the end ... 'a nicens little boy'? 'Confess!' 'Admit ... admit!' Or else 'Apologize,/Pull out his eyes,/Pull out his eyes,/Apologize!' Contrary to that 'noble company' of which we have seen him made one, our own first impressions from the passages quoted are likely to be that, where Catholicism is concerned, Mr Joyce is *not* 'a nicens little boy'. And with that impression we too would be in good company. Many of his first critical readers had that same impression. They saw him in *Ulysses* not so much re-presenting reality in interpretative *mimesis* as rubbishing it with mud, or at least darkening it in hostile obscurity. Eliot quotes one such critic to the effect that 'Mr. Joyce, with his marvellous gifts, uses them to disgust us with mankind'.[10] Another refers to '*Ulysses*, with its mocking *odi-et-amo* hodgepodge of the European tradition, with its blatant and painful cynicism, and its uninterpretable symbolism – for even the most painstaking analysis can hardly emerge with anything more than an appreciation of the multiple enmeshment of the motifs but with nothing of the purpose and meaning of the work itself.'[11]

Our question fits into a broader context and a wider interest of the moment. The religious dimension of literature in general is a current area of interest, or even a mode of approaching theology.[12] Further, Irish and Anglo-Irish lit-

10 In Kermode, op. cit., 176.

11 Erich Auerbach, *Mimesis: The Representation of Reality in Western Literature*, Anchor Books ed., 1957, 487; original German ed. 1946.

12 See e.g. George Steiner, *Real Presences*, London, 1989; William F. Lynch, *Christ and Apollo*, Mentor-Omega ed., 1963; Hans Urs von Balthasar, *The Glory of the Lord*, passim, and in particular vol. III: *Studies in Theological Style: Lay Styles*, Edinburgh, 1986; Paul S. Fiddes, *Freedom and Limit: A Dialogue between Literature and Christianity*, London, 1991.

erature is both very alive in itself and a live field of critical study. For obvious reasons national cultural identity is one focus of such study.[13]And for hardly less obvious reasons, another focus of study is the place of religion, and more specifically of Catholicism and attitudes to it, in that cultural identity.[14] Joyce is the classic and richest concentration of ore to be mined on both topics. So many Irish writers have had chips on shoulders, or at least one chip, the Catholic one. Joyce had the *two* chips, the nationalist and the Holy Roman Catholic one. And he had them not just on his shoulder but in his gut, providing a *double* irritant and focus for his 'morbid secretions' and the crystallization of the eventual pearls – if such they be. Who can forget, for instance, the Christmas dinner set-to in *A Portrait*, surely the classic dramatization of the classic theme of Parnell and Kitty, 'the Bishops and the Party', with 'the pope's nose' pronged up as a tasty extra? And classically too, Joyce could reject, or appear to reject, but never eject, the twin irritants from his system. 'I imagine Stephen said, that there is a malevolent reality behind the things I fear,' answering the question of why he feared 'a bit of bread', i.e. the Eucharistic Host, which might after all 'be the body and blood of the son of God and not a wafer of bread.'[15] 'I will not serve that in which I no longer believe, whether it call itself my home, my fatherland, or my church: and I will try to express myself in some mode of life or art as freely as I can and as wholly as I can, using for my defence the only arms I allow myself – silence, exile and cunning ... I go to encounter for the millionth time the reality of experience and to forge in the smithy of my soul the uncreated conscience of my race ... Old father, old artificer, stand me now and ever in good stead.'[16] Fightin' words. Yet when he came to write his all-encompassing 'universal particular', his 'concrete universal', his 'Day in the Life of Everyman', although he was in exile, the setting in which he chose to give it a local habitation and a name was the capital city of 'the old sow that eats her nine farrow', which happened also to be 'the – what ordinal was it? – the Xth city of Christendom', with all its endless 'minute particulars' – and in all their frequent tattiness too. The city's first citizen, so to speak, 'Mr. Leopold Bloom, ate with relish the inner organs of beasts and fowls ... Most of all he liked grilled mutton kidneys which gave to his palate a fine tang of faintly scented urine'. *Quelle vraisemblance*! And *quelle délicatesse* in the *mimesis* – in the fine tang of the faintly scented prose! But then, to keep our *question* in mind, there are fine odours too when sweet violets sicken.

---

13 See e.g. Robert Welch, *Changing States: Transformations in Modern Irish Writing*, London, 1993.

14 See e.g. Robert Welch (ed.), *Irish Writers and Religion*, Colin Smyth, 1992.

15 *A Portrait*, ed. cit., 244.

16 Ibid., 247 and 252; note the 'harmonics' of 'I will not serve', and 'old father, old artificer'.

Let us come to the particularities of that question, and most particularly the particularity that is Professor Lang's subject, Joyce and Catholicism, especially in *Ulysses*, but backed up by a run-in from Joyce's earlier writings. An approach, by the way, which Joyce should have appreciated, since one of his structural principles is precisely the *organic* development of the individual, *very* organic indeed, from womb to tomb, visceral even – it is not for nothing that Mr. Bloom's strange dietary preferences are such as we have noted, the inner organs of beasts and fowls. The question of Joyce and Catholicism has of course been much written about,[17] and Professor Lang introduces his own book by explaining why it is needed at all. In brief his explanation is that no previous examination of the question has come to adequately close grips with the evidence – the evidence being of *two* kinds: Joyce's texts, of course, but also the details of Catholic doctrine and ritual. (And let us say at once that under both aspects Professor Lang's book is very good indeed). Previous criticism he finds to be of three kinds. The first gives 'background', in aspects of Catholic doctrine and ritual, but pays too little attention to Joyce's text. The second does the opposite – focuses on 'religious elements' in the text, but without detailing how they relate to the doctrine and the ritual. The third does both, but within too limited a range. We know then what to expect from Lang's own book, and we are not disappointed.

As regards what we are to expect, this is a finely written book (despite its origins in a doctoral dissertation!), and so there is no point in trying to improve on the author's own statement of what we are to expect:

> This book attempts to go considerably further. It argues that the relation between *Ulysses* and Catholicism is even more extensive and complex than has been previously recognised. It identifies the specific rituals and doctrines Joyce has drawn upon, explores their precise meaning in the Church, and considers the structures in the novel which draw them together and give them new meaning. It proposes that *Ulysses*, which begins with a parody of transubstantiation, Catholicism's central rite, thereby begins to transubstantiate much of Catholicism. As the novel proceeds, it continues to appropriate the Church's symbolism, ritual, and doctrine. It engages in, and justifies, taking from religion and giving to art and humanity.

17 Apart from what we learn in Professor Lang's bibliography there is, for instance, Eamonn Hughes, 'Joyce and Catholicism', in Robert Welch (ed.), *Irish Writers and Religion* – an essay, by the way, more favourable to Joyce than is Professor Lang; there is also Daniel Murphy, *Imagination and Religion in Anglo-Irish Literature*. 1930–1980, Irish Academic Press, 1987.

Now there's a plain statement – if of what has oft been thought but ne'er so well expressed. And in the performance ne'er so well done either. 'Good man, Towser! Duck him! Come along, Dedalus!'

Lang provides the evidence not just from the fiction but, more domineeringly, from some very non-fictional statements of Joyce himself, or sometimes his brother Stanislaus – and here of course we have to make at least a token bow to the critical principle of judging by the writer's work and not by what he says about it. Lang quotes (p. 16) from a letter Joyce wrote to his future wife, Nora Barnacle, on August 29, 1904. 'Six years ago I left the Catholic Church hating it most fervently. I found it impossible to remain in it on account of the impulses of my nature. I made secret war upon it when I was a student and declined to accept the positions it offered me . . . Now I make open war upon it by what I write and say and do.' If no man is a hero in front of his valet, what are we to make of him in front of his wife? On p. 169 Lang quotes Joyce's brother, Stanislaus, to the effect that 'for his brother the Irishwoman was "the accomplice of the Irish Catholic Church, which he called the scullery-maid of Christendom ... ".' Of course we may say he is talking only of the Irish Catholic Church. But we don't know that he gave his allegiance to any other version of Catholicism. And in any case it is Catholicism as Joyce knew it in Ireland that provides the material in *Ulysses* – and elsewhere as well. And if he sees Irish Catholicism as merely a scullery-maid, to be attacked and parodied in 'open war', well then that is how he sees Catholicism, and that is the answer to our question. In which case, however, *Ulysses* is something rather less than the great universal epic of our time, i.e. if its subject is only, to coin a phrase, 'the mere Irish', and if its technique is the merely parodic. And what, paradoxically, would be more 'Irish' – not only at the popular and populist level but in a long literary tradition – what would be more 'Irish' than if the whole clotted and distended monster were one gigantic Irish 'take-off', an endlessly extended and endlessly more subtle variation on Irish 'buckleppery'! Wouldn't that be real fun. And come to think of it, if there is one episode better than another in *Ulysses,* it surely has to be the pub scene where all the windy boloney, all the hollow rare ould time, all the secret Celtic melancholic void masked over in the airy rodomontade that tourists mistake for the Irish gift of the 'talk' and the 'charm'[18] – the scene, I say, where all that flatus comes out of the pub scene in the persons of 'the Citizen' and his supporting cast of fellow citizens. 'And he took the last swig out of the pint, Moya. All wind and p ... , like a tanyard cat ... '. 'And the last we saw was the bloody car rounding the corner and old sheep face on it gesticulating and the bloody mongrel after it with his lugs back for all he was bloody well worth to tear him limb from limb.'

18 One may compare many less functionalized, more autobiographical scenes in Oliver St John Gogarty (the Buck Mulligan of *Ullyses*), *As I was going down Sackville Street* (Penguin Books ed. 1954).

'When, lo, there came about them all a great brightness and they beheld the chariot wherein He stood ascend to heaven ... And they beheld Him even Him, ben Bloom Elijah, amid clouds of angels ascend to the glory of the brightness at an angle of forty five degrees over Donohoe's in Little Green Street like a shot off a shovel.'

But to come back and be serious, according to Lang, Joyce was undermining Catholicism from the moment he began to write. Lang (p. 17) analyses his first short story, 'The Sisters', first published in 1904, and later rewritten for inclusion in *Dubliners*. Both in the story itself and in a letter of Joyce's about it, Lang finds hints of a simulacrum of the Mass. The hints turn on such details as the apparent inversion of the ritual at the Consecration, in particular the Elevation of the chalice. In the story the priest drops his chalice, and in any case it "contained nothing" – an empty rite therefore.

Lang goes systematically through the episodes of *Ulysses*, and, in his Introduction, he outlines the various Catholic doctrines and rituals woven into them. The range is extraordinary, starting with the Trinity itself. 'When Joyce lost his faith, the Trinity became a fiction, and later he would incorporate Catholicism's fictions into his. The persons of the Trinity haunt Joyce's fiction in the manner of offstage characters. To mention almost any aspect of the Church is to refer to at least one of them ... ' (p. 15). The detailed exposition of the point-counterpoint parallels between Joyce's trinities and that of Catholicism shows the quality of Lang's researches – and of course the extent of the 'research' done by Joyce himself, the 'fearful Jesuit' (*Ulysses*), who in the person of Stephen says of himself: 'I was born to be a monk' (*Portrait*, p. 225). For such exposition depends on reading the classic theological sources of Trinitarian doctrine, Aquinas (whom Joyce himself read) and, behind Aquinas, St Augustine, whose *De Trinitate* was the classic source even for Aquinas. It is an interesting question, not answered here, whether Joyce too read Augustine on the matter – or any matter. Hughes refers for instance to 'the formal correspondences between *A Portrait* and Augustine's *Confessions*'[19] but does not go further into the question of whether Joyce had actually read Augustine's *Confessions*. Few readers of both works can fail to be struck by the parallels between them. Parallels as basic as the genre itself – for surely the *Portrait* belongs among the classic 'Confessions' – and, although the tradition is a long one, 'classic' Confessions are few enough, and they start with Augustine.[20]

19 Art. cit., 116.

20 Even George Moore, Joyce's older contemporary, wrote his *Confessions of a Young Man*; and in fact some of the literary devices in *A Portrait* – and elsewhere – Joyce learned from Moore, though not from Moore's *Confessions*. As both works reveal – and both lives – Joyce and Moore had much in common, including destructive wit, even at the expense of their friends, the consequent making of enemies, and last but not least, the rejection of Catholicism – even if, unlike Joyce, Moore did not regard the loss of his Catholic faith as a loss of respectability too when he announced himself a

In content the *Portrait* and the *Confessions* share (inter alia) the characteristically 'confessional' concern with the dark underside of life that is sin, especially the sins of the flesh, all the darker for being set in the foil of the contrasting vision of ideal purity and radiance. 'A girl stood before him in midstream, alone and still, gazing out to sea ... Her image had passed into his soul forever and no word had broken the holy silence of his ecstasy ... A wild angel had appeared to him.'[21] And in both works there is not only the parallel of the general fact, but also the more striking parallel of the narrative concentration of it into one critical moment, Augustine's famous sixteenth year, which is also Joyce's time of 'crisis'.

Whether Joyce knew Augustine or not – and he could not read far in Aquinas without seeing him referred to – there is one other striking parallel between them. It takes us back to the Trinity, and into the master-ideas of both Joyce and Augustine. We should first explain the real dimensions of what the Trinity meant in Augustine's thought, and indeed in all the best of early Christian thought.[22] It was not just a theological conundrum. It was the ultimate creative and explanatory principle of all reality. It provided the final answer to the age-old Greek metaphysical quest for the ultimate ground of all reality, its *arkhē* in Greek, its *principium* in Latin – to be understood not in the temporal sense of beginning but in the transtemporal transcendent sense of the source and ground of all existents. And for the Christian, unlike the Greek philosopher, that ground is personal, active, creative – *ex nihilo* – and of course triune, although Neoplatonist philosophy did arrive at a trinitarian conception of the ultimate Ground of Reality.[23] Augustine is explicit and insistent on so interpreting the famous *in principio* of Genesis 1:1 and John 1:1[24] And – to anticipate where we are going – he also frequently refers to that creative *principium* as an *artifex*, a Maker, in other words an Artist. He goes further into interpretative detail. The three Persons of the Trinity

---

Protestant, quite the contrary – if one can have faith in any 'announcement'of Moore's! It should be added that they also shared the inability to get away in their writings from what they had rejected in their lives. A scene in the National Library in Oliver St John Gogarty, op. cit., ed. cit., 19, provides some evidence that Moore, and possibly therefore Joyce, knew Augustine's *Confessions*. The Librarian is speaking: 'St. Augustine, who, as you are no doubtless aware, 'endears himself to us by his mistress and his illegitimate child," I quote myself ... but George Moore, a frequenter of this library ... Moore has the Dark Ages in his mind so far as a sense of historical perspective went. Yes, there is a translation of the Confessions. What Latin! Only to be compared with Lyly's Euphues ... *Nondun amarem sed amare amabam* ... quite an obsession ... Do 1 bore you? Ah yes, the book will be with you in a moment.' We recall too that one of Moore's historical novels was Héloïse and Abélard – one of many works which show his concern with religious themes.

21 *A Portrait*, ed.cit., 1866.

22 See e.g. C. N. Cochrane, *Christianity and Classical Culture*, Galaxy ed., 1957, 360ff. and 409ff.'

23 See, e.g., Augustine's *Confessions*, VII 9, 13ff.

24 Out of many possible references see e.g. Augustine *De civ. Dei* X 24.

have each their appropriate role in the act of creation. And this corresponds with the triune nature of created reality itself. For 'there are three things especially we need to know about creation or any created thing ... : who made it, by what means he made it, and to what end he made it.'[25] The Greek answers are given in the corresponding tripartite division of philosophy, into metaphysics, ethics, and logic or dialectic.[26] But Christian revelation sees the answers in the respective roles of the three Persons of the Trinity. Who created things? God the Father. How? By what means? Through his *Logos* – Word.[27] To what end? Because they are good (Gen 1:31), which goodness, can be interpreted as corresponding to the Holy Spirit.[28] The same Trinity emerges in the answers to another related triad of ultimate questions: the source of the universe, the source of the light by which to comprehend it, and the source of the *beatitudo* that is the finality of human existence within it. The Father is the source of being. The Son is the source of the light of comprehension.[29] The Holy Spirit is the source of beatitude.[30]

Thus while there are endless actual opinions about the origin and nature of the universe, about the source and means of establishing the truth, and about the means of attaining that ultimate Good to which all our actions must be directed, nevertheless this diversity of opinion is all rooted in the three ultimate boundary-questions. 'For there is no doubt in anyone's mind about three points: that there is some cause of the universe, some method of knowing it, some final meaning and direction of human existence.'[31]

And then comes the analogy of the artist or master craftsman, the *artifex*. He too is a maker of things, a *poiētēs*. And in him too, 'three elements combine for the making of anything: natural talent (*natura*), theoretical training (*doctrina*), and practical application (*usus*). His natural talent is judged by his degree of genius (*ingenio*), his theoretical training by his knowledge (*usus*), and his practical application by its fruits.'[32]

This Trinitarian analogy between the 'creative' artist and the Creator God has been drawn even in modern times. It was drawn by Dorothy Sayers, the translator and student of Dante.[33] George Steiner draws it,[34] to the extent that he sees

25 *De civ. Dei*, XI 21; cf. XI 23f.

26 Ibid. VIII 6 ff, XI 25.

27 Understood as the *principium* of Genesis 1:1 and John 1:1, but also based on John 1:3: 'Through him all things were made.'

28 *De civ. Dei*, XI 23f; cf. Conf. XIII 5,6.

29 See John 1:5, 3:19, 14:6.

30 *De civ. Dei*, VIII 5, XI 25.

31 Ibid. XI 25.

32 Ibid.; cf. *De Trinitate* X II 17.

33 See Barbara Reynolds, *The Passionate Intellect*, London, 1989, 11f.

34 In *Real Presences*, 200ff.

aesthetic creation as at root a mimesis of the original divine Creator – an idea already contained in Plato's *Symposium* (208aff on the creative instinct). That idea has a profound scriptural basis in the conception of man as made in the image of God. Man as image of God is a master idea in Augustine – to such an extent that he sees even man's evil actions as really perverse attempts to play God.[35]

And that is precisely where Joyce seems to pervert the Christian tradition that he uses. That tradition was based not only on the specific Trinitarian basis we have shown, but also on the more general age-old philosophico-theological principle of the analogy of being. By that principle, higher and lower levels of being and action kept their place and were kept distinct, while at the same time they were unified into 'the great chain of being' by the analogies between them. Joyce will have none of this – on one reading of him anyway. He will be the captain of his soul, himself the new Daedalus and 'fabulous artificer', 'forging anew in his workshop out of the sluggish matter of the earth a new soaring impalpable imperishable being'.[36] He will be his own transubstantiating priest, 'a priest of eternal imagination, transmuting the daily bread of experience into the radiant body of everlasting life'.[37]As Lang comments (p. 18), he 'replaces the Catholic God with the idea that the literary artist is Godlike'. And in that of course Joyce is not unique. He is only the latest and most cunningly elaborated in a long modern line of replacers of religion by poetry, of the saint by the 'genius', of the Creator God by the 'creative' artist.[38]

It is in that context that we understand the full implications of some of Lang's statements and those of others about Joyce's use of the Trinitarian model. 'Joyce takes as a model for the artistic process not only God's creative activity but the Trinitarian relations. The Father's essence becomes "truth", the essence the artist has illuminated. The Son becomes "beauty", the aesthetic image. And the Holy Spirit becomes "joy", the feeling the artist experiences at the "instant of inspiration" ... ' (p. 20). On p. 45 he quotes Joyce himself to the same effect in an early essay on James Clarence Mangan. 'Beauty, the splendour of Truth,[39] is a gracious presence when the imagination contemplates intensely the truth of its own being

35 See e.g. *Conf.* II 6 – on the 'gratuitous crime'; cf. *De vera religione* XXXVIII, 69ff. on the roots of idolatry; and cf. Scripture again: '*You will be like gods*' (Gen 3:5), on the root of the original misdemeanour.

36 *A Portrait*, ed. cit., 184.

37 Idem., 226.

38 See e.g. Hans Urs von Balthasar, *The Glory of the Lord*, vol. V (Edinburgh, 1991), 296, in context, on 'the true Titan who administers the divine fire: "such a poet is indeed a second Maker", "a just Prometheus under Jove": the one who ... becomes himself a creator'.

39 That phrase too Joyce borrowed from 'the great tradition' – I have not noticed much recognition of the fact by commentators on a recent homonymous document.

or the visible world, and the spirit which proceeds out of truth and beauty is the holy spirit of joy.'

The Trinity is a high place to start from, but whether what someone has said of Catholicism be true or not, it is certainly true of *Ulysses* – a manger with fodder to suit every level of snout – down to tanyard cats in Dublin pubs, to Nighttown and Walpurgisnacht, to *The Irish Messenger* and devotion to the Sacred Heart. On whose foundress's name who but Joyce could perpetrate so vile a pun? Or on the devotion itself, who but Joyce could make so low a remark about how much lower down lies the real seat of the affections? To borrow a phrase from another organ, all human life is here. But Matthew Arnold used the same phrase to evoke the majesty of the collected works of Catholicism. Joyce's version of all that life is meticulously studied and evaluated in Professor Lang's richly sourced and limpidly written book.

One may conclude then with another borrowed phrase, the one with which Apuleius prefaced his equally doubtful tale, or rather – like Joyce too – a blue rosary of tales: 'Give ear, gentle reader, you'll enjoy it.' That is to say, you'll re-joyce, and maybe even re Joyce, if you are convinced by this book's thesis re Joyce. And among such gentle readers one thinks not only of the lay Joyceans but also of the many who have opted into the version of priesthood that Joyce rejected. Inevitably in this book there is constant reference to Catholic doctrine and ritual, not all of which they may be fresh on. And especially not on the ritual, for Joyce's Mass is of course Tridentine and pre-Vatican II – and in the Latin language. Who would once have anticipated a time when, before we get past the third sentence of *Ulysses*, we would need not only translation but explanation as well? *Introibo ad altare Dei.* Ah ... , yes ... yes ... Yes.

HOMILIES

THOUGHTS ON SUNDAY: THE END OF THINGS

I

The Scripture Readings for the beginning and for the end of November have the same theme. The Epistle for All Saints (Apoc 7:2–14), which describes the sealing of the elect with God's sign, is a parenthesis in a vision of the preliminaries to the end of the world: 'And behold there was a great earthquake ... and the heavens departed as a book folded up' (Apoc 6:12–14). The Gospel for the last Sunday after Pentecost (Mt 24:15–35)[1] answers the disciples' question on the signs to precede 'the consummation of the world': 'And then shall all tribes of the earth mourn; and they shall see the Son of man coming in the clouds of heaven ... ' (Mt 24:30).

November is the eschatological month in the Christian year. Eschatology looks to the End of things. Men do not always think of the end, but it is the end that shapes the meaning. For the Christian, it is not the butt-end of time, sand that runs out; it is a harvest gathered, from fields made bare, under the lowering sun.

Nowhere is the End more clearly looked to, more resoundingly expressed, than in the written word of the Christian revelation. The 'day of the Lord', the 'last days', are ever on the lips of the prophets. 'For behold the day shall come kindled as a furnace ... ' (Mal 4:1). Christ confirms its reality, as in the Gospel of the last Sunday after Pentecost – 'though of that day and hour no one knoweth' (Mt 24:36). The last book of the New Testament by the last of the Apostles, source of the Epistle for All Saints, is wholly composed of *apocalyptic* revelations.

'In all thy works remember thy last end ... '. Even primitive man without benefit of Christian revelation constructed the myth and symbol of natural religion. And they remembered the End above all at that season when the year comes towards its end and nature itself seems to die. They knew it did not really die. For the dying year hid away the seeds of new life, and spring would see resurrection. And in their harvest festivals all peoples have given thanks to the Life-giver, and seen there a symbol and a hope of their own destiny. The Hebrews had the Feast of Tabernacles. The Celts had *Samhain*.

1 [Editor: The Last Sunday after Pentecost is now, since the reform of the Liturgy after Vatican II, the 33rd Sunday on the Year.]

It is not accidental that the Church has chosen the month of *Samhain* to direct our minds more certainly to the last things – as expressed especially in our thoughts of the dead at this time. The year begins to pass through the death that is the door to spring. It is long since Christ ascended into heaven. Next month, we prepare for His coming. The month of the Holy Souls is appropriately an image of our own hopeful passage from life through death into life.

II

We speak of death as a passage to the next life, a door opening on another world. We naturally fear death. The body resists the last process to which its own laws subject it. The spirit holds back from the anonymity of unconsciousness. The soul does not easily accept that its sensitive instrument should be subject, even for a time, to the discourtesy of the earth.

No less perhaps than from those biological changes, we shrink from the Christian idea of death as a passage. There is a transition from the familiar world, if not into the unknown, then into the unexperienced. It is not to the Christian an entirely 'undiscovered country'; but knowledge does not always immunize against the anxieties that nature is heir to. Though we trust physical laws, every take-off is still an abandonment of ourselves.

Death is more than a take-off, an abandoning to a new element. It is a change in ourselves. 'We shall be changed', says St Paul, even while he consoles (1 Cor 15:52).

These are the sufferings of our state. But they are only part of the Christian's state. Ultimately of course they are 'swallowed up in victory'. And the Christian does not meet them with only the stiff stoicism of one who goes to the darkness with his own resources alone.

More important for the Christian, however, the physical facts of death itself have been modified. For him the relentless biological process has been spiritualized. For the body is holy. And its dissolution is not final. 'It is sown in corruption, it shall rise in incorruption. It is sown in dishonour, it shall rise in glory' (1 Cor 15:42–43).

So too the thought of death as the worker of change in us, as the transition to another existence, has lost its sting. Death remains the point where life is gathered to an overwhelming moment; in fact it does but complete what has already begun. For the Christian has already made a passage to a new world, undergone a radical transformation. In the language of St Paul, he has already died and been buried and risen again with Christ (Rom 6). Physical death completes, confirms, reveals. It does not begin a new process. 'The kingdom of God is within you' (Lk 17:21).

To elaborate: St Paul speaking of death contrasts Christian optimism with the hopelessness of his pagan contemporaries. Not all even of that pre-Christian world were totally without hope. But their hope was often little less sad than their despair. The gods they believed in were far off and silent – indifferent or powerless. Men were believed to be subject to the rule of mechanical Fate, of the heavenly bodies (Col 2:8), or the thwartings of demons. The body was the prison of a fallen soul. Hope was the hope of escape, ascent, return – unaided – to a lost world.

The Christian knows that God has *become* man, and has assumed the limitations of man's own existence in time and the world. Time and eternity, this life and the next, do not merely co-exist. Eternity has been inserted into time. The next life has been ingrafted in this. The next life begins by grace in this world. Death is not a break in continuity. It is a raising up to glory, a transfiguration of the life that is already in the Christian. But that life must be cultivated here. For time is the anvil on which the Christian forges his eternity. Death is the point of intersection of the two worlds. But as such it is only the supreme among a lifelong succession of crucial points. For at every moment the Christian lives and acts in two worlds. Every moment incarnates a value in eternity.

III

For his understanding of the next world the Christian does not depend on shadowy guessing, as did the world St Paul spoke of as having no hope – and for that matter most of those who lived with only the partial revelation of the Old Testament. 'As a cloud is consumed and passeth away: so he that shall go down to Sheol shall not come up ... ' (Job 7:9). Of the 'four last things' two shall make up that world. However little we may know of Hell or Heaven, we know they confirm our adherence at death to a choice already made. We cannot be indifferent to which it is.

The possibility of eternal loss once accepted, the imagination needs no straining to depict it. Not that the real is necessarily worse than the imagined; but here the real may be worse than the realistic. 'Depart from me, ye cursed ... '.

The conventional picture of heaven is less imaginatively compelling. One may sympathize with certain spirits who might feel a trifle *ennuyé* – if only for the lack of the good company which might be elsewhere. If the saints have become plaster images, heaven has become the painted backcloth. The language of the Apocalypse in the Epistle of the Mass for All Saints suggests something of the mystery and the incommunicable splendour of the reality. 'These that are clothed in white robes, who are they, and whence came they? ... These are they who have come out of great tribulation, and have washed their robes, and have made them white in the blood of the Lamb. Therefore they are before the throne of God ... and he that sitteth on the throne shall dwell over them' (Apoc 7:13–15).

Heaven is 'the glory to come, that shall be revealed in us' (Rom 8:8), for which the whole of creation 'groans in a common travail' (Rom 8:22). The saints are they who have won through – 'they shall speak of the glory of God's kingdom' (Ps 144:11).

The saints are not only that small number whose final sanctity the Church has been able to declare. They are 'a great multitude which no man could number, of all nations, and tribes, and peoples, and tongues ... ' (Apoc 7:9). They are all the numberless nameless ones 'of whom there is no memorial' because they lived hidden lives, but who pleased God because they were 'men of mercy whose godly deeds have not failed ... ' (Sir 44:10). We begin November by celebrating those indestructible generations. But within the universal community there is room for local loyalties. And on 6 November we honour the saints to whom Ireland owes this most vital tradition. 'Their name liveth unto generation and generation. Let the people show forth their wisdom and the Church declare their praise' (Sir 44:14–15).

'They shall see God.' Christ said simply (Mt 5:8). The mystics have wrestled with words and symbols in an attempt to adumbrate even the foretaste of that vision they have been granted in life. St Augustine has described a conversation with his mother as they looked out on the garden of their house at Ostia shortly before her death. They tried to rise to an understanding of that great mystery – 'what the eternal life of the saints would be like ... '. And as their minds climbed and they spoke of the eternal Wisdom, 'for one fleeting instant we reached out and touched it ... '. To hear the voice of God, all creation left behind and fallen silent, with nothing between ourselves and Him, 'just as in that brief moment my mother and I had reached out in thought and touched the eternal Wisdom', supposing this instant were to continue so that eternally 'this single vision entranced and absorbed the one who beheld it ... would not this be what we are to understand by the words "Come and share the joy of your Lord" ' (*Conf.* 9:10).

IV

'Eternal rest grant to them, O Lord: and let perpetual light shine upon them ... '(4 *Esdr.* 2:34–5). Nowhere are the words of the Church more beautiful, its music more full of feeling, than in the prayers for the dead. And the beauty and the feeling grow from the magnificent and strong consolation of the thought: that there is a state in the afterlife where the souls of the faithful can still be tempered to the perfection fallen short of in life. As we may hope that few souls face judgement fixed in the evil of a complete rejection of God's will for them, we believe in an intermediate state where those dimmed reflections of His image may be refined by the mysterious purgation of suffering for the final vision of the perfect Good. It is this thought more than any other that gives its atmosphere to the month of the Holy Souls. Aware of the gulf between God's perfection and the human failings even of the good, like Judas of old who found the stolen idols hidden on the slain of God's army. Church and faithful turn to prayer that 'the sins which have been committed may be forgiven' (2 Macc 12:42).

We know that sin must be expiated, that the anger of God is against all impiety and wrongdoing (Rom 1:17). But we do not best think of God's justice as that of a kind of supernatural inspector of weights and measures. His justice flows from His transcendent perfection. Only those can stand before Him who have fulfilled Christ's command, 'Be ye perfect as also your heavenly Father is perfect' (Mt 5:48). He who is the light of light to the blessed is also the burning fire of perverse wills. Even Moses was excluded from the Promised Land for a moment's hesitant faith. If the vision is to be of God Himself how much more imperative become the words; 'I am the Lord your God; be holy because I am holy ...' (Lev 11:44).

Nothing emerges more strongly from the Old Testament than this unapproachable holiness of God. The Israelites were forbidden even to touch the Mount of Sinai. They were slain who looked curiously into the Ark of the Covenant (1 K 6:19–20). And as He is holy so shall His people be 'perfect and without spot' before Him. But how wide a gap separates them. 'Can any man be justified compared with God, or he that is born of a woman appear clean? Behold even the moon doth not shine, and the stars are not pure in His sight' (Job 25:4–5).

And as it is happiness to possess Him, so it is punishment merely to be excluded from His sight. As the liberated soul flies towards the vision of God, so keenly does it suffer from its thwarting. The mystics have spoken of a state that may be analogous to the sufferings of the souls in Purgatory. St Teresa of Avila speaks of the extreme desolation that may come to those who have enjoyed the union of the higher stages of prayer – a crucifixion between heaven and earth because of absence from 'that Good that contains all good things within itself' ... There comes a distress so subtle and piercing that, placed as it is in this desert, the soul can say ... "I watch and am as a sparrow alone upon the housetop" (Ps 101:7).'

But this abandonment is a 'sweet martyrdom'. Through the Communion of Saints we can reach across to them. They know they are already standing before God's iconostasis. Their suffering is of love deferred. 'Afflicted in few things, in many they shall be well rewarded: because God hath tried them and found them worthy of Himself' (Wis 3:5).

V

'Tell us when shall these things be?' (Mt 24:3). The scene is the Mount of Olives. The occasion is Christ's prophecy to His disciples that of the splendour of the Temple spread below them 'there shall not be left ... a stone upon a stone ... ' (Mt 24:2). The answer to their question makes up the Gospel for the last Sunday after Pentecost.

It does not appear certain how far the answer refers to the coming destruction of Jerusalem, or also to the end of the world. But the words express the keen Christian awareness of the end with such power that St Paul in his letters, and the Church as here, have applied them to the second event.

The Christian is not bounded by the horizons of his individual world. As his charity extends to all men, so do his faith and hope beyond his own life to the destiny of all men, to the end of world and the gathering up of time and history. 'Heaven and earth shall pass ... ' (Mt 24:35). This faith gives him direction, not only in his own life but in the confusing spectacle of human affairs. Direction is towards an end, the end of history and of human choice, towards the full completion when Christ has put all His enemies under His feet and God shall be 'all in all' (1 Cor 15:28). Hence the emphasis in today's Gospel on the sign of the Son of man as the prelude to universal judgement. Not judgement alone. For direction also means sharing the cosmic optimism of St Paul who sees the creation that was cursed in man's fall now participating in his hope of delivery 'from the tyranny of corruption' (Rom 8:21).

'But hope that is seen is not hope.' And no optimism can release us from the lot that is ours to live surrounded by uncertainties. Certain knowledge does not deliver us from the need to watch in anxious uncertainty. For 'of that day and hour no one knoweth ... ' (Mt 24:36). The children of light are not taken out of the darkness, but forewarned not to be overtaken in false security ... The day of the Lord will come as a thief in the night. And 'when they shall say, peace and security, then shall destruction come upon them, as the pains upon her that is with child ... ' (1 Thess.5:3).

Ultimate optimism does not separate the Christian from the truth of evil, from the schooling of the persistent contest with it, from the temptation of apparent defeat. Christian optimism cannot be an easy naiveté, untrue to the depths from which men have cried. 'Because iniquity hath abounded the charity of many shall grow cold. But he that shall persevere to the end, he shall be saved' (Mt 24:12–13).

The Christian perspective on the end is not an escape from involvement in the trials of this time. It is the condition of the Christian life. Though the Christian's home is in heaven (Phil 3:20) it is here that we must make progress till Christ comes (Phil 1:11). Hence all through this time of emphasis on the last things, the Scriptures constantly shorten their depth of field to sharp-edged close-ups of the qualities and the duties of the Christian life – the Sermon on the Mount and Caesar's dues. It is in the soil of the earth the mustard seed is planted. It is in the dough the leaven is put to work. The Christian life is incarnate. The end is not at the world's end. It is now and at home.

HOMILY ON THE BEGINNING OF THE ACADEMIC YEAR[2] 9 OCTOBER 1996

Brevity is the soul of wit, saith Polonius, and most hearers of homilies will agree, I understand. Hence the advice of a former Maynooth Professor of the business – not to start from the Garden of Eden. But Horace saith: I labour to be brief and become obscure. Aye, there's the rub, especially in the age of the sound bite.

On the present occasion however, it should be possible to be both reasonably brief and reasonably clear, while doing justice to the occasion itself. In an academic context one may presume the validity of the Irish saying: *Ní beag nod don eolach*. Hence I take the liberty of opening with words spoken not in the Garden of Eden, but as recently as the year 1250, or thereabouts, by a professor of law announcing the order of his course for the academic year in the University of Bologna:

> I shall always begin the Old Digest on or about the Octave of Michaelmas [6 October], and finish it entirely, by God's help, with everything ordinary and extraordinary, about the middle of August.

So he did, and at the end of it he addressed his audience as follows:

> Now, gentlemen, we have begun and finished and gone through this book, as you know who have been in the class[!], for which we thank God and his Virgin Mother and all his Saints. It is an ancient custom in this city that when a book is finished Mass should be sung to the Holy Spirit, and it is a good custom and hence should be observed.

You will notice that, like some inaugural lectures to this day, the Holy Spirit was invoked at the end rather than the start of that academic year. As theologians and philosophers will know, to a Being beyond time it makes no odds whether He is invoked *before* or *after* in our temporal dimension. Neither does it make any

2 Scripture Readings: Wisdom 7:7–15
Psalm 8:2–6
John 14:25–26 and 16:12–15

difference to my reason for starting so much closer to the Garden of Eden than might seem reasonable.

My reason is to remind even myself just how ancient is the university rite of inaugurating the academic year with a Mass of the Holy Spirit. In other words we do so in Maynooth not just because throughout most of its history Maynooth has been an 'enclosed' Irish Catholic Seminary and Pontifical Athenaeum, and a Pontifical University. That of course would itself be no mean patent of nobility over the two centuries since 1795. But the larger and longer patent is that, in thus ritually inaugurating the academic year, Maynooth is continuing the great European university tradition since the beginnings of universities nearly a thousand years ago. In fact the ultimate roots of that tradition go back to more like two-and-a-half thousand years ago. For already the great pre-Christian philosophers in their Schools (to which Christianity owes so much) had the custom of starting the investigation of any great ultimate question with a prayer for light from some *divine* source of *sophia*, Wisdom.

In that context you can see the sense and the relevance of the Scripture Readings you have just heard. They are focused on Wisdom, *Sophia*, the range of the quest for it, and the light that we need to attain it. *Wisdom* of course is a word that does not always carry ideal connotations today. It often suggests rather the 'wisdom' of the marketplace – knowing the price of everything and the value of nothing! But let us not be shy of redeeming the word and its idea. It has a long and noble lineage dating from Plato, Aristotle, and the Old Testament, down the centuries to Cardinal Newman. It denotes that ideal supreme knowledge of supreme Reality in whose light the landscape of contingent realities may be ordered. Hence Newman called it 'philosophy, philosophical knowledge'. By which he meant not merely knowledge of philosophy, but a certain 'perfection or virtue of the intellect', an 'enlargement of mind', an 'illumination' of the multiplicity of reality and its sciences through seeing it from a 'centre'. 'That perfection of the intellect, which is the result of education, and its *beau idéal* ... is the clear, calm, accurate vision of all things, as far as the finite mind can embrace them, each in its place, and with its own characteristics upon it.' And of course Maynooth should be the last place to forget Newman's insistence that such an ideal of knowledge, such an 'idea' of the university, requires the contribution of Theology – whether she still regards herself as a Queen or not!

To turn – or return – to our Scripture Readings, I have neither the space nor the capacity to afflict you with an exegetical lecture. But, since we chose those readings to be the focus of our present occasion and theme, we must contemplate them a little.

Let us see them as a kind of triptych. In the centre panel Psalm 8: the primordial image of man looking out on the vastness of the cosmos and waking to the primordial philosophic wonder at the mystery-cum-paradox of its own immensity and its beholder's littleness. The latter is a paradox *within* a paradox: for the beholder is already the Pascalian 'thinking reed who is capable of the wonder and of the consequent question: faced with the vastitude of the starry heavens, 'what is man that You should spare a thought for him?' (v.4). 'An' as it blowed an' blowed, I often looked up at the sky an' assed meself the question – what is the stars, what is the stars? ... Ah, that's the question, that's the question – what is the stars?'

In the left and right panels of our triptych are two stages in the recognition of the source of an answer to man's questioning. The earlier stage is in Wisdom 7:7: 'I prayed, and understanding was given me; I entreated, and the Spirit of *Wisdom* came to me. I esteemed her more than sceptres and thrones ... '. The later stage is the coming in person of the One 'through whom all things came to be' (Jn 1:3). He is, further, the One in whom 'are hidden all the treasures of Wisdom and knowledge' (Col 2:3). For He is not only the Source but also the *Logos* – the ultimate 'Rational Principle' – of the universe that owes its being to Him.

Yet even He did not reveal all. He promised a further stage in the initiation into Wisdom – through the sending of the very *Spirit* of Wisdom, the *Holy* Spirit, the giver of those Seven Gifts that represent a scale of ascent from reverential fear of the Lord to the summit that is participation in his Wisdom. That is the theme of the Gospel Reading we have just heard. 'I still have many things to say to you, but they would be too much for you here and now. But when the *Spirit* of Truth comes he will lead you into *all* truth ... ' (Jn 16:12–13). And that is why the Mass for the opening of the academic year is specifically a Mass of the Holy Spirit.

The thoughts we have been thinking here point to high vertical peaks, and look out over vast horizontal plains. What are we to think of them on reflection? At worst they will be meaningless to the audience struggling to 'de-weed' their own private patches – whether the patch be their BA./BSc. 'subjects' or that chosen postgraduate patch of 'research' which will eventually qualify him or her to 'teach' within, the 'parameters' of his or her own 'specialty'. We need not be cynical definers of 'research' as 'knowing more and more about less and less' to recognize the contemporary pressures that lead in that direction. And to ignore them would amount to just beating our beautiful wings in the void.

But the good news is that it hath always been so – that is, ever since the Greco-Roman-Christian origins of the educational ideal, out of which Newman thought and wrote. Already in Greco-Roman times the degree of differentiation of 'disciplines' was such that, at the end of their exposition of the *idea* of overarching 'wisdom', the idealists had to confront the question of its *practical feasibility.* Indeed the problem is even in the mind of the author of one of the Wisdom Books of the Bible, Ecclesiastes, the pessimistic preacher who concludes with the warning that 'writing books involves endless hard labour, and that [conversely!] much study wearies the body!' (12:12). It is a logical conclusion from the principle he has enunciated much earlier in the Book (3:9–11). 'I contemplate the task that God gives mankind to labour at ... But though God has permitted man to consider time in its totality [or, 'has set eternity in man's heart'], man cannot comprehend the work of God from beginning to end.'

The problem is majestically evoked by Newman, in a meditation on the works and the beauty of God's creation and the demands made on us by the study of them:

> I look into the depths of space, in which the stars are scattered about, and I understand that I should be millions upon millions of years in creeping along from one end of it to the other, if a bridge were thrown across it. I consider the overpowering variety, richness, intricacy of thy work; the elements, principles, laws, results which go to make it up. I try to recount the multitudes of kinds of knowledge, of sciences, and of arts of which it can be made the subject, and, I know, I should be ages upon ages in learning everything that is to be learned about this world ... And new sciences would come to light, at present unsuspected, as fast as I had mastered the old, and the conclusions of today would be nothing more than starting points of tomorrow ...

So what then? The answer to the difficulty had already been given by the Roman Quintilian. In brief: it is only by aiming at the *ideal* that the best *possible* is reached. And already for the Greeks and the Romans the *ideal* was all the more urgent for the reason that the ultimate purpose and meaning of *sophia*/wisdom was not ideal, universal, 'objective' knowledge of reality merely for its own sake, but rather also for the sake of the ideal 'subjective' perfection of the human being – what Plato defines as 'the person foursquare in hand and foot and mind'. And meaning by that not merely an ideal of autonomous 'humanism', but that 'perfection of the intellect' (in Newman's phrase again) which has an ordered view not merely of the *truth* of things but also of truth's concomitant dimension of *value*. For it is by *values* that we order our *lives*. A fact to which we may adapt the familiar Gospel question: 'What does it profit a man to have [understood] the whole *world* and have lost or ruined his very self?'(Lk 9:25).

That is the 'wisdom' of Scripture. It is the 'wisdom' of Greco- Roman 'humanism'. It is the 'wisdom' of Christian humanism. It is the 'light of truth' for which Newman composed a prayer that he would 'like an inquirer to say continually':

O My God, I confess that Thou *canst* enlighten my darkness. I confess that Thou *alone* canst. I *wish* my darkness to be enlightened. (...) I will embrace whatever I at length feel certain is the truth, if ever I come to be certain. And by thy grace I will guard against all self-deceit which may lead me to take what nature would have, rather than what reason approves.

IN PLACE OF AN EPILOGUE

PRESENCES

STOKANE NATIONAL SCHOOL REUNION 1991

One of my earliest memories of Stokane National School is not within the alma mater itself, but on the road home from it. A white, dusty road between lush verges on a brooding June afternoon, with summer stillness all round, but inside my head the soporific buzz of a 'bee- loud glade'. We had been learning Yeats's 'Lake Isle', and I was drugged by its music ...

> I will arise and go now and go to Innisfree
> And live alone in the bee-loud glade.

It was the start of a long affair, with poetry in general but with Yeats in particular, and with the magic of the region, to which Yeats owes so much of his own magic. It is one of my debts to Stokane, one of those precious 'awakenings' on the way into life and the things of beauty its geniuses create.

Mention of life and its particularly remembered moments leads us into reflections. And, here again, at the other end of time, Yeats comes to mind. He visited a convent school once, in some sort of official capacity – as 'a sixty-year-old smiling public man'. Out of the thoughts that arose in him he made one of his greatest poems, 'Among School Children': 'I walk through the long schoolroom questioning... '. The occasion called up epiphanies from his own school years and from all the decisive stages that followed ... up to the present 'comfortable old scarecrow ... with sixty or more Winters on its head'. And the 'questioning' turns on the deepest reflections about what he has become, in body and spirit, at the end of the whole strange eventful history.

> O chestnut-tree, great-rooted blossomer,
> Are you the leaf, the blossom or the bole?
> O body swayed to music, O brightening glance.
> How can we know the dancer from the dance?

('That shook yeh!' – I can hear the current cant phrase with which Stokane would have put down high-sounding and mysterious ways of saying things ... .)

Dancing was not one of the accomplishments on the Stokane curriculum, although a lot of it was done at the time, especially in those ballrooms of the only romance people had in those days. And yet not in them alone. One of my memories of Stokane is the regular accounts of house-dances up the road, breathlessly retailed the morning after by one of my pals in the back benches. (I also recall his even more breathless account of a not entirely unrelated 'discovery'... I pass over what it was, but he was an enthusiastic rabbiter and, consequently a ferret-fancier .... .)

I used to envy my pals those house-dance nights of imagined high life and high kicking – if only over the broomstick. It made me feel I was not quite living it up myself. And truth to tell, I never did master many steps in the terpsichorean art – as my later schooling did enable me to call it. That later schooling, however, while it educated my head did not do the same for my feet. In those days the terpsichorean art was thought to have little to do with the road I took. Fashions change, alas, and very often now I am made to feel once more that I am not quite living it up. The lightest of light fantastic toes I have ever seen have been in the follow- up to, for instance, ordination breakfasts. I have even heard rumours of Parish Priests-Elect taking crash courses in the thing – poor retarded pre-Vatican II creatures like myself trying to catch up with *aggiornamento* and the signs of the times. Quite right, too. King David danced before the Ark of the Covenant. And in an old end-of-term custom known as a Free Class in the Maynooth that was, a clerical student once danced before myself – enthroned in front of him on the lecture hall rostrum.

But I digress. In Yeats (who also had the thing only in his head, and was tone-deaf to boot), dancer and dance are but metaphors for that human life that takes its first formal steps on the way from childhood to age, from innocence and ignorance to wisdom, within the walls of the primary school. What does that life mean? What has it 'blossomed' into – external appearance notwithstanding – by the time it is loaded 'with sixty or more Winters on its head'? It has become the inseparable unity of that duality that consists of the 'dancer' and his 'dance' – what we are in ourselves and what we have managed to 'make' out of what we are.

Naturally, that final compound is deeply coloured by our earliest formal educational influence, the primary school. Like so many institutions in Ireland the 'National School' began in dark and evil days. But it served well all the generations that trod, unshod, over the roads and the fields to school. That service was compounded for two elements, teachers dedicated to their work, and pupils who well-deserved the Irish term, *mic léinn*, sons of learning, deep dyed as they were with the traditional Irish regard for education and learning.

It is only fidelity to history to recall these things at a time when so many shapers of opinion forget or ignore them in favour of less-generous thoughts. There is the widespread idea that bigger is necessarily better, despite another growing realization – that 'small is beautiful'. There is the newly-fashionable sniping at our traditional educators – alleged cruelty, narrowness, undue Church influence etc. It is useful to read some less-blinkered history, accounts, for instance, of schooling in England of the same period, so much richer and better served but lacking neither in 'cruelty' nor 'Church influence'. In fact, it was an English man, a great theorist and historian of education to whom Ireland owes much, who wrote, concerning critics of Church influence that, ultimately, it is thanks to the Church's contribution to education that its critics can speak or write coherently at all. I refer, of course, to Cardinal Newman, as saintly as he was scholarly – shades of our island past.

To illustrate from my own case, when I left Stokane I could use the Irish language. (How I would love now to recover those school readers that had the illustrations by Jack B. Yeats). I knew grammar and syntax, parsing and analysis. Years later, when I set a question on parsing and analysis in a Christmas examination in Maynooth, I made several pages of notes from the result. As a New Year entertainment I devoted a lecture to reading them out to the authors. They were rolling in the aisles as they heard the play-back of their own performance. I once discovered a degree student of mathematics who had never heard of Euclid. I still recall another moment of 'awakening' in Stokane, when I suddenly tumbled to what the deuce it really meant that the sum of the angles made by a vertical on a horizontal line equalled one- hundred-and-eighty degrees (or words to that effect at this distance). And let us not forget Christian Doctrine. How well we were taught the Catechism in those pre-Vatican II days.

And not just by rote but its meaning as well. In recall, its clear language and rhythmic cadences still fall so pleasingly on the inner ear, unlike so much that we have had to read since.

Recalling the things we learned we recall the teachers who taught them, and gave us not only particular knowledge but also the foundations of general order in our minds. Their images float back out of the past... Miss Maye and Master Rouse, retired before my time, but still respected as dignified and appropriately magisterial figures. Mrs. Rouse (the Master's wife), my first teacher, who appeared to me (in the poet's phrase that I did not know then), 'old and grey ... and nodding by the fire', but in reality was all alert and quick to rebuke any disorder or slacking with an expression peculiar to her that I have never heard again: 'Suff on you!'

Mrs Rouse had high hopes of myself. One illustration amuses me still. I went to night-school in woodwork at one stage in my 'dance'. One summer evening I was setting out on my bicycle from the front gate when she and the Master came down the road in their pony and trap. She stopped to make talk with my mother, and enquired about my doings. Her shock was elegant when she discovered where I was going. 'I thought you'd be a doctor or a lawyer ... or something like that!' In the event I became neither, nor much of a woodworker, for that matter. But I like the pungent aroma of sawn timber, and I consider it not a mean part of education to have learned something about the art of using tools for their proper purposes, and of sawing timber ... 'straight and true to the face edge'. And come to think of it, there is that astonishment of the natives when Christ came back to Nazareth and preached so well; 'Surely this is the carpenter, the son of Mary ... ?' A lecture by her introduced me to some of the history and antiquities of Castleconnor.

Then there was Miss Hanlon – only recently gone to her reward. Fresh from the mint she came. Bright and elegant, polite and timid and tip-toeing. As well as her interest and dedication, she brought a touch of the exotic into our small world – pronouncing Irish after the Munster fashion.

And lastly, but mostly, there was John Murphy, only survivor now of my Stokane mentors, enjoying a long, ripe retirement into *otium cum dignitate*. John Murphy is the image of all images that embody the dedication of those teachers to their work. During the war years there was the petrol shortage. Day in, day out, Master Murphy pedalled the miles from Easkey to Stokane and back. Consequently, one of my fixed images of him has him astride his bicycle, wrapped in oilskins, arriving on time, flushed with pushing against wind and water.

John was dynamic and devoted, orderly and disciplined, and a *fear ann féin*. He, too, had expectations of me, and did not readily forgive my disappointing him at one stage by my performance in some examination or other. When I turned in a better one on a later occasion, I can still see and hear him read out the results and snap: '*Bhí sé in am duit, a Thomáis*!' Years later, after I had become neither doctor nor lawyer, nor carpenter but (from the bread-earning angle) another pedagogue, differing only in degrees from himself, he wondered what crime I had committed in some previous existence. I begin to see his point. But, once more with feeling, 'how can we know the dancer from the dance?'

As well as the good teachers, one remembers also the good companions. And in these liberated feminist times it is nice to be able to recall that they included 'lassies' as well as 'lads'. We did not know it then – nor Stokane itself for that matter – but Stokane, like every other similar place, was ahead of its time in regard to 'de-segregated' education! That jargon was to come later. The only real segregation was between the two school yards and that not always complete when it came to such occasional snatched pleasures as ring-a-ring-of-roses. In our own corral at lunchtime we, males, extracted the morning packed collation from our satchels and ingested such delicacies as the brown bread-and-butter that had a taste and aroma such as it never had on sea or land since then. On the strength of that, there was the brief possibility of some athletic prowess before the bell rang again. The high jump was easier then – *do bhí me luath a's tá mé mall*: Back in the classroom 'segregation''diminished. The 'quicker' could be designated occasionally to help the 'slower' without exception of persons. But that often served to reveal the tutor's own exceptions. And there goes poor old Yeats again:

> ... thereupon my heart is driven wild,
> She stands before me as a living child?

The heart stirs at one particular way in which some of the girls widened our male horizons. They went to town on Saturdays for their music lessons. In that way, coloured 'transfers' were discovered and became all the rage. The discovery led to a weekly import order – and out into the enchanted world of Sherwood Forest, Robin Hood and Maid Marion et al. As I write I learn that their story is currently the subject of two new Hollywood films. *Plus ça* change ... .

Outside that we had, of course, the normal blend – the ducklings and the daughters of swans, the placid and the fiery, the bright-eyed extroverts and the dark-pooled contemplatives with their shadows deep, the teases that teased and the Goldilocks that glistened. They come back in images – sloe-back eyes in an oval face framed in raven tresses, or the slow silver timbre of a reading voice.

All that, too, was education and 'awakening'. Often awakenings that, in later years of higher education, would give the key to some of the greatest things in literature. I think of Dante. Far from him we were reared in Stokane, but when wider horizons brought one to the greatest scholars of Dante [one knows that they] have never got that far – they never had benefit of the idylls of Stokane!

But the time passed and we all moved on and went our different ways. Our teachers grew old and passed on. Some of our companions passed on, too – some in the flower of youth, some in rich maturity, and one just as I write. But their memory and images have stayed, as permanent Presences, Presences, to revert to Yeats in his schoolroom:

> That passion, piety or affection knows,
> And that all heavenly glory symbolize ...

BIBLIOGRAPHY

PART I – ACADEMIC

ANTIQUITY

'Hellenic Humanism in the Book of Wisdom', in *Irish Theological Quarterly* 27 (1960), 30–48.

'Hellenism and Judeo-Christian History', in: *Irish Theological Quarterly* 28 (1961), 83–114.

'Total Tragedy in Homer's *Iliad'*, in *The Maynooth Review* 5:1 (1979), 71–83.

'Total Tragedy and the Epic of Gilgamesh', in *The Maynooth Review* 7 (1982), 3–16.

'The Myth of the Innocent Sufferer: Some Greek Paradigms', in *Proceedings of the Irish Biblical Association* 9 (1985), 121-35.

'Desired of All Nations', in *Studies in Patristic Christology: Proceedings of the Third Patristic Conference at Maynooth 1996*, edited by Thomas Finan and Vincent Twomey (Four Courts Press, Dublin, 1998), 1–22.

AUGUSTINE

'St Augustine', in *The Furrow* 38 (1987), 293–303.

'A Mystic in Milan: *reverberasti* revisited', in *From Augustine to Eriugena: Essays on Neoplatonismn and Christianity in Honour of John O'Meara*, ed. by F. X. Martin and J. A. Richmond (Washington, D.C., CUA Press, 1991), 77–91.

'Modes of Vision in St Augustine: *De Genesi ad literam XII'*, in *The Relationship between Neoplatonism and Christianity: Proceedings of the First Patristic Conference at Maynooth 1990*, edited by Thomas Finan and Vincent Twomey (Dublin: Four Courts Press, 1992), 141–54.

'St Augustine and the *mira profunditas* of Scripture: Texts and Contexts', in *Scriptural Interpretation in the Fathers: Proceedings of the Second Patristic Conference at Maynooth 1993*, edited by Thomas Finan and Vincent Twomey (Dublin: Four Courts Press, 1995),163–99.

EARLY IRISH CHRISTIAN LITERATURE

'Hiberno-Latin Christian Literature', in *An Introduction to Celtic Christianity*, edited by J. P. Mackey (Edinburgh: T&T Clark, 1989), 64–100.

'The Holy Trinity in Early Irish Christian Writers', in *The Mystery of the Holy Trinity in the Fathers of the Church, Proceedings of the Fourth International Patristic Conference, Maynooth, 1999*, edited by D. Vincent Twomey SVD and Lewis Ayres (Dublin: Four Courts Press, 2007), 131–50.

DANTE

'Dante and the Religious Imagination', in *Religious Imagination*, edited by J. P. Mackey (Edinburgh: University Press, 1986), 65–80.

'Poetic Imagination', in *Irish Theological Quarterly* 52 (1986), 66–80.

RENAISSANCE

'Some More Comforts: More and the Consolatory Tradition', in *Irish Theological Quarterly* 45 (1978), 205–16.

'International Thomas More Conference: Thomas More in His Time: Renaissance Humanism and Renaissance Law: Introduction to *Call for Papers*', in *Moreana*. 33, no. 127–8 (1996), 5–36.

'International Thomas More Conference: Thomas More in His Time: Renaissance Humanism and Renaissance Law: Programme', in *Moreana* 35, no. 133 (1998), 5–28.

'Homage to W. J. Kinsella', in *Moreana* 34, no131-2 (December 1997), 11–24.

'Erasmus: Letters 1535–1657: Review article on A. Dalzell and C. G. Nauert, *Erasmus: Collected Works in English, Vol. II: The Correspondence: Letters 1535–1657*, in: *Moreana* 32, no. 122 (1995), 71–97.

'Erasmus: Non in Dialectica?' Review article on M. Hoffmann, *Rhetoric and Theology: The Hermeneutic of Erasmus*, in: *Moreana* 33, no. 127 (1996), 133–50.

'Erasmus: Poems: "I lisped in Numbers": Review article on Clarence H. Miller and Harry Vredeveld, *Collected Works of Erasmus, Volumes 85–86, Poems* in *Moreana* 34, no. 130, (1997), 85–99.

ADDENDUM

'Texts without Comment', in *Irish Theological Quarterly* 48 (1981), 161–65.

PART II: OCCASIONAL ESSAYS

CONTROVERSIAL TOPICS

'Ireland and Europe: Cultural Implications of Unity', in *Social Studies*, Maynooth, 1 (1972), 267–77.

'The Burning of the Books', in *The Furrow* 23 (1972), 712–23.

'What is mortal sin?', in *The Furrow* 25 (1974), 227–31.

'Catechesis Then and Now', in *The Furrow* 29 (1978), 28–37.

'The Future of Maynooth: Ideals and Principles', in *The Maynooth Review* 4:1 (1978), 35–52.

"In front of our future": The Pope in Maynooth', in *The Furrow* 30 (1979), 691–96.

'Blood-dimmed Tide? Thoughts on the Apocalypse', in *The Furrow* 33 (1982), 659–66.

'Visions and Visionaries', in *The Furrow* 43 (1992), 147–57.

'The Canonization of Edith Stein', in *Irish Theological Quarterly* 64 (1999), 79–82.

LITERATURE

'A Poet in Glass, in *The Furrow* 41 (1990), 147–55.

'Ulysses and the Irish God', in *Irish Theological Quarterly* 62 (1996/7), 38–48.

HOMILIES

'The End of Things – Thoughts on Sunday', in *The Furrow* 14 (1963), 702–8.

'Homily on the Beginning of the Academic Year, 9 October 1996', in *Maynooth University Record* (1997), 11–15.

IN PLACE OF AN EPILOGUE

'Presences''(1991) [unpublished].

OTHER PUBLICATIONS

'Countryside in Autumn' in *The Silhouette* (1951), 12–13.

'"Through a mirror clear" – on nature poetry', in *The Silhouette* (1952), 32–6.

'"Stay, thou art so beautiful" – on Classics in the education system', in *The Silhouette* (1953), 54–9.

'The Dilemma', *The Silhouette*, Christmas (1954), 23-26.

'Digging up the Past', in *The Silhouette*, (Summer 1957), 42–8.

'An Aigne Linbh', in *Irisleabhar Mhá Nuad* (1970), 43–51.

Co-editor with Patrick Bastable et al., *St Patrick's Letters: A Study of their Theological Dimension by Daniel Conneely* (Maynooth: *An Sagart*, 1993) [contributed especially to the sections on the literary genre and Latinity of St Patrick].

ACKNOWLEDGEMENTS

'Hellenic Humanism in the Book of Wisdom' in: *Irish Theological Quarterly* 27 (1), pp.30-48. Copyright © 1960 by the author. Reprinted by permission of SAGE Publications, Ltd.

'Hellenism and Judeo-Christian History' in: *Irish Theological Quarterly* 28 (2), pp. 83-114. Copyright © 1961 by the author. Reprinted by permission of SAGE Publications, Ltd.

'The End of Things - Thoughts on Sunday' in: *The Furrow* 14 (1963), pp 702-8. Copyright © 1963 by the author. Reprinted by kind permission of the Editor.

'The Burning of the Books' in: *The Furrow* 23 (1972), pp. 712-23. Copyright © 1972 by the author. Reprinted by kind permission of the Editor.

'Ireland and Europe: Cultural Implications of Unity' in: *Social Studies,* Maynooth, 1 (1972), 267-77. Copyright © 1972 by the author.

'What is mortal sin?' in: *The Furrow* 25 (1974), pp. 227-31. Copyright © 1974 by the author. Reprinted by kind permission of the Editor.

'The Future of Maynooth: Ideals and Principles' in: *The Maynooth Review* 4 (1978), pp. 35-52. Copyright © 1978 by the author. Reprinted by kind permission of the Editor.

'Some More Comforts: More and the Consolatory Tradition' in: *Irish Theological Quarterly* 45 (4), pp. 205-16. Copyright © 1978 by the author. Reprinted by permission of SAGE Publications, Ltd.

'Catechesis Then and Now' in: *The Furrow* 29 (1978), pp. 28-37. Copyright © 1978 by the author. Reprinted by permission of the Editor.

'Total Tragedy in Homer' in: *The Maynooth Review* 5 (1979), pp. 71-83. Copyright © 1979 by the author. Reprinted by kind permission of the Editor.

'"In front of our future": The Pope in Maynooth' in: *The Furrow* 30 (1979), pp. 691-96. Copyright © 1979 by the author. Reprinted by kind permission of the Editor.

'Texts without Comment' in: *Irish Theological Quarterly* 48 (3-4), pp. 161-65. Copyright © 1981 by the author. Reprinted by permission of SAGE Publications, Ltd.

'Total Tragedy in the Epic of Gilgamesh' in: *The Maynooth Review* 9 (1982), pp. 3-16. Copyright © 1982 by the author. Reprinted by kind permission of the Editor.

'Blood-dimmed Tide? Thoughts on the Apocalypse' in: *The Furrow* 33 (1982), pp. 659-66. Copyright © 1982 by the author. Reprinted by kind permission of the Editor.

'The Myth of the Innocent Sufferer: Some Greek Paradigms' in: *Proceedings of the Irish Biblical Association* 9 (1985), pp. 121-35. Copyright © 1985 by the author. Reprinted by permission of the Editor.

'Poetic Imagination' in: *Irish Theological Quarterly* 52 (1-2), pp. 66-80. Copyright © 1986 by the author. Reprinted by permission of SAGE Publications, Ltd.

'Dante and the Religious Imagination' in: *Religious Imagination*, ed. by J.P. Mackey (Edinburgh: University Press, 1986), pp. 65-85. Copyright © 1986 by the author. Reprinted by permission of the Licensor through PLSclear.

'St Augustine' in: *The Furrow* 38 (1987), pp.293-303. Copyright © 1987 by the author. Reprinted by kind permission of the Editor.

'Hiberno-Latin Christian Literature' in *An Introduction to Celtic Christianity,* ed. by J.P. Mackey (Edinburgh: T&T Clark, 1989), 64-100. Copyright © 1989 by the author. Reprinted by permission of the Publishers.

'A Poet in Glass' in: *The Furrow* 41 (1990), pp. 147-55. Copyright © 1990 by the author. Reprinted by kind permission of the Editor.

'A Mystic in Milan: reverberasti revisited' in: *From Augustine to Eriugena: Essays on Neoplatonismn and Christianity in Honour of John O'Meara*, ed. by F. X. Martin and J.A. Richmond (Washington, D.C., CUA Press, 1991), pp. 77-91. Copyright © 1991 by the author. Reprinted by kind permission of the Publishers.

'Presences" [unpublished]. Copyright © 1991 by the author.

'Modes of Vision in St Augustine: De Genesi ad literam XII' in: *The Relationship between Neoplatonism and Christianity: Proceedings of the First Patristic Conference at Maynooth 1990*, editd by Thomas Finan and Vincent Twomey (Dublin: Four Courts Press, 1992), pp. 141-54. Copyright © 1992 by the author. Reprinted by kind permission of the Publisher.

'Visions and Visionaries' in: *The Furrow* 43 (1992), pp. 147-57. Copyright © 1992 by the author. Reprinted by kind permission of the Editor.

'Erasmus: Letters 1535-1657: Review-article on A. Dalzell and C.G. Nauert, Erasmus: Collected Works in English, Vol. II: The Correspondence: Letters 1535-1657 in: *Moreana* 122 (1995), pp. 71-97. Copyright © 1995 by the author. Reprinted by permission of the Licensor through PLSclear.

'St Augustine and the mira profunditas of Scripture: Texts and Contexts' in: *Scriptural Interpretation in the Fathers: Proceedings of the Second Patristic Conference at Maynooth 1993* (Dublin: Four Courts Press, 1995), pp.163-99. Copyright © 1995 by the author. Reprinted by kind permission of the Publishers.

'Ulysses and the Irish God' in: *Irish Theological Quarterly* 62 (1), pp. 38-48. Copyright © 1996 by the author. Reprinted by permission of SAGE Publications, Ltd.

'Erasmus: Non in Dialectica?' Review article on M. Hoffmann, Rhetoric and Theology: The Hermeneutic of Erasmus in: *Moreana* 127 (1996), pp.133-50. Copyright © 1996 by the author. Reprinted by permission of the Licensor through PLSclear.

'Thomas More in His Time: International Thomas More Conference 1998: Call for Papers' in: *Moreana* 127 (1996), pp. 5-36. Copyright © 1996 by the author. Reprinted by permission of the Licensor through PLSclear.

'Homily on the Beginning of the Academic Year, 9 October 1996' in: *Maynooth University Record* (1997), 11-1 5. Copyright © 1997 by the author.

Erasmus: Poems: 'I lisped in Numbers': Review-article on Clarence H. Miller and Harry Vredeveld, Collected Works of Erasmus, Volumes 85-86, Poems in *Moreana*, 130, (1997), pp. 85-99. Copyright © 1997 by the author. Reprinted by permission of the Licensor through PLSclear.

'Homage to WJ Kinsella' in: *Moreana* 131-2 (Dec. 1997), 11-24. Copyright © 1997 by the author. Reprinted by permission of the Licensor through PLSclear.

'Desired of All Nations' in: *Studies in Patristic Christology: Proceedings of the Third Patristic Conference at Maynooth 1996*, edited by Thomas Finan and Vincent Twomey (Four Courts Press, Dublin, 1998), pp. 1-22. Copyright © 1998 by the author. Reprinted by kind permission of the Publishers.

'Humanism, Law and Thomas More: International Thomas More Conference 1998: Programme' in: *Moreana* 133 (1998), pp. 5-28. Copyright © 1998 by the author. Reprinted by permission of the Licensor through PLSclear.

'The Canonisation of Edith Stein' in: *Irish Theological Quarterly* 64 (1), pp. 79-82. Copyright © 1999 by the author. Reprinted by permission of SAGE Publications, Ltd.

'The Holy Trinity in Early Irish Christian Writers', *The Mystery of the Holy Trinity in the Fathers of the Church, Proceedings of the Fourth International Patristic Conference, Maynooth, 1999*, ed. by D. Vincent Twomey SVD and Lewis Ayres (Dublin: Four Courts Press, 2007), pp. 131-50. Copyright © 2007 by the author. Reprinted by kind permission of the Publishers.